NEW YORK CITY

AND
NEARBY ATTRACTIONS

FODOR'S TRAVEL GUIDES

are compiled, researched, and edited by an international team of travel writers, field correspondents, and editors. The series, which now almost covers the globe, was founded by Eugene Fodor in 1936.

OFFICES
New York & London

FODOR'S NEW YORK CITY:

Editorial Contributors: CLIVE BARNES, LINDA D. CIRINO, FLORENCE FABRICANT, JOEL FISHMAN, DAVID FRANKEL, ELLEN GREENFIELD, JANE HERSHEY, MICHAEL IACHETTA, SPEIGHT JENKINS, G. E. KIDDER SMITH, GAIL LEVIN, ROBERT MARTIN, JOHN MAXYMUK, MICHAEL SHAIN, DENNIS STARIN, MARILYN STASIO
Editorial Consultant and Contributor: IRA MAYER
Editor: ALAN TUCKER
Editorial Associate: STEPHEN BREWER
Research: LISA MARRONGELLI
Illustrations: TED BURWELL, SANDRA LANG
Maps and Plans: DYNO LOWENSTEIN

FODOR'S

NEW YORK CITY

AND
NEARBY
ATTRACTIONS
1983

FODOR'S TRAVEL GUIDES
New York

All the following Guides are current (most of them also in
the Hodder and Stoughton British edition.)

CURRENT FODOR'S COUNTRY AND AREA TITLES:

AUSTRALIA, NEW ZEALAND
  AND SOUTH PACIFIC
AUSTRIA
BELGIUM AND
  LUXEMBOURG
BERMUDA
BRAZIL
CANADA
CARIBBEAN AND BAHAMAS
CENTRAL AMERICA
EASTERN EUROPE
EGYPT
EUROPE
FRANCE
GERMANY
GREAT BRITAIN
GREECE
HOLLAND
INDIA

IRELAND
ISRAEL
ITALY
JAPAN
JORDAN AND HOLY LAND
KENYA
MEXICO
NORTH AFRICA
PEOPLE'S REPUBLIC
  OF CHINA
PORTUGAL
SCANDINAVIA
SOUTH AMERICA
SOUTHEAST ASIA
SOVIET UNION
SPAIN
SWITZERLAND
TURKEY

CITY GUIDES:

BEIJING, GUANGZHOU, SHANGHAI
CHICAGO
LONDON
LOS ANGELES
MEXICO CITY AND ACAPULCO
NEW YORK CITY

PARIS
ROME
SAN DIEGO
SAN FRANCISCO
TOKYO
WASHINGTON, D.C.

FODOR'S BUDGET SERIES:

BUDGET BRITAIN
BUDGET CANADA
BUDGET CARIBBEAN
BUDGET EUROPE
BUDGET FRANCE
BUDGET GERMANY

BUDGET ITALY
BUDGET JAPAN
BUDGET MEXICO
BUDGET SPAIN
BUDGET TRAVEL IN AMERICA

USA GUIDES:

ALASKA
CAPE COD
COLORADO
FAR WEST
FLORIDA

HAWAII
NEW ENGLAND
PENNSYLVANIA
SOUTH
USA (in one volume)

MANUFACTURED IN THE UNITED STATES OF AMERICA
10 9 8 7 6 5 4 3 2 1

Contents

Attractions Near New York City

New York City Orientation

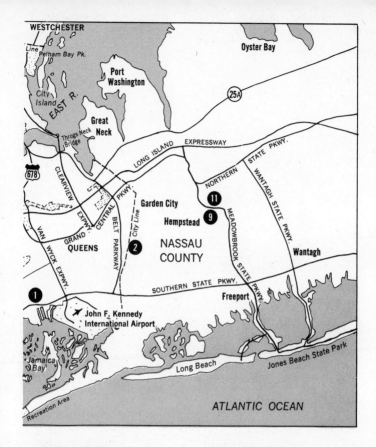

Points of Interest

1) Aqueduct Race Track
2) Belmont Park
3) Bronx Zoo & Botanical Garden
4) Brooklyn Museum &
   Botanic Garden
5) World Trade Center
6) Ellis Island

7) Governors Island
8) Meadowlands Sports Complex
9) Nassau Coliseum
10) New York Aquarium
11) Roosevelt Raceway
12) Shea Stadium
13) Staten Island Historic Museum
14) Statue of Liberty
15) Yankee Stadium

FOREWORD

Whatever New York City is—and we won't try to summarize it in this foreword, while so many fine writers have fallen short at it—it is the *ne plus ultra* of its type, the ultimate megalopolis. Visitors and residents alike feel this even when coming in on the Triboro Bridge from the Long Island airports at night or when flying over the city. The city holds forth both what is best and what is worst in the human panorama.

Fodor's New York City is designed to try to describe and explain the city to you, and to help you decide, once you're there, what you want to do and where you want to go. The book is intended to be your tool for making some order out of a chaos of possibilities. We have therefore concentrated on giving you the broadest **range** of choices the city offers, and within that range to present **selections** that will be safe, solid, and of value to you. The descriptions we provide are just enough for you to make intelligent choices from among our selections, based on your own tastes and pocketbook.

All selections and comments in *Fodor's New York City* are based on the editors' and contributors' personal experience. We feel that our first responsibility is to inform and protect you, the reader. Errors are bound to creep into any travel guide, however. We go to press in the late fall of the year, and much change can and will occur in New York City even while we are on press and during the succeeding twelve months or so when this edition is on sale. We cannot, therefore, be responsible for the sudden closing of a restaurant, a change in a museum's days or hours, a shift of chefs (for the worse), and so forth. We sincerely welcome letters from readers on these changes, or from those whose opinions differ from ours, and we are ready to revise our entries for next year's edition when the facts warrant it.

Send your letters to the editors at **Fodor's Travel Guides, 2 Park Avenue, New York, NY 10016.** Continental readers may prefer to write to Fodor's Travel Guides, 9–10 Market Place, London W1N 7AG, England.

NEW YORK CITY'S ETHNIC MAKE-UP

New York City must be considered in the context of the urban, suburban, and so-called exurban areas that surround it and of which it is the working center; this area has an estimated population of about 17,000,000 people, and is the most populous urban area in the world. (Mexico City is second and Tokyo third.)

The population of the five boroughs of the city itself is a little over 7,000,000. Of these, 1.1 million are Jewish (not an ethnic category, to be sure), and about two and a half million black. The figure for blacks includes those with heritages from Haiti, Trinidad, and other places in the Caribbean area. There are about 1.6 million Hispanic-Americans (Puerto Rico, Cuba, Dominican Republic, South America, Mexico). It is now difficult to estimate the Italian-American population, but it is presumed to be something less than a million, as is the Irish-American community here, many having moved out to the suburbs. Other noticeable ethnic presences are Greek, Indian, Chinese, Japanese, Korean (est. 110,000), German, Hungarian, and Russian.

Here are selected figures for registered *aliens* resident in the city:

Dominican Republic	75,000
Italy	46,000
China	43,000
Jamaica	38,000
USSR	20,000
India	15,000
England	14,000
Korea	14,000
Poland	9,000

The total of registered ("legal") aliens is 576,000, but the N.Y. City Planning Commission estimates that there are about 750,000 "undocumented" (illegal) aliens here, most of whom have not been included in any of the official population figures given above. There are 35,000 members of the foreign diplomatic community in the city.

FACTS AT YOUR FINGERTIPS

 WHEN TO GO. Ultimately, the answer to that question is "anytime." Whatever your interests—from grand opera to horseback riding, modern art to sea lore, the stock exchanges to the Statue of Liberty—there'll be more than you can possibly take in during any one visit, no matter what time of year you decide to go or how long you stay. In New York, even the natives (especially the natives, some might say) never see it all!

At one time, it seemed as though New York's cultural life was limited to the months between October and May, when the new Broadway shows opened, and during which span the Metropolitan Opera and New York Philharmonic held their formal seasons. That is no longer so. Today, there are Broadway openings in mid-July, while the hits of past seasons continue to run; the Met and the Philharmonic take to the city's parks for free live performances, and the number of visiting orchestras and opera and ballet companies can be staggering.

With the exception of a handful of holidays such as Christmas, New Years, and Thanksgiving, the city's museums are open year-round (they do have their regular day off during the week, of course), as are the parks for bicycling or cross-country skiing or viewing the fall foliage (in Central Park) or the springtime cherry blossoms (in Brooklyn's Botanic Gardens).

One word of caution, however: The weather in New York can go to extremes. Winter will be marked by a few sub-zero degree days, and summers find the temperature skyrocketing into the 90s (with humidity to match); spring and fall tend to be beautifully mild and dry—but then these seasons seem to be getting shorter every year, as blizzards blow in mid-April and Indian summers run into October. The best advice to a visitor: No matter how warm you expect it to be, carry an extra sweater (you may need it in air-conditioned places even if it's sweltering outside or in the evening for outdoor dining or concerts). Conversely, no matter how cold you fear it will get, bring something lightweight.

 PLANNING YOUR TRIP. We urge you to make your basic travel arrangements in advance, whenever possible. It is best to arrive in New York with hotel or motel reservations in hand, lest you find yourself competing with half a dozen major conventions that have booked up most of the rooms available throughout the city or having to pay for accommodations well beyond your needs or anticipated budget.

We also strongly recommend consulting a travel agent. There are numerous "package tours" for New York that provide air travel from your city of origin combined with hotel arrangements and sometimes with meals and theater tickets, and such packages tend to be far more reasonable than you could obtain

1

booking on your own. An agent will be familiar with the latest offerings and should be able to help you find one to suit your interests—whether you simply want air and hotel or whether you want some meals, or theater tickets, or a car as part of the deal. There is no fee for a travel agent's services beyond extraordinary telephone or Telex charges.

As will be explained in further detail later on, having a car in New York City, and in particular in Manhattan, is more of a bother than it is worth. If you insist on driving in New York and do not already belong to an auto club, now is the time to join one. They can be very helpful providing routings and emergency road service (if your car is a rental, the rental company will provide the latter). The most widely recognized is the *American Automobile Association,* 8111 Gatehouse Rd., Falls Church, VA 22047, with many offices around the New York metropolitan area. Members are entitled to free maps, among other publications, which are available at local offices or which may be ordered by mail. Like the AAA, *Amoco Motor Club,* 3700 Wake Forest Rd., Raleigh, NC 27609, *Exxon Touring Service,* 1251 Ave. of the Americas, New York, NY 10020, and *National Travel Club,* Travel Building, Floral Park, NY 11001, offer information, insurance, and tours.

It is a good idea to carry travelers checks and/or credit cards rather than a large amount of cash, though you may need some form of identification to cash travelers checks—and travelers checks are by no means universally accepted. Most major department stores accept one or another major credit card in addition to those they issue themselves. Gas companies, however, increasingly accept only their own cards—and as of mid-1982 some were begging to offer a small discount for cash payment!

Students and senior citizens will also want to carry suitable identification cards with them at all times, as many museums, some theaters, some hotels, and other institutions offer discounts for those who qualify.

 TIPS FOR VISITORS FROM THE BRITISH COMMONWEATH. Passports. You will need a valid passport and a U.S. Visa (which can only be put in a passport of the 10-year kind). You can obtain the visa either through your travel agent, or directly from the *United States Embassy,* Visa and Immigration Department, 24 Grosvenor Sq., London W1 (tel. 01–499 3443).

No vaccinations are required for entry into the U.S.

Customs. If you are 21 or over, you can take into the U.S.: 200 cigarettes, 50 cigars or 3 lbs of tobacco; 1 U.S. liter of alcohol; duty-free gifts to a value of $100. Be careful not to try to take in meat or meat products, seeds, plants, fruits, etc. And avoid narcotics like the plague.

Insurance. We heartily recommend that you insure yourself to cover health and motoring mishaps, with *Europ Assistance,* 252 High St., Croydon CRO 1NF (tel. 01–680 1234). Their excellent service is all the more valuable when you consider the possible costs of health care in the U.S.

Tour Operators. The price battle that has raged over transatlantic fares has meant that most tour operators now offer excellent budget packages to the U.S. Among those you might consider as you plan your trip are:

American Express, 6 Haymarket, London SW1.

Thomas Cook Ltd., Thorpe Wood, Peterborough, PE 3 6SB.

Cosmos, Cosmos House, 1 Bromley Common, Bromley, Kent BR2 9LX.

Cunard, 8 Berkeley St., London W1.

Jetsave, Sussex House, London Rd., East Grinstead RH19 1LD.

Page and Moy, 136–138 London Rd., Leicester LE2 1EN.

Speedbird, 200 Buckingham Palace Rd., London SW1.

Air Fares. We suggest that you explore the current scene for budget flight possibilities. Many of the main transatlantic carriers have stand-by tickets, available a short time before the flight only, as well as APEX and other fares at a considerable saving over the full price. Quite frankly, only business travelers who don't have to watch the price of their tickets fly full-price these days—and find themselves sitting right beside an APEX passenger!

Hotels. You may have need of a fast booking service to find a hotel room in New York. One of the very best ways to do this is to contact HBI-HOTAC, Globegate House, Pound Lane, London NW10 (tel. 01–451 2311). They book rooms for 58 individual hotels in New York and for most of the large chains (Holiday Inn, Hilton, Ramada etc.), so you can have a multiple choice with only one contact. HBI-HOTAC specializes in booking for business firms, but also deals with the general public.

Information. One excellent source of information is the *State of New York Division of Tourism,* 35 Piccadilly, London W1 (tel. 01–734 7282). Although they are not open for personal callers, they will be happy to let you have brochures and other information to help you plan your trip.

TOURIST INFORMATION. The *New York Convention and Visitors' Bureau,* street level in the modern skyscraper at the south end of Columbus Circle (58th Street and Eighth Avenue), has multi-lingual aides and several racks full of brochures about the city. You can also obtain bus and subway maps here. The Bureau is open Monday to Friday, 9 A.M. to 6 P.M., weekends and holidays 10 A.M. to 6 P.M. Telephone 212–397–8222.

The *New York State Division of Tourism,* 99 Washington Ave., Albany, NY 12245, is an even better-staffed office devoted to promoting tourism throughout the Empire State. Among its publications, available free for the asking, are *I Love New York Travel Guide to New York State* and *I Love New York Travel Guide to New York City.* The state's toll-free Vacation Information telephone number is 800–342–3810 or, if calling in the city, 949–9300.

Bus and subway information is available 24 hours a day by calling 330–1234.

PACKING. As mentioned, the weather in New York City can be surprising, so the trick in packing is to be prepared—without loading yourself down with unnecessary baggage. Common sense is the rule of thumb; a few layers of shirts and sweaters or a down parka will shield you from Wall Street's and midtown's fierce winter winds. In summer you'll want walking shorts or swim suits (the beaches are within a subway ride!). Generally speaking, woolen clothes and an overcoat are what you want in winter (preferably not thermal underwear, as indoor living spaces tend to be overheated); lightweight, wash-and-wear "business" and casual clothes for summer; and medium-weight outer garments plus a raincoat for spring and fall. As you create your checklist prior to packing, be sure to consider the type of trip you're planning. If you intend to dine at the city's four-star restaurants and attend the opera, you'll probably want to dress fairly formally. Otherwise, more casual attire will suffice just about everywhere. Pants suits and leisure suits do not go over big in Manhattan.

For the record keepers, precipitation averages 3.5 inches per month, except in July and August, when frequent thundershowers raise the typical rainfall to 4.25 inches. Snow is likely anytime between November and April. With some rare exceptions, usually as the seasons change, there is not a great variation in temperature in the course of the day. Average highs and lows by month, in degrees Fahrenheit, are as follows:

Jan. 26–39	Jul. 68–85
Feb. 27–40	Aug. 66–83
Mar. 34–48	Sep. 60–77
Apr. 44–61	Oct. 51–67
May 53–71	Nov. 41–54
Jun. 63–81	Dec. 30–41

Rest assured, if you run out of film or toothpaste or other everyday items, there'll be plenty of places to replenish your supply. Discount drug stores selling these and thousands of other items abound, often just around the corner from major hotels—and the discounts will be sizable when compared to what is charged for the same items at hotel counters.

WHAT TO DO WITH THE PETS. If you are going to New York City, leave them at home. The city's dog and littering laws are relatively strictly enforced by special inspectors, with high fines for violators. Moreover, most hotels are less than thrilled by the prospect of putting up pets.

WHAT WILL IT COST? This is perhaps the most difficult question of all to answer, and for most travelers, one of the most important to ask. Throughout this book we try to give you as many guidelines as possible to help you plan out your expenses in advance. But prices for accommodations, for food, for entertainment, and for all manner of services in New York City vary widely;

for this reason, the cost estimates given are often for a range. With hotel rooms, for example, the more you plan ahead, the easier it will be to obtain first-class arrangements at the lower end of the spectrum. In contrast, when going to the theater, it's the last-minute tickets picked up at the half-price booths in Times Square or the Wall Street area that yield the best "bargains."

Here, then, are a few general pointers on the two items that will make up the bulk of your budget once in New York—for those keeping an eye on what they plan to spend. More detailed information for budget and non-budget travelers follows in the Practical Information section:

Lodging. A West Side "tourist hotel" (clean but of minimal charm) in the 40s, near the theater district, will charge $50–$60 a night for a double; rates in the 50s for a somewhat classier environment are $15–$20 higher; and for the top Central Park South, Fifth Avenue, or East Side establishments, the rates begin at $100 a night—park views and suites running as high as $250. Again, tour packages can often get much lower rates, even for the top accommodations. Unlike elsewhere throughout the country, only a handful of Manhattan motels have free parking; these are noted in the hotel/motel listings. As most American hotels do not include breakfast as part of the tariff, you are best off going to a neighborhood coffee shop. There the scrambled eggs with bacon, potatoes, toast and beverage, for which a hotel will charge $12 and up, go for $3 or even quite a bit less. Besides, while business breakfasts are currently in vogue at New York's more fashionable hotels, the food served at them is almost universally scorned.

Food. The best way to eat economically and interestingly in New York City is to partake of the hundreds of small, family-run ethnic restaurants found all over the city. There are also numerous delicatessens and "food boutiques" to be found; at these you can purchase ready-made salads, cheeses, and cold cuts by the pound or by the portion—perfect for summertime lunches *al fresco* in the city's neatly planted "vest pocket parks" or for evening dining during outdoor concerts in the major parks or, for example, at the South Street Seaport. Many bars also serve free hors d'oeuvres from 5 P.M. to 7 P.M. weekdays. If you're looking to eat at the city's best restaurants but are still concerned with watching your budget, consider having your main meal at lunch (unlike most Americans), when the prices are lower than in the evening, or seek out those offering *prix fixe* before-or-after-theater dinners. Most establishments post menus in their windows; remember the prices of a few standard items such as coffee, soup, and side dishes with which to make comparisons, and see if complete dinners are offered as well as à la carte selections. Consider sharing appetizers and/or desserts (or sometimes main courses, even if there is a service charge for an extra plate). Insist on no ice in your beverages—you'll get 30–50 percent more to drink. If you enjoy a nightcap, have it at a local neighborhood bar rather than in the hotel bar or from room service; or keep your own bottle in your room. Ice is available for free just about everywhere.

Typical Expenses for Two People in New York City

Room at *moderate* hotel or motel	$75.
Breakfast	7.
Lunch at *inexpensive* restaurant	12.
Dinner at *moderate* restaurant	30.
Sightseeing tour	15.
Evening drinks	6.
Museum admission	6.
Public transportation	3.
	$154.

HINTS TO THE MOTORIST. We cannot urge you strongly enough to avoid bringing a car into Manhattan. There is very little street parking available (and violators are towed away literally within minutes), garages can cost as much as $15 for two hours in some neighborhoods, and getting stuck in daytime traffic that simply doesn't move in any direction can only lead to anger and frustration. During the day, subways and foot are unquestionably the most convenient and least time-consuming modes of transportation.

That said, if you still insist on driving in New York City (perhaps you're planning to spend much of your time outside Manhattan or happen to have brought a car as part of a longer trip), keep in mind: The speed limit is 55 miles per hour on highways, lower and as posted elsewhere; you must be able to prove that your vehicle is insured; and you must be over 18 years of age. Motorcyclists and their passengers must wear New York State-approved protective helmets and goggles or face shields. Campers and/or trailers are an even worse idea in Manhattan than are cars. Leaving them unattended on the street even where street parking is available is not advisable and space-conscious garages are frequently not apt to accept them. Specific road descriptions appear in the "How To Get Around" section of the Practical Information chapter.

DRINKING LAWS. Minimum age for the consumption of alcohol is 19, though some bars and restaurants limit service to those over 21. New York City bars may legally stay open until 4 A.M. except Sunday mornings, when they must close at 3 A.M. Some establishments get around this restriction by officially being designated social clubs; these may serve "members" any time. Beer can be purchased at supermarkets anytime except Sunday mornings (until noon). Wine and hard liquor are available at liquor stores only—which are not licensed to operate on Sundays.

RELIGIOUS WORSHIP. A listing of all of New York's religious institutions is subject for a book unto itself. The most comprehensive source of information is the Yellow Pages, which has separate listings for "Religious Organizations," "Churches" (broken down by denomination), "Synagogues," etc. For specific details about services in New York City, consult the Friday *New York Times.*

BUSINESS HOURS, HOLIDAYS, AND LOCAL TIME. New York State, like the rest of America, is on Standard Time from the last Sunday in October until the last Sunday in April. In April the clock is advanced one hour, for Daylight Savings Time, and in October is turned back an hour. The entire state lies within the Eastern Time Zone, which is 5 hours earlier than Greenwich Mean Time on local standard (winter) time.

Most businesses, banks, and many restaurants will be closed on the following holidays (the dates are for 1983): New Year's Day, Jan. 1; Washington's Birthday (observance) Feb. 14; Easter Sunday, April 3; Memorial Day (observance) May 31; Independence Day, July 4; Labor Day, Sept. 5; Thanksgiving Day, Nov. 24; and Christmas Day, Dec. 25.

In addition, banks and some businesses may be closed on Martin Luther King's Birthday, Jan. 15; Lincoln's Birthday, Feb. 12; Good Friday (from noon), April 1; Columbus Day (observance) Oct. 10; Election Day (partially) Nov. 1; and Veteran's Day, Nov. 8.

The annual St. Patrick's Day Parade occurs on March 17; this means that Fifth Avenue is closed from 42nd Street to 86th Street, the town is flooded with mobs of often unruly, drunken, or drugged teenagers, and normal activity in midtown Manhattan all but comes to a halt.

New York City having more Jews than Tel Aviv, it is inevitable that the city slows down considerably on the important Jewish holidays: Passover, starting March 29; Rosh Hashanah on Sept. 8; Yom Kippur on Sept. 17; and Hanukkah starting on Dec. 1.

Subways, buses, and trains provide less service on all official holidays and some of the lesser ones.

POSTAGE. At press time, rates for international mail from the United States are as follows: *Surface* letters to Canada and Mexico are at the U.S. domestic rate: 20¢ for 1 ounce or under, 37¢ for 2 ounces or under, but these rates actually get airmail carriage to those countries. Surface letters to other foreign destinations are 30¢ for the first ounce and 47¢ for up to 2 ounces. Airmail letters to foreign destinations other than to Canada, Mexico, and some Caribbean and South American countries are 40¢ ½ ounce, 80¢ 1 ounce, $1.20 1½ ounces, $1.60 2 ounces. Postcards (except for Canada and Mexico, which go airmail for 13¢) are 19¢ for surface mail and 28¢ for airmail to any foreign destination. Standard international aerogram letters, good for any foreign destination, are 30¢ but of course nothing may be enclosed in them. Postal rates are no exception in this period of inflation, so check before you mail, in case they have gone up since press time.

TIPPING. Tipping is supposed to be a personal thing, your way of expressing appreciation of someone who has taken pleasure and pride in giving you attentive, efficient, and personal service. Because standards of personal service in the United States are highly uneven, you should, when you get genuinely good service, feel secure in rewarding it, and when you feel that the service you got was slovenly, indifferent, or surly, don't hesitate to show this by the size, or withholding, of your tip. Remember that in many places the help are paid very little and depend on tips for the better part of their income. This is supposed to give them incentive to serve you well. These days, the going rate on *restaurant* service is 15 percent on the amount *before* taxes. Tipping at counters is not universal, but most people leave at least 25 cents, and 15 percent when it comes to anything over that. For *bellboys,* 50 cents per bag is usual. However, if you load him down with all manner of bag, hatboxes, cameras, coats, etc., you might consider giving an extra 50 cents or $1. In many places the help rely on tips for a goodly portion of their income. For one-night stays in most *hotels* and *motels* you leave nothing. If you stay longer, at the end of your stay leave the maid $1–$1.25 per day, or $5 per person per week for multiple occupancy. Detailed suggestions for restaurant tipping are included in the Practical Information section; suffice it to say here that 15 percent of the check—before taxes—is standard.

For the many other services you may encounter in a big hotel, figure roughly as follows: doorman, 25 cents for taxi handling, 50 cents for help with baggage; bellhop, 50 cents per day, more if you load him down with extras; parking attendant, 50 cents; bartender, 15 percent; room service, 10–15 percent of that bill; laundry or valet service, 15 percent; golf caddies, $1–$2 per bag, or 15 percent of the greens fee for an 18-hole course, or $3 on a free course; barbers and hairdressers 15 percent; shoeshine attendants, 25 cents; manicurists, $1. Masseurs and masseuses in clubs and hotels get 20 percent.

Transportation: Taxi drivers in New York *expect 20 percent.* Limousine service, 20 percent. Car rental agencies, nothing. Bus porters are tipped 25 cents per bag, drivers nothing. On charters and package tours, conductors and drivers usually get $5–$10 per day from the group as a whole, but be sure to ask whether this has already been figured into the package cost. On short local sightseeing runs, the driver-guide may get 25 cents per person, more if you think he has been especially helpful or personable. Airport bus drivers, nothing. Tipping at curbside check-in is unofficial, but same as above. On the plane, no tipping.

SENIOR CITIZEN AND STUDENT DISCOUNTS. Many attractions throughout New York City offer considerable discounts to Senior Citizens and students. Some may require special city-issued Senior-Citizen identification, but in most cases showing a driver's license, passport, or some other proof of age will suffice—"senior" generally being defined as 65 or over for men and 62 or over for women. Museums, first-run and neighborhood movie theaters, and even some stores will often post special Senior-Citizen rates. Those places offering student discounts are generally somewhat more stringent in their proof requirements—a high school or college ID, international student traveler card, or evidence of age may be requested. Unfortunately, there is no uniformity on these matters.

 HINTS TO HANDICAPPED TRAVELERS. *Access New York City* contains extensive listings for more than 400 public buildings in Manhattan, from hotels and museums to department stores and transportation services. It is available for $2 from The Junior League of New York, 130 E. 80 St., New York, NY 10021. Important sources of information in this field are: The *Travel Information Center,* Moss Rehabilitation Hospital, 12th St. and Tabor Rd., Philadelphia, PA 19141. *Easter Seal Society for Crippled Children and Adults,* Director of Education and Information Service, 2023 W. Ogden Ave., Chicago, IL 60612. Many of the nation's national parks have special facilities for the handicapped. These are described in *National Park Guide for the Handicapped,* available from the U.S. Government Printing Office, Washington, DC 20402. TWA publishes a free 12-page pamphlet entitled *Consumer Information about Air Travel for the Handicapped* to explain available arrangements and how to get them. Other publications giving valuable information about facilities for the handicapped are: the book *Travel Ability,* by Lois Reamy, published by Macmillan; the book *Access to the World,* by Louise Weiss, published by Chatham Square Press and available by mail from Access, Box 8B, 154 E. 29 St., New York, NY 10016 ($8.95 postpaid), and the annually revised guide *The Wheelchair Traveler,* by Douglass R. Annand, Ball Hill Rd., Milford, NH 03055.

METRIC CONVERSION.

CONVERTING METRIC TO U.S. MEASUREMENTS

Multiply:	by:	to find:
Length		
millimeters (mm)	.039	inches (in)
meters (m)	3.28	feet (ft)
meters	1.09	yards (yd)
kilometers (km)	.62	miles (mi)
Area		
hectare (ha)	2.47	acres
Capacity		
liters (L)	1.06	quarts (qt)
liters	.26	gallons (gal)
liters	2.11	pints (pt)
Weight		
gram (g)	.04	ounce (oz)
kilogram (kg)	2.20	pounds (lb)
metric ton (MT)	.98	tons (t)

Power

kilowatt (kw)	1.34	horsepower (hp)

Temperature

degrees Celsius	9/5 (then add 32)	degrees Fahrenheit

CONVERTING U.S. TO METRIC MEASUREMENTS

Multiply:	by	to find:
Length		
inches (in)	25.40	millimeters (mm)
feet (ft)	.30	meters (m)
yards (yd)	.91	meters
miles (mi)	1.61	kilometers (km)
Area		
acres	.40	hectares (ha)
Capacity		
pints (pt)	.47	liters (L)
quarts (qt)	.95	liters
gallons (gal)	3.79	liters
Weight		
ounces (oz)	28.35	grams (g)
pounds (lb)	.45	kilograms (kg)
tons (t)	1.11	metric tons (MT)
Power		
horsepower (hp)	.75	kilowatts
Temperature		
degrees Fahrenheit	5/9 (after subtracting 32)	degrees Celsius

 EMERGENCY TELEPHONE NUMBERS. For police, fire, or ambulance, dial 911. The Manhattan fire department may also be reached on 628–2900; the fire department also possesses medical emergency equipment.

INTRODUCTION TO
NEW YORK CITY

The Cosmopolitan Colossus

by **MICHAEL IACHETTA**

They call New York City "The Big Apple," and perhaps you wonder why.

The name was originally used in the 1920s and '30s by colorful people in the sports and entertainment world—particularly jazz musicians—as a way of saying, "I'm playing New York City; I've made it to the big time—the Big Apple." A variation on the same theme goes: "There are many apples on the tree, but when you pick New York City, you pick the Big Apple."

At least that's the explanation offered by Charles Gillett, president of the New York Convention and Visitors Bureau. He should know. Gillett is the sharpie who created and launched the Big Apple advertising campaign in 1971—a campaign that today lures approximately 17½ million visitors who spend over $2 billion annually in New York City.

The native New Yorker, whether born, bred, or transplanted here, thinks that the Big Apple is the greatest city in the world. And New Yorkers usually go out of their way to make sure visitors leave with the same impression.

With New York City attracting more visitors than any other city in the world, tourism is a major factor in its economy. The New York "attitude" may take some getting used to—that brusque, diffident manner that ignores everyone else on the street is basically a way to get a few extra moments of solitude—but most citizens in all five boroughs appreciate the never-ending parade of new arrivals who come here to explore the city's wealth of attractions.

Right from the start we'll admit that New York City *can* overwhelm you—with statistics alone: There are more than 100,000 hotel rooms in every price category; and over 350 theaters, 120 museums, 400 art galleries, and 37 single-spaced pages of restaurants in the New York telephone directory's business Yellow Pages. But statistics alone do not make up a city.

New York is, first and foremost, a gateway to America, and a swinging gateway at that—and has been almost since its birth. Endless succeeding generations continue New York City's tradition of ethnicity —from Chinatown to Little Italy, Yorkville, the West Side, all around the town. At its core, however, the Big Apple is much more than East Side chic and Madison Avenue slick, Brooklyn and Bronx street smarts and Queens and Staten Island middle-American open hearts. At the core of the Big Apple is the New Yorker, a very special breed, walking around to his or her personal version of "Lullabye of Broadway," no matter in which borough they live.

They may not go around humming "New York, New York, what a wonderful town" or singing that paean of praise to the Big Apple, "New York, New York," as Frank Sinatra does, but New Yorkers know that their city is a unique place. And a surprising number of our 8 million residents are anxious to help you get to know their city. Forget about the stereotype of the cold, blasé New Yorker. Are you in doubt about how to get from here to there? Is the subway map a maze of indecipherable colors, letters, and numbers? Just ask someone. But be prepared for the answer to come in any one of a variety of accents, depending on where you are.

Indeed, the average New Yorker can be an endless font of information. He or she can tell you all about "The Met," be it the Metropolitan Opera House, the Metropolitan Museum of Art, or the Mets baseball team. Of the Opera House at Lincoln Center they'll tell you of the moment when the dazzling crystal chandeliers begin to rise, signaling the start of a world-class opera, ballet, classical, or pop concert. Of the museum they'll tell of the New American and Chinese wings, the costume department, or the grand staircase and foyer by which you enter the building from Fifth Avenue. Of the Mets, who play out at Queens' Shea Stadium—well, they'll cheer on the local underdog team even if they try to steer you to Yankee Stadium instead, where you can catch the "Bronx Bombers," as the Yankees are affectionately known.

In short, whatever your taste, the Big Apple has something—and more—to satisfy it. But don't be tempted to bite off more than you can chew, especially at first bite. In other words, don't try to see and do everything at once. Break down your visit into manageable parts. First take a quick look at *Fodor's New York City* and decide what your "must see" attractions are, and give these high priority on your list of things to do. The book is organized so that you can conveniently group certain visits together—for example, the Statue of Liberty in the morning, the Wall Street area (including Trinity Church, the New York Stock Exchange, and Fraunces Tavern) in midafternoon, and the World Trade Center as close to sunset as you can time it make a full day of glorious sightseeing.

You may also want to decide right away whether you'll limit your excursions to Manhattan Island—as most tourists do—or whether you'll "take" the Bronx and Staten Island, too (as the song goes), or even Brooklyn and Queens; or take your visit borough-by-borough, neighborhood-by-neighborhood. This will save you a great deal of travel time on subways and buses or in cabs and automobiles, and you'll be fresh for the "real" business at hand: sightseeing, shopping, eating, and otherwise exploring the city.

Here, then, is a quick look at what the five boroughs have to offer, an appetizer of sorts before the movable feast that is the city as a whole. (Additional attractions and more detailed listings about those mentioned below are given in the appropriate sections of this book.)

We have to say, first of all, something that you seldom read about New York City: It is so frequently beautiful, especially in the spring and fall, though most prefer the fall, when the leaves color. The view of the midtown buildings from the Great Lawn up in Central Park is stunning and dramatic. Sunsets over the Hudson River (viewing from the West Side) can be spectacular, and the river is impressively majestic at all times.

There are those who call Manhattan the most exciting city in the world. But just as New York City is not the United States, Manhattan is not New York City. Indeed, Manhattan Island—you can prove to yourself that it is an island by taking a Circle Line cruise around it—is the smallest of the city's five boroughs. It is 13.4 miles long and only 2.3 miles across at its widest point, but it contains the artistic, financial, fashion, architectural, creative, and gourmet capitals of the world. We'll detail Manhattan's myriad offerings later, but the point for the moment is that while Manhattan is probably where you'll want to spend the bulk of your time in New York, visits to the other boroughs will help fill out your impressions of the city.

Almost everyone knows, for example, that Manhattan is at the heart of the nation's theatrical and musical activities. But the Brooklyn Academy of Music, known as BAM, has been one of the city's busiest performing arts centers since 1859. It is also the nation's oldest such complex, housing an opera house, a theater, numerous rehearsal areas, and several "performance spaces" that are used for small theatrical presentations and especially intimate concerts. Sarah Bernhardt played Camille here; Edwin Booth portrayed Hamlet, Pavlova danced *Swan Lake,* Enrico Caruso gave recitals. And all of their latter-day counterparts continue the august Academy's grand traditions.

Brooklyn may no longer have its own baseball team (the Dodgers moved to Los Angeles in 1958), but it would still rank as the fourth largest city in the country—if it were a city unto itself. Known to some as the "Borough of Churches" because of the number of its religious institutions—many dating back to pre-Civil War days—Brooklyn's highlights also include:

● The world's largest collection of Victorian brownstones in such neighborhoods as Brooklyn Heights (where literary figures Walt Whitman, Hart Crane, Arthur Miller, and Norman Mailer have lived);

● The Brooklyn Museum, bested only by those in London and Cairo for its Egyptian art collection;

● The extensive Botanic Gardens, with its special herb garden designed for the sightless;

● The Fulton Ferry, where Robert Fulton established his steam-powered ferry route from Manhattan in 1814 (recently refurbished and brought back into service for special weekend events);

● An endless variety of ethnic enclaves, with the Middle Eastern fare along Atlantic Avenue a particular standout from a culinary point of view;

● The city's most popular beach and amusement park—Coney Island and Astroland, respectively, where more than a million and a half people are likely to congregate on a hot summer Sunday;

● And, of course, the beautiful Brooklyn Bridge, spanning the East River from lower Manhattan. (The bridge has a wonderful pedestrian lane above the roadway, but it is scheduled for repairs and may be closed for a season or two.)

If Brooklyn is a borough of contrasts between industrial and shipping interests on the one hand, and 500-acre parks, miles-long beaches and well-preserved "olde New York" settlements on the other, Staten Island is the city's most rural area.

Staten Island (specifically, Tompkinsville) is where Giovanni da Verrazzano landed on April 17, 1524—the first European here.

An island of low, fertile hills and valleys, the borough—alternately known as Richmond—includes a wildlife refuge as part of Gateway National Park (parts of which are also in Brooklyn, Queens, and New Jersey) and much recreational parkland. The 80-acre Snug Harbor Cultural Center constitutes the largest single restoration project going on in the U.S. Voorlezer's House—known as the original Little Red Schoolhouse and built in 1695—is the oldest elementary schoolhouse still standing in the nation. It is part of the Richmondtown Restoration, which features buildings, furnishings and crafts of the 17th, 18th, and 19th centuries . . . and more.

Would you believe, for example, that the highest point on the Atlantic Coast between Maine and Key West is on Staten Island? That's Todt Hill, almost 410 feet above sea level. And would you believe that despite its considerable historical legacy, Staten Island is probably most famous for its ferry ride—a five-mile excursion across New York Harbor to the southern tip of Manhattan. Almost 320 million people a year make the round trip (many of them commuting just as easily as others might by bus or subway), as beautiful a nautical experience as the Big Apple offers. The tab? Twenty-five cents—round trip!

Geographically, Queens is New York's biggest borough. Its 13 parks cover 6,000 acres of land. It contains nearly 300,000 homes, features two of the nation's most famous tennis stadiums, and two of its leading thoroughbred racetracks. It is home to the New York Jets and Mets, giving the borough both a pro football and pro baseball team. Queens also boasts New York City's two commercial airports—John F. Kennedy on the southern shore and La Guardia on the northern shore.

Although the two airports are less than ten miles apart, those shores provide 196 miles of waterfront, with fine Atlantic Ocean beaches offering a cool respite from summer heat and humidity. The Queens Museum's star attraction is the 15,000-square-foot model of New York City that was originally featured at the 1964 World's Fair. And both that museum and the Science Museum are located on the former fairgrounds site.

The Bronx is the northernmost borough of New York. It is known as the "Borough of Universities" because it has ten institutions of higher education—more than most countries in the world. Its 42 square miles (23 percent of which are parkland) include a veritable Zoo's-Who in the Bronx Zoo. World-renowned for its collection of more than 3,000 animals representing over 800 species, the Bronx Zoo is newly renovated with a monorail and a tramway, and with "cages" simulating the animals' natural habitats. Nearby is the borough's other main attraction, the New York Botanical Garden, whose 250-acre expanse includes the 40-acre wilderness Hemlock Forest beside the Bronx River Gorge.

Because the Bronx is preeminently residential, many of its neighborhoods retain their original character. City Island, for instance, is a bit of seafaring New England tucked away on Long Island Sound—a nautical enclave of century-old houses and boatyards where America Cup-winning sailboats have been built. Other Bronx features:

- Mott Haven Historic District, with townhouses dating back to the Civil War era;
- Riverdale's fine country-style churches;
- The Van Cortlandt Mansion, dating back to before 1758, which served as headquarters for both American and British troops during the Revolution;
- And the wide avenue known as the Grand Concourse—a curving 4½-mile boulevard patterned after Paris' Champs Elysées, with the largest collection of Art Deco residences in the world.

For recreation-seekers the Bronx offers four 18-hole golf courses, the three-mile-long Orchard Beach, Pelham Bay Park, and an outdoor arena whose name tells all: Yankee Stadium.

By now you get the point that the Big Apple has more to offer than Manhattan's concrete canyons, skyscrapers, museums, theaters, nightclubs, restaurants, shopping districts, hotels, and pleasure palaces. If it is worth going beyond Manhattan's borders to sample what the rest of the city has to offer, there is still no denying that Manhattan is where most of the "action" really is.

Although most New Yorkers calmly ignore the fact, their hometown has been the political capital of the world for over a quarter of a century—ever since the United Nations set up headquarters here in 1952, on land that is international territory, donated by John D. Rockefeller for the purpose. But New York City is more than a political capital. It is the international marketplace of ideas, and the great catalyst of projects in publishing, advertising, entertainment, and finance.

Like Paris, London, and Rome, it is a capital of cosmopolitan thought with a large and diversified diplomatic corps whose members, many in colorful dress, add spice to the fashion parade. They also add glitter, excitement, sometimes mystery, to social functions and parties, and assure the reputation of the hostesses; their opinions and appearances add leaven to panel discussions on nationwide television broadcasts, and their thoughts often are recorded by energetic newsmen.

Even though it has only three major daily newspapers of its own, New York remains a world press center. Its columnists are read, via syndication, in papers all over America—and in some foreign countries. The faces and voices of television news personalities based in New York City are as familiar to Americans across the country as they are to viewers in the metropolitan area. The gossip that is generated by the comings and goings of people in the entertainment world is avidly read by newspaper readers all over the country. Who hasn't heard of Earl Wilson and his night-walking, night-stalking brethren? Similarly, and for less understandable reasons, the lives, loves, and leisure-time pursuits of New York area society, as minutely chronicled by an oversized corps of society writers, are of more moment to column readers in any town on the other side of the Hudson than is news of their own local school-board elections.

Equally important is the answer to the questions, what are the television, film, and Broadway stars and the international social leaders wearing this season . . . this month . . . this week? New York City is a world capital of fashion and glamour; *Women's Wear Daily* tells it first to the trade and the word spreads out from there.

It is true that the most beautiful women in the world can be seen strolling along Fifth and Madison Avenues, and that they will be dressed in the latest styles, some in quiet good taste, some in the bizarre fashions women's magazines contend "everyone" is wearing this year. (And a lot of New Yorkers are.) The Garment Center serves two masters: the average American woman—and the society leaders. The average American woman is the best-dressed "average" in the world because Seventh Avenue designers and manufacturers make it possible for her to dress smartly, even with chic, at budget costs. Helping the secretary, the department store clerk, the office worker dress well is the major burden of Seventh Avenue, for there are so many of these lovely women in the work force around the country, and their appearance—appealing, charming, attractive—has been a cause for comment by visiting foreigners. They are aided in their task, of course, by the cosmeticians, the hairdressers, milliners, furriers—and all the others who labor in the vineyard, the New York City vineyard, to make the American woman one of the best dressed in the world.

Society leaders insist on the innovations, the sometimes outlandish distinctive touches, that attract the cameras and columnists—and the designers serve them so well that it has now come to the point where women at a formal dress party may be wearing just about anything that seems new and different and still be dressed in style. And if some designs are shocking—what of it? It's grist for the fashion writer's mill, and likely to lead to a nationwide reputation for the designer.

As a shopping center, New York City is incomparable. To this market place, this giant bazaar, flow goods from all over the world, from a splendiferous new Rolls Royce to a carving set handcrafted by an artisan in a far-off village of Kashmir, from the latest Danish modern furniture to an antique candlestick holder from Yemen. New York City abounds in shops of every variety and size. There are the well-known department stores, such as Macy's and Gimbels, and the obscure grocery stores selling dried seaweed, bean curd, and other exotica essential to Japanese-style cookery. Almost anything that is available anywhere in the world can be found somewhere in New York City.

Start, for example, with the sidewalks of Manhattan's Fifth Avenue, from 34th to 59th Streets. Here, skyscrapers, traditional office buildings, and banks mix with the giant department stores and bookshops, jewelers, shoe stores, men's and women's haberdashers, specialists in crystal, porcelain, leatherware, tobacco products, toys, and more. Still more stores spread along the streets east and west of Fifth Avenue, especially on the main thoroughfares of 34th, 42nd, and 57th Streets. At Herald Square—where 34th Street meets Broadway and Avenue of the Americas (Sixth Avenue)—Macy's and Gimbels tower over opposite corners vying to bring shoppers the most of everything at the best of prices.

Due south of this famous intersection (which is the last stop on the Macy's Thanksgiving Day Parade route—an event televised all over the world) is the discount camera center. The prices here are so low that even Japanese tourists frequent the shops along West 32nd and 33rd Streets for "imported" bargains. To the north, on 47th Street between Fifth Avenue and Avenue of the Americas, is the diamond district. Eighty percent of the diamonds bought and sold in the U.S. are traded on this one block!

Still more shops stretch off Fifth Avenue from 49th to 51st Streets in the labyrinthine underground passages beneath Rockefeller Center's skyscrapers. West 57th Street is sprinkled with fabric shops and fashion boutiques and, as you head eastward, increasingly with art galleries and specialty shops. Second, Third, and Lexington Avenues, in the 50s and 60s, are for the *très chic,* what with Bloomingdale's—by far the city's most notoriously trendy department store—exclusive boutiques and haughty antique dealers.

Madison Avenue, also on the East Side, has its own shopping character from the mid-50s up to as far as 90th Street. The boutiques of leading international designers, galleries with the latest in contemporary art (as well as considerable pickings for more traditional tastes), and stylish houseware shops and restaurants fill to overflowing with the smart set.

Across town, on the Upper West Side along Columbus Avenue and Broadway (in both cases from about 66th to 79th Streets), tastes are a little less trendy. Returning down the West Side along Broadway or Seventh Avenue and into the 30s brings you to the garment district, where one third of all clothes worn in the U.S. are manufactured. A few more blocks south is the fur district, where some manufacturers sell retail as well as wholesale.

In shopping terms, Greenwich Village has lost much of its former distinction as a center for unusual crafts, handmade goods, and specialty shops. Nonetheless, a handful of established book and antique dealers, and even the occasional craftsperson have withstood the change in the Village's character—the book and antique people mostly centered around Broadway between 9th and 13th streets, the craftspeople sprinkled throughout the East and West Villages.

Over the past decade the warehouses and factories of SoHo—the abbreviation stands for "South of Houston Street"—have been converted into artists' studios and loft apartments upstairs, and art galleries, craft shops, and clothing boutiques on the lower floors. East of SoHo is Little Italy, where the best pasta, salami, espresso coffee and, especially along Mulberry Street and its immediate offshoots, the best genuinely Italian restaurants are to be found. Canal Street, the southern boundary of Little Italy and SoHo, is the street for appliances, hardware, and all manner of supplies for the do-it-yourselfer.

Canal Street is also the dividing line between Little Italy and Chinatown. On Mott Street south of Canal, you'll discover some of the best—and often least expensive—Chinese food in town, or anywhere. The service may be indifferent (waiters don't always understand English, and there's nothing leisurely about the pace), and the surroundings only a step removed from basic coffee shop, but the experience and shops are alone worth the visit.

The Lower East Side, particularly along Orchard, Eldridge, and Grand Streets, is a bargain hunter's paradise. Designer clothes, men's furnishings, towels, sheets, lingerie, handbags, shoes, children's clothing, wallpaper, yarns, and fabric are among the "finds" in small, crowded shops where discounts usually run to 20 percent off uptown prices. This is a predominately Jewish area, and many of the shops are closed on Saturdays—the Jewish Sabbath—but open for a full day beginning bright and early Sunday morning. It may not be wholesale, but the prices come about as close to that mark as you're likely to find anywhere.

In fact, "getting it wholesale" is one of many New Yorkers' favorite games—plants in the West 20s, lighting fixtures and restaurant/cooking supplies along the Bowery, Latin American foods on East 116th Street, Italian goods along Arthur Avenue in the Bronx, Middle Eastern specialties on Brooklyn's Atlantic Avenue. The New York City section in most local bookstores has several slim volumes with detailed information on Lower East Side and other discount/wholesale shopping areas.

But of all these things, clothing is the most important, and women from around the country, during visits, flock to the New York City stores and shops they have heard and read about in the national magazines.

And the crowds in New York's shops these days are being swelled by visitors from abroad who are discovering that the long-time relative decline of the dollar has made the United States a vacation paradise—the phrase that used to be used so often for the benefit of dollar-bearing Americans traveling in foreign lands. Oriental and European commercial and financial institutions have set up shop, too, in New York City; and in midtown Manhattan today you can see as many Japanese as you used to see Americans in Tokyo wandering around the Ginza.

Besides all this, New York City is a center of maritime commerce—and in fact is the second busiest port in the world (after Rotterdam).

Financier to the Nation

Despite the recent and widely publicized miseries of its own fiscal administration, New York is still the financial center to much of the world (the flood of foreign investment into America has captured attention of late); and its tradition for shrewd wheeling and dealing began in 1626, only seventeen years after Henry Hudson, an Englishman on a Dutch payroll, first explored it thoroughly. Peter Minuit, the first Dutch governor, thought he had put over a fast deal on the Manhattan Indians who had sold him the island for $24 worth of trinkets. But the Indians were the commercial ancestors of the sharpies who sold the Brooklyn Bridge to generations of credulous hayseeds—the friendly "First Americans" didn't even own the land they sold; their village was in Inwood, about twelve miles away, on the northern tip of the island.

Although the British first took the city as an act of war in 1664, they finally managed to hold onto it with the help of a shady deal involving the swap of New York for the Caribbean island of Curaçao, of all places. But while the Dutch had New York (it was Nieuw Amsterdam then, of course) they welcomed the first Jews to land in what is now the United States—twenty-three men, women, and children who were the forerunners of New York's present Jewish population of well over one million.

New York got its first newspaper in 1725, and ten years later freedom of the press was established in North America when its publisher, John Zenger, was acquitted of a libel charge. New Yorkers were split in their allegiance during the Revolutionary War; the city was a battleground during part of it, and Nathan Hale, a young schoolteacher given a spy assignment by George Washington, was hanged by the British near the present site of Grand Central Station. It was a battleground, too, during the Civil War, but the fighting then was between the police and New Yorkers rioting in protest against the draft laws. They've been exerting their right to protest ever since. Union Square became the focal point of the antiwar demonstrations of the late 1960s and early '70s, just as it was the heart of the Communist May Day parades during the Depression-ridden Thirties.

The United States experienced its greatest period of growth after the Civil War, and so did New York. The huge waves of immigration began to sweep in from Europe, and most of the wealth resulting from the winning of the West seemed to flow through New York. This was the era of the great millionaires: J. P. Morgan, the banker; Andrew Carnegie and Henry C. Frick, the steel men; and the transportation magnate, Commodore Cornelius Vanderbilt, whose nautical title derived from his operation of the Staten Island ferry. It was also the time of the newspaper giants: Horace Greeley, of the New York *Tribune,* James Gordon Bennett of the *Herald,* Joseph Pulitzer of the *World,* and then William Randolph Hearst and his *Evening Journal.*

New York was a big city in the Nineties, with a population 1,500,-000. But it really became a world metropolis on January 1, 1898, when Brooklyn, the Bronx, Queens, and Richmond (Staten Island) were combined with Manhattan to form Greater New York; in 1900, the expanded city's population neared 3,500,000.

In the early years of this century, the central city, trapped on Manhattan Island, found a new direction for growth—straight up. The skyscraper, architectural trademark of New York, started with the twenty-story Flatiron Building in 1902, and in 1913 the 60-story Woolworth Building became the tallest in the world. It held this title for seven years, until it was displaced by the 77-story Chrysler Building. The Chrysler's primacy lasted only eleven years, until 1931, when the 102-story Empire State Building became king. Even though a television tower brought its height up to 1,694 feet, it was surpassed in 1972 by the twin-tower 110-story World Trade Center in the downtown financial district. Sadly for New York though, it lost its world skyscraper championship in 1974, when the Sears Roebuck building was opened in Chicago.

The New York that draws and fascinates visitors is the city of gleaming skyscrapers and shining opportunity, and the way to come upon it is as the immigrants did it, from the sea. You can do this, no matter what part of the country you are driving from, by routing yourself into Elizabeth or Bayonne, New Jersey, crossing one of the bridges to Staten Island, and driving to the St. George car ferry, which crosses to the Battery. Then you'll come to Manhattan from the Upper Bay, with the Statue of Liberty and Ellis Island (where the immigrants were processed in the old days) on your left, and the military reservation of Governor's Island on your right. During the twenty-minute ride, the magnificent skyline of the downtown financial district will loom larger and larger directly in front of you, and you'll feel the full impact of this most dramatic city on earth.

Next best way to do it—and this takes more detailed arranging—is to fly into La Guardia airport (planes landing at John F. Kennedy airport generally do their circling too far away for a good view of the heart of the city) at twilight, when darkness creeps up from the city streets, and the lights go on in a million windows all over town.

These are the quickest ways to get a feeling for the glamorous and exciting New York—the New York of Broadway openings and experimental plays in Greenwich Village warehouses, of smart restaurants in the East Fifties, cooperative apartments on upper Fifth Avenue, and television production centers around Radio City; of advertising agencies and magazine offices on Madison Avenue; of Lincoln Center, Carnegie Hall and the art galleries along 57th Street; of all the power, wealth, energy and talent that, despite its faults and problems, still make The Big Apple the capital of the world.

The Visitor's New York

This is the New York of the visitor and of the eager, career-bound arrival—and of a relatively small proportion of the city's residents. But it is a city that millions of New Yorkers living in a thousand neighborhood communities in Upper Manhattan, Brooklyn, the Bronx, Queens, and Staten Island know little about. They still talk about "going to New York" when they're planning a visit to midtown Manhattan, and many do this only on such occasions as birthdays and wedding anniversaries. It's equally unfamiliar to the 400,000 commuters who come into the city five mornings a week and then return at night to hundreds of suburban "dormitory" communities in Long Island, northern New Jersey, New York's Westchester and Rockland counties, and southwestern Connecticut.

If Manhattan Island sounded small to begin with, the "New York" of the tourist and visitor is basically a smaller still rectangular piece of that land mass about a half-mile wide and about one and one-quarter miles long. Its boundaries are roughly 59th Street on the north, 33rd Street on the south, Third Avenue on the east, and Eighth Avenue on the west. Within this tight little area of less than a square mile are the two major railroad stations, all the airline offices, the bus terminal, all the major department stores and legitimate theaters, most of the night-clubs, almost all the well-known hotels, plus Times Square, Rockefeller Center, Carnegie Hall, Madison Square Garden, the New York Coliseum, and two of the tallest buildings on earth. Just outside its peripheries are Lincoln Center, Central Park, the United Nations headquarters, and the most expensive and elegant residential areas. Even though the visitor will make occasional forays to such outlying points as Chinatown and the financial district to the south, and the Metropolitan Museum of Art to the north, most of his New York will be in this one small section.

Unknown to him are the neighborhoods where New Yorkers live— the Inwoods and Yorkvilles, the Williamsburgs and Flatbushes, the Mott Havens and Morrisanias, the Flushings and the Ozone Parks, or the ghettos of East Harlem and Bedford Stuyvesant—which form the borderlands of the glamorous New York and which are the crucibles in which New Yorkers are created.

Because they are products of such crucibles, New Yorkers know how easy it is to get burnt here. So they are ever wary of the jostler, the pickpocket, the hustler, the hit-and-run thief, the modern-day equivalent of the conman out to sell you the Brooklyn Bridge. The sophisticated traveler, of course, is ever ready for some version of the hustle—and not just on the disco dance floor. So do be careful.

The Philosophic Cabdriver

Nonetheless, New York's problems somehow seem worse than those of other cities. Partly this is because of the city's size and the density with which its population is concentrated. Visitors (except possibly those from Tokyo) are invariably amazed at the crush of people traveling on the buses and subways during the height of the rush hour (8–9 A.M. and 5–6 P.M. If *your* schedule allows, we suggest avoiding public transportation at those times. Cabs, incidentally, are not easy to find at rush hour either (and most seem to disappear from the city's streets altogether at the first sign of rain).

To understand New York, the visitor must understand something of the New Yorker and his own perception that New York City life is a trade-off situation. Living in the city demands a certain willingness to put up with a variety of tensions—from air, noise, and street pollution to crowding to a deterioration of personalized services to small living quarters that often cost astronomical prices. But this is all in exchange for having full-time access to the greatest variety of cultural offerings in the world and, as the die-hard natives so willingly point out, it's all a matter of being a part of a city that is at the core of the political, economic, fashion, culinary, and other trends of the day.

That trade-off is also what forces the New Yorker into a very unique kind of insulation. Stop a passerby for directions on the street and don't be surprised if it isn't until the person has moved on a few steps that he turns to answer; New Yorkers are so accustomed to being asked for spare change and so wary of street thieves that they tend to just keep walking in all situations. Give them a few seconds to realize that the request was for help, though, and most of the time they'll respond graciously. Similarly, New Yorkers themselves will steal a few minutes on a subway ride for personal reflection, tuning out the noise and the crowd by tuning in to a personal stereo or simply by shutting their eyes or maybe even meditating. It's not that the New Yorker is unfriendly—it's more that he's forced to adapt to a life-style that is often at odds with a more traditional way of life, or at least the way of life with which most visitors are familiar and comfortable. Because there's more of just about everything here, there's also more competition to be seen, heard, and appreciated.

The cabdriver is a special kind of New Yorker. Added to all his other annoyances (and it should be mentioned that there are increasing numbers of female cabdrivers to be found) is the crowning frustration of New York traffic. "Gridlock" is a term new even to New Yorkers; it means that traffic is blocked in all directions at a given intersection. Cabs and trucks seem forever to be at the heart of these locked grids. This, together with the general never-easy flow of cars, the ever changing rules governing city streets, and the fact that many cab drivers are would-be actors, musicians, restaurateurs, and the like and really don't want to be driving a cab, help explain why cabbies are often so garrulous. As with any group of people, some are genuinely informative and obliging, while others (the best publicized) are out for the quick buck.

Whaddya Say?

In meeting and understanding native New Yorkers, the language barrier is not as formidable as it might at first seem to anyone whose impressions are based on having seen and heard New Yorkers in the movies. It must be recognized at the outset that the Jewish influence on the New Yorker is as important as the Irish influence is on the Bostonian. New Yorkers are likely to look upon their lives with the wry, sardonic, humorous cynicism that has formed part of the Jew's protective armor down through the ages. Perhaps this is why some television comic material sometimes sounds strange to audiences in Kansas City. The New Yorker's speech, threaded with Yiddish words that now have entered the local vocabulary for good, is likely to carry a rising inflection. Public relations men hailing from the Midwest, and not of the Jewish faith, think nothing of hanging over the bar in P. J. Clarke's calling each other "schlemiel," or accusing a client of having "chutzpah," a marvelous guttural-sounding Yiddish word that means "gall" and sounds like it. Common among New Yorkers is the practice of answering a question with a question, or answering a question with a shrug that employs all the facial muscles, the arms and shoulders, and even some back muscles.

While there are some quaint grammatical variations in the New York language, it's the pronunciation, the slurring together, the elimination of vital vowels and letters, that confuse the out-of-town listener. These accents are getting more homogenized with each passing day, but they still exist to a surprising degree.

Learning Native Customs

Despite this seeming barbarity of speech, many New Yorkers achieve an advanced state of civilized development, and the visitor seeking to acclimatize himself to New York would do well to adapt suitable local customs to his own needs. For example, New Yorkers have learned how to live with the fact that their city is probably the only one in the world besides Tokyo that suffers from *pedestrian* traffic jams.

This means no stopping at high noon on the sunny side of Fifth Avenue to tie shoelaces, no bunching up at street corners to talk with friends, and no milling around in front of theaters after the performance. Failure to observe these simple precautions could lead to a collision of bodies that would pile up and block all sidewalk traffic.

And beware of the push-boys. They are the men and boys who push the carts carrying clothes from one place to another in the Seventh Avenue garment district. They boldly thrust ahead, looking neither to right nor left, all the while shouting, "Watch it!" Jump when they come your way. The messengers on bicycle, tearing at full speed through red lights—and packs of crossing pedestrians—and usually going the wrong way on one-way streets are another danger.

Visitors wishing to observe the quaint feeding habits of New Yorkers can watch them eat on the run at a hot dog stand or counter restaurant, or at their leisure in a swank place in the East 60s. New Yorkers eating their fast-food lunch indulge in none of the niceties of Continental dining. Typically, hundreds of people are served between noon and 2 P.M. in establishments that will have only counter stools and too few

Manhattan Points of Interest

Points of Interest

1) Carnegie Hall
2) Central Park Zoo
3) Chinatown
4) Citicorp Center
5) City Hall
6) Cloisters
7) Coliseum
8) Columbia University
9) East Side Airlines Terminal
10) Empire State Building
11) Frick Museum
12) Gracie Mansion
13) Gramercy Park
14) Grand Central Station
15) Grant's Tomb
16) Guggenheim Museum
17) Hayden Planetarium
18) Lincoln Center

19) Madison Square Garden
20) Metropolitan Museum of Art
21) Museum of Modern Art
22) Museum of Natural History
23) N.Y. Convention Center (Constr.)
24) Pennsylvania Station
25) Port Authority Bus Terminal
26) Rockefeller Center
27) St. Patrick's Cathedral
28) South Street Seaport

29) N.Y. Stock Exchange
30) United Nations
31) Whitney Museum
32) World Trade Center
33) Museum of the American Indian;
    American Numismatic Society;
    Hispanic Society of America
34) Studio Museum of Harlem
35) New York University

waiters or waitresses. This is accomplished by feeding each patron in an average time of 15 minutes.

Fancy eating, which we now call dining, takes up to three hours, and at lunch time is indulged in by owners of companies, salesmen entertaining clients, public relations men, and well-to-do visitors. Headwaiters, captains, wine stewards, and just plain waiters hover around these guests brandishing huge menus offering delicacies from around the world. Dining well is one of the real pleasures of a New York City visit.

The City

This then is New York City; in population only the seventh-largest city in the world (Shanghai is first), and even so splintered into its own little cities; always a pacesetter, yet in some ways unbearably provincial; city of opportunity for the ambitious, the eager and the talented from all over the country, yet a stern testing ground where many fall by the wayside in face of brutal competition; a gourmet's paradise—and at the same time a city of greasy spoon restaurants; art center of the world, a city of symphony, opera, drama—a city of television watchers and street-corner cowboys; magnet for the starry eyed—magnet for the drifter, the junkie, the criminal; a city whose skyscrapers of concrete and glass startle, assault, sometimes titillate the senses—a city of many dirty streets, shabby buildings, unbearable traffic. In short, despite the gripes and complaints, it is what every New Yorker—born or adopted—really feels about his hometown: New York *is* the greatest city in the world. It may often be subconscious or only secret, but somewhere, somehow, every New Yorker is really proud that his city, in great measure, entertains, educates, finances, and clothes the rest of the nation—and a not inconsiderable part of the rest of the world.

NEW YORK'S SPECIAL PLEASURES

Essays on Its Arts, Entertainment, and Food

Many thousands of newcomers to New York City who come here on business or as tourists are captured by the city's less mundane delights. Others are drawn here for these special pleasures themselves.

Because these facets of the city are so central to its spirit, we have assembled here essays on ten of them: the New York of literary excitement, of the dance, theater, and classical music and opera—and the New York of jazz and pop music; of art and architecture, of the worlds of broadcasting and fashion. And, of course, the food of the world-famous Manhattan restaurants.

Each essay is written by a long-time New Yorker who is both an expert in his or her area and a well-known author, journalist, or critic. (More detailed information on the areas is offered in the Practical Information section later in the book.)

LITERARY NEW YORK CITY

by
LINDA D. CIRINO

Linda D. Cirino is co-author, with Susan Edmiston, of A Guide to
Literary New York, *reprinted by Damon Press, Box 224, Leonia, New
Jersey 07605. The book, on which this article is based, provides walking
tours of the literary places in each neighborhood in the city.*

In New York we can accompany Mark Twain in his white serge suit,
his white hair flowing, as he marches up Fifth Avenue, crowds abuzz,
to meet his friend Howells for tea. Standing near the Brooklyn Bridge
one can watch Walt Whitman stepping off Brooklyn Ferry and seating
himself beside the driver of a horse-drawn cab from whose perch he
observes the life of the city. At the South Street Seaport one can find
Melville's New York, when the harbor was alive with boats and no one
missed an after-supper walk along the river.

Each of us brings to the city a group of characters we know from
books we have read. It may be Stuart Little at the boat races in Central
Park or Irving's Diedrich Knickerbocker. Every visitor to the city adds
a personal dimension that augments enjoyment of it. Books we have
read and authors who have given us pleasure provide images that make
the city vibrate with life. So many New York scenes have been painted
in the literature of America's great writers. The chaos and variety of
New York life, the swarming masses of immigrants, the richness of
ethnic diversity—all elements the city still boasts—were sources for the
basic texts in American poetry and prose. No other place in America
can claim the number of famous writers in residence as New York. Poe,
James, Wharton, Dreiser, Lewis—there is hardly an American writer
who did not spend some time here.

Old New York

In the 1800s, when the New York life was small-scale and most of
the city was below 14th Street, rural refreshment abounded in the farms
of Midtown. Washington Irving, the first native-born writer to become
known abroad, began to write while he was living in a house on the
northwest corner of Ann and William streets, the site marked today

with a plaque. Irving Place, in Gramercy, is, of course, named for
Washington Irving, the Knickerbocker writer, but is really O. Henry
country. O. Henry, like others after him, believed that he was living
only a few doors from Irving's home, thought to be on the corner of
17th Street and Irving Place. This error is perpetuated today in the
bronze plaque on the building, though there is none on 46 East 21st
Street, the home of a nephew where Irving often did stay. A restaurant
occupies the first-floor parlor of O. Henry's home at 55 Irving Place,
where he spent hours at the window observing the passing scene of
Baghdad-on-the-Hudson. James Fenimore Cooper's residence at 145
Bleecker Street was "too magnificent for our simple French tastes"
according to Mrs. Cooper in 1833, though today one finds no proof of
it. Edgar Allan Poe moved to 85 West 3rd Street in 1845 to avoid the
heat of the downtown area.

Greenwich Village

On the north side of Washington Square you'll find most of the
fashionable early nineteenth-century homes that graced the square in
the days of Henry James and Edith Wharton; the Bohemian life was
lived in the blocks surrounding the square.

James was born at 21 Washington Place, a few steps from his grandmother's home on the elegant north side of the square, the atmosphere
of which he reproduced in *Washington Square* and other works.
Though Wharton lived on the square for only a brief time, she used it
as the setting of many of her books, which describe the life of the
aristocrats who frequented the place.

Before the First World War the area had attracted an intellectual
elite of political activists, poets, and writers interested in experimental
art forms and life styles. The staff of *The Masses,* a radical political
magazine, and the crowd that met at Mabel Dodge's salon on lower
Fifth Avenue lived in the Village; the poets and playwrights who were
associated with the Provincetown Players, where Eugene O'Neill got
his start, lived here, and major novelists, such as Theodore Dreiser and
Sinclair Lewis, came here to live and work.

The Parisian turn of the streets and old homes heavy with character
contribute to the charm of the Village. Edna St. Vincent Millay burned
her candle at both ends in an apartment at 25 Charlton Street and
captivated dozens of men who sat at her feet as she read her poems.
Critic and historian Edmund Wilson, one of her beaux, lived at 3
Washington Square North and later at 1 University Place. John Dos
Passos, author of *Manhattan Transfer,* reluctant to live anywhere for
very long, lived in the studio, originally stables, behind 3 Washington
Square North for a time in 1922, renting it from E. E. Cummings' wife

Elaine. Cummings, a long-time resident of the Village, lived at 4 Patchin Place from 1923 until his death in 1962, by which time he had taken over nearly all the floors in the house.

Thomas Wolfe came to teach at New York University in 1923 and lived a short walk away in Room 2220 of the Hotel Albert on University Place at 10th Street—now an apartment building. Wolfe describes his apartment at 13 East 8th Street in *The Web and the Rock,* but moves it to Waverly Place, and the apartment he shared with Aline Bernstein on 263 West 11th Street is described as being on 12th Street when he mentions it in the opening pages of *You Can't Go Home Again.*

Theodore Dreiser lived in every part of the city between his arrival in 1895 and the time he moved to California shortly before his death in 1945. His experience of the city provided background for his first novel, *Sister Carrie.* Dreiser's book is one of the first American novels in which the city appears as a protagonist.

Gay Street, a twisting alley that typifies the quaint image of the Village, appeared in the Broadway play *My Sister Eileen* written by Ruth McKenney, who lived there at number 14 with her sister, Eileen, who married Nathanael West, the New Yorker who later wrote *Miss Lonelyhearts.* Several doors down, at 18 Gay Street, Mary McCarthy lived while she worked as a drama critic for *Partisan Review,* the political magazine with radical roots and liberal fruit. McCarthy eventually moved to the more exclusive precincts of Sutton Place on the East Side, where she wrote *The Group* while living with Philip Rahv, an editor of *PR.*

72 Bank Street was the site of a lodging house for struggling artists, writers, and students, run by Marion Tanner, the model for Auntie Mame in the Patrick Dennis play of the same name.

Many of the restaurants where Village people met and drank and gathered after hours are gone, or are unrecognizable today, but Marta's at 75 Washington Place is still open under the same name and little changed from the time when Dos Passos, Elinor Wylie, and her husband William Rose Benét met there for dinner. There is a bar on 10th Street between Greenwich Avenue and Waverly Place, currently called the Ninth Circle, where Edward Albee found the title for his play *Who's Afraid of Virginia Woolf?.* He saw the words scrawled in soap on the mirror behind the bar and remembered them. The White Horse Tavern, at 567 Hudson Street, has treaded a line between working-class neighborhood bar and tourist attraction since the 1950s, when Dylan Thomas held court there. Norman Mailer used the White Horse as a living room for regular Sunday afternoon gatherings amid the sawdust. Though much changed from its heyday in the '40s and early '50s (it is now a Chinese restaurant), the San Remo café on the northwest corner of Bleecker and MacDougal was a hangout of the writers who lived in the area: James Agee, William Styron, as well as the Beats from the East Village—Allen Ginsberg, William Burroughs, and Jack Kerouac.

East Village/Lower East Side

In 1951, Ginsberg was the first of the Beats to move to the East Village, then called the Lower East Side. Nearly a slum, the East Village was a symbol of the Beats' rejection of the establishment literary scene, and the neighborhood also provided material for their work. Ginsberg, whose reputation for hospitality turned his home into a crash pad for his friends and struggling poets seeking advice, lived first in an apartment at 206 East 7th Street and later at 170 East 2nd Street. The area was in transition from the Jewish ghetto it had been to the Chinese/Puerto Rican/Italian mixture it is today. William Burroughs moved in with Ginsberg for a time, and Jack Kerouac was a frequent overnight guest when it was too late to go home to Queens. Kerouac also spent time at his girl friend's place at 501 East 11th Street, the setting of *The Subterraneans*. The building's inner courtyard was known as Paradise Alley. Ginsberg wrote *Kaddish* at 2nd Street and edited Burrough's *Naked Lunch* (originally titled *Naked Lust,* but misread by Kerouac—to Burrough's delight). LeRoi Jones, now Amiri Baraka, was part of the Ginsberg crowd, and lived at 7 Morton Street.

Norman Mailer lived at 39 First Avenue on the top floor of a tenement that had a kosher brewery on the ground floor. Dan Wolf, who later founded the *Village Voice* with Mailer and Ed Fancher, lived on the top floor of the house next door and would walk over the roof to visit Mailer.

Typical of New York's ability to accommodate a variety of literary styles, as well as life styles, is the fact that W. H. Auden, the English-born poet, lived in the East Village from 1953 until 1972—without consorting with the nearby Beat group. He lived at 77 St. Mark's Place, in the building where Trotsky printed *Novy Mir* in the basement.

The *Forward* Building at 175 East Broadway is the only link between today's Lower East Side area and the crowded, busy neighborhood that sheltered immigrants at the turn of the century. Abraham Cahan was editor of the *Forward,* and under him the Yiddish-language newspaper provided the Jewish community with advice and information for coping with American life. Cahan encouraged political participation and social adjustment, without neglecting the literary aspect. Isaac Bashevis Singer, the Nobel Prize-winning writer, began his career with contributions to the paper and still writes, in Yiddish, for the *Forward,* only later translating his stories for the English-reading public. Singer's home territory, however, is the Upper West Side, the eclectic area that is home to many of today's writers.

Upper West Side

When the Village became too expensive or too trendy, writers settled on the Upper West Side or the more posh East Side; some moved to the Hamptons on Long Island or to rural Connecticut.

Isaac Bashevis Singer has lived on the West Side, on 86th Street between Broadway and Amsterdam Avenue, longer than he lived in the Poland he writes about. He often eats at the Famous Dairy Restaurant on West 72nd Street, a vegetarian café like those that used to abound on the Lower East Side.

The fictional Glass family of J.D. Salinger lived in an apartment at 110th Street and Riverside Drive, not far from 390 Riverside Drive, where Salinger lived during his childhood.

Saul Bellow lived in New York during the fifties, and much of the scenery and feeling of the Upper West Side is captured in his *Seize the Day,* published while he was living at 333 Riverside Drive, in an apartment that had a river view only from the bathroom. Much of the action in *Herzog* and *Mr. Sammler's Planet* also takes place on the Upper West Side. Joseph Heller lives on West 80th Street, and Jack Gelber, whose play *The Connection* was a turning point in American theater, lives on West End Avenue in the 90s.

Writers today meet more frequently in the aisles of Zabar's delicatessen on Broadway between 80th and 81st streets than they do in literary salons.

Harlem

Arthur Miller was born on 111th Street, and before moving to Brooklyn lived in apartment 6B of the yellow brick building facing Central Park at 45 West 110th Street. Real-estate developers, who at the turn of the century were stuck with empty apartments after a building boom, opened the neighborhood to blacks from other parts of the city. Harlem became a middle-class black settlement. W. E. B. DuBois came in 1910 to edit the *Crisis,* a publication of the NAACP, and James Weldon Johnson, later NAACP executive secretary, and others came too. In the 1920s, a period that came to be called the Negro Renaissance, black writers were able to break into the white publishing world and find readers. Carl Van Vechten, talented white artist and writer, proved that books with a Negro theme would sell. His book *Nigger Heaven* (1926) began a flow from the pens of Harlem writers that did not stop until the drought years of the Depression. Claude

McKay's *Home to Harlem* (1928) set the scene, and the poems of Countee Cullen and Langston Hughes described the mood.

The social center of the Negro Renaissance was the mansion at 108 West 136th Street where A'Lelia Walker, daughter of the millionaire developer of a hair-straightening process, held court. For two years she ran a café where writers and artists could gather, calling it the Dark Tower, the name of Cullen's column in *Opportunity,* Charles Johnson's landmark Urban League publication. Today, the local branch of the public library, named for Countee Cullen, is on the site of the Walker mansion.

Around the corner is the new building that houses the Schomburg Collection, based on the donation by Arthur A. Schomburg, a Puerto Rican Negro who collected books on black history and literature. The Schomburg serves as a community meeting place and cultural center and offers a unique resource to writers.

The YMCA down the block has been a point of arrival for many of those attracted by the magic of Harlem. Ralph Ellison stayed there in 1936 and on his second day met Langston Hughes on the steps of the library. He arranged to be introduced to Richard Wright, who steered him from a career in jazz to the world of letters. Ellison, who still lives in the area, wrote *Invisible Man* while he was living at 749 St. Nicholas Avenue.

One of the few Harlem-born writers, James Baldwin was born across from the library at Harlem Hospital, Lenox Avenue at 135th Street. He chronicled his early life in *Go Tell it On the Mountain* and his play *The Amen Corner.* Baldwin met Wright after moving to the Village, and at the age of 24 he decided that "there was no point in my staying in the country at all. If I'd been born in Mississippi, I might have come to New York. But, being born in New York, there's no place that you can go. You have to go *out. Out* of the country." Since that time Baldwin has lived abroad, though his work is marked with the sensibilities he developed in Harlem.

In 1945, the Harlem Writers' Workshop was founded at the Harlem Y and served as a place for writers to read their work. Hughes read and Baldwin came, and the idea persists in the Harlem Writers' Guild, which meets at the Countee Cullen branch of the library on 136th Street. Contemporary writers Rosa Guy and John Oliver Killens organize and support the group.

Newspapers and Magazines—Midtown

The number of newspapers in New York is constantly dwindling, though the *Post* and the *Times* survive from the 1800s, when they shared Nassau Street, called Newspaper Row, with about a dozen others. William Bradford started the city's first newspaper in 1725 in Hanover Square (a plaque on the Cotton Exchange marks the site), the heart of the city at the time. William Cullen Bryant became editor of the *Evening Post* in 1825, James Gordon Bennett started the *Herald* in 1835, and Horace Greeley headed the *Tribune,* the first nationally distributed newspaper. Many of those whose reputations rest on more durable work wrote regularly for the newspapers. Walt Whitman, commuting on the (now-defunct) Brooklyn ferry, and Edgar Allan Poe, who came from Philadelphia to become editor and part owner of the *Broadway Journal,* described city life in short feature articles.

Bryant lived at 24 West 16th Street in a building that later was occupied by the offices of one of the "little magazines" that spent their brief lives igniting with their enthusiasm the creative spark of the city. In 1917, the *Little Review* moved from Chicago to 16th Street and continued its tradition of literary innovation. When the magazine printed James Joyce's *Ulysses* in installments, the first publication of the work anywhere, the editors were convicted of obscenity. Upstairs in the same building lived the struggling poet Hart Crane, who solicited the editors to publish his work. He later crossed the Brooklyn Bridge and lived in Brooklyn Heights, where he wrote his long poem, *The Bridge.* Also in 1917, the *Dial* which published quality criticism, poetry, and art, moved from Chicago to 152 West 13th Street. Marianne Moore, its editor from 1925 until it closed in 1929, lived at 14 St. Luke's Place, across the street from the Hudson Park branch of the New York Public Library where she had worked.

By 1914, H. L. Mencken and George Jean Nathan had taken over as editors of *Smart Set,* which brought Mencken to New York for frequent stops at the Algonquin Hotel, 59 West 44th Street, to meet with writers and discuss manuscripts. Eugene O'Neill, still living in poverty in the Village, had three plays appear in *Smart Set,* which also published some early F. Scott Fitzgerald stories. *Vanity Fair,* which included contributions from some of the *Smart Set* authors, had its offices at 19 West 44th and printed quality modern art and photographs in glossy reproduction, first-class fiction, and fashion. Robert Benchley was managing editor, Robert Sherwood drama editor, and Dorothy Parker caption writer. The three became the core of a group that began lunching regularly at the Algonquin, eventually taking over a large round table in the center of the room and collecting around it a group of wits who saved their *bon mots* to exchange over lunch. Most of the members were contributors to the midtown newspapers or magazines. Franklin P. Adams, the columnist F.P.A. for the New York *World,* Heywood Broun, sports writer for the *Tribune,* and Alexander Woollcott, drama critic, joined the original three, with a rotating group of extras that included Edna Ferber, George S. Kaufman, and Harold

Ross, who in 1925 founded the *New Yorker* magazine, which published many of the Round Table habitués. Its offices were at 25 West 45th Street, where *Smart Set* was headquartered. Now at 25 West 43rd Street, the *New Yorker* maintains its literary standards, innovation in comment and documentary on contemporary affairs, fiction, and poetry by quality writers, with cartoons and whimsical notes sprinkled throughout for zest. A revival of *Vanity Fair* is in the planning stages for 1983; it will attempt to reflect the contemporary scene with the verve and originality of the earlier version.

The *New York Review of Books* was conceived during a newspaper strike in 1963 at a dinner on the West Side shared by two West Side intellectual couples—Barbara and Jason Epstein and Robert Lowell and Elizabeth Hardwick—both couples living on West 67th Street in a row of studio duplexes on the north side of the street. The *New York Review of Books* has expanded its purview to political commentary that comes from a position on the left, from which it often finds itself in conflict with another group of West Side intellectuals who publish in Norman Podhoretz' neoconservative *Commentary*.

Book Publishing Today

The three-hour lunch, a publishing tradition, gives agents and editors the opportunity to strike a deal in relaxed surroundings. At the Four Seasons Restaurant, 99 East 52nd Street, lunch in the Grill Room, not the Pool Room, is a rare luxury indicating that a highly placed editor is the host. The 21 Club, 21 West 52nd Street, which dates back to the speakeasy days of prohibition, boasts plaques on the wall that memorialize frequent guests. "John Steinbeck, His Table" hangs near table number 8, "Benchley's Corner" identifies the location of tables 2 and 3 in the prestigious, visible section of the bar.

Today, editors and agents more frequently forego the long lunch and deluxe fare for the modern light lunch in Indian or Japanese spots near their offices. The dispersal of the publishing companies in recent years to locations outside midtown and the trend for fitness and *nouvelle cuisine* have modernized the publishing industry lunch. After hours, Elaine's, 1703 Second Avenue, and Nicola's, 146 East 84th Street, still attract established writers Joseph Heller, E. R. Doctorow, and others.

Manhattan
Points of
Literary Interest

LEGEND IS ON FOLLOWING PAGE

Points of Interest (for *Manhattan Points of Literary Interest* map on preceding page)

1) Hanover Square. The plaque on the Cotton Exchange building on the northwest corner of the intersection of Stone, Hanover, and William streets marks the site of William Bradford's *New York Gazette*, begun in 1725. Benjamin Franklin applied for a job, but was sent to Philadelphia where Bradford's son needed help on his paper.

2) The *Forward* Building, 175 East Broadway. In the heart of the former Jewish neighborhood, the Lower East Side, the *Forward* Building stands facing Straus Square. On the top of the building under the clock are the Hebrew letters for *Forward* and along the side the new owners have written Chinese characters.

3) 170 East 2nd Street. The apartment building where Allen Ginsberg lived when he wrote his poem *Kaddish*.

4) Washington Square. In this vicinity one can see the two faces of the Village. The elegant face is 7 Washington Square North where Edith Wharton lived, and the Bohemian is The Judson, Judson Hall at 51 Washington Square South where Edwin Arlington Robinson, the stereotypical struggling poet, lived. Nearby are other Village landmarks—147 West 4th Street, Volare's, formerly Polly's Restaurant, a gathering place during the twenties; in an upstairs room John Reed wrote *Ten Days That Shook the World*. At number 82 Washington Place at different times lived Richard Wright and Willa Cather. Mark Twain lived with his family at 14 West 10th Street in 1900.

5) St. Luke's Place, numbers 12, 14 and 16. In 1922 there were three famous American writers working shoulder to shoulder along the street. In the basement of number 14 Marianne Moore lived with her mother, working across the street at the public library; Theodore Dreiser occupied the parlor floor of number 16; Sherwood Anderson was at number 12.

6) The White Horse Tavern, 567 Hudson Street. Dylan Thomas, a serious drinker, came often when he stayed in New York. Norman Mailer and his *Village Voice* friends held court here on Sunday afternoons. Now, in warmer weather, the crowds overflow onto the tables with umbrellas on the street outside.

7) 241 East 17th Street, between Second and Third avenues. William Dean Howells, who had the habit of changing homes every year or so, lived here in the 1890s in a building facing Stuyvesant Square.

8) 35 East 19th Street. In this little three-story building Horace Greeley lived in the 1850s, his goat grazing in the backyard.

9) 149 West 21st Street, between Sixth and Seventh, in the middle of the block. In this patched up, "beat" looking building, one of a row of four, Jack Kerouac wrote *On the Road*.

10) Hotel Chelsea, 222 West 23rd Street. The polished plaques with lists of writers who lived there flank the entrance and the decorative wrought-iron fire escapes are still in place. More impressive from the outside than from the inside these days, this building, originally an apartment house, has sheltered more literary people than any other in the city. For example: O. Henry, Edgar Lee Masters, Thomas Wolfe, Arthur Miller, William Dean Howells, Brendan Behan, James T. Farrell, Mary McCarthy. This was Dylan Thomas' last address.

11) The New York Public Library, 42nd Street and Fifth Avenue. In this solid, dependable warehouse of information many writers have taken advantage of the Frederick Lewis Allen Room and the reading rooms, all places where writers meet. The card catalog room, with its wall of drawers, is a writer's first stop to be sure no one else has written the book they have in mind.

12) Algonquin Hotel, 59 West 44th Street. Mencken stayed at the Algonquin when forced to come to New York, and consulted with his co-editor George Jean Nathan who lived at the Royalton across the street in a top floor apartment from 1908 to his death in 1958.

13) Gotham Book Mart, 41 West 47th Street. "Wise Men Fish Here" is the motto on the sign outside, and writers have found obscure periodicals and books on the shelves here near their own works. Upstairs is the room where many parties have been held to celebrate the publication of new books.

14) St. Patrick's Cathedral, Fifth Avenue between 49th and 50th streets. F. Scott Fitzgerald and Zelda married here and honeymooned at the old Biltmore, before settling down near Central Park.

15) Barbizon Hotel for Women, Lexington Avenue and 63rd Street. This was a single girls' hotel where Sylvia Plath stayed when she was a young, single girl working for *Mademoiselle* magazine. In *The Bell Jar* she called it the Amazon.

16) 870 United Nations Plaza. The address of the successful writer Truman Capote, author of *In Cold Blood*.

17) Famous Dairy Restaurant, 222 West 72nd Street, kosher restaurant, closed Friday at 2 p.m. and all day Saturday. Isaac Bashevis Singer, who lives in the neighborhood, often partakes of the vegetarian fare of this local spot.

18) 84th Street (Edgar Allan Poe Street), between Broadway and West End Avenue. A plaque on the Alameda at 255 West 84th Street, just west of Broadway, commemorates Poe's residence here from March 1844 to August 1845, during which time he finished "The Raven." The fireplace mantel, where he carved his name, is now in Philosophy Hall at Columbia University.

19) Brooklyn Heights and Brooklyn. Marianne Moore moved from the Village to 260 Cumberland Street in the Fort Greene section in 1931. Richard Wright began *Native Son* while living with friends at 175 Carlton Avenue, and later, at 89 Lefferts Place, Wright worked on *Black Boy*. Arthur Miller

lived as a child at 1350 East 3rd Street and moved to the Heights in 1944, to 102 Pierrepont Street, where Norman Mailer was also living. Henry Ward Beecher preached from the Plymouth Congregation, on Orange Street between Henry and Hicks. Thomas Wolfe lived in Brooklyn Heights at number 111 Columbia Heights.

20) The Eldorado, 300 Central Park West, between 90th and 91st streets. In 1943 Sinclair Lewis requested an apartment with a view of all the New York bridges and a living room sixty feet long and twenty feet high. He moved into a duplex in this art deco building and described it as "a cross between Elizabeth Arden's Beauty Salon and the horse-stables at Ringling Circus Winter Headquarters: 29 floors up in the air and commanding a fair view of the Orkney Isles on the West, of Girard Avenue South on the North and West." This was also the nouveau-riche arrival point of Herman Wouk's Marjorie Morningstar.

21) 333 Riverside Drive, between 105th Street and 106th Street (Duke Ellington Blvd.). Saul Bellow lived here in the 1950s and had a view of the river from his bathroom.

22) 380 Riverside Drive, entrance on Cathedral Parkway (110th Street). This is the home of Salinger's fictional Glass family. Around the corner at 390 Riverside Drive, which has its entrance on 111th Street, Salinger himself lived.

23) West End Café, 2911 Broadway, between 113th and 114th streets. During the forties, Beat writers from Columbia used to hang out here, and at one time poetry readings were held regularly. It is still operating.

24) 200 Claremont Avenue, near Tieman Avenue and 125th Street. In 1919 F. Scott Fitzgerald was living here after his discharge from the army. Trying to make his way as a writer, he once had "one hundred and twenty-two rejection slips pinned in a frieze" around his bedroom.

25) 45 West 110th Street. Arthur Miller lived in apartment 6B as an infant.

26) 20 East 127th Street, also called Langston Hughes Place, between Madison and Fifth avenues. Hughes lived here with the Harpers, his adopted aunt and uncle, with a workroom on the top floor. Hughes once said, "Had I been a rich young man, I would have bought a house in Harlem and built musical steps up to the front door, and installed chimes that at the press of a button played Ellington tunes." He refused to consider living outside Harlem.

27) Salem United Methodist Church, 2190 Adam Clayton Powell Jr. Blvd., corner 129th Street. Countee Cullen, whose father was the minister of this church, lived in the parsonage. The poet, who later taught French in the New York public school system, married W. E. B. DuBois' daughter Yolande in this church in a ceremony that was exceptional for its drama and decoration. DuBois directed the rehearsal himself and 1,300 people watched the couple exchange vows while canaries in gilded cages provided accompaniment.

28) The new Small's Paradise, 2294 Adam Clayton Powell Jr. Blvd., near 135th Street. A "jump joint" in the twenties, DuBois celebrated his 83rd

birthday at Small's and Baldwin had a party there on publication of *Another Country*. Small's is a fixture in Harlem.

29) YMCA, 180 West 135th Street, near the corner of Adam Clayton Powell Jr. Blvd. Here was the stepping-off place for the many writers who came to New York from elsewhere, such as Hughes, Ellison, and many others. It is also a center for cultural activities.

30) Lenox Avenue and 135th Street. Several institutions here are cultural landmarks for most of those who come to Harlem. The Schomburg Center for Research in Black Culture at 515 Lenox is a new building housing a collection begun by Arthur A. Schomburg. Originally it occupied the building next door at 103 West 135th Street, still standing but not in use, designed by McKim, Mead and White. At 104 West 136th Street is the Countee Cullen branch of the public library on the site of A'Lelia Walker's mansion. Harlem Hospital, where James Baldwin was born, is across the street.

31) Hamilton Grange, 287 Convent Avenue, between 141st and 142nd streets. Alexander Hamilton lived in this country house designed by John McComb, in 1802, the period when wealthy families were building fashionable estates in place of the farms that had been there. The Grange is a small frame building dwarfed now by the large church on the corner and an apartment house. A statue of Hamilton stands in front and the building is open to the public.

32) 409 Edgecombe Avenue, at the top of Sugar Hill where the elite of Harlem lived. The view extends over the rooftops of the rest of Harlem across the river to Yankee Stadium in the Bronx. Walter White, executive director of the NAACP, Aaron Douglas, painter of the twenties, and others lived here.

33) Audubon Ballroom, 166th Street and Broadway. Malcolm X was shot while delivering a speech to his Muslim followers here. A battered sign is still on the marquee, but the building is run down and signs of its former elegance are nearly hidden by its current decrepitude.

34) Poe Cottage, Poe Park, Kingsbridge Road and Grand Concourse, the Bronx. Poe lived here from 1846 to 1848 in hopes that the country air would improve his wife's health.

THE THEATER WORLD OF NEW YORK

by
MARILYN STASIO

Marilyn Stasio, theater critic for the New York Post, *is an officer of the New York Drama Critics' Circle, the New York critics' professional organization. She is the author of* Broadway's Beautiful Losers.

To get a real sense of the way the theater permeates the life of New York City, you ought to catch the M-104 bus. Locally known as "the Broadway bus," the M-104 goes up Eighth Avenue and comes down Broadway, connecting the theater district with the Upper West Side of Manhattan. (Actually, this bus covers a lot of territory beyond these points; but as far as theater people are concerned, it self-destructs east of Broadway and north of 96th Street, once it takes them between home and work.)

Not everybody who works in the New York theater lives on the Upper West Side; but around 7 P.M. (headed downtown) and between 10 P.M. and 10:30 (going uptown) it certainly does look that way on the M-104. Every third person is either toting a dance bag or studying a script or humming under his breath or reading *Variety* or lugging a large musical instrument or circling audition notices in *Backstage* or clutching a *Playbill* and talking shoptalk with a friend. It's always showtime, folks, on the M-104.

Officially, the "theater district" refers specifically to that district—roughly between 42nd and 53rd streets, on the west side of Broadway—where one finds the legitimate houses where commercial stage shows are presented. But "the theater" is something that happens all around town.

Let's go back to that throbbing lifeline, the M-104. It's taking theater people to auditions, to classes, to conferences with agents and producers, to union meetings—and to the unemployment office. If we're traveling uptown, a lot of people will get off around Lincoln Center, which is one of those "magnet" districts that attracts theater professionals. Besides being the site of the city's major opera, dance, and music companies, the area offers professional facilities for people who make their living in all phases of the theater.

Juilliard, the city's renowned school for the performing arts, maintains its quarters within the Lincoln Center Complex. So does the High

School of Performing Arts, the center's newest addition. The country's main performing-arts reference libraries (music and dance, as well as theater) are housed in that modest-looking building behind the "reflection pool."

But these are only the obvious destinations that bring M-104 riders to the Upper West Side. Broadway dancers come to the area to take classes at the many small dance schools—from Melissa Hayden's classical ballet school to Luigi's jazz-dance studio—that line Broadway in this part of town. There are also a number of small Off-Off-Broadway theaters in the area—from the Richard Allen Center for black theater arts on West 62nd Street and the Second Stage at West 73rd Street all the way to the Equity Library Theater at 103rd Street—where theater artists practise their craft outside the commercial theaters. Television centers like the Reeves Studio and the ABC-TV Studios are still other Upper West Side meccas for theater performers who pay the rent between Broadway shows with lucrative assignments on TV commercials and sit-coms.

There's another, subtler reason for the heavy traffic on the M-104 going uptown. Ever since the Columbus Avenue renaissance transformed that artery into the city's liveliest new commercial and residential area, (between Lincoln Center and roughly West 86th Street) restaurants have been popping up everywhere. And restaurants have always been the young theater professional's main source of support between jobs. Those handsome waiters on roller skates and those smiling beauties toting your drinks at the outdoor cafes on Columbus Avenue are paying for their voice lessons and acting classes on your tips.

Whether they're gainfully employed in the chorus of *Annie* or waiting on tables to pay for their directing classes at Juilliard, members of New York's theater community also like to hang out together. On the Upper West Side you'll find them at places like Café Central, a favorite watering spot at West 75th Street and Amsterdam Avenue owned by actor Peter Weller, and Palsson's, a pleasant restaurant near West 72nd Street and Broadway that recently expanded its neighborhood appeal when it opened a popular cabaret show called "Forbidden Broadway."

The real business-end of the Broadway bus, however, is still its downtown destination: the theater district. You won't need much help finding the theaters; they're obvious. But you have to look sharp to catch a glimpse of the inner workings of the industry, even though it's all around you.

I always send my out-of-town visitors to the outdoor TKTS booth at Duffy Square, even if they already have their tickets for Broadway shows, for the simple reason that it's the best place in town for meeting people with a shared passion for the theater. It's always potluck at the booth, which offers limited numbers of half-price tickets for whichever Broadway shows happen to have unsold seats for that evening's performance. Since seasoned travelers usually nail their reservations down in advance, you'll find that many of the people on that long (but generally good-natured) line are locals; students and bargain-hunters mostly, but also theater professionals "on the entry level," whose gossipy shoptalk always brightens up the waiting time if you care to eavesdrop.

When the Theater Development Fund opened the TKTS booth ten years ago (June 1973), some Broadway producers set up a squawk, anticipating that discounting tickets would devalue their shows. But everybody got pally again once it was discovered that the booth boosted over-all business by creating the theatergoing habit in new audiences. On the pragmatic side, the booth also moves more than 25,000 tickets in an average week, which gives participating theaters more than $400,000 in weekly windfall income.

The high price of Broadway tickets is always a touchy issue with people in the business, and to the naked consumer it can seem a simple scandal that a ticket can cost between $20 and $40 (depending on performance and location). But the theater is and always will be a labor-intensive industry. It can't be automated, and its labor and materials are handcrafted, which puts the theatrical "product" in the rarified high-cost market of the hand-cut diamond and the hand-sewn shoe. With production costs hitting $3 million for a big Broadway musical (a straight play can come in for between $500,000–$600,000), a business with no recourse to normal cost-cutting measures can only pass the bill on to its consumers.

Besides stirring such thoughts, the TKTS booth also offers a great vantage point for surveying the offstage theater scene. That massive construction project gumming up 45th and 46th streets will someday emerge as the Portman Hotel, a 50-story, 2,000-room hostelry that raised a lot of bad dust within the theater community, mainly because two landmark theaters, the Helen Hayes and the Morosco, were sacrificed so men may ascend in elevators to wall-to-wall carpeting in the sky.

Having won this fight over those community dissidents who prefer to keep the buildings in their working district on human-scale, the real-estate forces have now got their eye on the rest of the area. The City's Board of Estimate recently approved new zoning regulations for midtown Manhattan that would encourage residential and commercial development west of Sixth Avenue. Protection has been promised for the 44 legitimate theaters that fall within this new zoning district, but the sidestreets between Sixth and Eighth avenues have been declared fair game. Better catch a look at them now, before they go down in a heap of rubble to make way for progress.

To the casual observer, these crowded little streets might look tacky, and at night they are pretty grim to behold. But for all their grimy faces, these narrow byways are an important part of the theater district, too.

Take 48th Street between Sixth and Seventh avenues. Grubby though it may look to developers who envision 50-story office towers rising in glory, the street happens to be the center of the theatrical music industry. Those old buildings are crammed with music stores, instrument repair shops, music studios, dance workshops, and small private schools. Daytimes, it's one of the liveliest, most colorful streets in New York City.

46th Street is another great, unappreciated thoroughfare. Down by the Sixth Avenue end stands an unprepossessing but historic pile of bricks that housed the High School of Performing Arts before its recent move to Lincoln Center and served as the inspiration for both the movie and TV versions of *Fame.* Across from it is the American Place Theater, the city's first underground theater and the scene of interesting experimental work. Mid-block, you'll find the offices of *Variety,* the legendary 75-year-old show-business newspaper. (Drop in and buy a copy, just to see a living stage set for *The Front Page.*)

At 165 West 46th Street stands the shabby, but nevertheless noble, Equity Building. Actors Equity, the powerful union that represents more than 30,000 theatrical professionals all over the country, owns the building and keeps its National Headquarters here. The rest of the building is a warren of small, busy offices housing talent agents, press agents, theatrical producers, casting directors, and other links in the complicated chain that support the New York theater industry.

Although some are a little bit grander and some a little cleaner than others, there are dozens of similar buildings scattered throughout these side streets. Across Broadway, in the blocks bounded on the west by Eighth Avenue, they are hunkered down between the theaters themselves—as are the industry hangouts, the restaurants, bars, and delis where theater people take themselves between showtimes.

The Gaiety on 47th Street draws the management crowd at lunchtime. (Many a deal has been struck over the pastrami sandwiches and pickled tomatoes.) But by curtain time, many of those industry moles who have spent the sunlight hours burrowed in their offices have managed to find their way to 45th Street.

On that busy street, Charlies' is a popular spot with the working crowd (and a good place to make contacts if you're temporarily between engagements). Once the shows are out, you can't hardly find the bar for all the chorus kids and stage managers jamming the place. The spillover goes next door to Barrymore's, which is the preferred noshery for stagehands and actors with moustaches (a personal observation, that). Depending on one's mood and finances, people in the business also patronize Joe Allen's, Jimmy Ray's, and the new J.R.'s.

Across "the alley"—Shubert Alley, of course—stands heart and home. Yes, everybody *does* go to Sardi's. It's customary to make jokes about the food and to grouse about one's table location, but when a nice check comes in, or some friend signs a contract, people always dash to Sardi's before the ink is dry. It's where we celebrate.

When you've had your ritual meal or drink at Sardi's, be sure to take a gander at the Sardi Building above it. It's a posher version of those small, no-nonsense office buildings on the other side of Broadway. Besides providing office space for various Broadway producers—including the powerful Shubert Organization—and meeting rooms for the theater's professional organizations, the Sardi Building also houses the handsome quarters of the Dramatists Guild and its parent body, the Authors League.

The Dramatists Guild currently represents close to 6,000 playwrights, only a fraction of whom actually get their plays done on Broadway. The rest of them write—and here's the tricky part—for a vast and amorphous body of Off-Broadway, Off-Off-Broadway, and experimental outpost theaters that constitute an important, if less visible, aspect of New York's theater.

All the larger and most active nonprofit companies (the Circle-in-the-Square and Joseph Papp's New York Shakespeare Festival, for example) are easily found by referring to local newspaper listings, especially the extended ones in the *Village Voice.* The Alliance of Resident Theaters/New York (325 Spring Street, New York, NY 10013; 212–989–5257) is a responsible information source on many of the 200-plus companies that function between SoHo and Harlem.

If you just want a taste of this infinite variety, trot over to Theater Row, on West 42nd Street between Ninth and Tenth avenues. This major project in urban restoration now houses 14 resident performance companies and eight theaters within a single city block, with many attractive restaurants and shops scattered among them. The big apartment complex across the street is Manhattan Plaza, another revolutionary development in that it was built specifically for the city's resident performing artists. On warm evenings, the sidewalk café outside Curtain Up! on 43rd Street seems to be the central gathering spot for residents and visitors alike.

However small it may be, a healthy and active theater can breathe new life into a whole neighborhood, and this is what is constantly happening all over Manhattan. In the middle of the garment district, the flower district, and even the meat-market district, you'll keep stumbling over little clusters of Off-Off-Broadway theaters with appropriate attachments (a café, a health-food store) close by.

Except for some major experiments like Theater Row, nobody really plans it that way; it's just the way it happens. In New York City, theater is all around you. Looking for it is half the fun.

THE DANCE CAPITAL OF THE WORLD

by
CLIVE BARNES

Clive Barnes, formerly the dance critic of The New York Times, *is now a drama critic for the* New York Post. *He is a member of the New York Drama Critics' Circle.*

New York is many cities and many things to many men. But to the dance lover, just as for the dancer, New York is quite literally Mecca. Its streets are paved with toe-shoes, modern-dance studios lurk in the avenues, and the press is full of news of dance and its dancers. Without doubt New York is the dance capital of the world—there are more dancers, more dance schools, more dance students, more dance companies, more dance performances, and more dance lovers here than in any other corner of the earth.

It was not always so. There are many reasons why American dance today stands matchless in the world—the simple fact that across the country we train more dancers than any other nation helps a lot—but one reason for our dance's richness is inherent in its special heritage. Dance—fancy classical or theatrical dancing—has been popular here since colonial times. In the early part of the last century the Austrian ballerina Fanny Ellsler caused an unbridled wave of balletomania across the country and, be it remembered, at the same time such American dancers as Augusta Maywood and the charmingly named George Washington Smith were having their fair share of success in Paris.

But the strength of American dance, its very uniqueness, derives from the combination of the indigenous American modern dance (stemming from the example of Isadora Duncan, and the teaching of the likes of Ruth St. Denis and Ted Shawn) with classic ballet. Classic ballet, after visiting these shores for centuries, really settled here in 1933, when the School of American Ballet was founded, first (but only briefly) in Hartford, Connecticut, and then in Manhattan. From this school originated one of the world's great ballet companies, George Balanchine's New York City Ballet.

Today most of the country's major classic ballet companies and virtually all of its leading modern-dance troupes make their homes in Manhattan. Let us be fair about this: One of the most remarkable aspects of the dance scene since World War II, especially during the last decade, has been the dessemination of dance, especially classic ballet, throughout the United States—the greening of American dance. Today major companies are to be found from coast to coast, from San Francisco to Boston. However, most of the top-echelon groups still call New York home and maintain their administrative offices and schools here.

By general consent there are six classic ballet companies in the world of such quality, scope, tradition, and intention that they are placed in a distinct group in world dance. Four of them are foreign; Moscow's Bolshoi Ballet and Leningrad's Kirov Ballet, both from the Soviet Union, Britain's Royal Ballet, and the Royal Danish Ballet. All four of these companies visit New York regularly, but the other two, New York City Ballet and American Ballet Theatre, live here.

New York also boasts three other classic companies of major international stature: the Joffrey Ballet, the Dance Theater of Harlem, and the Feld Ballet. The internationally accepted modern-dance companies that are alive and well and living in New York include the companies of Martha Graham, Paul Taylor, Merce Cunningham, Alvin Ailey, Alwin Nikolais, Murray Louis, the late José Limón, Erick Hawkins, Twyla Tharp, Laura Dean, Louis Falco, Dan Wagoner, Paul Sanasardo, the late Joyce Trisler, Pearl Lang, and, indeed, countless other groups, some well-established, some clinging fringelike onto the dance scene.

All of the classic companies maintain schools, as do most of the modern-dance groups—a notable exception being Paul Taylor. There are also many private classic teachers, including such well-known independent teachers as Maggie Black, Melissa Hayden, Finis Jhung, Robert Denvers, and David Howard. There are also independent schools such as the Harkness House for Ballet Arts, once the home school of the now-defunct Harkness Ballet.

As a result, New York provides a special magnet for the young dance student to come and study with some of the best teachers in the world, and in the most competitive pedagogic climate. For you can learn any kind of dancing here: ethnic dancing, jazz dancing, tap dancing—indeed, even belly dancing, the foxtrot or the waltz, or aerobic-exercise dancing.

But if these schools offer a promise of heaven to the serious dance student or even the dance professional searching for experience, they are less rewarding for the tourist. Few, if any, open their doors to strangers, although, if one writes with some cogently compelling reason, some schools might be prepared to receive visitors.

Nevertheless, even for the non-dancer and the non-student, the visitor will never lack for dance entertainment in New York. Dance is a year-round New York festival, although, interestingly, its most active period runs from about the beginning of April to the end of July, which is slap in the middle of the main tourist season.

During this four-month season in 1982, for example, it was possible to see Ballet Theatre, City Ballet, the Feld Ballet, The Royal Danish Ballet, the Netherlands Dance Theater, the Paul Taylor Company, the Alvin Ailey Company, the Merce Cunningham Company, the Martha Graham Company, and innumerable smaller troupes.

Where? In a sense, dance is a little like theater in as much as it is spread out all over Manhattan, but in its major offerings it is fairly centralized. Nowadays the most important places for dance are the two Lincoln Center theaters: the New York State Theater (home of New York City Ballet) and the Metropolitan Opera House (outside of the fall and winter opera season). Incidentally, even if there is no performance you want to see at Lincoln Center, a tour of the complete center is a visitors' must.

The City Center—the old Mecca Temple on West 55th Street—has now been refurbished and is one of New York's most important dance houses. It is the New York base of the Joffrey Ballet, and all of the larger modern-dance troupes give regular seasons there. There is also a smaller theater downstairs here, the Space at City Center, which plays host to smaller dance groups.

BAM, the Brooklyn Academy of Music (20 minutes from midtown Manhattan by subway, but a special bus service—details from the box-office—is also available) is a very important dance house. It is the New York home of the Pennsylvania Ballet, and dance companies, classic and modern, appear there throughout the year. Also in Brooklyn is Brooklyn College, which has a very important and prestigious dance series, specializing, like BAM, in companies from out of town and overseas. Another important location outside Manhattan is the Lehmann Center for the Performing Arts in Queens.

Back in Manhattan, the Feld Ballet has a new home; the Joyce Theater—devoted entirely to dance—has been recently rebuilt at the cost of more than $4 million on 8th Avenue and 19th Street. The Riverside Church, on Manhattan's Upper West Side, also has a long and lively dance season, often showcasing smaller groups. There are, of course, various workshops, labs, and studios with performances throughout Manhattan, and occasionally dance finds a theatre on Broadway, frequently either the Uris Theatre (where Rudolf Nureyev often performs) or the Minskoff Theatre.

Newspapers are useful in finding out about these performances, but the visitor should also make a point of checking *The Village Voice* and *New York* magazine. The two New York dance magazines, *Ballet News* and *Dance Magazine,* carry valuable advance information, as does

Dance News. European visitors are recommended to get the latest copy of the English magazine *Dance and Dancers,* which carries quite thorough New York listings—including advance repertory details not generally available anywhere else, even in the United States.

And, of course, your dance pilgrimage, should such it be, need not be limited to the formal dance companies. Many Broadway shows include a great deal of dancing, and a whole breed of Broadway dancer, known popularly as "gypsies," has grown up, with its own choreographers, such as Michael Bennett, Bob Fosse, and Tommy Tune, who mean almost as much in this world as George Balanchine, Antony Tudor, and Jerome Robbins mean in the more formal ranks of American dance.

New York—the dance capital of the world. You will see in any week of the year some of the world's greatest dancers and some of the world's greatest ballets in this wall-to-wall, month-to-month festival. Probably the one bad month for dance is August, but even then there will be a certain fringe activity—although probably not a major company.

And one last tip, on how to get tickets: When possible, book ahead directly with the theater by mail. When in New York, go to the box office itself; unlike Broadway, few seats are reserved for sale by ticket agents. Finally, always remember that there will probably be tickets returned just before the curtain and that your patience, and strong nerves, will almost certainly be rewarded by getting in. But watch out for scalpers; pay the box-office price and nothing but the box-office price. And enjoy.

NEW YORK AS THE MUSICAL BULLSEYE

Classical Music in the City

by
SPEIGHT JENKINS

Speight Jenkins, the host on the "Live from the Met" series on PBS, travels throughout the United States to lecture on opera. He is a contributing editor of Ovation *Magazine and is currently writing a book,* Opera Through the Eyes of Singers, *to be published by Alfred A. Knopf.*

New Yorkers often see their hometown as the center of many different worlds. One of these definitely is music. But is it an idle claim? True, a tremendous number of American musicians make their homes here, and quite a few foreign artists keep apartments in Manhattan as their headquarters in the Western Hemisphere. But the best testament to the significance of New York, not just in American but in world terms, comes from the mouths of the musicians themselves.

Birgit Nilsson, the famed Swedish dramatic soprano, has said that her success at the Metropolitan Opera in 1959, which resulted in a front-page news story in *The New York Times* and the *Herald Tribune* the next morning, made her the world's foremost Wagnerian soprano. She had succeeded all over Germany in the mid-50s, had sung in San Francisco and Chicago and even in England, but it was the acclaim here both from the audience and the media that made her the leader in her field.

Dame Janet Baker and Elly Ameling, two of the world's most beloved concert singers, have expressed similar feelings about New York and their successes here. Dame Janet particularly gives this city credit for her becoming known outside the British Isles. Why? What is it about New York that makes these artists and many like them so value success here? The density of people and the consequently larger and difficult-to-dominate halls are factors, as well as the pulse of theatrical excitement that defines the mood of the city. Another is the audiences.

Dame Janet discusses the New York audiences lovingly: "For a reserved English person to be able to communicate with a group of people as honestly warm gave me a tremendously enriched confidence to communicate with any audience anywhere. . . . You gave me openness and generosity, and you brought from me a quality which I found in myself and could use at home in a different way."

The English singer was specifically discussing the recital audience, traditionally one of the most intellectually attuned and restrained groups in this city. But all the audiences—from those who attend chamber music and lieder to the Puccini opera audience—are enthusiastic.

In past years New York audiences have been criticized, particularly by visitors from England, for too much talking, rustling, coughing, and general noise-making. No one has completely vanquished the crinkling candy wrapper or jangling bracelet, though now any offender will surely be loudly shushed, but the behavior over-all has improved considerably. There is now no talking during orchestral interludes at the opera, and contemporary pieces at symphony concerts are listened to respectfully, then either applauded or booed. Unfortunately, booing at the opera house has increased in recent years. Many find it necessary to express disapproval as violently as praise, a habit novel enough to fascinate most tourists.

Above all, the audience reaction in New York City is honest. The opera tradition in this city goes back to the Garcia family performances in the 1840s, and the Metropolitan Opera will celebrate a century of international-level opera in the 1983–84 season. Additionally, since 1891 Carnegie Hall has been one of the most acoustically perfect recital halls in the world, and the New York Philharmonic traces its lineage all the way back to 1842. With the tradition of performing comes the tradition of attendance, and over the years the New York subscriber has developed a finely tuned set of ears. Year in and year out, New Yorkers have heard the best, and they expect it. As a consequence, their reaction is not always—as is sometimes suggested—a reflection of publicity. Many is the audience that gives a huge hand to a favorite at the beginning of the concert or the opera and much less so as the evening progresses.

The subject of applause suggests those members of the audience who contribute the most feverishly to its volume, the standees. For years they have been described as the most knowledgeable members of the paying public. Many are very musical and aware. But a high proportion of this group is there to cheer a beloved singer or instrumentalist and will do so no matter how bad the performance is. Regular patrons tend much more to a show-me stance. This is why José Carreras, the Spanish tenor, said recently, "Every night at the Met is like a debut. The tension is unbearable."

Critics also make New York an important music center. There used to be ten newspapers. In the 60s, labor demands—mainly opposition to automation—cut the profit base to the point where many disappeared, and now the city has only three—the *Times,* the *News,* and the *Post.* The coverage of these three has dramatically changed over the past decade. Now the *Times* alone has thorough musical reportage, with the two tabloids reviewing only the most significant events. Even so, there is wider coverage here than in most cities, nor can the magazines be dismissed. That *Time* and *Newsweek* are published in New York means that the critics of those journals know best what is happening around town and can argue with their editors for its speedy inclusion. Add to them regular music correspondents for the Associated Press, the *Christian Science Monitor,* the *Wall Street Journal, Ovation, Musical America,* and several foreign papers, and one still has a formidable array of critics waiting to review what has happened. Additionally, critics from important papers around the country feel it incumbent upon them to come here once or twice a year to report on what is going on, a factor that cements the significance of music in New York in the eyes of the general U.S. audience.

The quality of criticism in New York has long been cussed and discussed. As a critic myself, I should not join the argument. But what can be said is that critics here have the tendency to be very exacting because they hear everything. If Horowitz plays in any given season, he plays here; after a five-year absence from the U.S., Birgit Nilsson returned first to the Met; and when the Soviet artists, currently not allowed by their government to perform in the U.S., return, they will surely come here first. The constant appearance of the best pushes standards higher and higher, and the New York reviews therefore have a reputation for severity not encountered elsewhere. They can also be more lenient; experience teaches that some scores never sound as perfect live as they do on records.

Not all of musical life is performance, and the tourist walking on Columbus Avenue (in the high 60s and 70s, the Upper West Side's equivalent of Madison Avenue in the 60s) is apt to see the most familiar faces of classical music. Most of them live in the area north of Lincoln Center—from 66th Street up to about 90th, from Riverside Drive to Central Park West. One finds, for instance, a building on Riverside in which two of the more famous violinists live side by side with the most famous American baritone, and another in which a world-renowned conductor lives cheek-by-jowl with a retired soprano and a very active tenor. Roughly the same area houses most visiting artists. Tourists might catch a glimpse of stars at the Mayflower (Central Park West at 62nd) or at any of the hotels on Central Park South, such as the Navarro, the Essex House, or the Hampshire House.

Some artists locate in New York because of the business aspects of the profession. Every important music management firm in the United States is located in New York, as are all the significant public-relations firms. The musician can easily transact his business here while he is rehearsing or performing. Additionally, he can more readily find the right instrument maker, the most thoroughly stocked music stores, and more teachers or coaches for any musical endeavor than anywhere else in the country.

The issue of teaching is too complex to investigate in detail, but World War II undermined the instrumental and vocal teaching tradition on the European continent. Many of the best pedagogues fled to New York City before the war and even more afterwards. Unlike many immigrants, most found it unnecessary to keep moving. New York was brimming over with excellent, promising young musicians eager to be trained, and there were plenty of places for them to perform. Such is still the case.

New York also has three of the most famous conservatories in the world—the Juilliard School of Music, the Manhattan School of Music, and the Mannes College of Music. Each has a large staff and many teachers who serve as instructors in particular musical disciplines. Juilliard, located in the Lincoln Center Complex, has the most financial support and publicity. Its graduates form a Harvard-type network throughout the U.S. music world, and a Juilliard diploma probably means more for teaching purposes than a diploma from any other musical institution. The instructors at the other schools, however, are equally distinguished, and the music students of each contribute to the constantly growing pool of well-trained musicians in this city.

19,000 active members of the American Federation of Musicians, Local 802 (instrumentalists), and 2,500 members of the American Guild of Musical Artists (singers and dancers) suggest the numbers of these talented performers who call New York home—a simple statistic that is a sure sign of the city's musical pre-eminence. Though many of these people work at regular musical jobs, there is always time to get together for informal sessions of chamber music or an evening of lieder.

Those musicians not belonging to an established orchestra or chamber music group are called freelancers. They make their living at the call of orchestral or vocal contractors. The contractor works as follows: If a modern Maecenas wants to present an evening of his works or those of a protégé in any New York hall, he or she need simply contact a contractor through the union or through other musicians, and within a few days he or she can have 40, 50, or even 90 well-trained musicians ready to play. There are enough jobs available from pick-up concerts of this sort and orchestras assembled for a particular soloist or conductor to provide good incomes for many of the musicians who live here. An even better money maker is the television commercial, which offers a built-in source of revenue to many instrumentalists. Many are filmed in New York; all use freelancers, and the pay and residuals are good. There are also Broadway shows.

The upshot of it all is that the tourist or the New Yorker who loves music is lucky indeed. On any normal Thursday night in February or March, a music lover might have to decide among a Metropolitan *Don Carlo* (with Mirella Freni, Placido Domingo, and Nicolai Ghiaurov, conducted by James Levine), a New York City Opera *Mefistofele* with Samuel Ramey, the New York Philharmonic playing the Mahler Third Symphony under Zubin Mehta, the Cleveland Orchestra under its new music director, Christoph von Dohnanyi, at Carnegie Hall, Claudio Arrau in a piano recital at the 92nd Street YMHA, and the Guarneri String Quartet in an all-Beethoven evening at Alice Tully Hall. Even if there is only one really hot performance on a given night, you can be sure that the artists will be giving everything they have to make the evening memorable. They are, after all, playing in New York.

POPULAR MUSIC IN NEW YORK CITY

by
IRA MAYER

Ira Mayer is popular music critic for the New York Post *and a contributor to various popular- and rock-music publications, including* Rolling Stone, The Record, *and* High Fidelity. *He also writes extensively about travel and pop-culture and is an editorial consultant to* Fodor's New York City.

New York represents the ultimate paradox for a musician: Given the city's vast number of clubs, concert halls, recording studios, theatrical productions, and advertising agencies, New York offers more opportunities to be heard and discovered than any other city in the world. And precisely because there are so many opportunities—and so much competition for them—it's more *difficult* to be heard and discovered in New York than it is in any other city in the world.

The often frenetic pace, the multifarious ethnic groups, and the variety of life-styles that constitute New York's personality blend together kaleidoscopically to foster a very special kind of creative environment that draws on blues and jazz and rock and country. Songwriter Doc Pomus, one of the traditionally minded Tin Pan Alley tunesmiths to make the transition to rock and roll with such classic anthems as "Teenager in Love" and "Save the Last Dance for Me," has the perfect metaphor for the mixed contrasts that influence New York's music scene. "There are two ways of looking at a tenement," he says. "One is to see a symphony; the other is to see a ghetto."

To put the size and scope of the New York music scene in perspective, consider that the local chapter of the American Federation of Musicians has approximately 20,000 members based here; the trade magazine *Pro Sound News* estimates that there are 200 recording studios nestled in lofts, office buildings, basements, and elsewhere within the city proper; *Fodor's New York City* lists more than 125 major clubs and bars featuring name talent regularly—and that's not counting the neighborhood places that have aspiring stars performing every night *or* the big-time concert halls. There are literally scores of record companies, including the headquarters operations of the CBS and Warner Communications labels—which together account for more than half of the United States' $4 billion in annual recorded-music sales—as well as many small "independent" labels that issue various special-interest albums and tapes. Midtown record stores such as King Karol, the Record Hunter, Colony, and Sam Goody vie for the title of best-stocked in the country; in fact, it's not unusual to find Elton John's limousine (to name just one star) parked outside Colony—or Elton emerging from the store having purchased several hundred singles at a clip.

Oddly enough, during the mid-'70s it sometimes seemed as though the entire music industry was migrating to California. The new glamor associated with pop stars was akin to that once reserved for Hollywood's favorite movie actors and actresses; pop and rock musicians wanted to share in that aura. The New York holdouts wagged their fingers and shook their heads. "You'll be back," they said. "You'll love the sun and enjoy the relatively relaxed pace, but in the long run it's New York that breeds creativity." Sure enough, most of the record companies and stars who moved westward a decade ago have now returned to make New York their home base. They missed the changes of season (including the infrequent winter blizzards that invariably mean good business for nightclubs and watering holes near the major hotels!) and the hectic pace. They'd fallen into a rut and needed "a dose of New York" to start the creative juices flowing anew.

That's an admittedly jingoistic interpretation, but New York is in fact the center of the popular (and, for that matter, classical) music industry. Tin Pan Alley doesn't exist any more—the Brill Building on Broadway near 50th Street, where songwriters from the Gershwins to Carole King turned out much of their work, houses far fewer song publishers than it once did—but there is virtually no form of popular music that isn't represented here, and much of the experimental work being done by new artists interested in everything from high-tech futuristic sounds to basic blast-'em-out rock and roll gets its start in the clubs, lofts, and studios of New York.

For those starting out, it's a decidedly anti-glamorous scene. C.B.G.B. and OMFUG, which is the best-known and most typical of the clubs for new right-off-the-street rock and roll bands, is a long, narrow, dingy bar with no sight lines and lots of walls for sound to bounce off of. With its postage-stamp size stage at the front, it's been a staple on the Bowery for more than 15 years and has repeatedly been the spawning ground for whatever the latest wave in rock and roll has been. Blondie, Talking Heads, Television—these and dozens of other bands have worked their way up through the ranks, graduating to the more establishment-oriented (and cleaner and more organized) Bottom Line and then to concerts and national tours. At the other end of the pop spectrum are the hotel rooms: the Cafe Carlyle on Madison Avenue, for example, where Bobby Short and Marian McPartland alternate their six-month terms at the piano, and where posh is the name of the game, at fittingly high prices.

Less formal even than C.B.G.B., but no less critical to the fabric of the city's musical life, are the hundreds of street musicians who have their regular outposts in the parks or on corners: steel-drum master Victor Brady, who can be counted on to be by the Bethesda Fountain at 72nd Street in Central Park summer weekends; the Dixieland bands, bluegrass quintets, solo saxophonists, even the occasional bagpiper— all of whom pass the hat to support their studies or supplement their salaries or, simply, to earn a living.

As for the record industry, even those major companies that aren't based here maintain sizable operations in the Big Apple, sure to check the local press for reviews when their out-of-town acts make it into one of the clubs or concert halls; a New York review helps sell a performer in the hinterlands, be it Fort Bragg, North Carolina, or Chicago. Similarly, while New York radio stations tend not to be very adventuresome when it comes to introducing new talent or records, it has been estimated that a hit in the rest of the country will sell an additional 100,000 copies if it finally makes it onto one of the area's major pop stations.

Still another important element in the New York music mix is the jingles industry. Advertising and Madison Avenue are all but synonymous, and the vast bulk of music written for and performed in commercials is created here. That's a whole subculture unto itself, with such artists as Barry Manilow emerging from the anonymity of writing, arranging, and performing on Coke and McDonald's ads to become internationally-renowned performers. Others never do make it quite into the foreground—though the residuals a singer makes on commercials can ease some of the pain of obscurity.

Broadway, alas, is not the source of many big standards anymore, but the Great White Way is still generating an enormous body of musical theater material (even if much of it doesn't survive more than a handful of performances). In recent years some pop artists have lent themselves to attempts at creating contemporary musicals, but when you get right down to it, even the "rock" musicals that have made it, such as *Grease, Evita,* and *Hair,* have come from composers and been performed by people coming from the theatrical tradition more than from the ranks of the music industry, this despite the infrequent efforts by a Linda Ronstadt to make the transition to musical comedy star, as that country rocker did in *Pirates of Penzance.*

The size of Broadway houses dictates, by union regulation, the number of musicians that must be employed for musical productions— regardless of what the score calls for. This has been a controversial issue in recent years, as costs for mounting Broadway musicals run in the $2–$3 million range, and producers are contractually bound to pay for players that aren't actually utilized (once termed "featherbedding" in the railroad industry).

Many of the most noted American songwriters, musicians, and performers are native New Yorkers; others have adopted the city as their home. Simon and Garfunkel, for example, were two Queens kids singing together in high school—and both have more or less continuously resided here. The Upper West Side is a veritable Who's Who in pop, with Simon, Diana Ross, Mick Jagger, Cher, Linda Ronstadt, and dozens of others comfortably ensconced along a few blocks in the upper 60s and lower 70s on Central Park West. (Alas, the Dakota on Central Park West at West 72nd Street is where John Lennon was brutally shot; his widow Yoko Ono and their son, Sean, still live there.)

For the most part, these superstars (as well as their lesser-known brethren) are active in the city. They hang out at Studio 54 when they want to dance their way to sunrise. They go to the Ritz when they want to catch the latest rage in new-wave bands, taking over the balcony tables reserved for guests of the house. They dine at the Russian Tea Room when they want to be spotted for the gossip pages. They go to neighborhood bars such as Chinese Chance at One University Place in the Village, where patrons are so accustomed to their presence that no one raises an eyebrow (let alone asks for an autograph or snaps a picture). They dine out in Chinatown, stalk the stalls at the Strand bookstore, go for walks in Central Park. By now you should have the impression that they live the life of the city—a little more cautiously, perhaps, in the wake of John Lennon's death, but clearly partaking of New York's distinctive style and culture, and using the city's offerings to build on their own talents.

Musically, the city flowers most distinctively at night—and very late at that. Pop concerts in the major concert halls usually start between 7:30 and 9, with a few scattered performances set for midnight (especially if an artist is playing two concerts a night). At the newer rock clubs and discos the doors often don't open until 10 or later, and shows at the likes of the Mudd Club and Peppermint Lounge have been known to start as late (or, have it as you will, early) as 3 A.M.! That trend was beginning to wane by mid-1982, as the economy took its toll and clubs sought to maximize the possible number of patrons. But late nights are a tradition among jazz musicians. Real aficionados would never think of going to a first set at 9:30 if they could make it to the 11 or 1 A.M. shows, and rock bands trying to trumpet their youthful anti-establishment position have co-opted that tradition for themselves. Three A.M. is a little extreme, but midnight or 1 A.M. are always likely to be popular.

John Kander's and Fred Ebb's words are a cliché by now: "New York, New York; if you can make it there you can make it anywhere." But as is so for most clichés, the words ring true, and especially so for those who are a part of New York's musical life. The opportunities are there, the competition tough, but the rewards for those who make it are unparalleled. Best of all, the challenge to be heard—or, for the fan, to discover someone new for yourself—is as much a part of the excitement as the music itself.

THE ARTISTS' NEW YORK
by
GAIL LEVIN

Gail Levin is an art historian and museum curator in New York. She has written books and organized exhibitions on Abstract Expressionism, Edward Hopper, and other topics and artists in American art.

Artists have found New York a hospitable city since the days of the Dutch settlement of Nieuw Amsterdam. New York's oldest surviving art institution is the National Academy of Design, founded in 1826 by painter and inventer Samuel F. B. Morse to serve as an art school and to organize annual exhibitions. Located since 1940 at the corner of Fifth Avenue and 89th Street, the National Academy still offers classes and presents a diverse program of exhibitions. The National Academy's conservatism and other factors resulted in the establishment of the Art Students League in 1875 and subsequently in many other splinter groups. The League, now at 215 West 57th Street, is still an active art school where many distinguished artists have studied and taught.

For the New York art world the end of the 19th century was a busy, restless time. One of the most prominent artists was William Merritt Chase, who taught at the Art Students League from 1878–1896 and who founded his own summer art school at Shinnecock on Long Island in 1891 and also one in New York in 1896 that became the League's rival. Chase's work can be seen in depth at the Parrish Art Museum in Southhampton near the Shinnecock Hills where he spent his summers and painted—in an American Impressionist style—the surrounding countryside with its picturesque fields and dunes. Chase helped to make the eastern end of Long Island the artist's colony it remains today.

By 1903, the progressive Robert Henri had become Chase's rival on the faculty at the school he founded in New York. Henri was an inspiring teacher who revived the realist tradition in American art and encouraged such students as Edward Hopper and George Bellows to paint life around them, resulting in some images that are quintessentially New York. John Sloan, who exhibited with Henri and six others as "The Eight" in 1908, was Henri's chief cohort in what became a struggle against the power of the Academy. Sloan's urban vistas captured the dynamism of early 20th-century New York. Some of the places he depicted can be visited today, among them the 19th-century tavern, McSorley's Ale House, at 15 East 7 Street (between Second and Third avenues), which since the Feminists' protests of 1970 now admits women, and the Washington Square Arch where, in 1917, Sloan along with French iconoclast Marcel Duchamp and others held a protest party to establish the secession of Greenwich Village from the United States.

For generations the Village was the home of many New York artists. Sloan lived at 88 Washington Place from 1915 to 1927, when he moved to 53 Washington Square, where he remained until 1935. Edward Hopper lived and worked on the top floor of the brownstone at 3 Washington Square North from 1913 until his death in 1967; his studio is now an office in the New York University School of Social Work. Many of the characteristic views in Hopper's realist paintings can still be found in the Village (and elsewhere in New York): Judson Memorial Church, across the square from the arch; rooftops punctuated with water towers and chimneys; rows of brownstone houses, often with their bay windows illuminated at night. Among the other artists and writers who lived or worked at 3 Washington Square North were Ernest Lawson and William Glackens of "The Eight," Thomas Eakins, E.E. Cummings, John Dos Passos, and Rockwell Kent.

From 1907, sculptor Gertrude Vanderbilt Whitney had a studio on Macdougal Alley where she held informal exhibitions of works by fellow artists. In 1914 she opened the Whitney Studio at 8 West Eighth Street, where she gave progressive and young artists exhibitions, and four years later she founded the Whitney Studio Club at 147 West Fourth Street. In 1923 the Club moved to the Whitney Studio on West Eighth Street, where evening sketch classes were held. In 1931, the Whitney Museum of American Art opened at the Eighth Street address. The Museum moved uptown in 1954, and subsequently to its current location at 75th Street and Madison Avenue. The old museum building on Eighth Street now houses the New York Studio School.

The Village has been the haunt of some of the most avant-garde artists in New York. During the 1910s, at 23 Fifth Avenue, Mabel Dodge held her famous "evenings," attended by radicals including future revolutionary John Reed, feminists, poets, and modernist artists such as Andrew Dasburg, Marsden Hartley, John Marin, and Francis Picabia. Further uptown at 291 Fifth Avenue, from 1905–1917, was Alfred Stieglitz's Gallery, known affectionately as "291" and officially as the "Little Galleries of the Photo-Secession." It was at "291" that Mabel first met many of the artists who attended her salons.

One of the most significant events for the New York art world was the great International Exhibition of Modern Art held in 1913 at the 69th Regiment Armory still at Lexington Avenue and 25th Street.

"The Armory Show" shocked the general public with modernist painting and sculpture by the leading European artists including Matisse,
Picasso, Duchamp, Picabia, and Brancusi and changed the course of
art in America. When Duchamp arrived in New York in 1915, he
eventually moved his studio into the building of progressive art patrons
Louise and Walter Arensberg at 33 West 67th Street.

During the late 1920s the "Fourteenth Street School" emerged, consisting of artists like Kenneth Hayes Miller and Reginald Marsh, who
had studios on Union Square. These artists, and Miller's student Isabel
Bishop, who still has her studio there, were attracted to the vitality of
this working-class shopping district—which was also a favorite place
for radical political activity, free speech, and assembly. Traditionalists,
these artists immortalized this spectacle, not as social commentators
but as keen observers of New York urban life.

By the late 1930s, another generation of burgeoning avant-garde
artists had populated the Village. Hans Hofmann, a German emigré,
had his own school at 52 West Eighth Street where he offered a modernist approach to art instruction. One of his former students, Lee
Krasner, eventually introduced him to Jackson Pollock, with whom
she was living at 46 East Eighth Street. These artists were to become
known as the "Abstract Expressionists." Their emergence as the vanguard coincided with the presence of many important European artists
living in exile in New York during the Second World War. Pollock and
Hofmann, as well as Mark Rothko, Clyfford Still, and others, showed
at Peggy Guggenheim's gallery, Art of This Century, at 30 West 57th
Street. Although this gallery with its Surrealist space designed by sculptor Frederick Kiesler no longer exists, West 57th Street today is still
one of the main gallery neighborhoods in the city. Among the places
frequented by the Abstract Expressionists was the Cedar Street Tavern,
then at 24 University Place and today under the same management at
82 University Place at 11th Street.

In 1945, Krasner and Pollock married and moved from New York
to The Springs section of East Hampton, Long Island, which soon
became the home of many other artists, including Abstract Expression-
ist painters Willem de Kooning and James Brooks, who still reside
there. Pollock's response to the area's natural beauty is found in *Ac-
cabonac Creek,* a series of paintings he showed in 1947, named for the
creek behind his home on Fireplace Road. Art exhibitions featuring
East Hampton's local celebrities can be seen at Ashawagh Hall in The
Springs and Guild Hall in East Hampton Village.

During the 1950s New York's vanguard artists shifted eastwards to
the area of the Village referred to as Tenth Street, since that block
between Third and Fourth avenues was at its center. By the mid-fifties,
artists organized many cooperative galleries to show their work there.

In the fall of 1948, Robert Motherwell, William Baziotes, Mark Rothko, and David Hare founded the Subjects of the Artist School in a loft at 35 East Eighth Street. Although it only lasted about a year, the Friday evening series of lectures by artists inspired many. For more than a decade beginning in the fall of 1949, just two doors away at number 39 East Eighth Street, the Club, founded by Franz Kline, Willem de Kooning, and others, held panel discussions. Today the center of artist activity has shifted to other areas, but the New Museum at 65 Fifth Avenue (at 14th Street) offers provocative exhibitions of contemporary art.

By the late 1950s a very different community of avant-garde artists grew up on the southern tip of Manhattan in lofts on Coenties Slip. This included pop artists Robert Indiana and James Rosenquist, as well as Minimalists Elsworth Kelly and Agnes Martin. Other artists had already begun to move to spacious disused factory lofts in a neighborhood of industrial decay called SoHo, the acronym for South Houston (pronounced HOUSE-ton) Industrial District. Throughout the 1960s the artist population there grew dramatically, and by 1968 the first SoHo gallery opened. By 1971, artists had won from the city the legal right to live and work in SoHo, and many galleries had located there. Real-estate values soared and the transformation of SoHo reached a new stage, attracting boutiques, chic restaurants, and young professionals, who enjoy both the ample living spaces and the atmosphere. The SoHo gallery scene is still the liveliest for contemporary art in New York, with West Broadway from Houston to Canal Streets the main thoroughfare for galleries and people watching—but less established artists can no longer afford to live there.

Following the development of SoHo, many artists settled in TriBeCa, the acronym for the triangle below Canal Street, extending west to the Hudson River and east to City Hall. Today many of the liveliest alternative spaces are found in TriBeCa, as well as a number of galleries. The alternative spaces includes the Franklin Furnace at 112 Franklin Street, an archives for artists' book works as well as a spot for artists' performances; the Alternative Museum, with an international program operated by artists at 17 White Street; Artists Space at 105 Hudson Street, which shows works of emerging artists not represented by private galleries; and the Clocktower of the Institute for Art and Urban Resources at 108 Leonard Street. TriBeCa now also has its own chic restaurants, including The Odeon at 145 West Broadway, with its refurbished Art Deco interior, where leading artists and dealers can be seen.

With galleries concentrated in SoHo, TriBeCa, on 57th Street and along Madison Avenue from the 60s through the 80s, anyone wishing to survey the New York art market must cover a large part of the city.

Today artists, who traditionally live where inexpensive space can be found, are settling everywhere from Long Island City in Queens to Hoboken, New Jersey. Neighborhoods, like artists, keep evolving—and that is part of New York's vitality.

MANHATTAN: SOME ARCHITECTURAL
PLEASURES

by
G. E. KIDDER SMITH

G. E. Kidder Smith is an architect and Fellow of the American Institute of Architects, but most of his professional life has been devoted to writing on the subject. His three-volume guide, The Architecture of the United States, *was published recently by the Museum of Modern Art and Doubleday. His* Pictorial History of Architecture in America *has inexpensively been republished in a single volume.*

In exploring the cornucopia of architectural delights of New York's essential borough, one can do no better than to begin where the city began, on that jutting tip of Manhattan known as The Battery (Bowling Green subway stop). Here, first the Dutch (1626), then the unresisted English (1664) set up shop. The Dutch legacy is now remembered by its log palisade (1653) memorialized as Wall Street, but alas, little remains of the structures which the two European powers erected; however, meticulously reconstructed models and dioramas can be seen in the Federal Hall Memorial Building (26 Wall Street) and in the Museum of the City of New York (Fifth Avenue at 103rd).

Not only did Nieuw Amsterdam/New York arise on this strategic point of land, the United States itself commenced life here, George Washington taking the oath of office (1789) as our first president on the spot where Federal Hall Memorial now stands. It will be recalled that New York was also the short-term capital of the new country. (The capital was moved to Philadelphia in 1790 before settling in Washington in 1800.)

Most of the structures from the distant past have long since vanished, not only in the The Battery–Financial District but in all of the city, indeed the nation. This fresh, brash new land has always looked forward—a philosophy epitomized by Henry Ford's statement that 'history is bunk'—and for several hundred years we have plowed under or built over many of those oft-sturdy witnesses of our background that constituted our historic stepping stones, a process often hastened by devastating fires. We are now fortunately more careful of our inheritance, for it can provide an enriching experience.

The most potent impact of the south end of Manhattan lies, however, not so much in its individual structures, aged or otherwise, as in its overwhelming density of buildings—those almost threatening phalanxes of skyscrapers marching down narrow streets, crowding out light and air, and rough-shouldering neighbors in grasps for maximum rentable space. At the noon hour of a workday the streets are frantic with men and machines; in the quiet of the weekend the area becomes a fascinating deserted world.

The following itinerary of architectural highlights is suggested; though of necessity limited in scope, and non-chronological, it is perhaps the simplest, and the interplay of disparate buildings counterpoints the vitality of each era. But before exploring the manmade ravines, take a bracing stroll around Battery Park, a key site—as would be imagined—for fortifications which, as 'recently' as the War of 1812, constituted the city's early harbor defenses. Castle Clinton in the park was once on an island, but was connected to the mainland by landfill after that war. Designed in 1807 by John McComb, Jr., the fort, with eight-foot-thick walls, subsequently served as a concert hall (Jenny Lind sang there), then was converted into an aquarium (1896), being fully restored to its original condition in 1975 by the National Park Service (open Weds. to Sun, 9 A.M.–5 P.M.). It is also from The Battery that one can take a ferry to Frédéric-Auguste Bartholdi's Statue of Liberty (1886; Gustave Eiffel, engineer) and another ferry to Staten Island (at South Street Station), the second excursion offering a marvelous and inexpensive perspective of Lower Manhattan.

The building of greatest distinction adjacent to the Battery is the Old Customs House (1909; Cass Gilbert, architect), holding down with élan the termination of Broadway. (Broadway is the city's longest avenue, stretching some 19 miles to Yonkers; it will form the downtown spine of this walk.) The Customs House stands at the peak of the city's Classic Revival, Beaux-Arts structures, because of its urban understanding, its monumentality, and its beautifully integrated sculpture. Daniel Chester French sculpted the four continents (the seated ladies) and a half-dozen sculptors the 12 historic trading cities above (the standing men). The Rotunda within, if open, should also be seen; its 1937 murals were painted by Reginald Marsh.

In progressing northward up Broadway, note the often handsome lineup of office structures (largely of the 1920s), many originally connected with shipping. Between Rector and Thames, and at the head of Wall Street, stands Trinity Church (1846; Richard Upjohn, architect), embraced by a beautifully planted cemetery (c. 1681). The church's interior may be on the dry side (its vaulting is suspended from wood trusses), but the exterior and 284-foot high steeple are compelling. Directly across the street at Number 1 Wall rises the 50-story Irving

Trust Building (1931; Voorhees, Gmelin, & Walker, architects), one of
the finest of the simplified, limestone-revetted skyscrapers of its period.
Note its window modulation and the angled Art-Deco touches.

A hundred yards to the east, at Wall and Nassau streets, stands
Federal Hall National Memorial, built as a Custom House (1842; Town
& Davis and John Frazee, architects), subsequently serving as Subtreasury, and since 1955 memorialized as the site where George Washington took office; his statue is by J.Q.A. Ward (1883). The building's
façade's proportions were taken directly from the Parthenon but with
a slight reduction. The interior now serves as a lively downtown museum. Federal Hall gazes down Broad Street at the Stock Exchange at
Number 8 (1903; George B. Post, architect), an opulent Classic-Reviv-
al statement topped by a pediment bursting with sculpted figures representing "Commerce," much of it by the aforementioned Mr. Ward.
Conducted tours—fascinating—are available business days.

Instead of immediately returning to Broadway, walk two blocks
north up Nassau Street (alongside Federal Hall; observe the power of
its flank) to Chase Manhattan Plaza. Chase Bank (1961; Skidmore,
Owings & Merrill, architects) rises 60 floors above its terrace with
unflinching rectangularity, its "meeting" with the horizontal being
notable. The plaza not only gives welcome openness to the area, but
because of it the bank itself could rise without setback—one of the early
urban tradeoffs made possible by the 1961 zoning regulations, by which
more open space at ground level on a building plot would increase the
number of full floors allowed for the building. A sunken landscaped
pool by Isamu Noguchi enables the visitor to look down into the
banking floor (entered off William Street), while Jean Dubuffet's 42-
foot high sculpture, "Group of Four Trees" (1972), acts as a superb
spatial "stopper" from the west and as a magnet from south and east.
Directly across Nassau Street stands the Marine Midland Building
(1968; Skidmore, Owings & Merrill, architects), a sleek-skinned, dark
counterpoint to Chase Manhattan. Its entry, at 140 Broadway, is
highlighted by Noguchi's brilliant orange-red cube balanced on a dia-
gonal. The entry plaza, plus the planted area along Cedar Street, allowed the building to rise an uninterrupted 52 floors. Completing a
trilogy of near-adjacent skyscrapers, all by SOM, is One Liberty Plaza
(1972) at 165 Broadway. The building's dark muscularity stems directly from its exposed steel framing. City building codes require fire-
proofing of steel—which can buckle under intense heat—and here
protection was achieved by flame-insulating shields wrapped around
the top and bottom of the enormous steel girders (some are 52 feet long
and almost 6 feet deep) but leaving the web (the vertical part) exposed.
The result is powerful, even aggressive, but it adds a new dimension to
the high-rise. The block across Liberty Street was acquired, cleared,

and made into a park so that the building could rise 54 floors without setback under the city's zoning laws.

Off Church Street, and directly west of One Liberty Plaza, loom the two 110-story high square towers of the World Trade Center (1980; Minoru Yamasaki & Associates, Emery Roth & Sons, architects). These brilliantly engineered towers—whose height surpasses the Empire State Building by 100 feet—decisively punctuate Lower Manhattan's madcap silhouette of high-rise idiosyncrasies. A U-shaped "frame" of eight-story buildings develops territoriality for the towers and creates a five-acre plaza on which all units focus. Sculpture by Masayuki Magare holds down the entry, with Fritz Koenig's bronze sphere and fountain in the center and James Rosati's ideogram left in the background. A splendid Calder stabile highlights the corner of Church and Vesey streets. The Observation Deck on WTC2 and the Windows on the World Restaurant (expensive . . . but try the bar) atop WTC1 offer heady views.

Returning to Broadway via Fulton Street, on the corner we find St. Paul's Chapel (1766; Thomas McBean, architect; tower 1794), Manhattan's only surviving pre-Revolutionary church. It is instructive to experience the 80-year difference between this late-Colonial house of worship and Trinity just down the street. St. Paul's London-inspired design radiates light and air via its large windows; Trinity's Gothic Revival opts for Medievalism. St. Paul's originally opened onto the river and Church Street.

Two blocks northward at 233 Broadway stands the famous Woolworth Building (1913; Cass Gilbert, architect), the tallest building in the world from 1913 to 1930—and still one of our finer-knit skyscrapers. London's "Gothic" Houses of Parliament were of architectural inspiration. Take a look at its refulgent lobby. Directly facing the Woolworth Building lies City Hall Park—once a common—with the competition-winning "French-Federal" City Hall near the center (1812; John McComb, Jr. and Joseph F. Mangin, architects). The prize money was $350. The Governor's Room museum on the second floor of this quietly civilized building is recommended.

One of the 19th century's greatest engineering feats—and one of New York's most memorable experiences—can be found just southeast of City Hall: the Brooklyn Bridge (1883; John Augustus Roebling and his son Washington, engineers). With a center span of 1,595 feet (more than 50 percent greater than any earlier bridge) the Brooklyn Bridge, whose centenary is 1983, remains one of the city's supreme landmarks. Moreover, it pioneered the use of caissons for working under water and the use of steel cables. Be certain to walk out on its elevated pedestrian level to feel enmeshed in its web of angled cables, Manhattan shining beyond. (The trip by car is less satisfying). At the Manhattan end of the bridge rises the imposingly arched Municipal Building (1913; McKim, Mead & White, architects; W.M. Kendall, designer). Very much of its Classic Revival period—this was a time of revivals as evidenced in the precisely contemporary Woolworth Building—the building exhibits sensitivity to its setting and to City Hall. The sculpture "Civic Fame" atop was sculpted by Adolph A. Weinmann. A mishmash of other civic structures, mostly concerned with the courts, lies just beyond (up Centre and Lafayette streets), with the lower edge of Chinatown a few blocks to the north and east.

Farther up Broadway and about a half-mile north of City Hall Park lies a unique section of New York. This SoHo (SOuth of HOuston) area is roughly bounded by Canal Street on the south, West Houston (pronounced "*Howston*") on the north, West Broadway to the west and Broadway and Crosby Street to the east. In recent years, SoHo has been "discovered" by artists seeking roomy work space, and the area is now alive with trendy shops and restaurants. Here one also finds a concentration of cast-iron buildings not equalled anywhere both for quantity and quality.

Cast iron as a structural building material (as opposed to a decorative one and for firebacks, etc.) was developed in the 1850s, and immediately became popular, especially for commercial buildings. Interior supporting columns could be small, while a façade of slender iron frames and large panes of glass admitted far more light into showrooms and work spaces than wall-bearing masonry. (Side walls and back were generally kept in brick and stone: they were cheaper and provided better fire protection.) Moreover, cast iron came in prefabricated, demountable, easy to erect units and—almost equally important—was able to reproduce an inebriating range of ornament at small cost. The material began to phase out in the 1880s and '90s with the introduction of far-stronger steel beams and columns. Greene Street, particularly near Canal Street, in SoHo is one of the most rewarding hunting grounds for cast-iron architecture, while the most famous single example—now, fortunately, a National Registered Landmark—is the former Haughwout Store at 488 Broadway and Broome Street (1857; John P. Gaynor, architect, with the Badger Architectural Iron Works). This former department store anticipated the skyscraper both in its use of cast-iron skeletal construction and as the first commercial building to install Mr. Otis' safety elevator. Moreover, its Venetian-inspired façades are superb.

At Broadway and 23rd Street stands the richly encrusted Flatiron Building (1903; D. H. Burnham & Co., architects), squeezed into a difficult triangle by Broadway and Fifth Avenue. Though only 20 floors high, it was for years the tallest and most famous office structure in town.

Switching now to Fifth Avenue (Broadway at midtown becomes

sadly cheapened) we hail at 33rd–34th Street the pharos of Manhattan, the Empire State Building (1931; Shreve, Lamb & Harmon, architects). Still elegant and proud—though outpaced in height by the World Trade Center—and always offering a marvelous vantage point, long may it serve as the city's trademark. The Observation Deck is open daily from 9:30 A.M. to midnight.

Fifth Avenue in spots develops a patrician quality from the mid-30s northward, and when it reaches 40th–42nd streets, we find one of the city's gems, the New York Public Library (1911; Carrère & Hastings, architects). Not only is the building itself possibly New York's greatest Beaux-Arts structure (its only peer is the Old Customs House), but the development of its relation to the street, which begins—with a garden —at the very edge of the sidewalk, is unequalled. The slightly elevated detachment of the Library's 390-foot-long parterre and the plantings behind provide a marvelous welcome to the building, which is set back 75 feet from the avenue. The main reading room on the third floor, though devious of access, is an airy chamber. Bryant Park (1884–1934), directly behind the library, provides a notable, small urban retreat (though not safe after dark).

Turning right (east) off Fifth Avenue at 42nd Street, one will encounter in a few blocks a clutch of the city's finer buildings. Foremost among these, opening onto Vanderbilt, Park, and Lexington avenues, is Grand Central Station (1913; Warren & Wetmore, Reed & Stem, architects; W.J. Wilgus, engineer). It is probably safe to say that no railroad station in the world—not even Rome's Termini (1950)—ennobles rail travel as handsomely as Grand Central's great concourse. In addition to solving—brilliantly—the complex task of handling X-hundred trains a day (600 in the 1940s), the station is a transportation nexus for the entire East Side of New York, with three deeply bedded subway lines and a vast network of underground connections to various hotels and office buildings. All of this is accomplished with dispatch and graspable simplicity. The exterior is commanding in spite of the embrace of elevated automobile ramps (1920), while the main interior is one of the city's great spaces.

Across Lexington Avenue from Grand Central pokes the multi-arced spire of the Chrysler Building (1930; William Van Alen, architect), alive with flashes of sun on its innovative stainless-steel roof. This 77-story, 1,046-foot high skyscraper, for a brief time the highest in the world, epitomizes the Art-Deco period of the '20s and '30s with its bursts of angles and its abstracted brick patterns of automotive features—plus radiator-cap gargoyles. Farther east at 220 42nd Street rises the Chrysler Building's precise contemporary, the Daily News Building (1930; Raymond M. Hood and John M. Howells, architects). Here a fresh simplicity and a prophetic series of sharply etched setbacks were pioneered, their climax shortly to be seen at Rockefeller Center on whose design team Raymond Hood played a decisive role. Just beyond Second Avenue on 42nd Street, but with main entrance at 320 East 43rd, stands the Ford Foundation (1967; Kevin Roche/John Dinkeloo, architects). When one uses the shadowed 43rd Street entry (preferable), one overlooks an exotic garden, generally sun-drenched and always intriguing, which steps down subtle terraces. Urban zoning demands that a certain proportion of a building site be left open, the amount depending on height, and when Roche/Dinkeloo proposed an enclosed garden 130 feet high, instead of an open court, the city rightly (for once) gave them a "variance" to do so. The court (Dan Kiley, landscape architect) also acts as a rallying point for the L of offices that open (literally) upon it, stimulating a "family" atmosphere for all concerned with the dispensing of the foundation's monies. Take a stroll in the carefully air-conditioned bower (open during business hours).

At the very end of 42nd Street at First Avenue rises the great slab of the United Nations Secretariat Building, with the less-great General Assembly at its feet (1950; Wallace K. Harrison, Director of Planning; Max Abramovitz, Deputy Director; Le Corbusier, Sven Markelius, Oscar Niemeyer, N.D. Bassov, members of Advisory Committee). The Secretariat's resolute geometry, with no breaks or setbacks, its blank end walls, the frank expression of its four utility floors (air conditioning, etc.), its curtain-wall skin with green-tinted glass (to lessen sun loads)—all these concepts were largely pioneered here. In short, a splendid building—and best seen (like most of the riparian architecture of NYC) from a Circle Line boat trip. Guided tours of the U.N. are conducted daily.

Returning to Fifth Avenue we find at 43rd Street a small bank—Manufacturers Hanover Trust—but one whose all-glass exterior changed forever the image of the "Classic" column-girt bank (1954; Skidmore, Owings & Merrill, architects). They even put the vault almost literally on the sidewalk. At 49th Street rises the most brilliant grouping of large buildings one will see anywhere: Rockefeller Center (1931–40; Reinhard & Hofmeister; Corbett, Harrison & MacMurray; Hood & Fouilhoux, architects). Each unit is respectful of the others and all to the central plaza. To develop a welcoming scale on Fifth Avenue, the two buildings leading to the plaza are only of six stories. Between them unfolds the promenade, seasonally flowered, and the ever-popular *Sitzplatz,* which debouches onto the sunken arena. Here, surrounded by the colorful flags of the members of the United Nations, and given accent by Paul Manship's gold-leafed statue of Prometheus (depicted on the cover of this book), one encounters a non-stop, open-air—and free—theater. Bright awnings fill this spatial nugget for outdoor dining much of the year, while ice skaters perform in winter. But whatever the season, the visitors themselves are part of this ingenious stage, the 70-story RCA Building acting as backdrop. On the Avenue of the Americas at 50th Street, the refurbished 6,200-seat Radio City Music Hall—an unforgettable theater of another kind—holds forth. The view from the Observation Roof on the 65th floor of the RCA Building is particularly sorcerous at dusk.

Holding down Fifth Avenue between 50th–51st streets, St. Patrick's Cathedral (1858–79; James Renwick, Jr., architect) takes brilliant urban advantage of its block-square site. The church itself has been criticized as being somewhat mechanical for "organic" Gothic architecture, but it is nonetheless impressive outside and smashing within. Note, on the exterior, that the "buttresses" do not "fly" to carry the roof thrust to the ground: they simply stand there unattached, the "vaulting" being supported by inner trusses.

The following list embraces a miscellany of buildings and two parks of interest, most of them a few blocks east of Fifth Avenue:

Paley Park (1967: Zion & Breen, landscape architects) at 3 East 53rd Street, though measuring only 43 by 100 feet, is a mid-city oasis of pure delight. Its waters add sparkle to the day, while muffling the noises from the street, and its 12 honey locusts establish an arbored "room" away from the cares of the day. Light refreshments are served except in January and February.

Lever House (1952; Skidmore, Owings & Merrill, architects), Park Avenue between 53rd–54th streets. The outstanding contribution of this company building (there is no rental space) lies in its airy liberation of site, with its elevated massing, walk-through garden court, and the 18-story office block rising at one side. Lever House's glass-walled architecture has been copied ad infinitum, but its land usage is unique.

Seagram Building (1958; Mies van der Rohe and Philip Johnson, architects), 375 Park Avenue. Diagonally across Park Avenue from Lever House and set back 100 feet from the street, the Seagram Building rises 39 floors with incredible dignity and graspability. Plaza and building—the horizontal and the vertical—have rarely in history been so superbly interwoven. Note that the granite pavement extends into the building and that the ground floor is precisely twice as high as those above. This building is not to be missed. (The Four Seasons Restaurant by Philip Johnson, entered from 52nd St., is one of the city's most posh; note the Lippold sculpture in the bar.)

Citicorp Center (1977; Hugh Stubbins & Associates, architects), Lexington Avenue between 53rd–54th streets. This startling skyscraper, its 48 floors blithely resting on a platform 115 feet in the air and with a full-grown church tucked beneath one corner, evolved because St. Peter's Lutheran Church, which owned a good slice of the property, would sell only if its parish could rebuild on the same site. The architects and engineers then evolved the brilliant solution. The three-story central interior space—the Market—is also impressive, with agora atmosphere alive with tempting shops and restaurants. It forms a spontaneous gathering spot, made possible by "incentive" zoning whereby rentable building height could be increased if public amenities were incorporated below.

At Madison Avenue and 75th Street rises the provocative mass of the Whitney Museum of American Art (1966; Marcel Breuer and Hamilton P. Smith, architects). Its upside-down, instepped façade arose through the imaginative desire to incorporate an open-air sculpture court across the front. The three upper floors, especially the taller one on top, provide some of the finest art-viewing rooms in the city. Moreover, they are admirably flexible in meeting the Whitney's main emphasis on temporary exhibitions.

On Fifth Avenue between 88th–89th streets we find Frank Lloyd Wright's only building in New York City, the famous, tantalizing and, in a way, outrageous Guggenheim Museum (1959). The building's forceful inner geometry and "dictated" ramp circulation (it has been called procrustean) tend, for some viewers, to dominate the art, but the inner space is so glorious that no one should miss it. Note the quiet, self-effacing entry, then the inner explosion of whirling ramps and the dazzling light shooting through the roof.

Lincoln Center for the Performing Arts (1959–68), 62nd–66th streets, Broadway and Columbus Avenue, anchors the entire West Side and acts as a key element in its rejuvenation. For most critics the classical allusions of the three main buildings are questionable: Avery Fisher Hall (1962; Max Abramovitz, architect); New York State Theater (1964; Philip Johnson, architect); and the Metropolitan Opera House (1966; Wallace K. Harrison architect). The Vivian Beaumont Theater (1965; Eero Saarinen & Associates, architect) and the Juilliard School of Music (1968; Pietro Belluschi, Eduardo Catalano, and Westermann & Miller, architects) get higher marks, while the activities all five buildings harbor are superlative. Conducted tours are available.

Whether approaching it from east or west, south or north, Central Park (1859–1876) forms the heart and lungs of New York City. Designed by Frederick L. Olmsted and Calvert Vaux, the park not only became the salvation of this city as it expanded northward, but the lesson of its superbly planned 840 acres was followed by many of the cities of the United States. As a consequence, the nation's concept of urban life marvelously expanded. The unkempt "pestilential" area transformed into Central Park had been rough terrain, dotted with swamps and squatters dwellings. Olmsted and Vaux, however, were not content merely to tidy matters up; every square foot was analyzed technically and esthetically before design decisions were made. Questions of topography, soil characteristics, drainage and water, circulation (pedestrian, vehicular, horse, bicycle) were only the initial concerns that preceded any thought of plants and trees. The result is one of the world's great urban statements: this city would be almost uninhabitable without it.

NEW YORK: THE VATICAN CITY OF BROADCASTING

by
MICHAEL SHAIN

Michael Shain is a reporter specializing in television for the New York Post. *He has been covering TV for over a decade, starting with* Broadcasting *magazine in 1971. He was written on TV for the* Village Voice, Penthouse, *and the* Washington Journalism Review.

A Florsheim shoe store now commemorates the spot where, nearly 80 years ago and quite by accident, the broadcasting business began. On 35th Street, where Broadway meets Sixth Avenue, 15-year-old David Sarnoff walked through the wrong doors in the lobby of the old New York Herald Building while looking for a copyboy's job. He came away that afternoon with a $5-a-week clerk's position for a telegraph company instead. Sarnoff rose, in the fashion expected of ambitious immigrant boys, to become the first president of the Radio Corporation of America (RCA), and thereby the first Caesar of a modern-day empire whose boundaries now lie somewhere between Archie Bunker's corner taproom and the orbit of Saturn.

Under Sarnoff, RCA existed to sell radio sets, the only plausible way of making a dollar in the broadcasting game at the time. He created the National Broadcasting Company (NBC) in 1926 to make sure something lovely and diverting would come out of those sets, to entice every family to want to own one.

And nothing sold sets like a couple of touring minstrel comedians named Freeman Gosden and Charles Cornell—Amos 'n' Andy. Andy was the feet-on-the-desk president and Amos the sole employee of the "Fresh-Air Taxi Cab Co., Incorpulated"—the epitome of the Depression-era strugglers making something grandiose out of not much at all. When they were on the air, movie theaters shut down their projectors, bar rooms emptied, and President Coolidge could not be disturbed at the White House.

"Amos 'n' Andy" and the shows that followed it—"Fibber McGee and Molly," the "Goldbergs," "Rudy Vallee," "Jack Benny"—were distributed over phone wires to an ever-growing chain of NBC affiliates from network headquarters at the Empire State Building, which had just been built on the site of the old Waldorf-Astoria Hotel.

By the time NBC moved uptown to the opulence of Radio City (not until recently have people begun referring to it properly as Rockefeller Center), the corporation was big enough to operate two separate, full-time networks—NBC Blue and NBC Red. But NBC no longer enjoyed a monopoly. The Columbia Broadcasting Service (CBS) was being run by an alarmingly young man from Philadelphia with a suave and skilled sense of showmanship and a rich father. Money from the family cigar business bought William S. Paley a controlling interest in CBS a year after the Wall Street crash. Paley's instinct for popular tastes put programs like "Jack Armstrong (All-American Boy)", "Gangbusters," and the "Kate Smith Hour" on the air from CBS headquarters at 485 Madison Avenue (now an insurance company building).

Throughout the 1930s, CBS could just about keep up with, but never surpass, NBC. It took Edward R. Murrow, a chain-smoking ex-newspaper man with the face of a hound, to show CBS as the equal of NBC. Murrow's vivid, rooftop reports of the Nazi bombing raids on London —the horrible footsteps of World War II sounding on America's front porch—seized the attention of the nation.

ABC, which was created at a single stroke by a 1943 government order for NBC to sell off one of its two networks, was strictly minor league well into the 1960s. Not until TV series like "Marcus Welby, M.D.," and "Happy Days" did ABC gain parity with its rivals.

Radio was a phenomenon when it was introduced in the mid-1920s. But television was practically a hysteria. In 1948 the number of TV sets in American could be counted in the hundreds. By the close of 1951 there were 15 million.

Some old radio hands made the step to television with grace—Jack Benny, Burns and Allen, Red Skelton, for instance. Television created its own personalities to replace those who could not: Milton Berle, Sid Caesar, and—most unlikely of all—Ed Sullivan.

Sullivan was a columnist for the New York *Daily News,* a raw-boned, unsmiling man who wielded enormous power in show-business circles. With the promise of juicy plugs in his column, Sullivan could lure just about any big-name performer he wished to the stage of his "Talk of the Town" show, produced from an abandoned Broadway theater on 54th Street that was eventually named after him. Around the corner is the deeply chic Studio 54 disco, where Perry Como, Jack Parr, and Jack Benny once did shows for CBS.

Because these glory days of radio and TV seemed to be evaporating so quickly, Paley endowed a Museum of Broadcasting (modelled in the image of the Museum of Modern Art, of which Paley is also chairman) in 1975. At One East 53rd Street, the Museum's two large theaters run special programs, continuous performances of maestro Arturo Toscanini's television concerts,.the Beatles hosted by Ed Sullivan, and Murrow's ground-breaking documentaries on Senator Joe McCarthy. In 1983, special retrospective exhibits on Walt Disney, the Muppets, and British television are scheduled.

Upstairs, 23 custom-built video consoles permit visitors to screen privately any of the 6,000 TV shows and 10,000 radio programs in its library—archives that range from the first and last episodes of "Charlie's Angels" and the "Mary Tyler Moore Show" to the full series of Public Broadcasting's "I, Claudius" and Kenneth Clark's "Civilisation" lectures.

Through its earliest years, television was "live," produced and broadcast on the spot from studios scattered up and down Manhattan's West Side. On the West Coast, "I Love Lucy" was being made with the same one-set, "live" look as the shows done in New York—but with an important difference: by putting Lucy on film, the show gained an immense new value—reruns.

The economies of film, and later video tape, chased producers out of New York and off to Hollywood. Much of the glamour left with them. What remained stoutly behind was the power to make decisions, the power to say "yea" or "nay" every spring when shows lined up for their annual renewals. These decisions of life (for one more season, at least) and death are dispensed from the three network headquarters, now clustered, like redwoods, along Sixth Avenue. NBC is at 30 Rockefeller Plaza on 50th Street, CBS at a stark and modern black-granite skyscraper on 54th Street (known unaffectionately in the business as "Black Rock," as in *Bad Day at Black Rock*), and ABC two blocks north on 54th Street.

Two things New York would not let go of were news and the production of soap operas. News is too important to a well-groomed corporate image (wasn't Walter Cronkite, in his placid way, the most recognizable symbol of CBS?) to farm out to California or even to Washington, D.C. and the soaps depended too heavily on the thorough supply of fresh Broadway theatrical faces—actors with the ability to work fast and in tight spaces—to fill out their large casts.

In a block-long fortress on 57th Street and 11th Avenue, CBS's Dan Rather slips behind the horseshoe desk bequeathed to him by Walter Cronkite to deliver the evening news at 6:30 P.M. every evening. Four doors away, in a powder blue studio, the stoney-faced hosts of "60 Minutes"—TV's single most popular (and profitable) program of the past decade—gather on Sunday evenings to present, live, the lead-ins to their slashy exposés of bureaucratic bumbling and consumer rip-offs. CBS's soaps, "As the World Turns" and "The Guiding Light," are also made there, in a set of studios on the 56th Street-side of the building.

Uptown, on West 66th Street just off Central Park, is ABC News headquarters. Some 200 local affiliates are fed (still by phone lines) the "World News Tonight" from an airless room chilled to the temperature of a meat locker to protect $15 million worth of electronic equipment from overheating.

Down the hall from where NBC anchorman Tom Brokaw reads his network's version of the day's events, on the fourth floor of 30 Rockefeller Plaza, is the cavernous, two-story studio built expressly for Toscanini and his weekly NBC Orchestra broadcasts. Three Saturdays a month beginning at 11:30 P.M., "Saturday Night Live," is broadcast from the room where Beethoven and Mahler once came back to life.

Beneath Brokaw's feet is the studio where "The Doctors," NBC's long-running soap opera, is turned out like Volkswagens off an assembly line, 30 minutes a day, 261 working days a year. In exactly the same fashion, NBC's "Another World" and "Texas" are made in an unspectacular brick warehouse across the East River, 10 miles away in the Flatbush section of Brooklyn.

Opposite ABC News' West 66th Street production center is a perfectly restored National Guard Armory—some Victorian architect's idea of what a medieval castle should look like—gutted on the inside and refashioned for "One Life to Live." Around the corner at 101 West 67th Street is the home of "All My Children." The "Edge of Night" is produced Monday through Friday on the second floor of an East 44th Street studio not far from the United Nations (and directly across the street from the new site of Costello's, an unofficial landmark and watering hole of New York reporters, where the tension of deadlines is chased away beneath original drawings by James Thurber painted on the walls).

The networks do not permit spectators on the sets of their soaps (or newscasts). Of course, no one objects if you care to stick around outside the studio entrances for a glimpse of the stars. But be warned: Your illusions are very much in peril. In their jeans, without make-up and wigs, most soap stars are altogether indistinguishable from the script girls and costume mistresses.

If you want to see those few New York shows that still use studio audiences—"David Letterman," "Saturday Night Live," Dick Cavett's interview program on PBS—write well in advance for tickets. And if you should spot a young person wearing a CBS "eye" button and hawking "free tickets," walk right up; CBS will be trying to muster an audience of otherwise innocent viewers to look at tapes of possible new series and sample their reactions. It's fun and takes only about an hour.

Perhaps you are immodest enough to think you've got a talent TV cannot do without? Then the networks have offices here in New York that will—at their own leisure—take a look. Acting hopefuls, understand, have practically no chance of breaking into TV this way (you need an agent). Still not deterred? Okay. Stuff an 8 x 10-inch glossy photo and a resumé of your acting experience into a big envelope, mark it to the Talent Department, and leave it at the reception desk on the ground floor at each of the three network headquarters.

Don't call them. They'll call you.

THE NEW YORK FASHION-ADVERTISING-PHOTOGRAPHY-FILMMAKING NETWORK

by
ELLEN J. GREENFIELD

Ellen J. Greenfield has been a reporter for Women's Wear Daily *in New York City and is a freelance writer specializing in business-related topics.*

Along Seventh Avenue, between 34th and 42nd streets, the grimy exteriors of the buildings and the rude jostling and jockeying of the workers almost hide the fact that here is the home of high fashion in the United States. Seventh Avenue—or Fashion Avenue, as the street signs point out—exerts its magnetic attraction to aspiring models and fashion designers throughout the country.

Blunt young men propelling racks of plastic-wrapped garments, loading-dock workers, truckers, millionaire executives, lithe, leggy models, trendy secretaries, offbeat or dapper designers, department-store buyers, beggars, bankers, and bargain hunters all crowd the streets of New York's Garment Center, as do students from the nearby Fashion Institute of Technology and Parsons School of Design, industry training schools.

The design rooms and showrooms of many renowned luminaries of the fashion universe are clustered here. Their names are often legendary: Oscar de la Renta; Calvin Klein; Ralph Lauren; Donna Karan and Louis Dell'Olio for Anne Klein; Perry Ellis; Geoffrey Beene; Mary McFadden; Bill Blass; Pauline Trigere. While they travel the world for new trends, ideas, and fabrics, many of them readily admit that New York provides the basis for their inspiration.

Surrounding the successful designers are a coterie of models, photographers, reporters, store buyers, and, of course, the beautiful people who wear the clothes.

Seventh Avenue activity, always bustling, reaches its frenzied peak twice each year—in April when the fall collections are shown, and again in October when the spring and summer collections make their appearances.

At these times thousands of store buyers, fashion reporters, and photographers from around the country descend on the avenue and move *en masse* from one dramatically staged and choreographed (and sometimes catered) showing to another. While invitations to most of the shows are a must, some designers may choose to hold their showings in large auditoriums such as that in Parsons School of Design. In that case, they may allow students and interested visitors to attend if advance reservations are made. If you admire a designer and plan to be in the city around the collection weeks, it can't hurt to call ahead and try to get a ticket.

While the clothes are, naturally, the central attraction, the models, or "mannequins" as they are sometimes called, often attain as much celebrity as the designers. Whether gliding down the runway, swinging into a pose for the camera, or rushing through the city streets carrying oversized bags of make-up and accessories, they look like long-stemmed beings from a more perfect planet.

New York is a mecca for beautiful young men and women who yearn for a career in modelling. They come here, portfolios in hand, to knock at the doors of some of the most influential modelling agencies in the world, including Zoli, Ford, Wilhelmina, Elite, and John Robert Powers. Most of the agencies have chic East Side locations in the fashionable Fifties. They are always on the lookout for new faces to add to their books, but they are also extremely discriminating and point blank in their evaluation of new talent—and with good reason. Top models can earn as much as $1,000 an hour for their work. Some, such as Brooke Shields, Cheryl Tiegs, Susie Parker, and Lauren Hutton, have managed to cross the boundary between commercial modelling and television or film acting. Even Dustin Hoffman, best known for his roles in such movies as *The Graduate,* started out doing commercials for Volkswagen!

The photographers who specialize in the New York fashion scene—Francesco Scavullo, Skrebensky, Richard Avedon, Irving Penn—have elevated their craft to an art form.

At the same time, newspapers such as *Women's Wear Daily* (often called "the Bible of the fashion industry") and *The New York Times* have their own photographers out on the streets here shooting new fashions "on location" or capturing trends from what the city's residents and visitors (from all over the U.S. and the world) are wearing.

Some freelance photographers, such as tall, bespectacled Bill Cunningham, have made candid street shots their forte. Anyone could be captured by their inquiring lenses, and you could find yourself amid the pages of *Women's Wear* under the caption "They are Wearing."

As the city real-estate prices skyrocketed in midtown, a group of younger, less established designers set up their studios and shops downtown in the SoHo area. There, large spaces and lofts once used for manufacturing are now devoted to a more flamboyant, outrageous, and sometimes humorous brand of fashion than is seen uptown. Clothing boutiques abound in SoHo, featuring the work of local designers, and they are worth visiting, along with the nearby art galleries.

But even the best of fashion and photography could not flourish without another industry indigenous to the city.

New York's Madison Avenue has become almost synonymous with the thriving industry that has invaded and changed the lives of people everywhere: Advertising. Advertising grew of age in New York beginning in the middle and late 1800s. Many of the earliest agencies—J. Walter Thompson, D'Arcy-McManus, N.W. Ayer, Albert Frank Guenther Law, Campbell-Ewald, Griswold-Eshleman, and Edwin Bird Wilson—still have offices here today and remain leaders in the field.

New York ad executives believe, and probably with good reason, that when you select your soda, beer, jeans, shoes, cigarettes, toys, or an airline, they have influenced your decision. New York agencies are responsible for more than $2 billion of the $5 billion per year the U.S. ad industry grosses in income.

It is estimated that some 3,000 to 4,000 ads and commercials are made here each year, compared with only about 1,500 in London and 1,000 in Paris. In fact, during the years when John Lindsay was mayor (1966–1973), New York became such a popular site for producing not only commercials but films and television shows that the city created a special post of liaison officer to facilitate police protection and cooperation with the media.

While "on location" shooting and production in the city has slowed somewhat in recent years, there are still plenty of places around town where ads and commercials are shot regularly.

Among the most popular sites are Grand Army Plaza at Fifth Avenue and 59th Streets; The Tavern on the Green in Central Park; the boat basin at 79th Street on the Hudson; Wall Street; the Lincoln Center plaza and fountain; Rockefeller Center; Washington Square in Greenwich Village; and the promenade in Brooklyn Heights, which boasts a splendid view of the New York skyline complete with several bridges and a spectacular sunset nightly (almost).

Just outside the city, on Long Island, the Phipps Estate on Old Westbury Gardens is reputed to be the most photographed mansion in the world. It was featured in a series of Johnny Walker Scotch ads, among many others. The beaches and coastline surrounding the city— especially the Hamptons and Fire Island, both on the South Shore of Long Island—are also prime locations for commercial photography.

You should not be at all surprised then while touring around the city, to walk onto the set for a film or commercial. The signs to look for: Several Winnebago recreational vehicles (used to house the "talent"), a number of trucks carrying huge lights, cameras, and coffee-guzzling stagehands parked nearby, miles of black cable criss-crossing the sidewalk and streets—and a large crowd of other curious spectators kept in line and out of the action by special-duty police. After you've seen New York, you will no doubt recognize some of the sights again and again on your television screen or between the covers of magazines you'll read back home.

There is one other aspect to commercial photography that is less obvious but still vital, and that is studio still-life work. In the studio is where all those gorgeous, tempting shots of products are made under the most precise lighting, camera angles, and exposure.

These studio shots are usually made with the utmost secrecy; an agency that discovers its photographer was too talkative about his technique might fire him on the spot. It is unlikely that a visitor to the city would ever find him or herself behind these closed doors, but a peek behind it would reveal some surprises.

For example, although some of the eye-appealing products you see in ads are the real thing, photographers are not above "faking" a better-looking model of a product.

What you see as a mouth-watering, moist-looking chocolate cake could, in fact, have been shot from a sculpture of a cake made from plastic or another foodstuff entirely. It is almost impossible to tell the real McCoy from a trumped-up model when a artful professional is at work.

Secrecy is the hallmark of the advertising industry, and no wonder. Agencies spend a great deal of their time "pitching" clients and trying to woo the best ones away from other agencies. Many, if not most, large U.S. consumer goods companies have headquarters or marketing offices in New York City. The competition can be fierce, cut-throat, and involve big money. Clients have been known to pay up to $750,000 for a single commercial. The winning of clients like these often involves elaborate theatrics and Herculean tasks on the part of agency executives, but the most successful ones are well-rewarded with considerable financial prizes and the acclaim of their peers.

Keep this in mind the next time you admire the slickness of a commercial or shun the crassness of an ad. When Ralph Waldo Emerson said "If a man has good corn, or wood, or boards, or pigs to sell, or can make better chairs, or knives, crucibles, or church organs, than anybody else, you will find a broad, hard-beaten road to his house, though it be in the woods," he had little idea of just how tortuous that road would be. The New York ad executive does.

FOOD IN NEW YORK CITY

by
FLORENCE FABRICANT

Florence Fabricant, a food and wine writer and restaurant critic who contributes regularly to The New York Times *and* Signature *magazine, has written for many other publications and is a daily participant in—as well as observer of—the New York food scene.*

New Yorkers are often puzzled to find "New York strip" steaks on menus in other parts of the country. They've never heard of such a thing.

The type of steak in question, a beefy, tender, well-aged, two-inch-thick cut of prime shell grilled to a turn, the *sine qua non* of the New York steakhouse that sets a standard elsewhere, *is* the standard here. Similarly, from the cornucopia that is the New York marketplace, where foodstuffs arrive by truck, rail, ship, and plane from all over the world, the restaurants select the finest produce, seafood, meat, poultry, game, delicacies, and condiments. Eventually, many of these products find their way into food shops and the home kitchens of New Yorkers, who are as likely to serve a Chinese stir-fry as they are Sunday morning bagels and lox. But the restaurants usually point the way.

It invariably begins in the chilly pre-dawn hours in the grim South Bronx at the Hunts Point Market or at the Manhattan foot of the historic Brooklyn Bridge at the Fulton Fish Market at a collection of brightly lit stalls where a bustle of activity contrasts with the quiet emptiness of the surrounding streets. A shipment of perfect, dewy raspberries or tiny, finger-sized zucchini specially raised in California stands out amid crate after crate of cabbages and oranges. The first succulent shad or delicate Maryland soft-shell crabs of the season attract more attention than piles of codfish or sacks of clams. Certain restaurants will be the first to know about these limited editions and will feature them on their menus that day.

New York City is a transportation crossroads and the nation's major port of entry, so the ingredients arrive daily from out of the way corners of the globe. Japanese yellowtail and the *maguro* tuna that are served in midtown sushi bars, dried mushrooms from China, pungent fish sauce from Thailand, a caravan of spices to enflame Indian curries, coffee beans from Kenya and Hawaii that will be roasted in Brooklyn, and vine-ripened Israeli tomatoes in mid-winter and sun-dried Italian tomatoes packed in olive oil all year are just a few of the items one can expect to find.

The elegant Quilted Giraffe restaurant sells $4,000 worth of imported French truffles a week; when the fresh herring are running, the Grand Central Oyster Bar flies them in from Holland; and it's not unusual to see Brie and German Black Forest ham on brunch menus in casual cafés.

But as available as imported exotica may be, a great deal of the food for New York tables travels a much shorter distance. Ducklings produced on Eastern Long Island are ordered fresh, not frozen, by a chef like Jean-Jacques Rachou, to serve with sauces of orange or green peppercorns at La Côte Basque and Le Lavandou. Rich bluefish that teem in nearby Atlantic waters in summer arrive in the market within a day, and prized scallops from Peconic Bay are the ones to look for from September to April. Hard clams from Great South Bay that are served on the half shell or go into the typically tomato-based chowder of Manhattan, Blue Point oysters from Long Island Sound, pheasants, quail and quail eggs from game farms in New Jersey, and Chinese vegetables such as bok choy and snow peas from truck farms also in the Garden State are available at the peak of freshness at any season.

Frequently, the restaurants make demands on producers or shippers that result in superior quality. That is the story of the "New York strip" steak. Although most of the beef that is sold in the United States today is shipped from the Midwest vacuum-packed in pre-cut sections, the top-of-the-line steakhouses that refuse to compromise on quality still select whole prime carcasses from wholesalers and packing houses located along a tangle of truck-choked streets on the West Side near 14th Street. The restaurateur stamps the ones he wants. The beef is held in temperature-controlled aging vaults until it has reached perfection.

An insistence on a dependable supply of fresh herbs has led growers in New Jersey and Pennsylvania to specialize and truck their crops directly to New York. Other nearby farmers find they have a market for sweet but extremely perishable local strawberries in June, tangy Macoun apples and curious purple broccoli in the fall. The Chinese and Japanese requirement for fresh *tofu* (bean curd) and bean sprouts has resulted in basement beansprout farms and tofu factories in Chinatown and in Queens, just as the need for certain vegetables and herbs such as chili peppers and coriander by both the Oriental and Hispanic communities has made them commonplace nearly everywhere, including the estimable Four Seasons.

Until recently, ethnic foodstuffs such as these were limited to certain neighborhoods. A trip to Chinatown was necessary for fresh ginger-root; the Lower East Side was the exclusive source for baked farmer cheese; Lebanese shops that line Atlantic Avenue in Brooklyn just beyond Brooklyn Heights were the only purveyors of cracked wheat and pita breads; a visit to the teeming stalls of La Marqueta beneath the elevated Conrail tracks in upper Manhattan would guarantee jicama, plantains, and chorizos; and the old-world side streets of the Little Italies of Manhattan, the Bronx, and Brooklyn were the only places to find shops that made fresh pasta.

But French chefs like Alain Sailhac of Le Cirque use fresh ginger now, fresh pasta can be purchased in cheese shops and department stores, and pita bread, farmer cheese, and plantains have become supermarket staples. Delicacies that once were obtained only from abroad are being produced here because there is a dependable market for them in New York. Thus belon oysters are cultivated in Maine, French haricot vert beans are grown in California, and morels mushrooms can be gathered in Michigan woodlands. All are served in New York restaurants.

Ice creams with nearly unpronounceable names that make them sound as if they are produced abroad—Haagen-Dazs, Frusen Gladjé, and Alpenzauber—are all local products that the rest of the country is beginning to discover. New Yorkers, like everybody else, prefer vanilla and chocolate ice cream but the third choice here is coffee, not strawberry. And a proliferation of ice-cream dipping shops has made it possible to have ice cream at any season in any part of the city. Like pizza and bagels.

The legendary New York appetite for bagels and lox has meant that 24-hour bagel bakeries are located in most neighborhoods, and more salmon is being sold than ever before. In fact, because sophisticated palates now insist on their salmon smoked, not just brine-cured the way traditional salty lox is made, it is possible to choose smoked salmon from Scotland, Ireland, the Pacific Northwest, California, Nova Scotia, or Upstate New York in quite a few Manhattan delicacy shops.

Lately, the bagel has encountered such serious competition from the croissant that Zabar's, a giant Upper West Side fancy-food market known for its breads, sells 20 times as many croissants as bagels. Swiss peasant breads, Russian health bread, pumpernickel raisin, French baguettes, Italian wheat and pepper breads, plain or sesame pita, marbelized pumpernickel and rye, buttery brioche, and golden challah are just a sampling of the variety that fills the New York breadbasket in restaurants and homes.

New Yorkers may complain that the corned beef and pastrami are not as good as they remember them, and nostalgic tears well up at the very thought of a knish. But cheesecakes are being baked in more flavors than ever before, barbecued ribs and onion loaf have made it north from Texas, and superb wines from small California wineries have enhanced the lists in restaurants of every stripe. The unanimous opinion of New York's restaurateurs, chefs, restaurant critics, and consultants is that the ingredients here have never been more varied or of better quality.

NEW YORK CITY

A Congregation of Neighborhoods

by ROSELLEN CALLAHAN and MICHAEL IACHETTA

Rosellen Callahan, former travel editor of the Woman's Home Companion, *contributed to many national magazines and was a past president of the Society of American Travel Writers. Michael Iachetta, a syndicated travel writer with the New York* Daily News, *is also a member of the Society.*

The time of day and the portal you choose to reach Manhattan make a world of difference in your lasting impression of the city. If you approach it at dusk, driving along the rim of the precipitous Palisades on the New Jersey side of the Hudson River leading to the high span of the George Washington Bridge or through the Lincoln Tunnel, the city is the most majestic, radiant, exciting sight you'll see in a lifetime of travel.

The jagged skyscrapers silhouetted against the dusky evening sky, their galaxy of lighted windows reflected in the rippled river, is indescribably overwhelming. The newcomer rarely completely recovers from this stunning introduction to the city. This is quite understandable when you consider that New Yorkers, and their New Jersey neighbors who live on the perimeter of Manhattan's skyline, have themselves never ceased to be awed by this magnificent vista.

If your route leads you by way of the under-river Holland Tunnel to New York—an unfortunate choice—you'll find yourself swept into a vortex of the city's tangled traffic and eddies of the bustling, jaywalking pedestrians bent on making the most of those seconds and splitseconds which stretch and stress their day. Coming upon the city this suddenly, your first impression could be a distracting combination of intensity, indifference, squalor, and splendor.

Seen from the vantage point of an airplane window, the city reveals itself as a cluster of odd-shaped islands tethered together by bridges. For New York is really a complex of boroughs: Manhattan, Brooklyn, Queens, the Bronx, and Richmond or, more commonly, Staten Island.

Yet, anyone who speaks of New York City means Manhattan. Even Brooklynites will say "we're going into the city," when in fact they live within the city limits.

Manhattan is only a little over twelve miles from tip to toe and less than three miles across at its widest point. Small in size, true—but you could spend a month exploring this island and never cover all the historic sites, hidden mews, jazz dens, restaurants, museums, ships, opera-concert houses, theaters, parks, and ethnic neighborhoods.

New York is a city that defies a pat description. Bustling, brash, complex, changeable, confusing—yes. Exciting, amusing, inspiring, rewarding—this, too. Unfriendly, indifferent, cold? Not really, if you spend time enough, give of yourself enough, in getting to know it.

It's been said that cities are one of the extraordinary creations of man and that New York is the master mold for the megalopolis. True or not, New York is without question the most magnetic city in the world, a unique blend of people of all races, religions, and cultures. "Melting pot" is the easy term once applied—but not everything melts.

What makes New York tick? Why is New York, well . . . New York? Why is there so much energy, in people in the arts as well as among the businessmen? To begin with, the major industries in New York that generate jobs and money are (in no order) finance, stock brokerage, consumer banking, commodities exchange, export-import, shipping, advertising, public relations, tourism, publishing, broadcasting, medicine, insurance, garment design and manufacture, printing—though the shops themselves have tended to move to New Jersey in recent years—and the performing arts, plus the services that have developed around these: lawyers by the platoon, designers, agents and their stables, messenger services, and so on. What makes New York tick? Simply, this is where deals are made. This is what the nervous energy, the seeming aggression stems from. This is why so many of the world's corporations have offices here, if not their headquarters. This is why the pop-music producers are coming *back* to the city after a wave of migration to Los Angeles. Office space and apartments are becoming harder and harder to come by here.

Some Americans, especially in the West and South, harbor fear of and dislike for New York City. This traces back to the Populism of the late 1800s that condemned "Wall Street" for crucifying "the toilers" on a cross of gold. In fact, the farm mortgages *were* largely held by Wall Street bankers, who *did* control the money supply to suit their needs, and who *did* control the railroads that *did* discriminate against farmers and ranchers. New York manipulated, and still does—and is seen by some still to be full of foreigners and loud-mouths as well.

New York's appeal has many facets. Good theater, great restaurants, exquisite shops, successful careers, financial gain, freedom, and privacy. It offers to each, whether visitor or resident, his own reward. It also demands much in return. The demands and rewards partly explain the frenetic pace of the city, the unremitting drive of the people, their seeming indifference to the stranger in their midst.

The Private Life of New Yorkers

To New Yorkers, privacy is precious and time is fleeting. Their ways of achieving privacy and hoarding minutes take many forms. For some it means learning to be oblivious to the suffocating crowds and ear-shattering noises around them by losing themselves in a private world of personal plans and thoughts. Best friends will pass each other by without a sign of recognition if they are late for appointments. Many will move about to the rhythms of their choice, listening to a Walkman as they make their way on the streets and subways.

Next-door neighbors in apartment houses may mumble a reserved "good morning" or "good evening," but will rarely engage in conversation for fear it will open the way to impromptu visits at inconvenient times. Yet, if they meet each other a long way from home, they are likely to fall into each other's arms like long-lost friends. Crowds in a subway or on the street may sidestep a stranger who has been felled by a heart attack and hurry on their way, lest they be involved in the time-consuming business of appearing as a witness.

Orientation Map of Manhattan

Lower Broadway, Wall Street area, and **White Hall** area are what New Yorkers call "downtown," by which they mean the financial district. Almost no residential.

Chinatown: Life out on the streets or in restaurants in full force. Little night life, though, in the bar and night club sense. Heavily residential, but in tenement buildings.

Little Italy: Residential area like no other in city. Restaurants, Italian food shops, cafés, and street life in full measure among shabby tenement buildings.

SoHo: A strange mix of artists-in-residence and light manufacturing. Restaurants and street life here and there. **TriBeCa** is similar but with more manufacturing and less street life, fewer residents.

East Village: Mostly lower-income residential in tenements, but mixed with light commercial enterprises. East portion is redolent of Middle-European immigrants who settled here. Hippies were centered here in 60s and 70s.

Greenwich Village: Primarily residential, and often quite expensive housing. New York University a big presence in central area. Restaurants, bars, night life, and stay-up late street life as overwhelming as ever. Attractive brownstone buildings, especially in the "West Village," which tends to be a bit stuffy.

Chelsea: An area in transition. Some artists' lofts and good housing, lots of not so good. Street scene is spotty and can be gamy.

Murray Hill: Predominately low-rise buildings, a mix of offices and residential housing, often quite good. The **Gramercy Park** area is similar but with more light manufacturing in loft buildings in the west—and artist and photographer lofts too. Restaurants and street life spotty, especially at night.

Garment District: Fascinating but hectic during the day, but not promising for ordinary visitors. Little residential, so deserted at night.

Theater District: Crowded with restaurants, too. Can be extra sinister late at night, after theater crowds have dispersed.

Midtown: *The* business district—but the east side of the area is heavily residential, with high-grade housing. Restaurants, night life, street life abound in spots throughout. Watch out for bicycles during the day. **Tudor City** is almost entirely residential.

Upper East Side: On its west side, the most expensive living space in the country—lawyers, doctors, stockbrokers, bankers. Slick. Mostly cooperative or condominium apartments. Exquisite brownstone buildings on sidestreets. Posh galleries too. Profusion of restaurants and night life is mostly in residential eastern half of area—young executives, singles, relatively few families—where rents are a bit lower, though still high.

Yorkville: Mix of expensive and inexpensive housing. Strong element of German and Central-European heritages.

Lincoln Center Area: Besides the Center, it is middle class residential, with plenty of restaurants and street life revolving around the Center.

Upper West Side: The far west and far east zones are middle- and upper-class residential, good but not quite as high-rent as the Upper East Side. Musicians, dancers, writers, actors, and middle-class families between Broadway and Riverside Drive. Broadway has bag people and looks seedy. Lots of restaurants, night life, street life on the two sides, up Broadway and Columbus Avenue, where the apartment buildings are largely cooperatives or condominiums. The Amsterdam zone is still mostly low-income tenements, but the area is in the process of being upgraded.

Morningside Heights: Its west side is the Columbia University/Barnard area.

Harlem is Harlem. **East Harlem,** sometimes called Spanish Harlem, also has an Italian element in spots.

The other areas of Manhattan—**Lower East Side, Bowery, Lower West Side,** and the northern parts of Manhattan—have little or nothing to offer most visitors.

The heavy population density of New York City is one of the most important factors in shaping the character of New York and the New Yorkers. When there are up to 2,000 people living on *one block* you can expect to find people passing each other in the street without continual and tiresome signs of recognition. And when just one of them drops a newspaper like *The New York Times,* the wind will make any street look like the worst slum street in five minutes. Although a lot of the best things about the city stem from the density—the street life, the nightlife, the array of restaurants and cafés, the excitement—so do many of the worst aspects.

But come a common catastrophe, New Yorkers, native-born and ex-outlanders, will offer the shelter of their homes, their help and counsel without stint. They are a conundrum, and even they cannot explain themselves.

A Bit of History's Perspective

Knowing a bit of New York's history will help you to understand the circumstances and pressures which have tempered the character of the city and its citizens.

Unlike New England whose settlers came to the New World primarily to escape political and religious injustices, Nieuw Amsterdam, as New York was named first, was settled by Dutch families in the employ of the West India Company, a Netherlands trading combine whose sole interest was carrying on a profitable trade with the Indians. From the start, they fared well. In their first year, they realized a profit of 250 guilders from the skins of beavers and otters alone. Considering that their governor, Peter Minuit, paid only sixty guilders, or roughly $24, worth of trinkets to the Indians in exchange for the island of Manhattan, it was an exceptionally good year.

From its earliest days—Giovanni da Verrazzano having discovered New York Bay in 1524, landing on Staten Island on April 17—the community welcomed the stranger. It needed the brawn and skill of the newcomer's hands to help build the village, and it cared little about his race, color, or religious beliefs. A French Jesuit who passed through in 1643 reported home that "there may well be four or five hundred men of different sects and nations . . . there are men of eighteen different languages." Eight years later another sect was added when twenty-three Jewish men and women arrived to seek sanctuary. A Virginian, who paused on his way to the English colonies north, also complained: "The people seem not concerned what religion their neighbor is of, or whether he hath any or none." And so it has remained throughout the centuries.

New York's geographic location—an elongated island jutting into a huge protected harbor, with a mighty river at its side coming from deep within the country's interior of untapped riches—foreordained her supremacy as the greatest commercial city in America.

New York also straddled a strategic slice of the Atlantic coastline, separating the English colonies of New England from Virginia and cutting off the westward expansion of Connecticut and Massachusetts. This, plus her commercial enterprise, nettled the British and in 1664, King Charles II presented his brother, the Duke of York, a little gift of "all the land from the west side of the Connecticut River to the east side of the De la Ware Bay," and sent a flotilla of warships to convince the Dutch colony's governor, Peter Stuyvesant, that surrender was preferable to annihilation. The practical, business-as-usual tradespeople urged the governor to surrender "in the speediest, best and most reputable manner." Nieuw Amsterdam passed into the hands of the British, was renamed New York, and the citizens went on about their business of trade and commerce.

The city learned early how to assimilate rather than be devoured. Long after the capitulation to the British, the Dutch clung to their traditions. The character of early New York became a composite of Dutch vigor and English tenacity. Trade remained the city's cachet, and has throughout the centuries. The ramifications of this have not been to everyone's taste; Emerson (from the vantage point of Boston) called New York "a sucked orange."

From the first, New York insisted upon and enjoyed a greater degree of religious liberty and political freedom than did most of the other colonies, and word of these special privileges spread abroad. The city's character reflected one bright new facet after another as wave after wave of political and religious refugees broke over its shores.

French and German Palatinates, fugitives from the religious persecutions of Louis XIV, sought sanctuary here in the early 18th century, followed by settlers from England, Ireland, and Scotland, who fled their homelands as the Stuart cause began to collapse.

Migrations ceased while New York suffered through seven bitter years of siege during the Revolutionary War. Again New Yorkers adjusted themselves to living under the threat of British guns, suffered a disastrous fire which destroyed the heart of the city, and played a waiting game, hoping that come what may, they would retain their individuality. By November, 1783, New York was part of the new Union and served as the nation's capital for the following six years.

"Loud, Fast, and Altogether"

Why didn't New York remain so? Its citizens may have decided that being the home of the national government would divert them from their historic role. A century and a half of history had tempered and forged New York into the nation's greatest city of commerce. Whatever the reason, New York passed the plum on to Philadelphia and got on with the business of becoming the "noisy, roaring, rumbling, tumbling, bustling, stormy, turbulent" city Walt Whitman found so disturbing.

In a way it always had been turbulent. Even in 1774, John Adams complained that "They talk very loud, very fast, and altogether. If they ask you a question before you can utter three words of your answer, they will break out upon you again, and talk away." There are grounds for complaint today in this respect.

It wasn't just rudeness, as John Adams felt, but rather exhilaration. The city has a way of stimulating the mind, crowding it with ideas, opinions, thoughts which refuse to be dammed up for long and come spilling out "loud, fast, and altogether." These are the very forces which have sent New York spiraling upward and outward.

The Erie Canal's completion in 1825 assured New York's monopoly of the nation's rich trade. Building burgeoned and the city's growth reached out to such scattered rural hamlets as Greenwich Village and absorbed them. By 1850 New York's population was well over a half-million and its real estate was valued at $400,000,000. Grand opera, concerts, and legitimate theater productions were adding the needed note of culture. Men were becoming millionaires and their wives were casting eyes abroad for titled mates for their daughters. Fifth Avenue soon would sprout with palatial residences and galas be given for visiting royalty. New York was, if ever there was, the pot of gold at the end of the rainbow.

Once again immigrants came to find it: Russian Jews fleeing the Tsarist pogroms; Italians escaping oppressive poverty; Irish Catholics who had coped with confiscation of their property and denial of religious freedom but could no longer battle starvation after the awful potato famine; and many more.

Their voyage often took ninety or more days. Jammed into the reeking holds of sailing ships with scarcely room enough to lie down, many succumbed to cholera. Those who survived the journey were often so weak they had to be carried off the ship. By the time the last of these "floating coffins" was retired, more than 23,000,000 immigrants had come through this gateway over a 40-year period.

Many headed for neighborhoods where immigrants from their homeland had already settled. Here they were able to buy familiar foods, join their own societies, read the news in their own language. Few ever learned to speak English.

Politicians preyed on their ignorance and poverty, manipulated their votes or, if need be, bought them with picnic excursions and food baskets. They were crowded into slums on the lower East and West sides, not too many cuts above their steerage experiences. Sweatshops paid slave wages for a 60-or-more-hour week. Advertisements for domestic help at one period often read "No Irish need apply."

Yet the ideal of America never dimmed. The immigrants were free and their children were free. Free to learn, to pull themselves up by their bootstraps and become lawyers, doctors, merchants, financiers, patrons of the arts, and senators. The fabric of New York is shot through with the sparkle, color, and tensile strength of these multitudinous ethnic-religious-political groups. They and their children and grandchildren have helped to make this city great.

In your wanderings throughout the city you will see remnants of these immigrant enclaves and find the imprint of their imagination on the skyscrapers of lower Manhattan, the elegant shops along Fifth Avenue, the bright lights of Broadway, the opera houses, concert halls, museums, and the home of the United Nations. The imprints of the Dutch and English are there, too. It is this pattern of people and events which has made New York the fascinating, cosmopolitan, polyglot city that it is. New York City has always been the most un-American of American cities—though Miami is now challenging it in this respect.

Sailing Around Manhattan

The best introduction to New York City, weather and season permitting, is to take a three-hour Circle Line boat around Manhattan. The Circle Line operates from Pier 83 on the Hudson, at 43rd Street and 12th Avenue, from April 1 to November 15. Boats leave approximately every 45 minutes beginning in mid-morning. The cost for adults in 1982 was $8.50, for children under 12 it is $4; for specific departure times call 563-3200.

As the boat pulls out of the dock, heading down the Hudson River, you pass Manhattan's lower West Side, which is undergoing fundamental—if controversial—changes and where the presently out-of-service West Side Highway is scheduled to be replaced. In any case, heavy construction is going on with the building of a convention and exposition center on 12th Avenue in the mid-30s and as the housing at Battery Park City (near the World Trade Center) gets under way. The ferry rounds the island's southern tip, giving a superb view of the Statue of Liberty and of the Wall Street skyline. Heading up the East River, you'll pass under three very different spans to Brooklyn: the Brooklyn,

Manhattan, and Williamsburg bridges. A glimpse of fashionable Brooklyn Heights is available and you may see, a mile or so upriver, the old Brooklyn Navy Yard.

Looking back to the Manhattan side, you'll have passed Chinatown and the Lower East Side and now be closing in on the United Nations Building at 44th Street and 1st Avenue. On your right will be the sometimes dormant Delacorte Geyser and Roosevelt Island with its new housing developments. The bridge overhead is the stolid Queensboro or "59th Street," and right next to it, the tramway linking Roosevelt Island with Manhattan. Farther up, you'll catch a glimpse of the mayor's residence, Gracie Mansion, built in 1799 by Archibald of that name.

Then it's upstream under the Triboro Bridge (it links Manhattan to Queens and the Bronx). After several smaller spans, you'll see on the right refurbished Yankee Stadium and the nostalgic traveler may look on the Manhattan side to a cluster of red high-rises and recall the fabled Polo Grounds, scene of many dramatic sports moments, that once stood on the site.

About a mile onward, the Hall of Fame for Great Americans still looks out from a Bronx hillcrest, once part of New York University's uptown campus (the entire school is now located in Greenwich Village). Today this outdoor colonnade designed by Stanford White is on the campus of Bronx Community College. Then, rounding the northern tip of Manhattan through the Spuyten Duyvil cut, the cruise slips past Columbia University's boathouse, Inwood Hill Park, and the Henry Hudson Bridge. Once again, you're on the Hudson River flanked on the west by the towering Palisades of New Jersey. On the east you'll see The Cloisters and the heights of Fort Washington Park as you approach the George Washington Bridge, Grant's Tomb, Riverside Church, the Soldiers and Sailors Monument. The midtown towers come into view as you head back to the dock past the rebuilt luxury-liner piers between 54th and 45th streets. It's a cruise you'll long remember.

Beginning at the Beginning

New York is an easy city to explore with the aid of a city map, which you can pick up at the New York Convention and Visitors Bureau at Columbus Circle, opposite the Coliseum. The bus systems and the more than 500 miles of subway tracks will take you to almost any sight you want to see. On occasion you may find a car more convenient for reaching widely separated attractions on fringes of the city, but for in-town touring a car is an expensive handicap. On-the-street parking is limited to very short periods and overtime parking can result in your car being towed away, costing $95 or more to recover. Garage parking is often difficult to find and can cost as much as $15 for two hours in midtown. You will find walking the most rewarding way to come to know the city and its people, to savor its flavor, and to make little discoveries of your own. In fact, New Yorkers themselves walk, and walk a great deal more than do the denizens of any other U.S. city. This is the key to the vitality of the city's amazing street life—and it continues to amaze even long-time New Yorkers. Here is what we have seen on the streets in the past few months (a selection): mimes, jugglers, magicians, flutists and violinists ("Music student needs help for tuition"), a team of "medical students" taking blood pressures, comedians, country-music groups, singers accompanied by music taped on a cassette player, trained dog acts, cats and monkeys dressed up in Victorian outfits, a man riding a bicycle and wearing a purple silk Musketeers suit and hat with purple feathers, bagpipers, blind beggars, crippled beggars, very healthy beggars, three-card monte conmen plying their three cards on cardboard boxes—this on Fifth Avenue!—and Renaissance troubadours—all of the above soliciting our money—and street vendors selling nuts and dried fruits, fresh-squeezed orange juice, parasols, handbags and gloves, luggage, bags of lavender, "solid gold diamond" rings (for $5!), tube socks ("For Mother's Day!"), real marijuana, phony marijuana, fruit, shish-kebab, Japanese dumplings and Chinese egg rolls, hot dogs (of course, with hot sauerkraut and/or onions), real New York egg creams, and giant inflatable vinyl frogs—with or without city peddler licenses. You can even play "speed chess" for a small fee at the corner of 42nd Street and Broadway, where the chessboards are set out atop garbage cans!

The Battery Park area, where the city's history began, is an excellent starting point for a day's walking tour of lower Manhattan. The bus and subway systems converge here at Bowling Green, the little "Green before the fort" where early burghers bowled on summer evenings. Within a small radius are some of the city's most historic sites.

To appreciate the strategic geographical situation of the city, which gave it a commercial advantage over all other cities, walk along the esplanade of Battery Park. It is a salt breeze-swept stroll which tycoons from Wall Street often take to help clear heads and quiet nerves when they are faced with multi-million-dollar decisions. Here you can watch a parade of luxury cruise liners and freighters steaming out to sea, tugs herding strings of barges, and ships of all flags anchored in the bay.

Look down to a point called The Narrows, where the Lower Bay funnels into the Upper Bay, and you'll see the 4,260-foot main span of the Verrazano-Narrows Bridge cinching the waist of the water between Brooklyn and Staten Island. It was at this point in 1524 that the Florentine navigator Giovanni da Verrazano, seeking a passage to Asia at the behest of King Francis I of France, discovered what he described as "this very agreeable situation located within two small prominent hills, in the midst of which flowed to the sea a very giant river."

While history does credit Verrazano with the first sighting of this magnificent harbor, the mighty river was named for Henry Hudson, an Englishman in the employ of the Dutch East India Company, who arrived eighty-five years later on another mission to "seek a new route to the Indies by way of the North."

Despite a long campaign by the Italian Historical Society of New York to make the Verrazano name better known—first by having The Narrows, and the bridge spanning it, named Verrazano—the Florentine is still not reaping the just rewards for his discovery.

The Statue of Liberty

There is one ferry which, until recently, has never been threatened with extinction. It is the ferry from Battery Park to the Statue of Liberty, probably the most symbolic structure in the United States, and certainly the most symbolic of New York.

A visit to Liberty Island is more rewarding if one knows beforehand a bit about the forces of friendship which inspired the statue, the genius of its construction, and the long struggle to make it a reality. That it stands in New York harbor is as much a miracle as was its completion.

The idea of the monument was first discussed at a small dinner party given by French historian Édouard de Laboulaye at his home in Versailles, shortly after the close of the American Civil War. It was to be a gift from the people of France to the people of the United States to commemorate the long friendship between the two nations—a friendship which dated from the American Revolution, when French aid to General George Washington helped to turn the tide of victory to the side of the Colonies.

The guests were prominent men in politics, letters, and the arts. One was Frédéric Auguste Bartholdi, a young Alsatian sculptor. Some of the guests had reservations about the idea. They held that it was impossible for gratitude to exist for long. They doubted that in an emergency France could count on America to remember the aid France had given and return it in kind. The idea went into hibernation for some years. When the idea was revived, it was decided that if a statue were to be constructed, it would be with the proviso that the French people would give the statue proper if the people of the United States would build the pedestal.

Bartholdi was sent to America to discuss the project with prominent philanthropists. During the ocean voyage he roughed out several concepts for the monument. But it wasn't until he sailed into New York's magnificent harbor that he conceived the idea of a "mighty woman with a torch" lighting the way to freedom in the New World. The perfect site was New York, the gateway to that world.

In France, public fêtes and lotteries were held to raise funds to build the statue. Gounod, the famous composer, wrote a song about the statue and presented it at the Paris Opera. Because the statue was to be a gift from the people of France, the government was not approached for financial aid, and it was seven years before the needed $250,000 was finally subscribed.

On this side of the ocean the proposed site for the statue stirred up old embers of hostility. Why, some states demanded to know, should they be called upon to donate money to finance the construction of a pedestal for a "New York Lighthouse"?

Piece by piece, the statue was taking form in France, while Americans continued to hassle and withhold contributions. To help kindle enthusiasm for the project, the 42-foot right arm and torch was exhibited in 1876 at the Centennial Celebration of American Independence held in Philadelphia. Public apathy could not be overcome. It looked as though construction of the pedestal never would be completed, and that the generous gift could not be accepted.

Joseph Pulitzer Saves the Statue

Philadelphia, Boston, San Francisco, and Cleveland offered to pay all the cost of a pedestal if the statue were presented to them. It was at this point that Joseph Pulitzer of the *New York World* launched a campaign to "nationalize" the project. In editorials he stormed at New Yorkers who failed to contribute according to their means; assailed the provincial thinking of citizens in other states who refused assistance because the statue was to stand in New York Harbor; called upon everyone to avert the shame of rejecting the most generous gesture one nation had ever made to another. The public's conscience was pricked and the campaign became a crusade.

Benefit balls, sporting events, and theatrical performances were held. Schoolchildren deposited their pennies and nickels in classroom containers. Contributions poured in from distant states. Completion of the pedestal was assured and the statue was packed, piece by piece, in 214 cases and shipped to New York to be assembled and mounted. The Statue of Liberty Enlightening the World was dedicated October 28, 1886, with these words by President Grover Cleveland: "We will not forget that Liberty has here made her home; nor shall her chosen altar be neglected."

The 151-foot statue is a monument to the herculean genius of its sculptor. To achieve the correct proportions of this mighty woman,

Bartholdi made a four-foot study model, then cast and recast it until it was thirty-six feet high. The statue then was divided into dozens of sections and each section enlarged four times. Liberty's eyes became two feet wide, her nose four feet long, her waist an ample thirty-five feet. On the mold of each section, copper sheets 3/32-inch thick were pressed and hammered into shape. Bartholdi had chosen copper for several reasons. It was light, easily worked, strong enough to withstand shipment, and impervious to the effect of New York's salty air.

The pedestal, one of the heaviest pieces of masonry in the world, towers eighty-nine feet above its foundation, the eleven-pointed star-shaped old Fort Wood. Alexandre Gustave Eiffel, the French engineer who constructed the famous Eiffel Tower in Paris, designed the framework which secures the statue to the foundation. Four huge iron posts run from the base of the statue to the top, forming a pylon which supports the weight of the whole structure. From this central tower a maze of small beams and iron straps were installed to support each section of the statue so that no piece bears the weight of the one above it. Thus, the statue is anchored to its pedestal, and the pedestal to the base in such a way that for a windstorm—and New York has severe ones—to overturn the monument, it would just about have to upend the whole island.

It is only a ten-minute ride from Battery Park to Liberty Island, and the ferry slowly skirts the monument so that you can take several closeup pictures. Once on the island, most visitors prefer to wander around on their own, and National Park Service guides are on hand to answer questions and provide you with a free souvenir pamphlet which details the history of the statue and the island.

In the base of the statue is the American Museum of Immigration. Circular in layout, the museum describes with multi-media exhibits such subjects as who settled this country, how they got here, what they brought with them (in addition to hopes and dreams), where they put down their roots, and how they fared.

Here, too, the poetic tribute written by Emma Lazarus is inscribed, its words making clear the symbolism of the Statue of Liberty:

> Not like the brazen giant of Greek fame,
> With conquering limbs astride from land to land;
> Here at our sea-washed, sunset gates shall stand
> A mighty woman with a torch, whose flame
> Is the imprisoned lightning, and her name
> Mother of Exiles. From her beacon-hand
> Glows world-wide welcome; her mild eyes command
> The air-bridged harbor that twin cities frame.
> "Keep ancient lands, your storied pomp!" cries she

With silent lips. "Give me your tired, your poor,
Your huddled masses yearning to breathe free,
The wretched refuse of your teeming shore.
Send these, the homeless, tempest-tossed to me:
I lift my lamp beside the golden door!"

An elevator takes you up ten floors to the balcony which runs around the top of the pedestal. On each of the four sides you'll find a sketch and description of the view before you, which makes it easy to identify Staten Island, the Verrazano-Narrows Bridge, Fort Jay, Governors Island, the Brooklyn, Manhattan, and Williamsburg bridges, Ellis Island, and the skyscrapers of lower Manhattan.

For the stout of heart and strong of limb there is a staircase which spirals up twelve more stories to Liberty's crown for a stratospheric view. You are not necessarily committed to go the whole way in one uninterrupted climb. Rest platforms are located every third of the way up, where you can also cross over and climb back down if you have a change of heart about making it all the way to the crown.

The Statue of Liberty Ferry leaves Battery Park daily every hour on the hour between 9 A.M. and 4 P.M. (5 P.M. on Sundays). The round trip costs $1.50 for adults, 50 cents for children 11 and under, which includes admission to the Museum of Immigration as well as the Statue itself. The elevator to the top is an extra 10 cents; the walk costs only the 12-flight effort. For further information: 732-1286.

Allow yourself at least two and a half hours for the ferry ride and tour of Liberty Island. It's worth the time.

Another historical site in the Upper Bay—and accessible by ferry from Battery Park (except in winter)—is Ellis Island. Its buildings were, from 1892 to 1954, the immigration processing entry point into the United States for over ten million people, primarily Europeans. The ferry operates between April 25 and November 1, leaving daily at 9:30 and 11:45 A.M. and 2:00 and 4:15 P.M. The price for adults is $1.50, for children under 11, 50 cents, and that includes a one-hour guided tour of the island. Phone: 732-1286.

Battery Park

On your return to Battery Park, you might find a circular stroll rewarding before continuing your tour of lower Manhattan. You'll discover statues tucked into bowers, and the handsome Marine Memorial is especially worthy of a few moments. Stand behind the memorial—an eagle on a black marble pedestal facing a corridor of huge granite slabs engraved with the names of those who gave their lives to the sea—and you will see the Statue of Liberty dramatically framed.

The Victorian-cupolaed gray building, with its gay red window-frames and bright green roof (near the park's exit), is the home of the city's fireboats. If you are lucky enough to be here on a day when a ship enters the harbor on her maiden voyage (admittedly a rare event), you'll see a fireboat or two saluting the liner with 200-foot plumes of spray.

The round brownstone building near the entrance to the park is Castle Clinton, built as a fort in 1811 to defend New York against any British attack. When the clouds of war cleared, the fort was ceded to New York City, transformed into Castle Garden in 1823, and served as a theater and public center. Here Jenny Lind, "the Swedish Nightingale," performed for $1,000 a night, an extraordinary fee in those days. From 1855 to 1890 the castle was used as the nation's principal immigrant depot, more than 7,000,000 "tempest-tossed" souls passing through its gate into a bright new world. When Ellis Island became the new depot, the castle served as the New York City Aquarium until a modern one was built on Coney Island. Today, Castle Clinton is a National Monument, and plans are underway to restore it to its original appearance.

New York is rather poor in ancient landmarks as compared to Boston and Philadelphia. Disastrous fires in the latter part of the 18th century and beginning of the 19th century took their toll of many historical homes and buildings. During the city's rapid rise as the nation's major metropolis, many fine old buildings were demolished to make way for the new. It wasn't until 1918, when Trinity Corporation decided to tear down the century-old St. John's Chapel to make way for commerce, that New York's civic pride was finally kindled. Public feeling ran high and protests were long and loud. Commerce won, however—as is usual in New York City—and the chapel came down.

It was a boom time, a period of fierce rivalry between moguls, and big buildings became an expression of this rivalry. As each tried to top the other, the old gave way to the new. In 1908 the Singer Building (now known as the Paul Building) at 561 Broadway, between Spring and Prince Streets, soared up to a record forty-seven stories. By 1913 the Woolworth Building, 233 Broadway between Barclay Street and Park Place, topped it by thirteen floors. The Equitable Life Assurance Society, 120 Broadway between Pine and Cedar Streets, covered an entire city block with a 44-story straight-sided building. Its ugly functional form jarred the city fathers into action, and New York's first zoning law was enacted in 1916. Buildings, they decreed, must have setbacks, a style which became known as the "wedding cake." (By a stretch of the imagination, the progressive bottom-to-top setbacks do resemble the tiers of a wedding cake.)

In your stroll through lower Manhattan you'll find many architectural forms. Opposite Bowling Green, at the intersection of State, Whitehall, and Bridge Streets, is the Customs House, an ornate Maine granite edifice studded with statuary by Daniel Chester French, which reflects the sprawling rococo period of building at the turn of the century. It seems a doughty dowager compared to the debutante across the way, the sleek new skyscraper at No. 2 Broadway, where many of New York's foremost brokerage houses have offices.

You'll find the streets down here are narrow, cut-up, and squeezed awry by the confluence of the Hudson and East rivers. If there is one place you'll need a street map to guide you, it is here. Yet, it is this crazy-quilt street pattern laid out by the first settlers which makes the scrambled spires so spectacular when viewed from a distance. Tucked into this granite-chrome-glass jungle are a few historic buildings which have managed to escape destruction or have been cleverly reconstructed.

Fraunces Tavern

One is Fraunces Tavern, at 54 Pearl Street (425–1776), a block east of the Customs House. Erroneously called "the oldest building in Manhattan," it is in fact an excellent reconstruction dating from 1907. Its square proportions, hipped roof edged with a light balustrade, regular window spacing, and white portico are perfect examples of the Georgian Colonial style favored in the early 18th century. Built of brick—which likely saved it from going up in flames during the disastrous fires of the Revolution—and turned from a residence into a successful business building (which staved off demolition)—it has had a long, colorful history. The original building was erected in 1719 as a residence for Étienne de Lancy, a wealthy Huguenot. His grandson turned it into a store and warehouse in 1757, and in 1762 it was sold to Samuel Fraunces, a West Indian of French and Negro blood, who renovated it, making it the Queen's Head Tavern.

Taverns in those days were more than food and drink emporiums. Captains of commerce, politicians, army officers, and fraternal groups often used them as meeting halls. It was at Fraunces Tavern that the Chamber of Commerce of the State of New York was founded in 1768 to help press the fight against the Stamp Act and the tax on tea. Here, too, George Washington called his officers together in the tavern's Long Room to bid them farewell.

It was a heart-wrenching leave-taking, one officer writing in his diary: "Such a scene of sorrow and weeping I had never before wit-

Points of Interest

1) American Stock Exchange
2) Bowling Green
3) Castle Clinton Nat. Monument
4) City Hall
5) Customs House
6) Federal Hall Memorial
7) Fraunces Tavern
8) Ferry to Staten Island
9) Fulton Fish Market
10) N.Y. Stock Exchange
11) South Street Seaport
12) St. Paul's Chapel
13) Trinity Church
14) World Trade Center

nessed, and I hope may never be called upon to witness again. It was indeed too affecting to be of long continuance—for tears of deep sensibility filled every eye—and the heart seemed so full that it was ready to burst from its wonted abode. Not a word was uttered to break the solemn silence that prevailed, or to interrupt the tenderness of the interesting scene. The simple thought that we were then about to part from the man who had conducted us through a long and bloody war, and under whose conduct the glory and independence of our country had been achieved, and that we should see his face no more in this world, seemed to me utterly insupportable . . . he walked silently on to Whitehall, where a barge was in waiting . . . as soon as he was seated, the barge put off into the river, and when out in the stream, our great and beloved General waved his hat, and bid us a silent adieu."

Fraunces Tavern is still a popular meeting place. The Sons of the Revolution in the State of New York purchased the property in 1904, faithfully re-created the original building, and today use it as their headquarters. A restaurant and bar occupy the first floor, and here, perhaps, you may see leaders of industry discussing million-dollar deals over lunch. But note: luncheon and dinner meals are served here from Monday to Friday only.

On the floors above you can view the Long Room, where Washington made his adieus, and wander through a small museum of relics from the Revolutionary period, paintings and prints depicting historical events, and such questionable Washington memorabilia as a fragment of broken tooth and lock of hair. The museum, like the bar and restaurant, is closed on weekends.

South Street Seaport

New York City gained much of its prominence and wealth as a major seaport. A nonprofit organization with a membership of more than 25,000 people established the South Street Seaport Museum, covering a four-block area around the former Fulton Fish Market in lower Manhattan, in remembrance of the city's early seafaring days.

The museum gallery is located at 16 Fulton Street, a book shop is located nearby (at the corner of Fulton and Water Streets), and a model ship and print shop are located at 207 Water Street, a short walk north from Fulton Street. Indeed, the popularity of the Seaport has spurred the city on to develop a mall and market in the area. Construction is underway.

The primary goal of the museum organization is to restore the historic buildings in the four-block area and several early vessels. Several such vessels are on view at any given time, such as the *Peking* or the *Wavertree,* a square-rigger built in 1885. Other vessels open to the public include the original *Ambrose Lightship*, built in 1904, and a hospital ship. To tour the ships is $3.50 for adults, $1.50 for children and students; Senior Citizens may board free. A covered Market Place features gift, craft and antique shops, and there is an assortment of food available—seafood as well as hamburgers served from different stalls. Table-and-chair eating also available. During the summer, there are many musical offerings at South Street, including a free jazz festival on weekends and folk, rock, and salsa (Latin) on other evenings. Square dancing and international folk dancing are also available here. For general information relating to the Seaport and its activities, call 766–9020.

Also one of New York's oldest and best seafood restaurants, Sweets, is in the South Street Seaport complex on Fulton Street near South Street—serving customers on a first-come, first-served basis. Open 11:30 A.M.–8:30 P.M. daily. Closed in July. Phone: 825–9786.

Wall Street

Wall Street, which is only seven blocks long, has become an inclusive name. When one says "I work in Wall Street," he usually is referring to the financial district in general. His office might be on Pine, Broad, or Cedar streets. Or he might say "I work on the street," which translates into "I work for a brokerage house."

The street, which follows what once was the walled northern boundary of the original Dutch colony, became a financial center soon after the Revolutionary War. The new Republic was $80,000,000 in debt and the first Congress, which met in a hall at the corner of Broad and Wall Streets, voted to issue stock to help pay the costs of the war. Trading was a new catch-as-catch-can business carried on by auctioneers in coffee houses and so disorganized that people were reluctant to invest. There was no assurance, they complained, that they could sell their securities when they wanted to. To give trading some semblance of order, a group of twenty-four merchants and auctioneers decided to meet each day at regular hours to buy and sell securities. They chose as their meeting place a shady spot under an old buttonwood (sycamore) tree which stood in front of the present 68 Wall Street. They were the first members of the New York Stock Exchange.

Today the Exchange has over 1900 member firms, and an average 45 million shares are traded daily behind the ornate façade on Broad Street, around the corner from Wall Street. Visitors are welcome to the second-floor gallery (weekdays until about 3:30) where you can look down on the Exchange floor and listen to a recording describing what all the frantic business is about. Guides take you on a tour and in the course of an hour demonstrate how a sale is recorded on tape. If you stand up in front, they may choose your name to demonstrate how a sale is run through. At another area there is a sort of animated Punch and Judy demonstration of how a Californian who wants to sell his stock is able to find a buyer in Boston and have the order executed through the Exchange.

Around the corner from the Exchange is a handsome Greek Revival building, on the corner of Wall and Nassau streets. It is the Federal Hall National Memorial, built in 1842 on the site of New York's first City Hall. It's quite an historic corner. Here, freedom of the press and freedom of speech were won by John Peter Zenger in 1735, the first Congress convened, and on April 30, 1789, General Washington inaugurated president. It was here that the Congress adopted the Bill of Rights.

The present structure served as customs house and subtreasury building and later housed the Federal Reserve Bank of New York. In a way, the handsome building is an anomaly. If architecture is your forte, you will wonder why a circular rotunda was placed in a rectangular building (and well you should). But such were the vagaries of the period of Greek Revival. Originally the plan was to build a Roman dome over the rotunda, set squarely in the middle of this Greek temple. The dome was never built, but the handsome rotunda remains.

Administered by the National Park Service, Federal Hall Memorial Museum, 15 Pine Street (344–3830), is filled with permanent exhibits. These include displays of early historical documents (you can purchase duplicates of many of them, including the Constitution and Bill of Rights) and miniature replicas in glass cases of momentous civil liberty victories. Pick up one of the headphones, push the button, and you can even hear the proceedings of the John Peter Zenger trial.

The low marble building across the street at 23 Wall Street is the home of the powerful J. P. Morgan banking company. If you study its façade you'll find the faded scars of the bomb which, in anarchist days, was meant for his son John Pierpont Morgan, Jr., but which killed several unfortunate passersby instead.

At the head of Wall Street, fronting on Broadway, is one of New York's richest landlords, Trinity Church. Its holdings—a land grant Queen Anne of England made to it in 1705 and bequests of large farms by early settlers—once extended along the Hudson River from about St. Paul's Chapel at Fulton Street to Christopher Street in the Greenwich Village area.

A History-Making Church

The present church building, erected in 1846, is the third one to occupy this site. The graveyard dates from even before 1697; much history is written on its headstones. If the gate is open you can wander along its tree-shaded paths to seek out the final resting places of Alexander Hamilton, Robert Fulton, and others who figured in the city's early history.

The church also contains an admission-free exhibit room. The showings cover a wide range of subjects, and there is no set schedule. It is best, therefore, to check with the church to see what exhibits are planned (285–0872). If you visit Trinity around the lunch hour, you might also stop in at the Trinity Church Coffee House directly behind the church at 74 Trinity Place.

Were it not for a favorable decision in the courts, Trinity would be just another poor parish today. After the great fire of 1776 reduced Trinity to a smoldering heap, a group of American revolutionists challenged her right to rebuild. They held that the fidelity of two of the church rectors to the loyalist cause had discredited the church; that its special status as the established Church of England in America under a royal charter was no longer valid now that the city had become part of the newly created State of New York; that the lands no longer belonged to her. Through passage of the New York State Act of 1784, however, Trinity was enabled to build chapels throughout the city with the income derived from her vast properties. It is the rentals from her large landholdings which have made Trinity one of the world's wealthiest corporations today. Leasing the land instead of selling it, Trinity was able to amass a fortune, as have other great land-holding institutions, such as Columbia University, owner of the property on which Rockefeller Center stands.

North of Trinity Church at Broadway and Fulton Street is one of the city's few remaining examples of Colonial architecture, St. Paul's Chapel, one of many Trinity built throughout the city. When it was erected in 1766, it stood in a field outside the city. Townspeople complained that it was much too far to go to church; yet it is only a five-block walk from Trinity. St. Paul's Georgian-Classic revival style bears a distinct resemblance to St. Martin-in-the-Fields in London, probably for good reason, since its architect, Thomas McBean, was a pupil of Gibbs, who built St. Martin. There is much to hold you here. There is a light, cheerful air to the interior which is rare in Colonial churches. Fourteen priceless Waterford crystal chandeliers glisten in the azure-tinted nave and galleries, providing an unusually elegant, if somewhat controversial, embellishment. Ever since these gleaming candlelight fixtures—they are wired for electricity now—were installed in 1802, parishioners have had some reservations about their propriety. Mumblings are still to be heard about their making the church look like a ballroom.

On either outer aisle you will find a handsome box pew. One was the special preserve of the governors who worshipped here in the comfort of upholstered chairs and draft-deflecting canopies. The pew on the left was also used by George Washington. Original William and Mary chairs in bright red satin brocade give the pew an air of elegance seldom seen in churches. Duncan Phyfe, whose cabinet shop was around the corner from the chapel, fashioned the handsome sofa you can see in the rear of the church. The altar, its railing, and a great deal of the ornamentation in the church is the work of Major Pierre L'Enfant, the designer who later planned the city of Washington, D.C.

St. Paul's congregation is probably the most scattered in the city. People who once lived in the area and were displaced when housing gave way to office buildings still return for Sunday services. They drive in from as far away as Long Island, Westchester, and New Jersey. Weekdays, the chapel serves as a quiet haven for office workers, who come to midday service or to sit on the secluded outdoor benches beside the peaceful cemetery.

Directly behind St. Paul's is the gigantic World Trade Center, operated by the Port Authority of New York and New Jersey. The Center takes up sixteen acres of lower Manhattan and stretches from Cortlandt Street on the east to West Street on the west and from Liberty Street on the south to Barclay and Vesey streets on the north.

From top (107 floors up) to bottom, the World Trade Center has become a major sightseeing attraction—and part of the lure is the food as well as the view. Its various dining rooms, cocktail lounges, private rooms upstairs, and its concourse-level dining room, bar, and café below have to be seen to be believed. And so does the view of the city from perhaps the most famous of the Big Apple restaurants, Windows on the World, and its less expensive counterpart, the Hors d'Oeuverie, a cocktail lounge and grill that is another part of the restaurant complex. They share the same view from the top: roughly 50 miles of New York City sea, river, harbor, sky, bridges, ships, planes, skyscrapers, and more—especially when the stars start staging their own light show.

Windows on the World (we'll use the apt abbreviation WOW) has been compared to an immense spaceship, an ocean liner—you name it and pick your own superlatives—for decor, design, and view. WOW's entrance has you walking along a mirrored reception chamber lined by huge rocks that offer a naturalistic counterpoint to the plants and flowers that seem to be everywhere. You are seated in multi-tiered dining rooms made to seem even larger by mirrors—but it is still the skyline that is the real view, no matter what a people-watcher you may be. And the people in WOW are privileged, "beautiful people." The main dining room is a private club Monday through Friday until 3 P.M., becoming a regular restaurant thereafter. The food doesn't match the view—but what could.

You can nibble on the hors d'oeuvres, sample the grilled entrées, or have dessert at the Hors d'Oeuverie, on the same level as WOW, or come for Sunday brunch. It is a lot less costly than WOW, a good place for snacks and drinks—and the view is equally spectacular. And when the evening sun goes down the Hors d'Oeuverie becomes one of the most romantic nightspots in town for nightcaps, dancing to a trio or piano, or just star-gazing in the adjoining City Lights Bar. The phone number for these 107th floor wining and dining spots is 938–1100.

Other worthwhile (and less expensive) stops at the World Trade Center are the Observation Deck, open from 9:30 A.M. to 9:30 P.M., with sunset an especially spectacular time to be there; the Big Kitchen series of deli-style fast-food emporiums in the main concourse of Two WTC, where the crowds at lunch hour are a sight to behold; and the Skydive Café on the 44th floor of One WTC. The latter is an inexpensive-to-moderately priced luncheon cafeteria with a bar that is also open after work. The Observation Deck costs $2.50 for adults, $1.25 for children 6 to 12 years old, and is free for Senior Citizens; telephone 466–7377.

City Hall

Return to Broadway and stroll up to City Hall. Almost any day of the week you are likely to see the welcome mat being spread out for a foreign dignitary, a group of VIPs, a newly-crowned beauty queen, a DAR delegation, or an award-winning actress. Many come to greet the mayor in legitimate roles. Others come seeking publicity. It's been the plaint of many a mayor that acting as the world's greatest greeter cuts deeply into the day's work of handling affairs for the city.

City Hall is both a museum and a municipal capital. Architecturally it is considered one of the finest public buildings in America. During the period between 1803 and 1811, when it was being built, construction costs rose to $538,000—a shocking amount in those days. The Common Council members, pinching pennies wherever they could, decided considerable money could be saved by using marble on the front and sides only. Brownstone would be used to face the back. After all, they maintained, most of the city's population lived south of the park and it would be a waste to use marble when it seldom would be seen. The city, they believed, would never grow much beyond City Hall. When the building was renovated in 1956, at a cost of $2,000,000, the outside was faced in limestone on all four sides, to afford equal respect to the citizens of each point of the compass.

The mayor's office in the west wing overlooks the triangular park where Dutch burghers once bowled and where, a century later, spunky

Revolutionists raised Liberty Poles and demonstrated against British rule. Even today it is not always a peaceful view. Demonstrators often congregate here to march and shout demands for a special action by the city fathers.

A handsome, curving double staircase leads to the Governor's Room on the second floor of City Hall. The elegant quarters, "appropriated as an office to His Excellency the Governor of the State," have been the scene of many gala, historic receptions. It had been traditional, even as far back as the Dutch and English rules, to set aside an area in City Hall for the governor's convenience. Today, New York's governor is not so honored. He is housed in an archaic monstrosity upstate in Albany with not one iota of the charm of the Governor's Room, which is now a showcase of antique furnishings and priceless portraits of early American heroes. One of the most notable items in the museum is George Washington's desk. Open Monday to Friday, 10 A.M.–3 P.M. Free. 566–5700.

On leaving City Hall, walk around to its rear and over to the tall-towered Municipal Building. A passageway through its arch will bring you out on Park Row, near the approach to the Brooklyn Bridge, the city's oldest span. From here, it is only a five-minute walk north to Chinatown.

Chinatown, Their Chinatown

Chinatown may come as a bit of surprise or disappointment, depending on your preconceived picture of it. Many tourists are drawn to the area in hopes of glimpsing the seedy side of life they've seen in class B movies and read about in mystery-thrillers. They are due for disappointment.

Long gone are the bloody fratricidal tong wars, knifings in the night, and the stealthy slipping of dead victims into the black East River waters. Gone too are the opium dens, where men made the world take on a rosy glow after puffing a pipeful of poppy seed. The tongs have turned into modern civic and fraternal organizations and the dens of iniquity have disappeared, though gangs of juvenile thugs (mostly immigrants from Hong Kong) have gained some notoriety recently.

Today, Chinatown is a colorful pocket of Oriental shops and restaurants catering to Chinese who live in other parts of the city, to local government department heads, Park Avenue matrons, Broadway stars, and out-of-town visitors (in short, to all lovers of good Chinese cuisine).

Chinatown is tiny, encompassing something like a dozen or so square blocks. Thousands of Chinese are crowded into tenements lining the narrow, crooked streets. Here, somehow, the tenements seem almost proper to their surroundings. Perhaps it's because pseudo pagodas crown their roofs, bright banners garland the streets, and temple bells and the singsong talk of venerable elders crowd out sounds of the 20th century. There is a faint aura of China's ancient civilization all around: emporiums which have modern adding machines but prefer to do their bookkeeping with the beaded abacus; apothecary and herb shops where family medicinal formulas are compounded. Stalls and shopwindows are piled high with exotic displays of condiments and herbs, snow peas, bean curd, shark fins, duck eggs, dried fungi, squid, and other ingredients used in the delectable Chinese dishes. In keeping with the Oriental theme, even the sidewalk telephone booths have been designed as tiny pagodas.

The juncture of Worth and Mott streets, across from Chatham Square, is the gateway to Chinatown. A Chinese Museum is located at 81 Mott Street, and for 75 cents weekdays or $1 weekends you can view exhibits of ancient Chinese coins, costumes, deities, and dragons. There are displays of flowers, fruits, chopsticks, and incense with explanations of their history and the symbolism attached to each. Push a button at the bottom of a musical instrument display case and a Chinese combo in native costume flashes on the screen to demonstrate how they sound. Youngsters especially enjoy the educational quiz, a game of thirty-eight questions along the lines of "Which city is farthest north, Peking or New York?" and "Who invented paper and printing, the Chinese or Egyptians?" You register your choice by pressing one of two buttons and by the end of the game you have a few nuggets of knowledge to confuse and confound your friends.

The museum also supplies you with a walking-tour map which is most helpful in identifying the Buddhist Temple, Christian churches, Chinese theaters, and other local attractions. Chinese characters and English appear on most signs. There are dozens of shops to browse through. Jade and ivory carvings, good-luck charms, slitted brocade dresses, tea sets, and sweets are to be had for generally lower prices than you can purchase them uptown. Open daily 10 A.M.–6 P.M. (964–1542).

You may hear little English spoken as you wander through Bayard, Pell, and Doyers Streets, though many of Chinatown's citizens can speak it if they please. Nor will you find them especially warm, restaurant owners and shopkeepers included. They maintain a cool dignity born of a culture which predates the Western by many centuries.

Dignity disappears when the Year of the Dragon (or Tiger, or any of the 12 in the Chinese horoscope) comes in, the whole town joining in the gay antics and colorful parades of fire-breathing monsters which mark the start of the lunar New Year at the end of January or beginning of February. Firecrackers explode everywhere. Huge dragons, unicorns, and lions prowl through the streets to scare away evil spirits. Old

Points of Interest

1) Bowery Mission
2) Chinese Museum
3) City Hall
4) Federal Court
5) Federal Office Building
6) Museum of Colored Glass & Light
7) Museum of Holography
8) N.Y. State Office Building
9) N.Y. State Supreme Court
10) Performing Garage
11) SoHo Repertory Theatre
12) Criminal Court
13) N.Y. County Court
14) Police Headquarters

and young dance along behind, shouting "Gun hay fat choy!" (Happy New Year with prosperity). Merchants offer gifts to the dragon and heads of lettuce sprouting dozens of dollars to be dispensed to the poor, for the dragon is an emblem of guardianship and generosity. It is a time when Chinatown is at its liveliest, most colorful best. Not even snow flurries can dampen the high spirits of the celebrants nor those from the outside who have come to watch and participate.

To the west of Chinatown is an emerging artist's neighborhood, christened TriBeCa ("Triangle Below Canal," bounded by the West Side waterfront—Greenwich Street—and West Broadway), which offers cheaper lofts for those driven out of SoHo by rising rents. There are a few interesting if gamy bars, restaurants, and night spots here.

The Bouwerie, the Bowery

Just north of Chinatown, in the shadow of the Williamsburg Bridge, is the Bowery. Once an Indian trail used by Peter Stuyvesant to ride to his *bouwerie,* or "farm," the thoroughfare grew into a fashionable amusement and theater center in the early 19th century, then went into a decline as people moved uptown to new neighborhoods. For almost a century the Bowery has been the "street of forgotten men."

You'll see them curled up in doorways or sprawled on the street, a newspaper or hat cushioning their heads, sleeping off an ever-present hangover. There are beds in the flophouses above the gin mills and pawn shops, but the bed that used to cost 25 cents a night now goes for $1.45 or even more. The men here live by panhandling and on the charity of such organizations as the Salvation Army.

The Army began operating in the area before the turn of the century. Their lassies were not especially welcome when they invaded the Bowery in 1880 to "Go for souls—and go for the worst." Their work to reform derelicts and teach them to lead useful lives was fought by saloon and dance hall proprietors, who felt the preachings were bad for business. The Army had no church nor meeting place; so they preached and sang on street corners until a reformed Harry Hill offered them the use of his bawdy, gaudy music hall for the salvation of souls. The Army's historian recalls: "Alcoholics and prostitutes—the poor and downtrodden and discouraged—soon found new hope and comfort . . . Not only souls were saved, but minds and bodies. Roofs were put over the heads of people who had no other home on earth. Hundreds were fed and clothed by the Army's busy soup kitchens." The lassies marched on to other areas of the city and thence to other areas of public service. Despite their efforts and the efforts of many other charitable service institutions, however, derelicts still take refuge there.

Where do they come from? Just about everywhere and from all stations of life. Some were born to be bums. Others were, perhaps, successful businessmen with fine families who could no longer cope with the pressure, competition, and demands of the commercial world. Whatever their motivation, they have found a solace of sorts in the anonymity of Skid Row. The ranks of the rehabilitated are thin.

The Lower East Side

Housing projects and artist's lofts are encroaching on their Bowery haunts, and within a few years the derelicts may have to move on to other doorways. Some already have made the move. You'll see them on the fringes of Greenwich Village and the East Village a little north of here.

Between the Bowery and the East River is probably New York's most integrated area. The entire city often has been called a "melting pot," but the mile-square east side area (bounded roughly on the south by Canal Street and on the north by Seventh Street) is, some observers feel, the most dramatic example of the blending of many races, religions, and cultures in the world.

Here, immigrants were crammed into ghettos and English was treated as a foreign language. Only those with the greatest stamina survived, and those with the greatest will succeeded in escaping from it. From here came Alfred E. Smith, a son of Irish immigrants, who became governor of New York State. Several sons of Jewish immigrants made the climb to success, too. Among them were Senator Jacob Javits, composers George and Ira Gershwin, comedian Eddie Cantor. A little Italian boy made it also—Jimmy Durante. The neighborhood also spawned its share of gangsters: a few are in jail, a few are living high.

While most shops all over the city are closed on Sunday, those on the Lower East Side bustle with activity. The Jewish Sabbath is observed on Saturday, while Sunday is a big shopping day down here. Grand Street, often called the "Street of Brides," is lined with one shopwindow after another of bridal gowns. The neighborhood now has a large Hispanic community, to add to the diversity.

The stalls on Orchard Street, a street so jammed with shoppers one can hardly wiggle through, display everything from clothing to kitchen wares. Bargaining is the way most transactions are handled, and customers should be wary to inspect merchandise—sometimes these stalls or shops deal in "seconds" in order to keep their prices low. Grand Street is for fine linens, the Bowery is for lamp stores, and Allen Street is the wholesale tie district—all featuring bargain prices.

The northwestern part of the Lower East Side, around Second Avenue and St. Mark's Place (an extension of East 8th Street) is still heavily laden with Middle-European ambience. But not unmixed: St. Mark's Place, formerly the spiritual headquarters of the Hippies, is now spiritual headquarters for the Punk Rockers. The cultural juxtapositions in this area must be seen to be believed.

Little Italy

Little Italy lies east of SoHo, just north of Chinatown, and south of Greenwich Village. Centered on Grand Street and its intersection with Mulberry and Mott streets, Little Italy is the home of Ferrara's, (195 Grand Street, 226–6150), the city's foremost Italian coffee and sweet shop, as well as dozens of Italian restaurants, imported-food shops, cafés, and clam bars—including the ever-popular Umberto's and Vincent's clam bars. These clam bars feature a special hot and spicy tomato sauce with mussels, conch or squid, dishes unavilable anywhere else in the city. Best times for sampling Little Italy's fare are its two major street festivals—St. Anthony's, held during the first two weeks of June, and the early September fête of San Gennaro. During these festivals the whole of Mulberry Street from Canal Street north is turned into a carnival, with food stands hawking calzone, sausage and pepper heroes, zeppola, and other standard southern Italian dishes. "Games of skill and chance" provide between-bite diversion. Chinatown seems to be crowding in on Little Italy from the south.

South of Houston (SoHo)

SoHo, on West Broadway (part of which was renamed La Guardia Place a few years ago), between Canal and West Houston streets, and off to the sides on Prince, Spring, and Broome streets, is an area with which many native New Yorkers aren't familiar. It is only in the last 15 or so years that (at first) artists and writers began moving into the area, bringing their imaginations to bear on buildings formerly used as warehouses and for light industry. They came because they liked what were then inexpensive rents for the lofts—often in need of plumbing and wiring but offering wide-open spaces—while gallery owners appreciated the high-ceilinged spaciousness of the old buildings, which allowed exhibit room to showcase the modern art and sculpture of today's genre. As rents rose, the area became fashionable among art patrons, jetsetters, and young professionals. So following the artists, writers, and galleries, a number of interesting and off-beat restaurants and bars came to be. Ironically, with few exceptions (the Bohemian Cupping Room Café on West Broadway, and O.G. Dining Room and Bakery on Thompson Street among them), most of SoHo's more unusual spots are far too expensive for the neighborhood's natives who work at art. On weekends and most weekday evenings West Broadway is thronged with people who come to SoHo to gallery-hop and browse at the poster shops and boutiques as well as to eat and drink.

Greenwich Village

Greenwich Village is not an entity but rather a collection of little villages. Its heart is Washington Square, at the end of Fifth Avenue, and its extremities reach out farther and farther each year. Roughly, it is bounded by Houston Street (pronounced "HOUSE-ton") on the south, 13th Street on the north, Hudson Street on the west—although much of the area between Hudson (the street) and Hudson (the river) has recently been restored and taken on a "Village" look. Its eastern boundary now extends to Lafayette Street and the vague beginnings of the East Village, where most of the real latter-day Bohemians have migrated. If the Village has a "Main Street," it is 8th Street (and up onto Greenwich Avenue), centered on Village Square at Sixth Avenue.

Rents in Greenwich Village have soared out of the reach of poor poets and struggling artists. Today's Village residents are largely career people—business executives, lawyers, doctors, teachers, successful writers and artists—who have been drawn by its small-town neighborliness and convenient location to the city's business centers. Others, tired of being bound by commuter train schedules, have come down from the suburbs and live in old houses they have renovated. You'll see little clusters of these tidy row houses on such tree-shaded side streets as Charles and Perry, Bedford and St. Luke's, their tiny rear gardens bright with blooms.

The Village is also home to a large segment of New York's Italian population. Their province south of Washington Square, really an extension of Little Italy, is a tangle of shops strung with tangy cheeses, breads, red peppers, garlic, bunches of oregano and rosemary. Housewives stream in from all parts of the Village to pinch the melons, poke through the tomatoes, and argue a bit about prices before making their selections.

In the early 20s the Village was a lively and bawdy place, a Montmartre in the midst of Manhattan. Painters and sculptors had discovered deserted lofts could be rented for a song. Poets and playwrights followed, crowding into the old buildings south of Washington Square, which became known as "Genius Row." They produced their plays in a theater converted from an old box factory, displayed their paintings in the park, scavenged for coal to heat their cold-water flats.

Since the turn of the century, it has been a center of creativity and intellectual curiosity that nurtured some of America's greatest writers and artists: Henry James, Edith Wharton, O. Henry, E. E. Cummings,

Maxwell Bodenheim, Rockwell Kent, and many others. Their haunts —cellar speakeasies, chile con carne joints, hole-in-the-wall restaurants, murky nightclubs with tawdry epicene shows—drew the curious uptowners who wanted a taste of *la vie Bohème*.

Many of their haunts are long gone, victims of urban renewal. Others remain as shrines to their talent and genius. This bawdy phase, however, is but one of many the Village has passed through, for its history dates back to post-Revolutionary days.

The first settlers fled to the Village during the yellow fever plagues which raged through the lower city from 1791 to 1798. Founded in haste on the site of an old tobacco plantation, the little village grew haphazardly and the streets meandered off in unplanned directions. The crazy-quilt street pattern contributes to the Village a quaint charm but drives uninitiated taxi drivers to distraction. One street changes its name in mid-block; another circles back and crosses itself; West 4th wanders across West 10th, 11th, and 12th and runs into West 13th; Little West 12th is four blocks away from its larger namesake. To explore the area, a detailed map is mandatory. Even then, it is difficult to find your way without asking directions. You'll find the Villagers friendly and willing to help you out of the maze.

Focal Point of the Village

Washington Arch, at the foot of Fifth Avenue, is the best point to start a stroll through the most colorful and historic Village areas. It is easily reached by a Fifth Avenue bus marked "8th Street," by 6th and 8th Avenue subway to West 4th Street station, or the BMT to 8th Street and Broadway.

Washington Square served as a potter's field for plague victims and public place for executions in the late 1700s. By 1823 it had been filled with 10,000 victims of the plague and the gallows. It had served its purpose and it was time for a change, the city fathers decided; so the plot was turned into a drill ground for militia. Eventually it became known as Washington Square Park, although most of its former greenery has today been changed to concrete.

Should you choose a Sunday in spring, summer, or fall for your stroll, you'll be treated to one of the town's best known free entertainments. The fountain in the square is a meeting place for jazz and bluegrass musicians, guitar-players, and pluckers of homemade instruments. Within their ranks you may run into a recording artist who has come down to play a session with a group of unknown troubadours just for the sheer fun of it. Sunday strollers are apt to include young parents with toddlers, a multitude of dog-walkers, and arms-around-each-other couples of all ages; in all manner of dress. Come Halloween on October

31 and the park is the end-point of a Mardi Gras-like costume parade that is both colorful and great fun.

The fountain is a good vantage point for viewing the red-brick, white-trimmed houses which line the north side of the square. Built around 1830, they remained a fashionable center of New York for a generation, sheltering members of old New York's aristocracy and a long-gone way of life so vividly described in Henry James's *Washington Square*, the novel which appeared on stage and in film under the title *The Heiress*.

Edith Wharton lived in the old Boorman house on the northeast corner of the square, a setting which inspired her novel *The Age of Innocence*. Down the street from her house, at No. 3, John Dos Passos wrote *Manhattan Transfer* and artist Norman Rockwell painted his own brand of "primitives." Rose Franken, author of *Claudia*, lived at No. 6 before this, while other, lovely patrician homes began to vanish.

Several, including the home of William Rhinelander Stewart, which stood on the northwest corner of Fifth Avenue, have been replaced by an apartment house. Fortunately, the building has been so constructed that it blends in with the remaining old houses. Only the building's first five floors are on the square and they are aligned with the roofs of the surviving houses. The red-brick facing and white trim of the new building blends with the old homes. The granite-colored upper floors are set back and front on Fifth Avenue, making that part of the structure seem completely divorced from the square. During construction of the apartment's foundation, workers found an underground stream. It was old Minetta Brook, which was buried by fill two centuries before. The brook surfaced and now bubbles up in a glass container in the apartment's lobby. It also spouts up in a fountain at No. 33, which is now a New York University residence hall.

The university, which has been here since the 1830s, owns and leases about four-fifths of the land around the square. In its original building, which stood at 100 Washington Square East, Professor Samuel F. B. Morse developed the telegraph and Samuel Colt invented the single-shot pistol.

When its student body began bursting the seams of the campus building on and around the square, the university reluctantly gave notice to the artists and writers along Genius Row. Loud outcries were to no avail, and the row of garrets has been replaced with the Georgian-style Law School at the southwest end of the square and the modern Roman Catholic Holy Trinity Chapel. Other modern N.Y.U. additions are the Hagop Kevorkian Center for Near Eastern Studies and the Bobst Library. Up the street, the tall brick-and-glass Loeb Student Center covers the site of Madame Blanchard's boardinghouse, whose

Points of Interest

1) Astor Place Theater
2) Bottom Line
3) Cherry Lane Theater
4) Circle in the Square Theater
5) Cooper Union
6) Jefferson Market Library
7) New York University
8) Palladium Theatre
9) Players Theater
10) Provincetown Playhouse
11) Public Theater (Papp)
12) Sullivan St. Playhouse
13) Theater De Lys
14) Village Gate
15) The New Museum/The New School (branch)
16) The New School for Social Research

boarders included Theodore Dreiser, Eugene O'Neill, Zona Gale, Frank Norris, O. Henry, and many other literary notables.

MacDougal Street Promenade

From here it's a short walk to MacDougal Street, which is called Washington Square West at this point. A few steps up MacDougal Street brings you to MacDougal Alley, one of the most charming back streets in the Village. Most of the little homes here were former stables and carriage houses of the elegant old homes on Washington Square North. Brightly painted, with doorways lit by gas lamps, they are among the most prized studios and apartments in all New York City. At the rear of the old homes on the east side of Fifth Avenue you'll find a similar cobbled street, lined by converted carriage houses, called Washington Mews.

Returning to the west side of Washington Square, passing the Law School, and walking on into the lower part of MacDougal Street, you will see the rebuilt Provincetown Playhouse, a pioneer off-Broadway theater made famous by the early works of Eugene O'Neill. This stretch of MacDougal Street is part of New York's "Little Italy," which has been invaded by a new breed of struggling artists who will sit you down on a campstool and paint your portrait, for a price, in short order. There are boutiques where you'll find witty, trendy, and ethnic clothes and jewelry; leather goods shops and fortune-reading ateliers; a few good restaurants; coffee houses (the latter now, alas, a Village rarity); and pizza and souvlaki eateries.

MacDougal Street leaves this mood behind as it crosses Bleecker Street, home of the Circle-in-the-Square Theater, which produced the early works of Tennessee Williams. The original theater group has now made the move uptown to Broadway and is operating at the Circle in the Square–Joseph E. Levine Theater, with an annual subscription season. On Thompson St. between Bleecker and Houston (a Dutch term meaning "house garden") is a row of well-kept, old brick houses where well-to-do professional people live. A similar row on Sullivan Street backs onto them and the private park between is shared by householders on both sides.

Turn back to Bleecker Street, head west across Sixth Avenue— officially known as the "Avenue of the Americas"—and you'll come to Father Demo Square and the Renaissance-style Church of Our Lady of Pompeii. Spend a minute or so in the church, for its lovely stained-glass windows and religious paintings are well worth the time. You are now at the beginning of the Italian shopping mart, which stretches from Sixth over to Seventh Avenue. The pushcarts have vanished from this colorful neighborhood, as have all but a very few produce stores.

But the aromatic fish stores, bakeries with their mouth-watering Neapolitan cakes and pastries, meat and cheese and grocery shops make this one of New York's unique streets, with a character and flavor all its own.

The Village's meandering streets can really defeat you at this point, but find Leroy Street and follow its bend to St. Luke's Place. Here you'll come upon a poplar-lined street of handsome Anglo-Italian houses, almost as elegant as those of Washington Square. Built in 1880, they have housed many a New York celebrity. No. 6 was once the home of New York's dashing mayor, Jimmy Walker. At an earlier time, it was the residence of the French Consul, and if you look to the left of the doorway you can still see, set in the wall, a title bearing the arms of the French Republic.

At the end of the street, turn right on Hudson and explore the streets which twist and turn off it: Morton Street, with its attractive but seedy houses, and Bedford Street, where Edna St. Vincent Millay and John Barrymore lived (at different times) in New York's narrowest house. It is numbered 75½ and is only nine feet broad, having been built in the driveway of the old Cardoza farmhouse.

Three of the most contradictory houses in the Village are found at the corner of Grove and Bedford streets. The house on the corner, a faded historic mansion, is backed up against a little doll house which is said to have been used for slave quarters a century ago. Next door, at 100 Bedford, is a gingerbread house known as "Twin Peaks." Local legend claims it was designed as a "dream house" by a Village artist, and that the sketches of his fairytale domicile caught the eye of financier Otto Kahn, who financed the dream. To many it is a nightmare.

Follow Grove Street to the point where it bends, and you will see the gate to Grove Court, a fenced-off cluster of small brick houses circling a shady garden. Grove Court was the home of O. Henry when he became affluent and it is the setting of his story *The Last Leaf*.

While you're following these winding streets, look for Commerce Street and the Cherry Lane Theater, the famous playhouse (converted from a box factory) which has given many a struggling playwright an opportunity to display his works. Follow Grove Street to St. Luke's Chapel on Hudson Street. St. Luke's was built by Trinity Church in 1822 and still maintains many of its old traditions. The church itself burned recently, but is being rebuilt. Wings of little brick houses jut out from St. Luke's. These old row houses also date from the 1820s and one was the boyhood home of Bret Harte.

Now, follow Grove in its eastward course, and before long you'll emerge into a nine-way intersection at Sheridan Square. The area around the square is studded with restaurants, shops, theaters, and cafés.

Meandering Mood

If you still are in the mood for meandering, pick up Waverly Place, and don't be startled when you find it meeting itself after awhile. Richard Harding Davis, who lived at No. 108, often walked in circles, too. Nearby is Gay Street, a crooked little path punctuated here and there with Greek Revival houses built in the 1820s. Ruth McKenney lived in the basement apartment of No. 14 with *My Sister Eileen*. A worthwhile detour, before you reach the square, is a walk along Bleecker Street, turning left from Grove and following it to where it comes to an end, at Bank Street and Eighth Avenue. This stretch of Bleecker, like much of the Village, is a designated landmark district, and most of the buildings along it date from the early 19th century. Some of the most attractive antique and gift shops in the city are along here. The White Horse Tavern, on Hudson Street, not too far from the end of Bleecker, was the favorite Manhattan drinking place of poet Dylan Thomas. Farther west, at West Street and Bank Street, on the waterfront, is Westbeth, the former Bell Labs building converted into an artist's community. A committee screens applicants so that only working people in the arts are offered apartments.

Follow Gay to Christopher, cross that street, and then follow it westward for a few blocks' worth of good window-shopping and browsing. The entire length of Christopher Street is the center of New York's large homosexual community. This route will take you across the Sheridan Square intersection again.

Village Square

Back at the Gay-Christopher intersection, turn right into the intersection that takes in Greenwich Avenue, 8th Street, and Avenue of the Americas. This is Village Square, one of the crossroads of the Village. The open-fronted vegetable stand to the right was once Luke O'Connor's Columbian Gardens, where back in 1896 young John Masefield, the late Poet Laureate of England, hauled beer kegs and mopped floors. Across the square to the north is a block of some historic interest. Patchin Place, itself a small courtyard of great charm, off West 10th Street between the Avenue of the Americas and Greenwich Avenue, was the site of E. E. Cummings' apartment for many of the later years of his life. Djuna Barnes also lived on Patchin Place. The iron-barred Women's House of Detention, across the street behind the Jefferson Market building, was demolished in late 1973. The property belongs to the city and there is doubt as to its ultimate destiny. Interested Village citizens have pushed for a semi-public park that would adjoin the neighboring Jefferson Market Courthouse, a cherished landmark since 1878. Its unusual Italian Gothic architecture is the work of Calvert de Vaux, one of the architects of Central Park, and Frederick Withers, who designed the picturesque gate of the Little Church Around the Corner. Its clock tower once served as the neighborhood fire lookout. Long unused, the Courthouse was refurbished inside and out and is now a branch of the New York Public Library.

Two major Village streets lead from this intersection in opposite directions. 8th Street between Fifth and Sixth Avenues changes personality yearly, it seems. Doorways and sidewalks are crowded and often trash-littered, especially on weekends, and shops, too, have changed radically over the years; garish snack shops and noisy record stores currently predominate. This single, busy block is still worth a visit—but a brief one. Going diagonally northwest between this intersection and Eighth Avenue is Greenwich Avenue, one of the more interesting promenades in the Village. Cafés, some good restaurants, eye-catching clothing shops (both trendy and classic), and interesting Villagers to look at make it a fun strolling route, and most of the neighborhood is out every weekend, bound on errands or the pursuit of pleasure. The farther northwest you go, the more conservative the shops and people seem. Greenwich Avenue is the Village in microcosm. The triangular vacant lot opposite St. Vincent's Hospital at Seventh Avenue and West 12th Street used to contain an apartment house inhabited by Village characters, where Edmund Wilson made his first home in the city.

The East Village

East Village, the new Bohemia, is more or less bounded by 14th Street on the north, the Bowery on the west, Houston Street on the south, and the East River. The area has inherited many of Greenwich Village's ways of the '20s. Here, every day is Freedom Day, and you'll see it celebrated in a variety of ways. This enclave of the disciples of unconventional living centers around Tompkins Square, seven blocks east of Washington Square.

Cheap rents first drew the poor painters and poets. Rooms and lofts could be rented for as little as $20 a month. Included, of course, were squalor and a lot of do-it-yourself decorating and repairs. There were other attractions, too. The new crop of artists and writers found the atmosphere lacked prejudice. Many residents live communally, sharing the work and expenses of their room and board.

The area abounds with talent, though many artists moved to SoHo or more recently to TriBeCa. Most of the area's new poets' works are published in underground magazines, mimeographed and stapled in someone's cellar, and distributed to friends and colleagues. Many an

avant garde theatrical production has been given a try-out at La Mama
E.T.C., 74A Fourth Street just west of Second Avenue. This small
coffee house-cum-stage is one of those theaters which is called not just
Off-Broadway but Off-Off-Broadway.

St. Mark's Place is the main promenade for the East Village. It is a
stretch between Third and First Avenues, the extension of East 8th
Street, and along it you'll see one or two emporiums that frankly
proclaim themselves "head shops," a reminder that just a few years ago
the East Village was one of New York's major outposts of the drug
culture. Hundreds of runaway teenagers flocked here to live in
anonymity and self-imposed communal poverty until sheer desperation
—or the police—sent them back to their parents. Some remainder of
this subculture still exists, and this is another area of the city where
old-time, immigrant-family citizens and the young, free-living newcomers are learning to coexist without too much antagonism.

On St. Mark's Place, there are also several clothing shops, mostly of
the wildly informal variety; boutiques with jewelry and leather goods;
record stores; and a popular movie house attracting buffs with its
program of cinema classics, mostly the old musicals. Between Second
and First, the architecture is considerably more attractive, and do note
the charming edifice that is the First German Methodist Episcopal
Church.

What was East Village before the invasion of the latter-day Bohemians? The square, named for one of New York's governors, Daniel B.
Tompkins, was a nice, quiet neighborhood of mixed cultures, people of
Ukrainian, Czech, German, Polish, Russian, Italian, Jewish, and, lately, Puerto Rican and Indian origins. Russian and Turkish baths, the
special delicacies in delicatessen, meat, and produce stores reflect the
heterogeneous ways of the neighborhood. Handsome churches of all
faiths—among them, St. Nicholas Russo-Carpathian, St. Brigid's-on-
the-Square, and St. Mark's Church-in-the-Bouwerie—have served generation after generation. The old-world ethnic composition of the area
also makes the East Village a good neighborhood for hearty, inexpensive dining.

This is the area Dutch Governor Peter Stuyvesant retired to after he
surrendered Nieuw Amsterdam to the British. It became a defense post
against the British in 1812, later a parade ground, then a recruiting
camp for Civil War soldiers and scene of draft riots, mass meetings, and
hunger strikes. Its tumultuous background is reflected in the area's
explosive temperament today.

The City Moves North

Fortunately there were enough parade grounds scattered around the city to break up the forward march of square block upon square block of brownstone houses. The city was lucky, too, in having a few imaginative builders.

One was Samuel Ruggles, who had bought a large tract of land between what is now 20th and 21st streets, extending east of Park Avenue South and west of Third Avenue. It is now known as Gramercy Park, center of one of the nicer residential areas in the city. In the early 1800s, when Ruggles bought the property, the area was far north of the city. His contemporaries derided his dream of turning this woodland tract into an English-type residential square and dubbed it "Sam Ruggles' Vacant Lot." The men of little vision lived to eat their words.

Ruggles divided the tract, making a square of forty-two lots that he set aside for a park, and the bordering area, which was carved into sixty-six building lots. The elite of New York were attracted with the promise that only those who built houses around the square would have the use of the park. Two golden keys to unlock the gate of the fenced-in park were given to each homeowner. The snob appeal made the venture an instantaneous success.

Mrs. Stuyvesant Fish, leader of society's "400," became a resident and many others followed. They included Cyrus W. Field, who was responsible for the first Atlantic cable; the illustrious architect Stanford White, whose career came to a sudden end when Pittsburgh millionaire Harry K. Thaw shot him for flirting with his ladylove (showgirl Evelyn Nesbit); James W. Gerard, the pre-World War I American ambassador to Germany; and wealthy philanthropist Peter Cooper. Shakespearean star Edwin Booth's home at 16 Gramercy Park is now the headquarters of the Players' Club, and the National Arts Club is housed in the mansion at No. 15, which once had been the home of Samuel J. Tilden, the man who was almost elected president.

The social register tenants are gone and the homes have been broken up into apartments occupied by decorators, writers, business executives, and wealthy widows. You'll see the lucky keyholders sitting in the park on a sunny afternoon, reading or watching the youngsters play quiet games. It is an oasis of peace and solitude, for no dogs, bikes, or swings are permitted.

Theodore Roosevelt's birthplace (28 East 20th Street) is now a National Historic Site. It is a fine example of a typical well-to-do Victorian home. The furnishings, including the scratchy horsehair sofa which menaced a small boy in short pants, are just as they were described later by T.R. in his autobiography. The home, and the adjacent museum of the relics Roosevelt collected during his years of adventuring, are open weekdays.

Nearby, the stretch of Broadway south of 23rd Street is the center of the photographers' loft district. North, at 1 East 29th Street, is a little church with a legend, a symbol of how time has worn down prejudice. When it was built in 1849, it was named the Church of the Transfiguration, but it has been known as "the Little Church Around the Corner."

It is filled with memorials, the most famous of which is a window dedicated to Joseph Jefferson, in his role as Rip Van Winkle, leading his shroud-clad friend, George Holland, to the church. In the post-Civil War period actors were socially unacceptable. On the death of Holland, when Jefferson spoke to the pastor of the church of his choice about funeral arrangements for his friend, the pastor turned him away, suggesting that he make arrangements at the "little church around the corner, where they do that kind of thing." It is now the actors' favorite church, and many a Broadway and Hollywood star attends services here. Of course, it is a favorite with brides, too.

The church on the corner of 29th Street and Fifth Avenue is the Marble Collegiate Church, designed by Samuel A. Warner and built in 1854 during the first phase of the Romanesque Revival boom which spread throughout New York. Its pastor is Dr. Norman Vincent Peale, author of *The Power of Positive Thinking*.

New York's Own Chelsea

The Chelsea area, on the west side across town from Gramercy Park, has let many of its historic landmarks slip through its fingers. Yet many writers find the remnants of its past gentility and the unfrenetic pace of Chelsea to their liking and the recent proliferation of cozy contemporary bars, moderately priced restaurants, and brownstone renovations has made it one of the up-and-coming neighborhoods of the city's "far west" end. Still a living symbol of the area's attractiveness to literary figures, the Chelsea Hotel, at 222 West 23rd Street, has been home to many celebrated writers. Thomas Wolfe and Dylan Thomas lived here and Brendan Behan wrote his book on New York in one of its apartments. Composer Virgil Thomson still lives there, though of late it has become a popular haunt of touring rock and roll stars.

The hostelry, a Victorian Gothic edifice with wrought-iron balconies, turrets, and chimney stacks, has been designated by the Municipal Art Society as one of New York's architectural monuments which should be preserved at all costs. In 1978 it was named a National Historic Landmark. If you should step into the Chelsea note the teakwood fireplace in the lobby and the bas-relief mural over it. It is the work of resident Rene Shapshak and depicts the arts—painting, drama, music, dance, architecture, literature, and sculpture. Harry S. Truman stopped by here many times when Mr. Shapshak was working on a bust of the former president. To the right of the registration desk is a staircase. Walk up a flight and you can see the hotel's famous web of wrought-iron railing ascending flight after flight to the skylight.

Across the street is the McBurney YMCA, the oldest "Y" in the city. Over the years its membership has included Lowell Thomas, Dale Carnegie, Arthur Godfrey, James Michener and Brendan Behan.

Chelsea's Night Before Christmas

The most notable of all Chelsea's residents was Dr. Clement Clarke Moore, who penned in 1822 the poem *A Visit from St. Nicholas,* more familiarly known today as *'Twas The Night Before Christmas.* Moore grew up on his grandfather's farm here, a spread which bordered the Hudson River and ran from what is now 19th to 23rd streets. The grandfather, Captain Thomas Clarke, had come to this country from England to fight in the French and Indian War. When his tour of duty was ended in 1750, he decided to remain, buy a farm, and build a mansion, which he nostalgically named "Chelsea" after the Chelsea Royal Hospital on the Thames, a charitable institution Nell Gwynne talked King Charles II into building for old, invalided soldiers. The lovely old mansion is gone; so, too, are Dr. Moore's house and the Grand Opera House where Josie Mansfield, Lily Langtry, and Edwin Booth performed.

The oldest building in Chelsea, which dates from 1785, is a two-and-one-half-story brick house with a steeply pitched roof and dormer windows at 183 Ninth Avenue, corner of 21st Street. Its ground floor now is occupied by a dairy store.

If you wander through 20th, 21st, and 22nd streets between Eighth and Ninth Avenues, you will see evidence of Chelsea's struggle to maintain its gentility. Many of the old brownstones have been tinted a lively pink, yellow, or blue. Their intricate wrought-iron balustrades gleam and their tiny front gardens are well tended.

The General Theological Seminary, with an entrance at 175 Ninth Avenue between 20th and 21st streets, stands on land which once was Captain Clarke's apple orchard. Dr. Clement Moore served on its staff as a professor of Hebrew. Its library, housed in a new building, is famous for its collection of rare theological books.

The rectory of St. Peter's Episcopal Church at 346 West 20th Street was built in 1831 on property donated by Dr. Moore. The adjoining Gothic Revival church was added in 1836; its parish house is a lively center of art festivals and dramatic productions. Visitors are always welcome.

This is the southern fringe of what was once "Hell's Kitchen"—20th to 50th streets, west of Eighth Avenue—an area which spawned such notorious mobsters as Mad Dog Coll and Owney Madden. It was predominantly Irish for many years, but with the coming of better times for the Irish and urban renewal, the Irish have moved elsewhere. The area now has a Greek (and slightly Turkish) atmosphere. Little nightclubs feature beautiful belly dancers, their spangles and beaded brass shimmering as they weave and wiggle to the mysterious tempo of wailing flutes and tinkling finger cymbals. Glasses of anise-flavored *ouzo* cast their spell over members of the audience, and now and again one will rise and slowly take up the controlled movements of a Greek folk dance. But the number of these clubs is dwindling.

Midtown Manhattan

Midtown Manhattan, which ranges roughly from 34th Street (the Empire State Building on Fifth Avenue marks the southern boundary) to 59th Street (Central Park begins there) and river to river, is a center of superlatives. The biggest buildings, best restaurants, most art galleries, brightest lights, greatest concentration of big business, largest complex of theaters, best bargain basements, most exclusive department stores, and the most specialized services are all here.

Here you can have your dog psychoanalyzed, then hire a professional dogwalker to take him for a stroll; pick up a glittery gown or mink stole for a pittance at thriftshops, where Broadway and TV stars leave them to be sold on consignment; swim and sun high in the sky on a hotel roof in the morning and ice skate in the afternoon at Rockefeller Center; buy a blue wig or a sable trench coat, if you care to.

You can see more and better French Impressionist art in a day's tour of museums and galleries here than you could see in Paris in all of a week. You can make a world tour of cuisine. Name any dish and it's yours: Brazilian, Japanese, Greek, French, German, Italian, Indian, Armenian, Polynesian, Jewish, Hungarian, Chinese, Spanish, Swiss, Belgian, Irish, Mexican, regional American. You can have breakfast at 5 P.M. or 5 A.M., for New York never sleeps.

It has been said that the forest of commerce in Wall Street reflects the purpose and push of dour, determined men. If so, then uptown New York, with its elegance, culture, countless diversions, and green acres, reflects the fruits of the dour men's labors.

The midtown shopping area is without peer in America. The most elegant, extravagant, and rare fabrics, furs, jewels, and accessories are displayed in profusion. Modish copies are offered to those of modest budget. The uninitiated are hard-pressed to tell the difference between the black Dior original and genuine strand of Oriental pearls on the dowager and the "authentic" copy and simulated pearls worn by the young career woman. Seventh Avenue, as a result, is a girl's best friend. The world's great concentration of garment manufacturers is right at her doorstep. The "rag business," as the trade affectionately calls itself, is concentrated in the west 30s, along Seventh Avenue. Fortunes are made and lost here, depending on the consumer's whim. Those dress houses which guess wrong twice in a row go bankrupt. Often you can profit from their mistakes and buy the unpopular models (they might be exactly to your taste) for less than cost in one of the bargain basements or cut-rate specialty shops in the neighborhood. The wholesale millinery firms are here too. Many have retail salesrooms on 38th Street, where you can also buy all the trimmings for a do-it-yourself creation.

Festive Fifth Avenue

Fifth Avenue is a festival all year-round, with a continuous showing of spectaculars. Its pioneers have fought to maintain its prestige and preserve its *haute monde* image. As far back as 1907, they formed the Fifth Avenue Association to do battle with any element which might threaten its lustre. At Christmastime, the street features tinseled trees, twinkling lights, bright garlands, and jolly St. Nicks. In springtime, awnings and entrances bloom with artificial flowers and perfume wafts onto the street to entice you inside. At night, windows are kept lit, offering the stroller an incomparable window shopping tour.

No matter what the season, the Empire State Building, on Fifth Avenue at 34th Street, remains a favorite attraction for natives and visitors alike. Perhaps because it held the title of tallest building in the world for so long, perhaps because it has been immortalized in so many films (not the least of which is *King Kong*), and perhaps because it gave New York its state title—"The Empire State"—it has retained a special place in people's hearts despite the fact that the World Trade Center stands a full 100 feet taller. It opened in May 1931 (it took only a year and a half to construct). Some 15,000 people work in the building and more than a million and a half people still visit its observatory annually for what remains a spectacular panorama of New York and its surroundings. This observatory, incidentally, is open nightly until midnight—two hours later than the one at the World Trade Center. Tickets cost $2.50 for adults, $1.35 for children under 12.

The merchants have done battle with the city fathers about parades on Fifth Avenue, which disrupted business. They won, up to a point. Today all parades except two—the Columbus Day and St. Patrick's Day parades—start at 60th Street, above the main shopping area. Despite their efforts to keep Fifth Avenue on the highest plateau, some

Midtown Manhattan

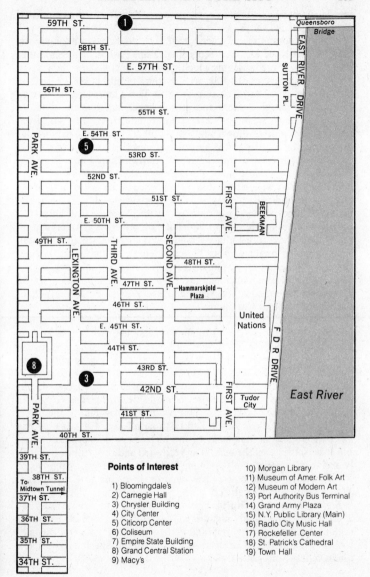

Points of Interest

1) Bloomingdale's
2) Carnegie Hall
3) Chrysler Building
4) City Center
5) Citicorp Center
6) Coliseum
7) Empire State Building
8) Grand Central Station
9) Macy's
10) Morgan Library
11) Museum of Amer. Folk Art
12) Museum of Modern Art
13) Port Authority Bus Terminal
14) Grand Army Plaza
15) N.Y. Public Library (Main)
16) Radio City Music Hall
17) Rockefeller Center
18) St. Patrick's Cathedral
19) Town Hall

interlopers have managed to open up tourist-trap linen-china-cameras-radios-gimcracks shops.

Midtown does not readily lend itself to cut-and-dried walking tours. It is an area to be explored according to one's whims and particular interests. There are museums which specialize in collections of modern art, contemporary crafts, folk art, costumes of all nations, re-runs of old silent movies, and lecture programs. There are scores of foreign tourist information centers and airline ticket offices with advice to inspire your next vacation. There are awesome views to be seen from observatories atop midtown's tallest buildings, a world to explore underground, a hundred little personal discoveries to be made if you venture off the beaten track. And, of course, there's the shopping. Virtually every one of New York's major department stores has a character of its own—a style that is manifested in the stores' own decor, in the merchandise they carry and in the people who shop at them. The accent is almost always on clothing—women's more so than men's, though Bloomingdale's gives equal if not preferential treatment to males—with furniture and household goods almost as an afterthought, something you might pick up "to complete the outfit" while passing through. Well, that may be an exaggeration, but here's a quick look at The Top Ten. Most, incidentally, have evening shopping hours on Thursdays throughout the year, and every night from the end of November through Christmas.

Altman's, at 34th St. at Fifth Ave., 689–7000, is where everyone's grandmother seemingly used to shop (back when Best & Co. was its main competitor)—and still does. They're attempting to update the look and feel of the store, and the merchandise is generally of top quality, even if a little staid.

Bergdorf Goodman, on Fifth Ave. at 57th St., 753–7300, is as starchily traditional as Bloomingdale's is modishly outrageous. If you're looking for a pure silk-lined fur nose-warmer, this would be the place.

Bloomingdale's, at 59th St. and Lexington Ave., 705–2000, is the place for high tech, high fashion, and high prices. The pace is frantic, the aisles (at least on the main floor) crowded and the attitude haughtily exclusive whether you're looking for the latest designer originals or for a colander in the housewares department or for an Oriental rug. Worth a trip just to sightsee!

Bonwit Teller, on 57th St. between Fifth and Madison aves., 764–2300, is the newest "old" member of the fraternity—recently reopened under a spectacular new roof (and behind gleaming glass and chrome) with four floors of the latest in women's fashion. Spacious and just a touch snobby, but with style.

Gimbels, across 34th St. and Broadway from Macy's, 736–5100, has the feel of a dingy bargain basement throughout, although the prices don't usually match the ambience.

Henri Bendel, on 57th St. between Fifth and Sixth aves., 247–1100. Don't turn your nose up until after you've passed the chocolate counter —one of the best in the city. Thereafter be prepared to shop among the elite (and that means salespeople as well as customers).

Lord & Taylor, at 37th St. on Fifth Ave., 391–3344, has the best Christmas windows of any store in New York. Forever being renovated, the mood is nonetheless old-style but sophisticated.

Macy's, at 34 St. and Broadway (Herald Square), 971–6000, retains its title as the world's largest department store under one roof. It has been modernized bit by bit over the last few years, with the popular Cellar (for housewares and gourmet foods) setting the tone for the rest of the store. Probably still the best all-purpose department store in Manhattan.

Ohrbach's, at 34th St. between Fifth and Sixth aves., 695–4000, is another bargain-basement-type store, but with a moderately contemporary feel and better than average merchandise (clothes).

Saks Fifth Avenue, at 50th St. and Fifth Ave., 753–4000, calls itself the "largest specialty shop in the world." It may well be, in its old-world, traditional way, a little dated, but it is always practical and reliable for the basics in clothing and other goods.

Three of the city's greatest attractions are in this midtown area: Times Square, where the Great White Way begins; Rockefeller Center; and the United Nations.

The Great White Way starts at Times Square, a point where meandering Broadway crosses 42nd Street and Seventh Avenue to form a tiny plaza which is anything but square in shape.

It is a monument to the vision and the gambling spirit of three men: Oscar Hammerstein I, an impresario who in 1894 sank a two-million-dollar fortune, and then some, into building the first theaters here; August Belmont, a financier who more than matched Hammerstein's gamble by extending the subway to bring the crowds uptown to the new theater district; and publisher Adolph S. Ochs, who built the Times Tower in 1904 as the new headquarters for his influential newspaper, *The New York Times,* and dedicated it with a night of revelry which has become a New Year's Eve tradition.

Theaters Move Uptown

Hammerstein's fellow impresarios knew a good thing when they saw it and moved their theaters uptown. With such a captive audience as Times Square offered, promoters of soft drinks, cigarettes, liquor, chewing gum, and two-trouser suits put up huge animated electric advertisements which outshone the sun.

Times Square became a symbol of facing life and making good. Dreams of becoming a dramatic star overnight, writing a musical hit, waxing a smash record, or marrying a millionaire swam in the heads of small town girls and small city boys who flocked to this street of dreams. For a special few, the dreams came true. Stars were born, fortunes were made, and millionaires wedded to their gold. Those who couldn't make the grade on Broadway took the ferry over to Fort Lee, New Jersey, and worked for the "flickers," a new form of entertainment legitimate actors deplored or ignored. The flicker performers made it big and went on to Hollywood, fame, and fortune.

The theater district has become tarnished quite a bit since the glamorous pre-Depression days when top-hatted stage-door Johnnies waited for their favorite Follies dollies, wined and dined them on the Ziegfeld Theater roof, and slipped a hundred-dollar bill under their plates for the privilege.

Broadway's Constant Lure

Times Square has taken on a midway bazaar-like look, with its soft drink and pizza stands, pinball and shooting galleries, racy lingerie and fake "fire sale" shops. Some of the old prestige theaters now feature X-rated movies and ladies of the evening roam the streets along with a hodgepodge of other derelicts and eccentrics. Within the radius of a few blocks in the 40s, however, there still remain numerous legitimate theaters, surely the greatest concentration of dramatic and musical productions you will find anywhere in the world (with the possible exception of London's West End). This tight little center of entertainment offers a rare opportunity for last-minute shopping. If you've neglected to order theater tickets in advance, make a tour of the box offices just before curtain-time and you might just be lucky enough to pick up a pair of unclaimed seats at regular prices. Or check with the Times Square Ticket Service office (the sign reads "TKTS") at 47th Street and Broadway, where tickets for cultural events from concerts to legitimate theater are usually available and always to be had for half the box-office price plus a minimal service fee.

Incidentally, right near this ticket mecca in the small triangular-shaped Duffy Square is a city-run visitors information center where you can pick up advice. The TKTS booth is open daily from 3 to 8 P.M. for evening performances, noon to 2 P.M. for Wednesday and Saturday matinees, and noon to 8 P.M. for all Sunday shows. Lines for first choice of the evening selections begin to form in late morning, much earlier for matinees. Telephone 354–5800. (There is a second TKTS booth down in the Wall Street area at 100 William Street, which is open Monday through Friday from 11:30 A.M. to 5:30 P.M. and Saturday from 11 A.M. to 3 P.M.; the lines here are generally much shorter than those uptown, and you may well save time making the extra trip downtown. Take the No. 2 or 3 IRT subway to the Wall Street stop—it shouldn't take more than 15 to 20 minutes each way.)

Times Square is the object of what seems to New Yorkers like a never-ending battle for upgrading. One major example of what appears to be a successful move in this direction is the Manhattan Plaza apartment/restaurant complex along the north side of 42nd between Ninth and Tenth avenues. The residential units are made available to performing artists only—primarily those involved with the nearby theater —who give a percentage of their income as rent. In response to the immediate filling up of the apartment building, a whole slew of restaurants sprang up in and around Manhattan Plaza, while the theaters on the south side of 42nd have been rehabilitated as legitimate Off-Broadway houses. As of press time, there was considerable controversy over another Times Square improvement plan known as the Portman Project. This has already involved the razing of three of Broadway's oldest theaters in order to make way for a new midtown hotel. Still, however else one may object to the strip shows and triple-X-rated movie houses in the area, it can't be denied that their neon lights burning 24 hours a day add, shall we say, color and spectacle.

For passenger ships, a series of three piers at 48th, 50th, and 52nd streets has been turned into a climate-controlled, modern terminal for cruise ships and the rare transatlantic liners. These piers provide not only more comfort and convenience for passengers but also excellent vantage points for tourists to watch the whole procedure of loading, unloading, and leave-taking.

The marble-and-glass building—formerly known as the Times Tower, then the Allied Chemical Building—located on the north side of 42nd Street between Broadway and Seventh Avenue, is still ushering in the New Year with a bright ball descending the flagpole on the building, reaching the bottom at the stroke of midnight.

The Avenue of the Americas

You might first like to stroll up Sixth Avenue, more accurately known as the Avenue of the Americas. Note the emblems of all the nations in North, Central, and South America hanging along the avenue. Like many areas of mid-Manhattan, it is changing as glittering new skyscrapers take the place of older edifices.

Bryant Park, located between 40th and 42nd streets behind the New York City Public Library, is a green and relaxing spot to visit and rest, if the dope-pushers and occasional crazies don't annoy you. Named in 1884 for William Cullen Bryant, poet and journalist, it is a gathering place for impromptu public speakers and their eclectic sort of audience. A couple of booksellers have opened bookstalls there. The park is also an excellent vantage point from which to view one of the city's more unusual skyscrapers. Located between the Avenue of the Americas and Fifth Avenue, with entrances on 42nd and 43rd streets and adjacent to the also intriguing new Graduate Center of CUNY, the Monsanto Building slopes gently upward, narrowing from its base to its towering roof, producing the rather uneasy effect of a hill carved from glass and stone. It was the city's first such structure and was designed by Gordon Bunshaft of the architectural firm of Skidmore, Owings & Merrill. A similar one curves inward from both 57th and 58th streets, also between Fifth Avenue and the Avenue of the Americas. Incidentally, this same firm also designed Lever House in 1952 at 390 Park Avenue, along with many other notable city buildings.

Midtown is where the famous private men's clubs, portrayed so often in the *New Yorker* cartoons, are thickest on the ground. Look for them as you stroll; by and large they are understated and easy to miss. A representative selection (look, but you can't enter unless you are a member): University Club, at the corner of Fifth Avenue and 54th Street; the Century Club, favored by men in the business of publishing; next to it, on 43rd Street between Fifth and Sixth Avenues, is the Princeton Club, looking like an electric-power substation; down the street toward Sixth Avenue is the New York Yacht Club, with interesting windows; the Metropolitan Club, at Fifth Ave. and 60th Street, in a building designed by McKim, Mead & White; the Harvard Club, 44th Street between Fifth and Sixth Avenues; the Racquet & Tennis Club, at 370 Park Avenue (53rd Street); and the Yale Club, across from the PanAm Building at Vanderbilt Avenue and 44th Street.

But back to Sixth Avenue. Walk north from 42nd Street and you'll see many other recently constructed buildings. At 1133, corner of 43rd Street, is the Kodak Exhibition Center, where you might stop in to see the exhibits in its downstairs gallery. Now a short detour east on 44th toward Fifth Avenue to the Algonquin Hotel and restaurant, still operating at No. 59. Behind its rather unimposing Renaissance façade many figures have wined, dined, and discussed the hours away: Dorothy Parker, Harold Ross, and Robert Benchley, among others. East on 45th Street is a concentration of the city's best hi-fi and electronics retail outlets. East on 46th Street, still off Sixth Avenue, is an array of Brazilian shops and restaurants. At 47th Street, you just might be tempted to take another detour east for a look at the block-long area known as the city's diamond center—it's obvious why when you see the countless glittering shop windows.

For the next three blocks on the west side of the avenue you'll be passing the three newest (early seventies) skyscraper members of the Rockefeller Center community. Between 47th and 48th streets is the 45-story Celanese Building, which was completed in 1973. The next block north contains the 51-story McGraw-Hill building. Here you should plan to take an hour out to see *The New York Experience* in the building's plush Trans-Lux Experience Theater. The production is a multiple-screen entertainment that surrounds the audience with sights, sounds, and multi-sensory special effects utilizing thirty-seven projectors and fourteen screens and quadraphonic sound. Included as a part of the presentation is an exhibit of Little Old New York, re-creating local city life as it was in the late 19th century. On 48th Street, between Sixth and Seventh Avenues, are musical instrument retail shops. The next block, on Sixth Avenue, between 49th and 50th streets, is the sleek 54-story corporate home of Exxon. This trio of buildings features open plazas and modern sculpture, where the weary sightseer can sit down with area office workers, especially at midday.

Radio City Music Hall, on the east side of the avenue at 50th Street, is a primary attraction, though its future is in doubt for financial reasons. It is the largest indoor theater in America, with a seating capacity of 6,000. When traditional seasonal pageants of the Nativity or the Glory of Easter are presented, the four blocks bounding the Music Hall are jammed with people who will wait for hours in sleet and rain to buy tickets for the presentation. If you want to take in one of these special pageants without waiting hours in line, it would be wise to write ahead for tickets. Two major television and radio network headquarters are located several blocks beyond—CBS, between 52nd and 53rd streets and designed by Eero Saarinen, and ABC at 54th Street. Both are on the east side of the avenue. (NBC's headquarters are one block south, in Rockefeller Center.)

On 55th Street, turn left and walk almost to Seventh Avenue if you want to pick up a pair of tickets at the New York City Center, 131 West 55th Street, which usually features ballet. Now that you're this far, you might also want to continue two blocks north along Seventh Avenue, swing east around the corner of 57th Street, and check out coming concerts at Carnegie Hall. New Yorkers have been grateful ever since the last-minute decision was made not to tear down this hall in the early 1960s, when Philharmonic Hall in Lincoln Center was being built.

Those of you with an artistic bent should backtrack to 53rd Street and turn east toward Fifth Avenue. On this one block you'll find the handsome sculpture garden and avant-garde works of the Museum of Modern Art, at 11 West 53rd Street, the Museum of American Folk Art at 49, and the American Craft Museum at 44. Another art excursion—one which will require your traipsing several blocks to Columbus

Circle at the southwest corner of Central Park—is to visit the statue at the corner of 59th Street and Broadway, Gaetano Russo's "Columbus," lending its name to Columbus Circle. On the park corner is architect H. Van Buren Magonigle's "Maine Memorial" with figures by sculptor Attilio Piccirilli. That massive building over to the northwest is the New York Coliseum, where public or trade exhibitions of varying interests are held.

Rockefeller Center

In our ramble up the Avenue of the Americas we've introduced you to several of the buildings that make up Rockefeller Center.

Rockefeller Center is a city-within-a-city; you could easily spend the whole day within its complex of twenty-one buildings. Many of its residents—it has a daytime population of 240,000—never leave its confines from their arrival in the morning until they go home. There is no need to, for the center has just about everything one could ask for. There are almost thirty restaurants, several shoe repair shops, drugstores, chiropodists, dentists, oculists, gift and clothing shops, bookstores, hairdressers, barbers, banks, a post office, movie theaters, schools, and subway transportation to all parts of the metropolis. Consulates of many foreign nations have offices in the center, as do airlines, railroad and steamship lines, and state and other travel information bureaus.

A shop-lined concourse, an underground passageway almost two miles long, ties together all its buildings and brings you almost to the doorstep of the Sheraton Centre and New York Hilton hotels. On rainy days, the concourse traffic is almost as thick as that of Times Square, but a lot drier.

It is the world's largest privately owned business and entertainment center and another monument to the courage and vision of the men who made New York City capital of the world. It was built because an opera house was not—a multimillion-dollar gamble on America's future during the height of the Depression years.

In October 1928, just before the big stock market crash, John D. Rockefeller, Jr., headed a civic drive to give New York a new opera house, arranging to lease from Columbia University the land on which part of Rockefeller Center now stands. The new Metropolitan Opera Company was to occupy the center of the plot and the remainder of the land was to be leased to private builders for commercial development. Before the grand design could get started, the opera company, plagued by legal difficulties and depressed funds, abandoned its plans for a new home and withdrew from the project. It left Mr. Rockefeller holding a long-term lease which committed him to a $3,300,000 annual rental. He was faced with a difficult decision: whether to abandon the development or go it alone? He decided to build.

The site of the center has an historic past. Until the turn of the 19th century, the area was part of Manhattan's "common lands," which stretched from 23rd Street northward. In 1801, Dr. David Horsack transformed twenty acres of these pasturelands into his famed Elgin Botanic Gardens; garden club ladies for miles around made pilgrimages to pick up ideas for their own plantings. When rising costs made the venture impractical, Dr. Hosack sold the property to New York State and a few years later the State Legislature turned over the property to Columbia College as an aid-to-education grant. At the time, the land was worth about $125 an acre. Today Columbia University receives millions of dollars a year rental for just the ground; its lease to the center runs until 2069.

The center gave a new life to the down-at-the-heels midtown area, changing it from a sprawling low-rent residential area to a soaring business and entertainment complex far in advance of the times. It was a pioneering approach to urban design. Skyscrapers were planned in relation to one another and fifteen percent of the land was set aside for a promenade of plantings and a breeze-swept plaza.

The Channel Gardens—six formal beds running from Fifth Avenue to the Lower Plaza—with their ever-changing seasonal plantings, draw millions of visitors. Artists, designers, and sculptors work year-round to devise new and dramatic floral patterns for the ten seasonal displays. The showings run consecutively, starting with thousands of lilies at Easter; tulips, hyacinths, daffodils, and other flowering bulbs in the spring; an all-azalea show; such perennials as foxglove, delphinium, and stock; summer lilies and snapdragons; marigolds and evergreens; tropical palms and bougainvillaea; begonias and coxcomb; chrysanthemums of every size and hue; and ending with the greatest Christmas tree of all. Even the rooftops of many buildings are landscaped, giving upper-floor tenants a soul-satisfying view of green foliage and brilliant blooms below.

The Lower Plaza, where you can ice-skate from the end of September through April and dine alfresco in the warm weather, is a kind of ceremonial town square where distinguished visitors are greeted, occasional concerts given, and special events commemorated with colorful ceremonies.

The 70-story RCA building, at 30 Rockefeller Plaza, faces one of the city's few privately owned streets. The three-block-long street, which bisects the center from 49th to 51st Streets, is closed once a year (on one Sunday in July) to protect Columbia University's ownership of this passageway.

From the Observation Roof on top of the RCA building you can see as far as Connecticut on a clear day. Smog and haze, however, make this a rare occasion. Still, you'll be treated to a spectacular view. A visit to the observatory is included in a guided tour of Rockefeller Center's highlights, a hour-long educational stroll which takes you to a landscaped roof garden, the interior of the Music Hall, the famous murals and art works scattered throughout the center, and along the concourse of shops of all nations. Along the way you might bump into a TV star or two. Another guided tour takes you behind the scenes at NBC's radio and TV studios. Separate tours of Radio City Music Hall are also available. Call 246–4600 for details.

When in doubt about what to see and where it is, visit the center's information booth in the main lobby at 30 Rockefeller Plaza, where you can also pick up tickets to television-show tapings. You might also consider an evening visit (sunset is best) to the Rainbow Room bar, which opens at 5:30 P.M., Tuesday through Saturday, and at 11:30 A.M. on Sunday.

Across Fifth Avenue at 51st Street is the Gothic-styled St. Patrick's Cathedral. Based on the design of the Cologne Cathedral in Germany, work on the Roman Catholic St. Patrick's commenced in 1858, it opened as a house of worship in 1879, and was finally completed in 1906. Constructed of white marble and stone, the church's towers ascend 330 feet. Thirty-foot pillars support the cross-ribbed Gothic arches which rise 110 feet inside, where stained-glass windows from France light the nave.

The United Nations

New York City grew from a metropolis to a cosmopolis in 1952, when the United Nations moved into its elegant new home overlooking the East River between 42nd and 48th Streets.

The hand of John D. Rockefeller, Jr., is imprinted on this monument to peace and brotherhood, for it was his offer of a gift of the 18-acre site that figured in the final decision to choose New York as the permanent headquarters for the UN.

Before the coming of the United Nations, the district was a crumbling conglomeration of ex-slaughterhouses, junkyards, and tenements. Today the area around the UN is studded with elegant structures and has become a showcase of new architectural design.

A bit of parkland makes the UN grounds—which are not U.S. territory—a pleasant place to stroll and watch the busy river traffic of freighters, tankers, and pleasure boats plying the East River.

The visitors' entrance to the United Nations Headquarters is at the north end of the marble and limestone General Assembly Building, at

45th Street and First Avenue. There is a museumlike quality to the vast lobby with its free-form multiple galleries, soaring ceiling, and collection of art treasures contributed by member nations.

Visitors are welcome to attend most official meetings and admission is free. Tickets are issued in the lobby fifteen minutes before meetings are scheduled to start. Because there is no advance schedule of meetings for any given day and since they may be canceled or changed at the last minute, the majority of tickets available to individual visitors are issued on a first-come, first-served basis.

At most meetings, speeches are simultaneously interpreted in the official languages—Chinese, English, French, Russian, and Spanish—and there are earphones at each visitor's seat with a dial system which permits you to tune in the proceedings in the language of your choice.

The decor and color schemes of the meeting rooms—General Assembly Hall, the chambers of the Security Council, Trusteeship Council, Economic and Social Council—have been chosen for their soothing, subdued qualities. Sometimes they work this magic and other times they fail. At times, speeches by delegates become so impassioned that visitors may be tempted to rise and shout "bravo." Be forewarned: protocol demands that visitors remain silent throughout all the proceedings.

Taking the hour-long guided tour through the headquarters buildings is the most satisfactory way to see all the meeting rooms, to learn the aims, structure, and activities of this world body, and to appreciate fully the art works and exhibits displayed. Tours leave the main lobby approximately every 15 minutes between 9:00 A.M. and 4:45 P.M., seven days a week. Most are in English, although you can request and reserve for other languages on the day you plan to tour. The cost is $3 for adults, $1.75 for students, and $1.25 for children. Phone: 754–7710.

If you would like to lunch with the delegates, stop by the information desk in the main lobby and ask about making a table reservation in the Delegates' Dining Room. Tables for visitors are in short supply and are assigned on a first-come basis. The earlier you make the reservation, the better.

On the lower concourse there is a coffee shop for a quick snack and lounges to rest your weary bones. Here, too, are several shops which offer the books, art, and handicraft products of the UN's member nations. Many a returning traveler shops here for some item he forgot or could not find while on a trip to Africa, Asia, Europe, or South America.

The sliver of land you see in the middle of the East River just to the north of the UN is Roosevelt Island (formerly Welfare Island) which once served as a prison stronghold. The riptides around the island acted

Plan of the United Nations

as prison "walls," for not even the strongest swimmer could navigate the 700-foot crossing to the mainland.

If one had money and influence there was no need for such a fool-hardy escape attempt. William Tweed, for instance, came and went as he pleased, though a prisoner. Tweed was the greedy political boss of New York who fleeced the city of $150,000,000 in the four years between 1867 and 1871. When reformers caught up with him and sent him off to a cell on Welfare Island, he arranged to live a life of ease. His ill-gotten gains bought him all the creature comforts. Gourmet meals were sent in from New York's finest restaurants. A masseur came in regularly to rub away his tensions. It's said he even had the prison bars replaced by a picture window. When life became too boring, Tweed managed to get a night off and a launch to take him over to the mainland for a round on the town. This kindly and loving care was enjoyed by Tweed and other moneyed mobsters and racketeers until the reformers once again bestirred themselves. The prison is gone now and in its place are two modern hospitals for the aged and chronically ill—plus the Delacorte Geyser, on the southern tip, which occasionally spouts a tall plume of an estimated 4,000 gallons worth of water per minute 400 feet into the air. There are also new housing units (many units are already occupied), reached from 59th Street and Second Avenue by a tramway over the East River (you may have seen it in Sylvester Stallone's movie *Nighthawks*).

Exploring Turtle Bay

As you leave the United Nations there are three general routes which you can follow, each one of which will lead you to fascinating aspects of the area extending roughly from 40th to 49th streets and from Third Avenue to the East River. It is known as Turtle Bay, whose name comes from the mid-18th century Turtle Bay Farm tract which bordered on a little cove of that name.

You can return to 42nd Street and head west. If you look up between First and Second Avenues you'll see some of the apartment buildings and hotels of Tudor City. If you've time, you might walk up the stairs along 42nd Street and enjoy this rather private little city of Tudor-style buildings around a small park. Go back down the stairs and you'll surely notice the building with the huge glassed-in garden near Second Avenue. That's the Ford Foundation Building and its offices are arranged in an L around this pleasantly leafy 130-foot-high arboretum. In the next block between Second and Third Avenues is the Daily News Building, home of one of New York's three daily newspapers. Step into the lobby here if you want to scan the latest weather charts or watch the huge revolving globe. Continuing westward you'll come to the

Chrysler Building at the northeast corner of 42nd Street and Lexington Avenue. When it was first built in 1930, its 1,048 feet made it the tallest building in the world. But it was soon topped by the completion of the Empire State Building in 1931. Now the twin World Trade Center towers are the highest in the city.

Westward again, between Lexington and Park Avenues on 42nd Street, is the steel-and-glass Grand Hyatt Hotel, a glistening high-tech structure (built over the skeleton of the old Commodore Hotel) standing in the company of the beaux-arts classically styled Grand Central Terminal, the Art Deco Chrysler Building and other similarly spectacular delights. Grand Central was built from 1903 to 1913. If you go inside the always-busy train station, you'll be able to take escalators directly up to the lobby of the Pan Am Building, a 1963 office skyscraper addition to the terminal. At the time it was announced much protest was raised since it would—and does—effectively block the vista up and down Park Avenue.

We said you had three alternative routes through Turtle Bay from the UN. Another would be to head north along First Avenue—past the pleasant UN grounds and the posh twin 32-story apartment towers of the United Nations Plaza. Your destination on this route is Beekman Place, where the townhouses on the two blocks between First Avenue and Beekman Place on 50th Street and along Beekman Place itself between 50th and 51st streets are gracious reminders of the 1920s. The roof of the Beekman Towers Hotel is also an excellent stop for a drink and a view of the Upper East Side.

The third jaunt is more circuitous and will serve to illustrate the dramatic juxtaposition of old townhouses and new office buildings that this city is capable of creating. Go north on First Avenue to 47th Street and turn left. Note the Holy Family Church and its pretty little courtyard on the north side of this divided street. This is where Pope Paul VI visited in 1965 in connection with a UN plea for peace. Next, a quick stop in the rock garden at Japan House (333 East 47th Street) is refreshingly tranquil. On the southeast corner of 47th Street and Second Avenue you might check out the current exhibit of alfresco, avant-garde sculpture in front of the rather conservative-looking office building. Continue on 47th Street to 747 Third Avenue, which is wonderfully imaginative with its undulating, multicolored brick walkways, circular outdoor phone booth, and benches and chairs. Look for the statue of a nude woman at the revolving doors.

Now turn right on Third Avenue, passing the Harcourt Brace Jovanovich building's uniquely designed bookstore, and cross Third Avenue on 48th Street to peek into the "citified" courtyard of the Buchanan apartment building. On the northwest corner of Lexington

Avenue and 48th Street in the Inter-Continental Hotel is the Caswell-Massy Co. Ltd., reputedly America's oldest pharmacy (1752).

A bit farther up Third Avenue is the giant Citicorp Center headquarters of the New York-based international bank. Opened in 1978, the center features a pedestrian mall. It is a refreshing change from the plain glass boxes that dominate the rest of the avenue. Indeed, Citicorp is so refreshing especially because it includes The Market, a multilevel international bazaar of restaurants and retail food shops that delight the eye as well as the palate of New Yorkers and tourists alike. The Market surrounds a sky-lit atrium and gives a village-square ambiance. There are tables and chairs where you may just sit and people-watch or picnic by bringing your own sandwiches or buying some at one of the eateries. If you time it right, you may even enjoy free entertainment, on Saturday mornings for children and daily for adults, from chamber music ensembles to jazz to poetry readings. (Call 559–4259 for schedule.) And if alfresco dining (or almost) in a stone canyon isn't what you have in mind, you can choose from a bevy of international restaurants that includes: The Greek taverna that is Avgerninos, the Italian Alfredo's, the Auberge Suisse, Les Tournebroches, and Richoux of London, a British coffee shop that is *veddy, veddy* Edwardian (with costumed waitresses). For sandwiches and desserts, consider Slotnick Daughters and for Scandinavian gourmet goodies such as herrings, salads and pâtés, consider Nyborg and Nelson. For spiritual nourishment, there is also a church—St. Peter's—in the building, and that church has staged some excellent plays of off-Broadway caliber. All of which combines to make Citicorp a nice place to visit for business or pleasure.

Up in Central Park

Central Park, a vast oasis of rural beauty in the midst of a concrete jungle of midtown spires, runs from 59th Street to 110th Street and from Fifth Avenue to Central Park West (an extension of Eighth Avenue). Masterfully designed by Frederick Law Olmstead and Calvert de Vaux, the park was designated a National Historic Landmark in 1965.

Before venturing into the park you might want to pick up some pamphlets and advice from the New York Convention and Visitors Bureau at Columbus Circle, just directly across the street from the park's entrance and from the Coliseum.

New York can thank its good fortune that there were men of vision in 1850 who insisted that this 840-acre spread be earmarked as a park. It was none too soon, for real estate developers were gobbling up huge hunks of land just to the south and turning them into bleak stretches of look-alike brownstone residences.

A stroll through the park will reveal the woodland terrain of New York as it might have been in the days of the Dutch settlers, long before dredges and bulldozers leveled the surrounding hills and rocky out-croppings to erect a fence of luxury apartment houses.

If you take a drive down through the park from the north end at dusk, just as the lights begin to sparkle in the windows and the last rays of the sun silhouette the spires at the south end, you will be rewarded with a most strikingly beautiful sight. These roads, however, are fre-quently closed to traffic to allow for strollers, bicyclers and joggers.

Or hire a carriage—they park across the street from the Plaza Hotel at 59th Street and Fifth Avenue—and take an old-fashioned leisurely turn around the ponds, lakes and woodlands. Should your horse slow down to a walk in some secluded section, don't be concerned about his being too tired to make it back. New York horses have never lost their sense of romance, and they know the likeliest settings for it. Rates are $17 for the first half hour, $5 for each additional 15 minutes. (Do make sure to agree on the rate before leaving.)

At this same corner of the park—a lively and interesting part of the city for people-watching—there are bookstalls open on nice days.

The park is a many-splendored mélange of fountains and ponds, statues and monuments, promenades and wooded paths. Park benches are lined with nannies gossiping away while their young Park Avenue charges swing and slide in the playgrounds. Joggers run year round while looking over their shoulders at oncoming traffic. On warm week-days, office workers find a favorite rock by the pond, spread out their lunches, and share them with the water birds. In the winter, they skate at Wollman Memorial Rink, currently being renovated. On Sundays, families come to picnic, play soft ball, pitch horseshoes, ride the merry-go-round, fly kites, row boats, ride bicycles on the curling, care-free drives, and absorb enough sun and fresh air to last them through another week of molelike living. The newest crazes in the park are skateboarding and roller-skating, and on summer weekends the park mall that stretches from the Bethesda Fountain overlook at 72nd Street down to 66th Street is populated with street performers ranging from Dixieland bands to magicians to stilt walkers.

Off the 64th Street entrance on Fifth Avenue is a small zoo with a splendid collection of birds, wild animals, and a sea lion pond. The animals are terrific "hams" and at feeding time, especially, they put on shows that rival the circus. For the small fry, there is another little zoo populated with domestic animals which willingly allow children to pat their heads and smooth their fur. (Adults are granted admission here only if accompanied by a child.) Near the Conservatory Pond at 74th

St. off Fifth Avenue are the statues of Hans Christian Andersen and
Alice in Wonderland.

On summer evenings you can attend outdoor performances of plays
at the Delacorte Shakespeare Theater. The theater accommodates
around 2,000—but get there in the afternoon to get in line for first-
come, first-served tickets. Enter from Central Park West or Fifth Avenue at 81st Street. Both the Metropolitan Opera and the New York
Philharmonic perform free in the park each summer as well.

The park is fringed with some of the world's great art and history
centers. You could spend a week on either side of the park and never
go any higher than the ground floors of these buildings.

Lincoln Center

Lincoln Center for the Performing Arts is an elegant four-block
cultural world, located between 62nd and 66th streets west of Broadway (actually between Columbus and Amsterdam Avenues). Get ac-
quainted with the buildings by taking one of the guided tours, or
wander around the open plazas and parks on your own. Tours leave
from Avery Fisher Hall every half hour between 10 A.M. and 5 P.M. daily.
The cost for adults is $4.25; Senior Citizens and students, $3.75; and
children $2.75. Call 877–1800. Standing on Broadway, the building you
see to the left of the large central fountain plaza is the New York State
Theater, home of the New York City Opera and the New York City
Ballet. On the right is Avery Fisher Hall, home of the New York
Philharmonic and the first of this $185 million complex to open (Sep-
tember 1962). Between the two is the Metropolitan Opera House, with
its two colorful Marc Chagall murals depicting motifs and themes
relating to music.

This is, of course, where The Metropolitan Opera company performs. It also has the Center's largest seating capacity: for over 3,700
people in its main auditorium. Tucked behind Avery Fisher Hall is the
charming Eero Saarinen-designed Vivian Beaumont Theater. And in
back, with an additional entrance on Amsterdam Avenue, is the Library and Museum of Performing Arts, a branch of the New York
Public Library. Also on these grounds is the Guggenheim Bandshell for
alfresco concerts.

Across 65th Street is the Juilliard School of Music campus, which
includes Alice Tully Hall, a Lincoln Center facility noted especially for
its chamber music presentations.

And, at the southern end of the Lincoln Center group is the midtown
campus of Fordham University.

Columbus Avenue from 67th Street to 83rd Street in the city's
newest "scene," with restaurants, bars, food shops, boutiques, roller-

Lincoln Center

Chinese Mission
to the U.N.

BROADWAY

66TH ST.

Juilliard School

← Alice Tully Hall

65TH ST. | Garage Entrance

Library
for the
Performing
Arts

Vivian
Beaumont &
Newhouse
Theaters

Pool

Avery Fisher
Hall

64TH

AMSTERDAM AVE.

Metropolitan
Opera House

○
Fountain

Guggenheim
Bandshell
& Damrosch Park

N
W—E
S

New York
State
Theater

COLUMBUS AVE.

62ND ST. | Garage Entrance

Fordham University
Branch Campus

Points of Interest

1) Beacon Theater
2) Boat Basin
3) The Coliseum
4) The Dakota
5) Fordham University
6) Hayden Planetarium
7) Juilliard School
8) Lincoln Center for the Performing Arts
9) Museum of Natural History
10) New-York Historical Society
11) Merkin Hall
(Goodman House)
12) Symphony Space

skate rental shops, and the special New York blend of show-offs, street musicians and mimes, and with-it people.

The Historical Society

If you are interested in tracing the history and growth of New York, visit the New-York Historical Society's headquarters at 77th Street and Central Park West. Here, there are exhibits which trace the city's history from the Indian tribes which lived in the area before the white man came, through the stories of Giovanni da Verrazano, Henry Hudson, and Peter Stuyvesant. There are displays depicting the English period before the outbreak of the American Revolution; the periods of strife and struggle during the Revolutionary War; and New York when it was the capital of the new nation. There are rare collections of just about everything which shows how New York's earliest residents lived and fared.

Across 77th Street is the American Museum of Natural History, founded in 1869 "for the purpose of encouraging and developing the study of natural science, advancing the general knowledge of kindred subjects, and of furnishing popular instruction." It has been operating for over a century and houses tens of millions of zoological, geological, anthropological, and botanical specimens that are studied by scientists, students, and scholars from all over the world.

A week wouldn't be enough to see all the exhibits, which cover close to twelve acres of floor space. To make the most of your visit, pick up a guide book and check off the exhibits you want to see first. Two of the museum's greatest attractions are the 94-foot life-size model of a blue whale on the first floor and the two huge halls' worth of dinosaur fossils on the fourth floor. Other highlights include the 64-foot-long Haida Canoe, made from the trunk of a single cedar tree; the Hall of the Biology of Man, which is devoted to the evolution, structure, and function of man as an organism; reconstruction of the extinct dodo; the exhibition of the Courtship of Birds; the collection of mammals; the Northwest Coast Indian Hall; the Hall of Man in Africa; and the demonstration-participation lectures in the People Center where onlookers are invited to try on costumes or play instruments, for example, of cultures around the world.

If your time is limited, you might find it worthwhile to rent an Acoustiguide, a one-hour tape-recorded lecture tour contained in a small portable case with ear plugs. The rental sets are available at the 77th Street entrance information desk.

A connecting passageway takes you to the Hayden Planetarium, at 81st Street and Central Park West, the department of astronomy of the American Museum of Natural History. Unless you have sailed the seas or lived in the unpopulated plains and mountaintops away from the bright lights of the city, you never have seen the heavens as they are shown in the planetarium.

The first part of the program is given in the circular Guggenheim Space Center, where a mechanized model of the solar system, forty-eight feet in diameter, is suspended from the ceiling. Here you learn about the motions of the planets and their moons.

The planetarium has numerous exhibits: murals of lunar landscapes, eclipses, and the aurora borealis; collections of meteorites (some weighing up to thirty-four tons); ancient Chinese, and German astronomical instruments. But the most popular exhibits of all are the five scales which register what your weight would be in outer space. A 130-pound person would weigh 113 pounds on Venus, but on the moon he would weigh 20 pounds, on Mars 47 pounds, on Jupiter 336 pounds, and on the sun 3,550 pounds. If you want to test your weight, count on waiting, for the lines are often long. Teenagers and young adults might also be interested in Laserium—the star show seen to the accompaniment of rock music. For information call 724–8700.

East Side Museums and Galleries

On the Fifth Avenue side of Central Park and on the side streets off Madison Avenue in the 60s and 70s is the city's greatest concentration of art galleries and museums. You might work your way up Fifth Avenue to 92nd Street, then over to Madison Avenue and down to the 60s.

A good starting point is the Frick Collection on Fifth Avenue at 70th Street, a splendid example of French classic architecture, formerly the home of Henry Clay Frick (who made millions in the steel industry). The mansion enclosing a peaceful glass-roofed courtyard and the private collection of the fine paintings, ornaments, and furnishings will give you an idea of the scale of living enjoyed by New York society before the income tax. (No small children allowed.)

Now head east to Madison Avenue and up to the 70s, where New York's art gallery district is centered. Many of the galleries which once clustered around 57th Street have moved up to these quieter surroundings; Christie's is on the East Side, over at 502 Park Avenue.

Also in this area are the Danenberg Galleries; the Graham Galleries, established in 1857 and reputedly the city's oldest; Perls Galleries, the distributor of Alexander Calder's works (he designed the cement and slate pavement in front); and the elegant Wildenstein Gallery, which presents important collections of Old Masters and French Impressionists. There are dozens of noted galleries, smaller and more intimate, besides these. In one afternoon you might be able to see more works of Renoir, Braque, Klee, Picasso, Redon, Chagall, Dufy, and Modigliani than you could in Paris.

In the midst of all this art is yet another great museum, the Whitney Museum of American Art, at Madison Avenue and 75th Street. The building itself, opened by Mrs. Flora Whitney Miller and Mrs. John F. Kennedy in September 1966, is at first startling. Given slightly less than one-third of an acre on which to build, architect Marcel Breuer was faced with the problem of creating ample exhibition and storage space for a vast collection of 20th-century American painting and sculpture which had completely outgrown the Whitney's old home on West 54th Street. (Its original home was on 8th Street in Greenwich Village.) Breuer's solution was to turn the traditional ziggurat (or "wedding cake") design upside down, with each of the second, third, and fourth floors projecting fourteen feet farther out over the street from the one below. New Yorkers' reactions were mixed, but the building has drawn students and architects from all over the world to study its design—more so, in fact, than did Frank Lloyd Wright's Guggenheim Museum.

Three blocks north and one west (on Fifth Avenue) is the Duke mansion, the former home of tobacco tycoon James Biddle Duke and his daughter Doris. Today it is the headquarters for the Institute of Fine Arts of New York University.

Across the way, facing Fifth Avenue between 80th and 84th streets, is the Metropolitan Museum of Art. The neo-Renaissance design of this imposing structure infringing on the reaches of Central Park was taken from the Columbian Exposition (Chicago World's Fair) of 1893. The museum houses one of the most comprehensive collections in the world. There are more than a million art treasures representing the work of fifty centuries. The whole of it cannot be enjoyed in one visit; so it would be best to study the floor plan and choose the galleries which hold the most interest for you. There are also Acoustiguides for rent here; the recorded tour takes approximately forty-five minutes. Its departments include Egyptian Art, Near Eastern Art, American painting, sculpture, furniture, armor, and arms. If you are interested in fashion, visit the Costume Institute, a favorite haunt of designers who come to study its period costumes.

Frank Lloyd Wright's Spiral

One of the most extraordinary buildings in New York is the Solomon R. Guggenheim Museum at 88th Street. The six-story spiral structure designed by the late Frank Lloyd Wright is worth a visit even if modern art doesn't interest you.

Eighty-sixth Street between Third and York Avenues is the center of old Yorkville, New York's German-American community, with

Upper East Side

YORKVILLE

Central Park

EAST RIVER

Roosevelt Island

Queensboro Bridge

Points of Interest

1) Alexander's
2) Bergdorf Goodman
3) Bloomingdale's
4) Christie's
5) Cooper-Hewitt Museum
6) Frick Collection
7) Gimbels East
8) Gracie Mansion
   (Mayor's residence)
9) Guggenheim Museum
10) Jewish Museum
11) Metropolitan Museum of Art
12) Rockefeller University
13) F.A.O. Schwarz
14) Sotheby Parke Bernet
15) Tiffany
16) Central Park Zoo
17) International Center
    of Photography
18) Whitney Museum
19) YM-YWHA

restaurants and shops featuring German food, records, and other items. Nearby are lots of Czech- and Hungarian-style restaurants, too.

At 91st Street and Fifth Avenue is the former home of steel tycoon Andrew Carnegie. This handsome Georgian mansion is now occupied by the Cooper-Hewitt Museum for design and the decorative arts. One block north is the luxurious former home of banker Felix N. Warburg, whose widow presented it to the Jewish Theological Seminary to be used as a museum. The Jewish Museum has become the repository of the most extensive collection of Jewish ceremonial objects in the United States and also is one of the three most important in the world, the other two being in Jerusalem and Prague.

From here, even though it's a short hike north, your Fifth Avenue museum touring would not be complete without a visit to the fine Museum of the City of New York at 103rd Street. The museum's collections are extensive and cover a wide variety of fields, reflecting both the city of today and yesteryear. Its decorative arts collection includes outstanding examples of costumes, furniture, and silver. The print collection numbers over half a million items of paintings, prints, and photographs of New York City. A theater collection contains what is reputed to be the most complete history of the New York stage ever assembled, while the toy collection covers the whole fun world of playthings—with its dolls and dollhouses of particular note.

Incidentally, if you have children in tow you might plan to visit on Saturday when, during the school year, special activities are planned, including puppet shows and "please touch" demonstrations.

The Upper West Side Above 79th Street

The Upper East Side and the Upper West Side are like two separate cities—and rival cities at that. Upper West Siders consider the East Side to be occupied by corporation lawyers, fancy surgeons, stockbrokers, the idle but boring rich, wealthy but superficial art collectors, and, over east of Lexington Avenue, carefully-dressed airline stewardesses and carefully-dressed ad-agency trainees on the make. Upper East Siders, for their part, consider the Upper West Side (except maybe Columbus Avenue just north of Lincoln Center) dirty and seedy, populated by bums and weirdos, multitudes of large Jewish families who crowd the countless delicatessens, ugly young men and women who work in publishing or champion unspeakable causes, skinny dancers, threadbare musicians lugging around instrument cases, and all accompanied by endless, passionate arguments about anything and everything.

One of the most scenic drives in the city is along Riverside Drive, which follows the Hudson River shoreline (inland of Riverside Park) from 72nd Street up to Inwood. The drive was another brilliant brain-child of Andrew Haswell Green, who was responsible for Central Park.

But Green, who had conservatively estimated the cost of the drive would run around $1,500,000, hadn't reckoned with Boss Tweed and his Forty Thieves. Tweed and boys liked the idea of building a park and drive; liked it so much that they made personal purchases of the land where the park was to be built and sold it to the city for a whopping profit. By the time the parkway was completed in 1885 the cost had zoomed up to $6 million.

At 79th Street, on the river, is the Boat Basin, a marina set alongside the Park promenade.

Along the route you will pass the boat basin where large yachts anchor. Next, at 89th Street, the Soldiers and Sailors Monument comes into view, a handsome Italian Carrara marble "silo" circled by twelve Corinthian columns. The 392-foot Gothic tower of the Riverside Church can be seen a mile to the north. Its 72-bell carillon is the largest in the United States and its range of tonal quality is superb. The largest bell, the *Bourdon*, weighs more than twenty tons, while the smallest weighs only ten pounds.

The rocky ridge that begins in Central Park rises gradually as it travels uptown through Harlem and Morningside Heights to the precipitous lookout at Washington Heights. Here one of the big battles of the Revolutionary War was fought, and this upper end of Manhattan is rich in historic sites and lore.

World's Largest Gothic Cathedral

Directly east, if you want to make a detour at this time, is the Church of St. John the Divine, on Morningside Heights (Amsterdam Avenue and 112th Street). Started in 1892, it will be the largest Gothic cathedral in the world when it is finally completed, which the church admits is probably another hundred years off!

At Broadway and 116th Street is the main entrance to Columbia University; on the other side of Broadway nearby are Barnard College and the Union Theological Seminary.

General Grant's Tomb is at 123rd Street, and at about this point Riverside Drive begins to skirt Fort Washington Park. At 155th Street you might want to make another short detour east to Broadway to visit a unique cultural center which houses four special-interest museums. Here you'll find the Museum of the American Indian–Heye Foundation, which has an outstanding collection of Indian art and relics of North and South America. The Hispanic Society of America has a museum of ancient and modern Spanish culture. At the American Numismatic Society, you can see a vast collection of coins and medals, and the country's most comprehensive library on the subject. At the American Academy of Arts and Letters, you can view the memorabilia of many famous artists, writers, and musicians.

Continuing north and east to 160th Street and Edgecombe Avenue, you'll come to the Morris-Jumel Mansion, one of the city's few remaining examples of pre-Revolutionary Georgian architecture. Built in 1765 by Roger Morris and later occupied by Madame Jumel, a wealthy widow who married Aaron Burr in his old age, the home has many exquisite architectural details. It has recently been turned into a museum devoted to the Revolutionary War period.

Heading north and west, pick up Fort Washington Avenue and follow it to Fort Tryon Park. This is the brow of Manhattan; from this vantage point, you have an uninterrupted view of the magnificent sweep of the Hudson River up to the Tappan Zee Bridge, the precipitous Palisades shoreline of New Jersey, the graceful arc of George Washington Bridge, and the far reaches of the Bronx beyond Spuyten Duyvil.

The Cloisters

Set in the midst of this woodland park is The Cloisters, a structure of unusual form and grace assembled from many sections of medieval European monasteries. Five different cloisters have been connected by a charming colonnaded walk and merged with a French Romanesque chapel, a chapter house of the 12th century, and a Romanesque apse which is on loan from the Spanish government.

The museum's medieval art treasures were gathered by George Grey Barnard and acquired by the Metropolitan Museum with funds provided by John D. Rockefeller, Jr. (Admission, by contribution, can be made either at the Met or at the Cloisters, and is good at both locations on the same day.) Among the museum's most notable treasures are the *Hunt of the Unicorn* tapestries, which are considered to be among the world's greatest.

At the time Mr. Rockefeller arranged for the purchase of the Barnard collection, he also bought the woodland area of Fort Tryon as the site for The Cloisters. To ensure an uncluttered vista across the Hudson on the New Jersey side Mr. Rockefeller also purchased a 13-mile strip along the Palisades and gave it to the Palisades Interstate Park Commission.

On the lowlands at the northernmost tip of Manhattan is the "Great Maize Land" of the fertile Inwood Valley, where Henry Hudson came ashore and shared a feast of oysters proffered by the friendly Indian tribe which later sold its homeland to Peter Minuit for a trunkful of trinkets. This little gem of a park is the last vestige of natural woodlands which once covered all of Manhattan island. Today you still can see fragments of centuries-old oyster shells as you wander through the park's forest of giant trees and along the banks of Spuyten Duyvil.

During the days of discovery, Spuyten Duyvil was a narrow, unnavigable creek which trickled between the Harlem and Hudson Rivers, separating Marble Hill from Manhattan's mainland. In 1895 a canal was cut through these flatlands, shortening the water route between the Hudson River and Long Island Sound, thus obviating the necessity of sailing way down and around the Battery to reach a berth on the Hudson River.

Within a stone's throw of Inwood Park are Columbia University's athletic fields and boathouse. On nearly any spring day you'll see oarsmen out on the Spuyten Duyvil practicing for a regatta, and in the fall, Columbia's home football games are played at Baker Field.

While you're in the neighborhood, you might want to drive down to see the Dyckman House, a museum at 204th Street and Broadway. When it was built in 1783, the wealthy Dyckman family owned most of the Inwood area. Today the little 18th-century Dutch farmhouse is squeezed between clusters of seedy apartment houses and shops, a sorry setting for such an historic gem. It has been beautifully restored by the city, is furnished with authentic pieces of the mid-18th century, and has an enchanting garden. If you ignore the surroudings, you will find it a rewarding visit.

Manhattan is a civilization on the sea and of the sea and it is from the water one fully appreciates its size, shape, and style. The Circle Line is a three-hour boat excursion around the island which reveals many of the city's characteristics one cannot observe while exploring on foot.

Outside Manhattan

As far back as 1833 there was a movement afoot to consolidate the villages around Manhattan into one Greater New York. Brooklyn, the big brother of the outlying areas, had been incorporated as a village for some time and doing very nicely on its own. In turning down the proposal to come under the wing of the bustling, brash, flourishing city of New York, its spokesman General Jeremiah Johnson echoes the sentiments of most Brooklynites with the statement that "Between New York and Brooklyn there is nothing common—unless it be the waters that flow between them. And even these waters—however frequently passed, still form and must forever continue to form an unsurmountable obstacle to the Union."

A half century later Andrew Haswell Green, having finished his big Riverside Drive project, looked around for something else to keep him occupied and hit upon reviving the Greater New York concept. The

Brooklyn Bridge had been completed in 1883 and Green decreed that the waters between New York and Brooklyn no longer constituted an "unsurmountable obstacle to the Union."

In 1889 he addressed the New York State Legislature and exhorted them to move on unification. By 1894 he had managed to place a referendum on unification before the voters of Manhattan, Brooklyn, Queens, Staten Island, and lower Westchester. The vote was a toss-up. The state legislature made up the voters' minds by enacting a bill for consolidation. On January 1, 1898, Brooklyn, Bronx, Queens, and Richmond (Staten Island) joined Manhattan to become Greater New York.

The Williamsburg and Queensboro Bridges, the Queens Midtown Tunnel, and miles of subway lines were built to bind the boroughs together, all save one: Staten Island, which could be reached by ferry only and remained a distant relative for fourscore years. Not until the Verrazano-Narrows Bridge was opened in 1964 was Staten Island brought fully into the fold.

The Rural Borough—Staten Island

Staten Island, the borough of Richmond, has always been the most rural area of New York City. Many of its families date back to the early 18th century, and its society is exclusive to the point of clannishness. One resident, whose family goes back to the 17th century, says that there was a time when the Vanderbilts were considered "common."

Cornelius Vanderbilt, who was born near Stapleton on Staten Island in 1794, was not to the manor born, to be sure, but he did have enterprise. At age twenty-three he started a ferry run over to the mainland and assumed the title "Commodore." Eventually he parlayed his ferry service into a railroad and hotel empire. His "rank" was given to the former Hotel Commodore on 42nd Street near Vanderbilt Avenue, which has reopened as a Hyatt hotel.

To this day Staten Island society is hard to crack, for the old families still have a tendency to stick together. Most of the old guard live up in the hills—Dongan, Emerson, Grymes Hills—in houses not exactly extravagant, but on property that has a long-time family background and a superb view of the Narrows. They are proud to point out that their Todt Hill, a 410-foot mound, is the highest point along the Atlantic coast between Main and Florida!

The island, an irregular triangle about fourteen miles long and seven miles wide, was given its name—"Staatenn Eylandt"—by Henry Hudson in 1609. It was a difficult piece of land to colonize for the original owners, the Unami Indians, were a wily lot. The Dutch started negotiating with the Unamis in 1630 and were repulsed with arrows and hatchets on three occasions before they finally were able to persuade the chieftain to sell the island. It wasn't long though before the Unamis were back to reclaim it. "They supposed by ye island by reason of ye war, by killing, burning and driving us off become theirs again," complained one colonist, Cornelius Melyn. The Dutch bought the island five times before they finally could call it their own.

When England took New Amsterdam in 1664, it appropriated Staten Island and made it a part of the province of New York. It was named Richmond County in honor of the Duke of Richmond, the son of King Charles II. Several disputes arose between the ducal proprietors from New Jersey and New York over which previous claims to the island's lush farmlands and timbered hills were still valid. It was a sticky decision to make.

The Duke of York, a man of great sporting spirit, chose a novel way of resolving the dispute. The property, he said, would be awarded to citizens who could circumnavigate the island in twenty-four hours. The first to accomplish the treacherous sail was Captain Christopher Billopp and in 1687 he was awarded the prize of 1,600 acres at the southernmost tip, which is now the village of Tottenville. The following year he built a fine mansion and it later became the scene of the famous conference Lord Howe called to determine the seriousness of American demands for independence. The Billopp Conference House at the foot of Hylan Boulevard has been restored and looks almost the same as when it first was built.

For more than a century and a half the island remained a farming area and preserve. In the 1830s fashionable bathing resorts sprang up on the north shore at Castleton, Stapleton, and New Brighton. New York socialites cruised over to spend the summer yachting, swimming, and picnicking on the beaches. Some were so taken with the bucolic atmosphere they built summer mansions and organized the Richmond Country Club, where they could meet for a stirrup cup and ride to the hounds.

For some reason Staten Island had a special appeal for Southerners, too. Many plantation owners spent their holidays here, and during the Civil War they sent their women and children to the safety of the isolated island.

The island's little scattered communities retained their rural, rustic atmosphere for almost a century more. Then came the dedication in 1964 of the Verrazano-Narrows Bridge, which opened the way from Brooklyn to Staten Island. Real-estate developers moved in, bought up many acres of farmland, and converted them into look-alike housing developments. Brooklynites have discovered that the island's beaches are a lot roomier than theirs, and now are creating weekend traffic jams.

Yet there are still miles of farm-fringed country roads, secluded parks, hilltop lookouts with superb views of Upper and Lower New York Bays, historic houses, zoos, and museums, which make a whole day's excursion around Staten Island most worthwhile.

That Wonderful Ferry Ride

Bridges link the island to New Jersey and Brooklyn. The most delightful way to reach it from Manhattan is by ferry from the South Ferry terminal at the foot of Battery Park. The inexpensive ride—25 cents round trip!—is a miniature ocean voyage past Governors Island, the Statue of Liberty, and other harbor highlights during the 15-minute run to St. George. The ferry transports passenger cars too ($1.75), and having your own car (or renting one) makes it easier for you to see all that the island has to offer. Ferries depart every half hour in each direction; during the Kool Jazz Festival in late June/early July, there are special rides featuring old-time Dixieland bands.

Staten Island Restorations

From St. George head for Stapleton and pick up Richmond Road. Drive through the Dongan and Todt Hills' areas of old estates and past the Richmond County Country Club on to Richmond. This is historically and geographically the center of the island and the site of a fascinating restoration called Richmondtown.

Richmondtown was called Cocclestown when it first was settled in the late 1600s, prompted probably by the quantities of oyster and clam shells left behind by the Indians. By 1730 it had grown into a compact little village with a dozen dwellings, a courthouse, jail, taverns, the Church of St. Andrew, and the center of the island's government. When the island was merged with the other boroughs into Greater New York, the abandonment of Richmondtown as the county seat left it without the incentives for change or expansion. It was a blessing in disguise.

Historically minded Staten Islanders recognized it as "a perfect setting for a life-sized model of an American town that would tell the story of the growth of such a village better than any number of pictures, exhibition cases and dioramas." You'll see the town taking shape under the auspices of the Staten Island Historical Society and the city of New York. Little 17th- and 18th-century cottages, cooperage, and basket-maker's shops, and other older buildings have been lifted off their foundations in villages around the island and brought here to form Richmondtown. The center of the settlement is the Museum of the Staten Island Historical Society, at Court and Center Streets, housed in a former county building built in 1848. The museum is small and its attendants—mostly volunteer workers—outdo themselves to make you feel welcome and show you around.

On display are assorted bits of Americana which show various aspects of how people worked and lived in centuries past. The community's 19th-century country general store is also popular. Ladies in bonnets and long gingham dresses tend store, selling old-fashioned licorice whips, horehound drops, taffy, and other delectables. The shelves are lined with ornate tea canisters and spice boxes. There are cracker barrels, old apothecary jars, a cigar store Indian, an old loom, and a spinning wheel. There is an assortment of irons that housewives warmed over a wood stove: small rounded ones for pressing ruffles, heavy cumbersome ones for bedsheets and workclothes. Behind an old barber chair you'll see an unusual collection of shaving mugs, each with its owner's name fired onto the ornate designs. A doctor's bleeding instrument is mixed in with a hodgepodge of other items usually found in the old general stores which served about every need of the community.

Ask one of the attendants for the brochure which gives the location and historic backgrounds of the various buildings clustered around the museum. There is the little clapboard Voorlezer's House, built about 1696 by the Dutch congregation as a church, schoolhouse, and a home for the *voorlezer* (church clerk). It is known as America's oldest remaining schoolhouse.

Treasure House, built by a tanner in 1700, is famous for the good fortune it bestowed on a later owner. About a hundred years ago when Patrick Highland took possession he found $7,000 in gold hidden in the walls. It's thought to be the cache of an overcautious or larcenous British paymaster.

The Guyon-Lake-Tysen House is one of the outstanding restorations. It was built about 1740 by Joseph Guyon and you can see his name marked in the mud coat over the dining room door. As each new owner took possession the house grew to meet his family's particular needs. You'll notice that the mantel in the dining room is of pre-Revolutionary design, while in the parlor, which was added later, the mantel is of the post-Revolutionary type.

Another restoration project on Staten Island is the newly opened (1982) Snug Harbor Cultural Center. It consists of 26 landmark historical buildings on 80 wooded acres along scenic New York Harbor. As of this writing, two buildings have been completed: the Newhouse gallery and Gallery III for the visual arts. It is hoped that by 1983 the 1,000-seat ampitheater and the Chapel (a 300-seat recital hall) will be done. The entire complex is ultimately envisioned as a center for the performing and visual arts from around the world.

If time permits, stop by the Jacques Marchais Center of Tibetan Art near the Lighthouse (338 Lighthouse Avenue), then pick up Amboy Road for a ride through a still somewhat rural area to the Conference House at Tottenville. On your return trip to St. George you can choose either Hylan Boulevard which skirts the shoreline or the inland Richmond Parkway which ultimately leads to the Victory Boulevard route to the ferry terminal.

The Indians Sold Brooklyn

Shortly after the West India Company settled Manhattan they sailed over to the "broken lands" southeast of the Battery to negotiate with the Indians for the purchase of the whole western end of Long Island.

Their first parcel in Brooklyn (Breuckelen—broken land) was acquired in 1636 and within a few years the company had brought over a number of Walloon families to settle along the Wall-boght (Wallabout Bay), the site of the Naval Shipyard.

Under the terms of "Provisional Regulations for Colonists," the company agreed to furnish them with "necessary supplies and clothes from the company's storehouses . . . at a reasonable price," which could be paid for in installments. The Colonists, in turn, were required to pledge that they would sell their farm produce and handicrafts to no one but the company's agents. They also were "bound to remain with their families for the space of six consecutive years at their destined place . . . and to faithfully fulfill their promises to the Indians and their other neighbors, whether in connection with trade or other matters."

The community grew and prospered quite separately from the earlier settlement of Nieuw Amsterdam. Brooklyn's colony burst the bounds of Wallabout Bay with the coming of Normans, French, and a group of English colonists from Massachusetts who had been excommunicated from the Puritan Church because they did not believe in the baptizing of babies. By 1643 the colonists had cleared and cultivated the lands as far as Gravesend Bay.

On Ilpetonga (high sandy bank) where the Canarsie Indians had lived in community houses (some of which were a quarter of a mile long), wealthy merchants built elegant homes. From the heights they could watch their clipper ships round Red Hook and berth at the waterside warehouses. To prevent the warehouses from marring their river view the merchant princes planted the roofs with lawns, flowering shrubs, and trees to form ingenious backyard gardens and shortcuts to the piers below. They called the area Clover Hill. Today it is known as Brooklyn Heights. With the coming of the Brooklyn Bridge and the subways, the patrician families fled the heights. Their homes have been partitioned into studios and apartments which are handsomely restored by artists, writers, and people who enjoy the Victorian atmosphere and one of the most exciting views in the world. This view alone makes a trip to Brooklyn worthwhile.

You can reach Brooklyn Heights by driving across Brooklyn Bridge and turning south, or by IRT Seventh Avenue subway to Clark Street. A stroll through the arboreal streets—Cranberry, Pineapple, Orange, Poplar, Willow—recalls a legend of old feuds. Before the Civil War these streets were named for prominent families. Local authorities were disturbed by the personality cult which wanted their names to go down in history by way of street signs. Overnight the family names were replaced with botanical street signs by the authorities. The families replaced their names and the battle of the street signs went on for weeks. Signs seesawed back and forth between families and fruit. The fruits and trees won in some cases and the families of Hicks, Montague, Pierrepont, and Remsen won in others. Miss Middagh, a supposedly staunch supporter of the fruit and tree campaign, also has a street named for her.

You'll find remains of Old World gentility in these streets. New Orleans-type wrought-iron balconies, stately pillared entrances, delicate scrollwork embellishments, ivy-covered brownstones, hidden mews of converted carriage houses similar to those of Washington Square make the 20th-century skyline across the river seem a mirage of the future.

Along Willow Street you'll pass a few of the older homes of the Heights. At 70 Willow Street is the van Sinderen House built in the Greek Revival style in the late 1830s. The three best examples of the Federal-style row houses of the early 19th century are found at 155–157–159.

An esplanade which extends from Remsem Street to Orange Street offers what photographic experts consider the most spectacular panoramic view of Manhattan. To the south, Wall Street's jungle of spires prick the clouds; parades of ferries, freighters, and barges ply between Buttermilk and East River Channels, often called the shipping crossroads of the world; the Statue of Liberty and the Verrazano-Narrows Bridge can be seen on the horizon. To the north, midtown's skyscrapers rise above the spidery spans of Brooklyn and Manhattan bridges.

Atlantic Avenue, nearby, is a center of Middle Eastern shops and restaurants toward its waterside end.

Fiery Sermons

Walking east from the esplanade you will come to the Plymouth Church of the Pilgrims on Orange Street, a severe, dark brick example of early Classic Revival architecture. Inside, its severity is softened with a series of memorial windows which trace the interesting history of Puritanism. It was here that the Abolitionist movement flared into a full-scale crusade.

Soon after the church was completed in 1849 Henry Ward Beecher began a series of fiery sermons and dramatic playlets on the evils of selling human souls on the auction block. William Lloyd Garrison, John Greenleaf Whittier, and other early Abolitionists also spoke from the pulpit. It was a bold program and one which inspired citizens throughout the country to raise their voices, even in cities where public discussions of slavery were not permitted. Abraham Lincoln worshipped here on two occasions in 1860 and took his stand against slavery in his historic speech at Cooper Institute.

Brooklyn—A City of Churches

Brooklyn was long known as the city of churches, and as you drive through the borough you will see spire after spire. It also has a fair share of institutions of higher learning, including Brooklyn College, Pratt Institute, Long Island University, and St. John's University. A half dozen parks, a world renowned museum, a botanic garden, and a huge aquarium offer a variety of diversions for all ages.

Flatbush Avenue, a few blocks from Brooklyn Heights, will lead you southeastward to the monumental Grand Army Plaza with its 80-foot-high memorial arch, often open to visitors on weekends and holidays and affording an interesting view of the harbor, the Manhattan skyline, and the local neighborhoods. A little beyond the Plaza to your left, onto Eastern Parkway and behind the Public Library, you'll come to Institute Park, where the huge Brooklyn Museum and the beautiful Botanic Garden are located.

The museum's collections of primitive and prehistoric art are world renowned: North and South American Indian handicrafts; works from Oceania, Indonesia, and Africa. There is a notable collection of American painting and sculpture from Colonial times to today. Its collection of Egyptian antiquities on the third floor is considered outstanding. One floor below is a fine collection of bronzes and porcelains from China, displayed in chronological order, as well as changing exhibitions from the museum's wealth of over 30,000 prints and drawings. Up on the fourth floor the costume galleries and the series of American interiors from the 17th century to the present are also of special interest.

The 50-acre Botanic Garden behind the museum, with more than 10,000 trees and plants, is especially noted for its Garden of Fragrance, one of the relatively few gardens in the world planted and maintained for the blind. The plants were selected primarily for their fragrance and shape, so that the blind might enjoy nature's beauty by the sense of smell and touch. Signs in braille are posted at the edge of each bed to aid the blind in identifying the flowers and plants. It is noted, too, for its Japanese garden, and there are acres devoted to wild flowers, herbs, roses, tropical plants, and groves of flowering shrubs.

To the south of the Botanic Garden is Prospect Park, a 500-acre expanse of woods, meadows, footpaths, bridle trails, and tree-shaded drives. The project was designed by the same men who had collaborated on Central Park, Olmstead and de Vaux. Here you can visit the Lefferts Homestead, a Dutch Colonial farmhouse which was built in 1776 and originally stood at 563 Flatbush Avenue. When the Lefferts family bequeathed it to the city, the home was moved to the park as a museum.

The Italianate villa which serves as the Brooklyn Park Headquarters (Prospect Park West between 4th and 5th streets) was once the home of railroad pioneer Edwin C. Litchfield. Built in 1857 from plans by Alexander Jackson Davis and called Ridgewood, it is said to have been one of the most elegant houses of its time and the center of Brooklyn social life.

A Day at a City Beach

Another summer day—make it a weekday when it's less crowded—can be spent in Coney Island. The island, which fronts on the Atlantic Ocean, once was a common pasture for early Dutch farmers. It became a fashionable beach resort in the mid-19th century when the enterprising Messrs. Eddy and Hart leased part of the island and built a pavilion. With the extension of the subway lines (BMT and IND), the island became accessible to all and now draws a half-billion people a year.

It was once a razzle-dazzle place with ferris wheels, carousels, roller coasters, tunnels of love, shooting galleries, penny arcades, sellers of pizza, hot dogs, saltwater taffy, and spun-sugar candy. Now Coney Island's number of amusements is diminishing, but it's still worth the excursion if only to get a taste of what the happy, gaudy, and thrilling heyday of this famous amusement park must have been like.

The New York Aquarium is here, too. Try to visit at feeding time: through portholes you can watch divers swim among the great white whales and feed them by hand; watch an attendant tickle an electric eel until it flashes and crackles a discharge of some 650 volts. You may see a pilot whale or seal which had gone astray and was given a home here. There are sea lions and seals, living coral, giant starfish, seahorses, octopi, and enough exhibits to keep you busy for half the day.

Another variation on the nautical theme is the fascinating Sheepshead Bay area. Take the Belt (also called Shore) Parkway east to Knapp St., head south a short way, then back west along Emmons

Avenue. This mini-port for saltwater fishermen comes spectacularly alive in the predawn hours and again in late afternoon. The amazing bustle, in which you're welcome to take part, involves the all- or half-day chartering of party or private-charter fishing boats. Even if you don't want to test the Atlantic fishing in person, the returning catch—you can't get 'em any fresher—is for sale at reasonable prices.

Back to the Shore Parkway and farther east still, straddling the Brooklyn–Queens border, and you'll be passing New York City's largest park, the Jamaica Bay Wildlife Refuge. It encompasses more than eighteen square miles (remember that Manhattan comprises only 22 square miles) of underwater island and tidal marsh terrain with 257 species of native birds. A permit is required for access to the wildlife area here; write the city's Department of Parks, Recreation and Cultural affairs. However, saltwater fishing is permitted.

Queens

Queens, covering 121 square miles, abuts Brooklyn to the south and west and Long Island to the east. The lines of demarcation are very vague. Even the native hardly knows at what point he is in Queens, Brooklyn, or Long Island. (The position of Manhattan is quite clear. It's across the East River, either over it via the Queensboro Bridge or under it via the Queens Midtown Tunnel.)

Queens is a borough of beaches, baseball parks, airports, golf courses, racetracks, yacht basins, and expressways to Long Island's beach resorts and suburban communities. The borough also has thriving manufacturing areas—especially Long Island City on the western edge—and distinct neighborhoods. Some of the large ethnic groupings are the Italians of Maspeth and Ridgewood, the Irish of Woodside, the blacks of Hollis and Jamaica, the Greeks of Astoria, the Jews of Forest Hills, and the Puerto Ricans of Corona and Elmhurst.

Until well into the 20th century Queens was a rural area. Henry Hudson had nosed the *Half Moon* into Rockaway Inlet on the south shore for a short look-see, then continued on to the Upper Bay and then to Albany in search of the Northwest Passage. Three years later Adrian Block sailed through Long Island Sound and, while navigating the roaring currents of Hell Gate on the northern extremity of Queens, didn't dare give the area a second look. He, too, was heading for Manhattan.

After the West India Company had sewed up the Brooklyn area, it approached the Reckouwacky Indians about selling a piece of their domain, in what was to become Queens, so it could continue its expansion program. Once the deal was consummated, towns sprang up all over the virgin flatlands.

By 1643 Flushing was inhabited by a small band of English Quaker refugees under the leadership of John Bowne. The same year a band of Englishmen from Hemel Hempstead had settled Hempstead, which is across the borough line in Long Island. Jamaica was chartered as a town by Governor Stuyvesant in 1656. They were followed by other English settlers and soon the area became known as Queens, in honor of Catherine Braganza, Queen of Charles II. It is not surprising, therefore, that during the Revolution, most of the people in Queens were British sympathizers.

Queens remained a loosely knit collection of small towns until the subway lines were extended to Jackson Heights, Flushing, and Jamaica. Today the borough has a population rivaling Brooklyn's, many of whom live in huge clusters of high-rise apartment houses.

There are only a few vestiges of its historic past. One is the Bowne House in Flushing (Bowne Street between 37th and 38th Avenues), which John Bowne built in 1661. For permitting Quaker meetings to be conducted in his home he was sent to Holland to be put on trial. His impassioned plea for religious tolerance won him a pardon and led to greater freedom of worship in the New World's settlements. His home is now a shrine to religious liberty.

Close by is the old Quaker Meeting House on Northern Boulevard between Main and Union Streets. It is one of the country's few remaining houses of worship dating from the 17th century. The meeting place was built in 1694 and has been in continuous use by the Society of Friends ever since, except for a time when it was occupied by the British forces during the Revolution.

Baseball, Tennis, and Racing

If horse racing, tennis, and baseball are your favorite sports, Queens is the place to head for. The National League's New York Mets (baseball) and the New York Jets (football) play at Shea Stadium in Flushing. The thoroughbreds run at Aqueduct in Jamaica. At the West Side Tennis Club in Forest Hills you can watch professional and amateur tennis tournaments.

For the less active pastime of strolling, sunning, and sightseeing, you might also plan on spending some time in Flushing Meadows–Corona Park in Corona. The site of both New York World's Fairs (1939–40 and 1964–65) with a few buildings of both expositions remaining, this area also contains a Hall of Science, a small zoo, a delightful aviary, a children's animal farm, and Louis Armstrong Stadium, site of the U.S. Open Tennis Championship.

The Bronx

It was a stroke of good fortune for New York City that The Bronx was slow in developing. When farsighted city officials began around 1870 to acquire lands to make Central and Prospect Parks they also turned their eyes northeastward across the Harlem River to the vast expanse of virgin forests and meadows of what was then called lower Westchester. They bought three parcels of land covering more than four thousand acres "to be held forever for the delight and well-being of the people of the city." In no other major city of the world has the country been kept this close to town (although at first glance the Bronx is hardly a "delight").

The history of the Bronx more or less parallels that of Queens. The Dutch West India Company purchased the area from the Indians in 1639 and two years later sold five hundred acres between the Harlem and Bronx rivers to a Scandinavian by the name of Jonas Bronck, later distorted to Bronx. He was joined by other colonists from New England and during the Revolution they, too, took the side of the Tories.

It wasn't until the mid-19th century that the area attracted any appreciable number of settlers. The Irish came in after the potato famine of 1840 to help build the Harlem and Hudson River Railroads. After the German Revolution of 1848 there was an influx of German farmers. They lived in small, independent settlements until 1874 when New York City enticed Kingsbridge, West Farms, and Morrisania to become wards of the city. Twenty years later they were followed into the fold by the townships of Westchester and parts of Pelham and Eastchester. Under the Greater New York Charter of 1898 these two annexations became the borough of the Bronx.

The lower Bronx is a cluster of unkempt neighborhoods and some are among the nation's most depressed areas. Its greatest claim to fame is Yankee Stadium; since its opening in 1923 it has been the home of the American League's Yankees and, from 1956 through 1972, of the football Giants.

Near the Stadium, under the Major Deegan Expressway, you can find the Bronx Terminal Market. A few years ago, it sold only to retail stores but that's changed. In one of those interesting experiments that makes living in New York a unique experience, groups of families began trying to save money by forming their own food co-ops and sending representatives to Bronx Terminal to buy wholesale lots of meat, fruit, and vegetables. Now these amateurs-turned-professionals compete with the Grand Union and A&P buyers for the best bargains.

The upper Bronx borders wealthy Westchester county and is a relatively open area with several college campuses—notably Fordham and

Manhattan Universities—surburban communities, parklands, and parkways.

Those visitors to New York who say, "It's a nice place to visit but I wouldn't want to live there," probably never have crossed over the border of Manhattan into the primitive forests of Van Cortlandt Park, nor ventured up to Pelham Bay Park's breeze-swept beaches (marred somewhat in recent years by an unsightly landfill mound growing out of a garbage dump) or across the bridge to City Island and its wide views of Long Island Sound.

The parks can be reached by subway, but the pleasantest and quickest way to go is by car. The most scenic route to Van Cortlandt Park in the northwestern part of the Bronx is along Manhattan's Henry Hudson Parkway, an expressway which skirts the Hudson River just beyond Riverside Drive, crosses over Spuyten Duyvil, and leads you right into the park.

Van Cortlandt's 1,132 acres are primarily for play and relaxation. There are hiking trails through its rugged, heavily wooded terrain, playing fields, a golf course, bridle paths, tennis courts, a small lake where you can rent a rowboat in the summer and ice-skate in the winter.

Van Cortlandt House

This was George Washington country. Van Cortlandt House, at the southwest corner of the park just off Broadway, served as the General's headquarters in 1783 just before he launched his final and successful campaign to retake New York City from the British. The house was built in 1748 by Frederick Van Cortlandt, a descendant of one of the early and influential Dutch families, who managed his estate along the lines of an independent principality. Slaves tended his livestock and crops; women spun his flax, wove it into cloth, and turned the cloth into garments. A score of skilled artisans embellished his living quarters and fashioned his furniture. He was lord of all he surveyed and his word was law. It is one of the few historic houses which remained in the hands of the same family for generations. It wasn't until 1899 that Van Cortlandt's descendants sold the estate to the city, which maintains it as a museum. (The mansion is not to be confused with Van Cortlandt Manor, at Croton-on-Hudson in Westchester County, which is also a museum.)

The mansion's unpretentious square fieldstone exterior in no way prepares the first-time visitor for the elegance of its Georgian interior. The spacious rooms are furnished with handsome English, Dutch, and Colonial pieces. Its huge fireplace is framed with blue tiles. The heart of the house, the kitchen, speaks a volume on the self-sufficient way of life that was lived here: candlemakers, spinning wheel, loom, soapmakers, handwrought implements, and caldrons large enough to feed fifty.

Another historic house of note in the area is the Poe Cottage, a short drive southeast at Kingsbridge Road and Grand Concourse. The little farmhouse was built in 1816 by John Wheeler and was the home of poet Edgar Allan Poe and his wife, Virginia, from 1846 to 1849. Before Virginia died here, Poe wrote some of his finest works: *The Bells, Ulalume, Eureka,* and *Annabel Lee.*

Gardens and Zoos

From Van Cortlandt Park it is about 20 minutes' drive east to Southern Boulevard and 200th Street, and the New York Botanical Garden's flower displays, which spread over 230 rolling acres of the northern half of Bronx Park. In its center is a forest primeval of hemlocks. This dense stand of trees is one of the very few virgin tracts to have survived the ax in the East.

West of Hemlock Forest is a turn-of-the-century museum building which houses an herbarium, library, auditorium, and exhibition halls.

Across from the museum is a four-acre garden with hundreds of rock-loving plants. A short stroll will bring you to the Enid A. Haupt Conservatory, renovated and reopened in 1979: an elaborate complex of greenhouses where orchids, poinsettia, and other brilliant tropical plants give New Yorkers a taste of southern climes during long winter months. Behind the Conservatory, you'll come upon the vast Rose Garden, where several thousand plantings of more than 160 rose varieties are displayed in formal beds and country-style clusters.

The Bronx Zoo—the southern half of Bronx Park, at Fordham Road and Bronx River Parkway,—is built with moats rather than iron bars to give the illusion of a walk through the African Veldt while elephants, deer, lions, ostriches, peacocks, and other wild life roam around at will. The 252-acre zoo is one of America's largest, and, for the foot-weary, there's an aerial tramway that passes directly over the African Plains, the Great Apes House, and Goat Hill, as well as a tractor train and monorail.

But don't forget to get off and explore the windowless World of Darkness with its nocturnal and cave-dwelling inhabitants. Another outstanding addition is the World of Birds, a series of oval aviaries connected by ramps. These contain, for example, a spectacular rain forest with a hundred species that are common to such environments in the New World. There is a forty-foot waterfall and rainstorms are simulated from time to time. There are exhibits of swamp birds, species from arid scrublands and African jungles. In The Treetops, five regional groupings are viewable only from above. Explanatory placards and drawings by artist Carlene Meeker show other facets of this World, such as the diets of various birds.

The children's zoo, the first in the country, has pigs, sheep, goats, a working beehive, and a chicken hatchery. Adults may enter only if accompanied by a child. There are pony rides, and for the more adventurous, there are even camels and llamas to ride. An outdoor restaurant and a dozen refreshment stands are spotted around the grounds.

Pelham Bay Park, a 2,000-acre jagged peninsula which juts into Long Island Sound, was part of the original 9,000-acre tract bought by English colonist Thomas Pell in 1654. Its rocky, rolling, wooded terrain is laced with bridle paths, picnic grounds, playfields, and the Pelham and Split Rock golf courses. On the sandy shores of the Sound is Orchard Beach, where you can rent bathing suits, towels, and a locker, roam the one mile crescent-shaped beach, picnic on 140 acres, visit the historic 215-acre Hunter and Twin Island Sites, or play paddleball or handball on the extensive recreational area fields. There are fishing facilities, too. Weekends bring out hordes of city dwellers, so it would be best to plan your excursion for a weekday.

The Bartow Mansion in the park is worth a visit. The handsome Greek Revival stone house was built in 1836, and today is the headquarters of the International Garden Club as well as a museum and landscape gardening exhibit.

A causeway connects the park with City Island, a busy center of boat building, rope and sail making, and pleasure boating. Fish fresh from the sea are served at the bustling waterside restaurants where you can watch sailboats get under way, their mainsails billowing before the wind as they head out to Long Island Sound.

In the beautiful residential section of Riverdale, in the West Bronx along the Hudson, is Wave Hill, at West 249th Street, whose spacious grounds—open to the public—include formal gardens, greenhouses, a herb garden, a beautiful and historic mansion house—Mark Twain, Theodore Roosevelt, and Arturo Toscanini have lived there—and a spectacular view of the Hudson and the Palisades.

Winding Up

New York is like a giant pastry shop. It offers hundreds of delectable delights, but they cannot be consumed all at once. One must return time and again to savor a dozen or so favorite selections each visit. Nor can each one be described in a guide if it is to be of a manageable size. These have been some of New York's pièces de résistance. You'll find many more listed in the New York City *Practical Information* section, which follows.

SIGHTSEEING CHECKLIST. No matter how you come to New York City, or how many times you've been here, your state of mind will determine the best approach for exploring the Big Apple. It is a world unto itself, and an incredible world at that. Even a recent Gallup Poll of typical American travelers attested to the fact that New York is the nation's "top city," and is considered the "most interesting" city in the U.S. with the "best food" and the "best-looking women." Those quotes cover a lot of ground, territory we'll cover in the following pages with historical background and suggested walking tours. However, before we get into helpful hints about how to get around the city, and what to look for, here is New York City's "Top Attractions Checklist" as compiled by the New York Convention and Visitors Bureau. We'll go into details later on, but for starters, this is the Bureau's list of must-sees:

(1) **The Statue of Liberty,** with an observation platform 22 stories above Liberty Island, offering a superb view of New York's bustling harbor. Don't miss the fascinating Museum of Immigration in the statue's base. Nearby is Ellis Island (open for tours, spring through fall) where millions of immigrants were processed.

(2) **The Empire State Building,** 1,472 feet high, is over 50 years old, but the sleek skyscraper of steel, limestone, and aluminum is as popular as ever. Each year millions of visitors enjoy the view from observation decks on the 86th and 102nd floors.

(3) **Rockefeller Center** is a city within a city, where you can ice-skate in winter and dine outdoors in summer. This midtown Manhattan landmark offers a superb guided tour to its varied delights. Nearby is the beautifully restored Radio City Music Hall Entertainment Center, where you can take in a musical extravaganza, Rockettes and all, in the world's biggest (6,000-seat) theater, a 1930s Art Deco marvel. A separate behind-the-scenes tour is available here, too. Also nearby, in the Center's McGraw-Hill Building, is a theater showing *The New York Experience,* a multi-media, multi-sensory show that helps put New York City into perspective.

(4) **Lincoln Center** is a vast performing-arts complex at 65th Street and Broadway that offers opera, symphony, dance, theater, films, a library—and a guided tour of the beautiful buildings that house them. From the Chagalls at the Metropolitan Opera House and the Henry Moore statuary seemingly climbing out of the reflecting pool outside the library to the Vivian Beaumont and Mitzi Newhouse Theaters, it is nothing short of a modern-day Acropolis minus the hills.

(5) **The World Trade Center** with its twin towers—each 110 stories tall—stands like a pair of soaring sentinels guarding New York's Harbor. On the rooftop "promenade" of the South Tower, you stand on the world's highest open-air observation deck (1,377 feet). On the top of the North Tower you can drink or dine at the elegant Windows on the World, the restaurant complex that offers New York's most spectacular view (although, not, alas, the city's most

spectacular food). Down below, on the concourse level, you'll find The Big Kitchen (budget and gourmet foods) and the Market Dining Rooms.

(6) The United Nations offers new sights, services, and activities for visitors taking in the imposing glass building seemingly rising out of the East River. The official meetings are open to the public, there is a one-hour guided tour (even all-day tours for small groups) and several more interesting stop-off points, including the post office, gift shops, restaurants, and gardens.

(7) New York's neighborhoods:
- Chinatown
- Little Italy
- Yorkville (German, Middle European)
- Greenwich Village
- SoHo
- Upper East Side
- Upper West Side
- Brooklyn Heights
- Forest Hills
- Richmondtown
- Riverdale

You can literally tour the world in one city. But plan your excursions carefully.

(8) The Great Museums: The Metropolitan Museum of Art and the Museum of Modern Art, the Frick Collection, the American Museum of Natural History, the Museum of the American Indian, the Museum of the City of New York, the New-York Historical Society, the Cooper-Hewitt, the Guggenheim, the Whitney, and the hundreds of galleries that make New York City the world's undisputed art center.

(9) Sports: The full gamut of sporting events can be observed at Madison Square Garden, Shea and Yankee Stadiums, the Flushing Meadows and Forest Hills tennis complexes, and the Belmont, Aqueduct, Roosevelt, and Yonkers racetracks. Baseball, boxing, hockey, soccer, football, tennis, track and field, horseracing—you name your game, New York City plays it.

(10) Times Square is the glittering "Great White Way" with its theaters, moviehouses, skyscrapers, and shops. If you can see only one play (make it *Amadeus*) one or musical (toss a coin between *Sophisticated Ladies, A Chorus Line* or *42nd Street*), your visit will be greatly enhanced.

(11) Houses of Worship offering food for the soul and impressive works of art and architecture include such landmarks as St. Patrick's Cathedral, the Cathedral of St. John the Divine (the world's largest Gothic cathedral), Temple Emanu-El, Riverside Church, Trinity Church and St. Paul's Chapel, and more than 2,500 other religious edifices.

(12) New York and American Stock Exchanges offer free tours during trading hours in the nation's marketplaces—the money capitals of the world. But beware of bulls and bears.

(13) South Street Seaport, an indoor-outdoor "museum" consisting of several blocks and three piers stretching along the East River waterfront at Fulton Street, near the site of the famous fishmarket. The entire area is being restored to its original appearance, as it was when South Street was one of the world's great ports for sailing ships. Among the attractions: a collection of historic ships, an old printing shop, a model-ships museum, the Fulton Market, the Titanic Memorial·Lighthouse, and some of the best seafood restaurants in town.

That's a baker's dozen sightseeing attractions to give you something to think about while you're deciding where to eat, shop, stay, or be entertained. One way—perhaps the easiest and most relaxing way—to get your bearings is to take a sightseeing bus tour or a Circle Line three-hour sightseeing cruise around the island of Manhattan. Or maybe even a sightseeing helicopter trip. How to find these places, sights and sites? When in doubt, write or stop by the Bureau at 2 Columbus Circle (59th Street and Eighth Avenue in Manhattan), NY 10019, which will even supply you with free folders on all the city's boroughs. And, of course, read on.

OUTSIDE THE CITY

Fire Island. From Memorial Day to late September, especially on weekends, the Fire Island beaches and beach communities are home for a good portion of New York City's business and creative people and journalists. Many of the summer rentals are taken by groups of singles or young married people. The ferry ride over and back—there is no other way to reach Fire Island proper than by water—is part of the experience.

The Hamptons. Farther out than Fire Island, the Hamptons have become widely popular only in recent years, drawing off some of what used to be the summer Fire Island regulars. Beaches in the Hamptons tend to be less accessible than on Fire Island, where all the ocean-side beaches are open to everyone, but the Hamptons seem to have a higher social cachet—or so the Hamptons regulars believe.

Sunnyside, below Tarrytown in the Hudson Valley, was the estate of Washington Irving.

Hyde Park, near Poughkeepsie in the Hudson Valley, was the home of Franklin Delano Roosevelt and is now a National Shrine. The house and library are open to the public.

West Point, on the west bank of the Hudson River, is open to the public, who can enjoy its museums, battle monuments, and other sights—including frequent parades.

Woodstock, New York, is the center of an art colony in the Catskill Mountains.

Western Connecticut and the Berkshire Mountains provide a taste of New England scenery and town life close to New York City. The best time to go is in October, when the foliage turns.

Princeton University, an hour by bus, train, or car from the city, is a peaceful gothic-style oasis compared with hectic Manhattan. Try to see the Graduate School and the Institute for Advanced Studies there.

The Jersey Shore is prime for fishing and the summer beach life.

Atlantic City, where you'll find the only legalized gambling on the East Coast and the attendant entertainment, is an interesting side trip from New York City, one that can be combined with sunning on the beach in season.

PRACTICAL INFORMATION
FOR
NEW YORK CITY

HOW TO GET THERE. By air: Virtually every major (and most minor) airline serves New York City. The three largest airports serving the city are *John F. Kennedy,* in southeastern Queens; *La Guardia,* in northern Queens; and *Newark,* in nearby New Jersey. A few private flights come in at *Teterboro,* in northeastern New Jersey. This choice of where your flight lands may be relevant, depending on where you are planning to stay in the metropolitan area. (For airport transportation, see *Getting Around,* below.)

By bus: The newly modernized Port Authority Building (8th Ave. at 41st St., 564–8484, Manhattan) is a fantastically busy place, with over 200 platforms where commuter and transcontinental buses alike load and unload. A few of the individual carriers who serve the region around New York City are: *Asbury Park-New York Transit; Garden State Coachways; Hudson Transit; Red and Tan Lines; Surburban Transit; Transport of New Jersey*—formerly known as *Public Service*— and *Lincoln Transit.* These all run from New Jersey.

From the Hudson Valley, try *Mohawk Coach Lines;* from Putnam and Dutchess Counties, call *Super Service.* The Berkshire area is connected to New York City by *Resort Bus Lines,* the Poconos by *Martz Trailways.* Of course, the busing giants, *Greyhound* and *Trailways,* have service to and from New York City from and to every region of the United States. Their passenger platforms are below street level in the terminal; those of the smaller lines are on the upper stories.

By car: The *Lincoln Tunnel* from New Jersey, and the *Midtown Tunnel* and *Queensboro Bridge* from Long Island, are the most direct arteries to mid-Manhattan. The *Holland Tunnel* from New Jersey, and the *Brooklyn-Battery Tunnel* from Brooklyn, reach lower Manhattan. The *George Washington Bridge,* from New Jersey, and the *Triborough Bridge,* from Queens and the Bronx, give access to upper Manhattan.

The *Brooklyn-Queens Expressway,* from Queens and Long Island, and the *Verrazano-Narrows Bridge,* from Staten Island, will get you to Brooklyn. The expressway, of course, continues on through western Queens, which may also be reached from the north via the *Triborough Bridge.*

From upstate New York and New England, the city is accessible via many highways, both free and toll. The *New England Thruway* leads to the Bruckner Traffic Circle in the east Bronx, from which you may go to Queens *(Bronx, Whitestone* or *Throgs Neck bridges),* Manhattan *(Bruckner Expressway and*

Triboro Bridge) or the west Bronx and Manhattan *(Cross-Bronx Expressway).* The *New York (Dewey) Thruway* extends via the *Major Deegan Expressway* (both I–87) to the south Bronx and Triborough Bridge. The bridge gives access to both Queens *(Grand Central Parkway)* and Manhattan *(Franklin D. Roosevelt Drive).*

By train: Long-distance *Amtrak* routes reach New York from Chicago and the West, Washington, Florida and the South, plus Boston, Montreal, and Toronto, and all terminate in the city at either Grand Central Station (42nd to 46th Sts. on Park Avenue) or Penn Station (31st to 33rd Sts., 7th to 8th Avenues, 212–736–4545). Suburban lines stretch about 75 to 100 miles north *(ConRail's Harlem* and *Hudson Divisions,* 212–736–6000) and east *(New Haven* and *Long Island Railroads,* (212) 739–4200, operated by the Metropolitan Transportation Authority*).* Both stations are quite good at giving out information; both have uncomfortable waiting areas. *PATH Train Lines,* (201) 963–2558, service Jersey City, Newark, and Hoboken into Manhattan, terminating at the World Trade Center or Penn Station. All the commuter roads are notorious for their erratic service, lack of punctuality, and frequent equipment failure.

 TELEPHONES: The area code for all five boroughs of New York City is 212. You do not need to dial the area code if it is the same as the one from which you are calling. Information (known as directory assistance) is 555-1212. When direct-dialing a long-distance number from within New York City, you must dial the number "1" (one) *before* you dial the area code and the number itself. An operator will assist you on person-to-person, credit-card, and collect calls if you dial "0" first. Pay telephones still start at 10 cents—one of the miracles of the modern world.

 HOTELS AND MOTELS. Manhattan is an island literally filled with hotels, or so it seems when a visitor is trying to make up his or her mind where to stay. From the chic super-deluxe establishments to the modest, more reasonably priced ones, there is an incredibly wide range of accommodations available.

Those accustomed to the hotel situation in almost all other parts of the United States may be taken aback by (1) the paucity of motels in the city and (2) the lack of or limited parking areas at those that do exist. Motels by design were intended for motorists, and most everywhere but New York you can park in front of your motel room or in an open lot nearby. That is rarely the case in Manhattan, where space is at such a premium that monthly parking spots in some neighborhoods cost in excess of $200—the equivalent of rent for a studio or one-bedroom apartment in some other parts of the country.

Nor will you find the simple, inexpensive roadside stopover motels that are otherwise the norm in the U.S.—the $13.95–$21.95 double rooms complete with color TV, outdoor pool, etc. In other cities, or on the road, you can usually pull into one of these places in late afternoon and get a room for the night. As in so many other things, Manhattan is the exception. As for room rates, the $13.95–$21.95 range is about what you'd pay for a single at the YMCA or YWCA (details below); and no matter how much or how little you anticipate paying, it is always best to have a reservation ahead. That way you're assured of a room awaiting you upon arrival and that the rate will be confirmed. While you might be lucky once hitting town with no reservation and finding a suitable room, you might just as easily arrive simultaneously with five or six mammoth conventions—with not a room to be had.

Another important suggestion in selecting a hotel or motel to suit your needs: If you have the luxury of planning ahead, consult a travel agent or, if you can get a copy ahead of time, the *Sunday New York Times Travel Section.* We've listed many hotels for you to choose from, including the range of rates for a *double* room—i.e., for two persons. Many of these hotels, however, offer special packages for visitors—particularly for non-expense-account sightseers. Most of these deals are built around weekend stays at reduced rates (when there are fewer businesspeople in town) and often include tickets to top Broadway shows, a bus tour, a bottle of wine or champagne on arrival, Sunday brunch (and the *Times*—a tradition among New Yorkers themselves) or other similar amenities.

Even if you have to pay a higher rate during the week, these weekend packages are definitely worth your consideration. In comparing them, however, be aware that in order to bring the numbers down to eye-catching appeal, some advertise the rate per person, based on double occupancy. Others give you the full weekend rate, all inclusive. Some are also available for one night, while others require longer stays. In other words, read the fine print carefully.

Because of the unique nature and diversity of New York City hotels and motels, we have tried to add a little extra detail to our general categories, and advise you to give consideration to geographic location as well as price and appointments. Getting around the city is time-consuming and expensive; thus a few extra dollars per night to be in the area in which you plan to spend most of your time (the theater district, lower Manhattan, the upper East Side, etc.) are probably well spent.

We've categorized our selection (it *is* only a selection) of New York's hotels based essentially on style, service, distinction of accommodations, and location. At the end of each individual listing we've included the range in price for a **double room for two people** as quoted at press time. You can expect that in most cases there will be very few rooms at the low end of the spectrum and many more at the higher end. In addition to these prices, there is also an occupancy tax charge included in your room rate (maximum $2), and the 8¼% New York City and State sales tax is added on to all hotel bills.

As a general guideline, our **super deluxe** category refers to the top hotels in Manhattan and, in fact, these few pinnacles of service and elegance rank with the finest hotels in the world. When the reality of the cost for such rarified atmosphere hits you—say, the $250 per night you'd have to spend for a double room overlooking Central Park at the Plaza—just remember that equivalent accommodations in London or Tokyo are almost double that price.

The **deluxe** hotels in our listing are only marginally less grand. The difference is one of history and tradition—either a slight fall from past glories or because they are so new and unproven—and is probably apparent only to those who cherish the nuance as much as the accommodation. These are all fine hotels and you can expect the maximum in service and comfort.

The **luxury** category is devoted to a select group of small- to medium-size hotels—most have 300 rooms or less—that aren't usually as centrally located as the super deluxe and deluxe establishments. Often they cater to business travelers, and their service therefore tends to be very personal. With few exceptions, the slight inconvenience of location (a plus for those who don't like being in the crush of things) is made up for by price and attention to detail. There are many excellent values in this grouping.

The hotels in our **first class** range include some more of the newer establishments and some of the convention-oriented "brand name" hotels that are also perfectly suitable for tourists. Their prices reflect the economy of today's world and while the accommodations are uniformly pleasant, they will often suffer from the sterile atmosphere that is so prevalent in contemporary large-scale hotels. This section also includes a few of the fine older hotels that have slipped from their former deluxe status. All hotels in this category will have a full range of services available, and such amenities as room service, television, and multiple in-hotel dining facilities are uniformly available.

The establishments included under **Motels, Chains** and **Simple But Practical** should be self-explanatory: serviceable places to rest your weary body at night but with little in the way of individuality or special services.

If you don't care where you sleep, the *New York Convention and Visitors Bureau* says there are always some rooms available somewhere, and they'll help you find one. Unfortunately the NYCVB closes at 6 P.M., so they are little help for late arrivals. And remember, prices quoted below are the range for a *double* room—one to be occupied by two people.

SUPER DELUXE

The Carlyle. 35 E. 76th St.; 744–1600. Located in one of New York's poshest residential areas, it is also handy to two of the city's best museums—the Metropolitan and the Whitney. All rooms are air-conditioned, suites have a pantry with refrigerator and some suites have private terraces and/or wood-burning fireplaces. The *Regency Room* offers elegant dining, and the *Bemelman's Bar* is decorated with murals by that whimsical artist himself. Bobby Short's piano often echoes in the Vertès-decorated Café Carlyle. There are 175 available rooms (the best are for full-time residents). Garage facilities. *$170–$195.*

Grand Hyatt New York. Park Ave. & 42nd St.; 883–1234. On the site of the old Commodore Hotel right next to Grand Central Station. This renovated masterpiece, done with lavish amounts of brass, glass, chrome and marble, features *nouvelle cuisine* at *Trumpet's* and a spacious lounge overhanging 42nd St. Summer rates are available. *$120–$180.*

Helmsley Palace. 455 Madison Ave. at 50th St.; 888–1624. Constructed above and around the landmark Florentine Renaissance-styled Villard Mansions, originally built in 1855, the Helmsley is extravagantly rich-looking and in a location central to just about everything. Alas, food and service are sadly not up to the mark of the setting, the lushly appointed rooms, or the locale. 875 rooms. *$135–$215.*

Marriott's Essex House. 160 Central Park South; 247–0300. Park Avenue has the reputation but Central Park South has the view, and is probably as attractive a location as can be found in the city. With 750 available rooms, the Essex House is one of the largest along this mini-hotel row, but it still manages to provide personal service along with its modern but Continental atmosphere. As is so for the other hotels along CPS, the Essex House is close to the Coliseum and Carnegie Hall, and not far from Lincoln Center or the theater district. *$125–$180.*

Park Lane. 36 Central Park South; 371–4000. A relatively new addition to the list of classic hotels on the southern boundary of Central Park, and one that quickly established itself as ranking right alongside them for dignity and service. There are views of the park, the skyline and, if you're high enough, the Hudson and East Rivers; a rooftop dining room; and a staff conversant in several languages. A favorite especially among knowledgeable foreign visitors. 640 rooms. *$115–$180.*

Pierre. 61st St. & Fifth Ave., opposite Central Park; 940–8100. This fine hotel, which opened in 1930, is primarily a residential hotel (cooperative apartments) and more than half of its 700 rooms are permanently occupied. Those which are not are available to transients, and these guests often occupy the highest echelons of society and celebrity. It's a favorite for entertaining, or you can be entertained in the *Café Pierre* or the *La Forêt* grill. *$190–$230.*

The Plaza. Fifth Ave. & 59th St.; 759–3000. The grandest hotel in the city has been on a major campaign to regain all its former glory, remodeling and touching up its public areas and redecorating rooms floor-by-floor. And even as the renovations have gone on, The Plaza has remained the most imposing and beautiful place to stay in New York. With Central Park on one side, and a small plaza complete with graceful fountain in front, this is New York's enclave of tradition and elegance in the European manner. None of the original 1907 flavor of this hotel has been lost. The 837 rooms are richly decorated, mostly in the French Provincial manner. Service is superb, the staff trained to the point of remembering guests' names—and using them. The Plaza's restaurants are famous in their own right, and include the staid *Oak Room,* the popular *Oyster Bar* (great for lunches and snacks), the *Palm Court* (where strolling musicians entertain during tea daily), the Hawaiian *Trader Vic's,* and the elegant *Edwardian Room,* where you dine by candlelight. *$135–$275.*

Regency. Park Ave. at 61st St.; 759–4100. French tapestries, Italian marble floors, gilt mirrors, guests such as Princess Grace, Audrey Hepburn, and Richard Burton (though the Beatles tried and never got in), and a garage ideally suited for 140 Rolls Royces—that's the level of elegance to be expected at the Regency. There are 500 rooms and suites, most decorated à la Louis XVI;

telephones and scales in every bathroom; kitchenettes connected to many of the suites; the excellent *Le Restaurant,* offering Continental fare with French influence; and an exclusive bar and cocktail lounge. The Regency does not cater to such crass things as conventions; it does cater to the elite in business, society, and entertainment. *$140–$215.*

Sherry-Netherland. 781 Fifth Ave.; 355–2800. Though somewhat less well-known than its neighbors, the Plaza and the Pierre, the Sherry-Netherland is a distinguished hotel with an aura of grandeur all its own. The accent is unquestionably Continental and the atmosphere as sedate and elegant throughout the hotel as at the darkly graceful Sherry bar. The rooms are lovely and the location chic. 375 rooms. *$125–$180.*

DELUXE

Berkshire Place. 21 E. 52nd St.; 753–5800. Since it was refurbished in 1979, the Berkshire Place has become a most popular haunt, largely because of the *Rendezvous,* an attractive bar and restaurant where the food is seriously lacking in distinction and highly over-priced, and the bright garden-like atrium in the foyer. The rooms are simple and modern, the ambience young-and-on-the-go but with good attention to detail in the service. 420 rooms. *$115–$180.*

Harley. 214 E. 42nd St.; 490–8900. Another new Helmsley hotel, close to the United Nations but catering to the executive. The Harley is sleekly modern with such unusual touches as phone extensions in the bathrooms. 790 rooms. *$105–$160.*

Parker Meridien New York. 118 W. 57th St.; 245–5000. New (March 1981) and big (600 rooms), the Meridien is opened by Air France's hotel subsidiary. Unique features include a health club, rooftop pool, squash courts, jogging track, and that it is in walking distance from Carnegie Hall and the Russian Tea Room. The house restaurant, *Restaurant de France,* features *nouvelle cuisine,* but considering its ownership, is an unfortunate representation of one of France's most notable exports. *$125–$180.*

Ritz-Carlton. 112 Central Park South. No phone number at press time. What was until recently the Navarro was scheduled to become the Ritz-Carlton in the fall of 1982, largely renovated and in keeping with the standards of the chain's other hotels around the world. Prices can be expected to reflect the change, but they will start at $125.

St. Moritz. 50 Central Park South; 755–5800. Another fine hotel on Central Park South, and although it is a little bit less expensive than the others, it doesn't sacrifice too much in the way of service or furnishings. Rooms are small but tastefully done, and the hotel is another favorite of foreign visitors. During the summer, the hotel sets up the *Café de la Paix* along the sidewalk. It may not be Paris, but the effect is still refreshing. 680 available units. *$90–$135.*

St. Regis-Sheraton. Fifth Ave. and 55th St.; 753–4500. The St. Regis represents the ultimate in Old World wealth and rococo elegance. John Jacob Astor IV built the place almost entirely of marble in 1904, intending it to be "not so much a hotel as a temporary home for those who are used to the best of everything, and who appreciate artistic surroundings." Although restoration of the hotel's full splendor is an on-going effort, many descendants of the famous "400," that original core of New York's social elite, still inhabit the St. Regis' 550 rooms. The hotel's luxury restaurants and bars are the *Oak Room,* the *King Cole Room* (which features excellent revues usually based on the work of Broadway songwriters), and *Astor's. $130–$185.*

UN Plaza. 1 UN Plaza, at 44th St. and First Ave.; 355–3400. Facing the United Nations, this is an ultra-modern tower with great views from all rooms. Indoor pool, health club, indoor tennis, sauna, the works. The jazzy bar and restaurant is all-mirrored (which may lead to bumped noses as you enter), and typical of the sometimes garish decor of the rooms. Small lobby, comfortable rooms (some interesting duplex suites). 290 rooms. *$115–$135.*

Vista International. 3 World Trade Center; 938–9100. Vista International's first property in the Continental U.S. is a flagship hotel in every sense. Located within walking distance of Wall Street and the entire southern tip of Manhattan's financial district, Vista is a sparklingly alive edifice with beautiful public areas, including the *Tall Ships* bar, the outstanding and friendly-but-formal *American Harvest* restaurant, and the less-imposing but equally satisfying *Greenhouse.* A fitness center and pool, racquetball court, full range of business services, free transportation to the theater district every evening, and a variety of special weekend packages (for those interested in everything from walking and bicycling tours to Broadway) are some of the ways this unusual hotel goes about making its culturally out-of-the-way location an asset. 825 rooms. *$90–$115.*

Waldorf-Astoria. 301 Park Ave. at 50th St.; 355–3000. Some hotels seem to improve with age, and the Waldorf is in some ways a prime example. It is certainly the most renowned of American hotels, and the very mention of its name conjures up images of luxury. To a certain extent the reality lives up to the image. The Art Deco Park Avenue entrance is imposing, and the rooms are decorated in a gracious style, but it has lost much of its Old World charm. The neatly redone *Peacock Alley* is a popular jazz piano haunt, tucked away in the still-regal lobby, and the Waldorf is invariably host to countless distinguished guests. *$110–$195.*

LUXURY

Adams on the Park. 2 E. 86th St.; 744–1800. Right off Central Park, and a few blocks north of the Metropolitan Museum of Art, the feeling is European— borrowed from its eastward neighbors in the German-influenced Yorkville section. The large rooms have excellent views and are well kept if a little out-of-date. It is partially residential. 180 rooms. *$80–$92.*

Algonquin Hotel. 59 W. 44th St.; 840–6800. Long a favorite for its warm hospitality and literary history (its bar—and drinks are also served in the comfortable lobby lounge—and restaurant continue to be the watering hole and outpost of the *New Yorker* magazine staff), the Algonquin prides itself on the traditions of Europe's finest family-owned hotels. The modern comforts are here, the location absolutely perfect whatever your purpose in town, and the rates surprisingly reasonable. Steve Ross, a pianist specializing in Broadway show music, serenades the supper crowds. *$89–$94.*

American Stanhope. Fifth Ave. at 81st St.; 288–5800. Its atmosphere is particularly gracious, and above all it features classic service. Shoes are polished if left outside the door at night; a baggagemaster will help guests arriving by ship clear their luggage through customs; and if the neighborhood—opposite the Metropolitan Museum of Art—seems a little out of the way, there's a free Rolls Royce shuttle service to 50th St. in the morning. Fine cuisine, elegant atmosphere in the *Saratoga Room.* And on a summer Sunday, having brunch outside at *The Terrace* as you watch the crowds amble to the Met is an experience you'll long remember. 275 rooms. *$135–$175.*

Doral Park Avenue. 70 Park Ave.; 687–7050. This hotel is a fairly recent addition to the ranks—an amalgam of a renovated hotel and a new building. The appointments are intended to be plush and there is definitely a predominance of luxury in all the rooms. It was decorated by Tom Lee, who was also responsible for the interiors of two sister hotels in Miami. Four blocks south of Grand Central Station. 200 rooms. *$95–$105.*

Dorset. 30 W. 54th St.; 247–7300. One of the lesser known of NYC's top stopping places, the Dorset is a very quiet, traditional hotel adjacent to the Museum of Modern Art and the corporate headquarters for such communications conglomerates as CBS, ABC, Capitol-EMI, and MGM. 190 available rooms. *$107–$140.*

Élysée. 60 E. 54th St.; 753–1066. This small hotel is elegantly tucked away between Madison and Park Avenues on 54th St. Its size permits the management to extend more than token service. Some individuality is maintained by assigning you a room having a name as well as a number, and the decor of each room varies. 110 units. *$95–$105.*

Gorham. 136 W. 55th St.; 245–1800. A small establishment very close to City Center, Carnegie Hall, the Museum of Modern Art and other midtown attractions. The accommodations aren't "luxurious," but they're relatively large, neat, and quiet. Most also have kitchenettes, and they're a bargain at the price. *$55–$70.*

Gotham. 700 Fifth Ave. at 55th St.; 247–2200. Closed for renovations at press time, but the new owners promise refurbished turn-of-the-century grace and elegance at this very central location.

Gramercy Park. 2 Lexington Ave.; 475–4320. Among the greatest beauties of London are its scattered parks and squares, forming oases in the city pattern. The namesake of this hotel is one of the few locations in the city that meets the London standard. The area is dignified and quiet. The hotel faces out on a small private park and is unpretentiously inviting. Yet many well-known rock groups stay here. Very comfortable bar. 500 rooms. *$75–$85.*

Kitano. 66 Park Ave. at 38th St.; 685–0022. New York's only Japanese owned and operated hotel, with half of its 80 rooms featuring Japanese decor. Good location, and a peaceful retreat with all the niceties of Oriental attention to detail. Excellent and beautifully done Japanese restaurant off the lobby on the second floor. *$85.*

Lombardy. 111 E. 56th St.; 753–8600. This ultra-smart hotel allows you a chance to stay in grand surroundings in a fine location. The rooms offer large distinguished accommodations, and Continental breakfast is included in the rates. Quite sumptuous, as is the outstanding French restaurant on the main floor, *Laurent.* 350 rooms. *$120.*

Mayflower. 15 Central Park West, at 61st St.; 265–0060. Unpretentious but most accommodating, this is the type of hotel New Yorkers wish they knew about to recommend for visiting friends. The views of Central Park are as good as from the south, and the feeling is simple friendliness. Close to Lincoln Center, Carnegie Hall, and the Coliseum but convenient via the Columbus Circle bus and train stations to just about everything. 240 available rooms. *$90–$125.*

Sheraton-Russell. 45 Park Ave., at 37th St.; 685–7676. Located on Murray Hill and a little removed from the heart of the city, the Sheraton-Russell offers a calm dignity that contrasts well with the trials of city life. The hotel is used mainly by businesspeople, but its generous rooms, some with fireplaces, should appeal to other visitors. 170 rooms, parking facilities. *$89–$150.*

Shoreham. 33 W. 55th St.; 247–6700. A small hotel just off Fifth Ave., the Shoreham presents a dignified appearance and is splendidly located for shopping activities, the Museum of Modern Art, and Broadway. The rooms are modest but clean and each has its own pantry. 150 rooms. *$64–$74.*

Tudor. 304 E. 42nd St.; 986–8800. On the East Side of the city and a part of the Tudor City apartment complex, this hotel is near the UN and not far from Grand Central. The area is pleasant, quiet, and refined, and so are the accommodations, which have been recently refurbished. 475 rooms. *$66–$125.*

Tuscany. 120 E. 39th St., 686–1600. This is a smaller luxury hotel also just south of Grand Central. All of its rooms are studios, complete with service pantries and other extras, such as bathroom telephones and color televisions. It is residential and transient. 270 rooms. *$110–$115.*

Westbury. 840 Madison Ave. at 69th St.; 535–2000. In many ways this is one of the better hotels in the city. The neighborhood surroundings are unimpeachable (especially for high-fashion shoppers, museum buffs, and gallery browsers), and the dignified tone of the hotel is intended to complement them. The furnishings reflect a grand style and the rooms are tastefully comfortable. Farther uptown than most, this hotel's personal attention and ambience more than make up for any inconvenience. 325 rooms. *$130–$185.*

FIRST CLASS

Barbizon-Plaza. 106 Central Park South; 247–7000. With the advantages of a view overlooking the park and central location, this large hotel is a bargain in its neighborhood. It is often bustling with tours and conventions, but relief from these can be found in the generally bright rooms. 800 rooms, garage facilities. *$75–$95.*

Halloran House. Lexington Ave. & 49th St.; 755–4000. (Formerly the Shelton.) Opened in 1978 following extensive refurnishing. Excellent midtown location. Affiliated with Howard Johnson reservation service. 650 rooms. *$108–$123.*

Inter-Continental New York. 111 E. 48th St.; 755–5900. (Formerly the Barclay.) Located half a block off Park Ave., one of this hotel's prime advantages is a degree of withdrawal from the bustle of the city while still being at the heart of the goings-on. This is an older, gracious hotel with pleasant, spacious atmosphere. Live birds frolic in the aviary in the lobby, restored to its original 1920s grandeur as part of a recent renovation. *La Recolte,* the restaurant, is a new incarnation of *The Barclay Restaurant.* 770 rooms, garage facilities. *$130.*

Loew's Drake. 440 Park Ave.; 421–0900. The Drake underwent a major modernization and restoration program in 1979, and the rejuvenation has been effective and tasteful. In addition to having pleasant surroundings the hotel is well located, with telephone and loudspeaker in each of the new bathrooms. There is also a lobby lounge, full concierge service and the new *Wellington Grill.* 640 rooms. *$125–$170.*

Loew's Summit. Lexington Ave. & 51st St.; 752–7000. The Summit has been completely redone in recent years. Ultra-modern guest rooms; lobby cocktail lounge; *Maude's* turn-of-the-century restaurant; Tower Suites; color televisions; refrigerators; phone in bathroom. ESP (Extra Special People) floor for those who want super-deluxe special services. Concierge. 770 rooms, garage. *$88–$103.*

Loew's Warwick. 65 W. 54th St.; 247–2700. The harried pace and uninspired lobby are misleading here. Once upstairs the rooms bespeak a simple, straightforward elegance. The hotel attracts people in the communications, advertising, recording, and fashion industries, but it has all that is necessary to appeal to the average appreciative visitor. The rooms are large and generally handsome. *Sir Walter's Restaurant* has long been a favorite of show people. 500 rooms. *$110–$120.*

New York Hilton. 1335 Ave. of the Americas; 586–7000. The Hilton name is becoming synonymous with large, fancy, modern (and impersonal) hotels; this one is no exception. One of the biggest and most popular among conventioneers and tourists alike, the Hilton can offer such conveniences as extra-long beds and heated bathroom floors. Central to everything in midtown. There is also entertainment in the way of jazz combos at *Sybil's.* 2,130 rooms. *$101–$160.*

New York Sheraton. Seventh Ave. & 56th St.; 247–8000. Standing in the lobby here is something akin to trying to meet somebody at the information booth in Penn Station. Tours are constantly arriving and leaving, the people who work at the hotel are rarely cognizant of which are which or who's who. Upstairs is as quiet as being in midtown ever gets and the rooms are attractive— some even luxurious. If you can get by without much in the way of service you'll be fine. 1,600 rooms. *$95–$125.*

New York Statler. 401 Seventh Ave., at 33rd St.; 736–5000. This is a huge (1,700 rooms), busy hotel directly across from Penn Station and Madison Square Garden and practically in the heart of the garment center. Very popular among businesspeople trying to get in and out of the city quickly, and among those coming into town for concerts, sporting events, or trade shows being held at the Garden. The rooms are unspectacular but comfortable. *$75–$114*.

Sheraton Centre. 801 Seventh Ave. between 52nd & 53rd Sts.; 581–1000. Formerly the Americana. The new owners have done more than refurbish—they've essentially redesigned the lower public floors and meeting rooms in order to make them more attractive and more practical. With 50 floors, the Sheraton Centre lacks warmth and the rooms tend to be small, but many opt for it simply because it is situated so close to the theater district. There are five restaurants, including a disco. *$99–$165*.

Sheraton City Squire. 790 Seventh Ave.; 581–3300. In recent years a number of motels have been built in the city, mainly on the West Side. They are uniformly modern and attractive. The City Squire is one of the better ones, and closer to the city's activities than most. An indoor swimming pool is also open to the public for a fee. 700 rooms. *$65–$125*.

Southgate Towers. 371 Seventh Ave.; 563–1800. Opposite Penn Station on 31st St., this large hotel is somewhat removed from the main attractions and tends to attract people doing business in the garment center directly to the south. Accommodations are suitable to most ordinary demands. 1,200 rooms, garage facilities. *$79*.

MOTELS, CHAINS, AND SIMPLE BUT PRACTICAL

Barbizon. 140 E. 63rd St.; 838–5700. Formerly a hotel for women only, the fashionably located Barbizon (right near Bloomingdale's) has reopened as a regular hotel, completely renovated and redecorated. *$50–$110*.

Bedford. 118 E. 40th St.; 697–4800. A small, almost inconspicuous hotel two blocks south of Grand Central, the Bedford offers pleasant rooms, all with serving pantries. It attracts mostly businesspeople. *$79–$99*.

Best Western Skyline Motor Inn. 725 Tenth Ave. at 50th St.; 586–3400. One of the first real "motels" built in New York. Quite far west but comfortable and within walking distance to most theaters. That walk late at night, however, is not suggested. Indoor pool, free parking. *$69–$76*.

Beverly. 125 E. 50th St.; 753–2700. Transient guests are usually business types, though tourists have found it increasingly well-suited to their needs. Some of the suites have pantries and terraces. Comfortable though not distinguished. *Kenny's Steak Pub* downstairs. 300 rooms. *$79–$109*.

Blackstone. 50 E. 58th St.; 355–4200. A good midtown address, convenient to the best of the city's shops, theaters, and movies. 200 rooms. *$70–$85*.

Chelsea. 222 W. 23rd St.; 243–3700. The Chelsea probably deserves a category unto itself—a study in contradictions, and totally unique among New York hotels. It was the first hotel in the city designated a historic and architectural landmark. It has a long history of sheltering creative talent—including the likes of Mark Twain, Thomas Wolfe, Dylan Thomas, Brendan Behan, Arthur Miller, Virgil Thomson, Ben Shahn, and Larry Rivers, to name a few. Some of the Chelsea's history is described in our *Walking Tours* section, and it is worth a brief visit even if you stay elsewhere. Today it is, shall we say, funky, attracting many rock stars who use it as home base when in New York. It is not for everyone. 400 rooms. *$45–$85.*

Doral Inn. 541 Lexington Ave.; 755–1200. (Formerly the Belmont Plaza.) One of several commercial hotels along Lexington in the upper 40s. There is nothing impressive about it, but it is comfortable and centrally located. Frequented by airline personnel and often the site of labor negotiations. 700 rooms. *$87–$94.*

Empire. 44 W. 63rd St. at Broadway; 265–7400. Located opposite Lincoln Center, you'd expect this once-flourishing hotel to be ritzy to the hilt. It is not. It is simple and modestly comfortable, popular for organized tours and among visiting musicians and performers. Weekly rates available. 600 rooms. *$60–$75.*

Excelsior. 45 W. 81 St.; 362–9200. A bit out of the way but convenient to bus and subway transportation—and unusually well kept for a hotel in this price category. *$43–$52.*

Executive. 237 Madison Ave.; 686–0300. More of a business person's hostelry, this is a small hotel for transients and residents a few blocks south of Grand Central. The atmosphere is modest, the rooms plain. Continental breakfast. 110 rooms. *$68–$78.*

Holiday Inn–Coliseum. 440 W. 57th St., between Ninth and Tenth Aves.; 581–8100. A bit off the beaten track, but the location avoids a lot of traffic for those arriving via the Jersey approaches to the city. Decor and room appointments conform to the standards of the chain. Rooftop pool and kennel. 600 rooms. *$89.*

Howard Johnson's Motor Lodge. Eighth Ave. between 51st and 52nd Sts.; 581–4100. Right in the heart of the theater district and a few blocks from "Restaurant Row." Color televisions, radio, in-room movies. Free guest parking. Cocktail lounge and restaurant. 300 rooms. *$67–$87.*

Iroquois. 49 W. 44th St.; 840–3080. Right next door to the posher Algonquin, this is an adequately serviceable family favorite. Weekly rates are even more attractive than the daily ones. *$45–$60.*

Lexington. 511 Lexington Ave.; 755–4400. This is a good hotel which was recently renovated. The rooms are more than adequate even if the decor is routine. If you care to trip the light fantastic Spanish-style, the *Chateau Madrid* supperclub is downstairs. 800 rooms. *$86.*

Mansfield. 12 W. 44th St.; 944–6050. The location is good, just off Fifth Ave., and not far from Times Square. The Harvard and Princeton clubs are virtually next door. There are no pretensions and the quarters are not for the fussy. The staff is particularly good for a hotel in this price range. 200 rooms. *$40–$48.*

Murray Hill. 42 W. 35th St.; 947–0200. A small hotel offering quiet in a busy neighborhood. Pleasant, large rooms. Near *Altman's* and *Lord & Taylor,* but not in the Murray Hill district itself. 140 rooms. *$50.*

Ramada Inn–Midtown. 790 Eighth Ave., between 48th & 49th Sts.; 581–7000. Center of the theater district. Color televisions, radio, in-room movies. Free guest parking. Cocktail lounge and rooftop restaurant. Rooftop pool (seasonal). 370 rooms. *$71–$91.*

Roger Smith. 501 Lexington Ave.; 755–1400. An unexceptional business-man's hotel near Grand Central. Its rooms are adequate and comfortable, though hardly distinguished. 200 rooms. *$71–$88.*

Royalton. 44 W. 44th St.; 730–1344. This quiet, dignified hotel is situated near the Harvard Club and the Algonquin. A favorite with visiting British business people. Good value for the price. 175 rooms. *$53–$95.*

Taft. Seventh Ave. and 50th St.; 247–4000. A very large old hotel a few blocks above Times Square and close to most theaters. The hotel is unpreten-tious—to be generous—and the rooms mostly modest. Its size makes it popular for meetings, conventions, and with travel groups. 1,300 rooms. *$55–$60.*

Travel Inn Motor Hotel. 515 W. 42nd St.; 695–7171. Almost beside the Manhattan-side Lincoln Tunnel exit, the location is particularly convenient for those entering the city from the west. Off the mainstream but convenient to the 42nd St. crosstown bus. Pool. Parking. 250 rooms. *$54–$60.*

Wales. 1295 Madison Ave.; 876–6000. The location on E. 92nd St. places guests in the heart of one of NYC's best neighborhoods, and close to the Metropolitan Museum of Art—though it is a mite uptown from the heart of the city. 100 clean and functional rooms, some with views of Central Park. *$35–$55.*

Wellington. 871 Seventh Ave.; 247–3900. Convenient to Carnegie Hall, the Coliseum, Broadway, and the Stage Deli. The rooms are contemporary but the hotel rundown. Provides most of the services of more expensive establishments to compensate. Used often by airline personnel. 700 rooms. *$54–$65.*

Windsor. 100 W. 58th St.; 265–2100. The accommodations here are consid-ered good but plain. No attempt is made to transport you to another world, but rather to give you solid comfort. Close to the Coliseum, Carnegie Hall, and Fifth Ave. 300 rooms. *$90–$100.*

Wyndham. 42 W. 58th St.; 753–3500. Modest though undistinguished, the Wyndham is close to Carnegie Hall, Fifth Ave., and Central Park. Functional rooms, no room service. A favorite among theatrical and musical folk. 225 rooms. *$76–$90.*

ROCK BOTTOM AND LOWER

Although a handful of establishments in the *Motels, Chains, and Simple But Practical* category offer accommodations in the $50-and-under bracket, we would find it difficult to recommend most others without telling you to look at what you're getting before you make a reservation—not usually a practical way of doing things if you're trying to plan ahead. Many YMCAs and YWCAs, however, have rooms at very reasonable rates—beginning with singles at $13 a night. Sometimes they are limited to students and other young people, but check with the individual Y for specifics. Also, as with regular hotels, it is essential to make reservations well in advance for weekends, holidays, and other peak periods. Among the possibilities in Manhattan (see the Yellow Pages for those in the other boroughs):

Allerton House, 130 E. 57th St.; $25 and up single, women only. *Martha Washington Hotel,* 29 E. 29th St.; $20 single, women only. *William Sloane*

House YMCA, 356 W. 34th St.; $18 single, $26 double; men and women. *West Side YMCA,* 5 W. 63rd St.; $19.50 single, men and a limited number of women. *Vanderbilt YMCA,* 224 E. 47th St.; $18 single, $26 double. Though they say they only accept men, they do also accept groups of women. *McBurney YMCA,* 215 W. 23rd St.; $15–$16 single, men only. *International House of New York,* 500 Riverside Dr.; $60–$75 per week, men and women. Accepts transient graduate students from May through August only.

THE OUTLYING BOROUGHS

Most of the hotels and motels outside Manhattan are grouped around two of the major metro airports—La Guardia and JFK, both of which are in Queens. Obviously the pace at these is going to be frantic, with guests constantly arriving and departing and with planes almost always buzzing overhead. Still, they are convenient for overnight stopovers, and those near JFK are also in close proximity to Aqueduct and Belmont racetracks. Prices indicated for the following generally reliable establishments are for doubles: **Hilton Inn at JFK,** 322–8700, *$71–$108;* **Holiday Inn of La Guardia,** 898–1225, *$87–$127;* **International TraveLodge at JFK,** 995–9000, *$77–$84;* **Howard Johnson's Kennedy Airport,** 659–6000, *$60–$65;* **Sheraton Inn La Guardia,** 446–4800, *$90.*

Two other nearby possibilities in the Bronx bear mentioning for their close driving proximity to the city: **Capri Whitestone,** 555 Hutchinson River Parkway at the Bronx Whitestone Bridge tollgate, 597–0600; and **Van Cortlandt,** 6393 *Broadway* at 256th St., 549–7272. Both have doubles available for under *$50.*

 HOW TO GET AROUND. For those using public transportation, a handy number to keep in mind is the *New York City Transit Information* phone, (212) 330–1234. Open 24 hours a day, they'll give you the best route from wherever you are to wherever you're going. If calling from a phone booth, however, have a few extra nickels ready—the wait "on hold" can be a while.

By subway: The city's extraordinary subway system is your best bet for speed-thrift-convenience—usually. Late at night, when waits between trains are much longer, safety is a problem. When traveling at night, stay at or near the center of the train. Police patrol is spotty, so the volunteer Guardian Angels group (look for them in their white T-shirts and red berets) do their civic best to deter foul play on the trains. The weekday rush hours, usually cruelly overcrowded, are particularly oppressive on very hot summer days.

Of course, you'll want to know what stop is closest to your destination. A pocket atlas—obtainable at book stores and in the magazine kiosk on the Times Square island (between 7th Ave. and Broadway, just north of 42nd St.)—superimposes subway routes onto the street maps. Once you've targeted the proper stop, check a map of the subway system—you can get one at any token booth or at the New York Convention and Visitors Bureau (at Columbus Circle). Subway maps also appear in the Yellow Pages for each borough. The map's main fault is that it is not drawn to scale. Rather, it enlarges areas such as downtown Brooklyn, mid-Manhattan and Jackson Heights, Queens, where many routes converge and mass changes from train to train occur at busy times. But it does help.

With the map you can utilize every stretch of track in the vast network. But remember to study it before you embark on a subway adventure. *Don't* grab a map as you rush to catch a train and expect to unfold and read it on a crowded platform en route. Use it patiently. You'll see, for example, that you can get from major terminals (Times Square; Roosevelt Ave.–Jackson Heights, Queens; Atlantic Ave.–downtown Brooklyn) to all but a few stops with no more than one change of train. And if you still have questions—about routes, schedules, rates—ask at a change booth or a conductor. Or call the Metropolitan Transit Authority, 330–1234.

A subway token costs 75 cents at press time. Reduced fares are offered Senior Citizens and the handicapped during certain hours. Note: You can use subway tokens on city buses, and get a free transfer, too.

Be cautious about using the subways after 7:00 P.M. If you must, stay on the platform in view of the entrance; on the train, travel in a middle car, near the conductor.

A trip to *Rockaway* (Queens) will cost an extra token each way south of *Broad Channel.* Staten Island has a surface train from the ferry at St. George to Tottenville.

Remember: Some trains have more than one route, depending on the time of day. It's all clearly explained on the map.

By automobile. While we urge all visitors not to attempt touring Manhattan by automobile, some people may wish to have a car at their disposal for trips to the outlying boroughs or for travel to other areas. It is worth noting that car-rental rates are considerably cheaper when you pick up a car at one of the airports than they are when renting from midtown locations operated by the same companies. Similarly, parking cars at centrally located midtown hotels is far more expensive than leaving them at lots and garages on the far west side of the island. Just make sure of the hours these garages are open so that you'll be able to retrieve your car when you want to. For short stays in the theater district, the Municipal Garage, which can be entered from 53rd and 54th Sts. between Broadway and Eighth Aves., is relatively inexpensive. In other garages, don't be surprised having to pay $8 to $15 for two hours' parking. Many restaurants (including Windows on the World at the World Trade Center) will "validate" your parking stub, entitling you to a discount or free parking at *designated* garages. The city itself attempts to discourage city drivers with a 14 percent parking tax added onto every bill.

Trying to drive around in Manhattan can be an educational, if searing, experience. The main drawbacks: heavy traffic, scarcity of legal parking spots, and very expensive garages—and unbelievable, car-wracking potholes. The police in Manhattan *will* quickly remove an illegally parked car from a zone marked "tow away," and it will cost at least $65 *in cash* to get it back. (You'll also get a parking violation ticket!) No excuse or plea sways the officers who man the West Side pier where cars are stored (these may be argued later in court), so prepare to pay. Better yet, don't drive or park illegally, or, best of all, forget about driving, except on weekends and holidays.

If you insist on driving, let's take the parkways first. *Manhattan's West Side Highway* is undergoing repairs south of 72nd St. and is closed south of 57th St. Its future is uncertain. North of there, it is sometimes referred to as the *Henry Hudson Parkway,* there is also inevitably traffic-snarling construction and/or repair work going on. It parallels the Hudson and meeting I–95 where the George Washington Bridge (to New Jersey) becomes the *Cross-Bronx Expressway* (to the Bronx and New England or to Long Island via the Triborough Bridge). The West Side Highway continues north, crossing the Harlem River into the West Bronx. It leaves the city above Van Cortlandt Park and goes through Yonkers into Westchester.

On the east side of Manhattan, with access to the Brooklyn Bridge, the *Franklin D. Roosevelt Drive* (also called *East River Drive*) runs from the Battery to 125th St. and to the bridges to Queens (Triborough) and the Bronx (Willis Avenue). The road still continues beyond 125th St., however, along the east side of Manhattan, under the name *Harlem River Drive.* On it, you can get to upper Manhattan (Washington Heights and Inwood sections) or cut off to I–95 (George Washington Bridge west, Cross-Bronx Expressway east). The F.D.R. Drive, being rehabilitated one portion at a time, is old, twisting, subject to dense traffic and, in a heavy rain, flooding.

The *Bronx* has three big, relatively new roads. The *Cross-Bronx Expressway* (I–95) passes through the Bronx at about 174th St. and has exits onto almost every major north-south avenue. From west to east, it also gives access to the *Major Deegan Expressway* (I–87, the southern extension of the Thruway).

The *Bronx River Parkway* (to White Plains and central Westchester) terminates at the new Bruckner Traffic Circle. At that gigantic interchange, you can go to New England via I–95 or eastern Queens via the Whitestone or Throgs Neck Bridges.

The Bruckner Circle also leads to another major highway in the borough, the *Bruckner Expressway,* which runs southwest to the Triborough Bridge. Use the bridge to reach Manhattan or Queens. If you don't take the Triborough, the same road also loops around the southern tip of the Bronx and heads up the west shore of that borough as the Major Deegan Expressway (I–87). It has exits for Yankee Stadium and for the Cross-Bronx Expressway, and moves out of the Bronx as the New York State Thruway, later passing by Yonkers Raceway.

The *Henry Hudson Parkway* runs up the west side of the Bronx, from Manhattan's West Side Highway, and leads to the *Saw Mill River Parkway,* among others.

Queens is accessible from the west by two highways. From the Triborough Bridge, the *Grand Central Parkway* runs through the northwestern communities of Astoria and Jackson Heights, passing La Guardia Airport and Shea Stadium. After an interchange with the *Long Island Expressway* (I–495), it dips south, touching Forest Hills and Kew Gardens, then bolts away to the northeast again, past Springfield Gardens and Queens Village. The Long Island Expressway runs fairly straight west to east from the Queens Midtown Tunnel (E. 36th St., Manhattan) as far as Rego Park (you'll see Lefrak City and other high-rise developments crowding in on both sides). Then it jogs northeast, connects via the *Grand Central Parkway* to Kennedy Airport and continues on to Nassau and Suffolk Counties. These two roads are the principal automotive corridors for commuters, shoppers and theatergoers from Long Island, and traffic is invariably formidable.

The main north-south highways in Queens are the *Brooklyn-Queens Expressway, Van Wyck Expressway,* and *Cross Island Parkway.* The first begins just east of the Triborough Bridge ("Brooklyn" exit from the Grand Central Parkway) and has interchanges with most major Queens thoroughfares as it passes over the mainly industrial western edge of that borough. The last exit in Queens is to the Long Island Expressway (L.I.E.).

The Van Wyck, important as the road to Kennedy Airport, connects with the *Southern State Parkway* for Nassau County. It intersects the Grand Central Parkway (which you must take to get onto the L.I.E.) and then becomes the Whitestone Expressway (I–678) through Whitestone and Bayside, Queens, on its way to the Bronx Whitestone Bridge. The Van Wyck is almost invariably— except, maybe, at 3:30 A.M.—snarled with traffic; leave early if you plan to use it.

The Cross Island starts in the north at the Whitestone Bridge and roughly parallels the north shore of Queens until it crosses Union Turnpike (a city street). Then it angles south past the Belmont Racetrack and traces the borough's eastern border until it is swallowed up by the Southern Parkway just east of Kennedy Airport. (Note: as your map will confirm, Southern and Southern *State* Parkways are not quite the same.)

Let's continue into *Brooklyn* with the Southern Parkway. Known as the Belt Parkway or Shore Road in Brooklyn, it girdles the entire borough along the southeast boundary around to the L.I.E. at the northwest. Major exits include Cross Bay Blvd. (to Rockaway), Flatbush Ave. (to Rockaway's northern tip, Breezy Point, Gateway National Park, and eastern Flatbush), Ocean Parkway (to Sheepshead Bay) and Cropsey Ave. (to Coney Island and Bensonhurst). Along the way, you'll see signs for the Verrazano-Narrows Bridge to Staten Island. The Belt Parkway, after passing under that huge span, continues up the west shore past Bay Ridge (exit at 65th St.) and Borough Park (exit at Prospect Expressway). Finally, it reaches downtown Brooklyn and the three main routes to Manhattan (Battery Tunnel and the Brooklyn and Manhattan Bridges). Having now changed its name to the Brooklyn-Queens Expressway, the highway passes over Williamsburg and Greenpoint. If you're heading in the opposite direction—*from* Queens—you'll have a chance to cut over the Williamsburg Bridge onto Delancey Street in Manhattan.

CITY STREETS

Manhattan has probably the most regular and gridlike pattern, except that the *Lower East Side* and *Greenwich Village*, two of its most interesting and vital neighborhoods, lie outside the grid. (Another confusing area for out-of-town drivers: downtown—the *Wall Street* area.) Almost all the east-west streets and most of the north-south avenues are one-way. The two-way streets are spaced rather evenly from south to north: Canal, Houston, 14th, 23rd, 34th, 42nd, 57th, 72nd, 79th, 86th, 96th, 106th, 116th, 125th, 135th, and 145th. North of that, the island is considerably narrower and the last really wide one is 207th, just about a mile from the upper end of the borough.

All the north-south avenues are parallel except Broadway, whose traffic winds from northwest (the 225th Street Bridge to the Bronx) to southeast *(South Ferry)*. Traffic on Broadway is one-way southbound below 59th Street, two-way above there. An attractive parallel alternative to the West Side Highway (which is invariably under construction and snarled with traffic) is Riverside Drive from 72nd Street to the George Washington Bridge.

Central Park offers a lovely interior roadway. It is beautiful, especially at night, when thousands of distant skyscraper lights are framed by trees. This road is closed to motorists on weekends during the day and occasional summer evenings for the benefit of the city's many bike-riders.

The table on the next page will help you find your way around town.

Brooklyn is accessible from lower Manhattan via three bridges. The most northerly is the *Williamsburg*, from Delancey St., followed by the *Manhattan* (Canal St.) and the *Brooklyn* (Chambers St.). Broadway will take you to Canal St. or Chambers St., and for Delancey, take Bowery, which is just a continuation of 3rd Ave. below 9th St.

Brooklyn is often said to be impossible to navigate (perhaps Thomas Wolfe had this in mind when he wrote his famous short story, "Only the Dead Know Brooklyn"). But this reputation is undeserved. Most neighborhoods there are also grids; problems arise only because they meet one another at odd angles (note the half-left turns in the routes outlined below). Brooklyn's most famous street, Flatbush Ave., runs diagonally from northwest (at the Manhattan Bridge) to southeast *(Marine Park, Floyd Bennett Airfield* and the Belt Parkway). Along the way it passes through *Prospect Park* and very near the *Brooklyn Museum*. From the opposite direction, southwest, corner of Prospect Park, three wide and well-maintained roads run almost due south toward the Atlantic: Ocean Parkway, Ocean Ave. and Coney Island Ave. About two miles farther east, Utica and Ralph Avenues trace parallel paths through *Crown Heights, Brownsville,* and *Flatlands.*

Routes across the breadth of Brooklyn are more complicated. The only continuous one is Atlantic Ave., from the East River to the Queens border, on the north edge of the borough. In the center, take 39th St. (eastbound exit from the Belt Parkway) across *Borough Park* to McDonald Ave. Turn right, then quickly left on Ave. F, which you follow to Coney Island Ave. Turn right and

KEY TO MANHATTAN STREET NUMBERS

Here is a handy guide to finding most addresses in Manhattan. To get the cross street nearest to a building number, just cancel the last figure of the building's number. Divide remainder by two and add the key number below. Result is approximately the nearest cross street.

Ave. A, B, C, D 3	8th Ave. 9
1st Ave. 3	9th, 10th. 13
2nd Ave. 3	11th Ave. 15
3rd Ave. 10	Amsterdam Ave. 59
4th Ave. 8	Columbus Ave.. 59
5th Ave.	Lexington Ave.. 22
1 to 200 13	Madison Avenue 27
201 to 400 16	Park Ave. 34
401 to 600 18	West End 59
601 to 775 20	Central Park West .... *
776 to 1286 .... *	Riverside Drive .... *
Avenue of the	Broadway
Americas .... Deduct 12	1 to 754 ... Below 8th St.
7th Ave.	754 to 858 ...... Deduct 29
1 to 1800 12	858 to 958 ...... Deduct 25
Above 1800 20	Above 1000 ...... Deduct 31

To find street numbers on cross streets commence as follows:

EAST SIDE		WEST SIDE	
1 at	5th Avenue	1 at	5th Avenue
101 "	Park Ave., Park Ave.	101 "	6th Ave.
	South or 4th Avenue		(Ave. of Americas)
201 "	3rd Avenue	201 "	7th Avenue
301 "	2nd Avenue	301 "	8th Avenue
401 "	1st Avenue	401 "	9th Avenue
501 "	York or Avenue A	501 "	10th Avenue
601 "	Avenue B	601 "	11th Avenue

*Exceptions: Cancel last figure of house number and add or deduct key:

5th Avenue		Riverside Drive	
775 to 1286 .... Deduct 18		1 to 567 .... Add 73
Central Park West .... Add 60		Above 567 .... Add 78

Example: 350 Park Ave. Cancel last figure (0), divide by 2, and add key number (34). **Answer: 51st Street.**

at Ave. J, turn left. This avenue runs block after block through the lovely and peaceful residential area of *Flatbush.* When you cross Utica Ave., start watching for Flatlands Ave., where you take a half-left. Flatlands keeps you on the crosstown route, becoming Fairfield in the *East New York* region. Follow on to Fountain, the border between Brooklyn and Queens. Take a left to Linden Blvd., then a right. In about a mile, Linden meets the Southern Parkway, west of *Kennedy Airport.* If you continue on Linden, you'll soon reach the *Aqueduct Racetrack.*

The southern tier of the borough contains the comparatively conservative communities of *Bay Ridge, Fort Hamilton, Bensonhurst, Sheepshead Bay,* and *Canarsie.* The route through here is, from the west, 86th St. to Stillwell Ave., where you take a half left onto Ave. U and follow it east to Flatbush Ave. near *Marine Park.*

It might be helpful to know about a few main streets in *Queens.* One route across the borough, west to east, begins with Metropolitan Ave. (exit from the southbound Brooklyn-Queens Expressway). It passes through a mostly industrial area at first, but soon becomes the main street in the *Ridgewood-Glendale* neighborhood you've probably seen in the opening of *All in the Family.* This is Archie Bunker "country." In *Forest Hills,* a block beyond 75th Ave., go left onto Union Turnpike, which angles northeast through *Kew Gardens, Flushing,* and *Bellerose.* It passes two of Queen's largest parks, *Cunningham* and *Alley,* before crossing into Nassau County.

The lower level of the Queensboro (59th St.) Bridge out of Manhattan lets the driver choose between the borough's two busiest roads, Queens Blvd. and Northern Blvd. The first runs east, connecting with Woodhaven Blvd. (to *Rockaway*), and the L.I.E., then curves south connecting with the Van Wyck Expressway (JFK Airport or the Bronx Whitestone Bridge) and leads onto Hillside Ave. (eastern Queens communities, *Hillside, Hollis,* and *Queens Village.*)

Northern Boulevard runs northeast past *La Guardia Airport,* the Grand Central Parkway–Van Wyck Expressway interchange, Shea Stadium and the *Flushing, Auburndale,* and *Bayside* areas. It is State Rte. 25A and continues into Nassau at *Great Neck.*

North-south through streets are scarce in Queens. In western Queens, use the Brooklyn-Queens Expressway; in east Queens, the Cross Island Parkway. In between, Woodhaven Blvd. runs from Queens Blvd. (at about 97th St.) south to *Rockaway,* becoming Cross Bay Blvd. en route. The Whitestone/Van Wyck Expressway combination goes from the Whitestone Bridge to Kennedy Airport at about 136th St. and thus serves *Whitestone, Murray Hill, Corona, Kew Gardens, Jamaica,* and *South Ozone Park.*

The Bronx is probably the most confusing of the four most populous boroughs. In the west Bronx, the main north-south roads are Jerome Ave. and Grand Concourse, the latter much broader and more attractive, but ending about 205th St. (The Grand Concourse serves as the east-west divider for the Bronx.) Jerome Ave. runs from *Yankee Stadium* all the way to Westchester, with driving made somewhat more "challenging" by the pillars of the IRT elevated subway line. In the center of the borough, the Bronx River Parkway begins at the Bruckner Expressway, goes into Westchester at *Bronxville;* White Plains Road is parallel, about ½ mile to the east; it too has an "el" structure.

There are only a few east-west roads. Tremont Ave. begins just south of the 179th St. exit from the northbound Major Deegan Expressway (I-87) and runs through many different neighborhoods, rich and poor, eventually leading to the Throgs Neck Bridge. Fordham Rd., beginning at the bridge from 207th St., Manhattan, runs cross-borough at about 190th St., passing *Fordham University* and the *Bronx Zoo.* As US 1, it continues east under the name Pelham Parkway and ends with interchanges for the Hutchinson River Parkway and New England Thruway (both lead to Westchester).

The Staten Island Expressway crosses that borough's northern tier, directly off the Verrazano-Narrows Bridge from Brooklyn to the Goethals Bridge for New Jersey. Other limited access roads are planned around the perimeter, but, for now, Hyland Blvd. is the most reliable route to the more rural sections, like *Tottenville,* in Staten Island. It connects to the interchange with the recently completed West Shore Expressway which crosses south to the Outerbridge Bridge.

By bus: Of course, buses are slower than subways (during rush hour, they crawl along). But the routes are varied and, since there are almost always stops every two blocks, you can often get closer to your destination than on the subway. Midtown bookstores will sell you a large-print map and explanatory guide; it should make the subway look easy by comparison. In *Manhattan,* there are routes on all north-south avenues and major crosstown streets, as well as several trips that zigzag along a wandering path through (and sometimes out of) the borough. Look on the front of an approaching bus for a sign hinting at its destination. But to know *how* it gets there, you'll need to ask the driver or consult the map. Free maps are also available on some buses, but your best bet for a free map is the Convention and Visitors' Bureau, the MTA booths at Grand Central or Penn Stations, or the Yellow Pages.

Buses also cost 75 cents (to ride you need *exact* change, a token, or a transfer); Add-a-Ride tickets, which at press time are free, allow you to transfer from one route to a connecting line.

By ferry: The famous nickel ride from the Battery to *Staten Island* now costs 25¢ (round trip). It is most glorious at night when city lights create a spectacular show. The trip takes about half an hour each way, the boat moves swiftly, has a snack bar and room for cars, and passes close to the Statue of Liberty.

From the airports: Some hotels serve the airport terminals with their own limousines, so check when you make reservations. There are usually plenty of taxis available. The fare to Rockefeller Center, for example, will be about $12 from La Guardia, $25 (tip included) from Kennedy if traffic moves steadily. *JFK Express:* Subway-bus service, connecting points in Manhattan and Brooklyn with Kennedy International Airport, is available for $4.25, one way plus 75¢ for subway entry. Travelers can board a specially marked subway train (look for a white airplane on a blue background) at its starting point at 57th St. and Sixth Ave., or at seven other express stops: 47th–50th Sts. and Rockefeller

Center; 42nd St. and 6th Ave.; 34th St. and Herald Square at 6th Ave.; W. Fourth St. and Washington Square at 6th Ave.; Chambers St. and World Trade Center; Broad and Nassau Sts.; Jay St. and Borough Hall in Brooklyn. The subway will terminate at the Howard Beach–JFK Airport station and passengers will be picked up by buses that will transport them to any of the airline terminals. Passengers leaving the airport can take the service into Manhattan for the same fare. The JFK Express operates at 20-minute intervals, seven days a week, from 6 A.M. to 11 P.M., from both terminals, and takes about one hour.

Helicopter service into Manhattan is available, weather permitting, from all three major area airports. Heliports are located on the East River at Pier 6 in the Wall Street area, at 34th St., and at 60th St. Bell (943–5959) and Metropolitan (883–0999) both serve the Wall St. Heliport; Island (895–5372) goes to all three East River landing strips, and Helicopter Travel Inc. (888–6363) goes to 60th St. All are also available for sightseeing, with Metropolitan offering special camera mounts on its choppers. The fares vary from $28 to $49.50, one way.

The Carey Bus Co. will bring you into Manhattan for $3.50 from La Guardia or $5.00 from JFK. The La Guardia bus makes stops at Grand Central Terminal (42nd St. and Park Ave., by the Grand Hyatt Hotel) and the East Side Airline Terminal (38th St. between First and Second Aves.); the JFK bus stops at the East Side Airline Terminal only. And of course the buses go back out to the airports—leaving from the East Side terminal—at the same fares, and stop at all terminals at the airports.

By taxi: The legendary garrulous New York cabbie is fast fading from the NYC scene. But there are still over 30,000 licensed cab drivers in New York: a complete cross-section of ages, races and education levels—and motoring skills and knowledge of city geography.

Some will try to help you and save you money; others will want to take advantage of your inexperience in getting around the city or of the fact that the weather's nasty. If you carry an atlas, you can discuss the route of a long or complicated trip before you set out. The driver, by law, may not refuse to take any "orderly" passenger anywhere in the five boroughs, Nassau, Westchester, or to Newark Airport (the last three destinations entitle him to twice the fare shown on the meter). Neither may he charge each passenger separately when there is more than one passenger. These rules, along with the phone number of the city's Taxi and Limousine Commission, (212) 747–0930, are posted inside each cab. On the back of the roof-light, you'll find the vehicle's medallion (identification) number. Sharing of taxis is permitted between New York's airports and certain midtown Manhattan hotels. Inquire at the airport or at your hotel.

The fair is $1 for the first ninth of a mile, 10¢ for each subsequent ninth. You also pay for waiting time (including red lights and traffic jams). The driver expects, because he usually gets, about a 15 to 20% tip. A larger tip is appropriate if your destination is an area far from where he can reasonably expect to find a return-trip passenger. The rider pays bridge, tunnel and/or highway tolls. Certain cabs are also entitled to a 50¢ surcharge per ride between 8 P.M. and 6

A.M. Those drivers permitted to charge the extra fee will have a sign indicating so posted in the passenger compartment.

Whenever you're traveling within the city limits— *including all five boroughs* —be sure the meter is running. Don't let cabbies try to offer you a "bargain" off-the-meter rate. Those bargains just don't exist. Officially, a driver cannot refuse to take you anywhere within the five boroughs, though in practice this isn't always the case—particularly if you wish to go to the far reaches of Brooklyn or Queens or into crime-infested areas such as the South Bronx. If you know you're headed far, it may well be best to phone ahead for a cab (regular meter rates apply except for "car services"); check the Yellow Pages of the telephone directory for companies and phone numbers. Hailing a cab on the street is simple: available cabs have the number on their roofs lit. A wave of the hand should flag them down. Take their advice with a grain of salt, though. As stated, some are genuinely proud of the city and feel as if they are ambassadors of good will. Alas, many also prey on those who don't know their way around.

More and more fleets and independent drivers are using two-way radio equipment to handle telephone orders. There may be an extra charge for this service if reserved in advance; ask the dispatcher on the phone rather than waiting until the cab arrives and trying to work it out with the driver. Some of the better-known radio fleets are: *Minute Men,* 899–5600; *XYZ,* 685–3333; *Scull's Angels,* 567–7777; *Intra Boro,* 845–1100; *Ding-A-Ling,* 691–9191; and *UTOG,* 741–2000.

By limousine: If you really want to do it up right, there's only one way to go—chauffer-driven car. *Carey Cadillacs* have a fixed price of $25 per hour or 95¢ per mile. A special airport fee system runs along these lines: from midtown to JFK is $40, and from JFK domestic terminals $45, international terminals $55, to midtown; all fees mentioned plus tips and tolls. *Fugazy Continental* has chauffeur-driven, six-passenger Lincolns with television and stereo for $26 per hour or $1.10 per mile, whichever is greater.

On foot: Several famous sections of Manhattan are easily seen on foot. They include, but are not limited to, Greenwich Village, Midtown, Wall Street, Lincoln Center, and the UN-Turtle Bay area.

 TOURIST AND GENERAL INFORMATION SERVICES. The *New York Convention and Visitors Bureau* at Columbus Circle (in the funny little skyscraper on the south side) has multilingual aides to assist you in making your sightseeing plans. At their headquarters, you can also obtain subway and bus maps, and information about hotels, motels, and restaurants, as well as seasonal listings of the city's special entertainment attractions. The Bureau is open Monday to Friday, 9 A.M. to 6 P.M. weekends and holidays 10 A.M. to 6 P.M. call 397–8222.

For the Rockefeller Center area, there is a *Guided Tour and Information Desk* at 30 Rockefeller Plaza. Open daily except Christmas Day, this is the starting point for multilingual guided tours and a good source of brochures about the city in a variety of languages.

There is also the *Times Square Information Center*, 42nd Street and Broadway, 221–9869, open seven days from 9 A.M. to 6 P.M. Here you can find maps listing many of the city's attractions in French, German, Japanese, Portuguese, Russian, and Spanish, as well as in English. Also, the Times Square Ticket Center (TKTS) at Broadway and 47th Street (354–5800) and at 100 William Street in Lower Manhattan (344–3340) sell Broadway and off-Broadway tickets at half-price on the day of performance.

New York magazine, published weekly and incorporating the listings sections from the old *Cue* magazine, does an excellent job of keeping a finger on the pulse of New York City. Weekly features include comprehensive information on cultural events, shopping, sports, street fairs, walking tours, museums and galleries, activities for children, and all manner of special events. *New York* also maintains a free ticket service information phone— 986–5872, Monday to Friday, 12:30 to 6:30 P.M.—which will advise you regarding ticket availability for theater, dance, and concerts.

New Yorker magazine, most famous for its literary efforts, also has excellent theater, music, dance and movie reviews, and listings (with brief, pithy commentary) of what's happening at art galleries, museums, nightclubs, opera, and ballet.

The city's daily papers—*The New York Times, New York Post* and *Daily News*—list current attractions, with the Friday weekend sections always geared to the most promising upcoming events. On Fridays, too, both the *Times* and the *News* list theater ticket availability through that Sunday. The huge Sunday *Times* is perhaps the best buy in town, though, with its "Arts and Leisure" and "Guide" sections overflowing with useful entertainment information and ads.

Of the city's varied weekly newspapers, the *Village Voice* is the one to consult for the latest on pop music, jazz, modern dance, and off- and off-off-Broadway theater.

Weather forecasts, time, traffic conditions, sports information, a jazz hotline, your daily horoscope, jokes . . . all can be obtained over the phone. For these and other numbers consult the White Pages of the telephone directory or dial 976–1000 for individual numbers.

 RECOMMENDED READING. A selection of books for visitors with specialized interests:

The American Institute of Architects' *AIA Guide to New York City*, by Norval White and Elliot Willensky (Collier), is a comprehensive guide to city architecture and history. The Landmarks Preservation Committee of the City of New York published a booklet, *A Guide to New York City Landmarks*, that is sold at most city bookstores and cultural institutions, such as museums and libraries, usually for one dollar.

The Street Book, by Henry Moscow (Hagstrom), is, as its subtitle suggests, "an encyclopedia of Manhattan's street names and their origins" and a good source of city lore.

Manhattan Menus (Manhattan Menus Inc.), revised annually, is a compilation of approximately 175 menus from a representative cross-section of New York eateries, complete with prices and specialties of the house. For serious *gourmands,* there is Seymour Britchky's *The Restaurants of New York* (Random House) for an almost bite-by-bite account of meals at an equally wide variety of establishments.

The Lower East Side Shopping Guide, by Alan Teller and Sharon Greene (Shopping Experience, Inc.), is an oversize pamphlet-type publication that gives a store-by-store account of the wholesale/retail shops along Orchard, Grand, and their surrounding streets. Other similar guides will lead to you warehouse and discount outlets throughout the metropolitan area.

The New York Walk Book (Doubleday) is the joint project of the New York–New Jersey Trail Conference and the American Geographical Society. It gives detailed information and maps for trails in all parts of the state, with a special section devoted to the five boroughs.

 SEASONAL EVENTS. If New York City is normally overflowing with more exhibits, shows, and galleries than even its natives can take in, it is also home to numerous annual special events that range from car shows to ethnic food festivals, from the Ringling Bros., Barnum & Bailey Circus to the St. Patrick's Day Parade. As a general rule (of course there are exceptions), you can expect outdoor happenings to be free, although the temptation to purchase food or merchandise at most street fairs and carnivals will be high. Indoor events at the Coliseum (59th St. and Eighth Ave.), Madison Square Garden (32nd St. and Seventh Ave.), the Seventh Regiment Armory (66th St. and Park Ave.), and Lincoln Center (64th St. and Broadway) usually require the purchase of tickets. Phone numbers cited below are all in the 212 area code.

January. *The National Boat Show* and the *Greater New York Auto Show,* both open to trade and public, take over the Coliseum, showing off the latest, sleekest designs. Both are very popular, and the crowds on weekends especially can be overwhelming. Call 757–5000. . . . The *Winter Antiques Show* is resident at the Seventh Regiment Armory late in the month, featuring some of the nation's finest dealers and their latest acquisitions. Call 288–0200. . . . The spectacular *Ice Capades* glide and spin at Madison Square Garden for a two-week stint. Call 564–4400. . . . Rounding out the month is the explosive *Chinese New Year,* which arrives at the first full moon after January 21 (Tet, in the lunar calendar). Fireworks, food, and fun mark this 10-day celebration. Call 397–8222.

February. The two-day *Westminster Dog Show* finds hundreds of competitors strutting their stuff at Madison Square Garden. Call 682–6852. . . . *Black History Week* is marked at the American Museum of Natural History, Central Park West at 77th St., by way of films, exhibits and discussions. Call 873–1300. . . . The *Start Your Own Business Show* at the Coliseum attracts aspiring entrepreneurs of all kinds. Call 757–5000. . . . *White Sales*—offering huge savings on towels, linens, and other merchandise—fill the major department stores with bargain-seekers on Washington's and Lincoln's Birthday weekends.

March. The Coliseum hosts two popular events: The *Sport, Camping, Travel and Vacation Show,* where you can buy direct from the exhibitors; and for stay-at-homers, the *Antiques and Garden Show.* Call 757-5000. . . . You don't have to be Irish to tag along in the *St. Patrick's Day Parade* on the 17th. Just follow the green stripe down the middle of Fifth Avenue and join the politicians and tens of thousands of marchers all decked out in green. . . . If that's not enough of a three-ring circus for you, get your tickets for the *Ringling Bros., Barnum & Bailey Circus* at Madison Square Garden. The good seats at the kiddie matinees sell out first for performances through the end of May. Call 564-4400.

April. The *Easter Parade* (admittedly, sometimes in March) starts at St. Patrick's Cathedral, Fifth Ave. at 49th St., immediately following the morning services. Put on your Sunday best and stroll uptown with the rest of the crowd. . . . For children, in the past there's been an *Easter Egg Rolling Contest* in Central Park, but the event has grown so popular, and the crush so bad, that its future is in question. Check the newspapers to be sure. . . . When the New York Knicks are contenders, the *pro basketball playoffs* can be seen at Madison Square Garden. Tickets are very difficult to get so try to reserve early. The same is true for the Garden's resident hockey team, the *Rangers.*

May. Parades abound: *Armed Forces Day, Brooklyn Bridge Day, Martin Luther King, Jr., Memorial Day* and *Norwegian Independence Day.* For dates and route information call 397-8222. . . . The street festival season gets underway in earnest with the *Ninth Avenue International Festival,* a multi-ethnic feast (plus much free entertainment) that stretches along Ninth Ave. from 37th to 59th Sts. Call 581-7029. . . . *The Park Avenue Antiques Show* is a week-long, nationally recognized display of American and European collectibles at the Seventh Regiment Armory. . . . The *Washington Square Outdoor Art Exhibit* sprawls out covering lower Fifth Ave. at Washington Square Park, Broadway, University, and La Guardia Place for three weekends beginning the last weekend in May. There's *some* good art to be found here, but most is pedestrian and uninspired. . . . *Memorial Day Weekend* is marked by parachute and acrobatic flying shows at Brooklyn's Coney Island. . . . Little Italy comes alive for the *Feast of St. Anthony* on Mulberry St. for the last weekend of the month. You'll be overcome by the luscious smells of sizzling calzone (oversize cheese-filled dumplings, deep-fat fried), grilled sausages, and fresh shellfish. Rides, raffles, and games of chance and skill are also featured. Call 226-2978.

June. The *Feast of St. Anthony of Padua* continues the Italian festivities a wee bit north on Sullivan St. between Houston and Spring Sts. Call 777-2755. . . . It's *Basically Bach* (with a few other well-tempered selections) at Lincoln Center's Avery Fisher Hall for six days—call 874-6770—while the free *Guggenheim Band Concerts* commence across the Lincoln Center Plaza in Damrosch Park. The latter run through August Wednesdays through Fridays, and Sundays, from 8 to 10 P.M. Call 867-8290. . . . George Wein's *Kool Jazz Festival* brings a large congregation of jazz musicians and fans together for 10 days (through July 4th) of concerts all around the city—in concert halls, on the Staten Island ferry, and in the parks. Call 787-2020. . . . The *New York Women's*

Jazz Festival overlaps the Kool fête for eight days. Sponsored by the Universal Jazz Coalition, call 924–5026. . . . *Shakespeare in the Park,* under the auspices of Joseph Papp's New York Shakespeare Festival Public Theater, brings the Bard free to the minions at the Delacorte Theater in Central Park (enter the park at 81st Street from either Central Park West or Fifth Ave.). The line for tickets, which are distributed on the day of performance only beginning at 6 P.M., forms early in the afternoon. Call 535–5630. . . . The *Metropolitan Opera* also brings free concert performances of complete operas to various city parks during the month. No tickets necessary, but you might want to stake out your space early, and bring a blanket and a picnic dinner. Call 755–4100. . . . *Museum Mile* finds Fifth Ave. turned into a pedestrian mall as the ten museums between 82nd and 105th Sts. open their doors for a special midweek evening. . . . The *Great Irish Fair* carries the spirit of St. Patrick into the summer with a two-day festival along the Brooklyn waterfront. . . . Parades mark *Puerto Rican Day* and a *Salute to Israel.* Call 397–8222.

July. The *Fourth of July* is America's Independence Day and the fireworks literally begin at 9:15 P.M., sponsored by Macy's Department Store and most recently emanating from barges on the waters around the Statue of Liberty. Check newspapers for best vantage points and for details regarding the *Fourth of July Harbor Festival,* the *Old New York Festival,* and the parachutists and aerobatics shows at Brooklyn's Coney Island. . . . It's *Mostly Mozart* at Avery Fisher Hall for the next six weeks, while Lincoln Center Plaza is given over to the *American Crafts Festival* for the first two weekends of the month. More than 300 craftsmakers sell their leather, furniture, glass, jewelry, and other wares with children's activities including mime, singing, magic and clowns. Call 677–4627. . . . Joe DiMaggio usually shows up for *Old Timers' Day* at Yankee Stadium. Call 293–6000. . . . More Italian-flavored street festivities are part of the nightly (for ten days) *Lady of Pompeii Feast* on Cornelia St. south of Bleecker St. in Greenwich Village. Call 989–6805.

August. The *New York Philharmonic* takes a portable stage to Central, Clove Lakes, Prospect, and other city parks for a series of alfresco performances. Blankets and picnics in order once again. Call 755–4100. . . . *Lincoln Center Out-of-Doors,* at that cultural center's Plaza, is a three-week marathon of free shows drawn from all the performing arts. Call 877–1800. It's the Mets' turn for *Old Timers' Day* at Shea Stadium. Call 672–3000. . . . The annual *Bluegrass Club of New York Amateur Band Contest* is held at the South Street Seaport Museum Pier. Call 687–9000. . . . The *U.S. Open* at the National Tennis Center in Queens' Flushing Meadow Park features top international pros competing for top national honors. Call 592–8000.

September. The *San Gennaro Festival* on Mulberry and Grand Streets is yet another chance to fill up on Little Italy's best goodies—for 11 nights running! Call 226–9546. . . . German-Americans celebrate *Steuben Day*—honoring one of the Europeans who aided the Colonists during the Revolutionary War—with a parade commencing on East 86th St. Call 397–8222. . . . *New York Is Book Country* is the theme on Fifth Ave. from 47th to 57th Sts. for one Sunday this month, with major publishers setting up kiosks in order to tout their authors' latest literary efforts. Some authors are in attendance, there are some publishing demonstrations, and street performers line the route. Call 752–9880. . . . The *New York Film Festival* previews art films as well as the latest soon-to-be-released Hollywood blockbusters for three weeks at Alice Tully Hall, Lincoln Center. Tickets are available—and often sold out—in advance. Call 362–1911. . . . The *TAMA Country Fair* and *Festival of the Americas* street fairs, with about 800 booths each, get one Sunday apiece on Third and Sixth Avenues, respectively. For TAMA information, call 674–5094; for Festival of the Americas, call 921–8122. . . . Brooklyn's Atlantic Avenue is turned into an *Atlantic Antic* for a celebration of Middle Eastern foods and crafts. Call 783–4469.

October. For walkers, parades: *Columbus Day, Pulaski Day, Hispanic Day,* and *Veterans Day* (for dates and routes call 397–8222); for runners, the 26-mile *New York City Marathon* begins on the Staten Island side of the Verrazano-Narrows Bridge and ends at Tavern-on-the-Green in Central Park. Hopefully, everyone starts and finishes on the last Sunday of the month. Call 758–6880. . . . The fall foliage season is the perfect time for a hike through any of the city's parks, with the Cloisters up at the northern tip of Manhattan island perhaps the most spectacular of all. . . . It's *United Nations Day* on the 24th, though there are no regular, official ceremonies. . . . *Old Home Day* at the Richmond Restoration, 441 Clarke Ave., Staten Island, finds the doors open to period houses throughout the area. Call 351–1611. On Halloween there is a colorful and somewhat bizarre *Halloween Parade* in Greenwich Village between Bank St. and Washington Sq., starting at about 5:30 P.M.

November. The *International Ski and Winter Sports Show* stops at the Coliseum with the latest fashions for the slopes. Call 757–5000. . . . *Macy's Thanksgiving Day Parade* is a thrill to see live as it wends its way down Central Park West (beginning about 8:30 from 77th St.), Broadway, and Seventh Ave. Everyone's wide-eyed as Snoopy, Bullwinkle, and other favorite cartoon characters march by as building-high balloons. Even Santa makes his first seasonal appearance! Call 397–8222. . . . As of Thanksgiving weekend, the windows at *Lord & Taylor, Altman's,* and *F.A.O. Schwarz* are done up with spectacular, moving Christmas displays. Go at night, if possible, for the lines during the day at Lord & Taylor especially can be long and deep. . . . The *National Horse Show* trots around Madison Square Garden for six days. Call 546–4400. The National Hot Rod and Custom Car Show appears at the Coliseum, noon to 11:00 P.M. on the Friday, Saturday, and Sunday following Thanksgiving. Admission charge.

December. The annual Christmas tree lighting ceremony at *Rockefeller Center,* 47th Street between Fifth and Sixth Ave., is always an event. Call 489–2947. . . . Tchaikovsky's *Nutcracker Suite Ballet* is the seasonal offering by the New York City Ballet at Lincoln Center's State Theater. The regular company is augmented by children from the School of American Ballet, and there are daily performances—which invariably sell out—for about three weeks. Call 870–5500. . . . For crafty holiday shopping try the *American Crafts Holiday Festival* at NYU Loeb Student Center, La Guardia Place and Washington Square South. Plenty of jewelry, clothing, furniture, glass, leather, and other goods. Call 677–4627. . . . And if you're lucky enough to be ringing out the old and ringing in the new in New York City, you can join the *New Year's Eve* revelry in Times Square as thousands watch an illuminated ball descend from the top of the

Allied Chemical building at the stroke of midnight. Alternately, there are midnight celebrations (complete with fireworks and live music) in *Central* and *Prospect Parks.*

 FREE EVENTS. Summer is especially full of outstanding free cultural offerings throughout New York City. Both the Metropolitan Opera (in late June and early July) and the New York Philharmonic (in late July and early August) travel the various city parks giving free performances—the Philharmonic concerts in Central and Prospect Parks usually augmented by fireworks accompanying the *1812 Overture* or some similarly suitable work. The Goldman Band concerts are held all summer long at the bandshell in Damrosch Park, in the southwest corner of Lincoln Center. Lincoln Center Plaza is also the scene of numerous free events, from the American Crafts Fair, held for two weekends beginning July 4th, to three weeks of daily performing-arts shows in August. A handful of Kool Jazz Festival concerts around the end of June are also free. At the Delacorte Theater in Central Park there are free Shakespeare productions, while the city's various other parks have extensive schedules of free dramatic, pop, jazz, classical, dance, and other offerings. (Call the individual parks or borough presidents' offices for full listings.)

The Mall in Central Park south of the 72nd St. transverse and the area north around Bethesda Fountain are always overflowing with street entertainers—musicians, mimes, jugglers, magicians, and the like—who perform summer weekends and holidays from about noon to dusk. Most, though, do pass the hat.

Fireworks can be seen weekly throughout the summer at Coney Island on Tuesdays and at Rockaway's Playland on Wednesdays. On the Fourth of July, Macy's sponsors a spectacular half-hour-long fireworks display from different parts of New York Harbor. And on New Year's Eve, rain or snow or bone-chillingly cold, Central and Prospect Parks shine from the glimmer of overhead lightshows.

Beginning with the Ninth Ave. International Fair in mid-May, city streets are given over to carnivals, street fairs, and festivals right through to the end of September. Strolling and entertainment are always free at these extravaganzas (the Ninth Ave. fair attracts half a million people annually; other smaller ones a few thousand on a single block) although there's always food, rides, and merchandise to be bought. Call the Mayor's Office of Street Activities (566–2506).

Many of the attractions in the *Museums, Historic Sites,* and *Walking Tours* sections of this book are free—with some additional museums asking only a voluntary contribution. Others that usually have fees, such as the Guggenheim and the Whitney, are free Tuesday evenings. Tickets for television shows—live or taped—are always free, and available at the Convention and Visitors Bureau, or frequently from station personnel stationed outside the NBC and CBS buildings. All of the city's parks, zoos, and gardens are free, with the exception that there is a charge at the Bronx Zoo Fridays and weekends.

Floral displays begin with those at Rockefeller Center's Channel Gardens on

Fifth Ave., but include Easter and Christmas displays in the Pan Am Building and a Spring Flower Show at One World Trade Center. At the Citicorp Center, there are daily (including weekend) popular and classical music programs in the Atrium, 153 E. 53rd St. Lincoln Center's Library of the Performing Arts, Amsterdam at 66th St., has free concerts on weekdays at 4:00, Saturdays at 2:30. Each Sunday at 5:00, there are jazz vespers at St. Peter's Church, 54th St. at Lexington Ave. Other new office buildings and culturally minded religious institutions also feature free performances, with increasing regularity; check the weekly entertainment pages of the Sunday *Times, Village Voice, New York,* and *New Yorker* for specifics.

Free outdoor art exhibits are common from spring to fall. Among the more famous are the Washington Square Outdoor Art Show, late May and early June, Greenwich Village; and the Brooklyn Heights Promenade Fine Arts Show, in May. The Canal Street Flea Market, 335 Canal St. (near Chinatown), is open Saturday and Sunday. Also in lower Manhattan is a self-guided Heritage Trail, which you can pick up anywhere, though Trinity Church at the head of Wall Street is as good a place as any to begin. The Manhattan Art & Antiques Center, 1050 Second Ave. (55th St.) has free admission to its complex of 72 shops, open every day. Up in Central Park, The Dairy (65th St., west of the zoo) has a free slide show every 30 min. from Tues. to Sun. There are also free guided park tours Wed., Sat., and Sun. at 12:30. Finally, you can tour a winery (the only one functioning in Manhattan) by calling at Schapiro's, 126 Rivington St., Sundays 10 to 6, every hour on hour. (Phone 674–4404 for weekday appointment.)

For other free tours, refer to the *Tours and Special-Interest Sightseeing* section, which follows.

TOURS AND SPECIAL-INTEREST SIGHTSEEING. Before you begin walking or busing around town, we urge you to take in *The New York Experience,* a multisensory film which will introduce you to the city and help you get your bearings. (Lower plaza, McGraw-Hill Building, 1221 Sixth Ave., between 48th and 49th sts., 869–0345.) Adults, $3.90; $2 for children under 12. Shows are daily every hour on the hour from 11 A.M. to 7 P.M.; Sundays, noon to 6 P.M.

General-interest bus tours are still available from midtown. *Gray Line of New York,* 900 Eighth Ave., 397–2600, offers 10 different tours covering uptown, downtown, and out-of-town. *Manhattan Sightseeing Bus Tours,* 150 W. 49th St., 245–6641, also has 10 tours. Reservations necessary. *Crossroads Sightseeing,* 701 Seventh Ave., 581–2828, covers many well-known Manhattan spots. *Short Line Sightseeing International,* 168 W. 46th St., 354-4740, also has good touring choices.

(Unfortunately, the city-sponsored, self-guided Culture Bus tours have been discontinued.)

If you want to skim the waters of the Big Apple, *Circle Line* cruises leave Pier 83 at the foot of W. 43rd St. and 12th Ave., 563–3200, approximately every 45 minutes beginning midmorning. Details of the sights en route are included in the introduction to the *Walking Tours* section, but it's a leisurely 2½- to 3-hour ride around the entire island. Adults $8.50, children $4.00. April–November. More intimate and adventurous are the daily sailings of the triple-masted schooner *Pioneer* from the South Street Seaport Museum Pier. $15 for adults, $7.50 for children and advance reservations (766-9020) are necessary. Riders are invited to help raise the sails and steer—to relax, picnic, and enjoy the view. Or you can take to the air via *Island Helicopter,* heliport at the foot of E. 34th St. on the East River, 683–4575. Flights day or night, from $15.00 per person. *The Petrel* is a sailing-yacht cruise of New York Harbor—great close-up views of the Statue of Liberty, Ellis Island, more—leaving from Battery Park 4 or 5 times daily, starting at 12 noon. Weekdays there is a lunchtime cruise, 45 minutes, for $5.50. Most cruises are 2 hours, and cost about $13.00. There are moonlight cruises leaving at 9:30 P.M. on weekdays and 8:00 P.M. weekends. 825-1976.

Still another unique perspective of Manhattan can be had by taking a hansom cab—horse-drawn carriage—through Central Park, down Fifth Ave., or wherever the spirit guides you. Carriages are always lined up at 59th St. and Fifth Ave., just outside the Plaza Hotel. The usual routes are a brief ramble through the park, or down Fifth Ave. for eight or ten blocks and back up Sixth Ave., but drivers will tailor a trip to your desires. It is not an inexpensive mode of travel, though, given the leisurely pace and the possibility of hitting traffic. Official rates are $17.00 for the first half hour, and $5.00 for each additional 15 minutes. And it is suggested to confirm the rate with the driver you choose before setting out.

Tours of some individual attractions in the city are also popular. These are described fully as part of the *Walking Tours* section but a brief reminder that they are available is in order. Among them: the *New York Stock Exchange,* 1 Wall St., 623–3000. Self-guided via automated narration and participant-activated exhibits. Mon.–Fri., 10:00 A.M.–4:00 P.M. Free; *United Nations,* First Ave. at 45th St., 754–7710. Hour-long tours are run daily, 9:00 A.M.–4:45 P.M. Adults $3, students $1.75, children $1.25; *Rockefeller Center* (enter 30 Rockefeller Plaza from 49th or 50th Sts. between Fifth and Sixth Aves.), (212) 489–2947. Tours include walk through NBC studios, Radio City Music Hall (when there's no performance) and general area, leaving the tour desk every 30 minutes from 9:30 A.M.–5:30 P.M. daily. Adults $3.35, children $2.85, senior citizens $2. *Radio City Music Hall,* 50th St. at Sixth Ave., 246–4600—call for schedule and prices; *Lincoln Center,* Broadway at 64th St., 877–1800—Avery Fisher Hall is the starting point every half hour between 10:00 A.M. and 5:00 P.M. daily, Adults $4.25, students and Senior Citizens $3.75, children $2.75.

For offbeat tours, contact *Adventure On A Shoestring, Inc.,* 300 W. 53rd St., 265–2663, and meet new people in unusual surroundings at budget-minded but imaginative events. You can visit clubs, restaurants, and theaters, escorted by the people at *Big Apple At Night,* 59 E. 54th St., 371–3455. *Discover New York* is a series of six Sunday-afternoon walking tours, sponsored by the *Municipal Art Society Tours,* 457 Madison Ave., 935–3969. Brooklyn Heights, Upper West Side, Upper Fifth Avenue are some of the areas on the itinerary; $5.00 per person. Other walking tours are listed regularly in the *Cue* section of *New York* magazine.

In addition to all of the above, and the museums, historic sites, and places to be seen on walking tours, all of which are described under those entries in this book, there are other fascinating places which don't fit into such convenient categories, yet deserve mention. Here are a select few:

Guinness World Records Exhibit Hall, Empire State Bldg., 34th St. and Fifth Ave., 947–2335. Over 200 exhibits, including moving light displays, replicas, etc., all from that wonderful book.

The city's police force is one of the best in America when it comes to human relations with the population they serve. You can look in on their training facility, the *Police Academy,* 235 E. 20th St., 477–9700, and also see a museum devoted to the history of the department.

Supreme Court of New York County and the *Criminal Court* are located at 60 and 100 Centre St., respectively. If a publicized trial interests you, or if you simply want to see the routine business of a court, they—and smaller courts—are open to the public.

The *Mormon Visitors Center,* Broadway & 65th St., 595–1825, features archeological exhibits in replica of artifacts from both Eastern and Western cultures. A diorama with talking mannequins relates the story of a contemporary Mormon family, a 19th-century pioneer family, and a *Book of Mormon* family of 2,000 years ago. Open seven days, 10:00 A.M.–8:00 P.M. Free.

You may not readily associate New York with the cotton crop, but it has the *Cotton Exchange,* 4 World Trade Center, 938–2650, one of the busiest futures markets in the world. If you call ahead, you can arrange for someone to meet you and briefly explain how the trading works.

If you're interested in—or puzzled by—our nation's fiscal and monetary policies, visit the New York *Federal Reserve Bank,* 33 Liberty St., 791–5000. You must call a week in advance to set up a tour, but they will then explain the Federal Reserve System and central banking, show you check processing and the gold vault.

Whether a new product on the market attains the Good Housekeeping Seal of Approval (*Good Housekeeping* being a major homemaking magazine) is determined at the *Good Housekeeping Institute,* 959 Eighth Ave., 262–6467. Morning and afternoon tours visit laboratories for appliances and chemicals, the needlework center, test kitchens and beauty clinic.

Gallery Passports, 1170 Broadway, 686–2244, organizes tours to artists' studios and lofts in the city and to other art attractions outside New York that can be seen in a day (Baltimore, Md., and Williamstown, Mass., for instance). Sept.–May.

The largest Black community in America is in upper Manhattan and the *Penny Sightseeing Company,* 303 W. 42nd St., 247–2860, offers a tour through Harlem. Ask especially about their special Saturday-night tours.

The largest theatrical community in America is in mid-Manhattan and you can glimpse its workings close up through *Backstage on Broadway,* 228 W. 47th St., 575–8065. The tour guides are professionals from all branches of the industry and the program draws praise from educators around the country.

Con Edison, New York's public utility for electricity, has installations all over the metropolitan area and several of these are visited by bus provided by the company. Con Ed's *Energy Museum,* 145 E. 14th St., 599–3434, displays the past, present, and future of electricity. Closed Sun. and Mon.

If you've never been in a transoceanic port before, the busy piers and luxury liners may prove fascinating indeed. The newspaper shipping pages list departure schedules, and if you call the line for its visiting policy (on ocean liners visitors are generally allowed about two hours before sailing), you'll be ready to stroll the decks while passengers board.

PARKS. These cover nearly a sixth of the city's land and provide welcome contrasts to its concrete canyons and crowded sidewalks. Vandalism and inadequate maintenance have taken their toll, but a spirit of preservation and renewal is increasingly in evidence.

The parks may disappoint those seeking pure pastoral beauty and restful solitude. They *are* beautiful—there's something very special about looking at the skyscrapers of Manhattan from a snow-covered Central Park, where cross-country skiers wend their way across the Sheep Meadow; or getting a feel of New England during the fall foliage season in the Bronx's Van Cortlandt Park. But New York's parks have gradually evolved into recreational and cultural areas, especially in summer.

If there's a promenade for strollers you can rest assured that there'll be street entertainers—musicians, magicians, jugglers, and even comedians—all along the route. More formally, both the Metropolitan Opera and the New York Philharmonic offer series of free park concerts during the summer, travelling from one borough to the next. And it is not unusual for these concerts to draw several hundred thousand fans a night. (Take a blanket, a picnic dinner, and arrive late afternoon for an 8:30 performance if you want to plant yourself within view of the stage.)

There are marathons, walk-a-thons, and races for men, women, children and handicapped in the different parks. There are weekend festivals sponsored by various ethnic, civic, and commercial organizations. The *Parks Department* sponsors drama, film, poetry readings, music and dance throughout the boroughs, with schedules available in local newspapers and magazines (see *Tourist Information* section). And of course there are miles and miles of trails for leisurely walking (not recommended for night), lakes for boating, bicycle lanes for two-wheel enthusiasts . . . and more.

Unique among Metropolitan New York parks is Gateway National Recreation Area, a federally administered park that stretches through parts of Brooklyn (Floyd Bennett Field, a former navy airstrip, is where numerous special events are staged), Queens (the Jamaica Bay Wildlife Refuge on Cross Bay Blvd. is a lure to birdwatchers from all over, while Jacob Riis Park is one of the city's most popular—and cleanest—beaches), Staten Island, and New Jersey. Ranger-guided tours, hikes, and educational programs are offered regularly all year round. Call the Park Authority for dates and times at 474–5606.

We must also reluctantly note that, with the exception of nights when there are special planned events, most of New York's parks are not very safe strolling areas after dark.

MANHATTAN

Central Park has 840 acres which include lakes for rowing (you may rent a boat, at the Loeb Boat House), stable and trails for horseback riding, dozens of baseball diamonds and playfields, a bocci green, a zoo, and a skating rink. (The Wollman Skating Rink was being renovated as of this writing, with its scheduled date of completion not available.)

The New York Shakespeare Festival makes use of the Delacorte Theater near the 81st St. entrances (from either Central Park West or Fifth Ave.) for free performances of the classics. (Tickets are given out on a first-come, first-served basis beginning at 6 P.M. the night of the performance only; the line for tickets starts forming in early afternoon.)

The Goldman Band Shell is in the Mall midway between East and West 72nd Street, and has frequent free concerts. The Mall itself is where most of the park's regular street performers congregate (best times for a stroll are Saturday or Sunday afternoons from May to October, from noon to dusk). North of 72nd St. is the Bethesda Fountain, another popular meeting place right by the edge of a lake. On nearby Conservatory Pond, you may see people maneuvering their battery-operated remote-controlled model sailboats in good weather; the boats are stored in a building to the east of the pond. A jogger's track and bridle trail circle the Reservoir in the 80s. The Metropolitan Museum of Art borders the park at Fifth Ave. and 82nd St.

Cars are banned from all park roads except the east-west transverses almost all but rush hours.

Riverside Park runs along the Hudson River beginning at 72nd St. and north through Harlem. Invariably less crowded than Central Park, Riverside is a neighborhood outpost, full of families and sunbathers. A favorite stroll is along the promenade by the 79th Street Boat Basin, where a number of yachts serve as full-time city residences.

Fort Tryon Park at the northern tip of Manhattan, high over the Hudson, runs south of the Cloisters. Besides the view of the Palisades across the river there is an attractive but somewhat wild garden area.

Battery and *Washington Square Parks* in lower Manhattan are small and don't even pretend to bring the country to the city. The latter, in fact, is mostly concrete. However, Battery Park gives a good harbor view and cooling breezes off the water in summer, while Washington Square is an active mingling ground for Greenwich Villagers. Some sing, play guitars, and smoke dope; some argue social issues, some play chess, and some romp with their children and pets. Washington Square is also the scene of a very New Orleans-like carnival every Halloween night (late in October).

Central Park — Reservoir

The Great Lawn

The New Lake

The Ramble

The Lake

Conservatory Pond

The Mall

The Sheep Meadow

Heckscher Ballfields

The Pond

CENTRAL PARK WEST

FIFTH AVE.

86TH / 85TH / 81ST / 77TH / 72ND / 67TH / 66TH / 65TH / 60TH

85TH / 79TH / 72ND / 66TH / 65TH / 60TH

Columbus Circle

CENTRAL PARK SOUTH

Grand Army Plaza

Points of Interest

1) Bandshell
2) Bethesda Fountain
3) Children's Zoo
4) Coliseum
5) Delacorte Theater
6) Frick Collection
7) Hayden Planetarium
8) Lawn Bowling Area
9) Loeb Boat House
10) Metropolitan Museum of Art
11) Museum of Natural History
12) New York Historical Society
13) Plaza Hotel
14) Police Station
15) Sailboat Storage House
16) Shakespeare Garden
17) Tavern on the Green
18) Wollman Memorial Rink
19) Zoo
20) Belvedere Castle

BROOKLYN

Prospect Park's northeast corner is right at Brooklyn's Grand Army Plaza, near the Brooklyn Public Library, Brooklyn Museum and Botanic Gardens. The park itself is more than 500 acres, with lakes, boathouse, riding stables, a Quaker cemetery, the historic Lefferts Homestead and Litchfield Mansion (both open to the public) and a bandshell at 3rd St. and Prospect Park South that is used for small jazz, pop, and classical concerts during the summer.

Also of interest: *Marine Park,* with its 18-hole public golf course.

QUEENS

Flushing Meadows/Corona Park is partially on the site of the 1964 World's Fair grounds, near La Guardia Airport and Shea Stadium. Housed in what was formerly the New York State Pavilion are the Queens and Science Museums, and a few rides and mildly "glamorous" playgrounds also survive. Top of the Park is a restaurant overlooking the park and its immediate surroundings.

Cunningham and *Kissena Parks* are, as is Flushing Meadows, in the central part of the borough.

Jacob Riis Park, best noted for its beach but full of picnic and play areas, is now incorporated into the Gateway National Recreation Area.

STATEN ISLAND

Clove Lake is the most popular of Staten Island's parks, with boating, fishing, horseback riding, and wooded paths. A short ride from the Staten Island Ferry terminal on a Victory Blvd. bus makes the park easily accessible to the visitor.

Although not actually a park, *Fort Wadsworth* is one of the quieter spaces in New York City. It is situated under the Staten Island end of the Verrazano-Narrows Bridge and commands an impressive view of New York harbor. To get there, take the Bay Street bus from the ferry terminal. On the grounds is the Fort Wadsworth Military Museum (closed Tues. and Wed.) which traces the history of the fort, which is still an active military post.

Other area parks include *Silver Lake, Latourette* and *Willow Brook.*

BRONX

The woods-and-flowers highlight of the Bronx is easily the *Botanical Garden,* with its 250 acres and thousands of trees, shrubs, and plants. Depending on the season, you'd want to look out for the rose, rhododendron, magnolia, or azalea gardens. (For further details see the *Gardens* section below.)

Pelham Bay Park is almost entirely surrounded by water and is the largest of the Bronx's public parks. Also especially scenic is *Van Cortlandt Park,* which includes the Van Cortlandt Mansion Museum—an 18th-century Colonial manor, furnished today just as it was when built in 1748.

ZOOS. New York has several zoological centers, but the *Bronx Zoo* (Fordham Road & Southern Blvd., Bronx; 220–5100) is something special. Over 250 acres, with more than 3500 animals, it is one of the largest in the world. It has recently been modernized and wherever possible the animals are not caged, which makes sections such as the African Plains most fascinating. A tractor train will allow for a quick survey, the Bengali Express monorail covers the Wild Asia area May through October, and a Skyfari cable car affords an overview of the entire zoo.

The Bronx Zoo is open 10:00 A.M. to 5:00 P.M. (5:30, Sundays and holidays; 4:30, November through January). Admission is free Tuesdays, Wednesdays, and Thursdays; $2.00 for adults, 75 cents for children, and Senior Citizens free at other times. There are nominal additional fees for the various rides. There is also a new children's zoo opposite the elephant house where admission is 80 cents for kids and 70 cents for adults! The Bronx Zoo can be reached via the IRT No. 2 or 5 trains to the East Tremont Ave. stop or by car at the intersection of the Pelham and Bronx River Parkways.

New York's other zoos can hardly rival the Bronx Zoo for size, in maintenance, or for educational value. Both the *Central Park Zoo* (including the *Children's Zoo*) (E. 64 St. & Fifth Ave.; 360–8213) and the *Prospect Park Zoo* (Empire Blvd. & Flatbush Ave., Brooklyn; 965–6587) are in the process of being rehabilitated. Also of possible interest are Staten Island's *Barrett Park Zoo* (614 Broadway; 266–8500) and Queens's *Flushing Meadow Zoo* (111 St. at 54 Ave.; 699–7239).

The *New York Aquarium* (Surf Ave. & W. 8th St., at Brooklyn's Coney Island; 266–8500) is filled with mammals, fish, and birds from the world's water environments. They are displayed and publicly fed to the delight of adults and children alike.

GARDENS. A youngster who grows up in New York City is sometimes called "a child of cement." As you have seen from our discussion of parks, it need not be so. And giving surprise to the visitor who expects to see no green in New York at all are the New York and Brooklyn *Botanical Gardens,* each ranking among the world's most beautiful public gardens. They have horticultural displays all year round, are open daily, and admission is free.

New York Botanical Garden, directly north of the famed Bronx Zoo, has brought pleasure to New Yorkers since 1891. Its 250 rolling acres contain some 12,000 different species of plants, some of which bloom on such specialized sites as Rhododendron Slope, Daffodil Hill, Azalea Glen, and Magnolia Dell.

There is also a spectacular 40-acre Hemlock Forest, virgin land unchanged since the days the Indians camped out there. Ancient hemlock, maples, giant oak, poplar, beech, hickory, ash, and tulip trees shade the forest floor. The Bronx River slices through this forest primeval, cascading over a falls not far from *Snuff Mill.* There you will find a post-primeval restaurant, the *Lorillard*

Snuff Mill, with dining terrace overlooking the river. There is a picnic area nearby.

The garden's 11 greenhouses feature a world of flowers: lush jungle blooms from Asia, desert plants from Africa, pineapple, oranges, and pomegranates from the tropics. There's also a plant sales area. Almost worth a trip to New York itself is the glass conservatory (inspired by London's Kew Gardens Conservatory).

The *Museum* (Italian Renaissance style) has displays explaining the evolution of plants and their use to man. The paleo-botanic exhibit has some 30,000 plant fossils, some of which date from the year 500 million B.C.

There are five acres of wild flowers, meadows, and rock gardens, and there is an herbarium with some 3,000,000 species. There are flower-bordered pools, 3 miles of roads, 15 miles of paths. There is an *Easter Show* in March, a *Rose Day* in June, and a *Christmas Show* in December. Call 220–8777 for general information.

To get there: Take New York Central Harlem Division to Botanical Garden Station; or, 6th Ave. Concourse-205th St. (D) subway train to Bedford Pk. Blvd. Walk east 8 blocks. By car, Pelham Pkwy. west from New England Thruway and Hutchison River Parkway; Bronx River Parkway to Mosholu Pkwy. Use Mosholu Pkwy. from Henry Hudson Pkwy.

The 50-acre **Brooklyn Botanic Garden,** directly behind the Brooklyn Museum, features two of the most beautiful *Japanese gardens* in this hemisphere. The pond-and-hill garden, built in 1913 by Takeo Shiota, is a landscape of symbols. The pond takes the shape of the Japanese character for the word "heart." There is a tori, or gate, in the pond; a shrine on top of the hill. And there are caves which echo the delicate sound of five tiny waterfalls.

The second Japanese garden, which was opened in 1963, is an exact replica of the 15th-century Ryoanji (Buddhist) Temple of Kyoto, one of the most famous abstract gardens of contemplation in the Far East. There is a replica of the viewing wing of the ancient Ryoanji Temple. The tennis-court-size garden area is filled with swirling patterns of gravel, and fifteen stones (imported from Japan) arranged in five groups. The original purpose of the starkly simple design: to draw the minds of monks into meditation.

Another unique feature of the Brooklyn Botanic Garden is its *Fragrance Garden for the Blind.* The plants, raised in beds, are specially selected for identification by taste, touch, or smell. The plaques describing the flowers are in Braille.

There is also a *Shakespeare Garden* (with the various plants and flowers mentioned in the Bard's works), a wild flower garden, a rose garden, a range of greenhouses, and an abundance of cherry trees which burst into sudden bloom in late April, retain their pink glory through early May.

Hours vary according to season; open seven days a week. Call 622–4433 for information.

To get there: From the East Side, take Lexington Ave. IRT subway downtown express marked Utica Ave. or Atlantic Ave. to Nevins St. Change to B'way 7th Ave. train. Ride to Eastern Parkway, also called Brooklyn Museum Station.

From the West Side, take B'way 7th Ave. IRT, downtown express marked New Lots Ave. or Flatbush Ave. Get off at Eastern Parkway. (Trip takes about 25 minutes from Grand Central Station.)

Japan House, at 333 E. 47th St., has both indoor and outdoor gardens. The gardens are a favorite relaxation spot for office workers on their lunch hour. There is also a library, art gallery, and auditorium here.

If you delight in strolling through quiet *formal gardens,* you'll be glad to learn that Gallery Passport, 1170 Broadway, 288–3578, often includes them in tours to spots in the city and the supporting areas, like *Boscobel* in Westchester. Bus transportation to the various attractions is included in the service.

Manhattan's own **Conservatory Gardens,** in Central Park near Fifth Ave. at 105th St., is just what the name suggests: a greenhouse featuring blooming plants, displays changing seasonally. It's about a 15-minute stroll uptown from the Guggenheim Museum.

The **Ford Foundation** at 320 E. 43rd St. has an indoor garden with a 160-foot ceiling. The garden is in the lobby on this impressive building and has all kinds of flowers, shrubs and vines. Open weekdays.

The **Queens Botanical Gardens,** 43–50 Main Street, Flushing, is a recent addition to the city's attractions. Noted for its summer rose garden and fall chrysanthemum show, the garden also offers a shop (reasonable prices) and popular horticultural programs. Environmentalists will be pleased to learn that this 30-acre Gardens is "planted" on a former garbage dump! *To get there:* IRT subway Flushing Line uptown to Main St. (the last stop); then take the Q44 bus, south on Main St., ask for the Botanical Gardens stop.

Also worth a visit is the **Wave Hill Center for Environmental Studies** in Riverdale, Bronx (West 249th St. and Independence Ave.). It offers an outdoor sculpture garden, greenhouses, and gardens (formal, "wild," aquatic, herb, rose), as well as concerts, lectures, etc. The view of the Hudson River and Palisades is spectacular. *To get there:* We recommend a cab or your car. The trip by subway-bus-foot is a trip itself (IRT Seventh Ave. subway, No. 1 train to 231st St. station; No. 10 or No. 100 City Line Bus from NW corner of 231st St. and Broadway to 252nd St.; cross Parkway Bridge, on foot; walk on 252nd St. to Independence Ave. The entrance to Wave Hill is a few blocks down the road—at 249th St.).

 BEACHES. By far the most famous of New York City beaches is **Coney Island**—a 3½-mile stretch of Brooklyn facing out on the Atlantic Ocean. Upwards of a million and a half people will descend upon Coney Island's breezy shores on a hot summer day. Yet for all its continued popularity, this is a sadly rundown area, of which author Mario Puzo has written, "There was a time when every child in New York loved Coney Island, and so it breaks your heart to see what a slothful, bedraggled harridan it has become, endangered by the violence of its poor and hopeless people, as well as by the city planners who would improve it out of existence. If I were a wizard with one last magic trick in my bag, I would bring back the old Coney Island."

Coney Island is not quite that bleak; it retains a certain tacky charm, with the idle parachute jump at nearby *Astroland Amusement Park* towering above the beach and boardwalk—and with what invariably seem like the best frankfurters, French fries, and cotton candy in the world. Coney Island remains an experience, safe certainly by day, if only by dint of the massive crowds that include representatives of every racial group and ethnic community in the city.

In addition to Astroland, the *New York Aquarium* is also nearby, and the side streets are dotted with some of the best Italian restaurants in New York (*Gargiulo's* on W. 15th St. is a garish, 500-seat remnant of Coney Island's bygone glory days; it also consistently garners raves for outstanding food and service).

The B, D, F, M, N, and QB trains all converge at Stillwell Ave., Coney Island; it is also accessible by car via the Belt Parkway, heading east from lower Manhattan by way of the Brooklyn Battery Tunnel. Take the Ocean Parkway exit south about ½ mile until you reach the waterfront. The main beach area and other attractions will be to your right. There are also express buses that go to the Coney Island area, which you can pick up at designated stops between Wall St. and E. 50th St. in Manhattan.

Almost as famous and easily as popular is **Jones Beach,** just beyond the city limits on Long Island. Jones Beach is more parklike than Coney Island, without Coney's array of distractions—with the noteworthy exception of the nearby *Jones Beach Marine Theater,* an outdoor arena where the stage floats in the water. (Evening performances only, always of big, brassy, well-known musicals.) The beach itself is usually very clean, despite the millions who come to bathe and swim there daily during the June to August season.

To get to Jones Beach by car, take either the Long Island Expressway or the Southern State Parkway to the Meadowbrook Parkway and follow the signs to the parking lots. Despite their size, these lots fill up quickly, and the area is then closed to further traffic. So if you're planning to make the one-hour trip (unmercifully longer on a hot Sunday), leave early in the morning.

Alternatively, leave from the Port Authority Bus Terminal (41st St. and 8th Ave. in Manhattan, 564-8484). There is continuous loading for this special service weekdays from 9:30 to 11:00 A.M. and weekends from 8:00 to 9:30 A.M. leaving for the beach. Return buses depart Jones Beach beginning at 5 P.M. weekdays and from 2:30 to 5:00 P.M. weekends. The fare is $4.00 each way. There is also a train-bus combination (advertised as $6.75 round trip adults, $4.40 children in the summer of 1982), involving the Long Island Railroad from Penn Station and a change to a bus at the Freeport Station.

Jacob Riis Park in Queens, named for the turn-of-the-century photographer and philanthropist, and recently incorporated into *Gateway National Park,* is another popular seaside resort. The beach and its waters are generally rated among the cleanest of any in the city and within the park's borders are an 18-hole pitch-and-putt golf course; numerous playgrounds for children of all ages; free tennis, shuffleboard, handball and squash courts; boardwalk; and some grassy, shaded picnic areas. It should be noted that the far eastern end of the beach has in recent years evolved into an unofficial nude sunbathing area popular especially among New York's homosexual community.

Riis Park has parking facilities for 10,000 cars, and is easily reached in about an hour via the Belt Parkway going east from Lower Manhattan. Take the Flatbush Ave. South exit and continue over the Marine Parkway Bridge onto the Rockaway Peninsula. Using public transportation, take the No. 2 or 3 IRT line to Flatbush Ave. in Brooklyn; at the Flatbush/Nostrand junction upstairs, take a bus marked Riis Park or Beach 116 St. (it's best to ask for the bus stop, as there are different lines running from every corner).

New York's beach lovers do run the risk of oil spills or shark alerts periodically closing their favorite haunts, but with the above, as well as *Orchard Beach* near City Island in the Bronx, and *Wolfe's Pond Park* in Staten Island, they're never at a loss for alternative sun-'n'-fun spots.

 BABYSITTING SERVICES. For parents who may be hesitant to bring their children to the Big Apple, there should be comfort in the fact that there are a number of reliable sources for babysitters here. Perhaps the best known is *The Babysitters Guild,* 60 E. 42nd St., 682–0227. Their prices will be steep by the usual babysitting standards, but their reputation is impeccable. Rates start at $4.50 an hour, and escalate depending on the number and age of children, and where the sitter is to work; for example, the fee for two children aged 8 and 10 staying at the Plaza would be $5.25 an hour. In all cases there is a four-hour minimum and an additional fee for carfare: $3.00 round trip during the day and until midnight, $5.50 after midnight. Rates for infants up to six months are higher because the Guild uses only people trained as baby nurses for children that young. In contrast, you can work out your own deal with sitters recommended to you by *New York University,* 720 Main Building, 200 Washington Place, 598–2971. Other sitting sources include *Barnard College Babysitting Service,* 606 W. 120th St., 662–7676/280–2035; *Cornell Nursing School Babysitting Service,* 420 E. 70th St., 472–8393; *Part-Time Child Care,* 19 E. 69th St., 879–4343; and *Stern College For Women,* 245 Lexington Ave., 481–0562.

 CHILDREN'S ACTIVITIES. There are very few places or activities in New York City that do not hold some fascination for youngsters or that can't be adapted to children's interests. Nonetheless, there are numerous things to see and to do that seem to have younger visitors especially in mind.

MUSEUMS

Most of the major museums have special programs designed for children of different ages, but none seem to garner wide-eyed enthusiasm more consistently than the *American Museum of Natural History* (Central Park West at 79th St.;

873–4225) and its sister *Hayden Planetarium* (can be entered from the Museum or separately at CPW and 81th St.; 873–0404)—the former with its life-size dinosaur skeletons and moon rocks, the latter with its changing sky shows and *Laserium* productions.

Laserium, produced by an outside organization in cooperation with the Planetarium, makes use of the Planetarium's star projectors but adds laser lights and music (sometimes rock, sometimes classical) for a multi-media assault that can be quite impressive. On Wednesdays, when the Museum and Planetarium are open until 8 P.M., you can time your visit to include *Laserium,* though that is quite a full day; remember, the Museum and Planetarium span two square city blocks, each with several floors—so be sure everyone is wearing comfortable shoes. Museum open daily 10 A.M. to 5:45 P.M., and until 8 P.M. Wednesday evenings. Suggested contribution: adults $2, children $1. Planetarium open essentially the same hours, though it's best to check the precise times of the sky shows. Admission is $2.75 for adults, $1.75 for students and senior citizens, $1.35 for children under 12. Check for *Laserium* times and ticket prices.

Also very popular among younger travelers are the *Museum of Broadcasting* (1 East 53rd St.; 752–7684), where the entire family can select old TV shows to watch together and explore the history of broadcast media; and the *Museum of Holography* (11 Mercer St.; 925–0526), with its unusual displays of three-dimensional light projections known as holograms.

Although one or another part of the *South Street Seaport Museum* (203 Front St.; 766–9020) is inevitably undergoing renovation, there are always some parts open and worth visiting. The Seaport is divided between traditional displays housed in a museum and a small fleet of schooners docked at the foot of South Street, several of which can be boarded and toured on your own. During the summer months, the Seaport's 110-year-old triple-masted *Pioneer* takes daily three-hour cruises in New York Harbor—and the 15 kids and adults on each trip are invited to help raise the sails and steer the vessel, or simply to picnic on the deck and take in the sights. This is a considerably different experience than the Circle Line's guided trek around Manhattan Island—but a most memorable one indeed. For a day-long trip, however, Circle Line offers roundtrip rides to Bear Mountain (about 50 miles north of Manhattan) and Hyde Park/West Point (90 miles north of the city).

FUN AND GAMES

Two stores offer puppet shows, free. *Barnes & Noble Sales Annex,* Fifth Ave. at 18th St., 675–5500, every Sunday at 11:00 A.M. and 12:30 P.M. Uptown, *F.A.O. Schwarz,* Fifth Ave. and 58th St., 644–9400, Monday–Friday, 2:30 P.M.

Puppet shows presented by independent companies include: *Alice May Puppets,* Origami Center, 31 Union Sq., 255–0469, November–May, Sunday at 2:00 P.M.; *Lea Wallace Puppets,* First Moravian Church, 154 Lexington Ave., 254–9074, Saturday, 2:00 P.M.; *Nicolo Marionettes,* New York Stage Works, 15 W. 18th St., 242–3967, September–mid-May, Saturday, 1:00 P.M., and Sunday, 1:00 and 3:00 P.M.; *Penny Jones & Company Puppets,* Greenwich House Music

School, 46 Barrow St., 924–4589, October–April, Saturday and Sunday, 3:30 P.M.;*Puppet Store,* 477 Atlantic Ave., Brooklyn, 625–3983, shows on weekends, 1:00 P.M., also sells puppets and books.; *Museum of the City of New York,* 1220 Fifth Ave., 534–1672, changes show every week, early November–April, Saturday, 1:30 P.M. Reservations for these and for the magic and other live performance shows listed below are always advisable and often necessary a few weeks ahead.

Magic Town House, 1026 Third Ave., 752–1165, features hour-long magic shows on Saturday, Sunday, and school holidays, 1:00, 2:30 and 4:00 P.M. (Shows for adolescents are held Saturday evenings.) *Mostly Magic,* 53 Carmine St., 924–1472 combines magic and comedy with audience participation, Saturdays at 3:00 P.M.

Original plays, fairy tales, and musicals are given at the following theaters: *Courtyard Playhouse,* 39 Grove St., 765–9540, Saturday and Sunday, Labor Day to June, 1:30 and 3:00 P.M.;*Henry Street Family Theater,* 466 Grand St., 766–9334, October–mid-April, Saturday and Sunday, 3:00 P.M.; *Off-Center Theater Company,* 436 W. 18th St., 929–8299, September–May, Tuesday, Wednesday, Thursday, and Sunday.; *Onstage Children Company,* 413 W. 46th St., 246–9872, mid-September–May, Saturday, 1:30 and 3:00 P.M.; *Thirteenth Street Theater,* 50 W. 13th St., 741–9282, Saturday, 1:00 and 3:00 P.M. Also check the Friday editions of the *New York Times* and the *Post* for extensive listings for that weekend.

ZOOS

Bronx Zoo, Fordham Road and Southern Blvd., 220–5100. There is a brand-new children's zoo opposite the elephant house where the admission is 80 cents for kids and 70 cents for adults! As for the main zoo—also recently renovated—rides include the Bengali Express monorail through the spectacular Wild Asia exhibit (where the animals roam free), a tractor train, and a Skyfari cable car. Open 10:00 A.M. to 5:00 P.M. (5:30, Sundays and holidays; 4:30, November–January). Admission is free Tuesdays, Wednesdays, and Thrusdays; $2.00 for adults, 75 cents for children, and Senior Citizens free at other times. There are nominal additional fees for the various rides.

Central Park Zoo, Central Park, E. 64th St. and Fifth Ave., 360–8213. Most of the animals are in buildings. It's a pleasant place to spend an hour or two, ride around in a pony cart, and have lunch at the outdoor cafeteria. Open every day, 11:00 A.M.–5:00 P.M. Free.

New York Aquarium, Surf Ave. & W. 8th St., Coney Island, Brooklyn, 266–8500. Over 3,000 varieties of marine life are shown in outdoor and indoor exhibits. The whale and dolphin show is very popular with children. Open every day, 10:00 A.M.–5:00 P.M. Admission.

Other good animal facilities include: *Jamaica Bay Wildlife Refuge,* Cross Bay Blvd., between Howard Beach and Broad Channel, Queens, 474–0613, open every day, 8:00 A.M.–6:00 P.M., free; *Prospect Park Zoo,* Empire Blvd. and Flatbush Ave., Brooklyn, 965–6587, open late June–Labor Day, 10:00 A.M.–

4:00 P.M., free; *Staten Island Zoological Park,* 614 Broadway, Staten Island, 442–3100, open every day, 10:00 A.M.–4:45 P.M., admission.

SIGHTSEEING

There is also, of course, the *Statue of Liberty,* which is reached by ferry from the South Ferry subway stop of both the IRT 7th Avenue and IRT Lexington Avenue lines. Children love to climb up the narrow, circular ramp to the statue's crown. An elevator can take you up to the first 10 stories, the last 12 stories are on foot.

The 102-story *Empire State Building* on Fifth Ave. between 33rd and 34th sts. is always popular. From the terraces of the 86th floor one can rent binoculars and look out across the whole city—and simply being in one of the world's tallest buildings is an unforgettable experience for a child. And don't forget the *World Trade Center* and the *RCA Building* at Rockefeller Center. A ride on the *Roosevelt Island* tramway at 59th St. and Second Ave. also provides still a different type of bird's-eye view of the Upper East Side.

Nostalgia Special, IND Subway, W. 57th St. and Ave. of the Americas, The B Line, 330–3060. A vintage subway train takes its passengers to the New York Public Transit Exhibit in Brooklyn and on to Rockaway Beach. Open Saturday, Sunday, and holidays, from Memorial Day weekend to Thanksgiving weekend. Admission.

Between Memorial Day and Labor Day, the city opens many outdoor pools for *swimming.* Van Cortlandt Park has one in the Bronx, Greenwich Village (Clarkson St. and 7th Ave.) in Manhattan, Flushing Meadows in Queens and Bedford-Stuyvesant (Kosciusko St. and March Ave.) in Brooklyn—but the area is rough. An indoor pool open all year is at 342 E. 54th St., Manhattan.

Several plots in the city have been protected from development and preserved as *nature areas.* Most notable are Wave Hill's 28 acres in the Bronx (675 W. 252nd St.) and the larger High Rock Conservation Center ‘on Staten Island (Nevada Ave.). Central Park's *Ramble* is a favorite for bird watchers; hilly and wooded, it lies just north of the 72nd St. lake and can be reached on foot in 10 minutes from the Museum of Natural History.

Toys and hobbies galore can be seen—or bought—at F.A.O. Schwarz (58th St. and 5th Ave.) and Polk's Hobby Shop (32nd St. and 5th Ave.), and Central Park has plenty of space, on weekdays, to fly kites or model airplanes.

Many of the sites covered in the essay "New York City: A Congregation of Neighborhoods," as well as those listed under *Historic Sites* and *Museums* will likely also prove exciting and memorable for children. And you might want to check the daily papers for such special events as the holiday pageants at Radio City Music Hall and the regularly touring circus, ice, Disney and Sesame Street shows that play Madison Square Garden.

OTHER SUGGESTIONS

Broadway and off-Broadway inevitably have some offerings popular among children—Broadway's *Annie* being one long-running example.

Radio City Music Hall's various spectacles are always designed as family entertainment, and the occasional concerts held there are usually also by big-name entertainers who appeal to all ages. Backstage tours here, as well as through the RCA television and radio studios across the street, or around Lincoln Center, give everyone a behind-the-scenes look at the technical side of New York theater.

Periodically throughout the year, the *Big Apple Circus* sets up its one-ring tent in parks around the city. Though small in scale, the company is wonderfully reminiscent of traditional European-style circuses. The clowns are exceptional (the enterprise was started as a school for circus artists by clown *extraordinaire* Paul Binder), and the trapeze and cycle acts are outstanding. Phone: 369–5110.

The *Ringling Bros., Barnum & Bailey Circus* comes to Madison Square Garden for the months of April and May every year. With a company of dancers to complement the high-wire acts, human rocket ship, and trained animals, it is a show that in recent years has regained much of the glamour and excitement that had been lost. Various other traveling ice, cartoon character, and fantasy shows can also be seen at the Garden throughout the year, though these are hardly unique to New York. Check the daily papers for current attractions.

At Christmas time, be sure to stop at the Fifth Avenue department stores to see the windows. Of special note are *Lord & Taylor,* at 39th St., *Altman's* at 34th St., and *F.A.O. Schwarz* at 59th St. If the children are old enough to go at night, that's your best bet—the lines are shorter and the atmosphere better, and you can linger to your heart's content. Moving indoors, the fifth floor at *Macy's* (34th St. at Seventh Ave.) is spectacular with Santa Claus in residence and toys galore. Also during the holiday season catch the Christmas tree at *Rockefeller Center.* Come April, the Easter Parade along Fifth Avenue and the egg hunt in Central Park are noteworthy. And Macy's Thanksgiving Day Parade, broadcast live around the world, can be watched in person all along the 2-½-mile marching route—from 79th Street at Central Park West, down around Columbus Circle, and southward on Broadway until it reaches the department store itself.

During the summer, the major city parks have bicycle and rowboat rentals, with roads generally closed to car traffic during non-rush hour times and on weekends for cyclers, strollers, and runners. Also, Coney Island's *Astroland Amusement Park* and Rockaway Park's *Playland* offer rides, "games of skill and chance," and miles of white sand beaches for sunbathing and swimming, plus midweek fireworks displays. July 4th is the time for Macy's spectacular fireworks show, set off from various points in New York Harbor and best viewed from Battery park on the west side of the island. Between Memorial Day and Labor Day, various city-run pools are open all over the city; check in the Parks Dept. listing at the back of the White Pages under "New York City Government Offices." An indoor pool is open year-round at 342 E. 54th St. in Manhattan.

Always a special treat is a real old-fashioned ice cream soda—best had at *Rumpelmayer's* (50 Central Park South), *Serendipity* (225 E. 60th St.), or the *Agora* (87th St. and Third Ave.). Further details on these and other possibilities are in the *Desserts* section, below.

PARTICIPANT SPORTS. The sports most participated in by New Yorkers are probably **jogging** and **bicycling.** Statistics bear this out, as do two major events created by interest in these two sports—the annual New York City Marathon (run through all five boroughs and a great way to sightsee on foot if your're up to covering 26 miles, 385 yards) and the 50-kilometer (31-mile) Bicycle Challenge 'round and 'round and 'round, etc.) Central Park. For the latter, participants are free to cycle one six-mile loop around the park or to go for as many as they can right up to the end. Both events draw international fields and are as much a circusy party as athletic competition.

The reasons for the popularity of jogging and bicycling are fairly obvious: They are relatively inexpensive, require no in-place equipment (just some park space), and their exercise and health value are intensified in the city environment, where the air is never better than "kind of pure" and so many people work inside sitting down. The reasons for the popularity of the New York City Marathon are not so obvious—but it must have something going for it because the cut-off number for participants is 16,000—and the waiting list to get into the run is usually over 20,000! In any event, the Marathon is always held on the third Sunday in October when the weather is usually fall crisp, cool, and clear. And the guiding spirit behind the race is the New York Road Runners Club, headquartered at the International Running Center, 9 East 89th St., New York, NY 10028, 860–4455.

Indeed, the Road Runners Club is a treasure trove of Big Apple running information for joggers of every speed. They can tell you about races scheduled while you are in town, or of the city's best running routes. These routes range from the obvious—such as the reservoir loop in Central Park or the scenic strip along the East River Drive leading to Randall's Island—to the not so obvious, such as the "Museum Mile" from 82nd to 104th Sts. passing ten museums along Manhattan's Fifth Avenue, or another lake loop in Flushing Meadows Park. The club even has a book filled with mapped running routes all around the city, yours for a nominal fee. For further information about running around the Big Apple, and for Marathon entry forms, write the Road Runners Club, P.O. Box 881, F.D.R. Station, New York, NY 10150. And if you are interested in running the Marathon, make sure to write early and to follow the instructions regarding earliest acceptable postmark.

The 50-kilometer cross-country tour drew 3,000 international cyclists, including a French exhibition team, for its first running in 1981. The number is expected to grow for the annual event, scheduled for the second week in July. For further information, contact the City of New York Department of Parks and Recreation, 360–8111.

Central Park in Manhattan and Prospect Park in Brooklyn have automobile roadways that are closed to cars and reserved for walkers, runners, and pedalers during daylight hours on weekends and often during non-rush hours weekdays. You can find plenty of places to rent a bike on the nearby side streets and avenues—check the Yellow Pages—or you can rent in Central Park at the Loeb Boathouse near the 72nd Street lake. You must bring some identification and at least $10.00–$25.00 or a major credit card as a security deposit. The bikes cost about $2.50 per hour, with special rates for the day, and a couple of brisk circuits of the park are certainly worth it for the activity and the view of the city and its citizens at leisure. Central Park is especially interesting for the various ad hoc music parties that fill the air in summertime, while Prospect Park is more of a family and community park.

There are plenty of informal participatory sports such as **softball, volleyball, soccer, rugby, frisbee,** or **pushball** in all the city's parks, and even the more formal league teams often look for "pick-up" players to substitute for their own absentees. In winter, cross-country **skiing** and **tobogganing** are popular in Central Park, while spring brings the **roller-skaters** out en masse. In good weather, there are a number of vans set up along Columbus Ave. in the 70s for renting skates, and on good days there is a shop near the corner of Columbus and 75th St. that rents skates also. In Central Park, most of the team games are played in the 60s and 70s, although there are many playing fields farther uptown as well. If you are brave enough to play rugby with total strangers, bring your own ambulance!

For general park information, call 360–8196; for free events information call 755–4100.

For a variety of inexpensive sports choices, from **handball** and **paddleball** to **swimming** and **jogging/exercise classes,** consider the "Y"'s way—a $5 daily guest membership offered by various YM-YWCAs and YM-YWHAs around town. Call the Y general information number (564–1300) for the address of the Y nearest you so you can check what they have to offer. Two handy Ys to keep in mind because of their location and facilities are the West Side Y at 5 West 63rd St. (787–4400) and the Vanderbilt (a k a Grand Central) Y, 224 East 47th St. (755–2410). The former has an indoor track, one of the best-organized running clubs in town, locker and shower facilities and pool, and is almost directly across the street from Lincoln Center and from Central Park. The Vanderbilt offers paddleball, handball, volleyball, sauna, swimming, and a convenient Grand Central Station area location close to the East River and the United Nations.

Increasingly, you'll come across Y-like health clubs and spas throughout the city, some with tennis and racquetball courts, pools, and extensive exercise rooms. Access to these is almost always by membership only, although you may be able to purchase a day-pass if you have a friend who belongs to one or another of the clubs. If on business, you might also be able to gain admittance through a company membership. Some hotels, including Vista International at the World Trade Center also have health club facilities that can be used by guests.

Chess and backgammon, and sometimes Go, are not exactly participant sports, but this is what is available at Chess Mart, 240 Sullivan St. at 3rd St., and the Chess Shop, 230 Thompson St. near 3rd St., both in the Village. These places, and the Game Room, 2130 Broadway at 75th St., stay open way into the evening.

There are plenty of **bowling alleys:** in lower Manhattan, Bowlmor (110 University Pl.) is for regular bowling most of the time, but adds a disco beat after midnight several times a week; in midtown, Times Square Lanes (1482 Broadway); check the Yellow Pages for other lanes.

Billiard Academies—or, if you prefer, pool halls—are similarly numerous, though not all for innocent visitors. *Magic Cue.*, 43rd St. and Broadway, is one of the few left in the Times Square area, and is well-kept. Elsewhere in Manhattan, you can cue up, in Inwood, near the Cloisters, at Guys and Gals (500 W. 207th St.). Brooklyn offers: in Flatbush, Action (2168 Albemarle Rd.); in Sheepshead Bay, near the charter fishing boat piers, Sheepshead Billiards (1710 Sheepshead Bay Rd.); in Bay Ridge, near the Verrazano-Narrows Bridge, Skytop Cue Club (512 86th St.) Queens locations include: in Little Neck, The Little Neck Recreation Center (250–21 Northern Blvd., Little Neck); in Forest Hills, Jacy's (96–42 Queens Blvd., Forest Hills). In Staten Island, you may play or take a lesson at Golden Cue (135 Canal St., Stapleton).

The city's numerous public **golf courses** are playable for a weekday green fee of $5.00, $7.00 on weekends. Phone ahead to get a "best guess" on how long a wait you'll have before teeing off. In Brooklyn, play at Dyker Beach (86th St. and 6th Ave.; 836–9722) or Marine Park (2880 Flatbush Ave.; 338–7113). In Queens, there's the Clearview in Bayside (202–12 Willets Point Blvd.; 229–2570), Douglaston Park in Douglaston (Commonwealth Blvd. & Marathon Parkway; 224–6566), Forest Park in Ridgewood (Interboro Parkway and Main Drive; 296–2442), and Kissena Park in Flushing (N. Hempstead Turnpike and Fresh Meadows Rd.; 445–3388). Staten Island's courses are Silver Lake (Victory Blvd. and Park Rd.; 447–5686), South Shore (Huguenot Ave.; 984–0108), and LaTourette (Forest Hill Rd.; 351–1889). The Bronx offers Mosholu-Booth (Jerome Ave. and Holly Lane; 822–4845), Van Cortlandt (Broadway near 242nd St.; 543–4595), and Pelham–Split Rock (City Island and Pelham Bay Park W.; 885–0838). There are two courses at the latter, and Split Rock may be the toughest challenge within the five boroughs. If a driving range would content you, Golf City in Whitestone, Queens, has over 100 tees and a battery of sport and game attractions suitable for a family outing. Golf City is at 140–15 20th Ave., reached via the 20th Ave. exit of the Whitestone Expressway, between Shea Stadium and the Whitestone Bridge; 746–4800. There are also large driving ranges and miniature golf layouts near the City Island Causeway in the Bronx and across from Floyd Bennett Field (near Gateway National Park and the Rockaways) in Brooklyn.

Ice-skating is popular, even fashionable, at the famous Rockefeller Center rink and the Wollman Memorial Rink (under renovation at press time) near 59th St. in Central Park. Other city locations are Sky Rink (450 W. 33rd St. in Manhattan, where the New York Rangers work out), Riverdale (236th St. and Broadway in the Bronx) and another Wollman Memorial, this one in Brooklyn's Prospect Park.

Roller-skaters gather in Central Park on a mall at about 70th St. due east of Central Park West—follow the skaters or the sound of blaring radios and tape players to find them. The most glamorous of New York's roller discos is Manhattan's Roxy (515 W. 18th St.; 691–3113), while the only banked rink is in Brooklyn at Sweet Ruby's (Wyckoff and Myrtle Aves.; 456–3300). When not occupied for rock concerts or flea markets, Skate Pier 84 (44th St. and 12th Ave., Manhattan; 244–4270) keeps you outdoors at the edge of the Hudson. Beginners flock to Greenwich Village's Village Skating (15 Waverly Pl.; 677–9690), while only the most experienced venture out to Brooklyn for the standard-bearing roller rink of them all, the Empire (200 Empire Blvd.; 462–1570). Check the Yellow Pages for additional neighborhood locales.

Fishermen can rent or charter boats to try their luck in the waters surrounding New York. Favorite launching points are City Island in the Bronx (Jack's Bait and Tackle) and the Sheepshead Bay area of Brooklyn (Bay End Dock Co. or Canarsie-Jamaica Marine at the Canarsie Recreation Pier, east of Sheepshead Bay). There are numerous other fishing excursions at both these locations.

Tennis courts maintained by the Parks Department are used by city residents, who purchase a season permit, valid from early April to the end of October, for $27.00; but visitors may buy individual $4.00 passes at the Central Park Courts (93rd and Central Park). These passes entitle the player to one hour of tennis on any of the city-run courts, a list of which may be obtained from the Parks Department. The Central Park courts are very popular, and players often have to wait an hour or two after signing in for a court, but at other locations, though they are sometimes tricky to find and not as well maintained, one can often sign in and walk right on to the court. For privately owned courts, rates vary considerably from summer to winter, often running as much as $10.00 an hour higher in the winter. The rates also vary according to the time-slot required: the hours before work, 7–9; lunch hours, 12–2; and the evening hours from 6–10, being generally most in demand and therefore most expensive. Prices per hour range from a low of $16 to a top of $25 for inexpensive courts, to a low of $27 to a high of $58 for the most expensive. (And many courts will be raising their prices soon.)

Courts in *Manhattan,* starting south and working uptown: *Wall Street Racquet Club,* foot of Wall St. at East River (952–0760); free parking; 9 new indoor Har-tru courts; low weekday rates. *Village Tennis Courts,* 110 University Place (989–2300); Acrycushion 6 surface courts; ball-machine practice courts; moderate. *Gramercy Tennis and Racquet Club,* 708 Sixth Ave. near 23rd St. (691–0110); new Elastraturf courts; moderate; major credit cards. *Midtown Tennis Club,* 341 Eighth Ave., corner 27th St. (989–8572); 8 Har-tru tournament courts; indoor and outdoor courts; limited back line space; moderate. *Tennis Club, Grand Central Terminal,* 15 Vanderbilt Ave. (687–3841); 2 Elastraturf courts; very expensive but luxurious. *Manhattan Plaza Racquet Club,* 450 W. 43rd St. (594–0554); new Elastraturf courts; excellent tennis pros; expensive. *Sutton East Tennis Club,* 488 E. 60th St. at York Ave. (751–3452); 8 clay courts; cramped space; moderate to expensive; open Oct. 26th to Apr. 5th. *Tower Tennis Courts,* 1725 York Ave. between 88th and 89th Sts. (860–2464); deco-turf indoor courts, limited side lines; expensive.

In the boroughs outside Manhattan the price range is considerably lower, being as low as $4.00 for open-air courts in the summer, and in the winter ranging from a low of $8.00 to a high of $23.00.

Brooklyn: Brooklyn Racquet Club, 2781 Shell Rd. (769–5167); 14 indoor and outdoor clay courts; free parking and babysitting; inexpensive. Parade Grounds Tennis, 305 Coney Island Ave. (633–5400); Har-tru surface courts; moderate to inexpensive. *The Bronx:* Stadium Tennis, 11 E. 162nd St. (293–2386); only open to transients in the winter, in the summer it reverts to a city court; 8 unevenly laid, rubberized cork surface courts; moderate to inexpensive. There are also courts in Van Cortlandt Park. *Staten Island:* Richmond Racquet Club, 2282 Forest Ave. (727–6787); Har-tru surface courts; open year round; $12 flat rate or 5-hour coupon book for $35. *Queens:* Sterling Tennis, 40–15 126th St, Corona. (446–5619); Har-tru courts; open-air in summer; inexpensive. Boulevard Gardens, 51–26 Broadway, Woodside (545–7774); indoor and outdoor clay courts; moderate to inexpensive. U.S.T.A. National Tennis Center, Flushing Meadows Park, Flushing (592–8000); this is the tennis complex where the U.S. Open Championships are played—there are 9 indoor and 24 outdoor courts, all in excellent condition; surfaces are Deco II; moderate to inexpensive.

Squash courts are available at the following Manhattan locations: Fifth Avenue Racquet Club (405 Fifth Ave.), Manhattan Squash Club (41 W. 42nd St.), Park Avenue Squash and Racquet Club (3 Park Ave.), Town Squash (151 E. 86th St.), and the Turtle Bay Racquet Club (541 Lexington Ave.). Manhattan's only platform tennis courts are at the Apple Platform Tennis Club, 215 E. 24th St. Because racquetball courts come and go as quickly as the ball flies off the wall at you, the Yellow Pages are your best source of information. Fees are generally somewhat lower than for tennis.

Some of the larger city parks maintain bridle paths for **horseback riding.** Near Forest Park, along the Brooklyn–Queens border, the nearest riding stable is Stanley's in Forest Hills (88–03 70th Rd.); in Staten Island, riding horses and horse-drawn hayrides are available at Clove Lake Stables (1025 Clove Rd.); the Bronx has the Van Cortlandt Park Riding Academy, in the northern tip of the park (Broadway and 254th St.); in Manhattan, the Claremont Stable (175 W. 89th St.) is right near Central Park; in Brooklyn, there are Prospect Park Riding Stables (51 Caton Place, off Prospect Park West) and Jamaica Bay Riding Academy (7000 Shore Parkway). All the stables listed also offer instruction. You can expect to pay $15–18 per hour, without instruction, but usually including a trail guide.

Some other sports opportunities in New York center around schools. Consult, according to your special interests, Offshore Sailing School, Aqua-Lung School of New York, Rohde's Academy of Fencing, A&L Scooter and Motorcycle, or Parachutes Incorporated.

SPECTATOR SPORTS. Baseball season, April through October, features the Yankees and Mets, and each schedules about 75 home dates, of which nearly half are night games. The Mets' ballpark is Shea Stadium, in Flushing, Queens (672–3000), while the Yankees play at their famous stadium in the Bronx, "the house that Ruth built" (293–6000). Tickets are available at many Ticketron outlets throughout the metropolitan area and a fairly good seat is usually not too hard to find unless the team is involved in crucial, late-season action. Caution: Shea Stadium can be uncomfortably chilly on spring and autumn nights. And the Yankee Stadium area isn't the safest place in the world, so don't linger too long after the game.

Pro football is a furious business, but New York's two pro football teams, the Jets and the Giants, are less furious than most and have been having more ups and downs than opposing linemen in recent seasons. Therefore general admission tickets to their Sunday National Football League games are usually readily available at Ticketron outlets and at the respective stadiums, even through both teams have hordes of regular season-ticket holders. The Jets share Shea Stadium with the aforementioned Mets—the result being they never play any home games until the Mets have finished their baseball schedule. Jets reserved seat tickets cost $9 and if you think it can get cold nights during baseball season, wait until the winter winds come howling in across Flushing Bay. Bring blankets, anti-freeze, hats, gloves—you name it, because, Baby, it gets cold outside when you root, root, root for the home team Jets. For ticket and game information call the stadium or 421–6600.

The pro Giants left Yankee Stadium for the greener pastures of the nearby New Jersey Meadowlands sports complex in East Rutherford, New Jersey. Tickets for games at Giants Stadium are also $9; phone (201) 935–8222. The season runs from September through January.

Yankee Stadium is most readily accessible via the IRT No. 4, and the IND D and CC subway lines to the 161 St. stop. Shea Stadium can be reached by way of the No. 7 Flushing line to the Willets Point–Shea Stadium station. The Shea parking lot (follow the signs from the Van Wyck Expressway or Grand Central Parkway) accommodates thousands of automobiles, though the traffic on both of these highways is always great. To get to the Meadowlands, see information in the *Jersey Shore* section below.

Basketball and **hockey** are the major attractions at Madison Square Garden, which stands above Penn Station at 32 St. and Seventh Ave. Known simply as "The Garden" to generations of athletes and sports fans, this 20,000-seat arena hasn't grown a real winner in recent seasons in either the Knicks—New York's pro basketball entry in the National Basketball Association—or the Rangers, the Big Apple's National Hockey League representative from Manhattan. Again, the result is that tickets are readily available on any given night, at prices ranging from $6 to $14 for Knicks games and $5 to $15 for Rangers games.

Both teams play a regular season that runs from early October to early April, excluding post-season playoffs that may go another six weeks. The regular season involves about 40 home dates. To find out who's battling either of these home teams call 563–8000. Parking near the Garden is difficult and expensive, so try using the IRT 1, 2, or 3 trains, or the IND A, CC, or E lines to Penn Station.

Diehard sports fans can catch more pro basketball action by venturing out of Manhattan to the Meadowlands to see the scrappy New Jersey Nets play their version of NBA ball (201–935–8888), while New York's best brand of hockey is played at the Nassau Coliseum on nearby Long Island, where the Islanders—

1980 and '81 Stanley Cup champions—skate through their NHL season (516–794–4100).

The Garden used to be famous for its **boxing** matches but has fallen on hard times of late for a variety of reasons. The *Daily News* still sponsors the exciting Golden Gloves programs each spring; the very lack of polish and ring experience guarantees action galore. And Madison Square Garden is still home for the final rounds of its post-season collegiate National Invitational Basketball Tournament, offering a Holiday Festival over the Christmas semester break that brings in excellent college teams and is occasional home court for such exciting local college squads as St. John's, Fordham, Manhattan, and Seton Hall. The Garden also hosts some prizefights, indoor pro tennis, prestigious track and field events such as the Millrose Games and entertainment events such as ice shows, the circus, rodeos, wrestling, horse shows, and even rock 'n' roll headliners who play the main arena (564–4400) as well as the smaller Felt Forum (563–8000).

Flat and harness tracks draw millions of **horse racing** enthusiasts each year. Thoroughbred racing takes place at Aqueduct Racetrack in Ozone Park, Queens, and Belmont Racetrack in Elmont, on nearby Long Island, with the season running from October through April at Aqueduct and from May through October at Belmont. Aqueduct is the largest thoroughbred racing track in the U.S., while Belmont is where the third and final leg of the "Triple Crown," the Belmont Stakes, is run to determine the nation's best three-year-old racehorse. Since post times vary seasonally it's best to check first with the New York Racing Association (212–641–4700) before heading out to the tracks. Working folks benefit from the night-time programs of standardbred harness races at Yonkers in Westchester County (914–968–4200; just over the New York City border at the edge of the Bronx), Roosevelt Raceway in Westbury (516–222–2000; on nearby Long Island), and the Meadowlands (from January through August), new home of the Hambletonian, in East Rutherford, New Jersey (201–935–8500). The Meadowlands also runs thoroughbred horses *at night* from September through December.

The New York City Off-Track Betting Corporation (OTB) is the nation's first government-run off-track betting operation. OTB offers betting programs from some of the best thoroughbred and harness tracks in America. It is a source of entertainment and sport for thousands of New Yorkers and visitors who want to get a bet down or just study the Damon Runyan characters who frequent OTB. There are over 150 branch offices throughout the city's five boroughs, many open seven days a week. Free admission. For further information, the New York City OTB phone number is 221–5624.

Tennis reaches its peak here in early September when the U.S. Open Tennis Championships are played at the USTA National Tennis Center, Flushing Meadows, Queens (212–592–8000). This is one of four titles which enjoys supreme status worldwide, and although tickets for the finals are scarce, you can catch most of the big names as they work their way through the early rounds. The prestigious tournament was recently moved from the West Side Tennis in Forest Hills (212–268–2300) which is still synonymous with the best tennis in the world. Forest Hills stages its own major pro tennis event in the early fall.

Golf tournaments are proliferating so fast that almost any area is a candidate for the next one, although the annual Westchester Classic in early June at the Westchester Country Club in Rye (914–967–6000) is one of the major steps on the Pro Golfers Association Tour (and really just a short drive away from one of the area's great amusement parks, Rye Playland).

You're probably aware of the sudden burst of interest in **soccer** in the U.S. This area's championship team, the Cosmos, are led by highly paid imported stars. The Cosmos play from April through August at Giants Stadium in the Meadowlands. Tickets cost $7 and $12 for adults, $4 for children, and information is available in New York at 265–8600.

College football, basketball, and **baseball** can provide some exciting moments on a highly skilled amateur level—as well as the opportunity to see some of the Big Apple's most beautiful campuses. Columbia University, for example, plays football against Ivy League rivals such as Harvard, Yale, and Princeton at antiquated Baker Field, Broadway at 218th St. in the colorful Inwood section of upper Manhattan. St. John's in Brooklyn, Manhattan in the Riverdale section of the Bronx, and Fordham in the Little Italy section off Fordham Road in the Bronx, play a very competitive brand of club- and small-college-division-level football, as does Wagner on rural Staten Island, Iona in Westchester, and Seton Hall in nearby New Jersey, where Rutgers plays the closest thing to a big-time football schedule in the metropolitan area.

All of the above-named colleges and universities have top basketball, baseball, and track and field programs and compete actively in such relatively minor sports as soccer, lacrosse, crew, and swimming. Indeed, Columbia is a perennial Ivy League soccer powerhouse. Most field women's teams in major sports as well. In fact, Fordham has become a national power in women's basketball.

LOTTERIES. At any given time, New York State will have several lotteries going, all benefiting local school districts across the state. Bets range from 50 cents up, with prizes as high as $1,000 a week for life. As of press time there are four regular lotteries being conducted: *Instant Winners, New York Numbers, Win 4* and *Lotto.* The "games" for each vary, ranging from scratch-and-match-the-pictures to genuine lotteries whereby individuals choose a series of digits and compare their number to one drawn at random. Tickets can be purchased at thousands of newsstands and candy stores, but winners for each game are drawn on a different basis. For example, for the lotteries mentioned above, winning numbers for New York Numbers and Lotto are drawn live on television—on Channel 5 in New York City at about 8:30 P.M. nightly for Numbers and Tuesday and Thursday for Win 4 and at about 10:15 P.M. on Saturdays for Lotto; Instant Winners tells you immediately after purchase what you have won in the preliminary rounds, with winners eligible for a grand prize drawing. Each day's or week's numbers are reported in the daily papers as well. Even if you don't win anything, you'll have an interesting souvenir—and you'll have helped the state's school system.

HISTORIC SITES. Wall Street Area and the Harbor:
If you are conducting your own walking tour of historical sites and sights, you might do well to start out where the city did—at the harbor. Henry Hudson, an Englishman employed by the Dutch East India Company, sailed his ship, the *Half Moon,* into the harbor in 1609 and the area's inclusion in what Europeans called the "New World" dates from then.

Battery Park. Time your explorations to arrive Tuesday at noon (from the end of June to early September) and your explorations can be accompanied by the brassy beat of a Battery Park Band Concert. A few of the historic sites of note (walking clockwise):

Shrine of Saint Elizabeth Ann Seton, 7 State St. Canonized in 1975, the first American-born saint, she once lived at 8 State St.

Jewish Immigrant Memorial. In front of the Staten Island Ferry Terminal, it commemorates the 23 Jewish men and women who arrived in Nieuw Amsterdam (then chiefly inhabited by Mana-hatta Indians) in 1654, and stayed to found several of America's most distinguished families.

Verrazano Statue. Honors the Florentine navigator who pre-dated Henry Hudson, entering the harbor in 1524. Despite the fact that he boldly took possession of "this island-bay, river, and all countries, rivers, lakes and streams contiguous and adjacent thereunto," his employer, Francis I of France, did nothing further about it, and the island, therefore, never was colonized by France.

Castle Clinton National Monument. Originally built as a harbor fort in 1811, it has been substantially restored as such. It has also served as the Castle Garden amusement center, where P. T. Barnum staged the musical "event of the century" by presenting Jenny Lind. Those who could not obtain tickets formed rowboat parties and listened to the Swedish Nightingale from the river. From 1855 to 1890 the ex-fort played host to some 7,000,000 "new Americans" as the country's chief immigrant entrance station. After that it served as a station for fishes—the city's aquarium—until 1941.

Bowling Green. This is the site, many believe, where Peter Minuit bought the island Manhattan from the native Algonquins. A century later, it was indeed a lawn where sportsmen played bowls. The original 1771 fence around the green is intact today.

U.S. Custom House. It was built by Cass Gilbert in 1907, when America was newly conscious of its central position on the world stage. This may account for the themes of the white marble sculpture: the great continents and commercial cities of the globe.

Fraunces Tavern (corner of Broad and Pearl Sts.). One of the few remaining restored Colonial buildings in the city. Built in 1719 as a handsome private house for Etienne de Lancey, it was bought in 1762 by a Frenchman, Samuel Fraunces, otherwise known as "Black Sam." He ran it as the Queen Charlotte, or Queen's Head Tavern, and it was there, in the second-floor dining room, that General Washington gave the farewell dinner to his officers. Souvenirs of the occasion can be seen in the third floor *Museum of the Revolution.* The ground-floor restaurant open for lunch and dinner weekdays, Washington's birthday. The Tavern once offered "first-class regular dinner for 25 cents, for gentlemen only." The prices are now somewhat more elevated. The entire Tavern is closed weekends. The Museum is open Monday–Friday, 10:00 A.M.–4:00 P.M. Free.

To reach Battery Park, take East or West Side IRT (local) to South Ferry. While at Battery Park you will no doubt want to visit the *Statue of Liberty.* The 151-foot-high lady, the world's best-known symbolic monument, may be visited via the special ferry which leaves from Battery Park every hour on the hour from 9:00 A.M. to 4:00 P.M. daily, with additional sailings Saturdays, Sundays, and holidays, April through October round trip fares for adults, $1.50; all children (11 years and under) 50 cents. For further information, call 248–8097. The boat trip takes 20 minutes; allow two hours for round trip plus inspection of the Statue. Refreshments and souvenirs available on boats. The Statue has been raising her torch over New York Harbor since 1886.

There is also a ferry from Battery Park to *Ellis Island,* the former immigrant-processing center, through which the ancestors of many, many Americans reached the New World. The ferry leaves the park 4 times a day (9:30 A.M., 11:45 A.M., 2:00 P.M., and 4:45 P.M.) 7 days a week. The cost is $1.50 for adults and 50 cents for children under 12. The price includes a guided tour of the island, which takes about 2 hours and includes the old buildings.

Lower Manhattan

A few old streets: Stone Street was the first cobbled under the orders of Nieuw Amsterdam's governor, irascible peg-legged Peter Stuyvesant, who also built a wall along the north edge of the settlement in 1658 as protection against the Indians.

Wall Street follows the course of that original wall. Several years later the first road was built (1668), linking the first colony to a suburban village called Nieuw Haarlem. The road was called Broadway. At 45 Broadway there is a tablet at the site of the first house built on Manhattan in 1613. Nearby is the historic *Trinity Church,* reputed to be the wealthiest single church in the world. In 1705, Queen Anne gave Trinity Parish a grant of land covering a substantial chunk of lower Manhattan; the church still owns much of it. Alexander Hamilton and Robert Fulton are buried in the graveyard. The church (built in 1845, the third on the site) and graveyard are open daily from 7:00 A.M. to 6:00 P.M. The Trinity Museum is open Monday–Saturday, 10:30 A.M.–3:30 P.M., Sunday, 12:30 P.M.–3:30 P.M. Admission to all is free.

Nearby is the *Federal Hall National Memorial,* on the site of the country's first capital, where our first President took his first oath of office. A statue of Washington stands on the spot today. The museum includes the Zenger Room, with documents relating to John Peter Zenger's fight for freedom of the press. Call for schedule of weekly concerts 264–8711.

In the busy City Hall-financial district stands *St. Paul's Chapel,* where Washington worshipped. You can see his pew in the north aisle. The church was also the site of a special service after Washington's inauguration. This handsome church was built in 1761–66, and is the oldest public building in Manhattan. It fills the block between Broadway, Vesey, Church, and Fulton Streets.

Some other Historic Sites in Lower Manhattan: St. Mark's-in-the-Bouwerie, at 10th St. at intersection of Stuyvesant St. and Second Ave., was consecrated in 1799. It stands on the site of a chapel originally built on the edge of Peter Stuyvesant's 300-acre farm (or—in Dutch—Stuyvesant's *bouwerie*). You can see Stuyvesant's grave, and a statue of him, in nearby Stuyvesant Park. Nearby Stuyvesant Town, a "city" within a city—35,000 call this middle-income development "home"—covers part of his river-front farm.

At the east end of Fulton Street is the *South Street Seaport,* an area undergoing restoration. Pier 16 has several tall ships, some of which the public may board and view; a museum with displays and folklore about the history of the Port of New York; and several shops in restored 18th- and 19th-century buildings with goods and services in the manner of the era.

Have lunch at nearby *Sweets* (corner of Fulton and South Street), one of the world's finest seafood restaurants, little changed in style or excellence since it was founded in 1845. To reach Sweets and/or the Fulton Fish Market, take IRT or BMT line, or Broadway bus to Fulton St. and walk east.

Civic Center

City Hall. The present structure was opened in 1812, restored in 1956. In 1824, Lafayette, the great French ally of the colonists during the Revolutionary War, was officially entertained here. You may sometimes see ceremonies on the steps in honor of a person or group that has performed a good deed. Also of interest is *The Governor's Room,* where period furniture and portraits of George Washington, Alexander Hamilton, and John Jay, among others, are on view. Open to the public, Monday–Friday, 10:00 A.M.–3:00 P.M. Free.

Nathan Hale Statue. West of City Hall, but still within the surrounding park, a statue commemorates the patriot whom the British hanged as a spy in 1776. As he prepared to ascend the gallows, he uttered his historic farewell, "I regret that I have but one life to give for my country."

Greenwich Village

The Village was the city's first residential suburb, started in the late 1730s when people fled "north" to escape the plague. *Washington Square* was designated as a potter's field and public execution ground. By 1826, when it became a drill ground for militia, some 10,000 bodies, victims of the plague or the gallows, had been buried there. Around this time the Square's redbrick, white-trimmed houses were built. The old *Boorman House* on the northeast corner was the home of Edith Wharton, William Dean Howells and Henry James.

Washington Arch, at the foot of Fifth Ave., was first built in 1889 when the city celebrated the centenary of Washington's inaugural. The present version was designed by the famous Stanford White, and built in 1895.

Two blocks over from the Square, at the corner of 6th and Greenwich Ave., is the *Jefferson Market Courthouse,* built in 1877 and more recently saved from the wrecker's ball and turned into a branch of the N.Y. Public Library.

There are many other historic houses in the Village—for example, *The narrowest house in the city* at 75½ Bedford St., whose tenants included Edna St. Vincent Millay and John Barrymore. But the only house in the district which you can visit is *The Old Merchant's House,* 29 E. 4th St., 777-1089. The house was built in 1830, was lived in by the same family, the Tredwells, from 1835 to 1933 when the last of the Tredwell sisters died, in her nineties. The house was bought by a grandnephew and presented to the city. Sundays, 1:00–4:00 P.M., group tours by appointment. Adults, $2.00; students and Senior Citizens, $1.00. *To get there:* take Third Ave. bus to 4th St.; or IRT Lexington local to Astor Place.

Another noteworthy old house not far from the Village is the *Theodore Roosevelt Mansion,* 28 E. 20th St. 260-1616. The Rough Rider was born and grew up in this typical upper-middle-class brownstone which is well kept up, and open to visitors. Daily 9:00 A.M.–5:00 P.M., except Monday–Tuesday, October–May. Adults, 50¢; children and Senior Citizens, free.

Midtown and Uptown

The Abigail Adams Smith Museum at 421 E. 61st St. 838-6878. One of Manhattan's last 18th-century buildings. Originally the carriage house for the home the then Vice-President John Adams had built for his daughter Abigail. A gem kept in perfect condition by the Colonial Dames of America. Guide on duty. Monday–Friday, 10 A.M. —4:00 P.M. Adults, $1.00; Senior Citzens, 50 cents.

Far Uptown: *Morris-Jumel Mansion,* W. 161st St. and Edgecombe Ave. This Georgian Colonial hilltop house was built in 1765. A year later, George Washington slept here for a night. His camp bed may still be seen. Here too Aaron Burr married the wealthy Mme. Jumel, then in her sixties, and soon divorced her. *To get there:* Fifth Ave. bus 2 or 3 to 162nd St.; or IND Eighth Ave. subway to 163rd St. (AA local). Tuesday–Sunday, 10:00 A.M. to 4:00 P.M. Adults, $1.00; students and Senior Citizens, 50 cents.

The Dyckman House, 204th St. and Broadway, was built in 1783, and was the farm residence of the wealthy Dyckman family, which once owned most of northern Manhattan. The only remaining Dutch farmhouse in New York City. *To get there:* IND (Eighth Ave.) subway (A) to 204th St. Tuesday–Sunday, 11:00 A.M.–5:00 P.M. Free.

General Grant National Memorial, Riverside Dr. and 122nd St., 666-1640. The Civil War general and two-term president is buried in the crypt, with photo and other exhibits also housed in the tomb. Open daily, 9:00 A.M.–5:00 P.M.; closed Monday and Tuesday, October–May.

The Other Boroughs

Brooklyn: *Brooklyn Heights,* a picturesque neighborhood of brownstone, brick, and old wooden houses high on a bluff overlooking New York Harbor, was designated New York's first "historic district." The New York Landmarks Commission calls the Heights "by far the finest remaining microcosm of our city as it was more than 100 years ago." Once a year the Brooklyn Historical Society conducts walking tours of some of the private homes, but even at other times you may wish to wander through the streets and trace the evolution of the New York townhouse: wooden and brick Federal style, Greek Revival, Gothic Revival (which came into style in the 1840s), Romanesque Revival, and Renaissance Revival. The Heights' *Lady of Lebanon Church* is the first Romanesque Revival building in the U.S. An esplanade reached by way of Montague Street, the residential area's primary shopping block, affords a spectacular view of the lower Manhattan Skyline and the New York Harbor.

Lefferts Homestead, Prospect Park, 965–6560. A homestead built in Dutch Colonial days. Call for schedule.

Bronx: *Van Cortlandt Mansion Museum* 543–3344. Built in 1748, this house, now run by the Colonial Dames, has furnishings and household goods which reflect both its Dutch and British owners. Tuesday–Saturday, 10:00 A.M.–4:45 P.M.; Sunday, 2:00–4:45 P.M. Adults, 75 cents, children, free. *To get there:* IRT Broadway subway to Van Cortlandt Park (end of line).

Poe Cottage, Poe Park, Kingsbridge Road, 881–8900. Edgar Allan Poe wrote many of his works (including *Annabelle Lee*) in this small cottage, which has barely been preserved as it was in the poet's day.

Queens: *Bowne House,* 37–01 Bowne St., Flushing 359–0528. The Society of Friends assembled in this old house. Built in 1661, it is today a shrine commemorating the struggle for religious freedom. Tuesday, Saturday, Sunday, 2:30 P.M.–4:30 P.M. Adults, $1.00; children 25 cents.

Staten Island: *Billou-Stillwell-Perine House,* 1476 Richmond Rd., Dongan Hills. Original section of this house was built prior to 1675, later additions date up through 1830.

Conference House, south end of Hylan Blvd., Tottenville 984–2086. Built in 1680. The only peace conference during the Revolutionary War was held here. Wednesday–Sunday, 1:00 P.M.–5:00 P.M. Adults, 50 cents; children, free.

 LIBRARIES. The *New York Public Library* consists of two branch networks, the first covering Manhattan, the Bronx, and Staten Island, and the second taking care of Brooklyn and Queens. Although beset by severe financial difficulties in recent years, the system includes a number of outstanding individual branches, some of which will be detailed below. The library operates an excellent home reference information service: 790–6161. There is also a "readers' advisor" service.

New York Public Library at 42nd Street

The crown jewel of the system, on Fifth Avenue from 40th to 42nd Streets, is, ironically, a private library open to the public—funded originally by the Samuel J. Tilden Trust and the Astor and Lenox libraries of the 1890s. The city contributed to its founding by donating the site and constructing the $9 million building that was to house the collections.

The *Main Branch*'s two-block-long Beaux-Arts façade, with twin lions perched alongside the steps leading to the entrance, is a symbol of New Yorkers' quest for knowledge. With a public card catalog containing 10 million entries, and more than half an acre of reading rooms, it includes resources for virtually every field of endeavor. Only the Library of Congress and Harvard's Widener Library are larger. No books are lent out at the Main Branch, but anyone, resident or not, may use the Main Branch's volumes within the confines of the building.

The 42nd St. library, however, is something of a museum as well as a research center. Sixteen years under construction, it opened in 1911, christened at the time by President Taft. The expansive marble foyer bespeaks extravagance in a way that is rarely seen in New York. In addition there are several galleries throughout the building, and such specialty reference rooms as the Manuscript, Art, Print, Oriental Language, Technology, and American History Rooms. Most of these are open to the public; for some, including the Manuscript Room, a special pass is needed. There are always two or three special exhibitions at the library in the lobby and along the second- and third-floor corridors—prints, books, or manuscripts—as well as the Berg Collection, which has large exhibits that change twice a year or so. The Berg specializes in literature, and, except for the exhibit area, is open to qualified scholars and researchers only. The Gottesman Gallery, right off the first-floor lobby, is scheduled to open in early 1984 for large special exhibits.

Several other midtown Manhattan branches are of particular interest, and worth noting here. These include the *Mid-Manhattan Library* (sometimes known as the Annex to the Main Building, at 40th St. and Fifth Ave.; whereas the 42nd St. Main Branch is purely a reference and research facility, the Mid-Manhattan Library is a less comprehensive research and reference collection—specializing in science, education, and business, though in the near future it will include history and sociology too—with some circulating titles); the *Library and Musuem of Performing Arts* at Lincoln Center (111 Amsterdam Ave.; there are really two libraries here: one, open to the public, for records, printed music, dance, film and drama books, and the other, open to qualified researchers by permission. This branch also has regular exhibits of performing arts materials such as set models, designers' sketches, music manuscripts, etc.); the *Donnell Library* (20 W. 53rd St., also strong on performing and fine arts and popular books in foreign languages); and the *Library for the Blind and Physically Handicapped* (166 Avenue of the Americas).

The number of other branches and the hours they are open have dwindled during the course of New York's various fiscal crises, so it is best to check with individual branches when planning a visit.

SPECIAL-INTEREST LIBRARIES

New York has numerous specialized libraries on almost all subjects. Some, listed below alphabetically by subject area, are open to the public. Others may be found by consulting the *Special Libraries Directory of Greater New York*, available at the Mid-Manhattan Library, 8 E. 40th St. If the library you are interested in is not open to the public, you may know someone in a professional association who is allowed in. In all cases, we suggest you call before going.

Advertising and marketing. *Batten, Barton, Durstine & Osborne Information Retrieval Center*, 383 Madison Ave., 355–5800, and *NBC Information Services*, 30 Rockefeller Plaza, 664–4444. It's best to identify yourself as a student.

Architecture, crafts, and design. *Fashion Institute of Technology Library*, 227 W. 27th St., 760–7695, and *American Craft Council*, 22 W. 55th St., 397–0600.

Banking. *C.I.T. Library*, currently 650 Madison Ave., but may move; 572–6500, and *New York Stock Exchange*, 11 Wall St., 623–3000, where an appointment is necessary.

Behavioral sciences. *American Society for Psychical Research*, 5 W. 73rd St., 799–5050, and *Kristine Mann Library*, 28 E. 39th St., 697–7877, the latter specializing in the work of Carl Jung.

Biblical studies. *American Bible Society*, 1865 Broadway, near Lincoln Center; 581–7400, where Bibles can be found in more than 100 languages.

Broadcasting. *Museum of Broadcasting*, 1 E. 53rd St., 752–7684. The latter includes a large videotape collection of historic TV broadcasts.

Business subjects. *American Institute of CPA Library*, 1211 Ave. of the Americas, 575–6200, and the *Brooklyn Public Library*, 280 Cadman Plaza W. An appointment is needed at the 80,000-volume library of the *NYU Graduate School of Business Administration*, 100 Trinity Pl., 285–6000.

Chemistry. *Chemists' Club Library*, 52 E. 41st St., 679–6383.

Civil liberties. *ACLU*, 132 W. 43rd St., 944–9800.

Economics and commerce. *Dun and Bradstreet*, 99 Church St., 285–7000 asks that you call ahead for an appointment. The same is true for *The Black Economic Research Center*, 112 W. 120th St., 666–0345. Also, *U.S. Department of Commerce*, 26 Federal Plaza, 264–3860.

Education. *Manhattan Community College*, 134 W. 51st St., 267–3527, has an extensive collection of non-white materials. *Children's Book Council*, 67 Irving Pl., 254–2666, is self-explanatory. If you're thinking of studying abroad, exchange programs are evaluated at the *Information and Reference Division of the Institute of International Education*, 809 UN Plaza, 883–8470.

Engineering. *Cooper Union*, on Cooper Square at E. 8th St. and Third Ave., 254–6300.

Flowers and plants. *Horitcultural Society of New York*, 128 W. 58th St., 757–0915.

Geography. *American Geographical Society*, Broadway and 156th St., 234–8100, and *Explorers Club*, 46 E. 70th St., 628–8383. An appointment is essential to the latter.

History and Genealogy. *New York Genealogical and Biographical Society,* 122 E. 58th St., 755–8532.

Industry and labor. *American Arbitration Association,* 140 W. 51st St., 484–4000. Data, laws, and court decisions in this field are at *Worker's Compensation Board,* 2 World Trade Center, 488–4141 and the *U.S. Department of Labor,* 1515 Broadway, 944–3435.

Insurance. *College of Insurance,* 123 William St., 962–4111.

Journalism. *NYU Bobst Library,* W. 4th St. at La Guardia Pl., 598–2450, has the morgue of the late *Herald Tribune.* Scholars preferred.

Medicine. *New York Academy of Medicine,* 2 E. 103rd St., 876–8200.

Music. In addition to the previously mentioned Lincoln Center and Donnell Branches of the Public Library, the *Wallace Library,* 799–5000, at Juilliard's Lincoln Center building requires advance arrangements. Also see the *Metropolitan Opera Association Archives* at Lincoln Center, 799–3100.

Public administration. *John Jay College of Criminal Justice,* 444 W. 56th St., 489–5183, has special collections on police work. *New York City Housing Library,* 218 W. 64th St., 581–4855, has literature on urban planning.

Publishing. *Oxford University Press Library,* 200 Madison Ave., 679–7300.

 MUSEUMS. Examples of everything beautiful that man has fashioned with his hands throughout the ages are on view in New York, much of it housed in buildings which are of great architectural interest themselves.

The fine arts lead, and such museums as the Metropolitan and the Museum of Modern Art are among the best in the world, but if the Old (or New) Masters don't move you, stimulation can be found in other museums. There are studies of nature and the stars, of man's history on earth, and more particularly, of his life in New York City. Smaller museums, or portions of larger ones, are devoted to coins, musical instruments, rare books, crafts and folk art, ships, interior decoration, clothing, textiles, medicine, historical figures—the list is endless. Once a year, usually in mid-June, the stretch of upper Fifth Ave. known as "Museum Mile" becomes a pedestrian mall between 6:00 and 9:00 P.M. From 82nd to 105th Sts., strollers are free to come and go at ten of the city's best-known museums, including the Metropolitan, the Museum of the City of New York, the Jewish Museum, and the Cooper-Hewitt. Admission to all is free that night, with street musicians, mimes, and clown troupes entertaining the walkers outside.

Lastly there often are exhibitions sponsored by banks, oil companies, and large industrial corporations, usually in the lobbies of their office buildings; or

Ground Floor

Museum Cafeteria

The American Museum of Natural History

Reception Center

Theodore Roosevelt Memorial

Junior Shop

Subway entrance Central Park West

1st Floor

Meteorites, Minerals and Gems

Education Hall

Biology of Man

Education Gallery

Eskimos

77th St. Entrance

Northwest Coast Indians

Naturemax Theater (Auditorium)

Parking Area

Gallery 77

Small Mammals

Mexico & Central America

People Center

Natural Science Center

Calder Lab

Man and Nature

Ocean Life & Biology of Fishes

North American Mammals

Planetarium

Birds of the World

Man in Africa

Biology of Invertebrates

Theodore Roosevelt Memorial

Biology of Birds

North American Forests

Central Park West Entrance

Akeley Gallery

Asian Peoples

African Mammals

2nd Floor

Asiatic Mammals

Theodore Roosevelt Memorial

Oceanic Birds

Central Park West Entrance

The American Museum of Natural History

3rd Floor

Eastern Woodlands and Plains Indians

Primates

North American Birds

Gallery 3

African Mammals

Reptiles & Amphibians

Central Park West

4th Floor

Earth History

Library

Fossil Fishes

Late Mammals

Early Dinosaurs

Late Dinosaurs

Early Mammals

Central Park West

you may find a display of anything literally from soup to nuts squirreled away in some corner of a school, church, YMCA, or firehouse—you name it.

The following New York City museums are all in Manhattan unless otherwise noted.

American Craft Museum I. 44 W. 53rd St.; 397–0630; **American Craft Museum II.** 77 45th St.; 397–0605. Exhibitions spotlighting contemporary craftspersons working in clay, glass, fiber, wood, metal, and paper are divided between the two locations. Museum I is open Tuesday–Saturday, 10:00 A.M. - 5:00 P.M., and Sundays and holidays, 11:00 A.M. - 5:00 P.M. Museum II is open Monday–Friday, 10:00 A.M. - 5:00 P.M. Admission is $1.50 for adults, 75 cents for children under 16, students and senior citizens. Children under 12 admitted free when accompanied by adult. One fee covers entry to both museums.

American Museum of Natural History. Central Park West at 79th St.; 873–4225. Billed as the world's largest natural history museum, where everything involving animal, vegetable, and mineral is dramatically highlighted, the American Museum of Natural History has an incredible array of marvels too numerous to be taken in on a single visit. (The museum's collections comprise some 35-million artifacts and specimens!) A few notables are the exquisite 563–carat (golf-ball size) Star of India star sapphire; one of only two dinosaur mummies known to exist in the world (part of the largest and most complete dinosaur collection anywhere); an enormous crosscut of a Giant Sequoia tree over 90 feet in circumference and dating back to 550 A.D.; and, of course, the 94-foot Blue whale, which hangs suspended in the first floor Hall of Ocean Life. The newest permanent attraction is the Naturmax Theater, with New York City's largest indoor screen (40 feet by 66 feet) and a special projection system that creates an incredibly realistic and spectacular film experience. The film schedule includes the soaring *To Fly, Living Planet,* and other giant-screen films guaranteed to leave audiences gasping in their seats. Call 496–0900 for times and admission fees. Another new treasure is the Garner D. Stout Hall of Asian Peoples, focusing on the rich cultures of Asia with 3,000 artifacts and artworks from the dawn of civilization to the present, many of which have never been shown to the public. It's a fascinating trip back into time, from 600,000 years ago when Peking Man inhabited China to the late 19th century when Western technology began changing traditional ways of life. Explore the Arab world, the Indian Subcontinent, the Himalayan Mountains, the Mongolian steppes; and be dazzled by the peerless Chinese jades, rare Tibetan religious tapestries, and exquisite Japanese ivory carvings. The Arthur Ross Hall of Meteorites showcases a wide variety of meteorites, rock samples from the moon, an audiovisual program showing the impact of meteorites, and a series of exhibits examining the origin and significance of meteorites. In other parts of the museum are exhibits on minerals and gems, birds, dinosaurs, fishes, invertebrates, reptiles and amphibians, shells, forests, ecology, mammals, and man. There are frequent lectures and movies, special exhibitions, a graduate-study program, three theaters, library (385,000 volumes represent one of the largest and most valuable research collections on natural history on this continent), laboratories, summer sidewalk café and cafeteria.

Special exhibitions for the Museum of Natural History during 1983 are: Nov. 22, 1982–Jan. 9, 1983, Origami Tree (in Roosevelt Rotunda); through Dec. 15,

1982, Natural History Photo Contest; Dec. 3–March 27, 1983, Star Gods of the Ancient Americas (Gallery 3); Jan. 22–May 15, Deep Ocean Photography; Jan. 18–May 15, Exploring the Deep Frontier (Oceanic); June 15–Sept. 25, African Textiles (Gallery 3); Sept. 24–Jan. 8, 1984, Francis Lee Jaques.

Open daily, 10:00 A.M.–5:45 P.M., and to 9:00 P.M. on Wednesday, Friday and Saturday evenings. Closed Thanksgiving and Christmas days. Suggested contribution: adults, $3.00; children, $1.50.

Hayden Planetarium, a separate division of the American Museum of Natural History, at 81st St. and Central Park West, 873–0404, presents its ever-popular Sky Show. A huge, star-filled dome brings the heavens to life via a Zeiss Projector and other dazzling special-effects techniques. The Guggenheim Space Theater, a circular area with 22 screens for projecting a wraparound slide presentation serves as an introduction to the Sky Show. Schedules vary, so call ahead.   Persons over 12 years, $3.25; students and senior citizens, with ID, $2.25; children under 13 years, $1.50.

American Numismatic Society. Broadway at 155th St.; 234–3130. The society advances numismatic knowledge as it applies to history, art, archeology, and economics. Exhibits include a large collection of coins and commemorative medals. Special emphasis is on the United States collection. Lectures on numismatic research are open to the public. Library, museum shop. Open Tuesday-Saturday, 9:00 A.M.-4:30 P.M., Sunday, 1:00–4:00 P.M. Free.

Asia Society. 725 Park Ave. at 71st St.; 288–6400. A $16.6-million, eight-story, red-granite building, designed by Edward Larrabee Barnes, is the new headquarters for this nonprofit educational group that concentrates on Asian affairs. Although not exactly a museum, the facility offers permanent exhibits accenting Far Eastern art. *The Mr. and Mrs. John D. Rockefeller 3rd Gallery* comprises three sections: an installation of South Asian stone and bronze sculptures, including art from India, Nepal, Pakistan, and Afghanistan; the Chinese section, displaying ritual bronze vessels, ceramics, sculptures, and paintings, along with a small group of Korean ceramics; and the Japan section, which houses ceramics, paintings, and wood sculptures. The second permanent exhibit is the Arthur Ross Gallery featuring Southeast Asian art—an important group of stone and bronze sculptures, mainly from Cambodia and Thailand. Temporary exhibitions are presented in the C.V. Starr Gallery on the ground floor three or four times a year.

The following exhibits tentatively scheduled for the 1983 season: through Jan. 1983, Arts of the Islamic Book (Collection of Sadruddin Aga Khan); Feb. 3–April 3, The Silk Route and the Diamond Path; May 5–July 31, The Dyer's Art in Indian Textiles; Sept. 15–Oct. 30, Emakimono (from Japanese Collections); and Dec. 10–Jan. 22, 1984, Korean Folk Painting.

Open Tuesday, Wednesday, and Friday, 10:00 A.M.-5:00 P.M., Thursday, 10:00 A.M.-8:30 P.M., Saturday, 10:00 A.M.-5:00 P.M., and Sunday, noon to 5:00 P.M. $2.00.

The Brooklyn Museum. Eastern Parkway and Washington Ave., Brooklyn; 638–5000. Flanked by the Brooklyn Botanic Gardens, this museum is a real find for museum lovers who enjoy viewing the sights but not battling the crowds.

Brooklyn Museum

Points of Interest

1) Sculpture Garden
2) Museum Shop
3) Main Lobby
4) Robert E. Blum Special Exhibition Gallery
5) Africa
6) The Americas
7) Oceanic
8) Community Gallery
9) Cafeteria
10) Himalayas/Southeast Asia
11) Japan
12) Korea
13) Library
14) China
15) India
16) Islamic Art
17) Print Gallery
18) Art School
19) Greek Art
20) Roman and Coptic Art
21) Lecture Hall
22) Auditorium Court
23) Coptic Art
24) Wilbour Library of Egyptology
25) Middle Kingdom and Dynasty XVIII
26) Monor Arts
27) Ancient Middle Eastern Art

28) Old and Middle Kingdoms
29) Predynastic Period
30) Old Kingdom
31) Funerary Arts
32) Egyptian Deities
33) Ramesside and Late Periods
34) 19th-Century American Period Rooms and Decorative Arts
35) Ceramics
36) Glassware
37) American Folk Art
38) 18th-Century Period Rooms: New England
39) American Folk Art
40) Metalwares
41) 18th-Century Period Rooms: the South
42) Special Exhibition Gallery
43) 20th-Century Decorative Arts
44) Jan Martense Schenck House
45) 17th- and 18th-Century Decorative Arts
46) Costumes and Textiles Gallery/Costume Theatre
47) American Painting III
48) American Painting II
49) American Painting I
50) American Painting IV
51) European Painting
52) Rotunda
53) Modern Painting

3rd Floor

Brooklyn
Museum

4th Floor

5th Floor

Though the museum is the seventh largest in the nation and houses a truly outstanding collection of artistry dating from ancient history to contemporary times, visitors are able to relax and enjoy the collection in an atmosphere of quiet peacefulness far removed from the hustle-bustle so often associated with many major museums. Perhaps most highly acclaimed for its world-renowned collection of ancient Egyptian art, the museum also has extensive collections of the primitive arts of Africa, Japan, and Indonesia, as well as American Indian primitive art. Also on view are the arts of India and the Orient, American painting and sculpture, prints, drawings, and watercolors (many by Homer and Sargent), costume collections, pewter, silver, ceramics, china (Wedgewood buffs will be pleased with the new Emily Winthrop Miles gallery, which contains a vast collection of the fine china), glass, and 28 completely furnished American period rooms—from Colonial days through the 20th century. Another standout not to be overlooked is the museum's outdoor sculpture garden; amidst the ivy, you'll find a vast array of ornamentation taken from Manhattan buildings, including one very life-like dragon who looks as though he could have flown directly from Tolkein's Middle Earth.

The 1983 schedule of exhibits for the Brooklyn Museum is: through Dec. 1982, From the Millicent Rogers Collection (evening wear accessories); Oct. 16–Jan. 16, The Genius of Charles James (original fashion designs); Nov. 10–Jan. 9, Realism and Symbolism in Scandinavian Painting, 1880–1910; Nov. 10–Jan. 30, Carl Larsson; Dec. 4–Feb. 6, Gene Davis: 30 Years of Drawing; March 19–June 19, The Great East River Bridge; through Sept. 1983, Marquetry (woodworking technique).

The museum has concerts, films, and lectures (write or call for a schedule), and there is a cafeteria in the building. The Gallery Shop sells folk art and handicrafts from over 65 countries. Open Wednesday-Saturday, 10:00 A.M.–5:00 P.M., Sunday, noon–5:00 P.M., holidays, 1:00–5:00 P.M. Closed Monday and Tuesday, New Year's Day and Christmas. Suggested contribution, $2.00 adults, $1.00 children under 12.

China House Gallery. 125 E. 65th St.; 744–8181. Classical Chinese art is exhibited at this facility operated by the China Institute in America, Inc. Open Monday-Friday, 10:00 A.M.–5:00 P.M., Saturday, 11 A.M.–5:00 P.M., and Sunday, 2:00–5:00 P.M. Free.

The Cloisters. Fort Tryon Park; 923–3700. A branch of the Metropolitan Museum of Art, this medieval art complex is perched on a hill overlooking the George Washington Bridge and the Hudson River. Constructed from the ruins of five French cloisters, some of the highlights include: 12th- and 13th-century Spanish frescoes; the extraordinary Unicorn tapestries; a Romanesque apse; a complete 12th-century architectural ensemble from a ruined abbey of Gascony; Romanesque wooden figure of the Enthroned Virgin and Child; the Bury Saint Edmunds Cross; stained-glass lancets from the Carmelite Church of Boppardam-Rhein; early Christian chalice of Antioch; an arcade from a Benedictine priory of Froville in eastern France; and scores of other priceless objects. It's well worth the trip uptown to this very peaceful retreat. Can be reached on the M4 bus, which goes up Madison Ave. in midtown. Open Tuesday-Saturday,

Plan of the Cloisters

Upper level

Books and Reproductions

Fuentiduena Chapel

St. Guilhem Cloister

West Terrace

Langon Chapel

Romanesque Hall

Pontaut Chapter House

Early Gothic Hall

Cuxa Cloister

Tapestry Room

Entrance Hall

Late Gothic Hall

Upper Driveway

Froville Arcade

Campin Room

Tapestries

Boppard Room

Hall of the Unicorn Tapestries

Gothic Chapel

N W E S

Lower level

Entrance

Lower Driveway

Treasury

Glass Gallery

Trie Cloister

Bonnefont Cloister

Gothic Chapel

10:00 A.M.–4:45 P.M.; Sundays and holidays, 1:00 P.M.–4:45 P.M., Sundays, from May to September, 12:00 P.M.–4:45 P.M.; closed Mondays. Suggested contribution: adults, $4.00; senior citizens and students, $2.00; children under 12, free.

Cooper-Hewitt Museum. 2 E. 91st St.; 860–6868. Founded in 1897 by Eleanor, Amy, and Sarah Hewitt as an adjunct to the Cooper Union (established by their grandfather, Peter Cooper), the museum collections were later entrusted to the Smithsonian Institution in 1967. In 1976, the Cooper-Hewitt opened in the historic mansion of American industrialist and philanthropist, Andrew Carnegie. The collection's accent is on decorative arts of all periods and countries, highlighting architecture and ornament drawings, prints, textiles, jewelry, ceramics, wallpapers, metalworks, woodworks, and specialized materials. Gallery space is predominantly made up of small, intimate rooms and hallways, many with magnificently carved Scotch oak or teak ceilings and walls.

The museum boasts the largest drawing and print collection in the U.S., and its textile department is one of the nation's most comprehensive. These materials are available as a research resource to the general public, and are of especial interest to designers, architects, and scholars, all on an appointment basis. An extensive reference and picture-research library is also open to the public by appointment. A lovely garden, true to Carnegie's day, provides a perfect escape from the city's hectic pace, while extensive book and catalog publications are available by subscription from the museum shop.

At press time, the following tentative schedule for 1983 special exhibits was available: through Jan. 2, 1983, Scandinavia Modern: 1880–1980 (history of Scandinavia in design); Nov. 23–Feb. 27, 1983, American Picture Palaces of the Golden Age. For further information concerning the Cooper-Hewitt's special exhibits, please call the museum desk. Open Tuesday, 10:00 A.M. –9:00 P.M., Wednesday-Saturday, 10:00 A.M.–5:00 P.M., Sunday, noon–5:00 P.M. Closed Monday and holidays. Admission, $1.50; senior citizens and students, $1.00. Free on Tuesday evenings, 5:00–9:00 P.M.

The Frick Collection. 1 E. 70th St.; 288–0700. In a word, the Frick Collection is magnificent. While most museums are simply a display area for works of art, the Frick has an elegant aura of an art lover's private home. Room after room is filled with masterpieces that make one's head spin. Even the most casual art-watcher will appreciate these works by the grand masters of art, including Renoir's *Mother and Child,* Vermeer's *Mistress and Maid,* Rembrandt's *Self Portrait,* Corot's *The Boatman of Mortefontaine,* and others by Fragonard, Bellini, Titian, El Greco, Turner, Whistler, Van Dyck—and the list goes on. Paintings, sculpture, exquisite furniture, decorative arts, stunning enamels, huge Oriental rugs—the Frick Collection has them all. Some highlights: South Hall—Vermeer's *Officer and Laughing Girl* and *Girl Interrupted at Her Music;* Boucher Room—Eight panels showing the *Arts and Sciences* painted by Boucher for Madame de Pompadour; Dining Room—18th-century British paintings of Hogarth's *Miss Mary Edwards,* Gainsborough's *Mall in St. James's Park;* Fragonard Room—Fragonard's *The Progress of Love,* 18th-century French furniture, including pieces by Riesener, Lacroix, Gouthière, Dupré, and Carlin, and Sèvres porcelains; Living Hall—Titian's *A Man in a Red Cap* and *Pietro Aretino,* El

The Frick Collection

EAST 71ST ST.

West Gallery

Enamel Room

East Gallery

Oval Room

Garden Court

Lecture Hall

North Hall

Library

Living Hall

Green Room

Sales

Reception Hall

Entrance Hall

Vestibule

South Hall

Fragonard Room

Boucher Room

Garden

Entrance

EAST 70TH ST.

Dining Room

Lawn

Terrace

FIFTH AVE.

Greco's *Saint Jerome;* Library—British portraits and landscapes by Gainsborough, Reynolds, Lawrence, Romney, and Turner.

To add icing to the cake, the building in which they are housed provides the sumptuous background necessary for such a collection. Overlooking Central Park (which can be glimpsed through the floor-to-ceiling French doors lining many of the rooms), the museum was the residence of Henry Clay Frick, the Pittsburgh coke and steel industrialist. A gorgeous indoor court, complete with fountain and tiered-glass ceiling, is the perfect resting place to sit and catch one's breath after seeing so many treasures. Be sure not to miss the Enamel Room with its 16th-century painted enamel dishes and triptychs, or the West Gallery, a huge room with a truly impressive display of art, among them Constable's *The White Horse,* and Bronzino's lovely *Portrait of Lodovico Capponi.*

A museum shop sells prints, cards, books, and detailed catalogs of the collection. Open September-May, Tuesday-Saturday, 10:00 A.M.–6:00 P.M., closed Mondays; June-August, Wednesday-Saturday, 10:00 A.M.–6:00 P.M., Sunday, 1:00–6:00 P.M., closed Monday and Tuesday, major holidays. Adults, $1.00; students and senior citizens, 50 cents. Sunday, $2.00. Children under 10 not admitted; those under 16 must be accompanied by an adult.

The Solomon R. Guggenheim Museum. 1071 Fifth Ave. at 88th St.; 860–1313. The ultramodern façade and interior created by Frank Lloyd Wright is the centerpiece for the modern works on display. The *Justin K. Thannhauser Collection* consists mainly of French works from the Impressionist and Post-Impressionist eras, including Pissarro, Manet, Renoir, Cézanne, van Gogh, Gauguin, Toulouse-Lautrec, and Degas, and heavily emphasizing works by Picasso and Braque. *Pioneers of 20th-Century Art,* another permanent collection gallery, contains a selection of 40 of the finest and most famous paintings of Kandinsky, Klee, Léger, Chagall, and many others. Artists represented in the *Peggy Guggenheim Collection* (in Venice) include Klee, Ernst, de Kooning, Gorky, Kandinsky and Pollock, among others. The main, spiral gallery is used exclusively for the temporary exhibits for which the Guggenheim is famous; check the newspapers or *New York* and *New Yorker* magazines. Special events include concerts, poetry readings, and lectures.

Special exhibits to come to the Guggenheim in 1983: Nov. 19, 1982–Jan. 9, 1983, Yves Klein (1928–1962): A Retrospective; Nov. 18, 1982–March 13, 1983. Selections from the Peggy Guggenheim Collection; March 11–May 8, Julio Gonzales; March 22–June 5. Charles Simonds; April 18–June 5. Aspects of British Art from the Guggenheim Museum Collection; May 20–Sept. 11, Acquisition Priorities: Aspects of Postwar Painting in Europe; Nov.–Feb. 1984, Kadinsky: Russian and Bauhaus Years, 1915–1933. Special events include films, lectures, poetry readings, and performing arts. For schedules, call 860–1356.

Taped or guided tours are available by appointment; 860–1363. The Guggenheim also offers an extensive bookstore, a café, and an outdoor terrace. Museum open Tuesday, 11:00 A.M.–8:00 P.M. Wednesday–Sunday and holidays, 11:00 A.M. –5:00 P.M., closed Mondays. Admission: $2.00; students and adults over 62, $1.25; children under seven, free; Tuesday evenings, 5:00–8:00 P.M., free.

Hispanic Society of America. Broadway and 155th St.; 690–0743. The famous Spanish masters, El Greco, Velasquez, and Goya are elegantly displayed here, along with collections of jewelry, sculpture, pottery, tiles, and textiles that reflect the history and culture of Hispanic people. Open Tuesday-Saturday, 10:00 A.M.–4:30 P.M., Sunday, 1:00–4:00 P.M. Closed Monday and holidays. Free, but contributions are appreciated.

International Center of Photography. 1130 Fifth Ave. at 94th St.; 860–1777. The only museum in New York City devoted exclusively to photography. Opened in 1974 and housed in a neo-Georgian landmark building that was once headquarters for the prestigious Audubon Society, the galleries display continuous, changing exhibits of works by such as Henri Cartier-Bresson, Alfred Eisenstaedt, Berenice Abbott, and others.

A tentative schedule of special exhibits to be held during the 1983 season is: Nov.–Dec., 1982, Bonjour M. Lartigue: the Work of Jacques Henri Lartigue; Jan.–Feb., 1983, The Frozen Image: Scandinavian Photography; March–April, Retrospectives of Norman Parkinson and Bill Brandt (as part of the Britain Salutes New York Celebration); May–June, Roy Stryker's Home Front—1940–1948; July–Aug., The American Image: Photographs from the National Archives—1860–1960; Sept.–Oct., Horst: A Retrospective—A Master of Fashion Photography; Nov.–Dec., Hiroshi/Hamaya: Japan—A Retrospective of Fifty Years.

The museum shop sells books, postcards, posters, and limited-edition prints. Also offered are lectures, courses, and workshops. Open Tuesday–Friday, noon–8:00 P.M., Saturday and Sunday, noon–6:00 P.M., closed Monday. Admission, $2.00; students and senior citizens, $1.00.

Japan House. 333 E. 47th St.; 752–0824. Headquarters for the Japan Society, organized in 1907 to bring the peoples of Japan and the United States closer together through the examination and appreciation of their respective cultures, this gallery features a wonderfully serene setting for exhibits from well-known Japanese and American museums and private collections of Japanese art. Other Japan Society programs special events include movies, lectures, classes, audiovisual presentations, concerts, and drama. Four exhibits yearly; the following tentative schedule was available at press time: Nov. 24–Jan. 16, 1983, Buddhist Sculpture; March 15–May 15, Kamban: Signs of Japanese Life. For further information concerning the exhibits, contact the gallery. Call 752–3015 for reservations for the performing arts. Open Monday–Thursday, 11:00 A.M.–5:00 P.M., Fridays to 7:30 P.M. Some weekends. Library hours: Monday–Friday, noon–5 P.M. Suggested contribution, $2.50.

Jewish Museum. 1109 Fifth Ave. at 92nd St.; 860–1888. Established in 1904, the Jewish Museum is dedicated to collecting and displaying art and artifacts that represent Jewish tradition spanning nearly 4,000 years. Elegantly housed in the former residence of the Warburgs (donated in 1944), the collection, one of the largest of its kind in the world, includes ceremonial objects, antiquities, paintings, sculpture, photographs, textiles, decorative arts, and more—all created by Jewish artists or containing Jewish material. Two exhibits had been scheduled at press-time—A Tale of Two Cities: Jewish Life in Frankfurt and Istanbul, 1750–1870, from Sept. 1982–Winter 1983; and Jewish Folk Art, Jan.–

May 1983. Events accenting Jewish themes include concerts, lectures, films, and workshops. The museum shop has an impressive range of items. Open Sunday, 11:00 A.M.–6:00 P.M., Monday–Thursday, noon–5:00 P.M. Closed Friday, Saturday, major Jewish holidays, and some legal holidays. Adults, $2.00; children and students with ID, $1.00; senior citizens, open contribution. Free guided tours; group tours by advance arrangement.

Library and Museum of the Performing Arts. 111 Amsterdam Ave. (Lincoln Center); 870–1630. A division of the New York Public Library, this library/ museum touches on just about every imaginable aspect of the performing arts. While the collection's subject matter is concentrated solely on the performing arts, the media involved can be expressed in anything from Katherine Cornell's makeup kit to holographic manuscripts of Bach, Mozart, and Stravinsky. Set designs, costumes, letters, records (the library has a circulating collection of over 30,000 records touching just about every Broadway show ever to hit the stage), paintings, models, posters, and lithographs are just part of the vast (and vastly entertaining) holdings. The Bruno Walter Auditorium has frequent performances, many of which are free to the public. Small fry can also get in on the fun with the world's largest children's library, which houses the Heckscher Oval Theater, an exotic puppet exhibit (shown at child height), and lots of interesting memorabilia including a slipper hand-embroidered by Mark Twain for turn-of-the-century child actress Elsie Leslie.

The Library's main exhibit for 1983 will commence in September 83 and run for six months. During this time, all available gallery space will be filled with materials commemorating the 100th anniversary of the Metropolitan Opera. Other special exhibits scheduled to be shown during the 1983 season are: Nov. 23, 1982–Jan. 15, Retrospective of Leslie Hurry (scenic and costume designs); Feb. 1–April 8, American School of Ballet; Feb. 14–April 22, Career of Violinist Joseph Szigeti; May 16–July 30, Drawings and Designs for Near Eastern Lutes. Frequent special programs for adults and children. Hours vary. Free.

Metropolitan Museum of Art. Fifth Ave. and 82nd St.; 535–7710. At the top of the grand staircase on the second floor of this venerable institution is a stunning eighteen-foot mural by the 18th-century Italian painter Tiepolo, whose masterpiece heralds the recently installed *European Paintings Gallery,* devoted exclusively to European paintings from the 15th century to the first half of the 19th century. All the great masters in the museum's general collection are housed in this one section, whose galleries have been refurbished and reorganized. Some representative works include El Greco's *The Miracle of Christ Healing the Blind,* Vermeer's *Portrait of a Young Woman,* Rubens's *Self-Portrait with Helena Fourment,* Rembrandt's *Aristotle with a Bust of Homer.* (See the accompanying *Plan of the Museum* for a more detailed breakdown of this gallery.)

The *Robert Lehman Wing* contains a special collection, primarily European old master paintings and drawings from the 15th to the 18th centuries, but some 19th and 20th. The *André Meyer Galleries* house the Museum's later 19th- and early 20th-century European paintings: from Goya and Delacroix through the Impressionists—and that is where these galleries are at their best—to the Post-Impressionists.

The fairly new *American Wing* is arguably the most impressively mounted of the Museum's permanent exhibits. It has room settings from the 17th to 19th centuries as well as painting, sculpture, and all sorts of other objects, including a lovely collection of turn-of-the-century stained glass from Tiffany Studios. It is a bit hard to find your way around the wing; basically, there is an inner structure (it faces the Engelhard Court) surrounded by an outer structure.

Even newer are the *Astor Garden Court* and *Ming Furniture Room* and the *Douglas Dillon Galleries for Chinese Painting,* marking the first phase in the permanent reinstallation of the museum's collections of Far Eastern art. The Astor Garden Court alone is worth a visit to the museum; it is a reconstruction of an actual 19th-century Chinese scholar's garden. It is on the second floor but can be reached only from below on the first floor.

The north wing houses the *Egyptian Galleries,* including the Temple of Dendur, a gift of the government of Egypt to the Met, brought over disassembled and then reassembled on the present site. During part of 1983 the Egyptian Galleries will be only partly open, as the exhibit is being redone.

The mammoth *Michael C. Rockefeller Collection of the Art of Oceania, Africa, and the Americas* is devoted entirely to primitive art spanning 3,000 years, three continents, and an array of islands in the Pacific. The collection's 1,500 objects represent a rich diversity of cultural tradition, and include sculpture of wood stone, terra cotta, precious and semi-precious stone, gold and silver.

Other galleries and collections are: *Islamic Art; Ancient Greek, Roman* and *Near Eastern Art; Twentieth-Century Art; Prints and Drawings; Far Eastern Art*—especially ceramics and sculpture; *Musical Instruments of the Past and of Non-European Cultures; European Sculpture and Decorative Arts; the Costume Institute; French and English Period Rooms; Medieval Art* (in impressive churchlike settings); *Arms and Armor;* and, of course, usually, two or three featured temporary exhibitions.

Major special exhibits scheduled at the Met during 1983 are (tentatively): through March 6, 1983, Rodin's *Gates of Hell;* Dec. 6, 1982–Sept. 1983, La Belle Epoque (a fashion exhibition); Feb.–mid-April, American Poster: 1890–1920; Feb. 15–April 17, 15th- and 16th-Century Italian Drawings; Feb 26–June 12, the Vatican Collection (reserved date and time tickets only, through Ticketron; $4.80); April 13–July, Constable's England; May 14–Sept. 25, World of Henry Moore; June 6–Sept. 4, Paintings by Charles Wilson Peale. Exhibits past this time have not been scheduled at press time. For further information on special exhibits, call 535–7710.

Visiting the Met can be frustrating. There are *always* galleries closed for reworking, and when you visit they will probably be the ones you wanted to see.

Be sure to inquire at the desk for audio cassette tours of selected galleries. And for the kids' enjoyment, pick up a few of the gallery hunt booklets, which contain the Met's version of an Easter-egg hunt.

The *Junior Museum,* on the ground floor, is undergoing construction which will result in an "education center," complete with studios, a library, and an auditorium. Children's exhibits and activities will be stressed. The *Thomas J. Watson Library,* for research, has more than 155,000 art books and 1,000

The Metropolitan Museum of Art

Ground Floor

(access from
main floor)

81ST ST.
Entrance

1) Auto Entrance
2) Public Garage
3) Elevator to Garage
4) To Garage
5) Junior Museum Library
6) Junior Museum Auditorium
7) Photography Sales
8) Slide Library
9) European Decorative Arts
10) Costume Institute

The Metropolitan Museum of Art

Main Floor

11) Greek and Roman Art
12) Library
13) Blumenthal Patio
14) European Sculpture and Decorative Arts
15) French Period Rooms (Wrightsman Galleries)
16) English Period Rooms
17) The Robert Lehman Collection
18) Medieval Art
19) Art and Book Shop
20) Gift Shop
21) Great Hall (the lobby)
22) Arms and Armor
23) Grace Rainey Rogers Auditorium

24) Membership Office
25) Egyptian Art
26) Concerts and Lectures Box Office
27) Sackler Wing/Temple of Dendur
28) The American Wing (28a is the Engelhard Court, 28b is the "inner" wing, and 28c is the "outer" wing)
29) Michael C. Rockefeller Collection of the Art of Oceania, Africa and the Americas (Primitive Art). 29a is Africa, 29b is the Americas, and 29c is the Pacific.
30) Portions of the Egyptian Galleries to reopen in 1983

The Metropolitan Museum of Art

2nd Floor

31) The American Wing (31a is the Engelhard Court—galleries for silver and glass overlook the court, 31b is the "inner" wing, and 31c is the "outer" wing.)
32) Islamic Art
33) The Andre Meyer Galleries
34) Greek and Roman Art
35) Ancient Near Eastern Art
35a) Assyrian Gallery
36) 20th Century Art
37) European Paintings
38) Great Hall Balcony
39) Far Eastern Art
40) Musical Instruments
41) Special Exhibition Areas
42) Sackler Exhibition Hall
43) Douglas Dillon Galleries for Chinese Painting
44) Astor Garden Court and Ming Furniture Room (access from main floor)
45) Acquisitions Gallery
46) Galleries for Drawings, Prints and Photographs

The Metropolitan Museum of Art
European Paintings Galleries

(This area is No. 37 at the top of the main staircase on the 2nd floor.)

1) Tiepolo
2) Reynolds, Gainsborough, Pannini
3) Giotto, di Paolo, Sassetta
4) Italian secular painting
4A) Pinturicchio
4B) Botticelli, Mantegna
5) Bellini, Mantegna, Tura
6) Botticelli, Lippi, di Cosimo
8) Titian, Tintoretto, Veronese
9) Moretto, Moroni, Correggio
10) Claude, Poussin
11) La Tour
12) Vermeer, De Hooch, Steen
13) Ruisdael, Cuyp, Van Goyen, Hobbema
14) Rembrandt, Hals, Vermeer
14A) Memling, Dürer

15) Rembrandt, Hals
16) Lawrence, Raeburn
18) Greuze, Chardin, Robert
21) Watteau, Boucher, Fragonard
22) Guardi, Hogarth, D. Tiepolo
23) Van Eyck, Van der Weyden
24) G. David, Bosch
25) Holbein, Cranach, Clouet
26) Bruegel, Cranach, Patinir
27) Rubens, Van Dyck, Jordaens
28) Van Dyck, Jordaens
29) El Greco
30) Caravaggio, Carracci, Reni, Rosa
31) Velazquez
32) Murillo, Zurbaran
39) Special Exhibitions

periodical items. In the southern wing of the museum, on the main floor, there is an indoor restaurant (serving so-so food). The museum also provides free lectures and films from time to time, plus subscription concerts and lecture courses on art.

In a way, the museum is also a sort of art supermarket, with these shops: A reproductions shop, for pendants, other jewelry, sculpture, and so forth, up to and including solid-silver reproductions of Early American silverware; a Christmas card shop; a children's shop; a regular—and very extensive—bookshop; and a poster shop.

Call or write for the museum's monthly calendar of events. Floor plans, friendly staff members, and special services are available. Note: Highlight tours are conducted weekends.

Open Tuesday, 10:00 A.M. to 8:45 P.M., Wednesday-Saturday, 10:00 A.M. to 4:45 P.M., Sunday and holidays, 11:00 A.M. to 4:45 P.M., closed Mondays, including Monday holidays. Suggested admission: $4.00 for adults, $2.00 for students and senior citizens. Members and children under 12 with an adult are free.

(In good weather and especially on weekends, there is almost always some sort of street theater going on for the tired museumgoers sitting on the steps outside the main entrance, usually mimes or magicians, plus, say, a brass quintet playing Gabrieli, and lots of hot-dog vendors.)

Pierpont Morgan Library. 29 E. 36th St.; 685–0008. The Library's collection is contained in a neo-Renaissance palazzo built in 1906 to house the already burgeoning collection of medieval and Renaissance manuscripts, old-master drawings, and rare books amassed by financier J. Pierpont Morgan. Since that time, the Library, located in midtown Manhattan, has become one of the city's classic landmarks. A treasure house of literary, historical, and artistic collectibles, the Library contains manuscripts dating back to the Middle Ages and on through the Renaissance, a comprehensive collection of bookbindings, many intricately wrought in precious metals and jewels, plus a good number of rare books dating from their original printings. The collection also includes such items as the Stavelot Triptych (reputedly containing fragments of the True Cross), and, on an historical note, Lord Cornwallis' letter to George Washington asking for surrender terms, which eventually led to our country's victory over England. Prominently displayed is the Library's newly acquired first printing, first state of the Declaration of Independence, the finest of 21 copies.

The walls of the West Room, formerly Pierpont Morgan's study, are clad in a vivid red-silk damask that provides a dramatic backdrop for the paintings, sculpture, stained-glass windows, furniture and intricately carved ceiling that adorn the room just as they did in Mr. Morgan's day. The East Room houses three tiers of bookcases extending from floor to ceiling. A scholar's reading room is open for study and research—accreditation is necessary, and the library asks visitors to abide by its very strict rules when using materials.

The exhibits are changed on a regular basis throughout the year. The 1983 schedule of exhibits is: Nov. 18, 1982–Jan. 30, 1983, The Last Flowering: French Painting in Manuscripts, 1420–1530; (musical manuscripts of) Stravinsky 1882–1971 and Haydn 1732–1809; Feb. 10–April 10, Symbolic Animals:

Monsters and Demons in Antiquity and the Middle Ages; same dates, Johannes Brahms; April 19–July 30, Holbein and the Court of Henry VIII, Drawings from the Royal Library at Windsor Castle; Sept. 1–Nov. 6, The Opera: 1600–1983 (a collection of original manuscripts, letters, and stage designs in conjunction with the 100th anniversary of the Metropolitan Opera).

Hours: Tuesday–Saturday, 10:30 A.M.–5:00 P.M., Sunday (except July), 1:00–5:00 P.M. Closed Monday, holidays, and August. Group tours available upon advance request. Contribution $2.00.

Museum of American Folk Art. 49 W. 53 St.; 581–2474. Weathervanes, whirligig toys that moved with the wind, paintings of people and landscapes, quilts, samplers, trade signs, painted and decorated furniture, and folk sculpture are found in the museum's collection of over 1,000 objects representing the nation's folk art heritage. The museum shop offers handmade items crafted in the folk tradition, postcards, and books on folk art. Open Tuesday 10:30 A.M.–8 P.M., Wed.–Sun., 10:30 A.M.–5:30 P.M., closed Monday. Admission: $1.00, students and senior citizens, 50 cents; children under 12, Free. Tuesday evenings 5:30–8. Free.

Museum of the American Indian—Heye Foundation. Broadway at 155th St.; 283–2420. Indians from North, South, and Central America are represented here with artifacts of hides and feathers, masks, totempoles, pottery, stone, jade and turquoise, and painted wooden sculptures. Children will gravitate to this exhibit. Open Tuesday–Saturday, 10:00 A.M.–5:00 P.M., Sunday, 1:00–5:00 P.M., closed Monday and holidays. Adults, $1.50; students and senior citizens, 75 cents.

Museum of the City of New York. Fifth Ave. at 103rd St.; 534–1672. A fascinating exhibit highlighting the history and culture of New York City—from a small Dutch town into the "Big Apple." Formidable portraits of New York's founding fathers look down on dioramas of historic scenes; a small-scale model shows the island of Manhattan when the "town" was walled off from the "country." There is a Fire Gallery with 18th- and 19th-century firefighting equipment, a turn-of-the-century streetcar, a history of the Stock Exchange, silver made by early craftsmen, ship models, period costumes, antiques, and six fully furnished rooms. The Dutch Galleries show a life-size reconstructed portion of Fort Amsterdam, and a multimedia show called "The Big Apple" is presented. From October to April, the museum's popular Sunday walking tours give visitors a chance to explore New York neighborhoods. Children's events include puppet shows, concerts, a "Please Touch" exhibit. Open Tuesday–Saturday, 10:00 A.M.–5:00 P.M., Sunday and holidays, 1:00–5:00 P.M., closed Monday. Free.

Museum of Modern Art. 11 W. 53rd St.; 708–9400. The museum (affectionately nicknamed MOMA) is currently completing a major expansion and renovation project that will significantly increase its gallery space—will, in fact, almost double it—and provide new services for its visitors and members. Because of the construction, the galleries as they had been set up over the past many years have largely been closed. During most of 1983, the entrance will be from what used to be the back of the museum at 18 West 54th St. Only two

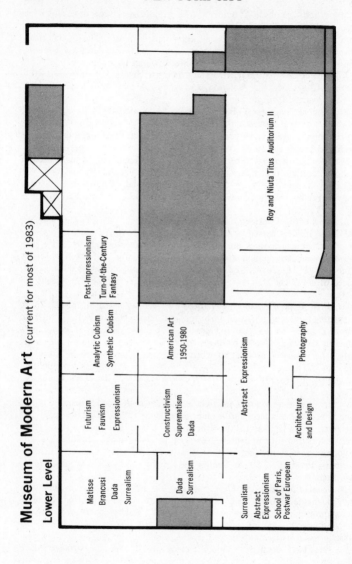

Museum of Modern Art (current for most of 1983)

Lower Level

Matisse
Brancusi
Dada
Surrealism

Futurism
Fauvism
Expressionism

Analytic Cubism
Synthetic Cubism

Post-Impressionism
Turn-of-the-Century
Fantasy

Dada
Surrealism

Constructivism
Suprematism
Dada

American Art
1950-1980

Surrealism
Abstract
Expressionism
School of Paris,
Postwar European

Abstract Expressionism

Architecture
and Design

Photography

Roy and Niuta Titus Auditorium II

THE MUSEUM OF MODERN ART IN 1983

During most of 1983, while full-scale construction and renovation of the museum's existing facilities are being completed, the museum's public program will take place in completed portions of its new West Wing. A selection of key works from its collections of Painting and Sculpture, Architecture and Design, and Photography will be on view on the lower level and a program of major temporary exhibitions will be displayed in new Ground Floor galleries. The entire museum will be closed for a short time toward the end of the year while its collections are rehung and inaugural exhibitions installed.

relatively small spaces will be open to the public, one for special exhibits and one for a sort of highly selective "best of" the museum's collection. This is in the new West Wing, the one currently under construction at press time. During 1983, the rest of the new West Wing galleries will be renovated and enlarged. The museum expansion should be completed by late 1983. Upon completion of construction, the entire museum will be closed to the public while its collections are rehung and its inaugural exhibitions installed.

When completed, the new configuration will include three public floors with permanent exhibits and two public floors for temporary exhibits, to total about twice the old gallery areas. The key to the new plan is the Garden Hall, a striking four-story steel-and-glass structure that will house a new system of escalators that will be a vast improvement over the old gloomy stairwells. Visitors will be able to look down upon the museum's Sculpture Garden through the glass wall. Next year's edition of *Fodor's New York City,* of course, will include complete floor plans of the completed project.

The Museum of Modern Art was founded in 1929 for the purpose of introducing to the public works of modern art—an area not then being covered at all by the Met. In acquiring works for the Museum, Alfred H. Barr, Jr., the first director, acted on the belief that art was not limited to painting and sculpture, drawings and prints, and extended the scope of the collections to include films, photographs, architecture, and design.

The museum's collections now include masterpieces of modern art from about 1880 to the present. In the new configuration the painting and sculpture collection will still be arranged more or less in chronological order, giving a sense of history and continuity to the art. The great movements of the late 19th and 20th centuries are all represented with outstanding, first-rate examples: Post-Impressionism, Cubism, Dada, Surrealism, Expressionism, Futurism, Constructivism, Abstract Expressionism, and more. Some of the most famous pieces of easel art on exhibit are van Gogh's *The Starry Night,* Matisse's *Red Studio,* Picasso's *Les Demoiselles d'Avignon,* Henri Rousseau's *The Sleeping Gypsy,* Jasper John's *Flag,* and Jackson Pollock's *One (Number 31, 1950).* The architecture, design, and photography collections are now probably the best in the world, including architectural models from Le Corbusier's studio, Edward Steichen photographs, Tiffany glass, posters, and so much more. Classic films have usually been shown at least once a day at the museum; the new setup will include not one but two auditoriums.

The following tentative schedule of special exhibits was available at press time: Through Jan. 4, 1983, The Work of Atget: The Art of Old Paris (photographs); Nov. 6, 1982–Feb. 8, 1983, Louise Bourgeois (sculpture). For further information concerning special exhibits, call 708–9480. Museum shops selling cards, books, posters, and reproductions are located in the lobby and at 37 West 53rd St. Information on Gallery talks is available from the museum desk. Open daily, 11:00 A.M.–6:00 P.M., Thursday, 11:00 A.M.–9:00 P.M. Closed Wednesday. Adults, $3.00; full-time students with I.D., $2.00; children and senior citizens, $1.00. Tuesdays, pay what you wish.

National Academy of Design. 1083 Fifth Ave. at 89th St.; 369–4880. Founded in 1825, the Academy's collection comprises works solely by American artists–Winslow Homer, Rembrandt Peale, Samuel Morse, Thomas Eakins, Reginald Marsh, George Grosz, Edwin Dickinson, and others—and ranges from the early periods of American art up to the present day. The collection represents only those artists who have been invited to membership, and since the requirements specify that the applicant submit a self-portrait plus a representative work of art, the Academy now boasts a vast holding of more American portraits than any other institution. Art genres represented are painting, sculpture, drawing, architectural drawing, engraving, prints, and photography. Exhibitions of the Academy's collection serve to document the considerable artistic activity in the United States throughout the 19th and 20th centuries.

Special exhibits may feature works from other countries, and those scheduled for the 1983 season are: Through Nov. 18, 1982, Samuel F.B. Morse: Educator and Activist; Nov. 4–Jan. 2, Battles and Leaders of the Civil War; Nov. 23–Jan. 23, Abbott Thayer Retrospective; Feb. 1–March 13., Three Centuries of Italian Still-Life; March 17–April 17, 158th Annual Exhibition (outstanding works by Academy members); April 28–June 15, Paintings from the Royal Academy; June 21–Sept. 4, Poland in the 19th century; Sept. 15–Oct. 30, Drawings of the French Revolution from Musée Carnavalet; Nov. 3–Jan. 1, 1984, Artists Portraits from the Collection of the National Academy of Design. Open Tuesday, noon–8:00 P.M., Wednesday–Sunday, noon–5 P.M., closed Mondays. Admission, $1.50. Free Tuesday evenings, 5:00–8:00 P.M.

New-York Historical Society. 170 Central Park W. at 77th St.; 873–3400. Founded in 1804, the museum showcases American history and art, with emphasis on the city's and state's contributions. The exhibits include fine American paintings, furniture, sculpture, and decorative arts such as original Audubon watercolors, Gilbert Stuart portraits, early American toys, old fire engines and carriages, and Hudson River school landscapes. It also has one of our nation's finest reference libraries of American history, housing over 500,000 volumes and many more manuscripts and prints. Open Tuesday–Friday, 11:00 A.M.–5:00 P.M., Saturday, 10:00 A.M.–5:00 P.M., Sunday, 1:00–5:00 P.M., closed Monday. Adults, $2.00; children, 75 cents. Tuesdays, contribution.

New York Public Library. Fifth Ave. and 42nd St.; 930–0800. Stored in what is certainly one of New York's finest architectural works are treasures far beyond what one normally thinks of in relation to a library. But the New York Public Library is no ordinary library. A Gutenberg Bible, early Shakespeare folios, the manuscript of Washington's Farewell Address (in his own hand), the Lenox Globe (one of the earliest global reproductions, dating from around 1510), and other rare books, prints, and manuscripts are all part of the Library's collection of things other than "just books." Frequently changed exhibits display selected portions of the Library's constantly growing holdings.

Some artworks to note are the four huge murals by Edward Laning on the second floor depicting the story of the written word from Moses and the tablets to the first printing press; *Kindred Spirits*, which hangs in one of the main hallways; and the gigantic *Blind Milton Dictating Paradise Lost to His Daughter*, located on the main stairway. Also of interest is the lion motif found throughout the library, even extending as far as the rather amusing lion water–fountains which dot the hallways. Plans are underway to renovate the Library's former main exhibition room (now office space), off the first-floor lobby, which fell into disuse during the Second World War when the Library put much of its collection into storage for safekeeping. This will be known as the Gottesman Gallery. Once renovation is complete (projected to be some time in 1984), the Library will be able to show a much larger selection of its vast holdings.

Special Collections are housed on the third floor: the Berg Collection, containing important editions, manuscripts, and autograph letters in the field of English and American literature; the Manuscripts and Archives Room; the Rare Book Room; and others. To use the materials in the Special Collections, a card of admission is required which can be obtained from the Office of Special Collections, Room 226.

Special exhibits tentatively scheduled for 1983 are: Through Nov. 1982, Rockwell Kent Centenary; Dec. 1982–Feb. 1983, 19th-century English Book Illustration and Victorian Publisher's Cloth; March–May, The Peace of Paris and Motion Picture Review Board; June–Aug., Festival Books and French Theatre Posters; Sept.–Nov., The Photographs of Alan Langdon Coburn; and Dec.–Feb. 1984, From Manuscript to Printed Book and Jewish Marriage Contracts.

Guided tours available Monday–Wednesday, 11:00 A.M. and 2:00 P.M. Open daily except Thursday and Sunday, 10:00 A.M.–6:00 P.M. Some divisions open until 9:00. Free. (See the plan of the Library in the *Libraries* section, above.)

South Street Seaport Museum. 207 Front St.; 766–9020. New York's historic waterfront has undergone dramatic restoration, and the museum, with its collection of historic ships and 19th-century buildings, is the centerpiece of activity. You can tour several old ships that are moored at the South Street pier, including the 378-foot, four-masted, square-rigged, oceangoing *Peking.* The museum shop (in Bowne & Co., Stationers) sells stationery, boat kits, and souvenirs. Concerts are held on the pier throughout the summer. Open daily, 11:00 A.M. –6:00 P.M., closed major holidays. Admission for vessels: adults, $3.50; students, $1.50; children under six, senior citizens, and members, Free.

Studio Museum in Harlem. 144 W. 125th St.; 864–4500. Making its home in the renovated Kenwood Building (with three times the exhibition space as the old location), the Studio Museum is hailed as the principal center for the study of Black art in America. The museum exhibits works by local and international Black artists, in addition to African jewelry and small artifacts, some of which is for sale. Special events include children's workshops, films, lectures, and poetry readings; call the museum desk for schedules. Located one-half block from the Lenox Ave. subway station (the West Side IRT 2 and 3 trains). Open Wednesday, 10:00 A.M.–9:00 P.M., Tuesday, Thursday, and Friday, 10:00 A.M. –6:00 P.M., Saturday and Sunday, 1:00–6:00 P.M., closed Monday. (Note: summer hours may vary.) Free.

Whitney Museum of American Art. 945 Madison Ave. at 75th St.; 570–3600. This museum contains the world's most comprehensive collection of 20th-century American art, with special emphasis on the work of living artists. Marcel Breuer's massive granite structure contains a sunken sculpture garden, lobby floor, three cantilevered gallery floors, and office space. There's a restaurant, and the museum shop sells catalogs, posters, and postcards on American art. Weekend lectures are popular.

Special major exhibitions scheduled at the Whitney Museum in 1983 include: Dec. 17–Feb. 27, Ellsworth Kelly: Sculptor; Jan. 13–March 13, Frank Stella: Prints 1967–1982; March 24–May 22, 1983 Biennial Exhibition; June 3–Sept. 18, An Aesthetic in the Making: American Art 1959–1963; June 16–Sept. 4, Grant Wood; Sept. 16–Nov. 27, Morris Graves; Dec. 7–Feb. 19, 1984, deKooning Drawings; Dec. 15–Feb. 26, 1984, deKooning Paintings; as well as the on-going exhibition 20th-Century American Art; Highlights of the Permanent Collection, and the installation of the Circus by Alexander Calder.

Open Tuesday, 11:00 A.M.–8:00 P.M., Wednesday–Saturday, 11:00 A.M.–6:00 P.M., Sunday and holidays, noon–6:00 P.M., closed Monday and Christmas day. Adults, $2.50; senior citizens, $1.25; children under 12 with adult, and college students with current I.D., Free. Free Tuesday, 5–8:00 P.M.

A SELECTION OF OTHER MUSEUMS
(All are located in Manhattan)

Abigail Adams Smith Museum. 421 E. 61st St.; 838–6878. Built in 1799 as a coachhouse and stable on a 23-acre estate, the structure has gone through many phases, functioning at various times as a country inn, a private home, and an office building. Abigail Adams, daughter of President John Adams, lived on the estate with her husband, William Stephens Smith, an aide to George Washington. As a museum its Greek Revival interior includes parlors, bedrooms, ballroom, library, music room, dining room, and kitchen, with authentic appointments from the early 1800s. The museum shop sells items from the Adams-Smith period. Open Monday–Friday, 10:00 A.M.–4:00 P.M. Closed holidays and August. Children under 12, free; adults, $1.00; senior citizens, 50 cents.

African-American Institute. 833 United Nations Plaza; 949–5666. Changing exhibits of contemporary and traditional African art. Monday–Friday, 9:00 A.M. –5:00 P.M., Saturday, 11:00 A.M.–5:00 P.M. Free.

Afro Arts Cultural Centre, Inc. 2191 Adam Clayton Powell, Jr., Blvd., between 129th and 130th Sts.; 831–4410. Artifacts from East, West, North, and Central Africa. Daily, 9:00 A.M.–6:00 P.M., for groups only. Adults, $1.75; children, $1.25.

Alternative Museum. 17 White St., below Canal St.; 966–4444. Mixed-media works by known and unknown artists, mostly of avant-garde nature. Wednesday–Saturday, 11:00 A.M.–6:00 P.M. Contribution requested.

American Academy and Institute of Arts and Letters. 633 W. 155th St.; 368–5900. Works by and about members, which include paintings, music, sculpture, and graphics. Research facilities open to accredited scholars, by appointment. Three annual exhibits open to the public; call for dates. Open Tuesday–Sunday, 1:00–4:00 P.M. Closed Mondays and holidays. Free.

American Institute of Graphic Arts. 1059 Third Ave. at 62nd St.; 752–0813. Competitive graphic design exhibits of both commercial and noncommercial origins. Monday–Friday, 9:30 A.M.–4:30 P.M. Free.

American Museum of Immigration. Statue of Liberty National Monument, Liberty Island; 732–1236. Part of the National Park Service, the permanent exhibit contains photographs, artifacts, and films depicting the history of American immigration. A comprehensive library also houses books and documents, and photographs from the collection of Augustus F. Sherman. By appointment; contact the librarian. Museum shop; handicap facilities. Open daily from 9:30 A.M.–5:00 P.M. Extended hours July–Labor Day. Sunday, 9:00 A.M.–7:00 P.M., Monday–Saturday, 9:30 A.M.–6:00 P.M. Free.

Aunt Len's Doll and Toy Museum. 6 Hamilton Terrace at 141st St.; 281–4143. Over 3,000 dolls and accessories, plus wind-up, mechanical, and tin toys. Tuesday–Sunday, by appointment only. Adults, $2.00, children, $1.00.

Bible House. 1865 Broadway at 61st St.; 581–7400. Among 40,000 volumes: two leaves from the Gutenberg Bible, fragments from the Dead Sea Scrolls, an 18-volume Braille Bible. Monday–Friday, 9:00 A.M.–4:30 P.M. Free.

Cathedral Museum. 1047 Amsterdam Ave. at 112th St.; 678–6913. Thirteenth- to 19th-century holdings from the collection of the Cathedral of St. John the Divine (the Cathedral itself well worth exploring). Monday–Friday, 11:00 A.M.–4:00 P.M. Closed Saturday, Sunday, holidays, and August. Free.

Center for Inter-American Relations. 680 Park Ave. at 68th St.; 249–8950. An affiliate of the Americas Society, this organization has exhibits concerned with the Western Hemisphere, from pre-Columbian to contemporary times. Tuesday–Sunday, noon–6:00 P.M. Free.

Drawing Center. 137 Greene St. near Houston St.; 982–5266. Group shows by promising unknown artists, and thematic shows by established figures, all based on work done on paper. Schedule varies seasonally. Free.

Fashion Institute of Technology. 227 W. 27th St.; 760–7848. Historic and contemporary displays of European and American fashions, textiles, furnishings, fashion illustrations, and photographs. Tuesday, 10:00 A.M.–9 P.M., Wednesday–Saturday, to 5 P.M. Free.

Federal Hall National Memorial. 26 Wall St.; 264–8711. It was near this site that George Washington delivered the first inaugural address of an American president. In the room bearing his name are miniature paintings, snuffboxes, and documents. In the Bill of Rights Room a diorama depicts the debate over that famous document. The John Peter Zenger Room honors the journalist-printer who founded the *New-York Weekly Journal.* Open September to May, Sunday–Friday, 9:00 A.M.–4:30 P.M., daily in summer. Closed major holidays. Free.

Firefighting Museum. 59 Maiden Lane near Nassau St.; 530–6800. Equipment, costumes, and assorted paraphernalia plus an extensive library that includes a photo file of old fire engines. Monday–Friday, 10:00 A.M.–4:00 P.M. Free.

French Cultural Service. 972 Fifth Ave. at 79th St.; 570–4400. Month-long shows by French photographers on view in the lobby of the former Payne Whitney family mansion. Monday–Friday, 10:00 A.M.–5:00 P.M. Free.

Goethe House New York—German Cultural Center. 1014 Fifth Ave. at 83rd St.; 744–8310. Exhibitions, films, video, lectures, readings, recitals offered on premises or at American partner institutes. Library with books, periodicals, and records. Tuesday and Thursday, 11:00 A.M.–7:00 P.M., Wednesday, Friday, Saturday, noon–5:00 P.M. Free. Write for the calendar of events.

Grey Art Gallery. 33 Washington Pl.; 598–7603. The New York University Fine Arts Museum is regularly given over to shows of mostly 20th-century fine arts; also, the Abby Weed Grey Foundation Collection of Contemporary Asian and Middle Eastern Art. Hours vary. Free.

Grolier Club of N.Y. 47 E. 60th St.; 838–6690. Rare books, manuscripts, and prints. Monday–Friday, 10:00 A.M.–5:00 P.M., Saturday to 3:00 P.M. October to June only. Free.

Institute for Architecture and Urban Studies. 8 W. 40th St.; 398–9474. Exhibits explore architecture in the context of the culture at large. Monday–Friday and some Saturdays, 9:00 A.M.–5:00 P.M. Free.

Interchurch Center. 475 Riverside Dr. at 120th St.; 870–3002. Displays pertaining to interfaith concerns. Outstanding permanent collection of Russian orthodox icons and church artifacts. Visiting arts and crafts exhibits. Monday–Friday, 9:00 A.M.–4:30 P.M. Free.

Intrepid Sea-Air-Space Museum. Pier 86 on the Hudson River at 46th St.; 245–0072. Unusually housed in a refurbished U.S. Naval aircraft carrier, this fascinating museum highlights episodes in Naval history from the Navy's origin in 1775 up to the present. It also features exhibitions revolving around the U.S. Air Force and space exploration programs. Exhibits are divided into four main theme halls spanning two full decks and several island bridges; these exhibits succeed admirably in taking the visitor back to the early days of technology and then far forward into the next century for a prediction of what the years ahead may hold. Open 7 days a week. June–September, 10:00 A.M.–8:00 P.M. (ticket office closes at 6:00 P.M.); October–May, 10:00 A.M.–7:00 P.M. (ticket office closes at 5:00 P.M.). Adults, $5.00; senior citizens, $4.00; children, $2.50. Call for group rates.

The Kitchen. 484 Broome St., SoHo; 925–3615. Continuous showings of new video and mixed-media works with the accent on the avant-garde. Tuesday–Saturday, 1:00–6:00 P.M. September–May only. Free.

J. M. Mossman Collection of Locks. 20 W. 44th St.; 840–1840. Historic survey of security instruments. Monday–Friday, 10:00 A.M.–4:00 P.M. Call in advance. Free.

El Museo Del Barrio. 1230 Fifth Ave. at 105th St.; 831–7272. Puerto Rican and Latin American fine arts. Tuesday–Friday, 10:30 A.M.–4:30 P.M., Saturday–Sunday, 11:00 A.M.–4:00 P.M. Voluntary contribution.

Museum of American Illustration. 128 E. 63rd St.; 838–2560. Contemporary, historical, solo, group, and theme shows drawn from the Society of Illustrators' 800-piece collection. Monday–Friday, 10:00 A.M.–5:00 P.M. Closed in August. Free.

Museum of Broadcasting. 1 E. 53rd St.; 752–7684. Enormously popular for its ever growing library of classic and contemporary radio and television programs, all available for individual screening. Tuesday–Saturday, noon–5:00 P.M. Suggested contribution: adults, $2.00, children under 13, $1.00.

Museum of Holography. 11 Mercer St. in SoHo; 925–0526. This museum, which was founded in 1976, is the first of its kind anywhere in the world. Holograms, which are pictures developed by laser light, create three-dimensional images. A permanent exhibit focuses on the history of the medium and its current state. A film called *An Introduction to Holography* is shown continuously in the 75-seat theater. Holographic portraits of people such as Andy Warhol, Joseph Papp, and William Buckley are on view in the New York Holofame. Open Wednesday–Sunday, noon–6:00 P.M., Thursday, noon–9:00 P.M. Adults, $2.00; children and senior citizens, $1.00.

Museum of Philosophy. 695 Park Ave. at 69th St.; 570–5142 or 265–5570. Lodged in the Hunter College Teacher Center, this is one of the new breed of interactive museums, known as such because of its "hands-on" exhibits in which the visitor is invited to participate in various philosophical experiments and displays. These explore the realm of metaphysics, and include holograms, experiments with perceptual illusion, video-taped lectures by well-known philosophers, skits on ethics, a series of computer exhibits, and also some lovely artwork such as photographs by Lotte Jacobi and the elegant calligraphy of William Metzig. Open Tuesday–Sunday, 1:00–5:00 P.M.; summer, Thursday–Sunday, 1:00–5:00 P.M.; closed Monday. Group tours arranged by appointment. Suggested contribution, $3.00; children, $2.00.

New Museum. 65 Fifth Ave. at 14th St.; 741–8962. Housed in a building of the New School for Social Research, but not a part of the school, this truly new museum—founded in 1977—shows art of the previous ten years by young artists who have had little exhibition exposure elsewhere. Monday–Friday, noon to 6:00 P.M., 8:00 P.M. Wednesday, Saturday to 5:30 P.M. Closed Sun. Contribution.

New York Fire Department Museum. 104 Duane St., near City Hall; 570–4230. Authentic firefighting equipment used during the 19th and early 20th centuries. Hand-drawn pumpers, engines, sliding poles, uniforms, and fireboat equipment are scattered throughout the museum. Children will love touring this old firehouse. Open Monday–Friday, 9:00 A.M.–4:00 P.M., Saturday–Sunday, 9:00 A.M.–2:00 P.M. Closed holidays. Free.

Pen and Brush. 16 E. 10th St.; 475–3669. Painting, sculpture, and graphic arts exhibits sponsored by the oldest professional women's creative arts organization in New York. Open daily except Monday, 1:00–4:00 P.M. October to May only. Free.

Puerto Rican Museum for the Arts. 3755 Broadway at 155th St.; 222–2966. Puerto Rican and Latin American fine arts on the campus of Boricua College. Monday–Friday, 9:00 A.M.–9:00 P.M. Voluntary contribution.

Theodore Roosevelt House. 28 E. 20th St.; 260–1616. Here is where our 26th President was born and lived during his formative years. The Greek Revival house contains memorabilia and historical items highlighting the Rough Rider's life. Such items include personal diaries, eyeglasses, relics of World War I, campaign buttons. Open daily, 9:00 A.M.–4:30 P.M., closed Monday and Tuesday. Adults, 50 cents; children under 16, free.

Schomburg Center for Research in Black Culture. 515 Lenox Ave. at 135th St.; 862–4000. A division of the New York Public Library, this is the largest museum and multimedia library in the world documenting the history, literature, and arts of Black people. Hours vary. Free.

Songwriters Hall of Fame. 1 Times Square; 221–1252. Pop music memorabilia ranging from Fred Astaire's hat and cane to the latest in electric guitars. Monday–Saturday, 11:00 A.M.–3:00 P.M. Free.

Theater Museum. 1515 Broadway at 45th St.; 944–7161. The theater district itself provides the natural home for New York's first theater museum, a satellite gallery of the Museum of the City of New York. Located in the arcade of the Minskoff Theater, this collection houses the most complete record of the New York stage. A few highlights: Mary Martin's original *Peter Pan* costume; Helen Hayes' first Oscar; all sorts of Ethel Merman memorabilia; and one of the world's most extensive Shakespeare collections, including set designs and costumes from various productions. A must for theater lovers. Open Tuesday–Saturday, 1:00–8:00 P.M., Sunday, noon–5:00 P.M., closed Monday. Suggested contribution, $1.00.

Urban Center. 457 Madison Ave. at 51st St.; 935–3960. Architectural and urban-issue exhibits and programs are housed in the North wing of the historic Villard Houses, at the foot of the Helmsley Palace Hotel. The bookstore specializes in architecture, urban design, and historic preservation. Hours vary. Free.

Visual Arts Museum. 209 E. 23rd St.; 679–7350. Five exhibits yearly, mainly of contemporary American art. Monday–Thursday, noon–9:00 P.M., Friday, 11:00 A.M.–4:30 P.M. Closed weekends. Free.

OTHER BOROUGHS

Bronx. *Bartow-Pell Mansion Museum and Garden,* Pelham Bay Park; 885–1461. The mansion, built in 1842, is a Greek revival restoration with sunken gardens, period furnishings, paintings, and a 200-volume library containing books on architecture, gardening, and herbs. Open Tuesday, Friday, and Sunday, 1:00–5:00 P.M. Contribution requested; children under 12 with adult, free.

Bronx Museum of the Arts, 851 Grand Concourse; 681–6000. This museum, founded in 1971, has a collection of Roman sculpture, decorative ironwork, and murals. Open Monday–Thursday, 9:00 A.M.–5:00 P.M., Sunday, 12:30–4:30 P.M.

Hall of Fame for Great Americans, W. 181st St. and University Ave.; 220–6450. Original bronzes of 102 prominent Americans are on display in the turn-of-the-century Stanford White edifice located on an important Revolutionary War site. This site is now on the campus of the Bronx Community College. (Call ahead to be sure of access). Open Monday–Saturday, 9:00 A.M.–5:00 P.M. Free.

Valentine-Varian House Museum of Bronx History, 3266 Bainbridge Ave.; 881–8900. Isaac L. Varian, mayor of New York City from 1839–1841, was born in this house, which was built in 1758 and was later the site of several Revolutionary War skirmishes. Indian and military artifacts, natural history displays, paintings, and prints and photographs tracing the history of the Bronx. Open

Saturday, 10:00 A.M.–4:00 P.M., Sunday, 1:00–5:00 P.M. Weekday tours by appt. $1.00 admission.

Queens. *Bowne House Historical Society,* 37–01 Bowne St.; 359–0528. Known for the *Flushing Remonstrance.* John Bowne, advocate of religious freedom when New York was still Nieuw Amsterdam, lived in this house built in 1661. It contains 17th-century furnishings, a pewter collection, and Bowne family memorabilia. Open Tuesday, Saturday, and Sunday, 2:30–4:30 P.M. School and adult groups by appointment. Admission.

Hall of Science of the City of New York, Flushing Meadow Park; 586–4004. Closed for renovation through 1983. Children almost always enjoy museums of science and technology; this one has a children's museum, cafeteria, and scientific toys for sale. The museum has a planetarium and an amateur radio station as well as collections explaining atomic energy, space science, and the environment. Open Wednesday–Friday, 10:00 A.M.–4:00 P.M., Saturday, 10:00 A.M.–5:00 P.M., Sunday, 11:00 A.M.–5:00 P.M. Suggested donation: adults, $1.00; senior citizens and students, 50 cents.

Queens Museum, NYC Bldg., Flushing Meadow, Corona Park, 592–5555, on site of 1964 World's Fair. This is the home of the Panorama, an 18,000 square-foot architectural model of New York City's five boroughs. Also exhibits major public and private collections, as well as the works of younger artists. Open Tuesday–Saturday, 10:00 A.M.–5:00 P.M., Sunday, 1:00–5:00 P.M., closed Monday Suggested contribution: Adults, $1.00; senior citizens, 50 cents; children, free.

The Store Front Museum, 162–02 Liberty Ave., 523–5199. Founded in 1971, this Black art and history museum has a collection of paintings, drawings, and sculpture by Black artists in the United States and abroad, including tribal art from Africa. A cultural center presents lectures, films, concerts and dance recitals. Open Tuesday–Friday, 9:30 A.M.–4:30 P.M. Free.

Brooklyn. *Brooklyn Children's Museum,* 145 Brooklyn Ave. at St. Mark's Ave.; 735–4400. A natural history museum designed especially for children with exhibits showing American Indian and other prehistoric cultures, fossils, mounted mammals, tame live animals, and a planetarium. Open Sunday, Monday, and Wednesday–Friday, 1:00–5:00 P.M., Saturday, 10:00 A.M.–5:00 P.M., closed Tuesday. Free.

Lefferts Homestead, Prospect Park, Flatbush Ave. near Willink Gate; 965–6587. The homestead was built in 1776 and contains costumes, textiles, and period furnishings. Open Monday–Friday, 9:30 A.M.–2:00 P.M., Saturday and Sunday, 10:00 A.M.–4:00 P.M. Free.

Long Island Historical Society, 128 Pierrepont St.; 624–0890. If your ancestors come from any of the four counties that make up Long Island (Kings, Queens, Nassau, or Suffolk), you might be interested in spending time in the reading room of this research library/museum, which has 125,000 volumes pertaining to local history and genealogy. The museum also has a collection of paintings, graphics, and costumes. Closed August. Open Tuesday–Saturday, 9:00 A.M.–5:00 P.M., July, Monday–Friday, 9:00 A.M.–5:00 P.M. Admission $1.00.

Staten Island. *Staten Island Museum* (formerly Staten Island Institute of Arts and Sciences), 75 Stuyvesant Pl.; 727–1135. Permanent science exhibits provide an introduction to the Natural History of Staten Island. The museum's changing fine arts exhibits contain paintings, graphics, and decorative arts which illustrate the history of Western Art. Open Tuesday–Saturday, 10:00 A.M. –5:00 P.M., Sunday, 2:00–5:00 P.M., closed Monday. Free.

Conference House Association, Conference House Park (7455 Hylan Blvd.); 984–2086. The only peace conference during the Revolution was held September 11, 1776, in a stone house constructed in 1675 known as the Conference House, or Billopp House, which now may be seen by guided tour. Open daily, 1:00–5:00 P.M., closed Monday and Tuesday. Admission $1.00, children 50 cents.

Jacques Marchais Center of Tibetan Arts, 338 Lighthouse Ave.; 987–3478. Here you may view examples of Tibetan and Buddhist art, study Eastern religions and philosophy in the 20,000-volume library, and meditate in one of the gardens. Closed November through March. Open April–November, Saturday and Sunday, 1:00–5:00 P.M., June–August, Friday–Sunday, 1:00–5:00 P.M. Admission $1.00, children 50 cents.

Richmondtown Restoration/Staten Island Historical Society Museum, 441 Clarke Ave.; 351–1611. This is New York City's only settlement restoration, representing three centuries of regional history and culture. The village, constructed upon 96 acres, consists of 25 historic structures including private residences, craftsmen's shops, a general store, a 1696 Dutch schoolhouse, and several municipal buildings. Thirteen buildings are open to the public and manned by authentically costumed interpreters who recreate the daily work activities and trades of an earlier way of American life. The Staten Island Historical Society Museum, displaying a fine collection of regional textiles, tools, household artifacts, and folk-art, will re-open early in 1984. Open May–June, September–November, Saturday, 10:00 A.M.–5:00 P.M., Sunday, noon–5:00 P.M.; July–August, Tuesday–Saturday, 10:00 A.M.–5:00 P.M., Sunday, noon–5:00 P.M.; closed December–April. Adults, $2.00; senior citizens, $1.50; Youth (6–18), $1.00; children under 6, free.

 MOVIES. Since 1963, the Film Society of Lincoln Center has produced what many regard as the most important film event in the country, the New York Film Festival, where many of the most innovative and critically acclaimed American and foreign films receive their first New York showing. It is the Big Apple's answer to Cannes, usually runs around two weeks from late September to mid-October at Lincoln Center and includes a "New Directors/New Films" annual series co-sponsored with the Museum of Modern Art. Tickets range from $4 to $6, opening and closing night are at Avery Fisher Hall, all other performances at Alice Tully Hall.

But New York is a year-around film festival. You'll hear many New Yorkers referring to movies as *films, flicks,* or *cinema,* and this art form is taken very seriously by fans, aspiring filmmakers, and professional critics. If two weeks pass and you haven't read about a W. C. Fields, Humphrey Bogart, or Marx Brothers Festival, better check to see if you're really in New York.

Movies are advertised daily in all the papers, but for a complete listing look to *New Yorker* and *New York/Cue* magazines, or to the Friday and Sunday *New York Times.*

There are at least five common formats for the presentation of movies here. First come the expensive ($5 or more) and prestigious East Side houses like the *Coronet* (993 3rd Ave. at 59th St.) or the *Beekman,* Second Ave. at 66th St.

Multi-screen neighborhood houses like *Loew's 83rd Street* (at Broadway) show features that have gained enough critical acclaim and made enough money in their first-run engagements to justify wide dissemination. They also host premieres of action-packed, star-studded "flicks."

Ten years ago, art film houses were known for foreign movies. Since film has come to be regarded as a kind of literature that can be experienced more than once, the situation has changed. Venerable theaters like *80 St. Marks* (8th St. and 2nd Ave.), the *Regency* (Broadway at 67th St.), and the *Bleecker St. Cinema* (Bleecker and La Guardia) have done well with old foreign and American classics and more recent works whose true values have surfaced since they first (sometimes unsuccessfully) came out. Some houses also have special midnight showings, on the weekend, of strange and often offensive cult films; read the listings carefully for these as they are frequently not advertised.

A fourth category includes museums, libraries, and churches that show films, often seldom-seen ones, in the course of retrospective examinations of great careers in the industry. Admissions are usually modest and the setting interesting beyond the film itself (such as the *Museum of Modern Art,* 53rd St. between 5th and 6th Aves., or the *Whitney Museum* on Madison Ave. at 75th St).

Finally, filmmakers not yet established in the big time want their work seen and occasionally have showings in out-of-the-way lofts or college buildings. They sometimes exhibit individually, sometimes band together in "collectives." Since they have little money for publicity, the best way to learn about a showing is to keep your eyes open for handbills and posters in Greenwich Village and near campuses around the city. Read the *Village Voice* for news of offbeat films.

Although ambitious plans for the facelifting of the Times Square area of Broadway are underway, some of its theaters are currently given over to X-rated films (this is true of W. 42nd St. and 8th Ave. as well). Those which are not, like the *National, Loew's State I* and *II,* show first-run action features—sure moneymakers. But colorful though the area may be, beware of the low lifes that infest some of the movie houses on this neon-lit strip.

There are some movie houses, however, that are as interesting as the movies they show because of their locale. The *Paris,* for example, at 4 W. 58th St., shows first-run foreign and art films right across the street from the venerable Plaza Hotel and Central Park. The *Harold Clurman,* 412 W. 42nd St., opens late in the afternoon, Mondays through Fridays, to show film retrospectives in a renovated theater in the heart of a new off-Broadway theater row on the spruced up West Side. The *Little Theatre,* in Joe Papp's Public Theatre complex at 425 Lafayette St., opens late in the afternoon to show old art films, giving one the opportunity to catch an off-Broadway play in the same building that evening. The *Thalia,* Broadway at 95th St., shows oldies but goodies and is an upper West Side institution, a liberal dowager of art-film houses, while the *Anthology Film Archives,* 80 Wooster St., way downtown, digs into its treasure trove to delight film buffs seeking the unusual. And smack in the middle, on the fashionable East Side from the 50s into the 80s, is a veritable Hollywood movie belt of first-run films in "piggy back" theaters, with as many as five different films playing in different showcases in the same complex.

 MUSIC. Manhattan is beyond serious dispute the most active musical city in the world, and the one with the largest population of professional musicians. (Most of them live and/or perform on the Upper West Side near Lincoln Center, where you will see many people carrying violins, cellos, and the like to and from lessons, rehearsals, and performances, and where it is not uncommon to hear tenors practicing scales as they do their grocery shopping.) Your only real problem is which performance to choose. In their daily entertainment sections, *The New York Times* and other daily papers list all the day's musical events—and Friday's papers include the entire weekend's goings-on, including church performances. The Sunday *Times* has the week's list.

Lincoln Center, Broadway at 64th St., is the musical heart of New York City, with *Carnegie Hall* (247–7459) its soul. Within the less-than-20-year-old Lincoln Center complex are *Avery Fisher Hall* (home of the New York Philharmonic, American Philharmonic Orchestra, the Mostly Mozart festival, and many visitng orchestra performances—874–2424); the *New York State Theater* (home of the New York City Opera—870–5570); the *Metropolitan Opera House* (base for that company as well as for many visiting ballet troupes—799–3100); *Alice Tully Hall* (probably the most acoustically perfect of the halls, and site of numerous chamber music recitals—362–1911); the *Juilliard School of Music* (799–5000)—one of the world's most respected institutions; and the *Guggenheim Bandshell* in the outdoor *Damrosch Park* (765–5100). Also part of the complex are the *Library and Museum of Performing Arts* (where some concerts and recitals are also held, especially for children—799–2200); and the *Vivian Beaumont* and *Mitzi Newhouse Theaters* (765–5100), which last two are currently not well utilized. The plaza at Lincoln Center is also the base for dozens of free concerts daily throughout the summer.

The various buildings opened one at a time, beginning with Avery Fisher Hall in 1964—then called Philharmonic Hall, but renamed after a donor contributed $5 million to have the acoustics adjusted. Interestingly, attractive as all the buildings at Lincoln Center are—the Met with its Chagall murals lighting up the plaza, the Calder sculpture that adorns Damrosch Park—designed by such recognized architects as Max Abramovitz (Avery Fisher) and Philip Johnson (State Theater, and later overseer of the reconstruction of Avery Fisher), they have almost all been beset by acoustical and structural problems. Avery Fisher and the Beaumont/Newhouse theaters have all undergone serious reconstructions, and the New York State Theater has just had its interior rebuilt for acoustics in the summer of 1982. Indeed, in Avery Fisher Hall, only the outside façade and general shape of the auditorium remain as originally constructed.

Thus New Yorkers, and musicians and fans around the world, were especially appreciative of the efforts to save Carnegie Hall (154 W. 57th St.) from destruction following the completion of Lincoln Center. It took great musicians like Isaac Stern to spearhead the campaign to save Carnegie when it was threatened with demolition in order to make way for yet another midtown office building. Opened in 1891 with a concert conducted by Tchaikovsky, it remains an acoustical marvel and leaves New York's musical heart and soul intact.

They say New York's longest running musical hit is the New York Philharmonic. The oldest symphony orchestra in the U.S., it is nearly 150 years old yet incredibly vital under music director and conductor Zubin Mehta, who gets the best out of the 106 extraordinarily gifted musicians in the orchestra. The Philharmonic season runs September through May at Avery Fisher Hall. Tickets cost from $5.00 to $17.50. The orchestra, of course, attracts outstanding guest soloists and conductors. And Avery Fisher Hall is the home of the Mostly Mozart Summer Music Festival, New York City's version of Tanglewood, with more than 40 low-cost concerts (about $8.00 for a reserved seat) from mid-July through late August. Basically Bach, another low-cost music festival, spills over from Carnegie Hall to Avery Fisher Hall and various churches in early June.

As it approaches its century mark, the Metropolitan Opera Company under James Levine has been tackling some 20th-century works, in addition to the Verdi and Puccini staples of the repertory. The casts are often all-star—from Placido Domingo to Shirley Verrett, Jose Carreras to Teresa Stratas—the productions grandly elegant, and the house itself, with its Chagall murals and cut crystal chandeliers, a spectacular setting for any event. The Met season runs from September through April, with about a dozen outdoor performances in city parks during June. Tickets range from $10–$65, with standing room and partial view seats also available.

Across the Lincoln Center Plaza, in the New York State Theater, the New York City Opera approaches its 41st year with vim and vigor under artistic director Beverly Sills—its prima diva not too long ago. Its seasons now run from July through November. Tickets range from $3.50 to around $25.00.

The differences between the Met and the New York City Opera (NYCO) are varied. Particularly under Miss Sills's leadership, the City Opera has tried to project an image as a nonelitist, less formal company, attracting a younger audience through a combination of (relatively) low ticket prices, efforts at presenting new American operas, stressing English language productions, and highly visible advertising and promotion. The Met, put most simply, remains a far more tradition-bound organization whose subscribers tend toward the musically conservative—which has made it difficult over the last few years for the company to experiment as much as Mr. Levine reportedly would like to. Still, the growing popularity of opera generally, largely because of exposure via National Educational Television broadcasts live from both the Met and City Opera, have helped introduce the form to a far wider audience that it has ever before had.

Alice Tully Hall in Lincoln Center's Juilliard Building is small, intimate, and perhaps the best acoustical building in the complex—a suitable home for the Chamber Music Society of Lincoln Center, which has commissioned over 30 compositions and has given 13 New York or American premieres since its inception in 1969. Also attracts outstanding performers, from pianists to vocal groups, as well as stages (usually free) performances by Juilliard students.

Many guest artists, composers, and visiting orchestras perform at various times at each of these Lincoln Center auditoriums and theaters. For information on performances and prices write for the Lincoln Center Calendar, Lincoln Center, 1865 Broadway, New York 10023. Tickets are also available by mail, but they should be ordered a month in advance. In the city, tickets are obtainable through Lincoln Center or at Bloomingdale's at Third Ave. and East 59th St., or through most Ticketron outlets. There are also occasional free outdoor performances at Lincoln Center, either on the plaza or at the Guggenheim Bandshell, in the summer.

For sheer musical variety and artistry, Carnegie Hall is hard to beat with instrumental recitals by the likes of Rudolf Serkin, Nathan Milstein, and Mstislav Rostropovich, visits by orchestras such as the mighty Chicago under Solti, the Cleveland under Maazel, the Philadelphia under Muti, the Boston under Ozawa, and an atlas of other famed orchestras as well as vocal recitals by world greats, from Baker to Fischer-Dieskau. Performances go on virtually year round. Tickets vary, from around $5.00 to $15.00.

The off-Broadway equivalent in the Big Apple music world may well be the 92nd St. YM-YWHA, 1395 Lexington Ave., which offers major chamber music and orchestral series as well as performances by individual artists of international stature and a fun series featuring Broadway tunesmiths performing and speaking about their work. Colleges such as Hunter and the College of the City of New York (CCNY) also offer programs featuring major musicians, as does Abraham Goodman House, 129 W. 67th St., sort of the off-off-Broadway of the music world. Town Hall, the famous old concert facility on W. 43rd St. near Sixth Ave., is undergoing a 5-year restoration; meanwhile, it will still offer concerts.

Here are some other possibilities:

Amato Opera Theatre, Inc., 319 Bowery. 228–8200. Two generations of Amatos have produced this showcase company for student and young professional singers.

The *Bel Canto Opera Company* is an amateur opera company performing at the Madison Avenue Baptist Church at 30 East 31st St. 535–5231.

The *Light Opera Company of Manhattan* (affectionately known as "LOOM") presents excellent Gilbert and Sullivan operettas throughout the year at their small theater at 351 E. 74th St. 535–6310.

The Manhattan and other borough parks have an extensive free concert series June through August. The New York Philharmonic performs twice each summer in the Sheep Meadow at Central Park and at least once in a park in every borough. So does the Met.

Free concerts are also offered at the *Greenwich House Music School* (IRT 7th Ave. subway to Christopher St. stop; ask for directions to 46 Barrow St.); *The Museum of the City of New York* (5th Ave. bet. 103rd and 104th St.; Sunday, October–May) and *The New-York Historical Society* (107 Central Park West, near 77th St., Sunday, November–April).

Check the listings in the music section of *The New York Times* Sundays for news of frequent concerts at the Metropolitan Museum of Art, the Guggenheim, the Nicholas Roerich Museum, the Brooklyn Museum, the Frick Museum, the concerts of live or recorded music on certain Sundays in the medieval splendors of The Cloisters (which are part of the Metropolitan Museum of Art but located uptown in Fort Tryon Park), and, usually, many other fine professional performances and recitals, each and every day.

The sound of music—usually free—fills some of the city's great churches. Some suggestions: St. Bartholomew's Episcopal Church, Park Ave. at 51st St., presents mixed choir concerts Sundays at 4:00 P.M. The beautiful Riverside Church, Riverside Drive at 122nd St., presents carillon concerts at noon Saturdays and 2:00 P.M. Sundays. St. Peter's Lutheran Church, in the Citicorp Center at 54th St. and Lexington Ave., has Jazz Vespers Sundays at 5:00 P.M. as well as interesting theater performances. And Trinity Church, at Broadway and Wall St., presents organ recitals on weekdays. (For more complete information, call the churches.)

The Library and Museum of the Performing Arts at Lincoln Center also showcases outstanding young concert artists, as do other branches of the New York Public Library. Check the Events Calendar of the New York Public Library, free at all branches. And don't overlook the Brooklyn Academy of Music (BAM), 30 Lafayette St., Brooklyn, the nation's oldest performing arts center, with its various chamber and orchestral series as well as performances by internationally acclaimed guest artists in its four theaters (where dance, theater, films, and children's programs are also staged). The BAM season usually runs from October through June. Tickets range from around $3 to $15.

POPULAR MUSIC

Pop and rock concerts are presented all over town all year long. The *Dr. Pepper Festival* runs from June to August, usually at the Wollman Skating Rink in Central Park, though it has spent two seasons at Pier 84 while the rink has been undergoing renovation. Some of the old-style former movie houses like the *Palladium* on E. 14th St. and the *Ritz,* a former ballroom, on E. 11th St., draw young people from the suburbs as well as the neighborhood and Manhattan. The biggest attractions, such as Bruce Springsteen or The Grateful Dead, can fill *Madison Square Garden, Radio City Music Hall,* or the *Bottom Line,* 15 W. Fourth St., for several nights. Other halls that play big-name pop, rock, or jazz headliners are Carnegie Hall, Avery Fisher Hall (Lincoln Center), and sometimes even Alice Tully Hall, also at Lincoln Center.

The *South Street Seaport,* Pier 16 at Fulton St. on the East River, presents pop, jazz, bluegrass and folk dance concerts throughout the summer, many for free or a nominal admission charge, and Save-Our-Ships concerts, on the waterfront from June through August in one of New York's more unusual but pleasant settings.

The *Kool Jazz Festival*, from around June 26 to July 5, percolates in Carnegie Hall, Avery Fisher Hall, and other places around town.

For events, dates, and times while you are in town, check the daily papers, *New York* magazine, the *Village Voice* or the *New Yorker*.

For information on other nonclassical music, that performed in club settings where drinks or meals are served, refer to the *Night Life* section later in the book. But nonclassical music thrives in New York in less formal places, such as "performance lofts" in SoHo and TriBeCa; read the papers carefully for the minute notices, or scan the handbills posted on poles and walls around the city.

 DANCE. New York is now the dance capital of the world, and the Metropolitan Opera House is perhaps the largest and most important impresario of ballet, with the entire Lincoln Center complex the vital nerve center that keeps the Big Apple on its toes. (You will see students of the ballet around Carnegie Hall on 57th St. and Broadway in the 60s, 70s and 80s, going to and from the many ballet schools there.) Three Russians help New York maintain its dance excellence: George Balanchine, Rudolf Nureyev, and Mikhail Baryshnikov.

It is Balanchine, of course, who built the *New York City Ballet* (NYCB) into one of the great ballet companies in the world, his dancers whirling through abstract geometrical patterns choreographed by Balanchine in plotless ballets whose very simplicity reflects the lines in the NYCB's home, the New York State Theater in Lincoln Center. With 110 dancers, the NYCB is the largest dance organization in the Western world. And it is Balanchine who has brought the proud traditions of Russian Imperial ballet to the New World and put them to work in creating the sleek, neoclassical, and decidedly American NYCB. Balanchine and the NYCB's other principal choreographer, Jerome Robbins, have created more than 160 ballets. These ballets are now regarded as *the* classic repertoire of the 20th century. The 1983 season will be the NYCB's 76th. The fall dates are November through February. December is reserved for Balanchine's Christmas classic, *The Nutcracker*. Tickets from $4.00 to $20.00.

Across the Lincoln Center Plaza, at the Metropolitan Opera House, the *American Ballet Theatre* (ABT) usually stages its fall season from October through November and its summer season from mid-April through June. ABT has made its reputation by becoming America's prime repertory company. They perform the great 19th-century classics as well as important works of the early 20th century and a regular crop of story and contemporary ballets.

While NYCB prides itself on being a "starless" company where dance is the true star under the first of America's great balletic émigrés from Russia, the legendary Balanchine, the ABT is nonetheless the Big Apple's—and America's—"star" ballet. The ABT is now under the leadership of its talented superstar, Mikhail (Misha) Baryshnikov, the latest of the dance defectors from Russia's brilliant Kirov Ballet, noted for its soft, lyrical style and its brilliant interpretations of story ballets. The dashing Misha and one of his leading ladies, Natalia Makarova, another defector from the Kirov, have managed to inject the Russian spirit into the American dance tradition that makes the ABT so special. Misha choreographs, too, a budding Balanchine. ABT tickets vary, from around $5.00 to $35.00 and climbing.

It was, of course, Nureyev, the first of the great Russian dancers to defect from the Kirov, who, with his superstar quality slowly dimming over the years, gave ballet its mass appeal in America. And it was the box office power of Nureyev's name that helped fill the Met when Rudi danced as visiting guest star with some of the world's best troupes—troupes first imported to America by another Russian great, the late impresario Sol Hurok. Hurok's death left a void. And the Met stepped into that void, acting as its own impresario to keep its house full during the summer months. But it is names like Balanchine, Nureyev, and Baryshnikov that bring the crowds in.

It is their popularity that helps keep both the State and Met filled with visiting dance companies when the NYCB and ABT aren't performing, and when the respective house opera companies aren't doing their thing. So it is possible for a dance aficionado to look forward to seeing, say, the athleticism of Russia's *Bolshoi,* the lyricism and story ballets of Germany's *Stuttgart,* the stateliness of the *National Ballet of Canada,* the pageantry of Britain's *Royal Ballet,* and the avant-garde leanings of the *Netherlands Dance Theater*—to name just a few of the great troupes that have come to the Big Apple in recent seasons.

But the troupers go beyond the classical greats. The Moorish-style City Center Theater at 131 W. 55th St., for example, which has been extensively renovated, is, along with several Broadway theaters, home for such world-class companies as the *Alvin Ailey* (with its haunting blend of spiritual, modern jazz and story ballet rising out of the Black experience), the up-and-coming *Harlem Dance Theater,* and the mod, hip, with-it *Joffrey Ballet* that dances classics as well as rock-inspired pieces. (The Joffrey is now partly based in Los Angeles.) *Paul Taylor* and his company fuse the classics with modern dance, humor and a marvelous athleticism; so do *Twyla Tharp, Murray Louis,* and *Alwin Nikolais* (who uses more lights than the hippest disco). New to the city is the Joyce Theater at 18th St. on Eighth Ave., where the *Eliot Feld* company is in residence. The theater hopes to become the base for many contemporary and avant-garde companies.

The Brooklyn Academy of Music draws all kinds of dance companies, too. Indeed, its *Ballet America* series is a national celebration of dance paced from October to June. Companies from Los Angeles, San Francisco, Pennsylvania, Cleveland, and Utah are among the visitors. In addition, *Martha Graham* and *José Limon* bring their respective companies here regularly.

The entertainment pages of the Sunday *Times* and the *Village Voice* are always full of dance events, ranging from those mentioned above to smaller presentations given in lofts, on college campuses, at churches and elsewhere, and ranging from avant-gardists such as *Merce Cunningham* to folk troupes from

Senegal and the Ukraine. In fact, a directory of Big Apple dance troupes lists over 140 companies in all!

Some things to keep in mind when buying tickets for performances at some of the more expensive houses: Dance has become very, very popular in recent years. The major companies sell out regularly, and in advance. If you can, write for your tickets ahead, or call and charge them to a major credit card to ensure seats for the performance you want. If you're planning to be here during Christmas season and want to take the kids to see *The Nutcracker* at the StateTheater, write as far ahead of time as possible. Despite a month of daily performances, *The Nutcracker* is invariably a hot ticket.

The best seats for dance at the State Theater are in the first ring, where you can look down and see the dancers' feet. Because there are no aisles down the center of the sprawling auditorium, you may get tired of climbing over people and vice versa if you sit in the center, so consider aisle seats at the ends of the row, or seats as near the aisle as possible. They cost less, too.

Because the acoustics are so bad at the Uris, dance home of many a visiting troupe, you may want to sit further back, in a lesser-priced seat that still affords a good view of the dancers. And because the glitterati sit up front at the Met doesn't mean you have to; dance and music critics have found the viewing and hearing is actually better farther back in the orchestra rows. The Dress Circle seats offer an excellent vantage point at considerable savings over an orchestra seat—an important consideration in these days when ballet tickets at the major houses are edging into the $40.00 and up category. Substantial savings can be made by purchasing an obstructed-view seat at the Met or State theaters.

Lastly, don't overlook the fact that discount ballet (as well as theater, symphony and opera) tickets go on sale the same day as the performance at TKTS booths (see the *Stage* section, below). If you have the time to wait in line, the savings are substantial—and you may hear dance fans discussing their own version of the who's on first theme—whether the NYCB's Peter Martins and Helgi Tomasson are better than ABT's "Misha" (Baryshnikov) and Fernando Bujones, or whether Natasha (Natalia Makarova) and Gelsey (Kirkland) of ABT are better than Suzanne (Farrell) and Pattie (Patricia McBride) of the NYCB. They used to compare the Yankees' Mantle, the Giants' Mays and the Dodgers' Snyder the same way in the old days. That's how big dance is in the Big Apple nowadays.

 STAGE. In the 1980–81 season at Broadway's legitimate theaters, more tickets were sold at higher prices than at any other time in Broadway history. And with 36 percent of the ticket buyers from outside the New York metropolitan area (11 percent were foreigners), all those numbers add up to Broadway being New York City's number one tourist attraction. And that's not even counting the tickets sold at the nearly 15 Off-Broadway theaters in the Greenwich Village area and the more than 230 Off-Off-Broadway showcases found everywhere from SoHo to the Upper West Side, from Chelsea to the

Bowery. As Ethel Merman sings it, there's no business like show business—and theatrical show business is obviously big business here.

At least part of Broadway's renaissance can be attributed to a combination of promotion and marketing campaigns undertaken by the League of Theater Owners and Producers, the city and the state. Most prominent among these is the effort to simplify ticket buying and, indeed, it is easier to buy Broadway tickets today than it ever has been. You can phone for reservations for a particular show from virtually anywhere in the world, charge the tickets to a major credit card, and have them waiting for you at the box office the night of the show. In the metropolitan area (and sometimes throughout the Northeast) you can purchase theater tickets and seats for other performing arts events at computerized Ticketron outlets (call 977–9020 for the location nearest you) up until the day before a performance. On the day of the performance, you can pick up last-minute seats to many plays, musicals, and other attractions for half price (plus a small service charge) at one of two TKTS booths—the first at Broadway and 47th St., the second at 100 William St., a few blocks north of Wall St. A third TKTS booth is scheduled to open in Bryant Park in 1983. And, of course, you can always go directly to the box office of the show you want to see and get tickets there.

Some facts and hints: The Times Square TKTS booth is open from 3:00 to 8:00 P.M. daily for evening performances, from noon to 2:00 P.M. for Wednesday and Saturday matinees, and from noon to 8:00 P.M. for both matinees and evening performances on Sunday. On William St. the hours are 11:30 A.M. to 5:30 P.M. weekdays for evening performances only, and from 11 A.M. to 3:00 P.M. on Saturdays, again for evening shows only. Lines at the Times Square booth can be very, very long. If you have very specific preferences you'd probably want to be on line by 10:30 or 11 in the morning for matinee tickets, by 2:30 or so for evening performances. Unless you happen to be touring the Wall St. area the same day you're planning to attend the theater, you're not likely to be near the William St. booth; nonetheless, it is often worth a little extra subway time to travel down there. The lines and wait (except at lunchtime) are shorter, and the selection just as good as uptown. On Saturdays especially, the William St. booth usually has no line. The TKTS booths, however, accept cash only—no credit cards, no checks. They handle many opera, ballet, concert, and off-Broadway attractions as well as those on the Great White Way.

You should also look into "twofers"—tickets that entitle you to buy two tickets for the price of one when presented at the box office for specified performances—and, if you're in town for an extended stay, the Theater Development Fund. Twofers are usually available at hotel desks, at restaurant cashier booths, and at the offices of the New York Visitors and Convention Bureau, 2 Columbus Circle. Sometimes they are even distributed while you're waiting on line at the TKTS booth. Or write in advance to Hit Shows, 303 W. 42nd St., New York, NY 10036, and enclose a self-addressed, stamped envelope. TDF, at 1501 Broadway, New York, NY 10036 is a membership organization through which you can obtain a book of "vouchers" entitling you to discounts at numerous off-off-Broadway presentations.

The emphasis here on half-price tickets is simple: Broadway prices have skyrocketed in recent years, and although tickets for equivalent presentations elsewhere—in Las Vegas or Tokyo or London—are often even more expensive than full price in New York, the $35 top-price seat for a Broadway musical is increasingly the norm, while one show imported from England during the 1981–'82 season had a $100 top-ticket (the "cheap" seats were to be $70) for a two-part, eight-hour show. Thus it is easy to understand why more than 20 percent of all theater tickets in New York are sold through the TKTS booths.

The best advice for getting in to see the biggest hits on Friday and Saturday nights is to write well in advance to the box office, or to phone a reservation via credit card. If you're writing, send a certified check or money order for the exact amount, give several alternate dates and enclose a stamped, self-addressed envelope. Tickets for these same hits are usually easier to get for weekday evenings and matinees, though the sooner you make your decision as to what you want to see and when you want to see it, the better chance you have of getting your first choice. For sold-out shows, you might try waiting at the box office around 6:00 P.M. the night *before* you want to see that show. That's when unused "house seats" (a handful of the best seats held by the management for VIPs) are put on sale. This is admittedly a risky bet. Many shows also sell standing room— usually on the day of the performance, at prices ranging from about $5 to $8. And if there's only one "must see" sold-out show for you, try a ticket broker. Brokers charge full price plus a commission, the latter *legally* limited to $2.50 per ticket, and all too often the hottest tickets go only to favored customers. Golden and LeBlang Theatre Ticket Services, 207 W. 45th St., 757–2300 "since 1894, the largest theatre ticket agency in the U.S.A.," is one creditable such service. Others are located at major hotels.

Picking a new show is as easy as ABC. Study the classified listings on the theater pages of the daily newspapers or in the *New Yorker* or *New York/Cue* magazines (the latter include concise capsule reviews of all offerings), where you'll find casts, telephone numbers, prices, curtain times, and theater addresses. The *New York Times,* especially on Sunday, has similar information. Ticket-availability boxes appear in the amusement pages of the *New York Times* and *Daily News* on Fridays. Hint to reading between the lines: When the availability chart says "all sections, all performances" or even "most sections," chances are you can get tickets to that show at the TKTS booth. For quick suggestions, scan the ads for major Tony Award winners—Broadway's equivalent of Hollywood's Oscars. Among recent winners that should be playing through the '82–'83 season: *Amadeus* (musings about Mozart), a stage remake of *42nd Street,* the burlesque revue *Sugar Babies* (starring Mickey Rooney and Ann Miller), *Dream Girls,* the Duke Ellington-inspired *Sophisticated Ladies,* the star-vehicle *Woman of the Year,* and the seemingly perennial pleasers *Annie* and *A Chorus Line.*

A recent trend on Broadway has been toward short-run one-man or one-woman shows featuring young talents such as Liza Minnelli, Neil Diamond, Bette Midler, Gilda Radner, and Peter Allen, and older standbys such as Lena Horne, Tony Bennett, and Andy Williams.

Many of the city's theaters themselves are handsome, steeped in theatrical history and designated city landmarks. Indeed, no visitor should bypass *Shubert Alley,* a narrow private walkway (open to the public) between 44th and 45th Sts. west of Broadway. It is named for the three famous producing and theater-owning brothers of the early part of the century, Sam, Lee and J.J. Shubert. Both the *Shubert Theater* and the *Booth* are on the alley (along with an "I Love New York" souvenir shop, restaurant, and ticket agency). At the foot of Shubert Alley on 44th St. is also *Sardi's,* famous theatrical hangout and site of numerous opening-night parties. Its walls are lined with caricatures of the famous Broadway personalities who have wined and dined there—though neither the food nor the service seems as pleasing to non-regulars as to those who are instantly recognized.

Broadway means different things to different people. To most, it means the New York City theater district situated around the bright lights of Broadway. But to theater people, it means a geographic entity of 36 square blocks bounded by Sixth and Ninth Aves. and 41st and 53rd Sts. In the theaters on those blocks are tried-and-true dramas and musicals and British imports on the main featuring the best talent money can buy. Since it costs around $1 million to stage a musical and about half that for a straight play, Broadway doesn't take chances and leaves the risk-taking on new and unproven plays to Off-Broadway (OB) and Off-Off-Broadway (OOB).

There are many differences between Broadway, OB, and OOB. For openers, Broadway performers work under an Equity (actors' union) contract for a basic minimum pay. The OB minimum is a lot less because the theaters are a lot smaller, the cost of mounting a play a lot less because of relaxed union regulations. And the OOB performers may be working for the experience, exposure, and contributions in everything from SoHo lofts to church basements to showcases in Queens short on scenery but long on desire.

OOB is, as the Off-Off-Broadway Alliance (OOBA) describes it, "alternative theatre—a place for testing potential, for experimentation and the discovery of new talent . . . the research and development division of the American Theatre. Pulitzer Prize winners *A Chorus Line, No Place to Be Somebody, Talley's Folly* and *Buried Child* are among the many works introduced in this arena for emerging artists." For information about OOB performances, read the *Village Voice* or contact OOBA, 162 W. 56th St. 757–4473. Keep your eyes open as you walk around, too. There are lots of theater endeavors not advertised on a regular basis, but you'll see posters or signs—such as the 78th Street Theater Lab's "BYOB Cabaret" (*literally* off Broadway). Churches frequently host such theater.

OB was born in much the same way when it started in the 1930s in Greenwich Village around the time when the *Provincetown Playhouse* on MacDougal St. began showcasing playwright Eugene O'Neill there. Bette Davis and Henry Fonda worked OB, so did Geraldine Page, Jason Robards, George C. Scott, and Coleen Dewhurst, and so did—and do—Meryl Streep, Dustin Hoffman and Al Pacino. Edward Albee and Lanford Wilson got their playwriting start there, Jose Quintero became an OB legend for his direction of O'Neill works there, and Brecht, Weill, Ionesco and Beckett got some of their first important U.S. exposure there. Indeed, Joe Papp's Public Theater complex there is a veritable supermarket of lively theater choices.

In brief, some of the best theater in America was—and is—presented OB in Greenwich Village theaters such as the *Cherry Lane, Circle-In-the-Square* (downtown), *Theatre de Lys, Roundabout, Public, The Negro Ensemble,* and *Circle Repertory* at less than half of Broadway prices. America's longest running show, *The Fantasticks,* has been playing for over 20 years at the *Sullivan St. Theater.* And the *Circle Rep, Manhattan Theater Club,* and *Hudson Guild*—all uptown—keep turning out hit after hit that move from OB proving grounds to Broadway. Newest members of this OB community—right on the fringe of Broadway itself—are the nine theaters of *42nd Street Theater Row,* between Ninth and Tenth Aves., across from Manhattan Plaza. Sadly, despite their relatively consistent quality and quest for innovation, just about all of these theaters and companies are in constant financial trouble, struggling from one production to the next, forever hoping to hit upon that one huge Broadway possibility—as *Chorus Line* and *Pirates of Penzance* were for *Joseph Papp's New York Shakespeare Festival Public Theater*—whose proceeds will finance other endeavors. Tickets for OB shows are usually about half the price of Broadway seats, and often less. They are even cheaper OOB.

Papp's theater complex on Lafayette St., near Astor Place, generates some of the most exciting theatrical events in the city. The various theaters play host to young playwrights honing their craft in workshop situations, to experienced actors and directors needing the feedback of a small intimately housed audience, to short-lived experimental works, jazz concerts, dance series, film retrospectives and anything related to the performing arts. Other reliable sources of interesting theater are the internationlly famed *LaMama Experimental Theater Club* (74A E. 4th St.), *Playwrights Horizons* (416 W. 42nd St.), the *American Place Theater* (111 W. 46th St.), *CSC Repertory* (136 E. 13th St.), *Jean Cocteau Repertory* (330 Bowery), and *New Federal Theater Group* (446 Grant St.). OB may also mean a trek even farther uptown—to the *Master Theater,* 103rd St. at Riverside Drive, or to the *Riverside Church,* 112th St. at Riverside Drive, where the *Equity Theater* presents dramatic and musical classics, or to the *Phoenix* at Marymount Manhattan College, 221 E. 71st St.

Central Park's *Delacorte Theater* continues to be home to summertime Shakespeare productions co-sponsored by the city and Joseph Papp's Public Theater. Tickets to these generally first-rate outdoor productions are free, distributed beginning at 6:00 P.M. on the night of performance. The line for tickets, however, begins forming early in the afternoon, so take a blanket, a book, and maybe a picnic for before the show. There are usually two productions each summer, running about a month each. The theater is set beside a rock-bounded lagoon near W. 81st St., and is accessible via the 81st St. entrances to the park from Central Park West or Fifth Ave.

Sitting in the Delacorte listening to Shakespeare's words will make you feel far removed from the pass-the-hat informality of OOB, from the OB of Greenwich Village, or the bright lights of the Great White Way. But it's all there for the taking, and all part of New York's great theatrical life. After all, the theater in Manhattan has to strain to outdo the everyday theater of the streets.

 SHOPPING. Whether or not you came to New York for the shopping, you probably won't be able to resist it while you're here. The city offers such a variety of stores, goods and services that, even if you don't buy, a shopping expedition can be exciting and fascinating.

First, though, you should know where to look for what you do want. The telephone book Yellow Pages are valuable guides (there is one volume for Consumers, another for Businesses). Or check the local newspapers and magazines for ads or articles on current sales. If you're not looking for something too esoteric, the major department stores (Macy's, Gimbels, Bloomingdale's) may surprise you with the completeness of their stock. Although a specialty store might have a collection that more exactly matches your tastes, the department stores have at least a little bit of almost everything, and after seeing some particular sections—both Macy's and Bloomingdale's for example, have lavish cookware departments—you may feel no need to look further. Many department stores now open their doors for Sunday shopping (Bloomingdale's is not one of them). The hours are usually noon to 5 or 6. Also, you need not have a store's own card to charge; many stores, including Bloomingdale's, Saks Fifth Avenue, and Macy's, now accept American Express and even Diners Club. So far, only Gimbel's and Alexander's accept MasterCard or Visa.

Nonetheless, it's fun to explore. Most of New York's serious shopping is done in the midtown area, between 34th St. and 60th or so—this corresponds to the "downtown" of other American cities. But other areas have valuable resources too. On the residential Upper West Side, from 72nd to 86th Sts. for instance, there's a concentration of quieter, neighborhood-type stores along Broadway, and the southern parts of Amsterdam and Columbus Aves. are now arcades of new, trendy shops and restaurants. This part of town has traditionally been the middle-class area of Manhattan, and though it's rapidly becoming fancier and more expensive, you'll still find some very civilized browsing there in the way of books, foodstuffs, antiques, and so on. The more fashionable Upper East Side, from the 60s through the 80s, is terrain for the serious collector of antiques and art (the auction houses are here, and the galleries of Madison Ave.) and for lovers of handsome boutiques. For bargains you really go downtown. For apparel, for example, a long stretch of Orchard Street from Houston Street south is the nearest the city comes to an old-fashioned marketplace. Don't go on Saturday, when many businesses shut for the Sabbath—though they do open Sunday—and don't be deterred by the countless small, poky stores—there are good buys here for those with the patience to look. *A. Altman,* for example, at 182 Orchard, is renowned for women's fashion.

But if shopping is at all a tourist attraction in New York—and we believe it is—there are two stores that ought to be on everyone's "must-see" list: Bloomingdale's and Macy's.

Bloomingdale's (705–2000), taking up the square block from 59th to 60th Sts. and between Lexington and Third Aves., is nothing less than a fashion showplace whether you're looking at designer dresses, Oriental goods (much of them imported from the People's Republic of China), or sheets and pillowcases. The main floor, with its walls upon walls of mirrors and stark lighting, is a chic open bazaar half given over to makeup, perfume, and fast-buy women's items, the other half a complete men's haberdashery. Informal and cheaper clothing is on the below-street-level floors, while the rest of the store features pretty much the kind of general merchandise you'd expect any well-stocked department store to have—only extravagantly displayed and with prices to match. You can receive personal shopping help in over 10 languages, and there are special services available to blind and physically disabled customers. Bloomies also specializes in large purchase shipments abroad. Usually closed on Sunday.

Macy's (971–6000), also a full block square from 34th to 35th Sts. between Seventh Ave. and Broadway, is more the everyman's department store. At Macy's the brand names and merchandise are familiar; it's not so much what the store carries as the depth of stock in virtually everything. The basement-level Cellar is the most popular part of the store, overflowing with housewares in what has been designed as a series of integrated boutiques. The Cellar also has a wonderful cheese counter (relatively reasonably priced) and a full stock of tinned, bottled, and otherwise prepared gourmet items (not so reasonably priced, though you can't beat the selection), and a small grocery with first-rate produce (very highly priced, but you won't find a rotten apple, or mushroom, in the barrel). The children's floors are indeed a wonderland from Thanksgiving through the New Year, with free shows and a spectacular decorating job. And the store is eminently reliable as far as shipping and/or delivering whatever you may purchase—from coffeemakers to carpets, parkas to pianos. The store also has one of the finest soda fountains in the city on the fifth floor. Macy's also features shopping assistance in French, Spanish, Italian, German, Japanese, and even Portuguese.

Moving essentially from downtown north:

May's, (677–4000), at 14th St. and Union Square (Broadway), provides a huge assortment of inexpensive merchandise. Certain items such as housewares, sheets, and such are at bargain prices, but the clothing is a mixed bag. A string of odd clothing and miscellaneous stores stretching along 14th Street to the west of May's are for the intrepid shopper only. Do not buy casette tapes, pantyhose or other merchandise in sealed wrappers; they may be irregulars.

On 34th St. between Fifth and Sixth Aves. there are a large number of shoe stores; plus *Gimbels,* 564–3300, (noted for bargain values), *Ohrbach's* (695–4000), (known for great fashion accessories at low prices as well as its own quality brands of menswear and hosiery), and one of the outlets of the chain called *The Gap,* selling men's and women's jeans and jeans-style fashions. Finally, at Fifth Ave., *B. Altman* (679–7800) is the last of 34th Street's department stores. This is a favorite of the middle-income shopper—respectable, always-acceptable merchandise is sold here; there is a fully stocked menswear department, along with excellent furniture, china, and glassware sections and fine foods. Altman's also has one of the best of the department-store dining rooms. The store also offers special personalized shopping assistance.

Fifth Ave. between 34th St. and 59th st. has long been known as a mecca for shoppers, although in recent years some of its more illustrious residents have folded their tents and been succeeded by less refined tenants. It is well to be suspicious, in fact, of several stores in this stretch selling cameras, electronics, carved "ivory," and such. But Fifth Ave. still offers an unusual number of fine shops of every description, and it remains a top attraction for visiting shoppers.

The traditional Fifth Ave. tour begins at 38th St., at *Lord & Taylor.* Here the Christmas-window decorations are a special treat, while the store itself is known for its fine clothing, especially that by American designers. They also offer special shopping services. At 50th St., *Saks Fifth Avenue* has long been a beacon of fashion and accessories. As you walk north along Fifth in the 40s and 50s, you'll notice that this is where many of the airlines have their offices, and also that this is good bookshop country (*Scribner's,* near 49th, and *Rizzoli,* near 56th, are the most handsome).

Henri Bendel (pronounced BEN-del by those in the know) on 57th St. just west of Fifth Ave.; 247–1100, is a small pearl of a store—set up in aisles of boutiques —known for its trend-setting women's fashions and for its always beautifully designed displays and windows. Just opposite it, on the corner of 57th St. and Fifth Ave., is *Bergdorf Goodman* (753–7300), chic and expensive; and a little farther east on 57th St. is the new *Bonwit Teller,* reopened after an absence and much reduced in size.

While in the neighborhood, consider *Alexander's* (593–0880), one block south of Bloomingdale's. This is another store noted for inexpensive clothing of all kinds, some of it very stylish; while it's somewhat chaotic and noisy, the values are good, offering special purchases and close-outs, some with famous labels, and Alexander's has a reputation for decent quality, if you are an aggressive shopper. It's also open most evenings until 9:00, making it ideal for a pre-movie browse.

Some of the stores we've named have branches scattered in other parts of the city. Shopping in midtown deserves some strategic thinking: Try to avoid the hours between noon and 2:00 P.M. (when office workers descend *en masse* to get their errands done) and weekends. Also crowded are the late-opening nights— usually Thursdays, when many of these stores will close at 9:00 P.M. If you prefer to avoid the midtown rush, find out if a branch is more convenient by calling the main office, or checking the ads in the newspapers, although stock and selection at the branches are rarely as good as at the flagship stores. Nearly all major stores (and even some of the smaller boutiques) extend their shopping hours for the Christmas season. If you happen to be in New York right after Thanksgiving, you'll find such stores as Bloomingdale's and Macy's open seven days a week, with shopping hours extended well into the evening. Lord & Taylor and Saks usually follow suit.

SPECIAL SHOPPING NOTES

As enticing as the larger stores are the hundreds of specialty stores are the signature of the city. The list below is partial, and concentrates on relatively "stable" stores that have been in business for some time. A further guide, as mentioned, is the Yellow Pages. If these fail, try calling a free service called Cityphone, 675–0900. Tell them what you're looking for—they'll try to find a source.

As you walk through the city, you may see some stores with the notation "To the Trade" on the door or window. Such stores sell goods at wholesale prices to business clients, and often do not accommodate the general public. However, some of them do occasionally open their doors for a special sale. Check the "Living" sections of the daily and Sunday papers or the "Sales & Bargains" column of *New York* magazine for announcements of the latter.

Sales tax in New York City at press time is 8¼%.

WOMEN'S CLOTHING

All of the well-known department stores previously mentioned dedicate much or all of their floor space and counters to wooing women. Competition is fierce; there are frequent sales and special offers, which are widely advertised in the local papers.

Generally speaking, the largest array of merchandise, and therefore the greatest range of choices, will be found in the larger department and specialty stores. *B. Altman's* (679–7800) on Fifth Ave. at 34th St., is best known for conservative styles, though it also offers fine traditional sport clothes. Very reasonable (and moderately modish) items are on the sixth floor. *Lord & Taylor* (391–3344) has a range of traditionally styled fashion which appeals to women of every age, including the young contemporary customer, male as well as female.

Saks Fifth Avenue (on Fifth Ave. and 50th St.) still touts the best in "carriage trade" fashion. It isn't cheap, but the labels are famous, and the store has a reputation for accessories. Recently, they've added several boutique annexes on E. 49th St., including an imaginative gift and gourmet department. There's also a chic active sportswear shop. *Bergdorf Goodman* (on Fifth Ave. at 57th St.) is indispensable for those who can afford its outstanding collection. It appeals to the young—and to their grandmothers.

It is only natural to center your shopping attention on the bigger stores; but you should also sample the fantastic range of boutiques around the city. Try walking along Madison Ave. between 60 and 78th Sts. or so, for a dazzling array of high-fashion shops nestled amid the galleries and salons. *Veneziano,* near 68th St. is a favorite of the members of the best-dressed list (prices are steep, as is to be expected in this area). Just south is *Halston,* one of the more famous names in the current pantheon. And at Madison and 65th St. you'll find *Betsey Bunky Nini,* for a younger look—the Betsey in the store's name is designer Betsey Johnson, though she is no longer affiliated with the place. *The Rubicon Boutique*

Midtown Shopping

CENTRAL PARK

Columbus Circle

CENTRAL PARK SOUTH

Grand Army Plaza

BROADWAY

SEVENTH AVENUE

(SIXTH AVE.)

AVE. OF THE AMERICAS

FIFTH AVE.

MADISON AVE.

VANDERBILT AVE.

Theatre District

EIGHTH AVENUE

Rockefeller Center

Times Sq.

Bryant Park

N.Y. Public Library

Herald Sq.

62ND ST.
61ST ST.
60TH ST.
58TH ST.
W. 57TH ST.
56TH ST.
55TH ST.
54TH ST.
W. 53RD ST.
52ND ST.
51ST ST.
W. 50TH ST.
49TH ST.
48TH ST.
ROCKEFELLER PL.
47TH ST.
46TH ST.
W. 45TH ST.
44TH ST.
43RD ST.
42ND ST.
41ST ST.
40TH ST.
39TH ST.
38TH ST.
37TH ST.
36TH ST.
35TH ST.
34TH ST.
33RD ST.
32ND ST.

The Big Stores

1) Bloomingdale's
2) Alexander's
3) F.A.O. Schwarz (toys)
4) Bergdorf Goodman
5) Tiffany
6) Saks Fifth Avenue
7) Brooks Brothers
8) Bonwit Teller
9) Henri Bendel
10) Lord & Taylor
11) W & J Sloane (furniture & antiques)
12) B. Altman
13) Ohrbach's
14) Macy's
15) Gimbels

The Areas

A Fifth Avenue: clothing, accessories, jewelry, silver, design, luggage & leather, bookstores—all, except tourist-trap electronics and camera shops, are very up-market in both quality and price.

B Madison Avenue: boutiques of all description, men's clothes, leather & luggage—like Fifth Ave., all up-market. Also on some sidestreets. Art galleries above 57th St.

C Lexington & Third Avenues: boutiques and shops, but less prestigious than those of Fifth and Madison Avenues. Some antique stores on Third.

D 57th Street: boutiques, art galleries, antique specialists—most quite prestigious and expensive.

E 34th Street Area: clothing shops, but distinctly non-posh.

F Gems and jewelry.

G Hi-Fi.

H Musical instruments.

I Brazilian imports.

at 849 Madison Ave. on 70th St. has one-of-a-kind romantic gowns made with vintage lace.

Right nearby, near 69th St., is *Jaeger International Shop,* where the tailored look finds its finest expression in some stunning sportswear. (Another Jaeger outlet is to be found just opposite Bergdorf Goodman, in the I. Miller store on 57th St. near Fifth Ave.) And near 71st St. you'll find *Saint Laurent Rive Gauche,* for the best Paris has to offer.

Back a little farther downtown, though still on the subject of Paris, the *Courrèges* shop is on 57th St. just off Madison Ave.; or for a change in manner, look at the sweetly English printed fabrics, clothing, and home accessories of *Laura Ashley,* on Madison near 63rd St. Finally, a midtown shopping expedition is not complete without a stop at *Martha Inc.* and at *Evelyn Byrnes,* two of the proudest and oldest names in New York fashion. The two stores are directly across from each other, at 58th St. and Park Ave.; an ample pocketbook is a necessity.

There are plenty of worthwhile places to visit besides the above shops, less mainstream both in style and in locale. On the Upper West Side try *Charivari for Women,* at Broadway and 84th St., for Italian and American clothes in the latest modes—very modern but also very handsome. *Charivari Sport,* one block north, offers once again very modern stylings; these, however, are more informal in nature, and the prices are relatively modest. Women in larger sizes will find beautiful clothes in natural fabrics at *Ashanti Bazaar,* 872 Lexington Ave. at 65th St.; also a good selection at the *Forgotten Woman* at 880 Lexington Ave. at 65 St. To see what the young of New York are wearing, this is a good place to stop, as is *Reminiscence,* in Greenwich Village on MacDougal St. near 8th St. This shop carries a range of now-fashionable "antique" clothing, as well as up-to-date stuff under its own label. And for the truly young-at-heart (or those prepared to be a little outrageous), *Fiorucci* is truly entertaining, at 125 East 59th St.

Accessories and such. For shoes, *Gucci* might be your first stop; it offers high-styled, high-priced shoes and other accessories and leather goods, and there is a branch on Fifth Ave. (Gucci follows the maddening Italian tradition of closing between noon and 2:00 P.M., when most New Yorkers are up and doing. Because Gucci items are great status symbols in Japan, and cost a good deal more there, you will often see clusters of Japanese visitors crowding the sidewalk outside the shop, waiting for the store to reopen after lunch.) *Charles Jourdan,* nearby at 55th St. and Fifth, can't be beaten for the latest Parisian shoe and boot designs—once again at astronomical prices. For more modest budgets, there's *Chandler's,* across the street, and *I. Miller,* at 57th Street and Fifth Avenue. Though its name may be less well known than the Fifth Ave. stores, *Maud Frizon USA,* at 210 E. 60th St., is a true competitor, both in styling and in prices; for fine shoes at low prices, good places to look are *Etiquette,* at 28 W. 38th St., and *Paul Ormont* at 59 Fourth Ave. in the Village.

Handbags, gloves, scarves, and the like can well be bought at the department stores that cater to women, for example Bonwit Teller or Saks. But one downtown handbag outlet is worth knowing about—*Fine & Klein,* at 119 Orchard St. The price range of the wide selection of bags here ranges from very low to very high, but even the very high items are somewhat discounted. *Lederer,* at 613 Madison Ave. near 58th St., also has a huge selection, and though these satisfy the most discriminating tastes, the prices are mostly within reach. A midtown bargain spot for top-quality handbags is *J.S. Suarez, Inc.* at 67 E. 56th St. They offer Coach and other fine brands at around 20–30 percent off list price. They also make their own creations. Purchasers of hats may enjoy *Whittall and Javits,* at 65 W. 37th St., or *I.J. Herman,* 15 W. 38th St., one of the last establishments left that do hat blocking.

Henri Bendel has a small but luxurious fur section, but the fur district proper is on Seventh Avenue, where *Varriale* is one of the more widely known names (call 247–1100 for an appointment). When buying furs you should comparison shop as far as possible, since you're probably making a sizable investment; in the same stretch of Seventh Ave. as Varriale, in the high 20s and low 30s, you'll find several more furriers, including *Balencia,* at 333 Seventh near 29th St., and *Aronowicz,* at 345 Seventh. Crossing town to the East Side, the *Fur Vault at Alexander's,* on Third Ave. and 58th St., is widely advertised and popular; the *Ritz Thrift Shop,* at 107 W. 57th St., offers fine used furs.

Bargain Shopping. Finally, there is the indescribable thrill of bargain shopping. Not just for a marked-down item (which can be a very good value at special season sales), but also for the designer dress you saw yesterday at an expensive midtown store and which you now find at a 50% to 75% reduction at a manufacturers' outlet.

Such shopping takes time and research. The advantage of an outlet, however, is that reductions occur at the very beginning of a fashion season. Often labels are cut out, but tags have code numbers veterans can identify as concealing a famous designer's handiwork. Stock can vary, and it may take several trips before you find precisely what you want. There may be slight irregularities in the stock, but *Loehmann's* (at Fordham Road and Jerome Ave. in the Bronx) and *Bolton's* (on Madison at 86th St., and at several other locations) are fascinating because you never know what they'll have next. Loehmann's, the grandmother of all the popular discounters, also has branches in Queens and Brooklyn.

Resale stores carry "gently used" things culled from the best private wardrobes—some of their merchandise may never have been worn. One well-known shop is *Resale Associates,* on Madison Ave. near 80th St. In a slightly different category *Damages* at 768 Madison Ave. offers very high style clothes for men and women at semi-high prices. Clothes are generally more "perfect" than not, but you should check for small imperfections. *Trishop,* on Third Ave. at 92nd St., and *Repeat Performance,* farther south on Third near 84th St., are two charity shops which regularly receive donations of fashionable clothes (some good-quality seconds, some perfect); this is not secondhand stuff, but comes direct from the department stores—you should look the clothing over before buying, but there is little here that is unsatisfactory. The *Ritz Thrift Shop,*

107 W. 57th St., has used furs. *Pushcart Trading Company,* 37th St. and Fifth Ave., has close-outs, special purchases, discontinued merchandise, household items, shoes, clothing, perfumes, toiletries, toys—the items change from week to week. Finally, *New Store,* at 289 Seventh Ave., near 27th St., has a large collection of designer lines and shoes at heavy discounts.

MEN'S CLOTHING

Barney's, Seventh Ave. and 17th St., calls itself the largest men's store in the world, and it's hard to see how it could have any competition. This is *the* center for menswear in the city—if only because so many different elements of gentle-men's garb are found here under one roof. Conservative styles, high-fashion tailoring, and the most modern fashions are all available, and in an enormous range of sizes. In addition, Barney's has occasional sales—very popular ones, and widely advertised. Very early on the first morning of a sale, the line of well-dressed men waiting for the store to open circles the block.

Brooks Bros. has been offering its wares to conservative New Yorkers since the beginning of the 19th century, and is still going strong at Madison Ave. and 44th St. The first floor contains an ocean of button-down shirts and striped ties, and the store is famous for its dignified high-quality suits; but you'll also find hats, haberdashery, sport clothes, and much else too. Still in the conservative vein are a series of stores in the same neighborhood, including *Chipp, Inc.,* at 14 E. 44th St., and the well-known name *Paul Stuart* (on Madison at 45th St.), for the slightly more adventurous. *F. R. Tripler,* on Madison Ave. at 46th St., is another long-established and reliable store.

Of course, all the major department stores have extensive men's sections.

In recent years, there has been a marked trend away from the stylish stores; the so-called "discount" men's outlet shops have taken a lot of the traffic away from their more impressive brethren. On Fifth Ave., in the area between 14th and 23rd Sts., you'll find a number of such places, of which perhaps the best known is *Harry Rothman,* on the corner of 18th St. The store has a good range of discounted suits, as well as sweaters, sport jackets, coats, and more. *Hampshire International,* nearby at 85 Fifth Ave., has similar stock at similar prices.

Part of the trend away from tradition has been toward stylish Italian clothes, such as those available at *Madonna* at 223 E. 60th St. *Charivari for Men,* 2339 Broadway at 85th St., also offers very handsome modern men's fashions. On the less formal side, jeans, workshirts, and western wear are an increasingly important element in men's fashion these days, and for that matter in women's too. Both sexes are catered to at *The Gap,* where the selection of jeans and related accessories is among the most complete in the city. There are several branches, the largest of which is at 86th St. and Third Ave. Downtown, *Hudson's* (105 Third Ave. near 14th St.) is the granddaddy of the so-called Army & Navy stores, though the merchandise here encompasses a far wider range than just military surplus. *Canal Jean,* at 304 Canal St. and on Broadway near Spring St., and *Unique Clothing Warehouse,* on Broadway near 8th St., both offer wilder, funkier, more diverse variants of jeans-style fashions. Both are city institutions, for inexpensive, trendy clothes.

While on the subject of Western-style clothing, let's talk shoes—or, rather, boots. *To Boot*, at 72nd St. and Columbus Ave., has a large selection of very fine cowboy boots, ranging from the straightforward to the ornate, and to be sold to both men and women; unfortunately, while the denims and shirtings of Western stylings may be bought relatively inexpensively, the same cannot be said of the footwear. To Boot also sells Western clothing.

More usual types of shoes may be bought all over the city, at branches of such chains as *Florsheim* or *Coward*. For distinctive stylings, try *Church's Shoes*, on Madison Ave. at 49th St.; this is a branch of the famous London bootmakers and offers elegant traditional footwear, but the price you pay for these traditional, but *very* durable and handsome, items is high. *Susan Bennis/Warren Edwards*, at 122 E. 55th St., offers unusual and fine-quality shoes for men and women, as does *Maud Frizon*, at 210 E. 60th St.; and *Barney's*, that great capital of menswear, has not one but two shoe departments. Lastly, *McReedy and Schreiber*, at 37 W. 46th St., is another popular shop.

A few expensive shops still specialize in what is popularly known as men's furnishings, and you had best visit these establishments with a thick wallet. Underwear, hosiery, ties, and shirts combine with sweaters, robes, and miscellaneous sportswear of the highest quality. *A. Sulka*, at 711 Fifth Ave. at 56th St., *Countess Mara*, at 110 E. 57th St., and *Alexander Shields*, at Park Ave. and 59th St., are good examples of this kind of store.

In New York City, men don't take a back seat even when it comes to the matter of haute couture. Designer fashions for men exist in virtually every major department and specialty store, and there are also high-fashion boutiques solely for men. Famous among these are *St. Laurent for Men*, at 543 Madison Ave. near 55th St., and *Pierre Balmain*, at 795 Madison near 68th St. St. Laurent in particular has fine shirts. And finally, of course virtually every men's department in the big stores such as *Bloomingdale's* or *Saks* is highly rewarding.

For renting good-quality, conservative, traditional formal wear, *Baldwin Formals*, 40 W. 56th St., and *A. T. Harris*, 419 Lexington Ave., near 44th St., should be satisfactory.

CHILDREN'S CLOTHES

All of the major department stores have children's sections that reflect their positions on the adult fashion ladder. Thus *Bergdorf Goodman* has elegant clothes in both the ready-to-wear and made-to-order categories. *Saks Fifth Avenue's* children's section is only slightly less posh. *Bloomingdale's* has very interesting clothes in a wide assortment, and *Alexander's* is the inexpensive (though good) end of the spectrum. Of all these stores, however, *Macy's* rates as the top choice, if only because of the size of its selection.

A great many boutique-style stores specialize in nothing but children's apparel, and they too cover the full spectrum of prices and styles. *Stone Free* alone carries a wide variety in its two children's stores, one on W. 72nd St. near

Columbus and the other at 1086 Madison Avenue near 82nd St.; not surprising-ly, the Madison Ave. branch is the more chic of the two, but both are unusual and appealing. (If these clothes appeal to you as you steer your children through Stone Free for Kids on 72nd St., there's an adult version of the store just opposite.) *Slithy Toves,* on W. 72nd between CPW and Columbus, features much unusual and handmade apparel for kids. *Cerutti,* at Madison and 68th St., received a measure of publicity from the patronage of Jackie Onassis, who reportedly purchased some of Caroline and John-John's gear there; the clientele is that affluent, and the prices reflect it. *Wendy's Store* is a delightful source of infant and toddler wear and toys, at 1046 Madison Ave., 80th St. For bargains, *Goldman & Ostrow,* at 315 Grand St. on the Lower East Side, is the real McCoy, or you could go a few steps down the block to *Rice and Breskin* (323 Grand). Or cross the river to Brooklyn and visit *Natan Borlam,* at 157 Havemeyer St. At this discount shop name brands are available at very low prices; open only Sunday through Thursday.

JEWELRY

Eye-catching, ready-to-wear, and conveniently centralized, high-fashion jew-elry in New York clusters around 55th St. and Fifth Ave. Within a ten-minute walk, the shopper encounters Van Cleef and Arpels (at Bergdorf Goodman), the highly esteemed Tiffany & Co., Buccellati, Fortunoff, Harry Winston, and Cartier. Along with the dazzling adornments that have earned them reputations as dazzlingly expensive, these stores also sell attractive items everyone can afford.

Tiffany's, at Fifth Ave. and 57th St., is almost as elegant as the reputation that precedes it, though there really isn't anywhere here to have breakfast. Even more elegant is the fabled *Cartier's,* at Fifth and 52nd St., where the mantle of wealth and privilege hangs heavy over its gilt and plush decor, but even Cartier takes a backseat in high prices to *Harry Winston's,* at 718 Fifth Ave. *Fortunoff,* a relative newcomer, has been very successfully advertised by Lauren Bacall, and prides itself on discounting brand-name items and stocking a vast array of not-too-expensive trinkets that make very welcome gifts. *H. Stern,* across 51st St. from St. Patrick's, has beautiful precious and semi-precious stones, and jewelry.

If you could use a change from Fifth Avenue's typically cool and sophisticat-ed sales transactions, shopping for jewelry can give you a great chance to do so. West 47th St., between Fifth and Sixth Aves., has been described more than once as the closest thing to a Middle Eastern bazaar to be found in New York—haggling included. This block is known as "the diamond district," and in shops packed with merchandise, where no time or expense has been wasted on decor, you can bargain over gems, gold, silver, and all kinds of semiprecious stones. Investigate *Bill Schifrin,* reputedly the world's largest purveyor of wedding rings, at Booth 86 of the National Jewelers Exchange. The whole block has an element of theater to it, and is well worth a visit, though the procedure of buying a stone here can be intimidating and chancy. It's best to go with a friend who knows diamonds.

LEATHER AND LUGGAGE

You will see any number of luggage shops tucked into the various corners of the city, and these are generally the best places to find bargains. *Innovation Luggage,* for example, has several branches, one of them at 42nd St. and Second Ave.; a walk down Orchard Street will furnish you with various displays of luggage, with *Altman's* (no relation to the department store), at 135 Orchard, among the better known. Sticking to the beaten path will involve higher prices, but willing buyers are apparently available in sufficient numbers to enable the more glamorous names to survive. *Gucci,* on Fifth Ave. at 54th St., has a worldwide reputation for its fine products, with prices to match. *Mark Cross,* just south of Gucci at Fifth and 51st St., is in the same class, as is *T. Anthony,* at 480 Park Ave. at 58th St. *Crouch and Fitzgerald,* at Madison and 48th St., is a handsome store that handles its own line of luggage, as well as *Louis Vuitton* bags (Vuitton also has its own outlet, on 57th Street near Madison); and *Dinoffer,* at 24 W. 57th St., is another of the city's reputable old names. The *Coach* company has opened its own boutique at 754 Madison at 65th St., where you can find the largest selection of their bags and portfolios. *Saks, Bloomingdale's, Macy's* and *Alexanders* all have sizable luguage departments, too.

COSMETICS, PERFUMES, AND TOILETRIES

One of New York's finest toiletry shops is *Caswell-Massey,* on Lexington Ave. at 48th St. This is a place that combines a certain modern flair with extremely long-established quality (the store dates back to the eighteenth century); the variety of soaps and all kinds of other liniments and miscellany is a delight. Ask for a catalog; it's wonderful reading. *Il Makiage,* at 107 E. 60th St., near Park Ave., is a cosmetics boutique with a fashionable Upper East Side air. Down in Greenwich Village, the *Soap Opera,* at 51 Grove Street, and the *Bath Stop* on Thompson St. have a wide range of soaps—as also, of course, do the relevant sections of the major department stores. The department stores are also where most New York women go to buy perfumes. Yet *Pushcart,* at Fifth Ave. and 37th St., has many famous toiletries on sale at all times, although stock may vary from week to week.

BEAUTY SALONS

There are a few establishments that can't be neglected—*Georgette Klinger,* for example, with its beautiful engraved doors at 501 Madison Ave. near 53rd St., is known for facials and skin care, as is *Christine Valmy,* at 767 Fifth Ave. (near 58th St.). *Cinandre,* at 11 E. 57th Street, is as fashionable for skin and hair as its neighborhood implies, and of course there are both men and women who will go nowhere else but *Vidal Sassoon,* at 767 Fifth Ave. (58th St.) for their hair. Many of the department stores, including *Bloomingdale's* and *Saks,* have their own salons. And a less famous, but well-liked, salon is *Monique of the Waldorf,* at 301 Park Ave., at 49th St. *Henri Bendel* even has a super-chic dental care salon, along with more traditional beauty services.

TOYS

The magnet for the majority of young and young at heart would have to be *F.A.O. Schwarz,* at Fifth Ave. and 58th St. Here, stuffed animals of a size that one would think would terrify a small person are instead immediate objects of delight; and every other conceivable game, toy, or member of a menagerie is available in some part of the store.

At least as famous is the toy department of *Macy's,* where most of the present crop of middle-aged, middle-class New Yorkers originally whet their acquistional appetites. Shelf upon shelf, counter upon counter—while most of the other department stores have representative departments devoted to toys, this has got to be the definitive department.

There are many dollhouse-and-miniature furniture retail stores in Manhattan; one is *Dollhouse Antics* on Madison Ave. near 92nd St.

Go Fly a Kite, at 1434 Third Avenue, is devoted to kites—from very simple ones to very expensive ones that one can't imagine being flown. Several stores specialize in model trains, including *Madison Hardware,* at 105 E. 23rd St., the *Train Shop,* at 23 W. 45th St., and the *Roundhouse,* at 14 W 45th St. *Polk's,* Fifth Ave. near 32nd St., features trains, plus boats and cars, models, radio-control equipment, and so forth.

Brentano's and *Barnes & Noble's* main stores also have interesting collections of toys and games for both youngsters and adults.

GOURMET FOODS AND EQUIPMENT

Whatever tastes in foodstuffs the visitor to New York may have, he can sate them here, and if he's not careful he'll develop a whole range of new ones too.

Probably New York's favorite delicatessen, and certainly its most often discussed, is *Zabar's.* This establishment occupies three storefronts, on Broadway at 80th St. On Saturday nights the store is open until midnight, and is jammed with New Yorkers who have picked up the bulky Sunday *New York Times*—on sale around 9:00 P.M. Saturday—and are now waiting in line to buy the fixings for a luxurious Sunday breakfast of smoked fish, bagels, cheese, and croissants, all sold here. Zabar's also has fine kitchen equipment, often at the best prices anywhere. They have sold their Cuisinarts at such a low price that for a time the company refused to sell them any. The fish counter—for whitefish, smoked salmon, sable, sturgeon, etc.—is usually especially crowded, and you must "take a number," but you'll also find meats, a slew of canned and packaged delicacies, coffees, fresh pasta, and much more. While you're on the Upper West Side, *Murray's,* at 2429 Broadway near 90th St., and *Barney Greengrass,* at 541 Amsterdam Avenue, near 86th St., are also renowned for sturgeon, lox, and the like. On the Upper East Side, *Caviarteria,* unsurprisingly, specializes in caviar (at 29 E. 60th St.), and more diversified stores include *Fay & Allen's Foodworks,* at 1241 Third Avenue near 72nd St., and *E.A.T.,* at 1064 Madison near 81st St. While you're looking at galleries in SoHo, take a peak at *Dean & DeLuca's,* 121 Prince Street. This place isn't cheap, but you'll find a range of high-quality pastries, cheeses, pâtés, olive oils, sausages, and you-name-it, as well as impressive-looking kitchen equipment. *SoHo Charcuterie,* at Sullivan and Spring Streets, is another must. Another such place in the Village is *Balducci's,* at Sixth Avenue and 9th Street, which in addition to all the exotica also stocks fine fruits and vegetables, meats, fish, and so on.

Ninth Avenue is the city's grocery store, and by walking down it between, say, 40th and 50th Sts., you'll find all kinds of good-quality meats, vegetables, pasta, and ethnic specialties. The *International Groceries and Meat Market* at 529 Ninth Ave. (at 39th St.) is packed with open sacks of grains and spices, along with the usual assortment of Greek, Spanish, and Italian gourmet items at good prices. Another top place is *Manganaro Foods,* at number 488 between 37th and 38th Sts. Italian foods are best located by strolling through Little Italy, in the area of Mulberry and Grand Sts., and stopping at any of several stores of which the *Italian Food Center,* at 186 Grand, is an example. Also, *Ferrara's* is nearby: for pastry and coffees. Farther north, *Todaro's,* at 555 Second Ave. near 30th Street, has a mail-order business in Italian foods and is justly respected. *Tanaka,* at 326 Amsterdam Ave. at 74th St., will provide you with Japanese foodstuffs; for Chinese, try any of the curious-looking stores on Mott Street or Mulberry Street south of Canal Street, in Chinatown. For Hungarian provisions, try *Paprikas Weiss,* at 1546 Second Ave. at 78th St., which not only has spices, jams, jellies, and imported candies, but can also provide such esoteric items as ready-to-use strudel dough. Indian spices can be found at a number of shops in "Little India," along Lexington Avenue between 26th and 30th Sts. In the way of coffee and teas, Zabar's has a famous name, and a very old but youthful-looking and expanding store is *Gillies 1840,* at Third Ave. and 84th St., plus other locations. Along Ninth Ave., try the tiny but well-stocked *Empire Coffee and Tea Company,* at number 486 between 37th and 38th Sts. In the Village at 109 Christopher St. near Bleecker, *McNulty's* has a wide range of teas and coffees too, as does *Cofféa,* 982 Third Avenue. The gourmet shops at *Bloomingdale's* and *Macy's* are also prime choices for fine and unusual spices, and their housewares departments are great places to find all kinds of cooking equipment. In cold meats, the store to measure all others by is *Schaller and Weber,* at 1654 Second Ave., near 86th St. Nearby, at 218 E. 86th St., is *Bremen House,* specializing in German foods. A good place for kitchenware is the *Cellar* in Macy's basement; alternatives are the chain of stores called the *Pottery Barn,* at several locations, which is noted for its good prices on a range of cooking equipment, and *Conran's,* at 54th St. and Third Ave. This last is an interesting place—downstairs is a range of modern furniture, while on the second floor are fabrics, rugs, and such, and pots, pans, earthenware in unusual shapes, utensils, spices, serving ware, and all kinds of other things unexpected in this sleek, modern setting.

There is, of course, much more to explore, but lastly, for those with a sweet tooth . . . *Godiva,* main shop at 701 Fifth Ave. near 55th St., makes well-known,

Manhattan Shopping

A Art galleries, swank boutiques, fine
  antiques, antiquities.
B Boutiques, ordinary antiques.
C Foreign food specialties.
D Sotheby Parke Bernet Decorative
  Arts Gallery.

E Second-hand books, antiques,
  auction galleries.
F Discount stores (clothes,
  accessories).
G Antiques, boutiques.

H Art galleries (contemporary),
  posters, boutiques.
I Italian specialties.
J Indian specialties.
K Chinese specialties.

L Tools and machinery.
M Jewelry.
N Clothing (trendy, funky, or casual).
P Restaurant equipment.

beautifully packaged (and expensive) chocolate; *Kron Chocolatier,* 764 Madison Ave. near 66th St., and at 506 Madison Ave. at 53rd St., is where many New Yorkers go for this indispensable substance. Or try the pâtisserie at *Dumas,* on Lexington near 88th St. For a snack, the best of the several chains of stores selling cookies is generally considered to be *David's Cookies,* at several locations, including Zabar's and Macy's. *Delices La Côte Basque,* at 1032 Lexington Ave. near 74th St., is famous for its pastries. Try the cheesecake at *Eileen's,* at 17 Cleveland Place (near the junction of Spring and Lafayette Sts.). And enjoy.

TOBACCO

Village Cigars, at 110 Seventh Avenue South, is a crowded little shop that has been around a long time at this busy Greenwich Village corner (Sheridan Square). *Nat Sherman,* at 711 Fifth Ave. near 55th St., is celebrated as "tobacconist to the world," and offers every conceivable type of tobacco. *J. R. Tobacco,* at 108 West 45th St., calls itself "the world's largest cigar store"—nobody has been heard to argue, and in addition to the merits of the selection, the prices are reasonable too. And one of the most respected names in the tobacco world, *Alfred Dunhill of London,* has a store at 620 Fifth Ave. in Rockefeller Center, and branches in both Macy's and Bloomingdale's.

For pipes, two places are recommended—*Barclay Rex,* at 7 Maiden Lane, downtown, and midtown, *Connoisseur,* at 51 W. 46th St. Both have large assortments of pipes and pipe tobaccos.

ART AND GALLERIES

There is really no easy way to compile a useful guide to New York's art galleries. You will have to do what New Yorkers do: once you've checked these listings in *The New York Times,* (especially the Friday, Saturday, and Sunday editions), *New York* magazine, or the *New Yorker* and marked the ones that seem most interesting at the moment, you start walking, either down Madison Avenue from 86th St. or across 57th St. and up Madison to 86th, stopping as you go.

But in recent years New York has developed another art center downtown, for balance. This is SoHo, an area of beautiful cast-iron architecture that was once a manufacturing and warehousing district. As industry moved out over the last decade, leaving behind large "loft" spaces with huge windows for plenty of light, artists began to move in; and it wasn't long before galleries followed them.

SoHo is now fashionable, handsome, and diverse, but the galleries are still there in quantity. In just one building, 420 West Broadway, you'll find five, including *Mary Boone, Leo Castelli,* and *Sonnabend.* Castelli alone has been associated with such modern figures as Jasper Johns, Robert Rauschenberg, Roy Lichtenstein, Andy Warhol, and Cy Twombly. Other galleries within these crowded few blocks include *O.K. Harris,* at 383 West Broadway, *Holly Solomon,* at 392 West Broadway, and *Vorpal,* at 465 West Broadway (Vorpal is known for its representation of prints by M. C. Escher, that proponent of visual paradox); but there is too much here, in the way of painting, sculpture, and other forms harder to find names for (but most of it super-modern), to list, and the best thing to do is simply explore this quite small, concentrated area.

Uptown, of course, the scene remains as strong as ever, and here too we can only name a few of the best known galleries. For contemporary art, for example, *Tibor De Nagy,* at 29 W. 57th St., *Marlborough,* at 40 W. 57th St., *Sidney Janis,* at 110 W. 57th St., and *Betty Parsons,* at 24 W. 57th St., all have worthy reputations; they specialize in painting, but usually handle sculpture too. For older art (interspersed with recent work), try *Knoedler,* at 21 E. 70th St., or *Wildenstein,* at 19 E. 64th St., among many others. If you're interested in a somewhat newer art form, try the *International Center of Photography,* at 1130 Fifth Avenue, or *Photograph,* 724 Fifth Ave., between 56th and 57th Sts.

For those less interested in investing, but looking for something nice for their walls, the major museums, such as the Guggenheim, the Museum of Modern Art, the Metropolitan, and so on, all have fine in-house shops offering reproductions of works in their galleries. For the Metropolitan, particularly, this is big business, and the stock runs not just to posters, but also to pottery, jewelry, and so forth. *Poster Originals* is a well-stocked poster shop that, cannily, has two branches: one on the Upper East Side, at 924 Madison Ave. near 73rd St., and one in SoHo, at 386 West Broadway. Not all the stuff here is cheap, but all is handsome.

Off the beaten track, the *Aaron Faber Galleries* at 666 Fifth Ave. (53rd St.) has an impressive collection of artists' hand-crafted contemporary jewelry in limited editions. There is usually an exhibition by one of the artisans on the second floor.

Contemporary prints (and some old prints), are the only offering at *Associated American Artists, Inc.,* 663 Fifth Ave. near 52nd St. For older prints, etchings, and illustrated books you might try, among many others, *Lucien Goldschmidt,* 1117 Madison Ave. at 83rd St., for the old-fashioned appeal of the shop if for nothing else. *Spaced,* 165 W. 72nd St., 2nd floor, is a gallery for architectural art; some of its material is exhibited in a first-floor café.

ANTIQUES

New York sports a huge variety of antique shops, and a lot of people spend a lot of time poring over a lot of objects, seeking finds. A word of warning: Prices in the city are usually higher than those offered in places farther outside the city; there are antiquers who make a point of not buying here, hoping to find better values elsewhere. But for both the serious collector and the amateur, there's simply so much in New York that browsing is worthwhile, and there's always the chance of a bargain.

The first place to start is at the auction houses. These are exciting, particularly if you've never been to one, and there's a rapid turnover of stock. Auction houses have sales on most days of the week, except Sunday. Check *The New York Times* for listings. As a general rule, Monday and Tuesday are exhibition days for midweek sales and Thursday for Saturday sales. No item, no matter how small, should ever be bought on the block without an examination at the exhibition.

You may think you are getting a bargain on the silver vase from 40 feet away, but if on closer scrutiny you find an inscription from some sporting society on the other side, you have only yourself to blame, for there is ample time to examine each lot carefully. If you are bidding for the first time, don't hesitate to ask a staffer for advice.

Sotheby's is probably the most well known of the auction houses, at 1334 York Ave. (72nd St.). *Christie's,* at 502 Park Ave. (59th St.), is claimed by many to be as good. It has a branch for Americana and other specialties at 219 E. 67th St., and is planning to open a "contemporary art" showroom. Smaller houses are *Phillips,* at two Upper East Side locations, and *William Doyle,* at 175 E. 87th St., among others. Goods on display at these establishments fall into varied categories, which at any one time may include fine art, jewelry, all sorts of furniture, porcelain, antique toys, and much more. At some of these houses the *buyer* must pay a commission; terms change, so we leave you to check for yourself. The top houses are closed for viewing Mondays, and some are closed Sundays also.

Having tackled the auctions, explore a few specific areas. Most of the best (and most expensive) shops are along 57th St. east of Fifth Ave., and on Madison Avenue in the 50s, 60s, and 70s. Smaller and less fancy shops are scattered all over, but the general concentration is on Third Avenue between 45th and 70th Sts. and the surrounding streets; Second and First Aves. within the same boundaries can also prove rewarding. Another antiques area is the area bounded by Broadway and University Place and 8th and 14th Sts. in the northern part of the Village. For example, *Ace Galleries* on University Place near 11th St. is an active auction house—a step down from Sotheby's, to be sure, but fun and less costly. Go—and you'll be sure to buy *something.* Other such auction houses—and there are many more—are *Tepper* at 110 E. 25th St., *Lubin,* 30 W. 26th St., and *Manhattan Galleries,* 1415 Third Ave at 80th St.

The Consumer Yellow Pages has a lengthy list of antique shops broken down into specific categories, and this is worth consulting before you start exploring an area which is quite widely dispersed.

There are, in fact, antique shops all over the city. Greenwich Village has a large concentration of stores—try walking down Bleecker Street between Christopher Street and Hudson, or look at oak furniture on Hudson Street between Bleecker and Christopher (those street names are accurate; they all criss-cross the area!). Second Ave. also has a lot of oak furniture, for several blocks south of 26th St. A store that seems to have a wide range of period furniture—English, Oriental, French—is *Gramercy Galleries,* at 52 E. 13th St. Provincial French furniture is well served in the city by *Pierre Deux,* at 369 Bleecker, *Le Vieux Monde,* nearby at 94 Charles St., and *Howard Kaplan,* at 400 Bleecker St. *Pat Sales* at 390 Bleecker offers American country antiques. And *Inglenook,* at 529 Hudson Street, offers antique American furniture, with a particular emphasis on wicker.

James Robinson, at 15 E. 57th St., has a worldwide name for antique silver; another source is *Wyler,* at 713 Madison near 63rd St. Try *Carol Ferranti,* at 888 Madison near 72nd St., for glassware and pottery, or *Leo Kaplan,* nearby at 910 Madison. *Second Childhood,* at 283 Bleecker St., is much loved for its collection of antique toys, which may include multi-shaped coin banks, dolls, hoops, books for children, and toy trains at any one time. Look for toy soldiers there, too. *The Antique Doll Hospital of New York*'s name is a bit misleading: they also buy, sell and appraise dolls, at 787 Lexington Ave. near 61st St. On the more serious side of the scale, *André Emmerich,* at 41 E. 57th Street, offers very high-quality pre-Columbian objects and such (there are also exhibits of modern paintings here) while the *Asian Gallery,* at 1049 Madison near 80th St., offers Far Eastern art and antiquities. *Atikoth* (16 E. 71st St.) and *Moriah* (699 Madison Ave. between 62nd and 63rd Sts.) trade in antique Judaica. For collectible clocks and watches, two establishments under the same roof are a best bet: *William Scolnick,* and *Joseph Fanelli's Clocks and Things,* both at 1001 Second Ave. at 53rd St. (This is a difficult and unusual field: "Not many people need ulcers," said the owner of one store that recently closed down its antique-watch operation.) The oldest autograph business in New York, at 25 E. 77th St., is *Charles Hamilton;* surprisingly, department-store *B. Altman* also has a reputable autograph section. *Mitsukoshi,* on the northeast corner of Park and 57th, has fine Japanese pottery and other arts.

Griffin & Howe have both new and used hunting arms as well as antique firearms, 589 Broadway near Houston. *Centre Firearms,* 51 W. 46th St., is another such place. Specializing in antique firearms is *Robert Brooks,* 235 E. 53rd St. *The Soldier Shop,* 1013 Madison Ave., has antique firearms as well as books on the military and antique miniature soldiers. *Hunting World,* 16 E. 53rd, has every imaginable accessory for the hunter—as well as prints, etc.

There are many places for antique clothing—some of it tatty, some very fine. *Reminiscence,* on MacDougal Street near 8th St., and *Trash & Vaudeville,* at 4 Saint Marks Place, both sell old clothes (and new, too) in as-new condition, to fit with younger fashions. *Unique Clothing Warehouse,* 718 Broadway, is another source. Leaving the Village for the more sedate Upper East Side, pay a visit to *The Best of Everything,* at 242 E 77th St., for clothing, jewelry, and accessories from the 20s through the 50s. On the Upper West Side, there are several possibilities on Columbus Avenue in the 70s and low 80s—a good place to browse, since there are also a number of pleasant antique furniture and memorabilia shops here (along with an increasing number of interesting places to stop for lunch).

Jacques Carcanagues, at 119 Spring Street in SoHo, offers beautiful Middle Eastern kilim rugs, and *Alexander,* at 410 Columbus Avenue, is good for Orientals.

The *Macklowe Gallery,* on Madison near 76th St., is one of several reputable jewelers where you can find both antique and contemporary stuff on and around Madison Ave., from the 40s through the 70s. Alternatively, you could visit the precious-stone and jewelry district along 47th St. between Fifth and Sixth Aves., where much antique gold, rings, and such are sold (although quality can vary widely).

You'll have to go through the Yellow Pages to find the shops that specialize in first-day covers, etc., but there are many good general stamp dealers, such as the long-established *J. & H. Stolow* at 915 Broadway (21st St.) and, rather rarified, *Stanley Gibbons* at 645 Fifth Ave. near 51st St. *Harmer*, 6 W. 48th St., conducts auction sales. And there are dozens of dealers grouped together downtown on Nassau St. *Stack's*, 123 W. 57th St., and *Harmer-Rooke*, 3 E. 57th St., are well-known dealers in coins (numismatics). *Macy's* at Herald Square (34th St.) has a good numismatic department; don't forget the auctioneers *Sotheby Park Bernet*, either, at 980 Madison Ave.

One more recommendation before leaving the subject of antiques—the *Old Print Shop*, at 150 Lexington Avenue, near 30th St., for a fine display of collectible prints, maps, and other visual Americana. And a word of warning—some art and antique galleries limit their hours or close altogether during the summer months, so if you're visiting at that time it's wise to check ahead. And good hunting.

BOOKS

New York is the capital of American publishing, and is blessed with an apposite number of bookstores. The chains—Dalton's, Waldenbooks—are represented here, but there are also countless more specialized establishments, some of them quite large; and even in the marketing of bestsellers, the chains have good competition.

An early stop for any book buyer should be *Barnes & Noble*, on both sides of Fifth Avenue at 18th St. The main branch, on the east side of the avenue, is known for its vast array of scientific and technical material, college textbooks, and general reference stuff, though you'll also find more entertaining matter here. Across the road, the Sale Annex has a huge selection of low-price remaindered stock in many categories; here, too, the current bestseller list is sold well below list prices. (Barnes & Noble branches throughout the city also offer this feature.) If the college books you wanted aren't at Barnes & Noble, try browsing through the several bookstores on Broadway in the area of 116th Street, near Columbia University.

Another good browsing place is Fifth Avenue from 47th St. to 57th St. Here you'll find not only branches of *Barnes & Noble* (discount) and *B. Dalton*, but also *Doubleday* (two branches), *Rizzoli*, the *Antiquarian Booksellers' Center*, *Scribner's* (the most elegant shop), and more. Turn west on 47th St. and you'll come to the *Gotham Book Mart*, a store with a long and prestigious history, the home away-from-home to eerie illustrator Edward Gorey, and still a favorite of New Yorkers in search of poetry, modern thought, and literature, and the unexpected. *Coliseum Books*, Broadway and 57th St., and *Books & Co.*, 939 Madison Ave., both also have good selections of new and in-print titles. The *McGraw-Hill Bookstore*, in the McGraw-Hill Building plaza at Sixth Ave. and 49th St., has a wide selection of technical and business books. Medical books may be found at the stores associated with the city's large medical schools (Cornell, Mt. Sinai, New York University), and also at *General Medical Book Co.*, 310 E. 26th St.

A real clue to the importance of books in the life of the city is the number of bookstores devoted to seemingly limiting specialties; these are some of New York's great pleasures. For example, the *Drama Book Shop,* 723 Seventh Ave. at 48th St., 2nd floor for theater books; the *Ballet Shop,* near Lincoln Center at Broadway and 64th St., for coverage of dance—plus memorabilia; or *Quinion,* at 541 Hudson St., for two subjects that go surprisingly well together; theater and cookery. *Murder Ink,* at 271 West 87th St., and *The Mysterious Bookshop* at 129 W. 56th St., specialize in mysteries; *Eeyore's,* at 2252 Broadway, is a children's bookstore; *Womanbooks,* 201 W. 92nd St., sells books by, about or for . . . women. For the military buff, the *Military Bookman* is at 29 E. 93rd St. The moviegoer might go to *Cinemabilia,* at 10 W. 13th St. For books on music, try *Schirmer's* or *Patelson's* (see *Music*).

There are a number of art bookshops, the best known of which are probably *Hacker,* at 54 W. 57th St., *Jaap Rietman,* 167 Spring St. in SoHo, *E. Weyhe* on Lexington Ave. near 62nd St., and *Wittenborn* at 1018 Madison Ave. (near 79th St.), 2nd floor. The museum stores are also worth trying for this specialty—especially the store at the Metropolitan Museum of Art—as is *Rizzoli* on Fifth Ave. near 56th St.; Rizzoli is also good for foreign-language material. The *Librairie de France* and the *Libreria Hispanica,* in Rockefeller Center at Fifth Ave. (and also downtown on Fifth, near the 18th St. Barnes & Noble) are probably the best sources for French and Spanish books. Books on the Orient are a specialty at *Paragon,* 14 E. 38th St.

For maps, globes, books on maps, nautical and navigation books, and charts: *Hammond,* 12 E. 41st St., and *Rand McNally,* 10 E. 53rd St. *Argosy,* at 116 E. 59th St., has antique maps (as well as a general selection of used books and sets). *Weitz,* Lexington Ave. near 91st St., also carries sets and fine bindings. New York has a very fine selection of occult bookstores, among them *Mason's* at 789 Lexington Ave. (61st St.) and *Weiser's,* Broadway near 8th St. in the Village. The *New York Astrology Center,* 127 Madison Ave. at 30th St., has books. See the Consumer Yellow Pages under "Book Dealers—New" for a complete guide to specialty bookstores by category.

Finally, older books. The *Antiquarian Booksellers' Center,* on Rockefeller Plaza, is a good place for the serious collector of rare books and first editions (or for the reader who would *like* to be a serious collector; some items here are quite expensive). See the Consumer Yellow Pages under "Book Dealers—Used & Rare" for a listing of other dealers and their specialties. At a less exalted level, but a very rewarding one: The hub of the used-book market is along Fourth Ave. between 9th and 14th Sts.—though it is shrinking. The best of them all, and not shrinking, is *Strand,* at Broadway and 12th St.; books here include, besides some rare books and the over one million used books, mint-condition reviewers' copies (at half price) and remainders, including art books at much-reduced prices.

Several shops carry large stocks of back-issue periodicals; two are *Jay-Bee Magazines,* 143 W. 29th St., and *A & S Book Co.,* 274 W. 43rd St. Some of the shops also carry celebrity photographs and old movie posters; check the Yellow

Pages. *West Side Comix,* 107 W. 86th St., has new, back-issue and rare comic books, as does *Supersnipe* at 84th St. and Second Ave.

The Complete Traveler, Madison Ave. at the corner of 35th St., specializes in travel guides and books about travel.

RECORDS

Immensely large selections from all major labels are the rule in New York City; two places where this is an understatement are *King Karol* and *Sam Goody,* both of them with various locations. The branch of King Karol at 126 W. 42nd is particularly vast—rock, folk, classical, jazz, it's all here. *Colony Records,* Broadway at 49th St., isn't cheap, but they have a fabulous selection of pop and show records. If your needs are current releases—cheaper in the U.S. than just about anywhere else in the Western world—try *Discomat* or *J&R Music* (at several locations), which sells its stock at well below list prices—it's better for popular music than for classical, and most of what you'll find here is fairly current. Also for discounted current LP's and out-of-print recordings. Walk along 8th St. between Sixth Ave. and Broadway; this is "L.P. Alley," and there's good browsing at any of the several stores along here, especially for domestic and imported classical recordings. *Discophile,* on 8th St. near Fifth Ave., imports classical records and "private" opera discs. *The Record Hunter,* at 507 Fifth Ave., near 43rd St., also concentrates on classical music and foreign labels.

If old Beatles singles and pop esoterica strike your fancy, chances are that the *House of Oldies,* at 267 Bleecker, or *Bleecker Bob's* on MacDougal at 8th St., will too. *Dayton's,* at Broadway and 12th St. (across the street from Strand Bookstore), has a stock of reviewers' copies of records in mint condition, at low prices, and also of out-of-print records, at collectors' prices. Most of the stock is popular; for hard-to-get classical stuff, try *Darton,* at 160 W. 56th St. Other secondhand disk shops are *Free Being,* 129 Second Ave., *Gryphon Bookshop,* 89th St. off Broadway, *Hall's,* 41 E. 7th St., *Golden Disk Records,* 239 Bleecker St., *House of Oldies,* 35 Carmine St., and *Ludus Tonalis,* 24 Eighth Ave. And if you're looking for a record that even the original issuing company doesn't have in its warehouse, try *The Record Exchange,* on Seventh Avenue at 55th St., but be prepared to pay what a serious collector would.

MUSIC AND MUSICAL INSTRUMENTS

First, walk along the section of 48th St. east of Seventh Ave., for about half a block. In this somewhat raffish environment, you'll find enough musical instruments, spread out over several shops, to equip dozens of orchestra—although the stock tends more toward brass instruments, electronic keyboards, guitars (both electric and acoustic), and the other necessities for rock and jazz than toward violins and cellos. They are here, too, though—specifically, at *Sam Ash,* 160 W. 48th St., one of the most well known and longest-established of these shops. Secondhand items are available on this street, but even the prices of the new pieces are often good, and Sam Ash and other leading stores such as *Manny's,* at 156 W. 48th St., and *Terminal Music,* at No. 166, advertise their discounts. Terminal also carries recorders (flutes) and recorder music.

Down a couple of blocks, the *Professional Percussion Center,* at 151 W. 46th St., exists to service the drum community. *Charles Ponte,* at 142 W. 46th St., specializes in wind instruments, and has an amazing assortment of reeds and tools for same, including the classical wind instruments.

In pianos (many people travel to Manhattan just to pick one out, and have it shipped home), the great name is, of course, *Steinway;* the company's imposing showroom is at 109 W. 57th St. The saleshelp is friendly even to browsers, though, since there's a two year wait for many of their models. *Baldwin* is at 922 Seventh Ave., and Yamaha is at *Ostrovsky,* 154 W. 56th St., next to Patelson's; Ostrovsky also has used and reconditioned pianos of all makes and ages. *A & C Pianocraft,* 149 Wooster St. in SoHo, is among the best for rebuilt Steinways. Call 254–1840 for an appointment—and be forewarned: the entrance is hard to find. *Jack Kahn,* at 158 West 55th St., has a variety of brands of pianos, including the Bosendorfer, and runs frequent sales. Zuckermann harpsichords (kits) are handled by *Harpsichord Building and Repair,* 12 E. 12th St., 12th floor.

Havivi, at 140 W. 57th St., has classical string instruments—and there are other violin and bow dealers in the same building. *Jacques Français* also deals in (rather up-market) violins, violas, cellos at the same address. For brass and woodwind instruments, *Giardinelli,* 151 West 46th St.—same building as the Professional Percussion Center—has a wide assortment, including lots of brass mouthpieces. Fine acoustic or "classical" guitars are sold at many specialist shops or workshops, among them *Juan Orozco,* Sixth Ave. and Spring St., *Noah Wulfe,* 115 W. 57th St. (also lutes), *Gurian,* 100 Grand St., and *Matt Umanov* at 273 Bleecker St. An unusual assortment of foreign and folk music instruments is to be found at *Music Inn* on W. 4th St. near Sixth Ave. in the Village; they have records too.

Having the instrument, you also need music to play on it. One of the most popular sheet-music shops is *Joseph Patelson's,* at 160 W. 56th St.—all their music and books on music are discounted 10 percent. Many serious musicians stop in here (it is right behind Carnegie Hall). *Frank Music Co.,* on an upper floor of a very arts-and-show-business-centered building at 43 W. 61st St., has a wide selection of classical scores and parts, but there is no browsing and you must know what you want. Then, of course, there is also *Schirmer,* at 40 W. 62nd St. near Lincoln Center, which stocks the sheet music of most of the classical-music publishers, and has books too. *Carl Fischer* has a retail outlet at Cooper Square, South of 8th St. For up-to-the-minute rock stuff, there are the sheet-music departments of the various branches of *Sam Goody;* Schirmer has pop and some rock, too, as does *Colony Records* at Broadway and 49th St.

PHOTOGRAPHIC EQUIPMENT

A tip on buying cameras—buy the Sunday *New York Times,* and turn to the back few pages of the "Arts and Leisure" section. A number of discount camera stores regularly advertise here, and it's a simple matter to find where you can get the camera you want most cheaply—prices are included in the advertisements. Make sure, however, that you're not comparing apples and oranges—that the camera advertised at a certain price also comes with the lens you want, and so forth.

There are many discount shops—so many, in fact, that it seems almost criminal to pay list price for a camera. Not all the stores are reputable, however, so shop carefully. One absolutely solid name is *Willoughby's,* at 110 W. 32nd St. This large, long-established shop has good—if not the best—prices, and a great deal of varied stock. Some equipment is also available on a rental basis. For many New Yorkers, Willoughby's is New York's photographic best bet. Another popular store is *Grand Central Camera,* near Grand Central Station at 420 Lexington Ave., and this too offers good discounts.

Hirsch Photo, at 699 Third Avenue at 44th St., discounts heavily and does a lot of developing work. *Fotomat,* with branches all over the city, is also popular for developing. *7 Hour Photo,* again with several branches, guarantees speed, whether it's color or black-and-white film to be processed. While on the subject of optics, *Dell & Dell,* at 19 W. 44th St., is an authorized dealer for Zeiss, Bausch & Lomb, and other fine makes of binoculars. Several manufacturers have showrooms, such as *Nikon's* in the "Channel" at Rockefeller Center.

SPORTING GOODS

A small number of New York stores will satisfy a large chunk of your sporting needs. Go to *Paragon* first. This store, at Broadway and 18th St., advertises itself as supplying equipment for tennis, hockey, camping, archery, squash, diving, golf, darts, skiing, skating (roller and ice), Ping-Pong, and more besides; the place is noisy and crowded, but that's only because it's popular, and because as a rule, the values are good. *Spiegel's,* at 105 Nassau St., and *Herman's World of Sporting Goods,* nearby at 110 Nassau and at various other locations such as 42nd St. between Sixth Ave. and Times Square, come similarly well equipped.

Try these stores before going to the more specialized places. *The Athlete's Foot,* with a number of branches around town, has a large variety of running and other sport shoes, as well as various sweatshirts and pants, shorts, and such. Fencers can resort to *Frederick Rohde's,* at 169 E. 86th St., or *George Santelli,* at 412 Sixth Ave. near 9th St. in the Village; a nice shop for fishermen is *Angler's Roost,* at 141 E. 44th St. All sorts of accessories and artifacts for and of interest to hunters are to be found at *Hunting World,* 16 E. 53rd St. If Paragon doesn't have all the camping gear you need, *Hudson's,* at 105 Third Avenue (13th St.), probably will, and *Kreeger,* at 16 W. 46th St., is another good source for backpackers; similarly, golfers may need to look no farther than Paragaon, but if they do they could try *Al Lieber's World of Golf,* at 147 E. 47th St. or *Richard Metz,* 35 E. 50th St. There are two important stores for riding equipment, quite close to each other— *H. Kauffman & Sons,* at 139 E. 24th St., and *Miller's,* at 123 E. 24th St.; both offer English and Western wear, saddles, boots, and all the necessary apparel. The *Scandinavian Ski Shop,* at 40 W. 57th St., is long established, and keeps selling skis all summer. *Peck & Goodie,* 919 Eighth Ave. near 55th St., has a superior line of ice skates and roller skates—and sells nothing else. *Goldberg's Marine* is the best-known of the city's suppliers of nautical and marine equipment for yachtsmen: 12 W. 46th St. *New York Nautical,* at 140–142 West Broadway, near Thomas St. in Tr.BeCa, is crammed with instruments (they also service), books, charts for the entire world, models, more. Besides general sporting shops (such as Paragon) which have diving equipment (scuba), there are a few specialists, among them *Richards Aqua Lung Center,* at 233 W. 42nd St. and *Scubaplus,* 201 E. 34th St.

ART AND CRAFT SUPPLIES

This is another field where much of your needs can be supplied at a few places. Go first to *Pearl Paint,* at 308 Canal Street. This five-story shop offers everything for the artist—canvasses, brushes, paper, pens, frames, easels, tables, stretchers, mats, and much more, including, of course, lots and lots of paint. The prices are good, and it's an interesting place to wander through, seeing the different kinds of people in the New York art community. Less exciting, perhaps, but equally good in their ways are such stores as *Sam Flax,* with several branches, *Arthur Brown,* at 2 W. 46th St. (this store advertises itself as having "New York's largest stock of artist materials"), *Lee's Art Shop,* at 220 W. 57th St., and *Charrette,* at 212 E. 54th St. and other branches (Charrette aims particularly toward the architect or professional draftsman).

Joseph Torch, at 36 W. 15th St., handles handmade papers. *David Davis,* at 539 La Guardia Place, is also recommended for its variety of pigments and quality papers. *Baldwin Pottery,* nearby at 540 La Guardia, should have all you need for ceramic work. *Fezandie & Sperrie,* 111 Eighth Ave., is a treasure house of pure powdered pigments. For those whose hobby is jewelry-making (or whose business this is, for that matter), a well-known name is *Allcraft Tool & Supply* —the main office is in Hicksville, Long Island, but the showroom is at 22 W. 48th St. Knitters will find yarns at any of several stores, including *Coulter Studios,* at 118 E. 59th St.; Coulter also stocks equipment for a number of fabric-related activities, such as weaving, needlepoint, and such. *Ladies Hobby Shop,* at 2350 Broadway near 85th St., is a small and friendly Upper West Side yarn store; *Design Point,* at 15 Christopher St., is a Greenwich Village equivalent specializing in needlepoint. *Alice Maynard,* 133 E. 65th St., *Erica Wilson,* 717 Madison Ave. near 64th St., and *Woolworth's,* 838 Madison near 70th St., all sell supplies for the knitter or needlepoint worker. And finally, for glass-workers, the best game in town in probably *Glassmasters Guild,* 621 Ave. of the Americas near 19th St. selling not only glass and the tools to work it, but also some rather nice finished pieces.

AND EVERYTHING ELSE

Finally, there's the large category of things that don't fit into any of our previous categories. A good entry to this field is *Hammacher Schlemmer,* at 145

E. 57th St. It's hard to describe this shop beyond saying that it sells gadgets—everything from the obviously useful to the intriguingly peculiar, from the clever corkscrew to the motor-powered surfboard. If anyone ever invents a better mousetrap, you'll find it at Hammacher Schlemmer.

While you're in the neighborhood, you might think about crystal. Both *Baccarat* and *Carole Stupell Ltd.* are on E. 57th St., at 55 and 61 respectively, and *Steuben* too is nearby at Fifth Ave. and 56th St., near *Tiffany* (which, in addition to its famous jewelry, also stocks crystal and gorgeous chinaware, some at surprisingly modest prices). At the more humble end of the china and glass scale, but still quite handsome and popular among New Yorkers for their good values, are the dinner services and barware stocked by the *Pottery Barn* chain, in several locations around town. There are regular sales, and the branch at 23rd St. and Tenth Ave. almost always has closeouts of good merchandise. *Stuppell China Outlet,* among others, carries discontinued chinaware patterns: 29 E. 22nd St. Discontinued silver flatware patterns are available at many places in the city; try *Golden Cockerel* at 82 Christopher St. (the Village), *S. Wyler,* 713 Madison Ave. at 63rd St., or *Panken & Thorn Antiques,* 207 E. 84th St.

New York has many shops selling unusual collectibles, such as beautiful and interesting mineralogical and fossil specimens (try *Astro Minerals,* 155 E. 34th St.; *Crystal Resources,* 130 E. 65th St.), and seashells (*Collector's Cabinet*—they also sell butterflies—153 E. 57th St.; *Seashells Unlimited,* 590 Third Ave.; *Captain Hook's* at 10 Fulton St.; *Glory of the Sea* at 124 MacDougal St. in the Village).

In addition to a whole range of gift ideas in the way of jewelry, china, and such, *Fortunoff* also stocks silverware (as, of course, does *Tiffany*). You could go somewhere expensive for your linen, towels, sheets, drapes, and such, but why, when you can go to the famous *Ezra Cohen,* at 307 Grand Street on the Lower East Side? Many New Yorkers shop nowhere else for these goods. *Liberty of London,* at 229 E. 60th St., is the New York outlet for the famous English fabrics, scarves and accessories, and *Tender Buttons,* with a large collection of antique and modern buttons, buckles, and cufflinks, is a good source for the trimmings. The millinery district, 38th and 39th Sts. between Fifth Ave. and Ave. of the Americas, has lots of outlets for wonderful ribbonry, silk flowers, beads, veils, trimming, and, of course, hats. *Sheru* on W. 38th St. (No. 49) is a good source of beads and crafts materials from around the world. *Simon's Hardware,* Third Ave. between 29th and 30th Sts., has one of the largest selections of decorative hardware in the country—so look here for those handles or hinges you can't find anywhere. There are good hardware stores all along Canal St. west of Chinatown; good selections of tools also at *Lilien Hardware,* 490 W. Broadway near Houston.

Not in the city, but in nearby New Jersey, is one of the nation's leading makers of astronomical telescopes: *Edmund Scientific,* 101 E. Gloucester Pike, Barrington.

Try *Capezio,* at several locations, for dance equipment. *Freeds of London,* an English firm, also has a boutique for dance gear (including toe and character shoes) at 108 W. 57th St. near Carnegie Hall. The best-known cutlery store is probably *Hoffritz,* with various branches, including one at 203 W. 57th St.; this establishment also sells barware, gadgets, and such. There are plenty of pet stores, but it seems a shame not to take a kitten or puppy off the hands of *Bide-A-Wee,* at 410 E. 38th St.; this is an animal shelter, not a business, and the prices are token, and tax-deductible. For classier dogs, try *Pedigree Pups,* at 969 First Avenue (they have cats, too). *Fabulous Felines* sells rare and unusual breeds: 133 Lexington Ave. And if you're not too far from home, you might be able to take away some tropical fish for your tanks at home; see *Fish Town USA,* Third Ave. near 34th St., and *Aquarium Stock Co.,* 31 Warren St., downtown, near City Hall. *Exotic Aquatics,* 272 Bleecker St. in the Village, also has snakes, lizards, and other animals not known to us! The flower district of the city is a few blocks of Sixth Avenue in the upper 20s—visit *Treemania* for unusual plants, or *Bonsai Dynasty* for those tiny trees in pots. (Visitors from outside the U.S. should consider the Customs regulations they may face on their trip home before buying plants or animals.)

There are several chess emporia in Greenwich Village; one of them is simply called the *Chess Shop,* at 230 Thompson St. near Bleecker. For a clock, go to *Tourneau,* at 500 Madison Ave. near 52nd St. *Bikes and Things,* at 377 East 23rd St., is an extremely well-equipped bicycle shop. A good, safe bet for stereo equipment is *Tech HiFi,* with several branches; there are a number of reputable hi-fi and advanced electronics shops, along with Tech, on 45th St. between Fifth and Sixth Ave. *Uncle Steve's* at 343 Canal St. has very good buys in electronic and hi-fi gear. To keep you healthy through all this, *Brownies* was a health food store before there was health food—it's at 91 Fifth Ave. near Barnes & Noble.

New York has a considerable number of places selling herbs, herbal teas, and herbal preparations: *Aphrodisia,* 28 Carmine St. in the Village (they also have books, as does *Samuel Weiser* at 740 Broadway); *Caswell-Massey* at 575 Lexington Ave.; *Good Earth* at Second Ave. and 72nd St.; *Kiehl Pharmacy,* 109 Third Ave.; *McNulty's, Paprikas Weiss,* and *St. Rémy* at 156 E. 64th St, which also features French fabrics and crafts, (see *Gourmet Foods* for addresses).

Finally, books, prints, drawings, photographs, and more on the ever-fascinating subject of New York City are to be found at *New York Bound Books and Urban Graphics,* 43 W. 54th St.

There's obviously an enormous amount that we haven't been able to touch, and that every visitor will discover for him or herself. But you'll find that no matter how well you know New York, there's always more to see. That makes the city tantalizing, but also somehow reassuring.

RESTAURANTS. There is really no single comment that can effectively describe the phenomenon of eating out in New York City. As the gastronomic capital of the United States—and by virtue of the international breadth of its offerings, of the world—it has by far more fine and distinguished restaurants than anywhere else in the country. Put at its simplest, there is a dining experience in the Big Apple to satisfy any palate (no matter how exotic one's tastes) and any budget.

No national nor ethnic cuisine is left out. Indeed, there are restaurants in New York offering various types of cooking not likely to be found anywhere else in the country—and we fervently suggest that you sample some culinary delight you may never before have had the opportunity to try. Such daring may well turn out to be a high point of your visit, though it may on the other hand engender a bit of future frustration as you contemplate the possibility of getting like preparations—say, a Thai whoefish with green chilies and onion—upon your return home.

You can cover the globe gastronomically in New York, spending as much or as little as you like. You can feast on steaks at the *Palm* or *Christ Cella,* paying dearly for every succulent bite, or you can opt for a reasonable facsimile at *Farnie's* or the *Blue Mill Tavern* for far less money. You can be transported to the far reaches of India at the delicately appointed *Raga* or *Shezan,* or you can head over to East 6th St. between First and Second Aves. where about a dozen friendly, inexpensive family-run eateries offer outstanding curries and tandoori specialties.

Most of the best restaurants in New York City center in Manhattan, and most of these are south of 86th St., so the bulk of our attention is focused on that area, although we have picked a few notables in the outlying boroughs for your additional consideration. Public transportation makes any corner of Manhattan Island, and most of the other boroughs, accessible, and the trip is frequently worthwhile. Enthusiasts of Middle Eastern cooking, for example, will do well to take a ride to Brooklyn's Atlantic Avenue section where there is a host of very good, modestly priced Lebanese restaurants (most owned by the Almontaser family, with the best of the lot, bearing the family name, at 218 Court St.; 624–9267). Similarly, many long-time natives swear that the *real* Little Italy of New York, with the best food at the cheapest prices, is on and around Arthur Avenue in the Bronx—at *Mario's, Stella D'Oro's, Il Boschetto,* and *Amerigo's* —not on Manhattan's Mulberry Street. The partisans battle on forever.

Time was, in fact, when you *had* to go way downtown to Chinatown or Manhattan's Little Italy for a good Chinese or Italian meal. Not any more. There are those who tell you the East Side svelte belt (starting aroung the Grand Central Station area off Second Ave. and heading uptown) has the city's best Chinese cooking, with rivals for the best of the best including *Uncle Tai's, David K's,* the *Sichuan Pavilion, Peng Teng's, Chef Ho's Hunan Manor,* and *Hunam.* True, they are expensive, which is why Chinatown still has its supporters. (By Chinatown they mean the six to eight cluttered blocks bordered by Canal St. on the north and the Bowery on the east with the boundaries spilling over into Manhattan's Little Italy itself.)

You name the style of Chinese cooking you want and New York has it, be it Cantonese, Shanghai, Peking, Hunan, Szechuan, Fukien, Taiwanese, or Mongolian. The same holds true for Italian cooking, whether you're looking for the staples of southern Italian Neapolitan cooking or the delicate flavorings of Florentine or Roman chefs. And again you have a choice of the more expensive restaurants (with the East Side's *Romeo Salta* or *Giambelli's* considered among the best of this breed), the tourist spots (such as *Mama Leone's*), or the moderately priced best of Little Italy (the *Grotta Azzura* taking top honors on that count for a savory balance between the quality of cuisine and price).

Indeed, the city is filled with ethnic pockets, and its restaurants spill over with the flavor of the Old World, Asia, the Orient. The far east 70s and 80s of Manhattan are known as the Yorkville area, and offer Slavic and German eateries galore. Greek and Thai restaurants have found a home north of the skin-flick houses on Eighth Ave. from 48th to 56th Sts. West 46th St. has taken on a decidedly Brazilian flavor, and mid-Manhattan looks like Tokyo East, with the smell of fish and tempura coming out of just about every other doorway. Astoria, Queens, is Greek restaurant heaven; so is Greektown around W. 27th St., with its bazoukis and belly dancers.

By now you get the point that we have eschewed the normal geographic divisions of Manhattan in favor of trying to whet your appetite with some suggestions that you might otherwise miss—especially if you were concentrating only on those restaurants in the immediate vicinity of your hotel—for that is the best way to get a real taste of the Big Apple. But there are a number of places worth singling out because they afford a spectacular view to go along with that taste of the Big Apple.

Most prominent among these is *Windows on the World,* the restaurant complex on the 107th floor of the World Trade Center (the eponymous restaurant offers expensive à la carte dining and a northerly view; the *Hors d'Oeuverie* has the southern exposure and serves only drinks and snacks). Others to consider for views from on high: the *Rainbow Room* at Rockefeller Center, *Top of the Sixes, Top of the Park* and *Nirvana* (both overlooking Central Park), and *The Terrace* at Columbia University. For the reverse view and a totally unique dining experience, journey to Brooklyn's *River Café,* at the foot of the Brooklyn Bridge, where you dine on a barge moored in the East River while drinking in the Manhattan skyline towering above you just across the water. The food at all of these restaurants, alas, can hardly compete with the view—and rarely does, although the River Café, on its better days, comes closest to the mark. You also pay dearly for what you see, even on cloudy days.

The vote for the most imaginative decor and cuisine might well go to the *Four Seasons,* where the decorations and menus change with—that's right—the seasons. The most expensive and sumptuous restaurant in a town filled with expensive and sumptuous restaurants would probably be *The Palace,* where meals come in three prices: $50, $95, and 50 per person. The *Coach House* draws consistent raves as one of the best for American-International cuisine. The arguments still rage between steak-and-chop lovers as to whether the East Side's aforementioned *Christ Cella* is better than *The Palm,* or whether *Gage & Tollner* and *Peter Luger* are better than either of them, even if it means crossing the East River to Brooklyn to get to them.

The range in price is as great as the variety of New York restaurant offerings —accounted for in matters of service, presentation, location, and decor as well as in who the chef is and what his or her capabilities are. This is so be the cuisine Chinese, Continental (that ill-defined hybrid of European and American influences), French, Indian, Italian, or otherwise. While a fine meal at an elegant restaurant can (and often does) extract a sultan's ransom from wealthy gourmands, it is also possible to have a nearly duplicate meal, served in more humble surroundings (and without a platoon of liveried attendants), at literally half the tariff.

In addition, there are a number of ways to dine at even the most expensive establishments without necessarily going bankrupt in the process. Many of the city's finest restaurants—and the Four Seasons heads the list!—offer special pre-theater dinners at prices that are a third to half less than the same meal ordered during prime serving periods. The menu selections are generally a little more limited, and you must usually be seated between 5:00 and 6:00 P.M., but service, preparation and surroundings are at the same high standards for which these restaurants are noted.

Then, too, lunches are often 10 to 20 percent cheaper than the same dinners would be, so having a big midday meal at *Lutèce,* for instance, at a prix fixe for approximately $16.75, affords the opportunity to dine at what is generally considered the finest classical French restaurant in the city at a fraction of what a similar three-course meal would cost à la carte in the evening. Another suggestion: Nowhere is it written that you must order courses as suggested on the menu at luncheon or dinner. If you are two or three people, for example, there is no reason why you can't order a selection of appetizers (which in at least some cases are scaled down portions of entrées), a salad, and a dessert—all to be shared. You get to sample several different items and the check—even if there is a "plate charge"—is within reason.

Increasingly popular all around the city is the leisurely weekend brunch—a late morning/early afternoon repast that is more extravagant than the usual breakfast but not quite as heavy as a European-style lunch. This, again, can be a good way to try some of the fancier restaurants at moderate cost; many offer special prix fixe brunches featuring classic omelettes and other egg dishes, as well as more exotic fare, with your choice of alcoholic beverage and tea or coffee included.

Remember that New York eats late; the better restaurants (except those near theaters or concert halls) don't get busy until 8 P.M., if then. If you insist on eating dinner as the second hand sweeps past six, you may be the only person in the place. Don't worry about going for dinner at 11:00 P.M.; lots of places will still serve. We've listed some that stay open much later.

In preparing the following lists of suggested restaurants, we've sought to provide a wide enough range of choices to fit every traveler's tastes and budget. And our listings do represent a *selection,* not a complete survey by any means, of places that will—we hope—enhance your visit to New York.

We regret, as you do, the prices that any meal costs everywhere these days, and the toll in New York is probably higher than anywhere else in the nation. But the following categories are the facts of life in today's dining out world, and we can only suggest that you mitigate each foray to some expensive temple of gastronomy with a sojourn to at least one or more modest sub-temple. As a rule of thumb, the higher the price, the more necessary reservations become. Dress codes vary, so check when making a reservation.

The price categories we use are approximate; figure for an average three-course meal (appetizer, main course with vegetable, dessert) at a given establishment, per person. This does not take into account the suggestions offered above for lessening the blow to the pocketbook, **nor does it include wine or drinks, taxes or gratuities.** As of this writing, meals are taxed at 8¼ percent of the total bill; for average service, most New Yorkers simply double the tax as a tip. For outstanding service you may wish to tip 20 percent, with another five percent for the maitre'd if he or she has been especially helpful.

Super Deluxe restaurants will cost $40 and up. **Deluxe** establishments will generally fit into the $35 range. **Expensive** dinners will usually cost about $25. **Moderate** meals should run about $15. A tab at an **Inexpensive** restaurant will cost an average of $10. Do not be misled, however, by traditional notions of super deluxe or deluxe. We have grouped the restaurants primarily by price category, and some very expensive places—particularly the *nouvelle cuisine* restaurants, and many establishments on otherwise abandoned SoHo streets—will hardly have the type of elegance one usually associates with such prices.

Today, credit cards, "plastic money," are a very acceptable commodity. Most—although not all—restaurants accept credit cards. These are indicated by the following abbreviations which appear at the end of the upcoming restaurant listings:

AE - American Express
CB - Carte Blanche
DC - Diners Club
MC - MasterCard
V - Visa

Where a listing says, for example, "No CB," that means that the restaurant in question accepts all credit cards except Carte Blanche. Because of the cost involved in processing credit card charges, some establishments offer a cash discount of 5 to 10 percent for cash-paying customers; others may request that you tip in cash.

During the summer, many restaurants are closed for vacation for as much as a month; call ahead to check.

We have arranged the restaurants according to general stylistic categories first (American-International, Steakhouses, Seafood, etc.) and then by national or ethnic cuisine rather than geographically, although we have endeavored to make specific references if a particular place is especially convenient to, say, the theater district or Lincoln Center. And we have broken down the sections within each cuisine by price category with entries in alphabetical order. This should simplify your comparisons as well as facilitate looking up information about a restaurant whose name you may know. But before we go to the formal listings, here are a few notes on additional places that don't fit the regular categories.

Fast food. Such internationally renowned operations as *McDonald's* and *Burger King* are alive and thriving all around New York City. *Kentucky Fried Chicken* is similarly well entrenched, with listings in the White or Yellow Pages of the telephone directory the best way to find the locations nearest you. When the budget is hurting, these are possible alternatives.

Pizza seems to be a major staple of New York eating habits. *John's Pizzeria,* 278 Bleecker St. near Seventh Ave. in Greenwich Village, has what many insist is the best pizza in New York. They sell whole pies only, and there is almost always a wait for a table—they take no reservations. Wine and beer, however, are available. *Amalfi Pizza* nearby at Bleecker on Seventh Ave. So., does sell slices. Every New Yorker has a different "best," it seems; try Sicilian style for a change.

Middle Eastern. Another very inexpensive and hearty fast-food alternative unique to New York is *Amy's,* again with branches all around town, serving Middle Eastern sandwiches and salads in bright, well-kept surroundings. You can bring your own wine or beer to most branches after 6:00 P.M. Street vendors also sell barbecued shish kebab that is usually pungent from a tenderizing marinade.

Chains. Other local chain-style operations with uniform outlets around the city include *Chock Full O' Nuts* (mostly in midtown office districts), *Zum Zum* (specializing in German *wursts* and beer), *Steak and Brew,* and *Roast Beef and Brew.* The last three offer free all-you-can-eat salads with the modest price of a meal and represent a good value for the money when you need a quick bite.

Cafeterias. Try *Dubrow's* (38th and Seventh Ave.) in the heart of the garment district. *Horn & Hardart* has one remaining coin-in-the-slot "automated" cafeteria at 200 E. 42nd St.

24-hour stops. People in New York do seem to be hungry at all hours of the day and night, and the selection among available offerings is only slightly less limited than normal if the time happens to be 4:30 A.M. or so. There are three reliable places on Second Ave. between 4th and 6th Sts.: *Kiev* (117 Second Ave.; 674–4040), an outstanding coffee shop great for hearty soups, blintzes, and fruit-filled pancakes that are almost like fritters; *103 Second Restaurant* (103 Second Ave.; 533–0769), which feels as though it were transplanted from SoHo, serving spicy, chunky chili, Continental meals and sandwiches, and breakfast at all hours; and the *Binibon,* at the corner of 5th St. (no phone), where you'll find inexpensive oversize salads the best bet. The *Empire Diner* (210 Tenth Ave., at W. 22nd St.; 243–2736) is a glorified candlelit boxcar with eggs and pasta and salads at any time—and with the crowd worth the trip particularly in the wee hours. Next door is *Factor's Find* (470 Tenth, at W. 23rd St.; 691–1708), which has a glass-enclosed café and a beautiful seating area near the bar (with bamboo tables and high-backed peacock chairs). The food is watered-down Continental, but by avoiding the more complicated concoctions you can do fine. The *Green Kitchen* (1477 First Ave.; 988–4163) and *Silver Star* (1236 Second Ave.; 249–4250) both serve a little of everything—they're more than a few steps above a coffee shop in quality and very reliable. *Mamun's* (119 MacDougal St.; 674–9246) serves up falafel (mashed chick peas deep fried) and other mid-Eastern sandwiches around the clock, while *Sarge's Delicatessen and Restaurant* (548 Third Ave.; 679–0442) has sandwiches right in midtown. *The Brasserie* (100 E. 53rd St.; 751–4840), a large but pleasant more-or-less Franch, well brasserie, is open 24 hours a day, seven days a week. Among the places included in the listings below, the *Stage Deli* is open 24 hours, while *Sardi's, On Stage,* the *Oak Room* at the Algonquin, and others in the immediate vicinity of Broadway at least serve post-theater suppers. So, too, do *La Folie* and the *Four Seasons*—the latter even featuring dessert and/or cheese in the bar area. Chinatown's *Hong Fat* and the far East Village's *Baltyk* are always open, and both *Palsson's* (158 W. 72nd St.; 362–2590) and the *Riviera Cafe* (225 W. Fourth St.; 242–8732) serve until 4 A.M. Throughout the city there are "Greek" coffee shops, known as such because so many appear to be owned by Greeks, not necessarily because they serve Greek food. They'll do well enough when it's a couple of scrambled eggs you want without having to travel very far.

Places with a view. There are lots of restaurants with good city views; we mention them in the individual entries. Here is a selection: *Top of the Towers,* Beekman Hotel, First Ave. at 49th St., offering drinks and music, has great views of the East River and the midtown skyscrapers. *Top of the Park,* Gulf & Western Bldg., Central Park West at 60th St., has a splendid view of Central Park. *Top of the Sixes,* 666 Fifth Ave., is smack in the middle of the midtown building cluster, as is the *Rainbow Room* at the top of the RCA Building in Rockefeller Center—but the Rainbow Room is higher. *Windows on the World,* in the World Trade Center on the 107th floor, has the best city view of all—by far. All the above are probably best just for drinks, but one that is especially good for the eats too, and not *too* expensive, is *The Terrace* in Butler Hall at Columbia University, at 119th St. a block from Broadway. The Terrace (French, dinner only) has a good view of the midtown skyline, chamber music, all in all, romantic. There are also good views of Manhattan from across the East River in Brooklyn, at the *River Cafe* or *Ferrybank.*

Brunch. We mention good brunches in the individual entries. Places offering Sunday brunch—usually starting at 11:00 A.M. or noon—are legion in New York. Many offer chamber music too. Saturday brunches are less popular. Carry your *New York Times* into the restaurant and look as if you've lived here all your life.

Dessert. Finally, if you turn to the last page of these listings, you'll discover our suggestions for desserts. These include notable ice cream parlors and pastry shops that just may lure you into forgetting lunch or dinner altogether.

AMERICAN-INTERNATIONAL

Super Deluxe

The Four Seasons. 99 E. 52nd St.; 754–9494. One of New York's most beautiful, ambitious, and interesting restaurants. As seasons change, so do menus and decor. The main dining room is dominated by a large, shimmering reflecting pool. Art work includes a Picasso, and changing floral displays constitute a veritable botanical garden. But the heart of the restaurant revolves around a series of gastronomic "events," featuring famous chefs from around the world preparing their most famous creations. Best seats are thought to be near the pool in the formal dining room, where prices can reach the stratosphere. The outside

Grill Room is a little less fancy and a lot less expensive. Knowledgeable New Yorkers who don't mind eating early take advantage of less expensive pre-theater dinner ($22.50 prix fixe as of this writing) from 5:00 to 7:00 P.M. Entrée choices are staggering in each case, as is the selection from one of America's most complete wine cellars. If the chocolate velvet for dessert is a once-in-a-lifetime experience, so is the restaurant itself. Closed Sundays. All major credit cards.

Windows on the World. 1 World Trade Center; 938–1111. A stunning and lavish restaurant with a wraparound view of the city that is suggestive of a ship's dining room—providing the ship is the *QE2* and she is perched atop the world's second tallest building, 107 floors up, where only the daringest crow's nest. Unfortunately, food doesn't always match the view—what could?—or the decor, which includes a rock-lined, mirrored reception chamber, a multi-tiered, multi-mirrored main dining room, a veritable acre of glass encompassing various-dining rooms, cocktail lounges and private rooms, lavish touches of brass, wood, plants and fresh flowers, and waiters resplendent in white uniforms with gold epaulets. The neighboring **Hors d'Oeuverie,** on the same floor and run by the same management, is an internationally minded cocktail lounge and grill that can be inexpensive if you eat and drink lightly while enjoying the sights and listening to the piano music. Reservations way in advance for Windows; not required for Hors D'Oeuverie, although there is often a wait at the latter for seats. All major credit cards.

Deluxe

Christ Cella. 160 E. 46th St.; 697–2479. Perhaps the largest piece of roast beef around, ditto the steaks, and everything else is similarly served in oversized portions. Decor on two floors is simple, but who cares, for this is generally considered the best steak and roast-beef house in town, although supporters of The Palm will give you an argument there—and have for years in a rivalry reminiscent of the Yanks and Dodgers. Closed Saturday/Sunday during July and August. All major credit cards.

The Coach House. 110 Waverly Place (the Village); 777–0303. A glowingly handsome English inn setting, where the best American dishes are served along with European classics in what many galloping gourmets consider the best all-around restaurant in the Big Apple, even though it does not exert itself for new customers. Open at 5:30 P.M. on Saturday, 4:30 P.M. on Sunday, closed Monday. All major credit cards.

Rainbow Room. 30 Rockefeller Plaza (Rockefeller Center); 757–9090. Classic Art Deco room dripping chandeliers, chrome, tables on multi-levels, and spectacular view of city from 65th floor of the RCA building. It also features name bands for dinner dancing—but food doesn't match mood, view or ambiance. The adjacent **Rainbow Grill** offers dinners, disco, and a mediocre imitation Vegas-Paris cabaret show with some nudity. All major credit cards.

Expensive

Café Loup. 18 E. 13th St.; 255-4746. A small, casual bistro in an unusual location, staffed by pleasant young people. The menu, chalked on blackboards, is more or less French—and the food is good. Major credit cards.

Chelsea Place. 147 Eighth Ave. near 17th St.; 924-8413. From the outside, the antique store at this address gives no hint that there's an exceedingly popular singles bar and restaurant literally "through the looking glass." You enter the eatery through what looks like an oversized armoir. There's a very pleasant glassed-in garden for dining year-round—well-removed from the bustle of the bar scene. The food is good yet overpriced in its class, but the setting and atmosphere are definitely unique. All major credit cards.

The Conservatory. 15 Central Park West at 61st St.; 581-1293. A relaxed, attractive spot for the Lincoln Center crowd. Diversified menu includes Mongolian lamb chops, shrimp scampi, and breast of capon piccata. All credit cards.

The Ginger Man. 51 W. 64th St.; 399-2358. Another favorite dinner locale among those attending performances at Lincoln Center. A well-decorated, pub-style establishment that is noted for its spinach salad and steaks. Check for musical entertainment. All major credit cards.

Greene Street. 101–103 Greene St. between Prince and Spring (SoHo); 925-2415. Good but not great food in a delightful setting— plants, catwalks, lots of space—in the interesting SoHo area. AE, MC, V.

Hurley's Steak & Seafood. 49th St. and Sixth Ave.; 765-8981. Jammed at lunchtime. Very popular with broadcasting and advertising folks—the NBC headquarters and studios are about thirty feet away. Major credit cards.

Joanna. 18 E. 18th St.; 675-7900. Trendy among those in the fashion and book-publishing worlds, Joanna dispenses everything from omelettes and snacks to *haute cuisine* in a partly Victorian, partly modern setting. The bar is always thickly populated, there's almost always a wait for a table (particularly at late hours), and the attitude is suitably haughty—though the food is consistently better than good. AE.

The Leopard. 253 E. 50th St., near Second Ave.; 759-3735. A fine, spacious dining room, with tables comfortably far apart, overlooking a plastic garden. Prix-fixe meals include all the wine you wish—and the wines are surprisingly good. The Continental-style food is not four-star, but neither are the prices. AE, DC, CB.

Maxwell's Plum. 1181 First Ave. at 64th St.; 628-2100. The bar is the mecca for NYC's single-and-mingle crowd. You can dine elegantly in the art nouveau, Tiffany-lighted dining area at the rear, where the menu is ambitious and interesting. The consummate New York City scene. All credit cards.

P. J. Moriarty's. 1034 Third Ave near 61st St.; 838-2438. A congenial place noted for the hearty American and international viands. The menu has new specialties each day, but the corned beef and cabbage is super special. All major credit cards.

Mortimers. 1057 Lexington Ave. & 75th, Upper East Side; 861-2481. Fancy and neighborhoody at the same time—upscale singles at the bar, older area residents at the tables. The food aspires to more than it attains. All major credit cards.

One Fifth. 1 Fifth Ave. in the Village; 260–3434. You won't get seasick in this first-class dining salon, a restoration of the *Caronia's* dining room. Continental cuisine, clam bar, piano music. Modern jazz in the front room late evenings. All major credit cards.

One If by Land, Two If by Sea. 17 Barrow St., between W. 4th St. and Seventh Ave.; 255–8649. In what was once a stable, this charming restaurant is a favorite more for its ambience and unusual layout than for its food—land is meat, sea is fish, get it?—though the food is all right if you stick to basics. There is no sign outside the place, so look for the street number. Not terribly casual in dress. All major credit cards.

Proof of the Pudding. 1165 First Ave. near 64th St. And an unpublished phone number, which should tell you something. On the singles axis at 64th St. No menu; waiters recite choices—sometimes they sing them. Would you believe veal Alaska? Music. No CB.

Tavern-on-the-Green. Central Park West at 67th St. (just inside Central Park); 873–3200. This long-time New York landmark has three beautifully appointed rooms with views of the park, and outdoor dining when weather permits. Specialties: salads, veal and beef dishes. Attentive service, so-so food, and be sure to have a reservation lest you be sneered away at the door. Live band for dancing on some nights. All major credit cards.

Moderate

Joe Allen's. 326 W. 46th St., in the theater district; 581–6464. A long-time theatrical hangout which means you probably won't get a table at prime time unless you're recognized at the door. Casual place, casual-style food and a good value if you can get it. MC, V.

Billy's. 948 First Ave. near 52nd St.; 355–8920. A neighborhood favorite among residents of the fashionable Beekman Place area. Has all the ambience of a Yukon saloon. Known for steaks and lamb chops. AE, CB, DC.

Bridge Café. 279 Water St.; 227–3344. Near the South Street Seaport and convenient to the financial district, though the restaurant itself is well hidden beneath the Brooklyn Bridge (on the Manhattan side). The kitchen experiments with unusual combinations—usually to good effect, as with a salad of watercress, avacado, and grapefruit—and there are superior soups and seafood. Very congenial, a little noisy, and excellent for Sunday morning brunch. No credit cards.

P. J. Clarke's. 915 Third Ave. at 55th St.; 759–1650. The most chic hamburger joint in town. A legend that is the special province of NYC's advertising and publishing set, though there's a branch for shoppers in Macy's Cellar. Good chili served in the bar area. No credit cards.

Crawdaddy. 45 E. 45th St.; 687–1860. New Orleans in New York: Creole dishes, gumbos, cheerful decor, live music evenings. Closed Saturday/Sunday. All major credit cards.

Gardenia Club. 482 W. 43rd St.; 594–8402. In Manhattan Plaza, the artist/ show business apartment complex. A rather romantic hideway, overlooking a pool. Chicken, simply prepared, is the specialty. Closed Mondays. AE, MC, V.

Gottlieb's. 343 Bleecker St. near W. 10th St. in the Village; 929–7800. A very relaxed and comfortable place, and the food somehow matches. No DC.

Hell's Kitchen. 598 Ninth Ave.; 757–5329. Good pre-theater stop for simple, hearty fare, though the menu is limited. Closed Mondays. AE.

Library. 2475 Broadway at 92nd St.; 799–4860. An eclectic menu—chicken gai yang, veal saltimbocca, barbecued baby back ribs—but the prices are reasonable and the relaxed Upper West Side atmosphere (yes, there are books on the walls) is enjoyable. Near the Symphony Space. Brunch with chamber music Sunday noon to 3:00 P.M. Major credit cards.

Lion's Rock. 316 E. 77th St.; 988–3610. Very good Continental-type food in a casual atmosphere, with an attractive open garden at the rear. Dinner only, but brunch on Sunday. Major credit cards.

Ma Bell's. 218 W. 45th St.; 869–0110. Fronts on famed Shubert Alley. You can order your choices via the phone at your table. Good for pre- or post-theater dining. All major credit cards.

Martell's. 1469 Third Ave. st 84th St.; 861–6110. French farmer's sandwich is a specialty at this Upper East Side boite, which advertises its "spirituous liquors." Sidewalk café in good weather. Good bar scene. All major credit cards.

Jim McMullen's. 1341 Third Ave. near 77th St.; 861–4700. Natural brick walls, no reservations. A hangout for models—Jim was one himself—the beautiful people and the sports crowd. Good seafood, first-class steaks. All major credit cards.

J. G. Melon. 1291 Third Ave. at 74th St.; 744-0585. This is fast food for the Beautiful People. The bar is a regular meeting place for New York's informal chic set. Hamburgers are fine, as are the Monte Cristo sandwiches. Also a West Side branch at Amsterdam Ave. and 76th St. (874–8291). No credit cards.

Palsson's. 158 W. 72nd St.; 362–2590. This extremely comfortable Upper West Side bar and restaurant is supposedly Icelandic, but the manager-owner is from a Romanian Jewish family and the chef is Chinese—but the food is good and reasonably priced: chicken tarragon, fish smoked to order, a few other well-chosen dishes—and the place really gets busy after 11:00 P.M. with show-business people. Cabaret upstairs. Major credit cards.

Simon's. 75 W. 68th St.; 496–7477. Simon's achieved instant notoriety when, a few weeks after opening, Walter Cronkite's friends threw a party to celebrate his retirement from the evening news. Thus are trends born—though this one has had no problem surviving its "instant stardom." All major credit cards.

Tastings. 144 W. 55th St.; 757–1160. An offshoot of the International Wine Center, Tastings usually offers upwards of 20 different wines for sampling by the glass or half-glass (for those who are really serious) on any given night. Best approach here is to create a meal from a variety of appetizers—either at the bar or in the modern, wood-plants-and-Italian-lamps dining room—and to let the liquid refreshment serve as the focus. Closed Sundays. AE, V, MC.

Texarkana. 64 W. 10th St.; 254–5800. Tex-Mex is something of a New York fad these days, and Texarkana caters to the trendiest of the faddists. Still, the ribs and smothered chicken dishes are very fine. The service in keeping with the attitude of the place. Reservations a must, and then expect a wait. AE.

Village Green. 531 Hudson St.; 255–1650. A stunning split-level restaurant, dark and romantic, with fresh flowers in abundance and a light hand in the kitchen. In winter, the upstairs bar faces a warming fireplace. AE, MC, V.

West Bank Café. 407 W. 42nd St.; 695–6909. Good ribs, chicken, salads, and quiches in the Manhattan Plaza apartment complex—excellent for after theater (be sure to have reservations). AE, MC, V.

Inexpensive

Buffalo Roadhouse. 87 Seventh Ave. South; 242–9082. Probably *the* Village favorite for hamburgers and beer, with an outdoor terrace during the summer and a wait for tables all year round. Good salads, too. No credit cards.

Elephant & Castle. 183 Prince St. and 68 Greenwich Ave.; 243–1400 and 260–3600. The Prince St./SoHo outpost is the newer, brighter, and livelier of the two, the Greenwich original a uniquely Village hole in the wall with great charm. Burgers, salads, and omelettes are what to count on—the kitchen isn't as adept at more complicated fare—with bar in SoHo, BYOB invited in the Village. Nice for brunch. All major credit cards at both.

Maestro Café. 58 W. 65th St. near Lincoln Center; 787–5990. Attractive decor, good "American-Continental" cuisine, lively service. Good for pre- or post-concert dining. All major credit cards.

Smoke Stacks Lightnin' Bar. 380 Canal St.; 226–2670. Good neighborhood hangout for hamburgers, salads, and quiches. Borders on TriBeCa punk-rock territory (the regulars are a colorful lot), but friendly. AE.

Ye Waverly Inn. 16 Bank St.; 929–4377. A Village landmark with three low-ceilinged, candlelit dining rooms—two with fireplaces—and a backyard garden. Down-to-earth American cookery that has been tired in recent years, though the pies and cakes are still homemade. No CB.

STEAKHOUSES

Super Deluxe

Christ Cella. See American-Continental.

Joe & Rose. 747 Third Ave. near 46th St.; 980–3985. They built an entire skyscraper around this humble-looking eatery. Food is hardly humble, though, and the steaks and corned beef and cabbage are specials. Like The Palm and Pietro's, this is a New York phenomenon, where the service and surroundings belie the prices—but the food doesn't. No menu. AE, DC.

Lobel's. 801 Second Ave.; 697–9500. The Lobels, best-known in New York for their Upper East Side butcher shop that caters to the rich and glamorous—at suitably uppity prices, opened this restaurant in mid-1982 within walking distance of the United Nations. Lunch and dinner Monday through Friday, dinner only Satursays. No CB.

The Palm. 837 Second Ave. near 45th St.; 687–2953. For the roughly two hundred ten million Americans who've been weaned on "New York cut" steaks, it's going to come as a rude awakening to discover that such a description has no meaning in N.Y.C. But if you are looking for just about the best piece of sirloin in town, this is the place. You should know that it's a madhouse at the prime dinner hours, and because of a non-reservation policy, an hour's wait is not the least unusual. We should also mention that the noise level is high and that the walls are decorated in a way that can only be described as vintage graffiti and that the waiters will do their best to antagonize you and get you in and out quickly. Yet beef lovers queue up gladly, and the double sirloin is a total delight. The cottage-fried potatoes and crisp onion rings are unequaled in the city, and the double lobster (carrying a tariff that may require payment in 30-, 60-, and 90-day notes) is simply splendid. A branch called **Palm Too,** 697–5198, directly across the street and serving the same food, tries to handle the overflow. Closed Sunday. All major credit cards.

Pen & Pencil. 205 E. 45th St.; 682–8660. Another steakhouse with an established (and highly vocal) group of supporters among the journalistic and entertainment crowd. In addition to grilled steaks and chops, a few Italian specialties can be ordered. All major credit cards.

Pietro's. See *Italian.*

The Post House. 28 E. 63rd St.; 935–2888. One of New York's newest and most comfortable steak houses. All major credit cards.

Smith and Wollensky. 201 E. 49th St.; 753–1530. Steaks, chops, roast beef, and lobsters are the basic items, and flank steak surrounded by vegetables is a feature. All major credit cards.

United States Steakhouse Company. 120 W. 51st St.; 757–8800. Owned by a friend of Mayor Koch, who may be seen here occasionally. Excellent steaks, chops, the works. Closed Sunday. All major credit cards.

Wally's Restaurant. 224 W. 49th St.; 582–0460. No frills in decor but excellent steaks, lobster, and some surprisingly good Italian dishes. Closed Sunday. Dinner only Saturday. All major credit cards.

Expensive

Broadway Joe's Steak House. 315 W. 46th St.; 246–6513 or 974–9832. This well-known old-timer has an open kitchen. Waiters recite the menu. Closed Sunday. AE, MC, V.

Downey's Steak House. 705 Eighth Ave. near 44th St.; 757–0186. In the heart of the theater district and a good choice for after-theater dining among performers and theatergoers alike. Particularly good Irish coffee. Closed Sunday. All major credit cards.

Elmer's. 1034 Second Ave. near 55th St.; 751–8020. With a name like that, it has to be good—and it is. All major credit cards.

Frankie & Johnnie's. 269 W. 45th St. off Eighth Ave.; 245–9717. Well worth the short climb to the second-floor dining room. Great steaks and potatoes served—but open until midnight for dinner only. All major credit cards.

Gallagher's Steak House. 228 W. 52nd St.; 245–5336. Near the theaters, it has a rugged, comfortable air, red-checkered tablecloths in the several dining rooms, and a large bar. Uncomfortably noticeable preferential treatment for regulars. All credit cards.

Kenny's Steak Pub. 565 Lexington Ave. near 51st St.; 355–0666. Favorite of the NYC professional footballer, who appreciates the generous portions of steak and prime ribs. The noise can sometimes sound like a stadium. Banana layer cake a treat. Dinner only Saturday/Sunday from 5:00 P.M. All major credit cards.

Le Steak. 1089 Second Ave. near 58th St.; 421–9072. Red meat prepared lusciously in the French style. Steak sautéed in garlic butter is indescribably good. A unique steakhouse open for dinner only. No CB.

McCarthy's Famous Steak House. 839 Second Ave. near 45th St.; 687–6131. A favorite of newsmen and sports figures, as well as of those who just love good steaks and chops. Pleasant surroundings for pleasant eating. Closed Saturday/Sunday. All major credit cards.

Old Homestead Steak House. 56 Ninth Ave. near 14th St.; 242–9040. The oldest steakhouse in NYC, established 1865, in the heart of the wholseale meat market. If you're especially lucky, you may hit them on the day each year when they roll back prices to those offered on the date of founding. Oversize steaks and lobster, and home-fried potatoes are the specialties. Hot shrimp balls are an unusual appetizer. All major credit cards.

Slate Steak House. 852 Tenth Ave.; 581–6340. Near the Coliseum. Big with the TV crowd. All major credit cards.

Moderate

Blue Mill Tavern. 50 Commerce St. in the Village; 243–7114. Tucked away amidst century-old buildings, and within walking distance of many Off-Broadway Village theaters. The management is Portuguese, and the food is good. All major credit cards.

Cheers. 120 W. 41st St.; 840–8810. Superb roast beef and more than ample portions. On the fringe of the garment and theater districts. All major credit cards.

Farnie's Second Avenue Steak Parlour. 311 Second Ave. near 18th St.; 228–9280. An unassuming neighborhood-type steakhouse that does its best to compete with its better-known and more expensive brethren. All major credit cards.

Inexpensive

Beefsteak Charlie's. Various midtown locations. Singled out mostly because of its low prices and "Small Fry" meals, which mean bargain prices for the kiddie korps.

SEAFOOD

Super Deluxe

Gloucester House. 37 E. 50th St.; 755–7394. Among the most extensive (and expensive) seafood menus in New York. Fabulous homemade biscuits. If you have an expense account this place will use it up for a month. All major credit cards.

Deluxe

John Clancy's. 181 W. 10th St. in the Village; 242–7350. Seafood, all fresh and all excellently prepared. Broiling is done over mesquite charcoal, á la Texas and West Coast. Must reserve days in advance. Dinner only, 6:00 to 11:30 P.M. Closed Sundays. Major credit cards.

Oyster Bar of the Plaza. Plaza Hotel, Fifth Ave. at 59th St.; 759–3000. If you want to combine Edwardian elegance with excellent seafood, this is the place. Full-course dinners will run high, but you can snack heartily very reasonably at the bar, as many New Yorkers do at lunch and after work. All major credit cards.

Expensive

Goodale's. 986 Second Ave. near 52nd St.; 755–7317. New England-style preparation is the signature of this owner-operated spot. Oyster stews and chowders are specialties. All major credit cards.

Joe's Pier 52. 144 W. 52nd St.; 245–6652. Huge, sprawling; music in lounge; city showcase for Broadway impresario Joe Kipness, who indulges his taste in seafood by pouring half the ocean's denizens onto the menu, which is not only extensive but satisfying. All major credit cards.

King Crab. 871 Eighth Ave. at 52nd St.; 765–4393. Gas lamps, track-lighting, young plants, old furniture and fresh fish, crabs, and interesting seafood combination. Open 7 days a week, dinner only Saturday/Sunday. AE, DC.

Marylou's. 21 W. 9th St. in the Village; 533–0012. A very handsome place on one of the Village's handsomest streets. The fish dishes are almost uniformly excellent. The clientele varies from night to night, but is often from the photography/fashion world. No lunch Saturday; only brunch on Sunday. Major credit cards.

Oscar's Salt of the Sea. 1155 Third Ave. near 67th St.; 879–1199. Stuffed lobsters are a particular specialty of this exceptional seafood restaurant, and virtually everything on the extensive menu is prepared perfectly. The only discordant note is the inevitable wait (often quite long) for a table. AE, DC.

Pesca. 23 E. 22nd St.; 533–2293. A beautiful, simply appointed restaurant with an open feeling. Some very unusual seafood dishes. The preparation tends to Latin-style—Italian and Portuguese. AE.

Sea Fare of the Aegean. 25 W. 56th St.; 581–0540. The decor is Mediterranean, and the food first-rate. Shrimp Santorini is a specialty, and the striped bass is also out of the ordinary. All major credit cards.

Sweet's. 2 Fulton St., downtown; 825–9786 or 344–9189. A landmark from the old clipper-ship days. Exceptional fish prepared in the traditional manner and considered the best seafood place in town—even though it takes no reservations and is usually crowded. It's in the Fulton Fish Market area and seems to get its fish fresh off the hook. Closed Saturdays, Sundays, holidays, and July. No credit cards.

Moderate

Broadway Bay. ("B'Way Bay" on the sign). Corner Broadway and 77th St.; 362–5234. Italian seafood specialties in a very casual Upper West Side atmosphere. The bar is especially casual—unprepossessing would be an understatement. All major credit cards.

The Captain's Table. 410 Sixth Ave. near W. 9th St., 473–0670; 860 Second Ave. near 47th St., 697–9538. Selections are broad and simple and the fish is fresh. Closed Sunday. AE, MC, V.

Dobson's. Columbus Ave. at 76th St.; 362–0100. This very large and understated restaurant is representative of the newly stylish Upper West Side, a dozen blocks north of Lincoln Center. The fish is fresh, the atmosphere casual—but not overly so. AE, MC, V.

Fishermen's Net. 493 Third Ave. near 33rd St.; 532–1683. Very reasonable. Daily specials with soup, salad, dessert—just like the old days. The wine list is poor. Look for the poem Ogden Nash wrote to and for the restaurant. All major credit cards.

Jane Street Seafood Café. 31 Eighth Ave. 2 blocks south of 14th St.; 243–9237. Narrow, intimate West Village setting with exposed brick and natural wood—and a gourmet touch in the kitchen. Slow service. AE, MC, V.

Janice's Seafood Place. 570 Hudson; 243–4212. Seafood with fresh vegetables—all handled with an Oriental flair. AE, MC, V.

Oyster Bar. Inside Grand Central Station, off 42nd St. at Park Ave., 490–6650. After being closed for several years, this shrine of good seafood is back again, with a booming business in its vaulted main room, in the quieter Saloon (532–1358) and the first-come, first-served sit-down counter. Several kinds of oysters, clams, and crabs at any given time, plus specials that include fish not seen often enough in New York. Main room is noisy but exhilarating. Closed Saturday/Sunday. All major credit cards.

Inexpensive

Milestone. 70 W. 68th St.; 874–3679. Superior seafood at reasonable prices in close proximity to Lincoln Center sounds like a fantasy, but Milestone fulfills the bill. The only real problem is that there's *always* a line. No reservations, no credit cards.

Paddy's Clam House. 215 W. 34th St.; 244–9123. A glorified clam bar that is a favorite with downtown shoppers and Madison Square Garden habitues. Good food served quickly but sloppily. Daily full-course meal specials. AE, MC, V.

Sloppy Louie's. 92 South St. downtown; 952–9657. Looks like a slum from the outside, but frequented by the button-down Wall Street crowd. Brokers sit at long tables to enjoy the fish landed across the street at the Fulton Fish Market. Also across from the South Street Seaport Museum. Tables are usually for six, so dining is a communal experience. No reservations. Closed Saturday/Sunday. No credit cards.

DAIRY

Inexpensive (See also Health Food)

B & H Dairy Restaurant. 127 Second Ave.; near St. Mark's Place (8th St.); 777–1930. Tiny coffee-shop-style place for good eggs, cheese, blintzes, pancakes. No credit cards.

Farm Foods. 142 W. 49th St.; 757–4971. The soups, blintzes, and fish are uniformly excellent. Centrally located for Broadway theaters, Radio City, Rockefeller Center. No credit cards.

Ratner's Dairy Restaurant. 138 Delancey St., near Essex; 677–5588. A legend in its own time on the Lower East Side for East European Jewish dairy cooking. No credit cards.

DELICATESSEN

Deli in New York is unique unto itself. A genuine deli sandwich here, as opposed to the kind that merely comes out of coffee shops, carries with it an entire set of expectations—pickles, peppers, and cole slaw not the least among them. The best corned beef or pastrami on rye in midtown will run an easy $7.00, while special triple-decker combinations such as chicken fat, salami, and roast beef, or tongue, turkey, and pastrami command $9.50 and up. That's expensive for a sandwich, but consider that one such sandwich at the Carnegie Deli (see below) will easily suffice for two people—and add a similarly shared side order of potato salad and you've got a feast.

Expensive

Kaplan's at the Delmonico. 59 E. 59th St.; 755–5959. Classiest of the lot, with fantastic deli sandwiches. AE, DC.

Inexpensive

Carnegie Delicatessen. 854 Seventh Ave.; 757–2245. By far the best deli in the city, according to deli maven Herb Hartig—and therefore in the world. The corned beef hash—always freshly prepared— is a minor New York miracle. The sandwiches are beyond overflowing, and all ingredients are first rate. Forever crowded and forever bustling and always worth a visit. An excellent choice for breakfast, too, if you're staying at the Sheraton Centre, Hilton, or other midtown/Broadway hotels. Open 6:30 A.M. to 4 A.M. No credit cards.

Fine & Schapiro. 138 W. 72nd St.; 877–2721. An easy walk to and from Lincoln Center—especially worthwhile on matinee days. Also Kosher Chinese delicacies.

Katz's Delicatessen. 205 E. Houston St.; 254–2246. A Lower East Side institution—cafeteria-style self-service that's a perfect treat after bargain-hunting on Orchard St. downtown. No credit cards.

Madison. 1175 Madison Ave. at 86th St.; 369–6670. Convenient to Upper East Side museums, this large, informal delicatessen restaurant offers a variety of sandwiches as well as appetizers, soups, smoked fish, dairy dishes, hot main courses, and Danish pastries. No credit cards.

Nathan's Famous. Broadway at 43rd St.; 594–7455. Having acquired fame and reputation at Coney Island, Nathan's in Manhattan now dispenses the same clams, scallops, oysters, pizza, barbequed beef sandwiches, and chow mein on a bun as at the original (still open) location. But Nathan's earned its nickname—"Famous"—with great hot dogs; and that's still its most popular item. Eat at stand-up counters, cafeteria-style at communal tables, or downstairs in the dining room. No credit cards upstairs; AE in the dining room only. Other branches now open–check the Yellow Pages. No credit cards.

Pastrami & Things. 297 Third Ave. at 23rd St.; 683–7185. Another Jewish delicatessen with a dining room and counter. The pastrami sandwiches are unsurpassed, and were chosen by *New York* magazine as the best in the city. Popular and crowded. No credit cards.

Reuben's. 244 Madison Ave. near 38th St., 867–7800; 770 Second Ave., 883–1193. "From a sandwich to an institution" is its boast, and justly so. No credit cards.

Second Ave. Kosher Delicatessen. 156 Second Ave. at 10th St.; 677–0606. Real kosher-style deli with all the trimmings—free pickles, cole slaw, waiters who invariably know what you want better than you do—and the unique offer of half sandwiches at half price. Easily among the best of the lot, and a bargain because of its out-of-the-way location. No credit cards.

Stage. 834 Seventh Ave. near 54th St.; 245–7850. This restaurant attracts a large after-theater crowd, but is nearly always bustling and noisy. Their sandwiches are packed with meat, the rye bread is superb, their appetizers tantalizing, and there is a variety of hot dishes, salads, and fish platters. Tables are for four, so if you're a couple expect company and surly-at-best service. Open 24 hours. No credit cards.

HEALTH FOOD

Inexpensive

Arnold's Turtle. 51 Bank St. in the West Village; 242–5623. Very popular small, informal Greenwich Village spot for fresh salads and simple vegetarian casserole dishes. No credit cards.

East-West. 105 E. 9th St.; 260–1994. Americanized, health-food oriented versions of classical Japanese dishes, a hybrid that's a little heavy on the brown rice but certainly original. One of the first "healthy food" restaurants in the city. No credit cards.

Grass. 1445 First Ave. at 75th St.; 737–3328. An alternative to hamburgers along singles-bar row. All major credit cards.

Great American Health Bar. 35 W. 57th St.; 355–5177; **II,** 15 E 40th St. 532–3232. Popular among diet-conscious shoppers stalking the exclusive women's department stores (Bendel, Bergdorf, Bonwit Teller) in the area. No credit cards.

Greener Pastures. 117 E. 60th St.; 832–3212. The salads and platters are a little more original than is usually the case, and the location is perfect when shopping at Bloomingdale's or catching an Upper East Side movie. No credit cards.

Healthworks! 153 E. 53rd St.; 838–6221. Flagship branch in Citicorp Center features salads galore plus yogurts, quiches and other light, interestingly prepared dishes. Also take-out. Other branches: 12 E. 36th St. (686–0401); 148 E. 57th St. (838–8370); 1345 Sixth Ave. at 55th St. (586–1980); 804 Madison Ave. at 68th St. (472–9300). No credit cards.

Spring Street Natural Restaurant. 149 Spring St.; 966–0290. One of the earlier revitalized SoHo outposts with something of a rustic, artsy New England feel to it, despite words like "macrobiotic" on the menu. Everything, however, is homemade. No credit cards.

University Produce & Restaurant. 71 University Place; 673–0634. At street level this is indeed a greengrocer; downstairs is an outstanding little restaurant which, while it does serve a few sandwiches that contain meat, is at its best with omelettes (ratatouille and Swiss cheese, fresh strawberries and sour cream, etc.) and bright, colorful, and unusual salads. Most items are $4.50—$5.50 and well worth it.

Vim & Vigor. 157 W. 57th St.; 247–8059. Expensive for what you get, but convenient to Carnegie Hall. No credit cards.

Zucchini. 1336 First Ave. at 72nd St.; 249–0559. Salads, soups, home-baked goods in a cheery Upper East Side setting. All major credit cards.

SOUTHERN

Moderate

The Cotton Patch. 1068 Second Ave. near 56th St.; 688–6595. Old country-barn decor, with fried chicken, ribs, and steak. All major credit cards.

Jack's Nest. 310 Third Ave. (23rd St.); 260–7110. Soul food in immaculate setting, featuring hot cornbread, barbecued ribs, chitterlings, Southern fried pork chops, AE, MC, V.

Inexpensive

Sylvia's. 328 Lenox Ave., 534–9414. In the heart of Harlem, and not recommended unless you can drive up and park in front of the door. Nonetheless, you'll find what is unquestionably the finest soul food in the city. A newly renovated luncheonette with but a few counter seats and a handful of booths, Syvia's Southern-fried chicken and stuffed pork chops (both under $4.00 including two fresh vegetables and cornbread) will be long remembered. No credit cards.

West Boondock. 114 Tenth Ave. near 16th St.; 929–9645. Sawdust on floor, down-home cooking, good live jazz thrown in for free. Saturday/Sunday dinner only. All major credit cards.

CUISINE BY NATIONALITY

AUSTRIAN

Expensive

Vienna '79. 320 E. 79th St.; 734–4700. The dining room is long, narrow, serene, decorated in non-Austrian motifs, and the food is what might best be termed *nouvelle* Austrian—from the Viennese fried chicken, veal goulash, and *Zwiebelrostbraten* (medium-size steak covered with deep-fried crisp onions) to the Wiener schnitzel, crêpes, and cream strudel. Dinner only. (An even newer sister restaurant, **Vienna Park,** is of equally high quality, located at 33 E. 60th St.; 758–1051.) All major credit cards.

BRAZILIAN

Deluxe

Casa Brasil. 406 E. 85th St.; 288–5284. On Wednesday this charming place serves *feijoada,* the Brazilian national dish. It includes rice, beans, many different kinds of meat, vegetables, fruit and several condiments. The rest of the week the kitchen turns out creditable Continental food; beef Wellington, purée of broccoli, tapioca with wine flavor. Bring your own wine and reserve at least a day in advance. There are two sittings per night, 7:30 and 9:30. The restaurant is small, popular, and closed Sundays. Cash or check, no credit cards.

Moderate

Brazilian Pavilion. 141 E. 52nd St.; 758–8129. Although the setting is modern, the interesting cuisine is traditional Brazilian with steaks Portuguesa (garlic!), shrimp Paulista, and Portuguese fish stew. The black bean soup is excellent; so is the dried codfish. Closed Sunday. All major credit cards.

Via Brasil. 34 W. 46th St.; 997–1158. On Manhattan's Brazilian street. The decor is a touch off-beat, but the grilled meats, especially the Brazilian-style marinated steaks, are superb. Major credit cards.

Inexpensive

Brazilian Coffee Restaurant. 45 W. 46th St.; 719–2105. In the heart of the theater district. *Feijoada* is on the menu every Wed. & Sat. Excellent Latin American specialties are available at all times. Appetizers may dissappoint but shrimp dishes and codfish are good. So is the guava compote with white cheese. The service is as informal as the ambience. Expect to see many Brazilians eating here at lunch. Closed Sun. All major credit cards.

Cabana Carioca. 123 W. 45th St.; 581–8088. Pleasant, friendly, and anything but elegant, but the food is relatively good and cheap by today's standards—especially the *caldo verde* (vegetable and potato soup) and shrimp dishes. Open

7 days a week for lunch and dinner. Service can be erratic. All major credit cards.

Chateau Bahia. 861 First Ave. at 48th St.; 753–2960. An attractive bar, a glass-enclosed section, and a large dining area in the rear. But the real attraction here is the seafood stew and the fish and shellfish dishes. It is open for lunch and dinner Monday through Friday, dinner only on Saturday, and closed Sunday. No CB.

Rio de Janeiro. 41 W. 57th St.; 935–1232. The dining area is dark, the decor somewhat barren, but the fish, shellfish, or chicken dishes can be interesting. *Feijoada* is served Wednesday and Saturday. Complimentary Brazilian-style appetizers are served with drinks. Closed Sunday. AE, MC, V.

BRITISH

Deluxe

Bull and Bear. Lexington Ave. and 49th St.; 872–4900. It's in the Waldorf-Astoria so expect it to be expensive. Everything is à la carte at both lunch and dinner, but the menu is large and so are the portions. Specializes in steaks, chops, and seafood. Open seven days a week for lunch and dinner. All major credit cards.

Cheshire Cheese. 319 W. 52st St.; 765–0616. Owned by two chaps from England, who also decorated their small pub most attractively. Small, candlelit dining room, jolly bar. Steak and kidney pie, roast beef with Yorkshire pudding, and imported Dover sole are headliners. À la carte. Closed Sunday, Monday, July, August, all major holidays, and Christmas through New Year's Day. Convenient to theater district. Excellent service. AE, DC.

Expensive

Charlie Brown's Ale & Chophouse. At 45th St. and Vanderbilt Ave. inside the lobby of the Pan Am Building; 661–2520. This pleasant pub, named after an old English inn, is handsome and has steak and kidney pie, mutton chops, Dover sole. Try a yard of ale here. Lunch, dinner, and after-theater à la carte. Lunch only on Saturday. Closed Sun. All major credit cards.

Ye Olde Chop House. 111 Broadway, near Wall St.; 732–6119. Much as it was in 1800, this restaurant is popular at lunch with Wall Street businessmen. Mutton chops, genuine Smithfield ham, seafood, and game in season are amply served up for hearty eating. Closed Saturday, Sunday and after 7:30 P.M., although they serve you if you arrive before closing. Also closed most major holidays. All major credit cards.

Moderate

Charley O's. 33 W. 48th St.; 582–7141. As much Dublin pub as London Tavern on an immense scale, it is one of the best restaurants in the Rockefeller Center area. The stand-up bar serves sandwiches, clams, oysters. The main dining area offers immense portions of ham, steaks, roast beef, pigs' knuckles, and more. It is closed Sunday, serves brunch on Saturday. There are branches in various other midtown locations. All major credit cards.

Inexpensive

English Pub. 900 Seventh Ave. at 57th St.; 265–4360. Shepherd's pie and burgers in a simple, dark setting directly across the street from Carnegie Hall. Popular among music-industry types. All major credit cards.

CHILEAN

Inexpensive

Chacareros. 76 W. 3rd St.; 473–8903. Typical and simple. House specialty: *empanadas,* what else? AE, DC, CB.

CHINESE

Super Deluxe to Expensive

David Kay's Chung Kuo Yuan. 1115 Third Ave., 65th St.; 371–9090. Perhaps New York's most luxurious Chinese restaurant, with a piano bar/aquarium upstairs and a flower-drenched main dining area downstairs. The food matches the ambience, from the pork with pancakes and the spicy beef in orange sauce to the Peking duck and back again to the squab soup. There's even a glass-enclosed private garden looking out on the street. Open seven days a week. Szechuan-style available upon request. AE, DC, CB.

Pearl's Chinese Restaurant. 38 W. 48th St.; 586–1060. Fairly small, with simple decor, it is a media favorite, especially with the publishing and broadcasting crowd who slurp up selections from 12 soups (the soup is almost a meal in itself). Best bets include the braised fish in sweet and sour sauce, the *moo shu* pork, and a variety of those steamed dumplings called *dim sum.* The food is filled with Cantonese nuances, from lemon chicken to pike. Closed Saturday, open for dinner only Sunday. No credit cards.

Shun Lee Dynasty. 900 Second Ave, at 48th St.; 755–3900. Many consider this one of the city's finest Chinese restaurants. The seasoning of these Mandarin and Szechuan dishes has been toned down somewhat, evidently in concession to American palates, but hot sauce is willingly served on the side. The sliced sautéed chicken, lobster ding, pan-fried noodles, or fried prawns are delicious specialties, but the menu includes many unusual and delectable items. The decor is colorful, with gold streamer room dividers and wood chimes overhead. Open seven days a week. AE, CB, DC.

Shun Lee Palace. 155 E. 55th St.; 371–8844. Decorated in what might be called Chinese Chippendale, the main room is a quietly lit and subdued Chinese/Hollywood set made up of alcoves, quiet corners, and large spaces, with a choice of tables or banquettes. The food is cross-China, a delicately tasty amalgam of Mandarin, Szechuan, Hunan, and Shanghai dishes. Indeed, all the Chinese classics are cooked here with finesse, from Peking duck through fried dumplings to baby spareribs. The chef will even produce Cantonese favorites on request, or any other you may request. This branch of the Shun Lee chain is open seven days a week. CB, AE, DC. The latest branch—**Shun Lee West**—recently opened at 43 W. 65th St., opposite Lincoln Center; 595–8845. AE.

Uncle Tai's Hunan Yuan. 1059 Third Ave. near 63rd St.; 838–0850. Adorned with hanging plants to resemble a garden (*yuan*), this handsome Hunan restaurant serves exciting and unusual Hunanese/Szechuan fare including venison in garlic sauce, sea bass in black bean sauce, and lamb in white sauce—all excellently prepared. Offerings here are often piquant and sometimes infernally spicy, sometimes sweet and sugary. It's a good idea to tell your waiter how you want your dishes cooked. Consider such specialties as vegetable pie wrapped in a pancake, the dry sautéed beef, the orange-flavored beef, carp, or fried noodles. Open seven days a week. AE, DC.

Moderate

Bill Chan's Gold Coin. 835 Second Ave. near 45th St.; 697–1515. Stunning dining rooms, a handsome bar and cocktail lounge. Both Mandarin and Cantonese cuisine is served. Tiny deep-fried frogs' legs are a delightful appetizer. Everything cooked to order, but most dishes tend to be bland and Westernized, although of top quality. Open seven days a week. Closed Thanksgiving, Christmas. All major credit cards.

Chef Ho's Hunan Manor. 1464 Second Ave. near 77th St.; 570–6700. Chef Ho started at Uncle Tai's, helped open David K's, and went to Fortune Garden —three of the city's better Chinese restaurants—before branching out on his own, with two partners. There are some 100 choices on the mainly Hunan and Szechuan menu that is almost uniformly excellent in this comfortable, carpeted, somewhat dressy storefront, where most of the attention goes to the food. Money is well spent here with the dishes mild to searingly hot—you specify— lightly sauced and beautifully presented. Open seven days a week. All major credit cards.

China Pavillion. 200 W. 57th St. near Carnegie Hall; 765–4340. Paintings, fresh flowers, fine food. All major credit cards.

Foo Chow. 1278 Third Ave. at 74th St.; 861–4350. This Upper East Side Mandarin restaurant offers over 100 entries, but try the *muk hsu,* a delicious dish of shrimp, meat, bamboo shoots, and vegetables wrapped in a kind of pancake. Peking duck is available with 24-hour notice. All major credit cards.

Fortune Garden. 1160 Third Ave. at 68th St.; 744–1212. Divided into two sections, a cheerful front half and a squarish second half, the restaurant captains take orders and the chef carries them out quite successfully, usually in the Cantonese-style, although the dishes can be spiced up Szechuan-style upon request. The kitchen is usually successful with beef and steak dishes, turns out interesting fish dishes—especially the whole sea bass in ginger sauce—and an excellent pork and pickled soup. The spring rolls and spareribs are exceptional. Open seven days a week. All major credit cards.

HSF (for Hee Seung Fung). 578 Second Ave. at 31st St.; 689–6969. The best-decorated of New York's smaller Chinese restaurants, HSF is a branch of an older Chinatown operation. Excellent *dim sum* (assorted dumplings which you choose from a succession of trolleys) for lunch. The room is oblong, the decor uncharacteristic of China, but the food goes a long way to make up for the lack of atmosphere. All major credit cards.

Hunam. 845 Second Ave. near 45th St.; 687–7471. The Hunam is generally acknowledged to be the progenitor of the cuisine of China's Hunan Province. (No one knows why they spell the restaurant's name with an "m.") It is also one of the city's best Chinese restaurants. Devilishly spicy items on the menu are thoughtfully marked, and the most important operative words for a first-time patron are "mild, please." Anyone whose Chinese eating experience has been limited to only traditional Cantonese cooking is in for a rare treat. AE, DC, CB.

Peng Teng's. 219 E. 44th St.; 682–8050. Owned by C. K. Peng and Philip Chiang, it features hard-to-find specialties from the cuisines of Peking, Szechuan, and Hunan. Mr. Peng, who owns six restaurants in Taiwan, is the guiding genius, with two dishes named after him (squid with hot pepper sauce and a special beef). Mr. Teng is the new head chef recently imported. Minced squab and water chestnuts steamed in a bamboo container for six hours is just one reason to go—the very popular "Dragon and Phoenix" (lobster and chicken) is another. On Saturday and Sunday, *dim sum* at lunch can be inexpensive as well as satisfying both to body and soul. The two main rooms can be noisy, but there are glass-enclosed private rooms to help mute the sound for large parties. Uncle Peng is the onetime chef of Chiang Kai-Shek, and who cares about the noise. AE, DC, CB.

Sichuan Pavilion. 322 E. 44th St.; 986–3775. Two spacious rooms, well-spaced tables, pleasant decor with pandas painted on the wall, and located right off the UN, the restaurant has numerous chefs specially brought over from China to make up one of the most interesting menus in New York—bar none. Of course, the menu lists in red (a New York Chinese-restaurant convention) the spicy items. One of the rarities is the numerous rabbit dishes. This is one of the city's newer Chinese restaurants—and certainly one of the better ones. The captains will help you with your ordering if you feel like experimenting off the menu. Open seven days a week. All major credit cards.

Szechuan East. 1584 Second Ave. at 82nd St.; 535–4921. Moderate-sized, moderately priced, but there's nothing moderate about the food—it is authentic, imaginative and spicy, with the captain or waiter available to help cool the cooking down. But don't. It's an adventure. Open seven days a week. AE, DC.

Inexpensive

Most of the restaurants listed below do not have liquor licenses, so you are welcome to bring your own wine or beer. However, it is advisable to call ahead to make sure this is the case, because the situation changes as pending licenses are granted.

Bo Bo. 20½ Pell St.; 962–9458. In Chinatown, tiny and unpretentious, but has a very good reputation for its authentic Chinese fare. Try the "house" dinner. No menu. No credit cards.

Chi-Mer. 11–12 Chatham Square; 267–4565. Excellent food, typically Chinatown atmosphere. One of the few places where you can get Peking duck without calling up in advance. All major credit cards.

China Bowl. 152 W. 44th St.; 582–3358. Serves most of the well-known Cantonese dishes and has moderately priced family dinners. Also American food. Pleasant surroundings and handy for theater-goers. AE, DC, CB.

Empire Szechuan Gourmet. 2574 Broadway at 97th St.; 663–6980. Exotic Chinese food cooked Szechuan and Hunan style in what is basically a storefront with red wallpaper, minimal decor, and a glass-enclosed alcove that extends onto the sidewalk. But the food—especially the shrimp, pork and chicken dishes—make this a great favorite with both the Columbia crowd and Upper West Siders. No credit cards.

Foo Joy. 13 Division St. off Chatham Square in Chinatown; 431–4931. For a delightful change from the popular Cantonese cooking, try their specialties from Fukien Province (adjacent to Canton). Fukien pork chops, steam-fried flounder, lemon chicken, or garlic spareribs are savory departures from the traditional. No credit cards.

Hong Fat. 63 Mott St.; 962–9588. This little Chinatown hole-in-the-wall specializes in noodles in many different forms. Many consider this New York's best Cantonese restaurant. Open 24 hours. No credit cards.

Hunan House. 45 Mott St., Chinatown; 962–0010. Subterranean but with two dining rooms and excellent pan-fried dumplings, orange-flavor chicken (not the usual sweet-and-sour concoction) and similar fare. You must emphasize if you want your dishes hot, though. AE.

Hwa Yuan Szechuan Inn. 40 E. Broadway; 966–5534. Slightly away from the main Chinatown district, in a large informal room almost without decoration, you can get some of the best Szechuan food in town. Known for its excellent soups, carp with brown sauce, double-sautéed pork, fried noodles with shredded pork and bean curd, home-style, it is well worth getting to know better because it keeps getting better. All major credit cards.

Peking Duck House Restaurant. 22 Mott St. in Chinatown; 962–8208. The house specialty—Peking duck—doesn't have to be ordered 24 hours in advance as at most places. It is priced around $20—a relative bargain because it compares favorably with the same dish at higher-priced restaurants. And it can be almost a meal in itself for a party of four. AE.

Say Eng Look. 5 E. Broadway; 732–0796. Our Peking (Mandarin) choice is a particular favorite with those who know their way around NYC's Chinatown. The name means "4, 5, 6" and refers to a particularly fine hand in Mah Jong. You'll notice that most of the patrons are Oriental, and we consider that an expert recommendation. It is also a favorite of NYC Mayor Ed Koch. Again, the decor is unimposing, the overall space small, and the atmosphere on the noisy side. But no lack of ambience can really detract from the *moo shoo* pork, Tai-Chi Chicken, or the deep-fried fish wrapped in bean curd or seaweed. There's also a whole pork joint in an incredible brown anise sauce. The specials are the dishes to go for here. So popular has this restaurant become that they've opened a branch across the street—*1–2–3*—to handle the overflow. Tell your waiter if you want your meal served in courses, however, or all selections will arrive simultaneously. Beer and wine available. V, MC.

Szechuan Cuisine. 33 Irving Place near Union Square (15th St., a block from Park Ave.); 982–5678. Gutsy, spicy food, where two can have a fiery meal for under $12, with choices including dried sautéed beef, kidney, ginger shrimp, and bean curd. No credit cards.

Szechuan Taste. 23 Chatham Square, Chinatown; 267–0672. Floor seemingly slants downhill but that doesn't tilt the menu, which is one of the city's best—and the lines to get in attest to its popularity. You may want to go easy on the hot stuff here. All major credit cards.

Szechuan West. 2656 Broadway near 101st St.; 663–9280. One of the original Empire chefs has branched out on his own—and very well. His crispy fried flounder tops a list of virtually untoppable hot dishes at bargain-basement prices, in a simple storefront where the grandeur is in the food. No credit cards.

Ying. 220 Columbus Ave. at 70th St.; 724–2031. Outstandingly spicy Szechuan food of unusual variety and taste—and resaonably priced. Often crowded. Near Lincoln Center. AE.

CZECHOSLOVAKIAN
Moderate

Czechoslovak Praha. 1358 First Ave. at 73rd St.; 988–3505. An excellent restaurant whose specialties include *svickova* (a marinated beef dish similar to sauerbraten), goulash, goose, and duckling. For dessert, *palacinky*—a thin pancake stuffed with prune or apricot jam—is excellent. In the heart of the city's "Little Czechoslovakia" district. No CB.

Ruc. 312 E. 72nd St.; 650–1611. Long established, so it must be doing something right, although its kitchen has a tendency to be uneven. The duck, roast pork, and goulash portions tend to be substantial and filling, and the price is right. Ruc serves dinner only from 4:00 P.M. on weekdays, and from noon on Saturday and Sunday. No MC.

Vasata. 339 E. 75th St.; 650–1686. Owned by the Vasata family (which has a famous restaurant in Prague), it has a devoted following for the crisp roast duck, chicken paprikash, and game in season. Neat, pleasant dining room and small bar. Imported wines. Complete à la carte dinner starting from 5:00 P.M. seven days a week from Monday through Saturday and from noon on Sunday. All major credit cards.

FRENCH
Super Deluxe

La Caravelle. 33 W. 55th St.; 586–4252. At the highest rank of New York restaurants, and among the top two or three French establishments in the entire city. A favorite with the social set at lunch. Very fashionable clientele in the evening, too. Elegant decor, top-notch wine cellar, attentive service, the latter especially so if you are known. This is one of those restaurants where the unrecognized diner can be treated rather cavalierly. (Tables near the entrance are considered the favored ones here.) Closed Sunday and the month of August. All major credit cards.

La Côte Basque. 5 E. 55th St.; 688–6525. Its reputation was made by its late founder, Henri Soulé, once also of the now legendary and defunct Le Pavillon. Stunning Bernard Lamotte murals enhance a totally handsome dining room. The cuisine is classic and can be superb. The service is a model of perfection. Closed Sunday. AE.

La Grenouille. 3 E. 52nd St.; 752–1495. A sublimely beautiful setting that complements a superb kitchen. The "in" place for lunch for expense-account diners. Often crowded, with the impact of the large number of diners accented by the proximity of one table to another. Classic French food as good as it exists in the city. Closed Sunday and holidays. AE.

Le Chantilly. 106 E. 57th St.; 751–2931. Large, stately, classical, and pretentious, but you can tell *toute le monde* it delivers when it comes to fish, lamb, veal, and desserts. Indeed, from soup to nuts, it is hard to beat—but at those prices, it should be. Open Monday to Friday for lunch and dinner, dinner only on Saturday, closed Sunday. All major credit cards.

Le Cirque. 58 E. 65th St.; 794–9292. Plush, haute cuisine restaurant with animals painted as humans in interesting circusy mural. Offers excellent service and meals to match from a menu that draws the beautiful people. The cognoscenti order a traditional yet offbeat specialty (traditionally not listed on the menu) of spaghetti primavera—one of the city's better versions of this trendy dish. The restaurant is located in the Mayfair Hotel. It is closed Sun. AE, DC, CB.

Le Cygne. 53 E. 54th St.; 759–5941. This is the best of the newer restaurants spawned by La Caravelle. Its imaginative and well-executed dishes include an unusual appetizer of mussels in mustard sauce and whole braised pigeon. The desserts, too, are excellent. The atmosphere can be somewhat stuffy. Closed Sunday and month of August. AE, DC, CB.

Le Madrigal. 216 E. 53rd St.; 355–0322. A favorite with the publishing crowd, this is one of New York's finest restaurants. Murals of 18th-century troubadours add a musical touch to this small restaurant. Closed Sunday; dinner only Saturday. All major credit cards.

Lutèce. 249 E. 50th St.; 752–2225. Probably the most ambitious and elaborate French food served in the United States. And almost as important, the pinnacle of perfection that has been achieved has not engendered the sort of pompous rudeness that is so much a part of the scene at other New York restaurants of this genre. The staff is almost uniformly pleasant, and aids immeasurably the consummate enjoyment of a unique dinner. The setting, in a former townhouse, is intimate and exquisite. If you only have the time (or budget) for one foray into fine French gastronomy, let us recommend Lutèce. Closed Saturday during the summer, closed Sunday throughout the year. All major credit cards.

Quo Vadis. 26 E. 63rd St.; 838–0590. Another superb restaurant of a singular standard. Gets its share of socialites who like the relaxed atmosphere in the two resplendent dining rooms decked with fresh flowers. Clams, oysters, eels in a special green sauce, and filet of beef in pastry crust are good samples of the haute cuisine. Fine wines and superb service. Steak and rack of lamb rank with the best around. Closed Sunday. All major credit cards.

Restaurant Raphael. 33 W. 54th St.; 582–8993. Considered by many to be the best argument for the *nouvelle cuisine,* Raphael hides behind elegantly understated doors, and is strictly by reservation only. Closed Saturday for lunch, and Sunday. Also closed the month of August. AE, DC.

Deluxe

Brussels. 115 E. 54th St.; 758–0457. Turn-of-the-century townhouse with walnut paneling, heavy chandeliers, and soft lights turning on to Old World ambience make Brussels *très haute,* posh, and perhaps a bit self-important. Belgian specialties—what else?—are features on a menu that also includes French haute cuisine and selected lofty Italian dishes. The food is first-rate, the atmosphere is rich and plush and the prices match. Superb wine list. Closed Sunday. All major credit cards.

Café Argenteuil. 253 E. 52nd St.; 753–9273. Notable are *quiche Lorraine, canard aux pêches,* and *bouillabaisse.* Fine wine cellar. One of the best purveyors of haute cuisine in the city. Don't miss the chocolate mousse in this small, très French bistro. Closed Sunday, dinner. All major credit cards.

Café Nicholson. 323 E. 58th St.; 355–6769. An unusual restaurant in an unusual locale under the Queensboro (59th St.) Bridge. Prix fixe dinner includes wine. Superlative chocolate soufflé. Added attraction is the Rolls Royce that whisks you back to your hotel. Tips included on your check. Ceiling fans, potted palms, and turn-of-the-century antiques help take your mind off the price. Open for dinner Tuesday through Friday. AE, CB, DC.

Chanterelle. 89 Grand St. in SoHo; 966–6960. Don't let the location—a seemingly deserted warehouse corner in SoHo—scare you off, because Chantarelle is celebrated as one of the most adventurous and interesting of *nouvelle cuisine* haunts—even if some of the more experimental taste combinations don't always work. Meals are served in a spare, spacious dining room under a tin ceiling in a landmark building. The staff is haughty but knowledgeable and the ambience the new chic. Dinner Monday through Saturday. AE, MC, V.

Claude's. 205 E. 81st St.; 472–0487. Deep-red panels, bright metal and glass provide a handsome setting in this elaborate restaurant located in two remodeled brownstones. Everything is à la carte and worth ordering, especially the beef, veal, and lamb dishes. Closed for vacation in July. Dinner Tuesday through Saturday in August, Monday through Saturday thereafter. All major credit cards.

Clos Normand. 42 E. 52nd St.; 753–3348. Has beautiful murals and tiles by Jean Pages to spark the handsome provincial decor of the dining rooms. The atmosphere is pure Normandy. *Canard* (duck) served with figs, and a classic crab quiche, are the specialties. You might also care to try the Norman cider. Closed Sunday. No MC.

La Cocotte. 147 E. 60th St.; 832–8972. A charming and unpretentious restaurant opposite Bloomingdale's. An excellent pâté is served, and there are also some very good veal dishes among 24 specialties offered. Closed Sunday. All major credit cards.

La Colombe d'Or. 134 E. 26th St.; 689–0666. Informal country atmosphere in a small establishment featuring *bouillabaisse, cassoulet,* and other Provençal specialties. Dinner only Saturday and Sunday. Closed Sunday in the summer. AE, DC, MC, V.

Hubert's. 102 E. 22nd St.; 673–3711. Elegant *nouvelle cuisine* in an attractively understated environment, with seafood a particular specialty. AE.

La Petite Ferme. Lexington Ave. at 70th St.; 249–3272. The owner/chef is the scion of Burgundian restaurateurs and hoteliers, and the food is simple and well-prepared. Reserve well ahead for a table at what looks like a prosperous farmhouse with a garden to boot. Closed Sunday. All major credit cards.

La Tulipe. 104 W. 13th St.; 691–8860. Housed in the street level of a brownstone on a tree-lined Greenwich Village block overflowing with Continental restaurants. This rather small, trendy place, however, surprises with its emphasis on good *nouvelle cuisine.* Dinner Tuesday through Sunday. AE, MC, DC, V.

Laurent. 111 E. 56th St.; 753–2729. Grand food in the grand French style of *haute cuisine,* with prices to match. AE, DC.

Le Chanteclair. 18 E. 49th St.; 355–8998. Authentic French cuisine is the hallmark of this small, cozy restaurant whose mural of La Place de La Concorde gives the feeling of a Paris café. Owned by the Dreyfus brothers, who dominated French auto racing in the 1930s. The veal and beef dishes are particularly good. Closed Sunday. All major credit cards.

Le Lavandou. 134 E. 61st St.; 838–7987. Because the restaurant is small, and the tables close together, it can get pleasantly hectic when crowded—and it usually is because the food is up to the best around. Closed Sunday. AE.

Le Manoir. 120 E. 56th St.; 753–1447. The elegant French provincial decor complements a superb kitchen whose dishes, though unpretentious, are often outstanding. The poached bass and chicken in red wine are excellent, and there is an interesting offering of desserts to go along with the ten main courses. Closed Sun. All major credit cards.

Le Périgord. 405 E. 52nd St.; 755–6244. One of the finest midtown restaurants. *Gratin de langoustines*—crayfish in a cheese sauce—is one of the specialties on the varied menu. Closed Sunday, dinner only Sat. (Sister restaurant, **Le Périgord-Park** at 575 Park Ave.; 752–0050.) All major credit cards.

Le Petite Marmite. 5 Mitchell Pl. off First Ave. 15 49th St.; 826–1084. Intimate and pleasantly appointed. Its location makes it a favorite of diplomatic laborers at the UN. Closed Sunday. All major credit cards.

Expensive

Black Sheep. 342 W. 11th St.; 242–1010. A tiny hidden jewel almost on the Hudson waterfront, where you'll start with crudites with aioli for consumption while pondering the menu, pâté of the day, soup, entrée, and dessert. The mimeographed wine list is unusually extensive for such a small place, and the owner's weekly suggestions are usually excellent values. Avoid Friday or Saturday nights, when everyone is hurried in order to accommodate second and third sittings. Exceptional veal, duck, and fish. Discount for cash. All major credit cards.

Château Richelieu. 48 E. 52nd St.; 751–6565. Elegant and friendly reception for newcomers as well as regulars. Excellent fish dishes as well as usual haute cuisine favorites. Traditional atmosphere and the kind of courteous service that used to be common in all superior establishments. Closed Sunday, most holidays, the month of August. All major credit cards.

French Shack. 65 W. 55th St.; 246–5126. One of the finest French establishments in the city at this price, with food that is far above average. The only objections are the crowds and the occasionally slow service. All major credit cards.

La Bibliothèque. 341 E. 43rd St.; 661–5757. French provincial food, but the best part is the place itself, with books on the walls—of course—and a magnificent view of the UN. Great for a midafternoon drink or snack. Outdoor dining in good weather. Closed Sunday. All major credit cards.

La Grillade. 845 Eighth Ave. near 51st St.; 265–1610. Its owners are all from Brittany, assuring authenticity in their many Breton dishes. The duck, as well as the roast lamb with flageolets, are especially good. Friendly service. Lunch and dinner Monday through Friday, dinner only Saturday/Sunday. AE, DC, MC, V.

La Petite Auberge. 116 Lexington Ave. at 28th St.; 689–5003. Pleasant inn-like surroundings. Standard bourgeoise cuisine, but good; nice specials. The management came from the nearby Mon Paris. AE.

Le Cheval Blanc. 145 E. 45th St.; 599–8886. The food is excellent at this family-run restaurant, and its bargain status at lunch generates quite a crowd. It's best, therefore, to sample the fare at odd hours. Must reserve. Be prompt, with no one missing from your party. Not so much of a bargain at dinner. Closed Saturday, Sunday, most holidays. No CB.

Le Moal. 942 Third Ave. near 56th St.; 688–8860. A long-time favorite, has pleasantly decorated dining rooms downstairs and upstairs. The family personally supervise the kitchen and the service. Provincial French cuisine has Breton overtones. The *moules marinière* are justifiably renowned. All major credit cards.

Le Paris Bistro. 48 Barrow St. in the Village; 989–5460. Next to the Greenwich House Music School, the restaurant is very comfortable, with garden dining in the back in season. *Steak au poivre* is a good bet. Dinner only. All major credit cards.

Le Vert Galant. 109 W. 46th St.; 582–7989. Very friendly, unhurried service in an elegant setting. Divine cheesecake, tender veal *piccata* and other house specials. Trio in lounge Wednesday through Saturday. Closed Sunday. All major credit cards.

Les Pyrénées. 251 W. 51st St.; 246–0044. Has a pleasant Gallic atmosphere and serves provincial French food. Though the menu is familiar, *quiche Lorraine* and ham in aspic are worth trying. A good choice for theater-goers. Closed Sunday. All major credit cards.

L'Olivier. 248 E. 49th St. near Second Ave.; 355–1810. In a converted brownstone, with cozy bar and tables downstairs (enclosed garden room in back in season), and a high-ceilinged room upstairs. Chef is owner. Try the *cassoulet* *maison.* Upper expensive range. Closed Saturday/Sunday. All major credit cards.

Mon Paris. 111 E. 29th St.; 683–4255. Small, unpretentious, and popular. Serves that relative rarity these days: unabashed *cuisine bourgeoise.* Closed Sunday in summer. AE, MC, V.

Raoul's. 180 Prince St. in SoHo; 966–3518. The spirit of a genuine French bistro despite the neon beer signs in the window and the falling-apart-at-the-seams decor (that contrasts sharply with the high prices). Friendly place where you can eat at the bar or at tables. Dinner only. All major credit cards.

The Terrace. 119th St. and Morningside Drive; 666–9490. On the top of Columbia University's Butler Hall, very good view of New York skyline, with good food and (usually) live chamber music. Good place for a romantic dinner. Lunch Tuesdays through Fridays, dinner daily except Mondays. All major credit cards.

Moderate

Crêpe Suzette. 313 W. 46th St.; 581–9717 or 974–9002. A little bistro that couldn't be plainer, but the food is well-prepared and portions ample. Breton crêpes are a specialty. Tiny bar, small wine list. Closed Sunday. AE, MC, V.

Delices La Cote Basque. 1032 Lexington Ave. (Upper East Side); 535–3311. Light luncheon fare—and a fine way to sample the parent restaurant's menu at (relatively) reasonable prices. AE, DC.

Le Biarritz. 325 W. 57th St.; 245–9467. An unprepossessing restaurant with copper cookware on the walls and fresh flowers at each table, and where the kitchen turns out excellent peasant soups and seafood. The seafood-stuffed crêpe Biarritz is superb. Open seven days but for dinner only Saturday/Sunday from 5:00 P.M. AE, DC, V.

Le Bistro. 827 Third Ave. near 50th St.; 759–5933. Small and informal, provincial in spirit. A blackboard menu lists specialties of the day. Closed Sunday, dinner only Saturday. All major credit cards.

Madame Romaine De Lyon. 32 E. 61st St.; 758–2422. Would you believe 500 different kinds of omelettes? Also fine salads and fresh croissants. Open only for lunch Monday through Saturday, 11:00 A.M. to 3:30 P.M. Closed Sunday, most holidays and month of August. No credit cards.

Pierre Au Tunnel. 250 W. 47th St.; 582–2166. Has unusual decor resembling an actual tunnel. It's small and unpretentious, and has the familiar French menu with different specialties added each day. Good choice when heading to the theater. Closed Sunday. AE.

Inexpensive

La Crêpe. Various locations around the city, one most convenient to midtown at 57 W. 56th St., 247–1136; another near Lincoln Center on Broadway at 67th St., 874–6900. Menu of 100 different kinds of crêpes is offered. Excellent place for an inexpensive lunch, a quickie dinner or after-theater snack. AE, DC.

GERMAN

Moderate

Café Geiger. 206 E. 86th St.; 734–4428. A retail bakery in front, Continental-style café and restaurant in back. All major credit cards.

Harvey's Chelsea Restaurant. 108 W. 18th St.; 243–5644. The look of a Victorian mansion, but the specialties of the house lean toward sauerbraten, knockwurst, and the like. There's nothing exciting about the preparation but reliability is a key reason why reservations are almost always necessary at this otherwise "local" establishment. No credit cards.

Kleine Konditorei. 234 E. 86th St.; 737–7130. Simple, homey dinner with everything from steak smothered in fried onions to different veal schnitzels ordered à la carte or as a dinner. Huge portions come adorned with several side dishes; friendly, informal service. AE, DC.

Inexpensive

Bavarian Inn. 232 E. 86th St.; 650–1056. Besides all the good, solid German fare and plentiful portions that you would expect from a *gemütlich* bar and restaurant (the restaurant rooms are open to the bar but raised above it), there is live zither music in the evenings. Major credit cards.

Ideal Lunch and Bar. 238 E. 86th St.; 650–1632. While this place looks like a shoe-repair shop converted to a lunch counter, it is by far the best food bargain on the Upper East Side "Since 1932." No credit cards.

GREEK

Moderate

Estia. 308 E. 86th St.; 628–9100. Fresh and simple Greek food, live music at 10:30 or so. All major credit cards.

Idra. 166 W. 4th St. in the Village; 691–5667. The atmosphere here is decidedly Greek taverna on both floors, enhanced by live entertainment. The menu features traditional Greek fare well-prepared and pleasantly served. No CB.

Molfetas. 307 W. 47th St.; 840–9594. Combination cafeteria-restaurant with simple decor, informal service, many lamb dishes and several simple fish dishes broiled with oil and lemon. Stock up on the Greek "caviar" (*tarama-salata*)—tasty stuffed grapevine leaves. No credit cards.

Pantheon. 689 Eighth Ave. near 44th St.; 664–8294. Lemon soup and macaroni-based dishes are good in this popular gathering place close to the theater district. Lamb dishes are plentiful but tend to be overcooked, so consider the homemade yogurt, fit for the dieting gods. No CB.

Sirocco, 29 E. 29th St.; 683–9409. Greek-Israeli restaurant with musical revue, Mediterranean dishes. $6.00 minimum except Saturday when it is $10.00. Closed Monday. No CB.

Inexpensive

Acropolis. 767 Eighth Ave. near 47th St.; 581–2733. Fish dishes good, lamb dishes ample, stuffed grape leaves abound and the price—cheap—is right if you are in the theater district. AE, DC.

Delphi. 109 W. Broadway; 227–6332. The turnover here from noon to midnight is such that with the exception of casserole dishes, everything is prepared to order—which is a surprise only given how inexpensive the meals are. Exceptionally friendly, and a little out of the way (except perhaps for those at the World Trade Center), Delphi is the sort of place those who know return to again and again. No credit cards.

Z. 117 E. 15th St.; 254–0960. Price not even withstanding, Z is often hailed as the best Greek food stop in the city. You might begin with the cheese-and-spinach appetizer—*spanakopita*—which is excellent at this pleasant, unassuming Greek restaurant where everything is served à la carte. The salads are superbly fresh and the lamb typically well prepared. Sandwiches, too, are offered and, weather permitting, there is dining in the garden. It happens also to be a favorite among budget-watching gourmands. Closed Monday. AE.

HAWAIIAN

Moderate

Hawaii-Kai. 1638 Broadway near 50th St.; 757–0900. Polynesian, Chinese, American cuisine in touristy South Sea setting. All major credit cards.

Trader Vic's. Plaza Hotel, Fifth Ave. at 59th St.; 355–5185. Touristy but respectable, as befits the Plaza. All major credit cards.

HUNGARIAN

Moderate

Csarda. 1477 Second Ave. near 77th St.; 472–2892. Bright, clean, uncluttered, with good food served tavern-style. Dinner only. AE.

Green Tree. 1034 Amsterdam Ave. at 111th St.; 864–9106. Hungarian food with a Columbian accent—Columbia University; that is—is served at this family-style place where the decor is virtually nonexistent but the meals are substantial. If you are looking for home-style chicken *paprikàs*, stuffed cabbage, or noodles stop by—but never on Sunday, when it is closed. No credit cards.

Red Tulip. 439 E. 75th St.; 734–4893. Small, simply decorated, crowded, and offering live music with dinner, this is a good spot for stuffed cabbage, chicken, varied paprika dishes and strudel. Closed Monday and Tuesday. AE.

Inexpensive

Magic Pan. 149 E. 57th St.; 371–3266. Both Hungarian and French crêpes served. Soup, salad, and steak kebab is also available. Lunch is liable to be crowded but the dinner hour is much quieter. AE, MC, V.

Tip Top. 1489 Second Ave. (between 77th and 78th Sts.); 650–0723. This small, family restaurant is an outstanding value—complete home-cooked meals can be had for $4.00 or less. Stuffed cabbage or goulash and noodles can be topped off with *palacsinta,* thin Hungarian pancakes filled with fruit. No credit cards.

INDIAN/BENGALI

Expensive

Gaylord's. 50 E. 58th St.; 759–1710. This stunning restaurant serves Indian food unlike any you've ever tasted. It is one of the few U.S. restaurants we know of with a real tandoori oven from which emerge succulent baked delights and a marvelous bread called *nan.* Among the individual delectables are lamb in spinach sauce, chicken with a yogurt curry, mint chutney and, most surprising, a dessert tray full of Indian goodies. Dinner is served seven days a week; lunch Monday through Friday. All major credit cards.

Nirvana. 30 Central Park South; 752–0270. The view from this penthouse restaurant overlooking Central Park is nothing short of spectacular. The window tables are romantic beyond belief but all are set beneath *shamianas,* multicolored tents, where you can feast on Indo-Bengali delights including tandoori and curries. The fare is likely to be no less spicy than the place is colorful so beware if yours is a tender palate. Unfortunately, spicy or not, the food is not up to the surroundings. All major credit cards.

Raga. 57 W. 48th St.; 757–3450. One of the most beautifully decorated Indian restaurants in America, occupying the site of the old Forum of the Twelve Caesars. Most well-known Indian specialties, including a superb assortment of breads, stuffed or otherwise. Ancient musical instruments are part of the decorative charm. Live Indian music some evenings. All major credit cards.

Shezan. 8 W. 58th St.; 371–1414. Lots of mirrors, chrome, glass bricks, and carpeted walls (from the designers who created the Four Seasons) meet you when you descend a flight of steps at the New York address for this famed London and Indian mini-chain. The food is uneven—too often prepared ahead and heated upon your arrival—but if you make your wishes known the Pakistani-Indian cuisine will come out first-rate. Waiters will also gladly oblige to help you order and share the likes of the shrimp and vegetable curries, tandoori chicken and lamb kebabs. Closed Sunday. Dinner only on Saturday. All major credit cards.

Tandoor India. 40 E. 49th St.; 752–3334. One of the most beautiful and best Indian restaurants in the city—even though the curries are toned down to suit the American taste. Try the tandoori chicken, Indian breads, *pakhoras* (vegetable fritters), and *samosas* (sweetened pastries). Sometimes a more economical buffet. Closed Sunday. All major credit cards.

Moderate

Akbar India. 475 Park Ave. at 58th St.; 838–1717. Tandoor (clay-oven) items are featured at this attractive restaurant serving food from the northern part of the country. They tone down the spiciness to suit the American palate but will spice the dishes up upon request. A mixed plate offers opportunity to sample a little bit of everything. Open seven days a week, dinner only on Sunday. All major credit cards.

Annapurna. 108 Lexington Ave. at 29th St.; 679–1284. A quiet, gracious restaurant serving a variety of authentic Indian dishes with chicken as a specialty. Major credit cards.

Bombay Palace. 30 W. 52nd St.; 541-7777. A large midtown restaurant quite popular with Indian businesspeople. There is a buffet lunch available as well as à la carte dishes. All major credit cards.

Nupur. 819 Second Ave., near 44th St.; 490–9126. Nupur boasts that it has "the most authentic Indian cuisine in New York City." That covers as much ground as India, but the Bengal chef tries to make the food live up to the slogan—and usually succeeds admirably, especially with the kebab and tandoori specialties, with hundreds of choices served up in what is basically a storefront restaurant: inexpensive brown leather chairs, rickety-looking tables, and tacky panelled walls. The money goes into the food, and it is money well spent. The restaurant is popular with U.N. personnel. There is an uptown branch at 1393-A Second Ave. between 72nd and 73rd Sts.; 772–7766-7.

Shalimar of India. 39 E. 29th St.; 889–1977. A wide selection of Indian cuisine ranges from hot curries (*vindaloo*) to mild cream-style curry(*murghum masala*), from *mulligatawny,* a spiced lentil soup, to a delicately flavored coconut soup. And the Indian breads are excellent. All major credit cards.

Inexpensive

Ceylon India Inn. 148 W. 49th St.; 730–9293. Has been deservedly popular for over forty years and noted for its curries and Indian specialties. Quiet, exotic setting in the upstairs restaurant. Special complete dinners at fixed prices and à la carte. AE, DC.

Kashmir. 10 W. 46th St.; 730–9201. Though plain, this is a pleasant place for Indian and Pakistani cuisine. Curries and tandoori chicken are among the specialties prepared by the owner-chef. Complete lunches and dinners as well as à la carte. But be prepared for some of the spicier food around. All major credit cards.

Madras Woodlands. 310 E. 44th St.; 986–0620. North Indian vegetarian dishes are authentically prepared and presented here. The staff is gracious, although your waiter will not advise you on ordering unless you ask him to (which for the unitiated can mean ordering several very similar dishes, or enough for twice the number of people dining, etc.). Hailed alike by U.N. delegates and the city's vegetarian population. All major credit cards.

Mitali. 334 E. 6th St.; 533–2508. One of about a dozen small, family-run Indian restaurants on the block (there are many more on First and Second Aves.), with excellent curries, typically ethnic decor and recorded music, and friendly, attentive service. AE, MC, V.

There are a number of very inexpensive but—for the price—quite good Indian fast-food shops on or around Lexington Ave. from 26th St. to 29th St., in "Little India." While some of them are quite shabby-looking, don't be put off, as they offer some of the best food bargains in Manhattan, among them **Shaheen Sweets** at 99 Lexington Ave. at 27th St.

IRISH

Moderate

Eamonn Doran. 988 Second Ave. near 53rd St.; 752–8088. Muzaked and carpeted, an Irish pub gone Continental. Exhaustive list of imported beers, pleasant food, good service. All major credit cards.

Tommy Makem's Irish Pavilion. 130 E. 57th St.; 759–9040. Folksinger Tommy Makem has taken over the Pavilion, gutted it, and decorated it with the work of contemporary Irish artist Jim Fitzpatrick and a gallery of portraits of famous Irish literary figures. The food is on the bland and overcooked side, and the menu is slim on Irish fare—but the draught beers are excellent and the ambience is warm indeed. Shows by Irish folk musicians and those of other nationalities are presented most nights at 9 and midnight. AE, MC, V.

Landmark Tavern. 626 Eleventh Ave. near 47th St.; 757–8595. With a pot-bellied stove and mahogany bar, this century-old tavern offers charm and an unpretentious bill of fare. Dine heartily on homemade soda bread, shepherd's pie, and Irish potato soup. No credit cards.

Inexpensive

Costello's. 225 E. 44th St.; 599–9614. Renowned with the newspaper crowd for good food, conversation. (This is a new location for the famous old joint with the Thurber murals.)

Limerick's. 573 Second Ave. near 32nd St.; 683–4686. Brick walls and decor that might best be described as Irish miscellaneous make this an American idea of a typical Irish pub. But they do feature corned beef and cabbage and authentic Irish soda bread. Closed Saturday during the summer and on holiday weekends. No lunch Saturday. All major credit cards.

Londonderry Pub. 134 W. 51st St.; 974–9077. Hearty pub atmosphere. All major credit cards.

McBell's. 359 Sixth Ave. near W. 4th St., in the Village; 675–6260. Red-checkered tableclothes, brick walls and antique lights make this not quite Dublin but more than just another Irish pub, especially if you stick to the simple fare such as Irish ham and bacon and stew served in a congenial atmosphere. No credit cards.

Rosie O'Grady's. 151 W. 51st St.; 582–2975. Irish and Continental specialties with kitchen open 'til 2:00 A.M., music seven nights. All major credit cards.

ITALIAN

Deluxe

Alfredo. 240 Central Park South (which is 59th St. across from the park); 246–7050. Northern Italian specialties that naturally begin with fettucine Alfredo. The location is relatively new, but its reputation for high quality is long standing—even if the reality does not often live up to that mark. Closed Sun. All major credit cards.

Barbetta. 321 W. 46th St. in the theater district; 246–9171. The most luxurious of the Italian restaurants, with its 18th-century furnishings and gorgeous crystal chandelier. Northern Italian cuisine, sometimes indifferently prepared, and the best of wines are featured—and have been for over 75 years. Beautiful cocktail lounge and bar. Outdoor garden dining in season, but ask for seating downstairs when reserving indoors. Many romantic triangles are cemented here. Closed Sun. All major credit cards.

Giambelli Albert. 238 Madison Ave. near 36th St.; 685–8727. The food is Northern Italian, delicate, refined, cooked with butter instead of olive oil, and light on garlic and tomatoes. The result is excellent pastas. Closed Sunday, and during the summer months, Sat. as well. All major credit cards.

Giambelli Fiftieth. 46 E. 50th St.; 688–2760. Good veal, fish, and pastas—but as expensive as the restaurant is ornate. Yet this Giambelli's is big with visiting Italian dignitaries and brass from Italy's tourism office, so they must be doing something right. Closed Sun. No DC.

Girafe. 208 E. 58th St.; 752–3054. On two levels, connected by a long, thin spiral staircase so it resembles its namesake, this restaurant provides a supperclub setting for savory pastas, especially the fettucine and carbonara. Closed Sunday. No CB.

Nanni Al Valletto. 133 E. 61st St.; 838–3939. An offshot of the excellent original Nanni's on 46th St. (697–4161), and somehow Nanni manages to keep on top of both places—but Al Valletto is much the posher of the two and less noisy (and with less character). Closed Sunday. All major credit cards.

Orsini's. 41 W. 56th St.; 757–1698. Presents northern Italian and Roman cuisine in an elegant atmosphere. The back room is most romantic, with love seats and candlelight. This restaurant has a very stylish following and many executives take their protegés here for a discreet late dinner. Closed Sunday. All major credit cards.

Pietro's. 201 E. 45th St.; 682–9760. The steaks here are as good as in any house and the Italian dishes also rank with the best. Housed in two crowded floors of a former speakeasy. The New York atmosphere here is not to everyone's taste. No credit cards.

Romeo Salta. 30 W. 56th St.; 246–5772. This remarkable restaurant in a spacious former mansion is handsomely decorated. The extraordinary pastas are conscientiously prepared and the veal Villa d'Este with eggplant is outstanding. A large menu offers a wide choice of carefully prepared and attentively served dishes. Closed Sunday. All major credit cards.

San Marco. 36 W. 52nd St.; 246–5340. Northern Italian cuisine in a small, smart room decorated with a display of wines. Veal and chicken dishes and made-at-the-table *zabaglione* are special, as are the sweetbreads in white wine. Closed Sunday. All major credit cards.

SPQR. 133 Mulberry St.; 431–7610. Elegant but hardly understated turn-of-the-century dining room in the heart of Little Italy, where classic Northern and

Southern Italian cuisine is served for lunch and dinner. Initials stand for *Senatus Populus Que Romanus* (the senate and people of Rome). Upstairs night club features dancing and name entertainment. Valet parking for dinner. All major credit cards.

Tre Scalini. 230 E. 58th St.; 688–6888. The mural of the Piazza Navona makes you feel as though you were in Rome, the pastas make you think you *are* there. It is a flashy modern dining room for Northern Italian cuisine that could hold its own on the Via Veneto. Closed Sun. All major credit cards.

Expensive

Amalfi. 16 E. 48th St.; 758–5110. Established 1927 and as Italian as the Amalfi Drive. All major credit cards.

Bruno. 240 E. 58th St.; 688–4190. Simple modern dining room with a country atmosphere—and outstanding pastas, from linguine matriciana with tomato sauce, prosciutto and onion, to trenette in pesto (basil) sauce. Closed Saturday, dinner only on Sunday. All major credit cards.

Capriccio Ristorante. 33 E. 61st St.; 759–6684. Family operated, featuring fuzi Angela—a flat pasta that is chief among the many pasta specialties. Closed Sunday, no lunch Saturday. All major credit cards.

DaSilvano. 260 Sixth Ave. south of Bleecker in the Village; 982–0090. Smartly trim storefront with excellent pasta dishes, from quill-cut penne in a Bolognese sauce to tortellini with a spicy meat filling. Very small place; must reserve. Dining out front in good weather. No credit cards.

Caffè da Alfredo. 17 Perry St., just off Seventh Ave. in the Village; 989–7028. Roman and Northern Italian dishes. The service is casual, in the spirit of the restaurant in general, but friendly and efficient. The special pastas, changed daily, are among the best in the city, and these should be prime among your choices. Reservations must be made a few days in advance, and you must be punctual. Bring your own wine. Jackets and/or ties are unnecessary. Closed Mon. (This is a better bet than the **Trattoria da Alfredo** of the same ownership, at 90 Bank St., 929–4400, which is closed Tuesdays and requires reservations weeks ahead. There is also the **Tavola Calda da Alfredo,** 285 Bleecker St. near Seventh Ave., 924–4789, which does serve wine.)

Eleonora Ristorante. 117 W. 58th St.; 765–1427. Northern Italian cuisine in a lavish theatrical setting celebrating the great Duse. After-theater suppers a specialty. Closed Sunday. All major credit cards.

Gian Marino. 221 E. 58th St.; 752–1696. Fair food from six provinces of Italy; popular among show-business folk. Closed Monday. All major credit cards.

Gino's. 780 Lexington Ave. near 61st St.; 223–9658. The food is good, though hardly extraordinary, yet this restaurant is very fashionable for models, fashion buyers, photographers, and their camp followers. Being seen is obviously more important than the quality of the cuisine. No credit cards.

Giordano's. 409 W. 39th St.; 947–3883. Northern Italian cuisine served in a supremely refined setting, with romantic alcoves for when the occasion demands, or a lone terrace table for when spring arrives (though the air here, given the restaurant's proximity to the Lincoln Tunnel, is particularly noxious). The pastas and veal come most highly recommended. All major credit cards.

Il Monello. 1460 Second Ave. near 77th St.; 535–9310. A restful setting for some of the best pasta on the East Side, especially the green lasagne, tortellini, and thin pasta strands in a Bolognese meat sauce. Closed Monday. No DC.

Il Mulino. 86 W. 3rd St. (in the Village); 673–3783. Not on the busiest thoroughfare, but one of the best Italian restaurants in the city. Great pastas—especially the mildly spicy ones—and unusual wine labels. The daily specials are truly special. A very European atmosphere. Closed Sundays. AE.

Il Nido. 251 E. 53rd St.; 753–8450. A stylish and currently very fashionable restaurant with provincial overtones—and some of the best ravioli and fettucine this side of Tuscany. The back room is noisy. Closed Sunday. AE, CB, DC.

Il Pescatore Veneto. 56 W. 56th St.; 245–9869. This restaurant does not, as you would expect from the name, specialize in seafood—nor even Venetian cuisine. Instead, this is a solid but middle-of-the-road Northern Italian place on the 56th Street restaurant row. Very comfortable and unthreatening. Closed Saturday lunch and Sunday; also, no Saturday dinner in summer. AE, DC, V.

Isle of Capri. 1028 Third Ave. near 61st St.; 223–9430. Generally acknowledged as one of the best Italian restaurants in the city, though it can be very uneven. A "trattoria"-style operation where the food's the thing. Sidewalk café. Closed Sunday. AE, DC, V.

Italian Pavillion. 24 W. 55th St.; 586–5950. Owned by the same people who run Quo Vadis and in the same league. Closed Sunday. All major credit cards.

La Strada East. 274 Third Ave. near 22nd St.; 473–3760. Friendly, informal atmosphere where you may enjoy well-prepared food that includes all manner of pastas, veal, beef, and some unusual dishes. Closed Sunday, dinner only on Saturday. All major credit cards.

Mona Lisa. 936 Second Ave. (50th St.); 421–4497. Dine in a skylight garden, with hearty cuisine, very good service. Closed Sun. All major credit cards.

Monsignore II, 61 E. 55th St.; 355–2070. Strolling guitarist, romantic ambience, good food. Closed Sunday. All major credit cards.

Nanni's. 146 E. 46th St.; 697–4161. Excellent Northern Italian cuisine that reaches its highest standards in the tortellini and chicken Valdostana. The same owner runs Nanni Il Valletto. Closed Sunday. All major credit cards.

Parioli Romanissimo. 1466 First Ave. near 76th St.; 288–2391. Small, gaudy, but terrific cannelloni and tortellini. Closed Sunday and Monday. AE, DC, CB.

Patsy's. 236 W. 56th St.; 247–3491. Noted for its Neapolitan food and friendly atmosphere. Simple, cheerful surroundings. Many different pastas, but the stuffed shells are unusual in this bright, two-story restaurant that offers choice of 35 main courses. Closed Monday. No CB.

Per Bacco. 140 E. 27th St.; 532–8699. Possibly because it is a bit out of the way, this Northern Italian restaurant (the Trieste region) is one of the unsung stars of dining out in New York; the daily specialties are the thing. Major credit cards.

Piccolo Mondo. 1269 First Ave. near 69th St., on the Upper East Side; 249–3141. Very good Northern Italian fare. The scampi here is among the best in the city. Overdecorated, though, and loud. All major credit cards.

Poletti's. 2315 Broadway at 84th St.; 580–1200. If there is such a thing as an Upper West Side style, this restaurant—along with Teacher's—exemplifies it. Pastas are made on the premises, and the pastas are what you should go for here—rather than the overpriced main dishes. All major credit cards.

Primavera Ristorante. 1570 First Ave., 81st St.; 861–8608. One of the best of the First Ave. storefront restaurants, especially the tortellini and fish dishes. Closed Sun. All major credit cards.

Roma di Notte. 137 E. 55th St.; 832–1128. Appeals to the eye. Stunning Roman decor in bar and cocktail lounge and dimly lit dining room. Dazzling array of appetizers, chicken Nero, rollatine of veal, fettucine are among many choices. They do a lot of cooking over a flaming rotisserie—none of which is terribly distinguished. All major credit cards.

Sal Anthony's. 55 Irving Place near 17th St.; 982–9030. Go up a few stairs into a large, spacious, well-decorated room and you enter a restaurant that serves as delicate a tomato sauce as can be found this side of Florence. Excellent pastas and eggplant. All major credit cards.

Salta in Bocca. 179 Madison Ave. near 33rd St.; 684–1757. A pleasant if undistinguished-looking dining room, where the excellent pasta is what catches your attention, especially the green-and-white fettucine casalinga. Very noisy, with tables close together. Closed Sun. All major credit cards.

37th Street Hideaway. 32 W. 37th St.; 947–8940. Italian-American specialties in John D. Barrymore's former townhouse. After-theater suppers until midnight. Closed Sunday. No V.

Trastevere. 309 E. 83rd St.; 734-6343. Small, intimate, rushed, named for a section of Rome renowned for its restaurants—and lives up to its name. AE.

Moderate

Alfredo the Original of Rome. Citicorp Center, 54th St. at Third Ave.; 371–3367. The name tells the whole story, but surprisingly, the pasta is excellent. Slightly hectic service at lunch, so try in evening. All major credit cards.

Angelina's. 41 Greenwich Ave. in the Village; 929–1255. A homey sort of place, unpretentious as far as decor and menu. The same à la carte menu is used for lunch and dinner. Veal parmigiana, shrimp marinara, and breaded pork chops are popular entrées. AE, DC.

Angelo of Mulberry Street; 146 Mulberry St.; 226–8527. Deep in the heart of "Little Italy." The pastas are a specialty, as is fish stew *(zuppa di pesce)*. All major credit cards.

Antolotti's. 337 E. 49th St.; 688–6767. Established in 1950 and improving with age. A conventional Northern Italian menu, generally well prepared. Good and friendly service. Clientele strongly other-boroughs. No lunch Sat. and Sun. All major credit cards.

Beatrice Inn. 285 W. 12th St.; 929–6165. From the outside this downstairs restaurant looks foreboding, but this is a genuine family-run affair in a surprisingly decorous setting—fresh flowers, brightly lit, and exceedingly friendly. The manicotti is outstanding, and the veal, chicken, and seafood dishes are on par with those at far more expensive establishments. Closed Sundays. AE.

Café Trilussa. 280 Bleecker St. off Seventh Ave. (in the Village); 929–9104. This small storefront restaurant, with unusual yet earthy dishes on a small menu, is the sort of new-style Village Italian restaurant many people come to New York for. The wine list is so-so, the food a bit uneven in quality, but the service and atmosphere are enjoyable. AE, MC, V.

Forlini's. 93 Baxter St. in the vicinity of Canal St.; 349–6779. Red sauce cooking with finesse. All major credit cards.

Grotto Azzurra. 387 Broome St.; 925-8775. One of the most popular Little Italy haunts, though some are put off by the prices relative to the simplicity of the décor and the sawdust on the floor. Still, the food is superior, though the best time to go is on a weeknight, when neither the kitchen nor the diners are quite so rushed.

Il Gattopardo. 45 W. 56th St.; 586–3978. Just as you'd expect a restaurant in Milan or Turin to look. Excellent service, very good food. Closed Sunday. All major credit cards.

Marchi's. 251 E. 31st St.; 679–2494. In an old brownstone, has a long-time reputation for its many-course dinner at fixed price. You eat whatever the host has selected for the day. Reservations accepted Monday through Friday only, closed for lunch and on Sunday. AE.

Parma. 1404 Third Ave. at 80th St.; 535–3520. With its plain piperack decor, Parma sets an informal mood that lets one get down to the serious business of wrestling with some of the best pasta this side of, well, Parma. Dinner only, daily. AE.

Patrissy's. 98 Kenmare St. in Little Italy; 226–8509. Friendly, informal, long-established Neopolitan restaurant, where everything is à la carte and you need a cart to carry off what you can't finish from their first-rate pastas. All major credit cards.

Pete's Tavern. 129 E. 18th St.; 473–7676. The manicotti is the best thing on the menu, the tomato sauce not the most subtle. This is the tavern made famous by O. Henry. Very simple setting, with outdoor café in summer. Wonderful old-fashioned bar. No CB.

Pronto Ristorante. 30 E. 60th St., 421–8151. Pasta made in front of your eyes; ultra-modern restaurant design and good Northern Italian dishes. Can be expensive. All major credit cards.

Rao's. 445 E. 114th St.; 534–9625. So tiny there were only six tables at last count, so out-of-the-way it is located in one of the city's most broken-down neighborhoods, but so "in" that the cognoscenti make the trip by car for some of the city's best homemade pastas. Dinner only. No credit cards.

Rocco. 181 Thompson St. in the Village; 677–0590. Neapolitan food, and very good—though the restaurant itself doesn't look very promising at first glance. Go here if you want the flavor of the Little Italy of times gone by. Major credit cards.

Trattoria. In the Pan Am Building. 45th St. between Vanderbilt and Lexington Aves.; 661–3090. Informal, though strikingly decorated with Italy's colors and posters. Outdoor dining—but on the least tranquil sidestreet in New York. Closed Saturday/Sunday. All major credit cards.

Via Margutta. 24 Minetta Lane in the Village; 254–7630. North Italian cuisine in neat, cozy quarters. The varied menu offers excellent shellfish, veal Margutta, and cannelloni Via Margutta. Wine served in attractive glass carafes. Complete lunches and dinners or à la carte. All major credit cards.

Inexpensive

Bleecker Luncheonette. Corner Bleecker and Cornelia; no phone. Literally a luncheonette with counter seats and a handful of tables. The menu is limited to equally few items, but everything is prepared to order and with a careful hand. The pesto is outstanding when in season, the meatballs the best around and the manicotti is heavenly. Yet to eat $10.00 worth here is a challenge; given the quality it would be a bargain at twice the price. Closes at 7:00 P.M., but if you're on line at 6:59 they'll still seat and serve you with a smile. No credit cards.

Guido's. 511 Ninth Ave., at 39th St.; 244–9314. Hidden behind the storefront Supreme Macaroni Company (where you can indeed buy freshly made pasta), this is a family-style southern Italian cooking—festive, well-prepared and served with a friendliness that is rare indeed. Don't be misled by the minimum $8.00 charge at dinner, because you'd really have to stuff yourself to surpass it by much. Great before theater, but be sure to have a reservation. No credit cards.

Luna. 112 Mulberry St.; 226–6322. From noon to midnight, this is possibly the most inexpensive *and* (relatively speaking) high-quality—and friendly—Southern Italian restaurant in the city. Don't expect to eat anything delicate or to while away the night lingering over a bottle of wine (the prices are low because the turnover is high), but do go for more-than-ample portions at very reasonable prices. And do go with the expectation of waiting on line for a table, as you may have to do. No credit cards.

Manganaro's. 492 Ninth Ave. near 38th St.; 947–7325. The best place in New York for overstuffed Italian hero sandwiches—eggplant parmigiana, mixed cold cuts, sausage and peppers. Bustling at lunch and closes at 7:00 P.M., but always worth the trip. Closed Sun. No credit cards.

Monte's. 97 MacDougal St. in the Village; 674–9456. Down half a flight of steps from street level, this restaurant has provided good, solid, bountiful, and unpretentious Southern Italian fare to the local Italian-Americans, New York University faculty and plenty of other New Yorkers for a long time—and at better than reasonable prices. Closed Tuesday. No credit cards.

Perretti. 270 Columbus Ave., at 72nd St.; 362–3939. Bright, glass-enclosed neon-lit dining room popular among neighborhood denizens and those headed to Lincoln Center. No reservations, so be prepared to wait. Pizza also served. AE, MC, V.

Puglia's. 189 Hester St. in Little Italy; 226–8912. This is a place for partying. Seating is at long, camp-style tables, the homemade wine served by the bottle (beer by the pitcher), the hearty Southern fare a mite greasy at times—but once the little old lady begins her sing-along routines (weekends only) you won't even notice. No credit cards.

Umberto's Clam House. 129 Mulberry St. in Little Italy; 431–7545. Site of the infamous Joey Gallo underworld murder but a favorite fresh seafood place. Very informal, with sidewalk tables in summer and open very late. No credit cards.

Vincent's Clam Bar. 119 Mott St. in Little Italy; 226–8133. The home of hot and spicy tomato sauce. Try your spaghetti with it, with scungilli or calamari—and you get one roll. Informal. No credit cards.

JAMAICAN

Moderate

Jamaican Seafood Restaurant. 432 Sixth Ave. near 10th St. in the Village; 982–3260. What you might expect, featuring a kind of Jamaican bouillabaisse, and all the trimmings, including plantains. All major credit cards.

JAPANESE

Expensive

Benihana of Tokyo. East: 120 E. 56th St.; 593–1627. Also **West:** 47 W. 56th St.; 581–0930 and **Palace:** 15 W. 44th St.; 682–7120. The show is what counts here, with a chef attending to every party (though parties are often grouped together) chopping, seasoning, and stir-frying over an open gas-heated grill. There's certainly better and more seriously traditional Japanese food around, but the spectacle involved is entertaining. All major credit cards.

Gibbon. 24 E. 80th St.; 861–4001. Combination of French and Japanese cuisines in a remodeled private house, with some dining on street level, but the main dining area is one flight up. Features good fish dishes. Open for lunch Monday through Friday, dinner seven days a week. All major credit cards.

Hakubai. 66 Park Ave. at 38th St. (entrance on side street); 686–3770. In New York's only avowed Japanese hotel, the Kitano. Very comfortable, uses very best raw materials for all dishes (the key to Japanese cuisine); everything is good here. All major credit cards.

Hatsuhana. 17 E. 48th St.; 355–3345. Small, very busy, specializing in raw-fish preparation and seafood. Totally authentic, but it is having trouble managing its success. Closed Sun. All major credit cards.

Inagiku. 111 E. 49th St. in the Waldorf Astoria; 355–0440. Excellent, authentic food in handsome restaurant, decorated in Japanese style—though a bit overstated. Same dishes available in three different areas—a special bar, grill room, and main dining room, with prices escalating accordingly. *Tempura, sukiyaki,* and seafood do Japan proud. Closed Sunday, dinner only on Saturday. All major credit cards.

Kabuki. 115 Broadway, downtown; 962–4677. This financial district restaurant typically attracts large Wall Street crowds for lunch, but the dinner is quiet, almost intimate. There are tatami rooms along one wall and regular Western tables in the center. Special banquet-style dinners and *donburi* lunches are offered. Serves lunch and dinner Monday through Friday. All major credit cards.

Kitcho of New York. 22 W. 46th St.; 575–8880. A favorite of the Japanese themselves. In addition to the usual *sukiyaki* and *tempura* fare so popular with Americans, there are a number of unusually prepared delicacies. Southern Japanese cuisine. Gentle, attentive service. Closed Saturday. Open 5:00 P.M. Sunday. AE, DC.

Nippon. 145 E. 52nd St.; 355–9020. Probably New York's most famous Japanese restaurant. Like a Japanese garden, complete with a stream. Tatami rooms or regular tables in an attractive setting. Unusual Japanese dishes are featured along with familiar *sukiyaki*. Cosy bar and cocktail lounge. *Tempura* and *sushi* bar for light meals. Closed Sunday. Dinner only on Saturday. All major credit cards.

Robata. 30 E. 61st St., 688–8120. Waterwheel, hanging plants, walls covered with reeds, and interesting Japanese murals approximate a Japanese farmhouse. *Robata* means "open fire." They broil fish over an open fire after you make your selection from the counter. Meat, too. All major credit cards.

Sagano. 3 E. 44th St.; 986–1355. Elegant and stylish décor—and very authentically Japanese—with elegantly served food in the Japanese style. With allegiances to Kyoto (southern Japanese) cuisine, there is the usual tempura, teriyaki, etc., but all of it top-flight. Closed Sunday; no Saturday lunch. Major credit cards.

Shinbashi. 280 Park Ave. at 48th St.; 661–3915. Tatami rooms where you sit on the floor, kimono-wearing waitresses, and Western-style items to go along with good Japanese beef or seafood grilled with vegetables make this large, somewhat austere place an interesting choice. Closed Sunday, dinner only on Saturday. All major credit cards.

Takesushi. 71 Vanderbilt Ave. at 45th St.; 867–5120. Yes, a sushi restaurant, and one of the very best in the city—if no longer *the* best (that honor goes to one we won't list because it is necessarily so small). Must reserve. Closed Sundays. Major credit cards.

Moderate

Hisae's Lobster House. 13 E. 37th St.; 889–9820. Japanese-style fish restaurant that is popular with devotees of seafood and the new low-calorie vegetable style of cooking. Good red snapper and sea bass make you forget about the noise. Art Deco tiles on the long bar near the entrance, and glass-topped tables that have never seen Tokyo. Closed Sunday. AE, MC, V.

Kamehachi. 14 E. 47th St.; 765–4737. Decor is not a feature of this restaurant, but good Japanese food is. There is a bar for sushi—raw fish on vinegar rice—and a complete selection of traditional specialties, including broiled eel and *tempura*. Closed Sunday. All major credit cards.

Lenge. 202 Columbus Ave., a bit north of Lincoln Center at 69th St.; 874–8278. Enclosed sidewalk café, *sushi* bar, tatami mat area. Good *tempura*, passable raw fish, unexceptional *sukiyaki*. AE, DC.

Miyokawa. 23 W. 56th St.; 586–6899. A delightful restaurant that is usually crowded with Japanese businessmen. Excellent *sushi* bar, *tempura*, and other specialties. Tatami (mats on the floor) dining is available. All major cards.

Nakagawa. 7 W. 44th St.; 869–8077. Authentic in decor and atmosphere. Divided into two sections, with a *sushi* counter and small tables up front and, down a few steps, more tables—but slightly larger. The food is authentic Japanese. AE, MC, V.

Rock Garden of Tokyo. 34 W. 56th St.; 245–7936. Kimono-clad waitresses cook your meals at tables with gas-flamed grills in the center. You can try your hand at it, too, in a food-preparation style called "Yakiniku." All major credit cards.

Saito. 305 E. 46th St.; 759–8897. A baker's dozen of main courses offered in three places—a *tempura* bar, a section where you can eat on the floor Japanese style, or one for dining at Western-size tables in *teriyaki, sukiyaki,* or *yakitori*. Closed Sunday, dinner only Saturday. All major credit cards.

Inexpensive

Bizen. 171 Spring St. in SoHo; 966–0963. The combination of art gallery (featuring works by Japanese artists), naturally woody setting, imaginative food preparation and unlikely music (usually Mozart or jazz) all at very reasonable prices is what SoHo as a residential neighborhood can be at its best. Relaxed and most pleasant. AE.

Dan Tempura House. 2018 Broadway, at 71st St.; 877–4969. From the outside it looks like a tacky Japanese coffee shop, but inside is a consistently satisfying restaurant most popular for its (obviously) *tempura* and seafood casserole-type dishes. For dessert: deep-fried ice cream—and it's wonderful, not just a gimmick. Convenient to Lincoln Center. AE.

Dosanko Larmen. 423 Madison Ave. at 47th St., 688–8575; 10 E. 52nd St., 759–6361; 341 Lexington Ave. at 39th St., 683–4740; 135 E. 45th St., 697–2967; 19 Murray St. near City Hall, 964–9696. Noodles in hot broth, with various trimmings, light and healthful. Super cheap. No credit cards.

Genroku Sushi. 366 Fifth Ave. near 34th St.; 947–7940. Sit around an enormous counter and pick your dishes off a perpetually moving conveyor belt. In addition to *sushi,* you can choose Japanese curry noodle and rice dishes, *tempura, sashimi, gyoza,* fried chicken, even soups and desserts. You are charged by the number of plates you take. Open seven days. Very cheap. No credit cards.

Mikado. 21 W. 39th St.; 840–7636. Small, attractive, specializes in *domburi* dishes, which consist of hot bowls of rice covered with various mixtures such as vegetables, shrimp, or chicken. Closed Saturday/Sunday. All major credit cards.

Sushi Ginza East. 4 E. 46th St.; 687–4717. Specializes in—what else?—*sushi* (seasoned rice topped with raw fish), but also serves sautéed beef and vegetables *(sukiyaki)* and good *tempura* (fried fish and vegetables). AE.

Taro. 20 E. 57th St.; 986–7170. A kind of Japanese McDonald's with noodles, filling the need for simple, tasty, low-priced meals served at round counters. It follows the concept of hundreds of similar restaurants in Japan, and serves *larmen* (noodle dishes) that come in soup, in fried dishes, or broiled with fish, chicken, or meat. Closed Saturday/Sunday. No credit cards.

JEWISH/KOSHER

Expensive

Lindy's. 50th St. at Sixth Ave.; 586–8986. The one-and-only, gone for a while, now revived and doing well. You come here for the cheesecake and the atmosphere—the rest of the food is carelessly prepared and overpriced. Not Kosher. All major credit cards.

Lou G. Siegel. 209 W. 38th St.; 921–4433. Serves authentic Jewish food under rabbinical supervision. The menu has *lungen* and *miltz* stew, stuffed derma, stuffed cabbage, meats, and poultry. Separate bar. No smoking after sundown Friday, closed Saturday. All major credit cards.

Moshe Peking. 40 W. 37th St.; 594–6500. A handsome restaurant only New York could spawn, featuring Kosher Chinese cuisine, including Peking duck, beef and veal. Closed Fri. sundown to Sat. sundown. All major credit cards.

Sammy's Roumanian Restaurant. 157 Chrystie St. on the Lower East Side; 673–0330. The waiters think they're comedians, but from the bowls of pickles and roast peppers on every table to the delicious chicken soup, blintzes, *karnatzlach* (a very garlicky sausage), and potted steak the food is not a joke. An experience, to put it mildly. AE.

Inexpensive

Ratner's. 138 Delancey St. on the Lower East Side; 677–5588. Strictly Kosher dairy (and listed under that heading, too). Sunday breakfast is the best time for a visit. A great place to take the kids. No credit cards.

KOREAN

Moderate

Arirang House. 28 W. 56th St.; 581–9698. If you like spicy grilled beef and the sourest of pickles, this is the place for you. Best example of Korean cooking in the city, but the atmosphere within is darkly mysterious. All major credit cards.

Myong Dong. 42 W. 35th St.; 695–6622. Long bar, semicircular banquettes, and all kinds of banquets, from soups, *sirhas mandoo gook,* to *jeyook kooi* (slices of pork). Closed Sunday. All major credit cards.

Woo Lae Oak of Seoul. 77 W. 46th St.; 869–9958. Perhaps the largest menu of all the city's Korean restaurants. *Bool koki*—strips of marinated beef cooked over small fire—pork ribs, baked short ribs, noodles, and all kinds of fish. No credit cards.

Inexpensive

Ho Shim. 120 W. 44th St.; 575–9774. Screens, artifacts, waitresses in Korean national costumes. A theater district location where you can get good noodles, *yakitori* (broiled chicken), marinated strips of beef, and fried fish. All major credit cards.

MIDDLE EASTERN

Moderate

Ararat. 4 E. 36th St.; 686–4622. Beautifully decorated establishment specializing in Armenian cuisine to match. Closed Sat., July and August. All major credit cards.

Balkan Armenian. 129 E. 27th St.; 689–7925. One of the oldest and most popular Armenian restaurants, offering such typical fare as stuffed grape leaves, egg-lemon soup, and a most unusual mushroom kebab. Short on frills. Closed Sun. All major credit cards.

Bosphorus East. 121 Lexington Ave. at 28th St.; 679–8370. The former owner and performer in a famous Istanbul restaurant and nightclub brought his knowledge of Turkish cuisine with him to New York and serves samples in a small, pleasant little place. Dinner only seven days a week. All major credit cards.

Cedars of Lebanon. 39 E. 30th St.; 725–9251. A variety of interesting and absolutely authentic Lebanese dishes in cavernous and poorly decorated surroundings. All major credit cards.

Dardanelles. 86 University Pl. 3 blocks south of 14th St.; 242–8990. Authentic Armenian cuisine in soft-lit quiet Village setting. Shish kebab, yogurt soup, stuffed mussels, and Oriental pastries are a few headliners. Greek wines are also available. Dinner only Saturday/Sunday. All major credit cards.

NORTH AFRICAN–MIDDLE EASTERN

Moderate

Keneret. 296 Bleecker St. at Seventh Ave.; 243–0866. Archetype Village atmosphere with very good couscous, moussaka. Dinner only. All major credit cards.

PERUVIAN

Inexpensive

Peruvian Restaurant. 370 W. 51st St.; 974–9099. Small menu in a small restaurant, with *ceviche, escabeche de pescado,* and other goodies. No credit cards.

POLISH

Inexpensive

Baltyk. 12 First Ave. at First St., one block north of Houston St.; 260–4809. Borscht, kielbasa with sauerkraut, pigs' feet, everything to delight a Slavic heart. Funky atmosphere. Open 24 hours. No credit cards.

RUSSIAN

Deluxe

Russian Tea Room. 150 W. 57th St.; 265–0947. A landmark right next to Carnegie Hall, and a favorite among musicians, dancers, movie celebrities, and other show-biz folk. Perhaps the city's richest food, and Christmas decorations all year long. Borscht, *blini* (pancakes with caviar), chicken Kiev, and (on Wednesday only) the legendary Siberian *pelmeny*. Russian cream for dessert if you can handle it. Watch out for the lethal concoctions brewed by the "Cossack" bartenders. All major credit cards.

Moderate

Russian Bear. 139 E. 56th St.; 355–9080. Unexciting versions of chicken Kiev, beef Stroganoff, etc. All major credit cards.

SCANDINAVIAN

Expensive

Copenhagen. 68 W. 58th St.; 688–3690. Danish specialties include open-faced sandwiches, a sumptuous *koldtbord* buffet with 100 hot and cold delicacies to choose from, including 26 kinds of herring. Aquavit and elephant beer to wash it all down—and the best coffee in town. All major credit cards.

SPANISH-MEXICAN

Expensive

Fonda La Paloma. 256 E. 49th St.; 421–5495. Hot and spicy Mexican dishes here are all prepared to order and courteously served in a pleasant atmosphere. The guacamole is without peer. Open seven days but only from 5:00 P.M. on Saturday/Sunday. All major credit cards.

Plaza España. 130 W. 58th St,; 757–6434. Authentic dishes in traditional surroundings. Try the garlic chicken. Closed Sunday, open for dinner only Saturday. MC, V.

Victor's Café. 240 Columbus Ave. at 71st St.; 575–8599. The place to go for the finest Cuban food in the city. The soups are excellent, fried beef with garlic and onions, and rice with seafood or chicken are equally delicious. Unusual on Sunday are Cuban hero sandwiches and roast suckling pig. Victor's is so popular it now has a theater district offshoot called **Victor's Café 52,** 236 W. 52nd St., 586–7714. All major credit cards.

Moderate

Cantina. 221 Columbus Ave. at 70th St.; 873–2606. Not slavishly authentic food, but a very popular Upper West Side hangout. Try the Mexican kitchen casserole if you are very hungry. No CB,DC.

El Coyote. 774 Broadway, 9th St.; 677–4291. Mexican cantina decor and best-selling combination platters. After 7:00 P.M. there can be a considerable wait at the bar. No CB,DC.

El Parador. 325 E. 34th St.; 679–6812. Small, plain restaurant that is so popular they leave you waiting for tables even when plenty are available. But the Mexican and Spanish cuisine are hailed by Latins. Try a Marguerita during the inevitable wait at the bar (that's the purpose, of course), which is a low-key singles scene in and of itself. Spanish wines and Mexican beers. Dinner only, à la carte. Closed Sunday. No credit cards.

Fonda Los Milagros. 70 E. 55th St.; 752–6640. Exciting Mexican dishes are served to the accompaniment of mariachi music. Try the *chiles rellenos* and *flautas de carne*. There are pre-theater and after-theater à la carte dinners. Closed Sunday. Dinner only Saturday. AE CB, DC.

Los Panchos. 71 W. 71st St. east of Columbus; 874–8006. Very accommodating neighborhood restaurant with outdoor garden for summer dining and a life-size stuffed burro at the bar. Food is simple but well prepared. All major credit cards.

Pamplona. 822 Avenue of the Americas near 29th St.; 683–4242. This bright, unimposing restaurant is among the best of those serving Spanish cuisine. Black bean soup is delectable, chicken dishes also commendable. Closed Sunday. No V.

Zapata's. 330 E. 53rd St.; 223–9408. Narrow, dim, dominated by a portrait of the revolutionary, but viva the good, heaping food portions that are reasonably well-seasoned. All major credit cards.

Inexpensive

Anita's Chili Parlor. 287 Columbus Ave. at W. 74th St.; 595–4091. Tex-Mex food inside, or at sidewalk tables to watch the Columbus Avenue madness. Service indifferent at best. No credit cards.

El Charro. 4 Charles St. in the Village.; 242–9547. Full selection of spicy Mexican fare available in this homey restaurant. The combination plates let you sample the usual variety of dishes such as *tortillas, tostadas, enchiladas,* and *tacos.* All major credit cards.

El Cortijo. 128 W. Houston St. between the Village and SoHo; 674–4080. A neighborhood restaurant whose Spanish fare consists of both meat and fish dishes. The *paella,* saffron-flavored rice with seafood and/or chicken and sausage, is good. All major credit cards.

El Faro. 823 Greenwich St., Horatio St. in the West Village; 929–8210. Don't be put off by the unappetizing exterior—or by the small, dark interior for that matter—for this is absolutely NYC's finest Spanish kitchen. Besides the obligatory *paellas,* there is a raft of other shellfish dishes called *mariscadas.* The sangría is the genuine article, and *natilla* is a special treat for dessert. Again, no reservations; can mean a lengthy wait. No credit cards.

El Tenampa. 304 W. 46th St.; 664–8519. Small, unpretentious, near theaters —and good. Closed Sunday. DC.

Rincón de Espana. 226 Thompson St. in the Village; 260–4950. Dinner only. No credit cards. And at **Rincón de Espana II,** 82 Beaver St., 344–5228, dress is as informal as food, which is good. Beaver St. closed Saturday/Sunday.

Tío Pepe. 168 W. 4th St.; 242–9338. From your vantage point on the sidewalk of this pleasant café you can watch the Village denizens while enjoying creditable Spanish fare and the music of a flamenco guitarist. Or choose the more intimate candlelit dining inside. All major credit cards.

SWISS

Expensive

Chalet Suisse. 6 E. 48th St.; 355–0855. A pleasing but pricey place for Swiss cheese fondue or fondue bourguignonne (cubes of beef you cook yourself in hot oil at the table). Other specials: onion and cheese pie, veal dishes, and roesti potatoes. Complete dinners and à la carte. All major credit cards.

Swiss Pavilion. 4 W. 49th St.; 247–6545. Opened when the 1939 World's Fair closed. Inviting atmosphere and serves many Swiss specialties, including veal and snails, as well as cheese fondue and fondue bourguignonne. Not the best value in town. Complete lunch and dinner. Closed Sunday. Bar. On a lower level, there is the **Fondue Pot,** which is more informal, noisier and somewhat less costly for basically the same food. All major credit cards.

Inexpensive

La Fondue. 43 W. 55th St.; 581–0820. As the name suggests, cheese dishes, and fondue in particular, are featured here. For those who demand meatier fare there is filet mignon. A charming, casual atmosphere, but luncheon eating is liable to be crowded and rushed. No credit cards.

THAI

Moderate

Thai Palace. 261 W. 54th St. No phone. Portions are small, like the restaurant, but a little bit goes a long way when the cooking is good—and it is better than that here. All major credit cards.

Siam Inn. 916 Eighth Ave. near 55th St.; 489–5237. Dozens of beguiling Thai specialties are skillfully presented by a shyly gracious and efficient staff in a cheerful modern dining room with decorative Thai accents. Close to the theater district, Columbus Circle, and Carnegie Hall—and gets very crowded during the pre-theater hours. AE, CB, DC.

Inexpensive

Bangkok Cuisine. 885 Eighth Ave. near 53rd St.; 581–6370. Rice with duck, pork with pepper, fish with curry. The usual mixtures which make Thai cuisine so delicious, yet hard to define, as though it were simply a mixture of Chinese and Southeast Asian (yet it is more than that). All major credit cards.

Pongsri Thailand. 244 W. 48th St., unlisted telephone. Within a month of opening became one of the most popular of Thai restaurants because of its spaciousness, gracious staff, modern theater-district setting and, especially, its seafood offerings. All major credit cards.

Thailand. 106 Bayard St. in Chinatown; 349–3132. The best of the lot, and one of the cheapest. Nobody does it better than they do here—but you'd better specify how hot you want your food done. Curries are authentic, fried fish and crab dishes outstanding, but the looks of this small, unpretentious restaurant leave a lot to be desired. Reservations a must. Closed Mon. No credit cards.

UKRAINIAN

Inexpensive

Ukrainian Restaurant and Caterers. 140 Second Ave.; 533–6765. A slice of the 1940s as you wend your way to what were once two little ballrooms and which now serve as the restaurant's dining rooms. The specialties are pierogi—stuffed dumplings—and blintzes (the east European version of crepes), both best eaten with mounds of sour cream. There's also an assortment of Polish-style sausages. Stick to the basics and you'll do very well. No credit cards.

YUGOSLAVIAN

Moderate

Dubrovnik. 88 Madison Ave. near 29th St.; 689–7565. Named for the resort town on Yugoslavia's Dalmatian coast, this pleasant restaurant offers an interesting though limited selection of Yugoslavian specialties such as *brudet* (a sort of chowder), and *cevapcici* (flavorful ground meat sausages). American and Continental dishes fill out the menu. Closed Sunday, dinner only Saturday. All major credit cards.

Portoroz. 340 Lexington Ave. near 39th St.; 687–8195. Rough brick areas, white walls. The restaurant is named for a resort area, looks like a country inn—near Grand Central Station—and serves good *sarma* (stuffed cabbage), interesting ground beef and pork dishes, and even some Italian main courses. Closed Sun. All major credit cards.

FAMOUS FOR EVERYTHING BUT THE FOOD

"Most Expensive Restaurant in the World"

The Palace. 420 E. 59th St.; 355–5150. One of the most opulent restaurants in the U.S.—which, not uninterestingly, went bankrupt once a few years back. The imaginative multi-course dinners feature such delicacies as Scotch salmon stuffed with caviar, and the pastries are made on the premises. As one would expect, there is an extensive wine cellar. Service impeccable. Very, very expensive ($50, $95 or $150—take your pick—per person prix fixe; drinks extra; dinner only; there is a service charge of 20%), but perhaps worth it if you want something to talk about back home, and if you're prepared for the splurge of a lifetime. Reservations necessary. Staff of almost 30 serves about 40 guests. Gold-rimmed plates, cut crystal, brocaded silk chairs, silver pots filled with flowers, and fine if not spectacular food. Closed Sun. All major credit cards.

Super Deluxe

Sign of the Dove. 1110 Third Ave. at 65th St.; 861–8080. A complete townhouse with terraces and a winter garden. The Sanctum Sanctorum is upstairs. Pretentious, and the food never measures up to the setting. No lunch Monday. All major credit cards.

"21". 21 W. 52nd St.; 582–7200. Great social cachet among high-class fixers, celebrity-chasers of all ranks, and slightly aging "beautiful people," and therefore in a category of its own. Somewhat difficult to enter unless you have reservations. Frequented by businessmen at lunch and "society" at night. Handsomely furnished dining rooms, a well-packed, convivial bar. Most-sought-after tables are downstairs, along the left wall. Located in several former townhouses, decorated with turn-of-the-century elegance, more a place to see and be seen—although food is good. Excellent wine cellar. All major credit cards.

Deluxe

Sardi's. 234 W. 44th St.; 221–8440. The place to see theater world celebrities, sometimes. The game here is to figure out why the personnel think the restaurant is any longer a special place, entitling them to treat ordinary customers in an offhand manner. Large dining room with convivial atmosphere has caricatures of the well-known as decoration. Best tables are thought to be those downstairs, near the entrance. Cannelloni alla Sardi is a special, for some reason. À la carte. Some 40 or so choices make for varied possibilities, but keep it simple. All major credit cards.

Top of the Park. Central Park West at 60th St. atop the Gulf & Western Bldg.; 333–3800. The view is terrific if you get a window table in the restaurant or the bar—the latter frequently noisy, ill-kept, overcrowded, and smokey. The food is not memorable because many of the items seem to be prepared in advance. Suitable if you want to look, eat, and run over to Lincoln Center. Dinner only. Closed Sunday. All major credit cards.

Expensive

Cafe des Artistes. 1 W. 67th St.; 877–3500. Amusing 1930s decor and famous Howard Chandler Christy murals on the wall may transport you to another time and place, though the food is at its best when most simply prepared. Try the duckling with pear, the gravlax, or the desserts bearing not too-fancy names. Reserve days ahead for dinner, but this restaurant has lots of regulars, so don't be surprised if even then you don't get a good table. However, no one will raise so much as an eyebrow if all you want is an appetizer and a salad—which often suffices here—or if you'd care to eat at the small but cozy back-room bar. Open seven days a week, with brunch on weekends. All major credit cards.

Elaine's. 1703 Second Ave. at 88th St.; 534–8103. The only legitimate reason for trying this restaurant, unless you know the proprietress, is to try to catch a glimpse of the large number of publishing and journalistic notables or non-notables who call it home. The food's ordinary at best, and mere mortals are treated shabbily, if not worse. A club, however, for the likes of Woody Allen, Gay Talese (who?), and visiting Hollywood pretty faces. Primarily Italian menu, some American dishes in what is more like a renovated saloon than a celebrity haunt. AE.

O. Henry's. 345 Sixth Ave. at W. 4th St.; 242–2000. Takes one back into the past with its Tiffany-style chandeliers, chopping block for tables, and waiters in butcher's coats and straw hats. Charcoal-broiled steaks and chops, plus a casual attitude toward food and guests equally, are the features of this Greenwich Village landmark. All major credit cards.

Toots Shor. 233 W. 33rd St. at Penn Plaza; 279–8150. A famous watering hole for New York's sporting fraternity, moved from its old midtown location to this relatively new spot opposite Madison Square Garden. Standard steak and chops fare, lively atmosphere. Closed weekends unless there are events of importance at the Garden. "Last of the Great Saloon Keepers" is no longer alive, but Toots' spirit lives. All major credit cards.

Top of the Sixes. 666 Fifth Ave. at 53rd St.; 757–8020. Provides a view of the city from its dining room and candlelit cocktail lounge. The menu is diversified with Continental overtones, but it is hardly haute cuisine. (In fact, most of the food tastes as though it were defrosted right from the Stouffer's freezer—which is the company that runs the restaurant.) All major credit cards.

Uzie's. 1442 Third Ave. near 82nd St.; 744–8020. Giancarlo Uzielli holds forth for pasta-eating beautiful people—but the food *is* good, if your ego is strong. All major credit cards.

Moderate

Asti. 13 E. 12th St.; 741–9105. A sing-along place, with waiters and customers getting into the act, whether opera or musicals. Also features a "Flying Pizza" act. Italian-style cuisine, but who's to notice? Closed Monday, July and August. All major credit cards.

Bianchi and Margherita. 186 W. 4th St. in the Village; 242–2756. If you enjoy music, especially opera, and don't care too much about its quality, you'll love this place, where waiter, proprietor, bartender, and customer join together (with luck) to sing duos, trios, quartets, sextets, even solos. The food is like the music—enjoy it and stop fussing. Closed Sun. All major credit cards.

The Cattleman. 5 E. 45th St.; 661–1200. Has to be seen to be disbelieved. A jam-packed bar, one room with an 1890 dining-car interior, another looking like a very elegant Crazy Horse Saloon, and so-so steaks, prime ribs, and tenderloin brochettes. All this, and a stagecoach to take you to the theater after dinner! Miss Grimble's cheescake. Bring appetite because portions are enormous. But quantity has little to do with quality. No CB.

Fraunces Tavern. 54 Pearl St., downtown; 269–0144. Original building dates from Revolutionary days (the present one only to the 1930s). Behind the white portico there's a restaurant for lunch and dinner and a museum filled with Early American memorabilia. It was here that George Washington feted his officers prior to assuming the first presidency. Quite convenient to Wall St. and for

George. But, while history was made here, few gourmet meals are. And swallowing the past can be tough. Closed Saturday during summer. All major credit cards.

Mama Leone's. 239 W. 48th St.; 586–5151. Known far and wide for the quantity, not quality, of food served in the complete dinners. Though the restaurant is large, the waiting line is usually larger, so make a reservation. The food isn't anything like it was when the original mama started cooking there in 1906. But strolling entertainers make up for the cafeteria-cum-trattoria style. All major credit cards.

Inexpensive

McSorley's Old Ale House. 15 E. Seventh St. near Third Ave.; 473–8800. One of New York's oldest landmarks, a drinking and dining institution for over 125 years. These last few years women have be permitted to enter. No credit cards.

OTHER BOROUGHS

BRONX

Expensive

Thwaite's Inn. 536 City Island Ave.; 885–1023. This old eatery dates from the Gilded Age, and is doing a roaring trade nowadays since New Yorkers are once again getting curious, then proud about the diverse neighborhoods that make up their city. In this case, City Island, jutting into Long Island Sound from the extreme northeast Bronx, is being rediscovered as a tiny, relaxed fishing "village." Thwaite's helps its own cause by turning out superb dinners, with lobster the logical and palate-pleasing specialty on this island that is a little bit of Cape Cod in the Bronx. All major credit cards.

Lobster Box. 34 City Island Ave.; 885–1952. A little "inland" from Thwaite's, this is also a focal point for City Island day-trippers. After all, who else but Lobster Box is going to offer a choice between fifteen or more preparations of lobster or shrimp? The baking is their own. If you can find a table on the terrace, a view of Long Island Sound is yours along with a scrumptious meal, although the nearby honky-tonk atmosphere of fast-food restaurants, custard stands, and an arcade gives the area a bit of Coney Island atmosphere. All major credit cards.

Anna's Harbor Restaurant. 565 City Island Ave.; 885–1373. A large restaurant, with Italian seafood specialties such as lobster fra diavolo (hot and spicy). AE, MC, V.

Between Thwaite's, near the beginning of City Island, and the Lobster Box, virtually at the farthest tip, are several seafood restaurants of slightly lesser quality—and slightly less expensive. These include the **Sea Shore** (885–0300) and the **Crab Shanty** (885–1810), both on the same main street from end-to-end of the island. All major credit cards.

Moderate

Amerigo's. 3587 E. Tremont Ave.; 824–7766. Began life as a pizzeria nearly half a century ago, now boasts two dining areas—one decorated in a Roman motif, the other with a back wall that becomes a waterfall. But it is the sauce, soups, pastas, and veal that make it Amerigo the beautiful—and one of the best in the North Bronx. All major credit cards.

Il Boschetto. 1660 E. Gun Hill Rd.; 379–9335. Unpretentious, small white building just off the New England Thruway—but as close to haute cuisine, Neapolitan-style, as you can get in the Bronx—especially the fish and veal dishes. Favorite of Bronx politicians noshing pasta. All major credit cards.

Mario's. 2342 Arthur Ave.; 584–1188. First-rate, unpretentious and adventurous Neapolitan cookery served up by the Migliucci family since 1919 in a style that has become famous throughout the Little Italy section of the Bronx and beyond. A favorite of *Times* gourmet writer Craig Claiborne. Octopus salad, *spiedini* (deep-fried mozzarella appetizers), striped bass, and beef and veal scaloppine among best dishes. Pizza may be the best in town, right up there with John's of Bleecker St. Ornate Bronx Renaissance decor. All major credit cards. Valet parking.

Within roughly 100 yards of Mario's, in the famed Arthur Ave. Italian shopping district, are three of the area's best Neapolitan restaurants—**Dom's** (no reservations, noisy, really little more than a bar but with a veal Française dish and a spaghetti and shrimp concoction that has regulars lining up from all over the city), the **Full Moon** (scungilli, calamari, pastas in what looks like a fast-food pizzeria), and **Ann and Tony's,** a family-style trattoria. No credit cards at any of these three restaurants—but good eating. And all within easy walking distance of the Bronx Zoo.

Stella d'Oro. 5806 Broadway near 238th St.; 548–2245. Family dinners Italian-style, with spaghetti à la Stella d'Oro the masterpiece, are graced with homemade pastas. The aromas from their nearby bakery may entice you to try some of their well-known egg biscuits. The restaurant is very near Van Cortlandt Park, so a visit to the area could also include a mansion tour, a Gaelic Football match, or some horseback riding. All major credit cards.

BROOKLYN

Super Deluxe

Peter Luger. 178 Broadway, near Bedford Ave.; 387–7400. Many insist Luger, lying in the shadow of the Williamsburg Bridge, convenient to Manhattan and the Brooklyn-Queens Expressway, is the city's most venerable steakhouse. There's no menu, and the waiter recites the day's offerings—but given the neighborhood, you should arrive by car or cab only, and have one called for the ride back. No credit cards except their own house account.

River Café. One Water St.; 522–5200. Astronomically priced American-International cuisine in a glorified barge sitting under the Brooklyn Bridge.

Spectacular waterfront view, less than spectacular food and service. Noisy. AE, DC, V.

Deluxe

Gage and Tollner. 374 Fulton St.; 875–5181. The unhurried pace of Brooklyn, before it surrendered its independence to New York City, is preserved here. The menu changes with the seasons, and you can expect delightful specials that follow nature's calendar. Try the Crab Meat Virginia. The owners have preserved the 1879 landmark building's original decor, too. All major credit cards.

Lisanne. 488 Atlantic Ave.; 237–2271. French classic and *nouvelle cuisine* surprisingly well-prepared in an attractive, skillful restaurant that features a changing menu and extraordinary desserts. Closed Mon. Bring you own wine. AE, MC, V.

Expensive

Ferrybank. One Front St.; 857–3137. Seafood and southern American fare are the specialties at what was, in fact, once the bank by the Brooklyn/Manhattan ferry. Elegantly brassy, with tables on the main floor and an overhanging balcony, Ferrybank was started by disenfranchised waiters from Gage & Tollners, and is giving both G&T and the River Café some needed competition.

Moderate

Bamonte's. 32 Withers St. in Greenpoint section; 384–8831. In business over 80 years, so whither thou goest, this is one of the city's best Italian neighborhood restaurants. MC, V.

Bay Ridge Seafood Center. 8618 Fourth Ave.; 748–2070. Where the men and women who work at the Fulton St. Fish Market go for seafood. Need more endorsement? Just be prepared for a wait despite the restaurant's size. All major credit cards.

Charlie's. 348 Flatbush Ave.; 857–4585. Victorian charm and simple American-Continental food. A favorite for Sunday brunch. All major credit cards.

Della Rocco's Pier 69. 18 Bay Ridge Ave.; 745–9384. In business since 1894, so despite a mixed-bag decor, they must be doing something right—especially with the veal dishes, and the delicious fresh fish. All major credit cards.

Henry's End. 44 Henry St.; 834–1776. Popular Brooklyn Heights spot with solidly prepared Continental dishes as well as better-than-usual hamburgers and salads, and excellent desserts. All major credit cards.

Gargiulo's. 2911 W. 15th St.; 266–0906. A wide, spacious setting for some of the city's best Neapolitan cooking—it is a favorite of *Times* food critic Mimi Sheraton—in which pasta in the noodle category is homemade. Ravioli and fettucine dishes are classics, veal is good. Italian politicians love it as much as votes. Great atmosphere for kids, too. All major credit cards.

La Villa Storica. 225 9th St.; 788–5883. Restored 1840s Victorian mansion converted into an intimate restaurant, with five dining rooms and Corsican cuisine. Once seated, the table is yours for the night to savor a six-course prix fixe dinner, ($14–$17). All major credit cards.

Raintree. Prospect Park W. at 9th St.; 768–3723. A bit of SoHo comes to Park Slope by way of the restoration of a one-time soda fountain—the marble fountain counter has been converted to a bar—into a casually elegant Continental eatery. Piano music weekend evenings. AE.

Inexpensive

Junior's. Flatbush & Dekalb Aves.; 852–5257. Best-noted for its prize-winning cheesecake, Junior's is a wonderfully gaudy orange-and-white deli, serving overstuffed sandwiches, charcoal broiled hamburgers, and dozens of desserts. AE.

Brooklyn's Atlantic Ave. and Court St. (the two cross each other) have a big concentration of Middle Eastern restaurants, most owned by the Almontaser family and its various offshoots. Among the best, all serving essentially similar menus heavy on lamb and curry dishes, are: **Almontaser,** 218 Court St., 624–9267; **Adnan,** 129 Atlantic Ave., 625–8697; **Near East,** 136 Court St., 522–4188; and, a mite more expensive than the others, **Sinbad,** 172 Atlantic Ave., 624–9105, where there is live belly dancing Friday and Saturday nights.

QUEENS

Moderate

Cognoscenti consider it a toss between **Caesar's** (97–12 63rd Rd., 459–2828, major credit cards) and **La Stella** (102–11 Queens Blvd., 459–9511, closed Monday, AE, DC) as to which is the borough's best Italian restaurant. Flip a coin, but don't rule out **Manducati's** (13–27 Jackson Ave., 729–4602, no credit cards), a Long Island City neighborhood restaurant that is as good as most Neapolitan trattorias—and reason enough to consider making a culinary pilgrimage to Queens.

Jahn's. 17–03. Hillside Ave.; 847–2800. In the residential Richmond Hill area not far from Kennedy Airport or Forest Hills tennis, this beloved landmark is famous for old-fashioned ice-cream desserts. Every sweet tooth in Queens is enthralled by it, and you get a free ice cream soda on your birthday, no matter what your age. No credit cards.

Steinway Brauhall. 28–26 Steinway Ave.; 728–9780. Hearty German food served up off Northern Blvd., near the Steinway piano factory. Closed Monday. V, MC.

STATEN ISLAND

Inexpensive

Jade Island. 2845 Richmond Ave.; 761–8080. Don't let the shopping-center location fool you: the food's excellent and invitingly served. There's a smorgasbord Monday and Tuesday, but the main efforts go into the Polynesian and Chinese items. After other mall stores close, parking should be a breeze. All major credit cards.

DESSERTS. Perhaps inevitably, the best ice cream sundaes in New York are the biggest nuisance to obtain, and the prices are equal to those for a meal. Nonetheless, who can resist when the craving strikes? **Dave's Luncheonette** at Canal St. and Broadway downtown is an oversize coffee shop known near and wide for the best egg creams in the world. An egg cream, you ask? Nothing more than flavored syrup, milk, and seltzer, but legend has it Dave's knows the secret of the spoon. Very reasonable (a favorite among eat-on-the-run cabbies), very good and pretty much out-of-the-way.

Among the chain operations, there are a number of **Howard Johnson's** scattered throughout the city (three in Times Square) but we'd be less than candid if we didn't mention that they've been completely eclipsed by the burgeoning **Baskin/Robbins, Haagan Dazs, Seduttos,** and **Bassetts** specialty shops, while the California **Swenson's** chain has an outlet on 65th and Second Ave. (expensive, and the service is deplorable). It's getting so you can't go around the corner in New York without tripping over one or more of these ice-cream supermarkets, and the choice of flavors is mind-boggling.

Agora. 87th St. and 3rd Ave.; 369–6983 is an old-fashioned ice cream parlor in elaborately Art Deco setting that is attached to a clothing boutique. Sundaes and ice cream sodas are especially good, served with mounds of real whipped cream. The "Flat Iron Building" is a specialty—pound cake, chocolate ice cream, hot fudge, and whipped cream prepared in the shape of its namesake. Other food is available, but why bother? All major credit cards except CB.

Macy's. 34th St. and Seventh Ave.; 695–4400. Yes, the world's largest department store happens to have one of the best ice-cream parlors in the city on the fifth floor. Beautiful green-and-white patio setting and great sodas. AE.

Rumpelmayer's. 50 Central Park South in the St. Moritz; 755–5800. More of a tradition than a good ice-cream parlor, the stuffed animals and bright setting are always pleasing for kids. All major credit cards.

Serendipity. 225 E. 60th St., 838–3531. A celebrity ice-cream-parlor-cum-boutique, where you're likely to encounter Barbra Streisand or Cher slurping and splurging. Expensive even by New York standards (a banana split for $5.00!), but most preparations are enough for two or three.

In the boroughs, look for **Jahn's** various branches in Brooklyn and Queens; **Once Upon a Sundae,** 7702 Third Ave., 680–6532 (with original 1890s set-up) in Brooklyn; and **Hoft's,** 3200 White Plains Road, 654–5291, in the Bronx.

Moving briskly from ice cream to pastry, first and foremost is **Ferrara's,** the bastion of Italian sweets nestled at 195 Grand Street (226–6150) in the middle of "Little Italy." All sorts of specialties are available (most served with piping-hot cups of espresso or cappucino), and there are some nifty items to take away with you. The line for tables is long on weekends, but the setting is uniquely festive. Also strikingly attractive with brick and glass walls, marble counter and enclosed garden, and with outstanding cheesecake, is **Café Biondo,** 141 Mulberry St., 226–9285, around the corner from Ferrara's.

Another, more imaginative, way to enjoy great desserts in a civilized manner is to go to some of the best restaurants— **Four Seasons,** for example—later in the evening, such as after a concert or the theater, and tell the maître d'hôtel that you want only dessert. This particular restaurant even encourages dessert-only patrons. At others, if business is tapering off, they'll be happy to oblige. **Slotnick's Daughter,** 153 E. 53rd St. in the Market at Citicorp Center; (935–1744) offers the opportunity for people-watching while sipping a variety of imported coffees, ice-cream drinks, or sampling pastries and sandwiches. **Eclair,** 141 W. 72nd St. (873–7700) is part restaurant, but the real lure is the outstanding Austrian pastries. Similarly, **Cakemasters** at Third Ave. and 65th and at 122 W. 72nd St. is a bakery-cum-café. Up by Columbia University (diagonally across from the Cathedral of St. John the Divine) is the **Hungarian Pastry Shop,** 1030 Amsterdam Ave. (866–4230), with excellent pastries and breads at prices catering to the predominantly student clientele.

 COFFEEHOUSES (CAFÉS). One of the pleasures of touring the Village is to stop into one of the numerous Italian-style coffeehouses for a cup of just about any sort of coffee or tea—in cooler weather—or some Italian ices in the summer. In the Continental tradition, these are places where you can sit . . . and sit . . . and sit. There are almost always tables outside on the sidewalk in even halfway decent weather, or at least the café will open onto the sidewalk. You will probably stumble onto your own favorite, but just in case, here are a few good ones: **Café Reggio,** 119 MacDougal St.; **Le Figaro Café** at the corner of MacDougal and Bleecker Sts. (one of the best known, closed for a while and reopened a few years ago); **Caffé Borgia,** across the street from Le Figaro; **Caffé Dante,** south of Bleecker St. on MacDougal; **Bruno Bakery,** 506 W. Broadway, South of Bleecker, a bit off the main track; **Caffé Lucca,** at 228 Bleecker St. at Sixth Ave.; and **Café Sandolino,** on Barrow St. between W. 4th St. and Seventh Ave. (more of a student/seedy poet place, with light food, no outside tables). **Pane e Cioccolato,** Waverly Place at Mercer St., is a hangout for New York University students (the university is all around it). The **Cornelia Street Café,** on Cornelia between Bleecker and W. Fourth St., is on a relatively quiet side street and so may be even more relaxing than these others.

Cafe de la Paix (—a bar in the St. Moritz Hotel at Sixth Ave. and Central Park South—59th St.) is probably the nicest midtown people-viewing spot, though you may get tired of looking at the double-parked limousines.

On the Upper East Side, on Fifth Ave. and 81st St. across from the Metropolitan Museum, there is the **Terrace Café** (actually a restaurant/bar) in the American Stanhope Hotel—fun when the museum is open, not so much fun when it isn't.

NIGHT LIFE. When a Broadway baby says good night, it's usually early in the morning, as the song says. And there are plenty of ways to make it through the night in New York City, with bars and lounges permitted to stay open and serve liquor until 4:00 A.M. every night except Saturday (in reality Sunday morning), when closing time is 3:00 A.M. Increasingly, too, the big-name discos stay open considerably past that hour—consider that many don't even open until 11:00 P.M. or midnight—and during the last year there has been a revival of semi-legal after-hours clubs. The latter either require an actual membership fee that can be used repeatedly, or *call* their fee at the door a membership fee, thus attempting to convince the authorities that they are private clubs (for which there are no restrictions on how late they can serve). The after-hours places actually do sometimes advertise discreetly in the *Village Voice*, catering to a young, high-paying, jet-setting crowd. And then there are the night-life happenings you just come upon, such as recently at an unlikely spot, "Rose," a Thai restaurant-cafe near 77th St. on First Ave., where four young professionals were doing a concert version of *Oklahoma!*

But most New York night life is of a more traditional nature, even if the styles and venues have changed and the hours have gotten later. The classy old hotel nightclubs are gone—the Persian Room at the Plaza, the Empire Room at the Waldorf, the Maisonette at the St. Regis—as are the big, flashy comics-and-kickline places such as the Latin Quarter and the Copacabana (though the Copa has been reincarnated as a disco). The accent today is on discos, hip cabarets, trendy rock and roll clubs, and country-in-the-city real or fake honky-tonks. And while you can still find quality entertainment at a handful of hotels and other fashionably appointed addresses, most of New York's night life seems to be housed in converted theaters and moviehouses, spruced up Art Deco ballrooms, one-time warehouses—even a former men's clothing store in the heart of Times Square that has a dance floor big enough to hold more than 2,000 people comfortably!

The rules as far as dress (and everything else—but we'll get to the rest in a moment) are concerned are probably what you'd expect—jackets and ties for men at the more traditionally-minded establishments, glitter and everything you've got at the big name discos, and casual-but-neat just about everywhere else. Admissions, cover charges and/or minimums, and show times very from place to place, and sometimes from night to night at a given club depending on whether or not there is a live performer and on who that performer is. Call to check, and to find out what the policy is for reservations; some places will accept phone reservations, for others you may have to purchase tickets ahead. Such uncertainty is typical of the current night-life scene, where the in spot one moment is closed the next; where the hot spot to see and be seen one night is forgotten by morning. Many clubs have a bar from which you can watch or at least hear the act without paying a cover or minimum; check.

Some places stand out as the ones to go to if you have only a few nights on the town. We'll single them out first and then provide a longer but still *selective* list broken down into various categories—jazz, pop/rock, cabaret, disco/dancing, country, floor shows, hotel rooms and piano bars, comedy/magic. Once in town, consult the *New Yorker* for comprehensive capsule listings of who's appearing where, and the *Village Voice* for the most complete advertising section devoted to night life. While the outlying boroughs have their share of popular bars and entertainment, all the serious night-life spots are centered in Manhattan; even for Brooklynites, a big night out involves a trip into "The City."

Key to credit card information following each listing:

AE = American Express
CB = Carte Blanche
DC = Diners Club
MC =MasterCard
V = Visa

CREME DE LA CREME

Bottom Line. 15 W. 4th St.; 228–7880. An intimate 400-seat club where rock-and roll bands, jazz ensembles, folk and bluegrass musicians are the norm —but were classical flutist Jean Pierre Rampal, modern dancer Laura Dean, and avant-garde composer/pianist Phillip Glass are also to be found. As New York's foremost showcase club, the Bottom Line numbers among its past finds the likes of Bruce Springsteen, Ashford & Simpson, Meatloaf, and numerous others who've gone on to international fame. These days "graduates" sometimes return, but the emphasis remains firmly rooted in presenting the best new talent under the most professional circumstances. Salads, hamburgers, and pizza are available. Tickets generally range between $6.50 and $10.00, depending on the act, with shows at 8:30 P.M and 11:30 P.M. weekdays, 9 P.M. and midnight Fridays and Saturdays. No credit cards.

Café Carlyle. At the Carlyle Hotel, Madison Ave. and 76th St.; 744–1600. Bobby Short, considered the piano man's piano man for his mastery of the Broadway classics, alternates in six-month stretches with the jazzier Marion McPartland—and either way you are transported to a quieter, more humane world. All major credit cards. Food available.

Greene Street. 101 Greene St.; 925–2415. Greene Street will give you a taste of contemporary SoHo chic—a restaurant and cabaret two stories high, giving a rare New York feel for spaciousness. Its soaring walls, 10 skylights, fieldstone bar, tropical trees, pink and green mural, and tiered dining tables are a perfect setting for just about any kind of music—and the entertainment policy indeed runs from jazz to a cappella oldies groups. AE, MC, V.

Hors d'Oeuverie. 1 World Trade Center; 938–1111. More intimate for dancing than the Rainbow Room, and with an even more breath-taking view, the Hors d'Oeuverie features a light jazz trio that alternates with a solo pianist beginning at 7:30 P.M. You *can* be entertained cheaply here—the cover charge is a mere $2.50, and you can limit yourself to one drink ($3.00 to 4.00), but the temptation is to partake of the hors d'oeuvres, for which you are charged by the small plateful. Also, on weekends and during holiday seasons, get there early or you'll be subject to a long wait just to get into the elevator—a 107-story climb. All major credit cards.

King Cole Room. At the St. Regis Sheraton, Fifth Ave. and 55th St.; 753–4500. The only remaining old-style hotel-room nightclub with name entertainment in the city, the King Cole Room offers revues of Broadway showtunes by the likes of Rodgers and Hart, Gershwin and Porter, sung by performers of the caliber of Mimi Hines and Larry Kert. Consistently high-caliber, small-scale productions in a smartly gracious setting. All major credit cards. Food available.

Rainbow Room. 30 Rockefeller Plaza; 757–9090. Dance atop the RCA Building to name big bands under the direction of Bobby Rosengarden or Panama Francis, among others. The Art Deco splendor drips chandeliers and plush red walls and floors—and a spectacular 65th-floor view of the New York skyline. The food has slipped, although the kitchen still comes up with respectable American-International fare. (Entertainment at the **Rainbow Grill** across the hall has sunk to imitiation Vegas-Parisian revues with some nudity.) All major credit cards.

Studio 54. 254 W. 54th St.; 489–7667. Certainly New York's—and possibly the world's—most notorious disco. Housed in a former television studio and the subject of many headlines (about its original owner's skimming of cash from the nightly receipts) and even more rumors. Steve Rubell, the man who made most of the headlines, was also the one responsible for creating the atmosphere inside. Yet despite the abusive manner in which clientele were (and are) selected from among those lined up on the street to get in, Rubell was a master at making sure the mix inside the club had just the right balance—genuine characters, Wall Streeters, media stars, tourists, and partyers. Though Rubell and his partner are no longer the actual owners (following conviction on charges of tax evasion), the club has reopened and life at the disco just as it always was. Admission can range from $6.00 to $25.00 (and up for benefits), and drinks are about $3 and up. No credit cards.

For jazz aficionados it's more difficult to pinpoint one outstanding place. Details will follow in the listings, but consider **Eddie Condon's** or **Jimmy Ryan's** for Dixieland and mainstream sounds uptown on W. 54th St., or the **Village Vanguard, Sweet Basil,** or **Seventh Ave. South** for all styles in Greenwich Village. The **Blue Note** has reopened, on W. 3rd St.

Here then is a broader but still selective look at some of the better night spots in the Big Apple, broken down by category. "Inexpensive" refers to places where the cover and/or minimum total less than $5.00; elsewhere, figure on $10.00 *or more* per person.

JAZZ

At jazz clubs in particular you can often sit at the bar and still have a full view of the stage; this can be a big saving when there are cover and/or minimum charges at the tables.

Angry Squire. 216 Seventh Ave. near 23rd St.; 242–9066. Pleasant nautical setting with small intimate booths. Duos and trios with a modern edge. Music weekends only. Food. Inexpensive. No credit cards.

Blue Note. 131 W. 3rd St.; 475–8592. Same name, new club, with lots of mirrors and slatted wood and a stage accommodating trios and quartets most comfortably. Three shows nightly by quality acts even if the name value isn't always great, with dinner served from 7 P.M. to 2 A.M. Admission varies; around $6. All major credit cards.

Bradleys. 70 University Pl.; 228–6440. Smoky and always crowded, it's the typical jazz bar, with the emphasis on reflective piano-bass combinations. Inexpensive. All major credit cards.

Cookery. 21 University Pl.; 674–4450. Loud and boisterous, the restaurant seems an excuse to bring back oldtimers such as Alberta Hunter. AE, V, MC.

Crawdaddy. Vanderbilt and 45th St.; 687–1860. Music to go along with the New Orleans decor and food, with name artists always in residence. All major credit cards.

Eddie Condon's. 144 W. 54th St.; 265–8277. Small-band jazz with a '40s ambience and decent food—part of the latter-day "swing street" (transplanted from the 52nd St. of old). AE, DC, MC.

Fat Tuesday's. 190 Third Ave. at 17th St.; 533–7902. Popular singles hangout (especially the bar and the street-level restaurant) with mainstream and contemporary artists downstairs. Dining. Closed Mon. AE, MC, V.

Ginger Man. 51 W. 64th St.; 399–2358. Harlem-oriented rhythm-and-blues across the way from Lincoln Center. All major credit cards.

Gregory's. 1149 Third Ave. at 67th St.; 371–2220. Low-key jazz as background to friendly conversation. Stride piano Sundays from 5. Inexpensive. All major credit cards.

Griff's Plaza Café. Third Ave. at 37th St.; 867–7179. Continuous sets from 8 P.M. Tuesdays through Fridays, from 9 P.M. Saturdays, with mostly old-time mainstreamers on hand. No admission fee. All major credit cards.

Hanratty's. 1754 Second Ave. at 91st St.; 289–3200. Stride, bebop, and singers of surprisingly good quality (including the occasional familiar name). The sister club of the same name on the Upper West Side sometimes also has music. Inexpensive. AE.

Jazz Forum. 648 Broadway near Bleecker St.; 477–2655. Loft popular among moderately "outside" players. Inexpensive. No credit cards.

Jazzmania. 40 W. 27th St.; 532–7666. Jam sessions with name participants are the constant order with top-dancing jazz brunches a frequent novelty. No credit cards.

Jimmy Ryan's. 154 W. 54th St.; 664–9700. Dixie, swing, and bebop on the street popular for same. Inexpensive. AE.

Jimmy Weston's. 131 E. 54th St.; 838–8384. The restaurant is a popular hangout for sports celebrities, the bandstand in the far corner given over primarily to piano mainstream trios. All major credit cards.

Knickerbocker Saloon. 33 University Pl.; 228–8490. The spirit of old Charlie Knickerbocker lives in atmospheric dining room where jazz wafts in from the bar. Noisy but comfortable with simple American fare. AE, MC, V.

Lush Life. Corner Bleecker and Thompson Sts.; 228–3788. *The* hot new jazz room, with the emphasis on modern sounds and well-known musicians placed in unusual combinations—Cecil Taylor with a big band, jazz brunches, etc. All in a comfortably packed setting with Italian/Continental fare available.

Marty's. 1265 Third Ave. near 73rd St.; 240–4100. Mel Tormé is a regular at this stylish supper club, and that should say it all. Food. Expensive. All major credit cards.

Michael's Pub. 211 E. 55th St. at Third Ave.; 758–2272. Atmospheric olde English roome with solid mainstream jazz and occasional jazz-based revues. Continental food. Expensive. All major credit cards.

Mikell's. 760 Columbus Ave. at 97th St.; 864–8832. Neighborhood supper club featuring pop-oriented rhythm-and-bluesers. All major credit cards.

Other End. 149 Bleecker St. in the Village; 673–7030. Rock usually, but appearances by the likes of Stephane Grappelli and others with some frequency. No credit cards.

Peacock Alley. Waldorf-Astoria, Park Ave. at 50th St.; 355–3000. A cozy piano (and sometimes duo/trio) hideaway where the music plays from 6:00 P.M. to 2:00 A.M. All major credit cards.

Red Blazer, Too. 1576 Third Ave. at 89th St.; 876–0440. Some say the big-band revival such as it is emanated from here thanks to regular weekday stands featuring a variety of local ensembles. It may be true. Large and always busy with a slightly touristy flavor, and Dixieland on weekends. AE.

Saratoga. 995 Fifth Ave. (in Stanhope Hotel); 744–8714. Flutist Herbie Mann and his Family of Mann are in residence in this classically stylish supper club whenever they're not on the road (about six months of the year). Sets at 10 and 11:30 P.M., with a $10.00 music charge. Dinner and late night supper until 1 A.M. All major credit cards.

Seventh Ave. South. 21 Seventh Ave. S., above Houston St. in the Village; 242–4694. Easy-going upstairs room (no cover at the bar downstairs) owned by the sax- and trumpet-playing Brecker Brothers, and popular among their pop-funk-jazz friends. V.

Star & Garter. 105 W. 13th St.; 242–3166. Light, airy room that's intimate and friendly. Mostly mainstream combos accompany moderately priced Continental meals. AE.

Storytowne. 41 E. 58th St.; 755–1640. Not quite Bourbon St., but big and brassy in the Dixieland fashion. All major credit cards.

Sweet Basil. 88 Seventh Ave. S. just south of Christopher St. in the Village; 242–1785. Knotty pine walls adorned with jazz memorabilia and a wide range of mainstream and contemporary musicians make this one of the most consistently pleasing establishments around. Sunday brunches feature trumpeter Doc Cheatham. All major credit cards.

Village Gate. 160 Bleecker St. in the Village; 475–5120. Once a mainstay on the jazz circuit, the concerts are only intermittent these days, but always featuring name players. MC, V, AE.

Village Vanguard. 178 Seventh Ave. S. in the Village; 255–4037. The prototype jazz club—downstairs, smoky, with lousy sound system and cramped quarters. And everyone loves it just as it has been for 40 years. Proprietor Max Gordon can usually be spied napping at a center table. No credit cards.

West Boondock. 114 Tenth Ave. at 17th St.; 929–9645. Out of the way—take a cab to get here—but a staple for soulful music and inexpensive soul food. The music's free and always high quality even though the names are rarely known. All major credit cards.

West End. 2911 Broadway at 111th St.; 666–8750. If you first discovered jazz while in college, you'll feel perfectly at home at this haunt frequented by Columbia and Barnard University students. Inexpensive.

West Village Club. 577 Hudson St.; 255–2788. Contemporary feel, brick walls, fireplace, very friendly Village crowd. Duos and trios, mostly contemporary and mainstream. Food. Moderate. All major credit cards.

Zinno. 126 W. 13th St.; 924–5182. Restaurant with light mainstream entertainment to accompany the menu. AE.

POP/ROCK

Bottom Line. See *Crème de la Crème*.

CBGB & OMFUG. 315 Bowery near 3rd St.; 982–4052. New York punkers and new wavers from Blondie to Talking Heads to whoever-the-rage-is-today all served their apprenticeship here. Loud, long, and narrow—and the going can get a mite tough. Always call for set times—but don't necessarily believe what they say. No credit cards.

Danceteria. 30 W. 21st St.; 620–0790. A rock-and-roll club with a history of different locations and perpetual conflict among its owners. The bands tend to be the loudest and newest, and the club personnel treat customers like lepers. Interesting layout, though, with three floors: first for live bands and dancing, second for dancing to recorded selections, third for dining, drinking, and watching experimental videos. $6.00–$7.00 during the week, $8.00–$10.00 on weekends. No credit cards.

Eagle Tavern. 355 W. 14th St.; 924–0275. Bluegrass, old-timey string band and folk music brewed here Wednesdays and weekends. Very inexpensive. No credit cards.

Folk City. 130 W. 3rd St.; 254–8449. Once the spawning ground for the folk-protest movement of the '60s, the glory days are clearly over—though some of the old-timers occasionally return for old time's sake. Inexpensive. No credit cards.

Great Gildersleeves. 331 Bowery at 3rd St.; 533–3940. New, hard-rocking outfits come in for one night at a time, playing in a tacky, cavernous environment. Inexpensive. No credit cards.

Home. 1748 Second Ave. at 91st St.; 876–0744. A neighborhood bar where the back room is given over to studio musicians and other pros who are working out new, mostly rock-oriented acts. MC, V.

J.P.'s. 1471 First Ave. at 76th St.; 288–1022. Popular record-business hangout with a handful of performers appearing on a rotating basis—and with major name concert acts dropping in after their shows to jam. All major credit cards.

Kenny's Castaways. 157 Bleecker St. in the Village; 473–9870. Folk-based rockers and old-time blues shouters are the mainstay with owner Pat Kenny's ever-jovial presence the place's biggest asset. No credit cards.

Mudd Club. 77 White St. in TriBeCa; 227–7777. A hard-rocking disco with live bands, but nothing gets going until 1:00 A.M. at the earliest. Then again, the audience is really the show. No credit cards, and they're selective about whom they admit—lest the crowd get "too straight."

Other End. 149 Bleecker St., in the Village; 673–7030. Formerly the Bitter End, and home to many a '60s folk singer, at least some of whom continue to return to the brick-walled, cozy club. Also still noted for its share of "discoveries"—most recently Steve Forbert. No credit cards.

Peppermint Lounge. 100 Fifth Ave., just north of the Village; 989–9505. For the young and adventuresome, the new "Pep" is three floors of the latest in new wave rock, many of the bands coming from England. Downstairs there's a post-punk cabaret; the main floor is for the headlining groups and dancing; and the upper balcony is for watching rock videos or observing the dance floor. Courtesy and friendliness are not part of the game here, so be prepared for hostility at the entrance and people stepping on your toes inside. No credit cards.

Ritz. 119 E. 11th St.; 254–2800. A 1935 ballroom (in an 1889 building) restored to its original Art Deco glamour and, as of this writing, the most popular rock club in town. Video (on a 30' x 30' screen) and dance music before and after shows—the latter featuring everything from rockabilly to jazz, new wave to reggae. Downstairs is all dance floor (only a few banquettes along the walls provide seating), and the balcony is usually reserved for visiting VIPs, so be prepared to stand. No credit cards.

Speakeasy. 107 MacDougal St.; 598–9670. A folk music club run cooperatively by the local community of folk musicians, ranging from "names" such as Dave Van Ronk to a host of newcomers. Informal, inexpensive (usually $1.00–$3.00), and high calibre performers. No credit cards.

Tramps. 125 E. 15th St.; 777–5077. The one spot in the city regularly featuring traditional blues artists such as Otis Rush and Big Joe Turner. No credit cards.

Trax. 100 W. 72nd St.; 799–1448. Same owner as J.P.'s and same description fits. All major credit cards.

CABARET

Applause. 360 Lexington Ave. near 40th St.; 687–7267. Singing waiters and waitresses take their turns on stage. All major credit cards.

The Duplex. 55 Grove St. near Seventh Ave. in the Village; 255–5438. A split-level West Village club popular among latter-day torch singers who try to turn their sets into mini-revues. No credit cards.

Freddy's. 308 E. 49th St.; 888–1633. Christine Jorgensen made a "comeback" here, and that sort of explains the tone of the place. All major credit cards.

Greene St. See *Crème de la Crème* above.

Les Mouches. 260 Eleventh Ave. near 28th St.; 695–5190. Many a Broadway star comes in after the final curtain to try his or her hand at a solo act—and the names have been known to include Chita Rivera, Eartha Kitt, and Jaye P. Morgan among others. Disco dancing too. All major credit cards.

Mickey's. 44 W. 54th St.; 247–2979. Everything from *angst*–ridden singer/songwriters to supper clubby country bands and serious Dixie stompers. No V.

Onstage. 349 W. 46th St.; 581–0222. Mostly singers and small combos for the after-theater crowd. Hopping until 4:00 A.M., with kitchen open until 2:00. All major credit cards.

Once Upon A Stove. 325 Third Ave. near 25th St.; 683–0044. Skits and revues in the upstairs room. All major credit cards.

Palsson's. 158 W. 72nd St.; 362–2590. Attractive second-floor room that seats about 50 people, with some additional space at the bar. Revues used to change every few weeks, but lately there has been only one show, *Forbidden Broadway,* which looks as if it will run forever, updated annually. Reservations a *must.* The kitchen stays open until last call at 4:00 A.M. Cover charge at tables *and* bar. All major credit cards.

Playboy Club. 5 E. 59th St.; 752–3100. Various lounges and show rooms, some with name entertainment, others strictly for conversation and/or dancing. For keyholders only, but keys can be purchased at the door. Plans call for relocating, but not before a suitable replacement site is found. All major credit cards.

S.N.A.F.U. 676 Sixth Ave. near 21st St.; 691–3535. Ever on the lookout for unusual entertainers—from civil servant Quentin Crisp to torch singers and rock bands with a visual and/or comic twist. All major credit cards.

SPQR. 133 Mulberry St. in Little Italy; 431–7610. Attractive upstairs nightclub in one of Little Italy's fancier restaurants, catering to the adult audience with crooners such as Julius LaRosa, Enzo Stuarti, Bobby Vinton. Dance floor, and dancing between sets. All major credit cards.

Sweetwater's. 168 Amsterdam Ave. near 67th St., north of Lincoln Center; 873–4100. Mostly singers—and a pleasant stop-off following Lincoln Center performances. All major credit cards.

FLOOR SHOWS

The days of extravagant Las Vegas and Parisian-style floor shows in New York, once available at the Latin Quarter and Copacabana, are gone. The few that remain are not very good attempts at scaled-down versions of these lavish spectacles, and cater almost exclusively to tourists. For those who insist, we list them herewith, but given the prices most such establishments charge, we suggest that Broadway's *Sugar Babies* and *42nd Street,* both offering the old-style entertainment, are far better buys for your money.

Bianchi & Margherita. 186 W. 4th St., Village; 242–2756. Not the usual type of floor show at all—instead, you get live opera while you savor your veal piccata. The food's only fair, but the experience is fun. All major credit cards.

Chateau Madrid. 48th St. and Lexington Ave.; 752–8080. Continental and Spanish cuisine in this Hotel Lexington nightspot. Energetic Latin American shows with resident chorines and flamenco dancers. Nightly at 9:30 P.M. and midnight, except Saturday (8:30 and 11:30 P.M., 1:45 A.M.). **Flamenco Suite** offers dancers, singers, and guitarists from 10:30 P.M. Closed Monday. All major credit cards.

Club Ibis. 151 E. 50th St.; 753–3471. Continental restaurant with exotic decor—but you can't eat decor. The 9:30 and 11:30 P.M. shows (Saturday: 8:45 and 11:30 P.M., 1:30 A.M.) help take your mind off the food when the Ibis girls are in good form. Upstairs room features belly dancers, Middle Eastern musicians, etc., from 10:30 P.M. Downstairs it's headliners such as Phyllis Diller and Eartha Kitt. All major credit cards.

El Avram. 80 Grove St. near Sheridan Square in the Village; 243–9961. New York's only long-running Kosher nightclub is housed in a Spanish-designed room that offers belly dancers, singers, comedians, and dancing. Except for the mixing of national influences (Israeli, Spanish, Italian, and Greek) this is the stereotypical nightclub you'd expect to find anywhere but in New York. No DC.

Ipanema. 240 W. 52nd St.; 765–8025. Brazilian nightclub that tries none too successfully to transform Manhattan into Rio. Jazz on Wednesday, disco other nights. Closed Tuesday. All major credit cards.

La Chansonette. 890 Second Ave. near 48th St.; 753–7320. Singer Rita Dimitri re-creates the world of Piaf, Brel, and Aznavour to the accompaniment of guitarist/husband/real-estate person Stanley Brilliant. Pleasant French restaurant features trio for dancing Tuesday-Saturday, and Russian gypsy music Monday. All major credit cards.

Riverboat. 350 Fifth Ave. (Empire State Bldg.); 736–6210. Dance bands and American cuisine, with an "all you can drink" package including steak, dancing and show (such as it is) for about $25.00. Closed Monday. All major credit cards.

Sirocco. 29 E. 29th St.; 683–9409. Israeli songs, belly dancers, bouzoukis, and revues with Middle Eastern food to match. Shows at 10:00 P.M. and 1:00 A.M. except Monday. AE, CB, DC.

DISCO/DANCING

Adam's Apple. 1117 First Ave. near 61st St.; 371–8650. Two floors for dining and dancing. American cuisine, bar, lounge, sidewalk café, open seven days till 4:00 A.M. All major credit cards.

Bond's. 1526 Broadway, Times Square; 944–5880. Disco dancing in what was once a men's clothing store. Multi-tiered, and usually featuring locally popular black disco artists. No credit cards.

Cachaca. 403 E. 62nd St.; 688–8501. Jazz sambas of Brazil alternate with recorded Brazilian and American disco music between sets featuring authentic Brazilian pop music with singer and trio. A supper club that really goes for south-of-the-border atmosphere. Disco swings into high gear after 11:00, open nightly except Monday from 8:00 P.M. to 4:00 A.M. AE, CB, DC.

Copacabana. 10 E. 60th St; 755–6010. Minus chorus girls but retaining some of its old glamour. The Copa is making a comeback at its original site, with upstairs cabaret shows and disco downstairs from 10:00 to 4:00. Closed Tues. All major credit cards.

La Folie. 21 E. 61st St.; 765–1400. Small, elegant French restaurant with disco from 10:30 on ($5.00), or have dinner (four courses for around $40.00) and have disco charge waived. Closed Sunday. All major credit cards.

Le Cocu Discotheque Francaise. 152 E. 55th St.; 371–1559. Light show to turn on to reflected off stainless-steel dance floor from 10:00 to 4:00 nightly except Monday. MC, V.

Les Mouches. See *Cabarets*.

Onde's. 160 E. 48th St.; 752–0200. Split-level supper club with good international food and a solid trio playing for listening/dancing from 8:00 nightly except Sunday. A pianist performs in the lounge. All major credit cards.

Rainbow Room and Grill. See *Crème de la Crème*.

Régine's. 502 Park Ave. at 59th St.; 826–0990. Mirrors reflect subdued lighting in this playpen for beautiful people with a good (if overpriced) restaurant open Monday/Saturday 8:00 to midnight. Disco action from 10:30 P.M. to 4:00 A.M. Closed Sunday. All major credit cards.

Roma di Notte. 137 E. 55th St.; 832–1128. Dine on Italian food in a private cave, dance to music of toga-clad musicians on marble floor from 7:30 to 1:30. Closed Sunday. All major credit cards.

Roseland. 239 W. 52nd St.; 247–0200. New York's largest dance hall features two live orchestras for continuous dancing nightly Wednesday to Sunday, with matinees Thursday/Saturday/Sunday and disco nightly from midnight Wednesday to Saturday. Has 700-seat restaurant-bar, featuring American cuisine. Admission varies from $5.00 to $7.00. AE, V, MC.

37th St. Hideaway. 32 W. 37th St.; 947–8940. Dining-dancing from 7:30 in actor John Drew's former townhouse, with performers usually including singer, trio. All major credit cards.

Underground. 860 Broadway, at 17th St.; 254–4005. A dramatically striking environment on two levels, with brick walls, mirrors, neon lightning bolts, and spectacular bowls of live flowers. The crowd, alas, tends to haughty and pretentious, and the guards at the door tend to behave with all the finesse of bulldogs. Sundays are usually for homosexual audiences. $5.00 to $15.00, depending on the "event" taking place. No credit cards.

Wednesdays. 210 E. 86th St.; 535–8500. Disco/bar/restaurant complex that resembles underground European street festival in the form of a block-long underground village with sidewalk cafés, bistros, wine-and-cheese shops, gaslights, trees, huge drinks, American food and all kinds of night-life entertainment. Closed Monday. Cover charge from $4.00 to $6.00 depending on night. All major credit cards.

Xenon. 125 W. 43rd St.; 221–2690. The "innest" of the "in" discos as of this writing, though Studio 54 is at least as much of a headline maker. Yes, you are likely to spy Mick Jagger or Tennessee Williams or Diana Ross or Cher on the dance floor, picking up the beat from a $100,000 sound system with bizarre lighting effects to match. They're catty at the door—that's part of the mystique —and if you happen to arrive for one of the club's frequent special "theme party" nights the admission will zoom from the regular $12.00 to $25.00 or more. Drinks start at $4.00. No credit cards.

COUNTRY

City Limits. 125 Seventh Ave. S. at 10th St.; 243–2242. An enormously friendly place to party western-style to live bands. Just make sure you have your dancing boots on and save room for some chili. The action begins at 10:00 P.M. nightly, and be forewarned: This is a big place but *very* popular. No credit cards.

Cody's. 16th St. and Sixth Ave.; 620–0377. Modern two-tiered singles bar (plus food) with strong country influence via live bands from 9:30 on. No credit cards.

Lone Star Café. 61 Fifth Ave. at 13th St.; 242–1664. The official Texas embassy in New York City, though the bands veer to blues and rock as often as to country. Still, the food and ambience are as close to Southern-fried as two New York owners are ever likely to make it. Great chili, ribs, and salads, too. All major credit cards.

O'Lunney's. 915 Second Ave. at 48th St.; 751–5470. The first New York country bar has the most genuinely Western feel to it—the sort of place where women in beehive hairdos and men in ten-gallon hats feel right at home. Live music that's always good for dancing from 9:00 P.M. nightly—sometimes on two floors. All major credit cards.

Also check **Bottom Line, Other End,** and **Ritz.** All sometimes present name country acts.

COMEDY/MAGIC

Catch A Rising Star. 1487 First Ave. near 78th St.; 794–1906. See young new comedians the same time Johnny Carson's talent scouts do—with big-name graduates frequently dropping in to test new material. Some singers change the pace, with the festivities beginning about 10:00 P.M.and the cream of the crop usually going on between 11 and 1. Always a fun night, no matter how bad the acts get. All major credit cards.

Comic Strip. 1568 Second Ave. near 82nd St.; 862–9386. Essentially same format as Catch—nonstop parade of up-and-comers—and frequently with the same acts shuttling between these clubs and the West Side's Improvisation. The fun begins about 9:30 P.M. No credit cards.

Dangerfield's. 1118 First Ave. near 61st St.; 593–1650. The "Can't get no respect" man does a stint himself several months out of the year, but mostly the stage is given over to promising newcomers—and Dangerfield has demonstrated a good ear for laugh-provoking talent over the years. Showtimes 9:30 and 11:15 P.M. Monday to Friday, 9:00 P.M. and midnight Saturday. Special Sunday showcase at 9:30 P.M. All major credit cards.

Improvisation. 358 W. 44th St.; 765–8268. Before there was Catch or the Comic Strip, the Improv, as it is fondly known, was giving birth to the careers of Richard Pryor, Robert Klein, David Steinberg, and others. They all return to see who the latest finds are as well as to tell their latest stories. Still the most Bohemian of the comedy rooms, and popular for after-theater entertainment and snacking. No credit cards.

Magic Town House. 1026 Third Ave., 61st St.; 752–1165. Matinee performances for children and teenagers, evening buffet shows (bring your own bottle) for drinking age teens and young adults. Reservations a must. No credit cards.

Mostly Magic. 53 Carmine St. in the Village; 924–1472. Magic and comedy are paired with audience participation Saturdays at 3:00 P.M. for children, with periodic special programs for adults. Reservations necessary. No credit cards.

HOTEL ROOMS AND PIANO BARS

Algonquin Oak Room. 59 W. 44th St.; 840–6800. Pianist Steve Ross holds forth, recreating the spirit of the '30s, '40s, and '50s from 9:00 P.M. Wednesday to Saturday and from 5:30 P.M. Sunday. Especially popular for after-theater supper buffet. Reservations suggested. All major credit cards.

American Stanhope. See Saratoga Room, under Jazz.

Beekman Towers. 3 Mitchell Place at 49th St. and First Ave.; 355–7300. Great East River and UN views, and sweepingly gentle piano music to go with them. No cover, no minimum, no hurry. All major credit cards.

Bemelman's Bar. Hotel Carlyle, Madison Ave. at 76th St.; 744–1600. Romantically private, usually featuring Barbara Carroll's equally intimate piano playing. All major credit cards.

Café Carlyle. See *Crème de la Crème.*

Carnegie Tavern. 165 W. 56th St., directly behind Carnegie Hall; 757–9522. Dark-brown walls that have a coppery glow and a glassed-in sidewalk café are especially special when the likes of Ellis Larkin is at the piano. Monday to Saturday, 8:00 P.M. to midnight. All major credit cards.

Conservatory. 15 Central Park W. at 61st St.; 581–0896. Very pleasing, relaxed café/restaurant in the Hotel Mayflower, with harpists nightly from 8:30. Convenient to Lincoln Center and the Coliseum. All major credit cards.

David K's. 1115 Third Ave. at 65th St.; 371–9090. While most people come here for gourmet Chinese food of the first order, some also stop by regularly for pianist Hugh Shannon, who inhabits the lounge Tuesday to Saturday from 9:00 P.M. AE

Downey's. 705 Eighth Ave. at 44th St.; 757–0186. Steakhouse with name pianists in the bar area. All major credit cards.

Front Row. One Times Square at 42nd St. and Broadway; 695–1880. This is the cocktail lounge of the Act I restaurant overlooking the lights of the Great

White Way. Piano music from 7:00 P.M. to midnight. Closed Sunday. All major credit cards.

Grand Hyatt of New York. Park Ave. at 42nd St; 883–1234. Piano music for dining at **Trumpet's** restaurant. All major credit cards.P.M. to 1:00 A.M.

Helmsley Palace. 455 Madison Ave. at 50th St.; 888–1624. Pianists nightly in **Harry's New York Bar** from 6:00 P.M. until midnight. All major credit cards.

Harley. 214 E. 42nd St.; 490–8900. Another **Harry's Bar,** with another pianist performing from 5:30 P.M. to 1:00 A.M.

Hilton Hotel. 53rd St. and Sixth Ave.; 586–7000. Light jazzy fare trios and quartets at **Sybil's,** quieter piano music in the **Kismet Lounge.** All major credit cards.

Le Vert Galant. 109 W. 46th St.; 582–7989. Excellent French restaurant with pianist-singer in the lounge Wednesday to Saturday from 7:30 P.M. All major credit cards.

Monkey Bar. 60 E. 54th St. in the Hotel Élysée; 753–1066. Johnny Andrews has been at the piano here Monday to Saturday from 5:30 to 7:30 P.M. since 1941. Enough said. All major credit cards.

New York Sheraton. 870 Seventh Ave., 55th St.; 247–8000. Dancing from 9:30 P.M. to 1:00 A.M. at **Sally's** turn-of-the-century cabaret, which is sometimes given over to hour-long revues. Pianist in the **Falstaff Room** (No Shakespeare) from 5:00 P.M. to 1:00 A.M. All major credit cards.

Parker-Meridien. 118 W. 57th St.; 245–5000. Piano players nightly at **Le Patio** from 5:30 P.M. until 1:00 A.M.

Piano Bar. Broadway and 68th St.; 787–2501. Pleasant after-Lincoln-Center haunt in spacious, friendly quarters. All major credit cards.

Pierre Hotel. Fifth Ave. at 61st St.; 940–8185. Class acts such as Bucky Pizarelli's trio inhabit the **Café Pierre** for listening, dining, drinking, and dancing from 8:00 P.M. on. All major credit cards.

Plaza Hotel. Fifth Ave. at 59th St.; 759–3000. The Grand Dame of New York hotels has a trio for dancing in the stately **Edwardian Room** Tuesday to Sunday from 6:00 P.M. to 12:30 A.M., and piano and violin in the classic **Palm Court** from 5:30 to 11:30 P.M. All major credit cards.

Polo Bar. Westbury Hotel, Madison Ave. at 69th St.; 535–2000. Quietly elegant piano music Monday to Saturday 5:30 to 11:30 P.M. All major credit cards.

Regency Bar. Regency Hotel, Park Ave. at 61st St.; 759–4100. A bit stuffy, perhaps, but intimate and with international overtones in the repertoire of the alternating pianists. Nightly from 6:00 P.M. All major credit cards.

St. Moritz Hotel. 50 Central Park South; 755–5800. Piano music at both **Café de la Paix** (Tuesday to Saturday from 5:30 P.M.) and **Harry's Bar** (nightly from 6:00 P.M.). All major credit cards.

St. Regis-Sheraton. 2 E. 55th St.; 753–4500. **King Cole Room,** see *Crème de la Crème.* Also, quartet for dancing in **Astor's** from 9:00 P.M. to 1:00 A.M. Tuesday to Thursday, to 2:00 A.M. Friday and Saturday. All major credit cards.

Sheraton Centre. 52nd St. and Seventh Ave.; 581–1000. New Orleans atmosphere and dancing nightly in the **French Quarter,** piano in **Caffè Fontana**

(Continental restaurant), another piano in the posh eatery **Rainier's,** and a cabaret with dance music in **La Ronde.** All major credit cards.

Sherry Netherland. 781 Fifth Ave. at 59th St.; 355–2800. A pianist plays in the **Petit Restaurant.** All major credit cards.

Sign of the Dove. 1110 Third Ave. at 65th St., 861–8080. Show tunes from pianist Lynn Mulinax are far more worthwhile than the food at this overpriced and underqualified Continental restaurant. All major credit cards.

Spindletop. 254 W. 47th St.; 245–7326. Broadway-area restaurant serving Continental food and background piano music from 5:00 P.M. All major credit cards.

UN Plaza. 44th St. and First Ave.; 355–3400. Various pianists play from 6:00 P.M. to midnight in a mirrored maze with muted lights called—what else?—the **Ambassador Lounge.** All major credit cards.

Village Green. 531 Hudson St. at Charles St. in the West Village; 255–1650. Piano music in the upstairs bar/lounge—the second floor of a tastefully appointed Greenwich Village restaurant. AE, MC, V.

Village Corner. Bleecker St. at La Guardia Pl.; 473–9762. Interesting, intimate Village spot where the entertainment is nowhere near as tacky as the surroundings might suggest. No credit cards.

Vista International. 3 World Trade Center; 938–9100. The **Vista Lounge** just above the lobby is where the piano is situated, though the music carries to the front reaches of the Greenhouse and American Harvest restaurants. Music from 5:30 P.M. until midnight.

Waldorf-Astoria. Park Ave. and 50th St.; 355–3000. **Peacock Alley:** see *Jazz.* Also, piano bar in the **Hideaway** from 8:30 P.M. All major credit cards.

 BARS. No one can drink in every one of Manhattan's bars—and live. Even if someone were to try, the number of places going into business and out of business would soon make the attempt meaningless. What we now offer the visitor to New York City is a *selection* of Manhattan bars, with an attempt to differentiate them by their qualities and their locations.

But we can take no responsibility for the results. Bars, even more than restaurants, are a very personal matter—especially to New Yorkers. Two seemingly similar bars, side by side, will each have its regular customers who will express disdain for the other place. Our descriptions, too, must be subjective to a great degree; "lively," for example, may mean different things to a football player than to a librarian.

Those who like well-appointed drinking places, where most of the clientele are well dressed, behave in a dignified manner, and have generally arrived at comfortable station (or age) in life, would be well off at the good midtown hotel bars, many of which have been mentioned in the *Night Life* section, above. These are in the Plaza Hotel *Oak Bar* class. Piano bars, which tend to be restrained, are covered there, too. At the (almost) other end of the scale are the neighborhood bars, with names like Dottie's Pub and McGowan's Tavern. These are where the doormen and cab drivers drink, and where you will be 100 percent certain of getting into a conversation, whether you want to or not. In this group are the chains—*Martin's, Blarney Stone,* and others—where you will also find quite good and *cheap* food counters, with hot pastrami and the like.

That leaves all the rest in the middle. With the exception of a few ethnic bars, we have chosen to cover our selection of bars by geographical area, and to give you some idea of where each place fits in the spectrum.

Now to the subject of Manhattan's famous (infamous?) singles bars. Whereas it is possible for man and woman to meet in, say, a commuter bar in Grand Central Station, the phrase "singles bar" seems to belong to mysteriously designated places where everyone knows he or she is in a singles bar. Beyond that we can say nothing more definite, and can only mention which ones are clearly "singles"—though there are numerous borderline bars. By far the majority of the purely "singles" bars are on the Upper East Side. And in some parts of town the night of the week is important; Monday is usually the slackest day—but, well, not always. Peak hours vary, too, much too irregularly to be given here. Also, the character of the clientele may change radically from, say, early evening to the late evening. There is a belief in some quarters that singles bars wax and wane like mushrooms. Not true. Most of the places we'll mention here have been doing business for over a decade.

New York bars may stay open, legally, until 4:00 A.M. every night except Saturday (Sunday morning), when they must close at 3:00 A.M. Many places, however, close earlier; ask. At some places, when there is a particularly enjoyable crowd at closing time, the bartender will lock the doors and keep serving.

For a little amusement, ask any New York bartender about what happens here when the moon is full.

Enjoy some or all of the emporia below, but a word on New York street sense: Don't steam unsteadily out of a bar late at night and stroll off into a quiet side street; you'll make yourself a mark. And don't think there is necessarily safety in numbers, unless the numbers are in the vicinity of double digit. Better take a cab and be safe, until you develop your own street sense.

Tipping the bartender has unfortunately become an established custom here at most middle- and upper-class bars, so leave something in some proportion to all your drinks, but not necessarily 15 percent.

Visitors from Great Britain or Europe should keep in mind that American spirits are distilled to a higher proof than in the Old World. In other words, the booze here is stronger. On top of that, most New York bartenders put a lot more than the standard Continental shot (measure) into their concoctions, often serving what would be a double or even a triple. But beware of Bloody Marys and other concoctions with strong mixers; all too often, and even in "nice" places, these are light on the liquor.

In almost all of the bars below you can also eat, if not London broil, at least hamburgers and sandwiches. If the food is of special note, we'll say so. Remember, too, that New York likes to eat *late.*

WALL STREET AREA

This area pretty much empties out of people after work hours—but not entirely. Some stay to drink and socialize. *Harry's at Hanover Square,* 1 Hanover Square (a block south off Wall and Pearl Streets) gets a very big crowd after work. *Pig 'n' Whistle South,* at 15 Trinity Place, is another crowded spot, as are *Rosie O'Grady's South,* at 211 Pearl St., and *Jim Brady's,* 75 Maiden Lane. The latter two may have Irish music later in the evening.

TRIBECA/SOHO

TriBeCa (TRIangle BElow CAnal St.) comes as close as any area south of 110th St. to being Manhattan's *terra incognito,* though if things take their usual course the artists and designers who now enjoy the lower rents and large loft spaces here will soon be displaced by well-heeled dilettantes seeking an artsy ambience. Coats and ties and dresses and high heels are distinctly uncommon in bars here (and, to a lesser degree, in SoHo). Things usually don't liven up till well after 9:00 P.M.

Begin your TriBeCa bar tour at a typical TriBeCan place: *Raccoon Lodge,* Warren St. east of West Broadway, where there is an excellent juke box, a pool table, and where you drink your beer right out of the bottle, country style— though the bartender is likely to be a punk lady with a red dress and orange and green hair. Don't go before 11:00 P.M. *Morgan's Bar & Restaurant,* Reade St. near Hudson, has outdoor tables that are very pleasant at sunset in the summer. The bar inside, however, smells like the burial chamber of the Cheops Pyramid. If there is a pool game going on at *Barnabus,* 155 Duane St., and you don't have a seat at the bar, you may find yourself doing a lot of moving to keep out of the shooting line. Continuing north more or less along the Hudson St. axis—which will eventually bring you right up into SoHo, if you turn right on Franklin then left on West Broadway—you come to *Puffy's,* 81 Hudson St., a bar in the Raccoon Lodge vein, but friendlier. On West Broadway near Franklin is Teddy's Restaurant, an Italian late-night steakhouse that looks like a set from "Kojak" and sits improbably among the warehouse buildings. This is a fancy place where it is unwise to make loud Mafia jokes. Farther up the street is the very fashionable Odeon Restaurant, where uptown people come to eat their meat and fish with kiwis. For your bar tour, we don't recommend a stop at either of these two places. But you should have a last drink, before leaving TriBeCa, at *Magoo's,* a nice restaurant as well as a relaxed, comfortable bar at the northern edge of the area, 21 Sixth Ave. at Beach St., near Canal St.

Cross Canal St. on West Broadway and you are in SoHo (South of Houston St.), which, with its tight concentration of lofts, restaurants, bars, clubs, art galleries, and boutiques, is much more on the beaten path than TriBeCa, and many of the folks you see will be the so-called "bridge-and-tunnel" crowd from Long Island and New Jersey—but persevere, because when the sun goes down in SoHo, especially on the weekdays when the locals have the place more to themselves, the bars here can be interesting. The newish *Grand Street Bar,* east

A **Chinatown.** Few bars and clubs, lots of restaurants.
B **Little Italy.** Some bars, lots of cafes and restaurants.
C **SoHo.** Bars, restaurants, cafes, street happenings.
D **Greenwich Village.** You name it, they've got it here, on and off the streets.
E **Times Square Area.** Theaters, movie houses, both straight and porn; bars, restaurants; drug sales on the street. Sleazy and dangerous, especially along 42nd St. and after theaters close.
F **Midtown.** Centered on Fifth Ave. and 57th and 59th Streets. A place for strolling in the early and middle evening; look at shop windows and the other

people. A fairly well-heeled group of strollers. 56th St. between Fifth and Sixth
Aves. is "Restaurant Row." Some bars, lots of restaurants in entire area. Some
street activity.

G **Midtown.** Second, Third and Lexington Aves. Lots of restaurants. Lots and
  lots of bars. Nightclubs here, too, and discos.
H **Upper East Side.** The three singles streets: First, Second and Third Aves.
  Restaurants, bars, clubs, discos.
I **Lincoln Center.** Also part of the Upper West Side. Bars, restaurants, clubs,
  discos. Lots of street life and mummery.

of West Broadway, has live music evenings. The *Broome Street Bar,* at the corner of West Broadway, is probably the best-known SoHo bar, though you'll come out smelling like a hamburger. Other recommended stops are *Berry's,* 180 Spring St.; *Central Falls,* 478 West Broadway; *Spring Street Restaurant,* 162 Spring, which is probably the most typical SoHo bar; the *Wine Bar,* 422 West Broadway; and the place with the roomiest bar of all, *Mama Siltka's,* 468 West Broadway. Most of these bars have a special SoHo feeling that comes mostly from the architecture of the old commercial buildings that house them.

This is not true, however, of *Frank Dowd's Rozinante Tavern,* corner of Sullivan and Spring Sts., which is more of a mix between the new SoHo and the old Little Italy. (Across the intersection from Dowd's is an excellent pizzeria, Napoli Pizza, which has tables outside for eating and drinking in good weather.) The bar at *Raoul's,* 180 Prince Street, though little more than a passage through the restaurant's front room, affords a priceless sight of SoHo's punk *demimondaines* mixing with Wall Street lawyers. The bar on the southeast corner of Prince and Thompson—it has no legible sign—is one of the raunchiest, seediest joints in the area; you're on your own here.

GREENWICH VILLAGE/CHELSEA

Whereas SoHo's bars seem centered on one relatively small stretch of one street, West Broadway, the Village bars are nicely spread out, both in geography and in the type of clientele. The oldest is probably *McSorley's Old Ale House,* 15 E. 7th St., which until a few years ago banned women from its seedy delights. Go here, if for no other reason than to see what saloons looked like in New York a hundred years ago. This used to be a hangout for Village wise men; there was even a book written just about the place. Nearby, opposite the Public Theater (the old Astor Library) is *Lady Astor's.* The decor here is of interest, the building being formerly an Astor family townhouse (mansion) property.

More in the middle of the Village, we recommend a stop at *Kettle of Fish,* 114 MacDougal St., where you will find a dart board and a usually satisfactory mix of genuine Village residents and N.Y.U. students. *Knickerbocker Saloon,* University Place at 9th St., has an older crowd, with jazz combo evenings. *Chinese Chance,* 1 University Place, caters to N.Y. University students and artists. Nearby, on Waverly Place near Greene St., *Garvin's* is a pleasant, open bar in a pretty good restaurant. *One Fifth Avenue's* bar (actually two bars) at 8th St. east of Fifth features conversation that seems to have been written by Woody Allen. The food here is somewhat more pretentious than at most places in the neighborhood; live music in the front room later in the evening. A prime hangout for neighborhood lip artists is the *Cedar Tavern,* 82 University Place. (The Cedar used to be a real artist's hangout when it existed in a couple of other locations to the west.) At Fifth Ave. and 13th St., now minus the hideous giant iguana sculpture that used to stand on the roof before neighborhood killjoys forced its removal, endures the *Lone Star Café* ("Too Much Ain't Enough," says the banner across the façade), Texas' challenge to Manhattan.

Moving toward the so-called West Village: At 331 W. 4th St. is *Julius,* probably New York's oldest overt gay bar. At or near Sheridan Square (Seventh Ave. at Christopher and W. 4th Sts.) are the *Lion's Head,* 59 Christopher, and the nearby *55 Christopher Street;* both are dingy outposts of the local Literati. The *Duplex,* 55 Grove off Seventh Ave. at Sheridan Square, has great sing-alongs later in the evening, in a semi-gay environment. *The Riviera Café,* right across from Sheridan Square, is a good place for people-watching. A block or so south on Seventh Ave., on the east side of the street, resides the *Buffalo Roadhouse,* with scarcely a sign to identify it. You can eat and drink outside in good weather. Many of the outrageously dressed characters here seem to be off-duty stockbrokers, but it's an interesting place nonetheless. Across the street and down Barrow St., near the corner of Bedford St., is a wooden-slatted door that gives into a little courtyard. At the other side of the yard is a door with a little barred window in it. This is the back entrance to *Chumley's,* an old Village hangout, and, on Sundays, often the site of poetry readings. The "front" entrance, with no sign, is just as hard to find.

If you liked the Cedar Tavern, the Lion's Head, and Kettle of Fish, try the *Corner Bistro,* at 331 W. 4th St., near Abingdon Square, where Eighth Ave. starts off Hudson St. On Hudson St., at 11th St., is the *White Horse Tavern,* one of Dylan Thomas' favorite saloons. *Cody's,* on the west side of Sixth Ave. between 15th and 16th Sts., is a country-and-western bar and a singles spot, too. Going into Chelsea, we recommend a stop at the *Chelsea Place Restaurant,* 147 Eighth Ave. near 17th St. There is what seems to be a junkshop in front, but in the back is a busy bar (with entertainment) and restaurant.

MIDTOWN

The midtown area has the widest variety of bars of any one part of the city; our review simply starts at the south and works north.

Pete's Tavern, Irving Place at 28th St., was probably one of O. Henry's drinking spots. The bar itself is a work of art; tables outside in good weather. *Caliban's,* Third Avenue near 25th St., is a comfortable brick-wall sort of neighborhood bar—and the neighborhood in question is an interesting mix of types. *The Back Porch,* Third Ave. at 33rd St., has tables outside in good weather for drinking or dining. *Arthur's Inn,* 34th St. between First and Second Aves., with a skylit "garden" area in back, and *El Parador*—a fine Mexican restaurant on 34th St. east of First Ave.—are both very mildly singles bars, and are close to a group of first-run moviehouses on 34th St. So is *Brew's,* a sawdust-on-the-floor emporium on 34th St. between Lexington and Third Aves. *Kitty Hawk's,* at 565 Third Ave. near 37th St., is something of a singles bar, too, though in a low-keyed way. The big thing here seems to be the video games.

We have mentioned the very good hotel bars. One of the coziest is the little bar—the Blue Bar—just inside the entrance to the *Algonquin Hotel,* around to the right. Throughout the midtown area, you will find that bars near the big companies' offices will be filled with—surprise!—people from those companies. For example, find the bars nearest the CBS building on Sixth Avenue and you'll find broadcasting people. Some bars attract all sorts of hotshots, though, such as *Charley O's* at 33 W. 48th St. (plus good eats), or, for the slightly lower-ranked: *The Office Pub* on 55th St. east of Sixth Ave.; *Paul Revere's Tavern,* Lexington Ave. near 48th St. (mature advertising folks; very convivial at night, with piano music); *Maude's,* Lexington Ave. at 51st St. (a slightly younger ad crowd); *Molly Mog's,* 65 East 55th Street; and the king of them all, *P. J. Clarke's,* 915 Third Avenue at 55th St. (Get some chili from the little grill near the front door.)

Charlie Brown's, in the Pan Am Building at the top of the escalators from Grand Central, has some singles action after work (all ages, it seems). *Goose & Gherkin Ale House,* 50th St., west of Second Ave., and *Knicker's,* on Second Ave., near 49th St., are agreeable places; Knicker's features facilities for chess and backgammon, all comers. *The Landmark Tavern,* Eleventh Ave. at the corner of 46th St., is in a somewhat grim neighborhood, but the bar is, in fact, a landmark, is well kept up, and is fun. Try it for Sunday brunch if you aren't otherwise adventuresome. *Mimi's,* 984 Second Ave. at 52nd St., is probably the best place in town for grown-up folks to mingle and have a good time. It's even busy on Mondays, with a sing-along piano bar. *O'Neal's at 57th Street* is a very comfortable place; the bar sometimes sees discreet single action. Nearby, the *Carnegie Tavern,* in and behind Carnegie Hall at Seventh Avenue and 56th St., is a very pleasant place for a pre- or post-concert toddy; live music, too.

LINCOLN CENTER AREA

O'Neals Baloon is right across the street from Lincoln Center at 63rd St. The drinks are expensive but the place is busy and interesting. The name was originally to have been O'Neal's Saloon, but some city department objected, so to save money—and annoy the city—the owners merely exchanged a *B* for the offending *S.* Now there are lots of "saloons," such as *The Saloon* at Broadway and 64th St., a barn of a place. The bar has all the character of a baggage pick-up area in an airport. *The Ginger Man,* a small bar in a pleasant restaurant, is around the corner a few steps east on 64th St.

Going up Columbus Avenue from Lincoln Center, the bars come fast and usually furious. To single out just a few: *Stephen's West Side Wine Bar,* 103 W. 70th St., and *Vintages,* Columbus and W. 70th St. (why two nearly identical wine bars need to face each other is another question). There is another wine bar/café at Columbus and 74th, *Il Cantone,* with drinking in a "wine cellar" in the basement. *Palsson's,* 72nd St. between Broadway and Columbus—nice restaurant at back, too, as well as a modest cabaret upstairs. After 10:30 P.M. is attracts show-business types. *Nanny Rose,* Columbus at 74th St., a quiet bar scene, but here you can draw on the paper coverings on the tables, crayons being provided; *Ruelles,* newly expanded and a bigger circus than ever, at the corner of Columbus and 75th St., open to the street at two sides, with tables on the sidewalk—you won't find many West Siders here, because it attracts the sort of people who think Ken and Barbie look lifelike; the infamous *Tap-a-Keg,* which advertises in neon over the front, "A Hell of a Joint"—and it is (the intergalactic bar in *Star Wars* was modeled after this place); the *Museum Café*, at Columbus and 77th St., is well situated, being across the street from the Museum of Natural History grounds, but it is less fun than it seems.

UPPER WEST SIDE

The *All-State*, on 72nd St. just east of West End Ave., is a dive, but very friendly and very cheap, patronized by the younger working people of the neighborhood. Almost next to Zabar's Delicatessen, on Broadway between 80th and 81st Sts., is *Teacher's*, a very well designed and comfortable bar and restaurant (with mediocre food). There is a clone of Teacher's, *Teacher's Too*, one block to the north. *Café Central*, Amsterdam at 75th St., is a compact gathering and meeting place for the relaxed set, who may draw on the paper table covers as at Nanny Rose. The tiny partitioned bar area is frequently jammed with "singles." One block up is the relatively tranquil West Side branch of *J. G. Melon*, in a nice old-style bar setting. *Shelter*, at Broadway and 77th St., looks and feels like a singles bar, and, with Café Central and Ruelles, is maybe the closest the Upper West Side can come to a singles bar. *Marvin Gardens*, on Broadway between 81st and 82nd Sts., typifies the Upper West Side's ability to mix races, creeds, religions, ages, and anything else. *Hanratty's*, Amsterdam and 95th St., is on a less-than-good block, but somehow its pleasant character attracts Upper West Side literary folks. *The Abbey Tavern*, off Broadway on 105th St., is a long-time spot for Columbia hangers-on; and the *West End*, 2911 Broadway almost opposite Columbia University, is the headquarters for the college's drinking class.

UPPER EAST SIDE

Now we are in Singles Country. The bars that are pure-and-simple meeting places we will label as such, but up here the singles are really where you find them. Many of the latest "in" singles spots aren't listed here: too new. But follow the crowds and you spot them. Note that some of these singles places actually charge admission on certain days, usually weekends; we do not attempt to list which charge, or when, or to tell you why you should pay such a charge anyway—we don't know why.

First Avenue

The most famous singles strip is on First Ave. between 61st and 65th Sts. The first and one of the most well known of all is *Thank God It's Friday*, in its bright blue building at 61st St., now a rather staid place. Nearby is *Adam's Apple*, and one block north is *the* most famous singles bar, maybe in the world: *Maxwell's Plum*, which, surprisingly, is also an excellent restaurant; the two coexist in one space by the expedient of the bar being raised on a platform in the middle of the restaurant.

Skipping ten blocks to the north, there is a whole string of bars, each of which is wholly or partly a singles place: *Finnegan's Wake* (73rd St.); *September's* (75th St.) for the young; *Grass* (75th St.) for the possibly even younger; *Wilson's*, across the street from September, is new and currently popular; *Boodles* (at 77th St.) has a 30-ish customer; and *Samantha's* (78th) for somewhat more mature clientele.

Off First, toward Second Ave. on 79th St., is *Sugar Mill,* which has the loudest jukebox in town. As conversation is impossible, singles must converse by telepathy. Heats up late.

Second Avenue

Hudson Bay at 76th is a pleasant, quiet neighborhood place. *Mad Hatter,* between 77th and 78th Sts., is less quiet, with a singles aspect; it is a favorite jock hangout, especially for rugby players. *Court Street,* between 80th and 81st Sts., has dancing later in the evenings. *O'Melia's* (81st St.) caters quietly to a more mature neighborhood crowd, as does *Red Blazer,* between 81st and 82nd Sts.; the latter has music, and is an old, if somewhat dull, standby. *New York Boat Yard,* at 81st St., is for the younger set, while *Dorrian's Red Hand* (84th St.) and *Drake's Drum* (between 84th and 85th Streets) have been solid neighborhood standbys for years.

On 84th St. between Second and Third Aves. is *Brandy's,* a seedy-looking dive that is another survivor, with music nightly. Brandy's, with its gay overtones and extremely casual, nonthreatening atmosphere, comes close to being a European-style *boite,* and is a welcome relief from the plastic macho so common on the Upper East Side. *Pedro's,* 251 E. 85th between Second and Third, looks even more downscale than Brandy's, but turns out to be quite a meeting place for Manhattan's Deep South contingent.

In the vicinity of the corner of Second Ave. and 88th St. stand three bars of special note. *Eric* has a slightly sinister decline-of-the-West feeling; live music in the evenings. *Elaine's,* across Second Ave., is fun if you are a nationally famous figure in the arts or politics. Otherwise, you'll be a lot happier across Second Ave. at *Rathbone's,* a rather jock-ish place run by a former British professional soccer player; nice food at reasonable prices.

Third Avenue

Now we are on the Champs d'Élysée of the Upper East Side bar circuit. *Rusty's* at 73rd St., and *Churchill's,* a few doors to the north, are both for the over-30s. *J. G. Melon,* at 74th St., is likewise a nice but hardly madcap place. *Harper,* between 74th and 75th Sts., is mostly a restaurant, but the bar scene is considered attractive by the sort of young or used-to-be young people who read *Vogue* or *GQ* magazines. And if Harper isn't smug enough for you, do try *Jim McMullen* between 75th and 77th for the ultimate in nervous Third Avenue quasi-chic. *Ravelled Sleave,* between 78th and 79th, is a long-established preserve for preppies of all ages; and a very pleasant place withal. This is the bar that a few years ago received a bequest from a finally departed regular, so that the surviving regulars could drink for free; the fund has been depleted. *Auctions,* at 80th St., is open to the street in good weather; usually packed with fairly well-dressed friendlies.

Willie's, at 81st St., is a no-nonsense neighborhood bar (and grill), whereas *Hoexter's Market* between 81st and 82nd Sts., as much a restaurant as it is a singles bar, is anything but no-nonsense, being a competitor of Jim McMullen's. (Both of the latter ask men to wear tie and jacket.) *Martell's,* on the corner of 83rd St., is one of the solidest all-purpose bars on the Upper East Side. There is a large restaurant as well, and tables outside in good weather. *Oren & Aretsky,* between 84th and 85th Sts., is another Jim McMullen look-alike, frequented by politicians and sports stars, as well as carefully dressed nonentities.

Other Upper East Side bars are: *Peartree's,* First Ave. at 49th St., at the bottom of the Beekman Tower, where underemployed models act as waitresses; also a singles crowd, but later in the evenings. Up at the top of the building is the *Beekman Tower Bar,* a wonderful—and romantic—place for viewing the city at night. Across the street from Peartree's, on the other side of First Ave., is *St. John's,* a slick bar and restaurant that attracts the younger singles of this neighborhood. Up First Ave. a bit, at 53rd St., is the *Mayfair,* a gathering place for the executives who make their homes in this very affluent part of the city.

ETHNIC BARS

The ones we recommend happen to be mostly of the Irish persuasion: *Donovan's Cafe,* 1604 Third Ave. at 90th St., has decor you'd expect to have found in Leadville, Colorado, in 1861, and on some nights the only customers will be a nice lady and her dog—but on other nights, especially weekends, it is a mob scene, with lots of palaver. *The Green Derby,* 978 Second Ave. near 52nd St., makes an attempt to serve Guinness on tap—the right way. *Flanagan's,* First Ave. between 65th and 66th Sts., has a good, solid kind of person for trade, plus Irish music, especially on weekends. *The Eagle Tavern,* 355 W. 14th St., has country and Western, Irish and Scottish music on weekend evenings, and, every Wednesday evening, an open jam session. *John Barleycorn,* 209 E. 45th St., has Irish music. *Jim Brady's* and *Rosie O'Grady's* we've mentioned in the *Wall Street* section. Finally, a German neighborhood bar in New Yorkville: The *Bavarian Inn,* on the south of 86th St. between Second and Third Aves.

Chances are that the bar you end up liking best isn't even listed by us. That's the way it is with New York City. Enjoy.

Attractions Near
New York City

FIRE ISLAND AND THE HAMPTONS

"Out East" from Manhattan

**by DENNIS STARIN
and ROBERT MARTIN**

*Dennis Starin, a year-round Hamptons resident, is a travel writer who
has contributed to* The New York Times, Signature, *and* Smithsonian
*magazine, among others. Robert Martin is an editor and writer on Long
Island's largest newspaper,* Newsday.

Shaped like a gigantic 1,723-square-mile fish, Long Island nudges
Manhattan with its head and stretches its tail some 130 miles northeast-

ward to Montauk Point. The western two-thirds of the island has increasingly become a bedroom community for New York City commuters, although a growing number of light industries has given the island's population of over seven million residents a sense of regional identification.

Of the four counties on Long Island, two are boroughs of New York City. Queens County is the borough of Queens and Kings County is the borough of Brooklyn. Between them they have more people than the entire city of Chicago. Nassau County—the center segment of Long Island—and the western half of Suffolk County are less citylike, with houses clustered lawn-to-lawn rather than wall-to-wall.

Fire Island

Fire Island, a barrier island just off Long Island's South Shore, has some of the world's most beautiful public beaches and is just an hour's ride from New York City by train or car (twice that in heavy traffic), plus another half hour by ferry. Although it is 32 miles long, Fire Island is only about half-a-mile wide in most places. Most of the island has been designated a national park, Fire Island National Seashore, part of which includes the Sunken Forest, a natural wonder of dense trees growing in a fertile glade below the sea level near Sailor's Haven. About 15,000 people live on Fire Island during the summer, and as many as 30,000 more flock there on sunny days to enjoy its clean sands and thundering surf. The island is easily reached from Long Island by taking a ferry across Great South Bay from Bay Shore, Sayville, or Patchogue, but don't think of renting a car when you get there: Except for access highways to parks at the tips of the island, there are no roads. While this may seem an inconvenience to some, it has preserved the island's primitive charm. The small communities that dot Fire Island are semi-isolated, both from the rest of the world and from each other, and each has developed its own distinct character.

The fragile nature of its ecology has much to do with the protective attitude most islanders have about the place. But even more than this, perhaps, Fire Island represents a primitive retreat from the hectic pace of modern life where life has been stripped to the essentials and where commercialism is vigorously discouraged. Most Fire Island communities have no public restrooms or other such facilities—such as for changing clothes—and eating on the beaches is not allowed. Although a barefoot style prevails, the islanders can hardly be described as hut dwellers. Pole-mounted shanties coexist with million-dollar beach houses, as designer bikinis are as commonplace as cut-off jeans. The island supports over a dozen distinct communities, some clustered side by side, others separated by long stretches of beach. The social and age mix cuts across all lines. The communities of *Saltaire* and *Point o'-Woods,* for example, are made up of older, wealthier and more conservative residents than those who inhabit *Davis Park.* While *Ocean Bay Park* has a reputation as being the island's singles center, *Ocean Beach* and *Seaview,* on the other hand, are family-oriented and have large teen-age populations. The ferry slip at Ocean Beach regularly disgorges tons of equipment brought over by day-trippers, even though the town has two supermarkets, ice-cream parlors, hardware stores, several restaurants and clothing boutiques, and other support services. Prices tend to be somewhat higher than on Long Island. The communities of *Cherry Grove* and *Fire Island Pines* are the home bases of a mixed, but predominantly gay, society from the New York theater, arts and fashion worlds. Lavish—and stunningly beautiful—homes, lavish parties, lavish food, and haute couture are the bywords there. An influx of singles at *Kismet* and *Davis Park* has brought about such summertime activities as wet T-shirt contests, disco marathons, and nude sunbathing. Nudity on the beaches is also *de rigueur* in Cherry Grove and Fire Island Pines.

Throughout its history, Fire Island has suffered repeated devastations by storms, fire, slave-traders, and rum-runners. But none were as threatening to its continued existence as the invasion in the fifties and early sixties by real-estate developers intent on exploiting its resources for commercial gain. Efforts to protect the island from further development led to the establishment of the *Fire Island National Seashore* in 1964. At present, visitors can enjoy public facilities at *Robert Moses State Park* at the western end and at *Smith Point County Park* at the eastern end. Both parks are reached by toll bridges from the mainland. In addition, the National Park Service maintains facilities at *Sunken Forest, Sailor's Haven, Watch Hill,* and *Smith Point West.*

Fire Island National Seashore is something more than the usual public beach. Here you have a chance to explore a scene formed by nature, rather than by man. The unspoiled seashore remains as essentially intact as it was when Isaac Stratford of Babylon set up a whaling station at Whalehouse Point in 1653. To help preserve this natural resource, visitors are given a number of "don'ts" regarding the disturbing of plant and animal life and are requested to keep off the fragile dunes. You may, however, enjoy surf fishing, swimming, strolling through the Sunken Forest, or relaxing on an uncluttered section of beach. Guided nature walks are offered in summer, park rangers give free guided tours at Watch Hill and Sailor's Haven.

Facilities at Sailor's Haven park include a marina, guarded swimming beach, ferry terminal, snack bar, visitor center with information and exhibits, picnic area, nature trail, restroom, change rooms and showers, pay phones, and dog walk area. Similar facilities are available at Watch Hill in addition to a 20-unit campground (reservations required: 597–6633). The Smith Point West facility features a small visitor center with information and exhibits, interpretive activities, and a nature trail.

Boating on Fire Island takes its character from shallow, breezy Great South Bay, and the most suitable boats are thus small, shoal-draft and capable of being beached or even carried home. Board boats such as the Sunfish are extremely popular, and it seems likely that the new breed of Windsurfer-style sailboards will be even more so. For larger craft, most towns have marinas accessible to residents, but transient boats are discouraged, except in the two marinas operated for Fire Island National Seashore.

Hotel and guesthouse accommodations are available in a few communities. The facilities typically consist of room and bath with few amenities. On Fire Island the litterbug is considered Public Enemy No. 1. Local ordinances are strictly enforced.

Suffolk County

The eastern third of Long Island has retained miles of the unspoiled beaches, secluded coves and open spaces immortalized by its native bard, Walt Whitman. When New Yorkers speak about the island, they are usually referring to "out east"—a loosely defined area of farmlands, summer homes, and beach resorts situated along the north and south forks of the island's east end. Hoping to preserve the area's wetlands and open spaces from encroaching urban sprawl, east enders are making efforts to create a fifth county, "Paumanok," the Indian name of Long Island.

Organized in 1683, Suffolk County is one of New York State's ten original counties. More than 80 miles long and 20 miles wide, it encompasses the five west end towns of Huntington, Smithtown, Babylon, Islip, and Brookhaven, and the five east end towns of Riverhead, Southold, and Shelter Island on the north fork; Southampton and East Hampton on the south fork.

Southampton was settled in 1640 by a group of English colonists from Lynn, Massachusetts. When they arrived at North Sea Harbor, one of the pilgrim women is said to have exclaimed: "For conscience sake, we're on dry land!" The landing site became known as Conscience Point and is designated by a plaque mounted on a large boulder. With the help of the friendly Shinnecock Indians, the settlers planted their crops and soon reaped the harvests of land and sea. In those days the island was inhabited by 13 tribes whose territories extended from the lands of the Canarsies in the west to those of the Montauketts in the east. Today only descendants of the Shinnecocks survive. While their ancestors were known far and wide for the quality of their wampum beads, modern Shinnecocks are engaged in a number of occupations, including the growing of shellfish on a solar-powered sea farm. An annual Pow Wow featuring authentic Indian dancing, crafts, and food is held on their 400-acre reservation in Southampton during the Labor Day weekend and is open to the public. Throughout Long Island scores of Indian place names survive: *Sewánhaka* High School, Lake *Ronkónkoma,* the towns of *Massapéqua* and *Spéonk,* the *Níssequogue* River, *Nescónset* Highway, and *Masháshimuet* Park in Sag Harbor.

A Foodfaring People

Long Island is justly famous for its potatoes, ducks, and bay scallops. The first two are really foreign imports introduced to the new world in the last century. Potato farming had its start "up island" during the late 1800s, when Polish immigrants preferred to try their luck with the island's soil rather than brave Manhattan's teeming masses. After World War II, however, the housing boom gobbled up thousands of acres of prime farmland. At present the only remaining potato farms are on the east end, with Riverhead being both county seat and potato capital of Long Island. Surprising as it may seem, Suffolk is the leading agricultural county of New York State in dollar volume. And while the potato is still undisputed king, east end farmers grow sizable quantities of cauliflower, cabbage, strawberries, and Oriental vegetables for the Metropolitan market. In business for only a few years, the Hargrave Vineyards at Cutchogue, a short distance from Riverhead, has been producing a local vintage with much success. At an Eastport processing plant Long Island's famous ducklings are dispatched, plucked, frozen, and shipped throughout the country. The duck was introduced to Long Island in 1873 by a Sag Harbor sea captain who brought nine of them here from China. The birds took readily to their new surroundings and flourished. Today there is scarcely a restaurant that doesn't include the beautiful duckling on its menu. In fact, one Southampton restaurant, John Duck Jr., is named after the delectable bird and has likewise flourished since 1900.

Ask east enders which is their favorite time of year, and the answer is invariably: Fall. It is then when summer's hoards have dwindled to a precious few and when baymen take to their boats to dredge the Peconic Bay's nutrient-rich eelgrass beds for the prized bay scallop. At the many oyster festivals and old-fashioned clambakes held throughout the area during October, you can watch shuckers in action deftly opening shellfish with a flick of their knives. The tiny blue dots radiating along the outer edges of the scallop shell are actually eyes. Only the white adduct or muscle is eaten, however. Through careful manage-

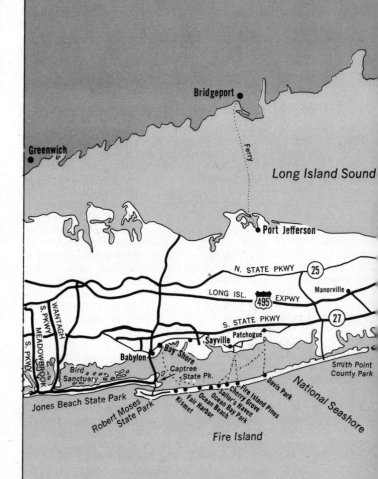

Long Island Resort Areas

Bridgeport

Greenwich

Long Island Sound

Ferry

Port Jefferson

N. STATE PKWY (25)

LONG ISL. 495 EXPWY

Manorville

S. STATE PKWY (27)

Sayville   Patchogue

Babylon   Bay Shore

Smith Point County Park

Captree State Pk.

Bird Sanctuary

S. PKWY
WANTAGH
MEADOWBROOK
S. PKWY

Fire Island Pines
Cherry Grove
Sailor's Haven
Ocean Bay Park
Davis Park
Ocean Beach
Fair Harbor
Kismet

National Seashore

Jones Beach State Park

Robert Moses State Park

Fire Island

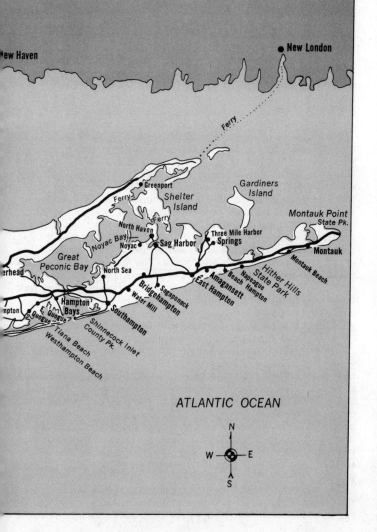

ment baymen and marine biologists have begun to revive the island's once-flourishing oyster and clam industry.

The Hamptons

No matter where he hails from, the first-time visitor out east is bound to experience a feeling of déja vù—that haunting suspicion of having encountered the place before. There is nothing mysterious about this, however, since the Hamptons and their residents—both the native-born descendants of the first settlers as well as more recent pilgrims—have been photographed, talked about and written about at great length. Even a partial listing of notable Hamptonites would include a good many stars and superstars of the literary, art, and theater worlds. The Hamptons are at once chic and sophisticated, while at the same time conservative and surprisingly naïve, depending, of course, on which part of the Hamptons you're talking about. The much-touted Hampton "look," therefore, is largely in the eyes of the beholder. There are "in" places and "out" places and a scorecard is sometimes needed to tell one from the other. An Amagansett disco that was packing them in a few summers ago unaccountably became "out" and you could have rolled the proverbial bowling ball the length of its bar without knocking over a single glass. Strangely enough, a former Southampton bowling alley was converted for use as a elaborate disco and is currently one of the area's most popular night spots. You're likely to find a best-selling author or two at Bobby Van's in Bridgehampton and will recognize one of your favorite movie stars on East Hampton's Newtown Lane. Déja vù encounters are a part of the Hampton scene. But chances are you have come out east not to meet celebrities, but to pursue the good life that has been attracting generations of east end pilgrims since the anonymous goodwife set foot on Conscience Point.

Not long after the Civil War the south fork was rediscovered by wealthy New Yorkers who found its ocean breezes, rolling farmlands, and quaint villages to be ideal watering places in which to spend their summers. Credit for the discovery must go as much to Walt Whitman's idyllic ballads extolling the virtues of this paradise regained as to the eastward expansion of the Long Island Railroad. The first summer people stayed in boardinghouses or roomed in private homes. Resort hotels soon followed. One of the earliest, the Howell House, was built in Westhampton Beach in 1866. The ravages of time, fire, and a disastrous hurricane in 1938 have left few examples of these early watering places.

The millionaires who came to Southampton and East Hampton built their summer homes on a grand scale, often importing not only marble, stone, and precious woods, but the skilled craftsmen who wrought them into regal showplaces. Throughout the older estate areas of both communities you can glimpse vistas of sprawling Tudor manors, splendid Victorian and Newport-style beach "cottages" and lavish villas, surrounded by magnificent gardens and emerald-green lawns.

While the real-estate boom has continued unabated, and condominiums often seen to sprout in the wake of the plow, there are still open stretches of farmland between ocean and woodland. From early to mid-June you can stop at a number of strawberry fields and pick your own. A month later will find acres of potatoes in snow-capped blossom, and all along the byways are the native charmers of blue asters, purple sumac, Queen Ann's lace, and the ubiquitous goldenrod. The colors and textures of land and sea are somehow intensified in the ever-changing light of the east end sky. This quality was discovered by generations of artists who came here for a summer of painting and remained for a lifetime. Approaching Southampton from the east via the old Montauk Highway, which becomes Hill Street in the village, you pass a cluster of ramshackle cottages almost hidden behind a jungle of wisteria. The place, now occupied by private residences, is known as the Art Village. It was here that William Merritt Chase founded the first summer art colony in the country back in 1892. Other painters soon followed, including Winslow Homer, Howard Russell Butler, and Charles Hawthorn (who later founded the Provincetown Art Colony). Many of Chase's works are in the permanent collection of the Parrish Art Museum on Jobs Lane. In the 1950s a second generation of painters, spearheaded by Jackson Pollock, settled in the Springs, a then secluded and entirely unfashionable section between East Hampton and Gardiner's Bay. His widow, Lee Krasner, lives and works there today, as do Willem deKooning, Balcomb Greene, Jimmy Ernst, and other noted artists. Major exhibits are held year round at Guild Hall in East Hampton and at summer galleries throughout the east end.

The Hamptons include all of the villages and hamlets within the townships of Southampton and East Hampton. In spite of some obvious similarities, each of the Hamptons has its own atmosphere and attractions. Westhampton Beach is the gateway to the Hamptons and is also the place to go for a shopping tour of interesting boutiques and specialty shops. Main Street is a broad shopping plaza punctuated by inviting alleyways where one can browse through art galleries and gift shops or pause for a light refreshment. By night, especially on frantic weekends, it is a mecca for under-40 singles. Several dance emporiums strike up the band as early as brunchtime on weekends, attracting a young and largely "preppy" crowd. The night spots open at various times, some dispensing with the usual cover charge before 10:00 P.M. But the action seldom begins before midnight, when the more popular establishments are jammed to capacity. At least a dozen disco clubs are situated along the Montauk Highway between Westhampton and points east. For the less energetic, Westhampton Beach has two cinemas, beach and tennis clubs, a golf course, and enough restaurants to suit every budget and taste.

Before dark you might want to take in one of the best shows in town. And it's for free. A drive along Dune Road will bring into focus an architectural kaleidoscope of houses ranging from stately homes of an earlier era to ultra-modern condominiums and fantastic geometric constructions that seem to defy the laws of gravity. Parking regulations are strictly enforced throughout the Hamptons. Daily and seasonal permits for beach areas are sold at most village offices and at some parking lots. By way of contrast, follow any of the tree-lined streets that meander through the nearby hamlets of Remensburg, Westhampton, and Quiogue. Nostalgia buffs will find the rose-covered cottages, picket fences, and authentically restored country farmhouses that have all but disappeared from the American scene. Don't miss the annual House and Garden tour through some of the area's finest homes. Other summer events of note are an outdoor art show, crafts show, and a mid-August flea market. Check the local papers for times and dates.

To the east are the quiet-as-clam villages of Quogue and East Quogue. Before continuing, a word about clams. We have it on the best authority that both *Quiogue* and *Quogue* are derived from the Indian word, *Quaquanantuck*—which refers to an area of soggy marshland that squishes underfoot. Such a place is the natural habitat of the round clam, known locally as a *quohog*.

Back on the mainland and to the north is Suffolk County Airport, which provides service for air taxis, executive jets, air charters, sightseeing trips, and general aviation.

As you continue east along the Sunrise Highway, or follow the parallel Route 27A (Old Montauk Highway) from Quogue through Hampton Bays, the flatlands and pine barrens give way to the Shinnecock Hills in slowly rising mounds. As the Sunrise crosses the Shinnecock Canal, you'll be met with a sweeping view of the Shinnecock Bay to the south and Peconic Bay to the north. East of the canal Route 27 is also marked County Road 39, but it is most often referred to as the North Highway or the Southampton Bypass. The canal represents both a physical and social dividing line between the heart of the Hamptons ahead and the neighboring towns to the west. The Shinnecock Hills played an important role in the development of Southhampton as a summer "colony"—a term still preferred to the more commercial implications of "resort." While today's Southampton millionaires take to the discos, restaurants, and tennis clubs for recreation, the founding colonists built private and exclusive clubs where they played the gentlemanly sport of golf. Across the highway from Southhampton College stands the magnificent clubhouse of the Shinnecock Golf Club, built in 1883 and considered the oldest in the country. A few miles behind it lies the National Golf Club, built several years later to rival the best clubs in Scotland and England.

Founded in 1963, Southampton College sprawls across 110 acres. Among its 33 buildings is a 254-year-old windmill. In addition to an extensive program of summer courses, workshops, seminars, camps for children, study and travel events, the college sponsors a number of cultural programs for students and area visitors. For some families with children, the summer program makes it possible to combine study and recreation. Prior arrangements must be made with the Residence Life Officer. The campus is regularly served by the Long Island Railroad, Hampton Jitney service from New York City and local villages, and Sunrise Coach Lines from East Hampton, Riverhead, and Greenport. In addition, the college runs a free shuttle bus service to the ocean beach and town every afternoon.

The Shinnecock Canal is also crossed by Route 27A just past Hampton Bays. Formerly called "Good Ground," Hampton Bays is an unpretentious fishing village, attracting families as well as singles and retired persons. Here you can rent or charter a boat, join an open party boat for a day, half-day, or night of bay fishing, or simply buy some fresh bait and try your luck canalside. One of the Hampton's largest discos, OBI East (Oak Beach Inn), lies a clam's throw from the canal. For many years this grand old establishment was known as the Canoe Place Inn and run as a fashionable resort hotel boasting a grand ballroom. During the duck shooting season Babe Ruth and other famous sports figures were frequent guests.

Southampton

Long recognized as one of the world's most fashionable summer resorts, Southampton has retained the patina of its Colonial heritage and the indomitable stamp of old money in the face of dramatic changes wrought by real-estate development and the march of progress. Its accessibility to New York via good roads, train and jitney bus service have combined to make Southampton a village for all seasons. It can boast of miles of open shoreline along the ocean and bays, well-known clubs, restaurants and shops, good schools, historic churches, a superb art museum, library and historical museum, and an excellent hospital. This very attractiveness, however, has also caused its remaining farmlands and white-elephant estates to fall victim to condominium sprawl.

The best way to explore the village is on foot. A walking-tour map detailing places of interest is available without charge at the Chamber of Commerce Building on Main Street. On Jobs Lane there are fashionable boutiques and art galleries along with a well-patronized thriftshop, eating places, and gourmet shops, and the beautiful Parrish Art Museum with its tree-shaded grounds and statuary. Herrick's hardware store and Hildreth's department store have been in business at the same Main Street location for well over a hundred years. Some of Long Island's most famous restaurants are in or near the village.

It's easy to miss the restored mill from which the neighboring village of Water Mill takes its name. As you enter the village on Route 27, make a sharp left turn onto Mill Pond Road opposite the Villa Maria estate. At the Old Water Mill Museum you will find an imposing array of Colonial hand tools, spinning wheels, looms and milling equipment; and if you happen to be there when Mrs. Barton McGuire, the museum director and resident miller, is at work, you can watch locally grown corn, wheat, and rye being ground into flour. The mill apparatus contains a pair of 2,400-pound grinding stones and is powered by a 1½-ton waterwheel fed by water from seven ponds north and west of the village. Classes in such old-fashioned crafts as potting, quilt and rug making, woodcarving, and early-American stenciling are taught in the museum throughout the summer. An annual crafts fair is held on the second Saturday in July.

Such descriptive street names as Butter Lane and Lumber Lane reflect Bridgehampton's ties with the land. This is still very much a farming community and its Main Street, like that of Water Mill, consists of a few shops, bars, and restaurants clustered along a stretch of Route 27. The village nevertheless supports six churches, a Community House (often used as a summer theater), a museum, library, and public school. Near the corner of Ocean Road at the far end of town you will find a lovely old windmill, which villagers hope to restore. The mill was actually built in Sag Harbor in 1820 and later moved to Bridgehampton. The road to the left of the War Memorial is the Bridgehampton–Sag Harbor Turnpike and was once a toll highway used to ship farming produce from Sagaponack and other south shore villages to the "Harbour of Sagg."

Sag Harbor National Historic District

Unlike its Hampton neighbors, Sag Harbor has always been a workingman's town. Built on industry rather than tourism, it has a hometown look and blue collar atmosphere that has attracted writers rather than painters to its shores. It was here that James Fenimore Cooper found inspiration for his sea tales, where John Steinbeck spent his last years, where Lanford Wilson writes his prize-winning plays, and novelist Velda Johnston creates her stories of romance and suspense. During the mid-19th century Sag Harbor ranked with New Bedford and Nantucket as a leading U.S. whaling port and is duly mentioned in *Moby Dick*. In the days of the tall ships Sag Harbor was a lusty and boisterous place. Its streets bustled with merchants, coopers, ships' chandlers, and sailors speaking a variety of languages. In 1845 there were 35 bars on Main Street alone, not to mention an untold number of brothels tucked away in a red-light district. Today there are still drinking men's bars that are suitably seedy and where the out-of-towner is not especially welcome. Back then, the rowdies were made to toe the line, however, since the majority of ships' masters, crewmen, and villagers were a God-fearing lot. The well-known hymn tune "Jesus Saviour Pilot Me" was written by the Rev. Edward Hopper, minister at the Old Whalers Presbyterian Church (the one that lost its steeple in the hurricane of '38). Whaling voyages often lasted for years at a time and when an inbound ship was spied approaching the harbor, perhaps by an anxious wife or mother keeping watch from a widow's walk, it was the custom to run up a flag on the old Beebe windmill (the same mill that stands in Bridgehampton). The cry would go out: "Flag on the mill! Ship in the bay!"

Swashbuckling adventures were part of the local scene even before the whaling era. During the Revolutionary War the British fleet was anchored in Gardiner's Bay following their victory in the Battle of Long Island. In May 1777, a daring commando operation was carried out by a Col. Meigs and 130 Continentals who rowed across the Sound from Connecticut to Peconic Bay. From there they conducted a pre-dawn raid on the British garrison quartered on the site of the American Hotel on Main Street. The raiders set fire to 12 enemy ships, captured a number of Redcoats, and returned to the mainland without the loss of a single man.

A number of firsts: In 1789 Sag Harbor was declared the first U.S. Port of Entry in New York State. The first Custom House in the state was also here and can be inspected in restored condition at the corner of Main and Garden Streets. Long Island's first newspaper, the *Long Island Herald,* was published here in 1791. Its editor, David Frothingham, had the misfortune of backing Aaron Burr in his dispute with Alexander Hamilton, was arrested on a libel charge and disappeared under mysterious circumstances. Frothingham's wife continued publishing the paper for several years, no doubt becoming the first newspaperwoman in the United States and setting a local tradition. Today the village supports two hometown newspapers, both published by women.

With the California gold rush of 1849 and the drilling of the first oil well in Pennsylvania ten years later—reducing the need for whale oil—Sag Harbor's heyday came to an end. A number of light industries flourished for a while, but prosperity as the villagers had known was to be a thing of the past. Today, several light industries and the building trades provide employment for the whalers' descendants. The majority of young people, however, must seek their fortunes on distant shores as in the days of old. It is ironic that as the Hamptons developed into fashionable summer resorts, Sag Harbor declined into a virtual ghost town by the 1940s, since few could afford to make alterations to their century-old houses. The result, of course, is that today Sag Harbor homes can boast of a preserved and well-cared-for look instead of the simulated appearance so often found in historic restorations. Throughout the village you will find excellent examples of Colonial, Federal, Greek Revival, and Late Victorian styles. A walking-tour map is available at the Windmill Information Center on Long Wharf. House tours are conducted by the Friends of the Library several times a year, and a two-day Whalers Festival is held during the second weekend in June. Classes in sailing, scuba diving, and wind-surfing are conducted at Long Beach in nearby North Haven.

To reach the north fork from Sag Harbor, take Route 114 through North Haven to the Shelter Island ferry. Continue on Route 114 to the Shelter Island–Greenport ferry.

East Hampton and Montauk

East Hampton is reached via Route 114 from Sag Harbor or Route 27 from Bridgehampton. It is no idle boast that East Hampton has been described as "America's most beautiful village." At the intersection of Route 27 and Main Street you come upon a tree-shaded village green and lily pond that is Currier & Ives. In the background stands a venerable English-style country church and an ancient cemetery. Among its crumbling stones is one designating the resting place of Lion Gardiner, New York State's first English settler and Lord of Gardiner's Island. In the vicinity are two well-preserved homes, now run as museums, the Mulford Farm and the Home Sweet Home residence of composer John Howard Payne. Farther along Main Street you pass Guild Hall and the John Drew Summer Theater, the east end's cultural center. Across from it are the village newspaper office, library, and Clinton Academy museum. The shopping district lies along Main Street and Newtown Lane. East Hampton restaurants are plentiful and tend to be on the expensive side, and if restaurant reviews are to be relied on, price is not always an indication of quality. As an alternative you might try one of the many church suppers, benefit barbecues, or cocktail parties held throughout the summer, where food is usually abundant, prices reasonable, and may include entertainment and the chance to meet local celebrities. Check the newspapers for times and places. Past Newtown Lane Route 27 forks into North Main Street to the left of the village windmill. The remaining stretch of Route 27 goes to Amagansett and Montauk. North Main again forks into Three Mile Harbor Road and the Springs Fireplace Road. Both lead through miles of woodland and newer residential areas. According to local history, travelers to Gardiner's Island would light a signal fire at road's end to summon a boat from the island. The privately owned island is not open to the public. A number of good restaurants with reasonable prices can be found in the Three Mile Harbor area.

Amagansett has fully recovered from its status as the "in" place for swinging singles during the 1970s. Today it appears to attract a jogging crowd whose healthy good looks are an inducement to wholesome living. An interesting assortment of shops can be found in the Amagansett Square shopping mall, including a gallery devoted entirely to leather art. In spite of its tiny size the village boasts two museums: the Amelia Cottage and Carriage House on Route 27 and the East Hampton Town Marine Museum at Atlantic Avenue and Bluff Road (turn right at the Main Street flagpole). While marine buffs inspect whaling artifacts and displays of tides, navigational devices and vintage baymen's boats, children will delight in exploring a landbound outdoor fleet that includes the pilothouse of a real tugboat, a ship's hold, and the various nautical gear a sailor might use on board ship. Courses in wooden boat building are conducted several times a year.

A long stretch of road crosses the Napeague dunes before you reach the easternmost village of Montauk. Wild cranberries, beach plums and blueberries grow here in profusion. The road divides between a low road that follows the original Montauk Highway along the ocean, and a high road with an overlook where you can pause for breathtaking views of the Atlantic Ocean and Block Island Sound. Montauk is a place of rugged beauty where the emphasis is definitely on fishing. First-time visitors are surprised, however, at finding a seven-story city-style office building in the middle of town, awkwardly at odds with its surroundings. Vacant except for a real-estate office occupying the ground floor, it was built in 1927 as Carl Fisher's headquarters. Fisher was a wheeler-dealer millionaire who had hoped to repeat his earlier feat as builder of Miami Beach by transforming Montauk into a colossal summer resort. His plans included lavish estates and a deep-water port to accommodate ocean liners for his fellow millionaires, as well as 25-foot-wide lots to be sold to the working classes who would arrive by railroad. The great depression of 1929 put an end to his schemes, but not before he had erected the beautiful Montauk Manor on a spectacular hilltop setting. The Manor was run as a luxury hotel until well into the fifties. Since then it has stood like a white elephant, defying several attempts to convert it to condominium use.

Montauk's most famous landmark, however, is the ancient lighthouse that has stood watch at land's end for 200 years. Its construction was authorized by George Washington in order to make the passage round the point less hazardous to navigation. Over the years the shoals around Montauk have become a graveyard for ships, which is also one of the reasons they provide some of the best fishing action along the entire East Coast. In summer the Montauk "fleet" swells to over 1,000 boats of every category. Charter boats carry sportsmen to the blue Atlantic for marlin, giant tuna, and swordfish, while party boats take anglers to the offshore haunts of blues, porgies, weaks, and flounder. Even during winter dedicated anglers brave mountainous seas for deep-water cod. Surfcasters will find plenty of action with stripers all along the Montauk shore. A number of sightseeing cruises, moonlight sails, and a passenger ferry to Block Island are available at the fishing docks. There are a number of good restaurants in the Westlake Drive area and prices are, for the most part, reasonable. Gosman's Dock is laid out along the lines of a New England village and includes an assortment of specialty shops, a retail fish market, outside clam bar, and waterfront restaurant. Oddly enough, Montauk had one of the earliest cattle ranches in the United States. Teddy Roosevelt also camped his Rough Riders here and you can still follow those early trails on horseback. Riding facilities are at Hidden Echoes Ranch and Deep Hollow Ranch.

The lighthouse is open for inspection by groups of 10 or more and includes a museum room filled with nautical artifacts and lighthouse lore. Admission is free, but since the facility is an active duty station of the United States Coast Guard, prior arrangements must be made. Write:

Commanding Officer: Light Station Montauk Point
P.O. Box 321
Montauk, NY 11954

PRACTICAL INFORMATION FOR LONG ISLAND

HOW TO GET THERE. This string of towns along the South Shore of Long Island begins with Westhampton, about 30 miles beyond Bay Shore. Then comes Westhampton Beach, Hampton Bays, Southampton, and East Hampton.

THE HAMPTONS

By car. From Manhattan and points west, take the Long Island Expressway

(495) east to exit 68. Go south on William Floyd Parkway to Route 27. East on Sunrise Highway to the Hamptons and Montauk.

By air. *US Air* from major cities to Long Island-MacArthur Airport in Ronkonkoma. *East Hampton Aire* operates scheduled year-round air-taxi service between La Guardia Airport and East Hampton Airport. Tel. (516) 537–0560.

By train. Train service on the Long Island Railroad is frequent—at least on weekends—but it is often late and can be uncomfortable. From Manhattan fares range from $8.40 (Westhampton) to about $9.75 (East Hampton). Travel time is just over 2 hours for the former to almost 3 hours for the latter. There are also stations in Jamaica, Queens, and downtown Brooklyn.

By ferry. There is excellent and frequent service across Long Island Sound from Connecticut. Ferries from Bridgeport come into Port Jefferson Tel. 473–0286; those from New London dock at Orient Point Tel. 323–2525. Connecting ferries to the South Fork operate from Greenport to Shelter Island and North Haven.

By bus. *Hampton Jitney* operates year-round coach and minibus service between East Side Manhattan and the Hamptons; also an airport connection in Queens with flights from JFK and La Guardia. Tel. (516) 537–3880, (516) 653–4659, (212) 895–1941.

FIRE ISLAND

By car. *Robert Moses State Park:* Southern State Pkwy east to exit 40. South on Robert Moses Causeway (toll). *Smith Point Park:* From Manhattan and points north, take the L.I. Expressway east to exit 68. South on William Floyd Pkwy to Smith Point Bridge (toll). From Brooklyn, Verrazano Bridge, points south, take Southern State Pkwy to exit 44 east. Sunrise Hwy to William Floyd Pkwy and Smith Point Bridge.

The drive to Bay Shore, for example, from Manhattan can take anywhere from just over an hour to more than double that, depending on what time you leave. Long Island's culture is centered around the automobile and on summer weekends people take to the road early. On Friday nights it is even worse because New Yorkers are heading for their weekend retreats. Allow plenty of time.

Ferry service (passengers only) is provided from the towns of Bay Shore, Sayville, and Patchogue, as follows:

Communities serviced:	**Bay Shore Terminal**
Seaview	Long Island Expwy east to Sagtikos Pkwy South; left
Ocean Bay Park	lane exits onto Southern State Pkwy. Get off first
Ocean Beach	exit: 5th Ave.- Bay Shore, go south. Turn left on
Kismet	Main St., right on Maple St. (4th Ave.), follow to
Dunewood	end.
Saltaire	
Fair Harbor	

Sayville Terminal

Cherry Grove
Fire Island Pines
Sailor's Haven
(Sunken Forest)

Long Island Expwy east to Sagtikos Pkwy South; left lane exits onto Southern State Pkwy. Get off at Sunrise Hwy East exit, right off Sunrise onto Lakeland Ave. Go 2 miles to 2nd traffic light (Main St.), follow green and white signs to ferry terminal.

Sandspit Terminal (Patchogue)

Davis Park
Leja Beach
Ocean Ridge

Southern State Pkwy to exit 44 east. Sunrise Hwy to S. Ocean Ave. Turn right on S. Ocean to Maiden Lane/Brightwood St.

National Seashore Terminal (Patchogue)

Watch Hill

Follow above directions to S. Ocean Ave. Cross railroad tracks, turn right on Division St. Pass the railroad station, turn left on West Ave. The terminal is behind the bowling alley.

By train. Take the Long Island Railroad to Bay Shore, Sayville, or Patchogue. With the exception of the National Seashore Terminal, which is a short walk from the railroad station, a taxi is necessary to reach the ferry terminals. Train fare from Manhattan is about $5.00 and travel time is about 2 hours.

By air. *Watair Express, Inc.* operates seaplane service from the Marine Aviation Terminal in downtown Manhattan. Flying time is ½ hour. (516) 981–4634. Air taxis from other locations include *Gold Coast* (212) 885–1875, *Jersey City Seaplane* (201) 332–6105, *Pelham Airways* (212) 828–0420, and *Suburban Seaplane* (212) 895–6855.

TELEPHONE. The area code for Long Island (Nassau and Suffolk counties) is 516. This area code applies to all telephone numbers listed here.

TOURIST INFORMATION SERVICES. *The Long Island Tourism Commission,* MacArthur Airport, Ronkonkoma, NY 11779. *Fire Island National Seashore,* 120 Laurel St., Patchogue, NY 11772. *Long Island State Park & Recreation Commission,* Belmont Lake State Park, Babylon, NY 11702. *Suffolk County Department of Parks, Recreation and Conservation,* Montauk Highway, West Sayville, NY 11796. Up-to-date listings of hotel, motel, and guest house accommodations are available from Chambers of Commerce at 74 Park Place, East Hampton, NY 11937; 324–0362; Box CC, Montauk Hwy, Montauk, NY 11954; 668–2428; 76 Main St., Southampton, NY 11968; 283–0402; 123A Main St., Westhampton Beach, NY 11978; 288–3337.

HOW TO GET AROUND. Most of the Hamptons and Long Island South Shore communities facing Fire Island have telephone-ordered radio-taxi services. But the only efficient way to get around on Long Island—except on Fire Island, where there are no roads—is by car. If you don't have one available, rent one.

Long Island's highways will get you the length of the island but most of them alternate between limited-access sections and double-duty stretches as the main streets of towns and villages. They usually have names as well as numbers, so asking directions may elicit a confusing, though well-intended answer. By all means, have a map along.

Towns on the South Shore are served directly by State 27A, called Merrick Road in the western half of the island, Montauk Highway in the eastern, a winding, busy thoroughfare. A bit to the north, but requiring less perseverance, is State 27, called Sunrise Highway. It runs as far out as Southhampton, then joins State 27A for the last lap to Montauk. The Southern State Parkway, with no consistent numerical designation, runs from Kennedy Airport to East Islip.

Down the center, you brave the Long Island Expressway from Manhattan to Riverhead. Thereafter, take State 25 to the north fork and Orient Point or State 24 southeast for a link-up in Hampton Bays with State 27 to Montauk.

STATE AND NATIONAL PARKS. Long Island has 21 state parks scattered along its north and south shores, and in between. *Jones Beach State Park,* in Wantagh, Nassau County, is one of the largest and most beautiful ocean parks on the East Coast. Its attractions include 5 miles of ocean beach, a 2-mile-long boardwalk, heated swimming, diving and wading pools, sit-down and fast-food restaurants, and scores of activities for children and adults. A spectacular Broadway show is featured at the Jones Beach Marine Theater throughout the summer. Facilities for use by handicapped persons are available at all L.I. state parks. *Captree* has both "open" and charter fishing boats. *Heckscher State Park* in East Islip, *Hither Hills,* near Montauk, and *Wildwood* at Wading River on the North Shore have campsites. Most parks have hiking trails, bridle paths, picnic areas, and refreshment stands. At the 160-acre *Montauk Downs State Park* facilities include a clubhouse, golf and tennis pro shop, locker rooms, restaurant, catering service, 18-hole golf course, driving range, 6 fast-dry tennis courts, swimming, diving and wading pools. Entry fees run from $1.50 to $2.00 per car. For further information and a full listing of camping and recreational facilities on the Island, contact: The Long Island State Park and Recreation Commission, Belmont Lake State Park, Babylon, NY 11702. *Fire Island National Seashore.* Marinas at Sailor's Haven and Watch Hill, nature walks at both. New campsites at Watch Hill. The Sunken Forest at Sailor's Haven is one of nature's wonders.

NATIONAL WILDLIFE REFUGES. Target Rock National Wildlife Refuge. Target Rock Road, Lloyd Neck, Huntington, NY 11743. This refuge serves as headquarters for the complex of refuges on Long Island and is located 15 miles east of New York City, 8 miles north of Huntington, off West Neck Road at the east end of the Lloyd Neck Peninsula. Established in 1970, this lovely 80-acre estate, donated to the Service by the Eberstadt family, will be a focal point for marine and ecological research, conservation education, and environmental interpretation. Warbler migrations coinciding with the peak of the rhododendron blooming season make this garden spot highly attractive in the third week of May. The area, due to its size, can be open only to limited public use and only for nature study purposes. A formal Environmental Education Program for students and teachers has developed at this site. Advance reservations are required for use of the interpretive trails because no more than 50 visitors can be accommodated at one time.

The following six refuges are under administration of Target Rock Refuge:

Amagansett National Wildlife Refuge. Located 4 miles east of East Hampton on Long Island, just off the Montauk Highway (Route 27) along Bluff Road. Established in 1968, it consists of 36 acres including 1,342 feet of barrier beach and the associated dune complex along the Atlantic. The property has special significance in the protection of a small segment of unspoiled beach and dunes. With interesting vegetation it has great value for environmental study of beach and duneland ecology. Public access is allowed along the shore for sport fishing, hiking and photography. A Special Use Permit is required for entrance into the fragile dunes.

Conscience Point National Wildlife Refuge. Near North Sea, Long Island (Suffolk County). Its 60 acres were bequeathed to the Service by the former owner in 1971. The area consists of open fields, meadows, woodlands, and about 15 acres of brackish marsh. It is an attractive area for nature study and is expected to be used in environmental education programs.

Morton National Wildlife Refuge. Located on Noyack Road, near the junction of Millstone Road, Long Island, off Route 27, between Little Peconic Bay and Noyack Bay. Donated in 1954 by Elizabeth Alexandra Morton, this 187-acre refuge serves as a resting area for waterfowl and shorebirds. A 2-mile trail to the north tip of Jessups Neck provides a delightful setting for nature study and photography. Interpretive facilities are available.

Oyster Bay National Wildlife Refuge. Located 12 miles east of New York City in Long Island Sound, adjacent to the town of Oyster Bay. Established in 1968, it comprises significant portions of the marsh and open bay areas of Mill Neck Creek, Oyster Bay, and Cold Spring Harbor. This 3,117-acre refuge is of special value in the protection and management of migratory birds and its preservation will be of value in the perpetuation of the existing ecology of the adjacent tidal wetlands and bay bottom. Portions of the area adjoining the refuge are used extensively for pleasure boating, fishing, swimming, waterfowl hunting, and commercial shellfishing. Access is limited.

Seatuck National Wildlife Refuge. Located near Islip, and established in 1968, this 10-acre refuge is subject to the life estate of the donors and is not open for public use. The area contains valuable habitat for migrating waterfowl, songbirds, shorebirds, and resident mammals. This refuge will serve as a valuable environmental studies site in future years.

Wertheim National Wildlife Refuge. In Brookhaven on Long Island. Established in 1947, it consists of 2,191 acres of brackish marsh, salt marsh, fresh meadows, and uplands. The Carmen River, recognized as a state scenic river, passes through the refuge. The area is a valuable waterfowl and shorebird habitat, containing one of the last natural esturine environments remaining on Long Island.

MUSEUMS. Amagansett: *Town Marine Museum.* Atlantic Ave. and Bluff Road. A see-and-touch museum with interesting and informative exhibits of marine life, fishing and whaling lore. Children's playground.

East Hampton: *"Home Sweet Home."* James Lane. Colonial saltbox, circa 1660, in which John Howard Payne composed his famous tune. The lovely Gardiner windmill (not open to public) stands next door, as does the *Mulford Farm.* A companion saltbox filled with fine antiques including English Staffordshire china brought over by the original owner.

Sag Harbor: *Suffolk County Whaling Museum.* Main St. Collections of whaling artifacts, scrimshaw. The beautiful 1845 Greek Revival mansion was built by Minard Lefever. The building outshines the collections therein.

Old Custom House. Across from Whaling Museum. The restored home of Henry Packer Dering, who was postmaster here in 1794 while moonlighting as the customs collector for the Port of Sag Harbor.

Fire Museum. Sage and Church Sts. Here you will see some of the accoutrements firemen used to save the village from ravishing fires in 1817, 1845 and 1877. The State's first chartered Volunteer Fire Company was organized here in 1819.

Southampton: *Parrish Art Museum.* Jobs Lane. Permanent collection of Renaissance art; sculpture garden with classical Roman and Greek statuary; an American art section changes exhibits frequently; one of the most beautiful museums anywhere.

Southold: *Indian Museum.* Bayview Road. Indian artifacts and archeological digs. Presently open Sunday afternoons only.

Riverhead: *Suffolk County Historical Society Museum.* Near County Center Bypass at W. Main St. Excellent collections of Indian artifacts and Colonial antiques. Changing exhibits feature various aspect of life in Southampton Town over the centuries.

Water Mill: *Old Water Mill Museum.* Old Mill Road near Rte. 27. The 1644 mill has been restored to working condition. Freshly milled flour and cornmeal can be purchased. Show-and-touch exhibits of looms, spinning wheels, farming implements, old American handtools. Gift shop.

West Sayville: *Suffolk Marine Museum.* West Ave. at State 27A. Permanent and changing displays depict the lives of South Shore baymen.

 WHAT TO DO WITH THE CHILDREN. *Long Island Game Farm.* Manorville, L.I. Expressway, exit 70. An animal wonderland where children can walk among small animals that roam free. Sea lion shows, monkeys galore, snack bar, and picnic area.

Hampton Bays Amusement Park, Hampton Bays. Rte. 27A. A commercial fun city for kids, with rides, games, and a video arcade.

Playground activities: Most Hampton towns offer programs from swimming and sailing lessons to arts-and-crafts projects. There are also roller-skating rinks in Hampton Bays and Southampton. Tutors and babysitters advertise in the local papers.

 TOURS. The Long Island Railroad offers a variety of reasonably priced day-long tours. The tours leave from Penn Station, Brooklyn, or Long Island's Jamaica Station. Their "Around Long Island Tour" includes the train to Westhampton, a bus ride to Greenport, and ferry rides to Shelter Island and Sag Harbor, a visit to Montauk Point and return. The National Park Service runs free guided tours through the Sunken Forest on Fire Island. In addition to do-it-yourself walking tours, guided field trips, house and garden tours and visits to well-known artists' studios are held throughout the Hamptons area from spring to fall. Check the local papers or contact the East End Arts and Humanities Council, 133 E. Main Street, Riverhead, NY 11901; Tel. 727–0900.

 MUSIC. A *Bach Aria Festival* is held at the State University of New York at Stony Brook sometime in late June and early July. Call (516) 246–3511 or 246–5678 for information. Summer theaters include *John Drew* at East Hampton, and the *Jones Beach Marine Theater*—the latter offering musical extravanganzas. Summer band concerts are held on Tuesday nights at Marine Park in Sag Harbor against a background of twinkling harbor lights. Admission is free; bring blanket or camp chairs.

 SPORTS. *Swimming. Jones Beach State Park,* Wantagh Pkwy, where millions splash in the cool Atlantic surf or saltwater pools on hot summer days. *Hither Hills State Park,* Montauk, offers bathing, fishing, and picnicking. Superb *public beaches* at East Hampton, Fire Island, Patchogue, Quogue, Sayville, Shelter Island, Southampton, and Westhampton Beach, all on the Atlantic side. Most beaches on Long Island Sound are private.

Charter boats for *deep sea fishing* are available at many East-end ports. Party boats operating out of Hampton Bays and Montauk offer half-day, full-day, and night fishing trips to Peconic Bay, L.I.Sound, and offshore reefs. The Shinnecock Canal at Hampton Bays affords landlubbers a chance to try their luck for flounder, snapper, and weakfish; bait and tackle shops are nearby. Marine facilities and small boat rentals are available throughout the Hamptons.

Horseback riding. Sears Bellows Riding Stables, Route 24, Hampton Bays; beach and trail riding at Hidden Echoes Ranch and Deep Hollow Ranch, Montauk.

Skating. Skatehampton, County Road 39A, Southampton; 283–9109.

Golf. Bridgehampton, *Poxabogue Course,* 9 holes, greens fee $4–$4.50. Commack, *Commack Hills Course,* 18 holes, fee $6–$10.

 HOTELS AND MOTELS can be found in all categories from no-frills roadside cabins to luxurious oceanfront resorts with kitchenettes and maid service. Most are filled during the summer, especially in August, and may require a minimum stay and advance deposit. Bed and breakfast in private homes in the Hamptons can be arranged for stays of two nights or longer. *Lodgings Plus* offers budget ($26–$48), moderate ($54–$74) and deluxe ($76–$96) accommodations. Rates are for singles, $10 more for a second person in room. Telephone (516) 324–6740 or (212) 828–9589, or write Box 279, East Hampton, NY 11937; Visa, MasterCard. *Hampton Hosts* offers a fixed rate of $40 single, $55 double in season, $5 extra per child. Telephone (516) 324–9351 or (212) 689–1920, or write Box 507, East Hampton, NY 11937; All lodgings provide bedroom, private or semi-private bath, and Continental breakfast. For the East Hampton area, a list of guesthouses is available at the East Hampton Chamber of Commerce, 74 Park Place, East Hampton, NY 11937.

AMAGANSETT

Sea Crest. *Deluxe.* Montauk Hwy, Napeague section, 48 units, all oceanfront. Heated pool, 2 tennis courts. One-week minimum stay during season. Deposit required.

Ocean Colony Motel & Tennis Club. *Expensive.* Montauk Hwy, Napeague section. 400-ft. private ocean beach; 2 pro tennis courts (free). Studios and suites with kitchenettes, 1- and 2-bedroom cottages. Pets accepted. Off-season rates April 15 to June 19 and September 11 to October 15.

Gansett Green Manor. *Moderate.* Box 799, Main St. Walking distance to ocean beaches and village; guest rooms, studios, and 1-bedroom efficiencies with kitchens; 1- and 2-bedroom cottages; laundromat; pets accepted conditionally. April 1 thru December 26.

The Mill Garth. *Moderate.* Windmill Lane. Complex of apartments and cottages in country garden setting; walking distance to ocean. All accommodations have kitchens, private entrance, and daily maid service. Open all year.

EAST HAMPTON

Holiday Acres Motel & Cottages. *Expensive.* Montauk Hwy.; 324–0565. Motel efficiency units, 1- and 2-bedroom cottages; outdoor grills for each cottage, picnic tables. Off-season rates.

The Hunting Inn. *Expensive.* 94 Main St.; 324–0410. Old World inn that dates back to 1699. Quiet location, spacious grounds, restaurant, cocktail lounge.

Michael's. *Expensive.* Maidstone and Park Roads, off Three-Mile Harbor Road; 324–0725. Fine seafood, steaks, and Continental dishes. Very plain decor; casual dress. Best to reserve. Major credit cards.

East Hampton House. *Deluxe.* Montauk Hwy, 1 mi. E. of village. Individual patios, heated pool. One-week minimum stay in season. Deposit required.

Hedge's House. *Deluxe.* Restored 18th-century inn. 14 guest rooms, each with private bath. En Brochette restaurant on premises. Outdoor dining patios.

Dutch Motel. *Moderate.* 488 Montauk Hwy. One- and 2-room efficiencies and apartments. Maid service, laundromat, cable TV, pool. Restaurant on premises. Open all year.

Three Mile Harbor Inn. *Inexpensive.* 324–9857. Cottages with kitchenettes, sleeping 2 to 4 persons. Cocktail lounge, walking distance to Bay. Group rates available.

FIRE ISLAND

Overnight accommodations on Fire Island are scarce and sometimes impossible to come by on short notice. Some communities have no overnight facilities for travelers whatsoever. Where accommodations exist, most hotels require guests to sign up for two nights (Friday and Saturday) on a weekend; reservations for summer weekends should be made at least three weeks ahead.

Dune Gate Motel. *Deluxe.* Kismet; 583–8565. 29 units near ocean, includes kitchens, bathrooms, tennis court. No credit cards.

Clegg's Hotel. Ocean Beach; 583–5399. Simple but practical, 14 rooms rented by the season, with some vacancies for transients. No credit cards.

Houser's Hotel. Ocean Beach; 583–5387. Simple but practical, 12 rooms, restaurant and bar. Visa, MasterCard.

Jerry's. *Expensive.* Ocean Beach; 583–8870. 168 Cottage Walk.

Flynn's Hotel. Ocean Bay Park; 583–5000. Simple but practical, rooms for 125 guests near the ocean. Most major credit cards.

Belvedere Hotel. *Expensive.* Cherry Grove; 597–6448. 20 double rooms. Visa, MasterCard.

Beach Hotel. *Deluxe.* Cherry Grove; 597–6600. 60 rooms, most major credit cards.

Fire Island Pines Hotel. *Deluxe.* Fire Island Pines; 597–6500. 28 rooms on the harbor, swimming pool, coffee shop. Most major credit cards.

Leja Beach Casino. Davis Park; 597–6150. Simple but practical, 10 rooms, restaurant, bar, disco. No credit cards.

HAMPTON BAYS

Allen's Acres Resort Motel. *Moderate.* 728–4698. 62 motel and efficiencies. Private patios, 2 pools, coffee shop, cocktail lounge, and restaurant. Boating/fishing dock.

Hidden Cove Efficiency Motel. *Moderate.* 33A West Tiana Rd., 728–6767. Kitchenette efficiencies, cable TV, pool, barbecues, recreation area, bike rentals, pool. Tennis nearby. Weekly, weekend, off-season rates. Open all year.

SAG HARBOR

Baron's Cove Inn. *Deluxe.* 725–2100. Motel, marina and restaurant. All rooms with picture windows overlooking harbor. TV, pool, sundeck.

Whaler's Motel. *Expensive.* Long Island Ave.; 725–2420. 9 units on waterfront. Open April through November.

SHELTER ISLAND

Dering Harbor Inn. *Deluxe.* Winthrop Road, 2 blocks east of NY 114; 749–0900. 29 air-conditioned units, all overlooking the harbor. Some with fireplaces and some kitchenettes. Café, bar, entertainment, and dancing. Pool, tennis, and boat dock. Closed November through April.

Pridwin Hotel & Cottages. *Expensive.* Shore Road, 1½ miles west off NY 114; 749–0476. 40 hotel rooms and 11 cottages. Private patios and balconies. Private beach. Café, bar, entertainment, and dancing. Water sports and golf privileges. Hotel closed October through May.

SOUTHAMPTON

The Sandpiper. *Deluxe.* North Hwy, Shinnecock Hills; 283–1940. Motel units, cottages, and efficiencies. Private beach, tennis, pool. Off-season rates. Open all year.

Southampton Inn. *Deluxe.* 91 Hill Street at First Neck Lane, 1 block west of State 27A; 283–6500. Luxury accommodations in Tudor-style inn. Tavern on premises. Tennis, pool, spa.

Squaw Island Resort. *Expensive.* North Sea Road; 283–3333. Family-style resort, private beach, playground, tennis, pool.

Hampton Heritage. *Moderate.* Route 27; 283–4220. Air-conditioned units, cable TV. Off-season rates. Open all year.

MONTAUK

Montauk has more than 78 motel facilities ranging from moderate to super-deluxe categories. Reservations are a must during the summer. Most motels offer off-season and special package rates after September 15th.

Montauk Yacht Club & Inn. *Deluxe.* Star Island Rd, off West Lake Dr.; 668–3100. A full-service Inn-Marina-Executive Conference Center and Spa complex on Lake Montauk. Two fine restaurants with music nightly. Indoor and outdoor pools.

Atlantic Terrace Motel. *Expensive.* Rte. 27; 668–2050. Family resort on the ocean. Heated pool, recreation room, and lounge. Continental breakfast is included.

Harborside Resort Motel. *Expensive.* West Lake Dr.; 668–2511. 21 units with kitchenettes. 2 professional all-weather tennis courts. Barbecue area, pool, adjacent to marina. 1 mile from Montauk Downs Golf.

WESTHAMPTON BEACH

Dune Deck. *Deluxe.* Dune Rd.; 288–4100. 86 rooms, pool, ocean beach, tennis courts. 20 percent discount on weekly rates. Breakfast and dinner included.

Westhampton Bath & Tennis Club & Resort. *Deluxe.* Dune Rd.; 288–2500. Luxurious bath and tennis club. Spacious rooms and suites. Restaurants, cocktail lounge, and coffee shop. Olympic-size pool and sauna, private beach and marina. 10 tennis courts.

 NIGHT LIFE. The Hampton disco scene is without doubt the liveliest on the East Coast. Fire Island discos are unrivaled anywhere. Cover charges vary and may not apply until 10:00 P.M. Some are restaurant-discos, others disco-bars.

FIRE ISLAND

The Monster, Cherry Grove. *The Ice Palace,* Cherry Grove. *The Pavillion,* Fire Island Pines. *The Inn,* Kismet. *The Out,* Kismet. *Maguire's Bay Front Restaurant,* Ocean Beach. *Flynn's,* Ocean Bay Park, for singles.

WESTHAMPTON BEACH AREA

Scarlett's, Westhampton Beach.; 288–9739. *Club Marakesh,* Westhampton Beach; 288–2023. *JK's TO,* Beach Road & Montauk Hwy.; 288–9368. *Neptune Beach Club,* Dune Road, East Quogue; 653–6921. *The Barge,* Dune Road, East Quogue. *The Mad Hatter,* Montauk Hwy, East Quogue; 653–6885.

HAMPTON BAYS

La Plage, Foster Ave. *OBI East,* Off Sunrise Hwy, Exit 65 south at Montauk Hwy.; 728–4121.

East Side Comedy. In Southampton Inn, 91 Hill St.; 283–6500. Name comedians, in a dinner-theater type set-up. Light food. $10.00 cover. Open Memorial Day to Labor Day, Thursday to Sunday nights; shows at 10:30 P.M. except at 8:30 P.M. Sunday. Reserve. Major credit cards.

SOUTHAMPTON

Great Scott, Tuckahoe Lane and Rt. 27; 283–5090. *LeMans,* intersection of Rtes. 27 & 27A; 283–8800. Fabulous disco in converted bowling alley. Celebrity hangout.

WATER MILL

27 East Supper Club, Montauk Hwy.

BRIDGEHAMPTON

Woodshed Saloon, Montauk Hwy. west of Bridgehampton. Live country-and-Western music Friday and Saturday.

WAINSCOTT

The Swamp caters to a gay crowd.

 DINING OUT. Fresh seafood from local waters and produce grown on nearby farms are featured at most restaurants and prepared in a variety of cuisines that reflect the international tastes of Hamptonians. Prices are generally on the expensive side and reservations are recommended, especially on summer weekends. Price categories may be interpreted as follows: *Deluxe,* $12.50 and above; *Expensive,* $10.00–$12.50; *Moderate,* $6.50–$10.00; and *Inexpensive,* below $6.50.

AMAGANSETT

Ashley's. *Expensive.* Amagansett Square; 267–6508. N.Y. café-restaurant serving breakfast, lunch, and dinner. Indoor/outdoor dining.

Gordon's. *Deluxe.* Main St.; 267–3010. Pretentious service, good food. By reservation only.

The Lobster Roll. *Moderate.* Montauk Hwy at Napeague; 267–3740. Simple but good. A popular place for lunch.

Lobsters Unlimited. *Moderate.* Main St.; 267–8893. Take-out seafood dinners.

The Inn at Napeague. *Deluxe.* Montauk Hwy.; 267–8103. Mediterranean specialties.

The Lobster Roll. (see Montauk')

BRIDGEHAMPTON

Bobby Van's. *Expensive.* Montauk Hwy.; 537–0590. Popular with the local literati. All major credit cards.

H.S.F. (Hee Seung Fung). *Expensive.* Montauk Hwy. East end branch of famous N.Y. City Chinese eatery. All major credit cards.

Candy Kitchen. *Moderate.* Montauk Hwy. Old-fashioned luncheonette, famous for its Sunday breakfast and homemade ice cream. The Hampton Jitney stops at its door.

EAST HAMPTON

Laundry Restaurant. *Deluxe.* Race Lane; 324–3199. Dinner nightly, lunch on weekends. Credit cards.

The Palm at the Huntting Inn. *Deluxe.* Main St.; 324–0411. East end branch of posh N.Y.C. restaurant. Closed Tuesdays. American Express.

1770 House. *Deluxe.* Main St.; 324–1770. Continental cuisine in elegantly restored home. Guest room available. Credit cards.

Buoy Restaurant. *Moderate.* Montauk Hwy. east of village; 324–9010. Closed Wednesday. MasterCard.

Il Monestero. *Moderate.* N. Main St.; 324–8008. Italian specialties. Visa, MasterCard.

FIRE ISLAND

The Kismet Inn. *Moderate.* Kismet; 583–8443. Popular established seafood restaurant.

Le Dock. Fair Harbor; 583–5200. French restaurant.

Leo's Place. Ocean Beach; 583–8088.

Maguire's Bay Front Restaurant. *Moderate.* Ocean Beach; 483–8800. Oldest and largest restaurant on Fire Island, seats 375 indoors and on deck. Dancing. Most major credit cards.

Matthew's Seafood House. *Expensive.* Ocean Beach; 583–8016. Overlooks Great South Bay.

The Schooner Inn. Ocean Bay Park; 583–8498.

The Skimmer. *Moderate.* Ocean Bay Park; 583–8438. Italian food. No credit cards.

The Monster. *Moderate.* Cherry Grove; 597–6888. Restaurant, disco, nightclub. No credit cards.

The Pavilion. *Expensive.* Fire Island Pines; 597–6677. Restaurant and late-night disco. Dining on covered deck overlooking harbor. Continental food. Most major credit cards.

The Pines and Dunes Yacht Club. *Expensive.* Fire Island Pines; 597–6131. Tables on deck overlooking harbor, most major credit cards.

Leja Beach Casino. *Moderate.* Davis Park; 597–6150. Overlooks ocean. Disco. No credit cards.

HAMPTON BAYS

Judge's. *Expensive.* North of Montauk Hwy. on the canal; 728–1717. Credit cards.

Chart Inn. *Moderate.* On the canal; 728–1111. Credit cards.

Fish Net. *Moderate.* Montauk Hwy. east of town; 728–0115. Good seafood. No credit cards.

Villa Paul. *Moderate.* Montauk Hwy.; 728–9552. Italian-American cuisine. Credit cards.

MONTAUK

Gurney's Inn. *Deluxe.* Old Montauk Hwy. east of village; 668–2345. Ocean-front dining in large resort-spa complex. Credit cards.

Gosman's Restaurant. *Expensive.* Westlake Drive overlooking Montauk Hwy; 668–5330. Indoor/outdoor dining in nautical setting. Dockside clam bar. Jammed on weekends. No credit cards.

The Anchorage. *Moderate.* Westlake Drive; 668–9394. Open year round. Credit cards.

Gatsby's. *Moderate.* In-town ice-cream parlor and dessertery; family game room.

Kenny's Tipperary Inn. *Moderate.* Flamingo and Westlake Drive. Sidewalk café, entertainment nightly.

Il Capuccino. *Moderate.* Main St.; 725–2747. Northern Italian cuisine. Visa, MasterCard.

The Paradise. *Moderate.* Main St. Ice-cream parlor and family-style restaurant. Breakfast, lunch, dinner.

SAG HARBOR

American Hotel. *Deluxe.* Main St.; 725–3535. The *hautest* cuisine in town, with prices to match; renowned for its wine cellar. No credit cards.

The House on Otter Pond. *Deluxe.* Jermain Ave.; 725–9710. Continental menu; cabaret entertainment. Credit cards.

The Foxes. *Expensive.* Noyac Rd.; 725–0810. Good food, friendly atmosphere. A local favorite. Serves early-bird breakfast at 3:00 A.M. on weekends. Credit cards.

George Studley's Long Whart. *Expensive.* 725–0176. Indoor/outdoor dining with spectacular harbor view. French cuisine and seafood. Credit cards.

The Salty Dog. *Expensive.* Noyac Rd. at Long Beach; 725–0840. Waterfront dining amidst nautical trappings. Credit cards.

The Baykerry. *Moderate.* Bay St. across from Yacht Club; 725–9613. Vegeterian restaurant with imaginative specialties. Closed Mondays, Tuesdays.

SOUTHAMPTON

Herb McCarthy's. *Expensive.* Bowden Square; 283–2800. A Southampton institution since 1938. Credit cards.

Lobster Bill's. *Expensive.* North Sea Rd. at Conscience Point; 283–8986. Waterfront seafood restaurant.

Lobster Inn. *Expensive.* Sunrise Hwy. at Rte. 27; 283–9828. Very crowded, especially on weekends. Credit cards.

Barrister's. *Moderate.* Main St.; 283–6206. Popular with the brunch crowd. Credit cards.

Irene's. *Moderate.* Rte. 27 west of village; 283–8555. Chinese cuisine. Credit cards.

WESTHAMPTON BEACH

Club Pierre. *Deluxe.* Beach Rd. and Main St.; 288–4046. Restaurant français.

Kruggerand. *Expensive.* Montauk Hwy. and Seabreeze; 288–9009. Japanese cuisine.

Palmer's Place. *Moderate.* Montauk Hwy.; 288–9723. Daily specials. Credit cards.

THE HUDSON VALLEY

Majestic Homes on a Lordly River

by
JOEL FISHMAN

Joel Fishman is Travel Editor for the Gannett Westchester newspapers.

The Hudson River Valley is one of the most scenic and historic regions in the country. Just a short distance from New York City are sights and sites that date to pre-Revolutionary War times. Open for public tours are the grand estates of eighteenth- and nineteenth-century millionaires whose fortunes included the priceless beauty around them. Here, too, are such attractions as the Franklin Delano Roosevelt Home and Library at Hyde Park, and the nearby Vanderbilt Mansion.

Whether you prefer to take day trips from New York City or to explore the region at length, the Hudson Valley is a destination for all seasons. Spring brings the flower festivals at the Sleepy Hollow Restorations in Westchester. Summer is ideal for a visit to the region's wineries and perhaps a buying expedition at one of the many crafts fairs. Fall is punctuated by the crisp air and the crunch of shoulder pads during football games at West Point. Winter can mean the solitude of cross-country skiing in a state park or the companionship of fellow country-inn enthusiasts gathering by a fireplace.

From the days when the mighty Hudson was the only highway and settlements sponsored by the Dutch patroons outcropped its green banks, the Hudson River Valley has been a celebrated attraction. Along its shores occurred many important events during America's founding days. Historic sites are dotted along the banks and to the traveler it sometimes seems as if there isn't a town that doesn't have at least one old house to which the natives can point with pride as a place where George Washington once slept.

During the Revolutionary War, the Americans exerted their utmost efforts to retain control of the Hudson, both because it was a lifeline of supplies for them and because in British hands it would have been an open gateway to the interior. Battles and maneuvers took place almost continuously along its length, so it is quite possible that Washington really did sleep at most of the places that claim the distinction. A vital place was West Point, standing high upon the inside curve of a sharp bend in the river; cannon placed there could sweep the water in both directions. The Point was so vital that the rebellious colonists tried to block the river to British ships both there and a few miles below by stretching heavy iron chains from shore to shore. Some of the 300-pound links of those chains may still be seen in the museum of the U.S. Military Academy. The outcome of the war might have been different if Benedict Arnold had succeeded in his plot to surrender West Point to the British.

Progress Up the Hudson

Two early 19th-century events were of the greatest importance to the Hudson. The first occurred in 1807 when Robert Fulton steamed up the river from New York to Albany; the second in 1825 when Governor DeWitt Clinton opened the Erie Canal, stretching from the river at Albany to the Great Lakes at Buffalo. With the way to the entire northern part of the United States open, and with the means to move passengers and goods quickly and inexpensively, there was no stopping New York's growth. The picturesque sailing vessels vanished, but business and population boomed.

Art and literature took note of the Hudson. Washington Irving published his tales and a whole Hudson River School of artists began to paint the valley. In the late 19th and early 20th centuries, more stately mansions, some of them literally palaces, were erected upon the hilltops.

More recently, bitter controversy has raged between environmentalists, who wish to preserve the natural splendor of the Hudson from further indignities, and those who would make continued use of its industrial and commercial potential, even at the expense of its scenery. Pollution has killed shad fishing, once a profitable local industry. Major attacks on the pollution problem have been made during the past decade, but there is still a long way to go.

In 1609, Henry Hudson and his crew were the valley's first admiring sightseers. Today, modern expressways like the Governor Thomas E. Dewey Thruway and Taconic State Parkway whisk travelers within easy reach of myriad historic sites and vacation attractions. In the Sleepy Hollow country around the Tappan Zee Bridge, according to legend, Dutch ghosts and goblins still wander on misty nights. You can visit Washington Irving's whimsically designed stone mansion Sunnyside; handsome Van Cortlandt Manor, its lawns and gardens appearing just as they did during the Revolution; and Philipsburg Manor and Gristmill, headquarters of Frederick Philipse's vast 18th-century landholding.

In an area rich in Revolutionary landmarks, history comes alive during drills and demonstrations at New Windsor Cantonment in Vails Gate, or at Miller Hill Restoration, with its diagrams and rails marking the progress of the 1776 Battle of White Plains. World-famous also are the United States Military Academy, clinging to a bluff above the river, the smart precision of the corps of cadets parading on the old grounds of West Point, and President Franklin D. Roosevelt's home, grave, and library at Hyde Park.

Awaiting sightseers elsewhere are such contrasting activities as a stroll through Oriental Gardens in North Salem, mock battles of World War I aircraft in Rhinebeck, or tours of such extravagant mansions as Lyndhurst in Tarrytown, Olana in Hudson, and Boscobel in Garrison. The Hudson Valley also has a multitude of state parks where vacationers can enjoy swimming, boating, camping, and hiking.

Today, the lower Hudson Valley, especially Westchester County just north of New York City on the east side of the river, is one of the wealthiest suburban areas in the United States.

The Hudson Valley

Kingston

Rhinebeck

9 W

Vanderbilt Mansion

Hyde Park

FDR Natl. Historic Site

Poughkeepsie

To Woodstock and Catskills

Hudson River

DUTCHESS COUNTY

NEW YORK

84

Newburgh

9

PUTNAM COUNTY

West Point

87

202

17

THRUWAY

N.Y. STATE

ROCKLAND COUNTY

Bear Mt. State Park

9 w

PKWY.

WESTCHESTER COUNTY

Peekskill

Harriman State Park

TACONIC STATE

684

CONNECTICUT

PALISADES PKWY.

NEW JERSEY

287

CONNECTICUT TURNPIKE

White Plains

Greenwich

Yonkers

95

LONG ISLAND SOUND

80

New York City

N E W S

0   20

Miles

The Heart of the County

White Plains is the county seat of Westchester. In 1776, Washington outwitted a stronger and fresher force of British troops in the Battle of White Plains, re-enacted yearly in October. Here it was that the Declaration of Independence was adopted and the State of New York formally organized. The sightseer can visit Washington's headquarters in the Elijah Miller House and see demonstrations of colonial crafts, as well as various Revolutionary War relics.

In Croton-on-Hudson, Van Cortlandt Manor, a restored 18th-century Dutch-English manor house on twenty acres of what was once an 86,000-acre estate, stands as one of New York's three Sleepy Hollow Country Restorations. Today it is the scene of demonstrations of spinning, weaving, and dyeing in early June, and of old crafts and country tasks in September, but once it was a welcome place for travelers to obtain food and lodging. The family entertained Franklin, Lafayette, von Steuben, and Rochambeau in the Manor House, now considered one of the most authentic extant restorations of early America.

East Bank of the Hudson

Take US 9 north along the Hudson to State 9D, and follow it past the Bear Mountain Bridge to Garrison. Here, be sure to visit Boscobel, one of the finest examples of Federal architecture in North America. High above the Hudson, this mansion commands a sweeping southward view of the majestic valley. Said to have been designed in 1805 by Robert Adam, it was scheduled for demolition in 1960. A local restoration society saved it, however, and moved it fifteen miles north to its present site.

Ahead on State 9D lies Beacon, a proud place that toots its own horn each June on Beacon Day, and lights up with fireworks and a big parade. Here, the Brett Homestead, built in 1709, has period furnishings and a formal garden. The Mount Beacon Incline Railway rises to where fires were lighted to warn Washington of the movements of British troops, giving the city its name.

Vassar, Roosevelt, and Vanderbilt

State 9D joins US 9 at Wappingers Falls, and from there it's on to Poughkeepsie (pronounce it p-KIP-see), the habitat of Vassar girls (and boys) and the Smith Brothers of coughdrop fame. Poughkeepsie was state capital for a short while, and it was here that the Federal Constitution was ratified. Clinton House, containing historical pictures, Revolutionary War material, and antique furniture, served as headquarters for George Clinton when he served as New York's first governor.

A few miles further on is Hyde Park, with its National Shrine, the home of Franklin D. Roosevelt. Every year, thousands pay tribute to the late President who, with his wife, lies buried in a corner of the grounds. The house and library, containing many mementoes, photographs, and papers of FDR, are open to the public.

Just up the road is the 700-acre estate of Frederick Vanderbilt, with its fifty-room mansion built in 1895 by noted architect Stanford White. A fine example of the ostentation of the 19th-century millionaires, it is rich in Italian Renaissance and rococo effects. Presently, it is administered as a National Historic Site, and contains many valuable furnishings and objets d'art.

In West Park, off of US 9W, is the 175-acre John Burroughs State Park. This area, known as "Slabsides," was the summer retreat of Burroughs (1837–1921), a leading naturalist-philosopher of his day. On Slabsides Day, the third Saturday in May and the first Saturday in October, tours are conducted through Burroughs' large log cabin where he lived and wrote during the summer.

Rhinebeck, a bit north along the river, is the home of the Old Rhinebeck Aerodrome, the world's largest collection of individually owned antique aeroplanes (up here, nobody says "airplanes"). On nice summer Sundays, there are aerial shows, and mock battles between the various World War I planes recapture the thrill of old-time flying.

Berkshire Gateway

Hudson, named after Henry, was once an important port, and the town just barely missed being named New York's capital years ago. Today it will interest fire buffs as the home of the American Museum of Fire Fighting, which has a large collection of pictures, trophies, flags, and equipment, including 18th-century hand pumpers and 19th-century horse-drawn steam pumpers. Just outside Hudson on US 9 is Olana, the estate of Hudson Valley artist Frederic Church. Created completely by Church, Olana is the total environment, designed as a work of art leaving nothing to chance. The state-owned Historic Site, built in Persian style, contains many fine Church paintings in its thirty-seven rooms. Situated on a hill commanding a spectacular view of the Hudson below, Olana was once described by its owner as "the center of the world."

Further on is Kinderhook, birthplace of President Martin Van Buren and site of an elegant Federal-style residence, the House of History, Benedict Arnold Inn, Ichabod Crane Schoolhouse, and the Van Alen Homestead, scene of *The Legend of Sleepy Hollow*. A little east, on

State 66, is Old Chatham. The Shaker Museum here houses exhibits in a complex of six buildings to preserve and display the beauty and simplicity of the Shaker sect. Although there are few Shakers left today, an annual festival takes place in early August, and demonstrations of Shaker crafts are given every September.

West Bank of the Hudson

At this point, we are ready to cross the river to the west side and head back south.

Newburgh is rich in Revolutionary history. Here are headquarters used by Washington at the end of the Revolution when he created the Order of the Purple Heart, officially disbanded the Army, and announced the end of the war. Just outside the city, down State 32 in Vails Gate, is New Windsor Cantonment, a reconstructed army camp where Washington's men met, dined, and where he worshipped with his officers. Here, too, he dissuaded a group of officers who plotted a coup against the young Continental Congress. Guides here wear Revolutionary uniforms, and visitors enjoy picnicking. Outside here, on State 94, are the headquarters of Revolutionary War General Henry Knox, the heaviest man on Washington's staff.

Follow State 94 into Washingtonville for a visit to the Brotherhood Wineries, the oldest winery and largest wine cellar in the United States. A tour of the winery includes sampling of the finished product. Nearby, in Monroe, on State 208, the Museum Village in Orange County has a collection of authentic houses and items of antiquity, with an old country store selling penny candy the way it used to be.

Back to US 9W and West Point. The U.S. Military Academy is open to visitors, with its parades, battle monuments, museums, and other sights. The Storm King Highway, just above it, is one of the most scenic highways in the east, and a drive along that road will give a good indication of why the area held such strategic importance during the Revolution. Just south is Bear Mountain State Park, which has almost every facility for outdoor fun including a zoo, swimming pool, boating, ice skating, ski slopes and jumps, and an excellent restaurant.

Crossing the Hudson at the Tappan Zee Bridge, we arrive in Tarrytown, where the Rockefellers live at their sizable Pocantico Hills estate. In North Tarrytown, you'll find the Old Dutch Church of Sleepy Hollow, where Washington Irving is buried. The church itself dates from the 17th century.

Washington Irving Country

Just across the street from the church is a fascinating place, Phillipsburg Manor, which has recently undergone major renovation. This early 18th-century gristmill and trading center complex, once the headquarters of a 90,000-acre estate, has an operating water-powered mill and a two-story 17th-century stone house. Regular demonstrations of weaving, spinning, and candle-dipping are given.

Below Tarrytown, Irvington boasts the unusual Sunnyside estate home of Washington Irving, whose tales of the Hudson River Valley have made the area familiar to millions.

PRACTICAL INFORMATION FOR THE HUDSON RIVER VALLEY

HOW TO GET THERE. *By car:* The Governor Thomas E. Dewey Thruway, to the west of the Hudson River, and the Taconic State Parkway to the east are the fastest north-south routes through the Hudson River Valley. State Routes 9 West and 9 parallel the Thruway and the Taconic but run closer to the river, affording more interesting scenery at a slower pace. In Westchester County, I-95, also called the New England Thruway, runs near Long Island Sound through New Rochelle and Rye and on into Connecticut. The Boston Post Road (US 1) parallels the Thruway. Take the scenic Saw Mill River Parkway or the functional Major Deegan Expressway for the western part of Westchester; and the Bronx River Parkway or the Hutchinson River Parkway for points in between east and west. The Bronx River Parkway turns into the Taconic State Parkway near Valhalla. I-87 travels north from the Major Deegan Expressway, crossing the Hudson River at the Tappan Zee Bridge. I-684 goes north-south from White Plains past Mount Kisco and Bedford Hills, leaving the county near Croton Falls.

By train: ConRail and Amtrak have service from New York City's Grand Central terminal to Westchester County and through the Hudson River Valley.

By air: Air North, Command, and Air Florida at Westchester County Airport in White Plains. *Command Airways* has commuter service to Dutchess County Airport in Poughkeepsie.

By bus: Poughkeepsie and Kingston are the primary bus depots in the Hudson River Valley, but most towns have scheduled, if less frequent, service. Among the bus lines serving the area are: *Adirondack Trailways, Hudson Transit* and *Mohawk. Greyhound* has service to White Plains in Westchester County. For specific schedule and fare information contact your nearest bus station or your travel agent.

TELEPHONES. All telephone numbers listed are area code (914) except where indicated.

TOURIST INFORMATION. Hudson River Valley Association, 150 White Plains Rd., Tarrytown, NY 10591; 631–8405. Westchester Tourism Council, 148 Martine Ave., White Plains, NY 10601; 682–7591. Dutchess County Visitors Bureau, 41 Main St., Poughkeepsie, NY 12601; 485–4690.

HOTELS AND MOTELS. Lodging prices are seasonal and generally are higher the closer you get to New York City. Many suburban hotels cater to a business clientele during the week and offer lower-priced packages on weekends. The categories for this region are: *Expensive,* $60 and above; *Moderate,* $35–$60; *Inexpensive,* under $35.

ARMONK

Ramada Inn. *Expensive* on weekdays and *moderate* on weekends. On I-684 at exit 3, four miles from Westchester County Airport; 273–9090. Restaurant, cocktail lounge and pool.

BEAR MOUNTAIN

Bear Mountain Inn. *Moderate.* Rustic resort hotel on the park grounds; 786–2731. Dining room and cocktail lounge.

BREWSTER

Heidi's. *Moderate.* On Rte. 22, one mile from I-684; 279–8011. On 10 landscaped acres with pool and picnic area.

CANAAN

Berkshire Spur. *Inexpensive.* Rte. 22 at New York State Thruway exit B3; (518) 781–9998. Pool and free coffee in rooms. Convenient to Tanglewood.

CENTRAL VALLEY

Gasho Inn. *Inexpensive.* Rte. 22, two miles east of New York State Thruway exit 16; 928–2277. Twenty-acre complex with Japanese gardens and restaurant in a 16th-century Samurai farmhouse.

FISHKILL

Holiday Inn. *Moderate.* I-84 at US 9; 896–6281. Heated pool, live music on weekends.

HAWTHORNE

Hawthorne Circle Quality Inn. *Moderate.* Rte. 9A; 592–8600. Barbecue facilities, pool, and spacious grounds.

HILLSDALE

Swiss Hutte. *Moderate to expensive* (includes Modified American Plan). Three miles east of Rte. 22 and 10 miles east of Taconic State Parkway; (518)

325–3333. Closed in April and November. Restaurant is closed Mondays in May. Heated pool, ice skating in winter.

HYDE PARK

Golden Manor. *Inexpensive.* Rte. 9 across from FDR's home and library; 229–2157. Large pool and new sauna. Some efficiencies.

Dutch Patroon. *Moderate.* Route 9; 229–7141. Pool and large gardens.

KINGSTON

Sky Top. *Moderate.* Rte. 28 at New York State Thruway exit 19; 331–2900. Spacious grounds on a mountaintop overlooking the Hudson River Valley. Pool and steam bath.

MOUNT KISCO

Holiday Inn. *Moderate.* Saw Mill River Parkway at Kisco Ave. exit; 241–2600. Heated pool and shops. Lounge entertainment. Popular with singles.

Kittle House. *Moderate.* Rte. 117; 666–8044. Country inn with restaurant and spacious grounds.

NEWBURGH

Ramada Inn. *Moderate.* 1055 Union Ave., two miles west of junction of I-84 and New York State Thruway; 564–4500. Nightly entertainment and heated pool.

Super 8 Motel. *Inexpensive.* Rte. I-84, exit 75; 564–5700.

NEW PALTZ

Mohonk Mountain House. *Expensive.* 255–1000. Large Victorian-type hotel resort on a 2,500-acre estate. Tennis, horseback riding and hiking. Many unusual "theme" weekends. Rates include meals.

NYACK

Tappan Zee Town House. *Moderate.* Mountain View Ave., off exit 11 on New York State Thruway; 358–8400.

West Gate Motor Lodge. *Moderate.* Rte. 59, off exit 11 on New York State Thruway; 358–8100.

POUGHKEEPSIE

Po'keepsie. *Moderate.* US 9, three miles south of downtown; 452–5453. Pool. Near two large shopping centers.

Best Western Red Bull Motor Inn. *Moderate.* 576 Douth Rd, off Rte. 9; 462–4400. Pool, patio, entertainment, and dancing.

RHINEBECK

Beekman Arms. *Moderate.* 876–7077. Believed to be the oldest hotel in the country and has operated since 1700. Reservations required for weekends. Hotel is booked far in advance for craft fairs and state fair.

TARRYTOWN

Hilton Inn. *Expensive* during the week and *moderate* on weekends. Rte. 9 near the Tappan Zee Bridge; 631–5700. Restaurants, entertainment, and pools.

Marriott. *Expensive* during the week and *moderate* on weekends. 631–2200. The newest luxury hotel in Westchester. Popular meeting place for area workers and singles.

WEST POINT

Hotel Thayer. *Moderate.* 446–4731. Historic hotel on grounds of the military academy. Rooms overlook the Hudson River.

 SEASONAL EVENTS. Rhinebeck is the site of two of the most important fairs in the Northeast. *The Fair at Rhinebeck,* formerly the Northeast Crafts Fair, is one of the largest crafts fairs in the country. Even more competitive than the exhibitors who must audition to gain entry to the show are the patrons who vie for the privilege of purchasing the items. The fair is held the last weekend in June; 255–0039. The *Dutchess County Fair,* held the third week in August, features harness racing, livestock competition, and rides; 876–4001. Both events are held on the spacious county fairgrounds.

 CAMPING OUT. Hikers and backpackers may camp on any state-owned land in the forest preserves and state reforestation areas. There are more than 20 organized camping areas in the Hudson Valley. Following are some of the most popular sites:

Taconic State Park. Camping facilities are located in Copake Falls, near the Massachusetts border, and at Rudd Pond, two miles north of Millerton off Route 22. No dogs are allowed and there is a seven-day minimum stay during the peak season. Tickets may be purchased at Ticketron outlets or by calling (518) 329–3993 for Copake Falls and (518) 789–3059 for Rudd Pond.

Harriman State Park. The camping facilities in this multi-purpose park are located at Beaver Pond on Route 210, five miles west of Stony Point. There are 220 sites with tables and fireplaces, but there are no electric or sewer hookups. Tickets may be purchased at Ticketron outlets or by calling 947–2792.

Hudson Valley KOA Campground. Plattekill. Midway between Newburgh and New Paltz. Near West Point, Hyde Park, and winery region. 564–2836.

PARKS. *Franklin D. Roosevelt State Park* (formerly Mohansic). Yorktown Heights. Water sports, hiking, and nature trails. Cross-country skiing in winter. Adjacent to the Taconic State Parkway. 245-4434.

Ward Pound Ridge Reservation. Cross River. Nature museum, hiking trails, and arboretum. Cross-country skiing in winter and outdoor entertainment series in summer. 763-3493.

Clarence Fahnestock Memorial State Park. Cold Spring. Boat rentals, bridle paths, hiking, and fishing. 225-7207.

James Baird State Park. In Pleasant Valley, nine miles east of Poughkeepsie. Golf, roller skating, archery, and swimming. 452-1489.

Bear Mountain State Park. Fort Montgomery at Palisades Parkway and Route 9W. Pool, boat rentals, and hiking trails. 786-2701.

Margaret Lewis Norrie State Park. Staatsburg. Camping and picnic grounds and a yacht basin that is a haven for some of the grandest pleasure craft cruising the Hudson River. 889-4646.

Taconic State Park. The park extends for 15 miles along the New York-Massachusetts border from Millerton through Copake Falls. The Rudd Pond area in the south offers fishing, hiking, camping, and water sports, and the Copake sector in the north adds cabin and cottage rentals. Both have skiing and snowmobiling in the winter. The Rudd Pond telephone number is (518) 789-3059 and the Copake Falls number is (518) 329-3993.

Lake Taghanic State Park. Ancram. Beach, boat rentals, hiking, and ballfields. (518) 851-3631.

Tallman Mountain State Park. Sparkill. Hiking trails, picnic areas, pool, and ballfields. Part of Palisades Interstate Park complex. 359-0544.

HISTORIC SITES. The *U.S. Military Academy at West Point* is perched on the Hudson's west bank. The most popular tourist attraction in the Hudson Valley, its highlights include the museum with the largest general military collection in the Western Hemisphere; Fort Putnam, a fully restored Revolutionary War fortification; and the chapel, noted for its organ and stained glass. Parades are held in late April and May and again in the fall, and the spirit of the academy is most visible (and audible) during football games. Tailgate picnics are as much a part of the tradition as saluting the officers. The barracks and academic buildings are not open to the public. An information center located just inside the main gate provides information on daily activities. For further information call 938-4658.

Hyde Park, Franklin Delano Roosevelt's home from boyhood through adult life, was heavily damaged by fire in January 1982, and full repairs are not expected to be completed until late 1983. Plans are for rooms to be reopened to the public in stages. The third floor rooms, where the damage was the greatest, will be the last to reopen. To compensate for the curtailed program, guides will conduct tours of the open areas and the grounds. The adjoining library and museum contains displays, papers, and exhibits, such as ship models and photographs of the First Family. President and Mrs. Roosevelt are buried in the rose garden. Hyde Park and the library and museum are open daily from 9 A.M. to 5 P.M., except Christmas and New Year's. Admission is $1.50 for visitors 16 to 62 and free for everyone else. Further information is available by calling 229–9115.

Separate from the Roosevelt home but part of the same admission package is the *Vanderbilt Mansion National Historic Site*. The opulent Beaux-Arts style mansion features a marble entrance hall, grand staircase, and a collection of antique clocks. Hours and admission are the same as for the Hyde Park site. Both are located on Route 9.

The *Jonathan Hasbrouck House*, 84 Liberty St., Newburgh, has been designated a National Historic Landmark because it was the last headquarters for General Washington during the Revolutionary War. The house contains war relics and period furniture, and a separate museum has exhibits relating to the defense of the Hudson highlands. The property is open weekends only from January to March and Wednesday to Sunday the rest of the year. Admission is free. 1982 and 1983 are bicentennial years and several special programs are planned. For further information, call 562–1195.

 MANSIONS AND RESTORATIONS. Situated along busy Route 9 in Westchester are three properties known collectively as the Sleepy Hollow Restorations. The settings and furnishings gracefully recall the 18th and 19th centuries, and all three can be visited in one day.

Sunnyside, author Washington Irving's estate in Tarrytown, evokes the elegance of the Victorian era. The creator of such classics as *Rip Van Winkle* and *The Legend of Sleepy Hollow* entertained many guests, who marveled at the serenity and majesty of the Hudson River Valley. Modern guests can picnic under the shade of centuries-old evergreens, stroll flower-bordered paths, and relax by the "Little Mediterranean," the pond Irving designed to complete his estate.

Four miles north in North Tarrytown is *Philipsburg Manor,* an 18th-century trading and agricultural center. Dutch emigré Frederick Philipse built a gristmill, barn, and stone house on the banks of the Pocantico River near where it meets the Hudson. The manor has been restored so it looks like it did between 1720 and 1750, the period of its greatest commercial importance. Costumed guides tend to the numerous tasks, such as grinding corn and wheat and tending to the sheep. A new barn was built in the spring of 1982 to replace one destroyed by fire the previous summer.

Van Cortlandt Manor in Croton was also built by a wealthy land owner. Restored to the way it appeared between 1770 and 1814, the estate features a brick-paved "Long Walk," flanked by an expanse of flowers, fruit trees and vegetable gardens. At the east end is the Ferry House and kitchen, a familiar stop for travelers along the Old Albany Post Road.

The three restorations listed above are open daily from 10 A.M. to 5 P.M. year-round except Thanksgiving, Christmas, and New Year's. Admission to each is $4 for adults; $2.50 for senior citizens and children six to 14; and free for children under six. A combination ticket for two properties is $7 for adults and $4.50 for senior citizens and children six to 14; admission to all three costs $10 for adults and $6.50 for seniors and children six to 14. Information about the restorations is available by calling 631–8200.

Also located on Route 9 is the Gothic Revival mansion *Lyndhurst.* Built for William Paulding, a mayor of New York City in the 1830s, Lyndhurst was best known as the summer residence of railroad magnate Jay Gould. The 67-acre estate overlooks the Hudson River and the mansion contains furnishings of the period. Financial problems have made the future of the estate uncertain and at press time the mansion was open for tours only on Sundays. The grounds also serve as the site of a popular outdoor concert series in the summer. Further information is available by calling 631–7766.

Just north of Garrison on Route 9D is *Boscobel,* one of the finest examples of Federal architecture in the country. Built by States Dyckman, a Loyalist during the American Revolution, the mansion is furnished in the early 19th-century style, and visitors are rewarded with an outstanding view of the valley. Boscobel is closed in January and February and is open daily except Tuesday the rest of the year. Hours vary during the seasons. Admission is $4 for adults and $2 for children six to 14. Further information is available by calling 265-3638.

The *Olana State Historic Site* on Route 9G in Hudson is a 37-room home built by Frederick Church, a Hudson River School artist. The Persian-Moorish villa features restoration gardens, nature walks, and picnic areas and is open from Memorial Day through the last Sunday in October, Wednesday to Sunday. Call (518) 828–0135.

 MUSEUMS AND GALLERIES. Beacon. Madame Brett Homestead, 50 Van Nydeck Ave. Oldest home in Dutchess County; formal garden and period furnishings. Open mid-April to mid-November, Thursday to Sunday 1–4 P.M. Admission $2 for adults and 50 cents for children under 19. 831–9827.

Cold Spring. Historic riverfront village with 19th-century antique, craft, and specialty shops. Most are closed Monday or Tuesday. 265–2100.

Hudson. American Museum of Fire Fighting, Harry Howard Ave. Antique fire-fighting equipment, including a fire engine from 1725. Open April to November daily from 9 A.M. to 5 P.M. Free. 828–7695.

Katonah. Katonah Art Gallery, 28 Bedford Rd. Westchester's "living museum" presents new exhibits every six to eight weeks. Emphasis is on modern art, but other styles are represented. Open Tuesday to Sunday. Free. 232–4988.

Monroe. Museum Village, Rte. 17. A rural crossroads village of the 1800s, the outdoor museum contains more than 30 buildings including a schoolhouse, general store, crafts shop, and natural history museum. Open daily except Monday from May to October from 10 A.M. to 5 P.M. Adults, $4; children and senior citizens, $3. 782–8247.

Newburgh. Storm King Art Center, Old Pleasant Hill Road. Contemporary sculpture in a 200-acre garden setting. Open daily except Tuesday from mid-May to October. A $2 donation is requested. 534–3115.

North Salem. Hammon Museum and Oriental Stroll Gardens, Deveau Rd. (off Rte. 124). Annually changing exhibits on the humanities. The three-acre site contains 15 varieties of gardens, a lake, pool, and plantings designed to refresh the spirit and please the eye. There is a pleasant terrace restaurant on the grounds. The gardens are open mid-May to late October from Wednesday to Sunday and the museum is open May to December. Admission is $2 for adults and $1 for children for the museum or garden. 669–5135.

Rhinebeck. Old Rhinebeck Aerodrome, Stone Church Rd. (off Rte 9). Antique planes from the "classic era" of 1900 to 1937. Air shows are held on weekends and visitors can arrange for rides in open-air cockpits. Open mid-May to October daily from 10 A.M. to 5 P.M. 758–8610.

Staatsburg. Mills Mansion, Mills State Park (off Rte. 9). A 65-room neoclassical mansion designed by Stanford White and furnished in Louis XV and XVI styles. Open Memorial Day to the last weekend in October from Wednesday to Sunday. Free. 889–4100.

WINE COUNTRY. The Hudson River Valley is the oldest wine-growing district in the United States. The nation's first commercial winery was established in Croton about 150 years ago, and the Brotherhood Winery in Washingtonville is the oldest operating winery in the country.

The area wineries range from "mom and pop" operations to large, commercial ventures. Among the specialties are Kosher and Lambrusca wines and French hybrid and vinifera production. Several wineries make a visit a festive occasion. In addition to the organized tours during which guests learn about the full wine production process, guests may indulge in such activities as cross-country skiing and sleigh rides in the winter and medieval pageants and grape stomping in warmer months. All tours conclude with a sampling of the products.

Although the vintners take their profession seriously, there is time for some gentle digs at the elitism that sometimes intimidates novices. The owner of one vineyard, for example, has labeled one table wine "Hamburger Red."

Following is a list of the seven major Hudson Valley wineries. The first four offer organized tours and the others generally welcome visitors who call for appointments. Because operating hours change with the seasons, visitors should call ahead.

Brotherhood Winery. Washingtonville. Tours are conducted from February through Thanksgiving, but the winery is open year-round. Admission charge. 496–3661.

Hudson Valley Winery. Highland. Open year-round for tours except Thanksgiving, Christmas, and New Year's. Admission charge. 691–7296.

Royal Wine Corp. Milton. Open on Sundays only from January 1 to April 1, Sunday to Friday the rest of the year. Free from January to May, admission charge rest of the year. Closed on Jewish holidays. 795–2240.

Cascade Mountain Vineyards. Amenia. Open daily for tours and for demonstrations of alternate energy facilities. Free. 373–9021.

Benmarl Vineyards. Marlborough. Not open for public tours, but those interested in development of eastern wines can call 236–7271 for an appointment.

Cagnasso Winery. Marlborough. Visits by appointment only May through December. 236–4630.

Clinton Vineyards. Clinton Corners. Visits by appointment only Fridays through Mondays. 266-5372.

 DINING OUT. Whether your taste runs to fast food or feast food, you're certain to find something to your liking in the Valley. Dining facilities range from charming country inns to spacious hotel restaurants, and there are several specialty establishments to please the most adventurous and demanding patrons. Many of the higher-priced restaurants offer luncheon menus for considerably less. The Sunday brunch phenomenon has spread up here from New York City and is a pleasant way to conclude a weekend in the area. Restaurant categories are as follows: *Deluxe,* $25.00 and above; *Expensive,* $17.50–$25.00; *Moderate,* $10.00–$17.50; and *Inexpensive,* under $10.00. Included are appetizer or soup, entrée, and dessert. Not included are drinks, tip, and tax.

ARMONK

Covingtons. *Moderate.* 465 Main St., one mile east of exit 3 on I-684; 273–5700. Handsome English-style restaurant with seafood and fish specialties. Lunch, dinner, and brunch on weekends.

BEDFORD

La Cremaillere. *Deluxe.* North St. in Banksville; 234–3306. Located near the Connecticut border, the restaurant is housed in a landmark building dating to 1750. The classic French cuisine is complemented by one of the most comprehensive wine cellars in the country. Lunch Tuesday–Saturday; dinner Tuesday to Sunday.

BREWSTER

The Arch. *Expensive.* Rte. 22; 279–5011. French country inn serving price-fixed dinners. Some menu selections—including dessert souffles—carry a surcharge. Dinner only; Wednesday–Sunday.

Capriccio. *Expensive.* Rte. 22; 279–9834. Located on a wooded six-acre estate, the colonial home features beamed ceilings, stucco walls, and an impressive stone fireplace in one of its two dining rooms. Pasta and veal are the specialties.

Lunch, Monday and Wednesday to Saturday; dinner, Monday and Wednesday to Sunday.

CANAAN

Shuji's. *Moderate to expensive.* Junction of Rte. 20 and 22; (518) 794–8383. Japanese food served in a former mansion. Diners have a choice of the tatami rooms, where seating is on the floor, or the conventional dining room. Dinner only, Tuesday–Sunday.

CARMEL

Dreamwold. *Deluxe.* Gypsy Trail Rd.; 225–3500. A Tudor manor house set on 32 acres. Diners may enjoy cocktails on the terrace and coffee and liqueurs in the intimate drawing room. Price-fixed menu; dinners only, Wednesday–Sunday.

COLD SPRING

Plumbush. *Moderate.* Rte. 9D; 265–3904. Rambling Victorian house with several dining rooms. Swiss-inspired cuisine. Lunch, Monday-Saturday; dinner, Monday-Sunday, Sunday brunch.

CORNWALL

Cornwall Inn. *Moderate to Expensive.* Rte. 218; 534–2212. French menu. Lunch and dinner daily.

CROTON FALLS

Mona Trattoria. *Expensive.* Rte. 22 near exit 8 on I-684; 277–4580. Large, Gothic-revival style house; Mona specializes in Bolognese dishes. Dinner only, Wednesday–Sunday.

DOVER PLAINS

Old Drover's Inn. *Expensive.* Old Drover's Inn Rd., just east of Rte, 22; 832–9311. Quaint 200-year-old building with original tap room and antique furnishings. Game specialties. Lunch, Monday, Thursday, and Friday; dinner Thursday–Monday.

FISHKILL

Harrald's. *Deluxe.* Rte. 52, Stormville; 878–6595. A small restaurant with menu selections written on blackboards and given loving descriptions by dining room personnel. Six-course price-fixed dinners. No credit cards. Dinner only, Wednesday–Sunday.

GARRISON

Bird and Bottle. *Expensive.* Nelson's Corners, Rte. 9; 424–3000. Restored Colonial dining room. Very cozy in winter. They smoke the trout and sausage themselves. Lunch, Wednesday–Saturday; dinner, Wednesday–Sunday; Sunday brunch.

HARTSDALE

Auberge Argenteuil. *Expensive to Deluxe.* 42 Healey Ave.; 948–0597. Paintings and antiques grace this converted house. Splendid wine cellar. Specialties include seafood and game appetizers. Lunch Monday–Friday; dinner daily.

HILLSDALE

L'Hostellerie Bressane. *Deluxe.* Junction of Rtes. 22 and 23; 325–3412. Antiques and 18th-century atmosphere. Classical background music to match the French cuisine. Dinner only Wednesday–Sunday. Closed Monday and Tuesday except in July and August.

MILLBROOK

Daniele's. *Moderate.* Franklin Ave. on Rte. 44; 677–3393. Continental menu with large portions. Italian murals on the walls. Lunch and dinner daily.

NEWBURGH

Beau Rivage. *Moderate.* 538 River Rd., five miles north of Route 9W; 561–9799. Continental and American dishes served in a Colonial house overlooking the Hudson. Lunch and dinner Tuesday–Sunday.

NORTH SALEM

Auberge Maxime. *Deluxe.* Ridgefield Rd. (Rte. 116); 669–5450. French Provencial-style inn specializing in puffed pastry dishes and delicate sauces. Lunch and dinner daily except Wednesday.

OSSINING

Dudley's. *Moderate.* 6 Rockledge Ave.; 941–8674. Casual dining in an airy room filled with greenery. Lunch Tuesday–Saturday; dinner Tuesday–Sunday; Sunday brunch.

PATTERSON

L'Auberge Bretonne. *Expensive.* Rte. 22; 878–6782. Spacious dining rooms in a Colonial house. Candlelit atmosphere for French Provincial specialties. Lunch and dinner daily except Wednesday.

POUGHKEEPSIE

Culinary Institute of America. *Expensive.* Rte. 9; 452–9600. The CIA is the nation's chief training ground for serious chefs. The Escoffier Room restaurant is the final test for the students, who prepare and serve the meals. Lunch and dinner Tuesday–Sunday. Reservations should be made several weeks in advance.

Treasure Chest. *Moderate.* Rte. 9; 462–4545. The Dutch-Colonial home provides an inviting décor for diners. Lunch Monday–Friday; dinner Monday–Saturday.

PURDYS

The Box Tree. *Deluxe.* Junction of Rtes. 22 and 116; 277–3677. Warm and intimate dining. Traditional French cuisine with exceptional soups and appetizers. Dinner only daily except closed Monday and Tuesday from October through April. No credit cards.

RHINEBECK

Beekman Arms. *Moderate.* Beekman Square on Rte. 9; 876–7077. Lunch and dinner daily and Sunday brunch.

SOMERS

Silvano's. *Moderate to Expensive.* 232–8080. Cozy dining areas dominated by a fireplace. Pasta specialties. Dinner only Tuesday–Sunday.

SOUTH SALEM

Le Chateau. *Expensive.* Rte. 35; 533–6631. An English Tudor house with a large formal reception area. Traditional French cuisine in a romantic setting. Lunch and dinner Tuesday–Sunday.

Horse and Hound. *Expensive.* Spring St.; 763–3108. A blackboard lists such game specialties as boar, buffalo, and pheasant. Fall is the best season here. Price-fixed dinner daily and Sunday brunch.

WHITE PLAINS

Bengal Tiger. *Moderate.* 144 E. Post Rd.; 948–5191. A tent-like setting with Indian tapestries and sculptures. Buffet lunches and a la carte dinners and lunches. Lunch, Tuesday–Saturday; dinner, Tuesday–Sunday.

YORKTOWN HEIGHTS

Damiano's. *Expensive.* Rtes. 118 and 202 in Granite Springs; 248–7200. Northern Italian specialties using the freshest of ingredients. Hot and cold appetizers include traditional and innovative selections. Dinner only Tuesday–Sunday.

 ENTERTAINMENT AND NIGHT LIFE. Perhaps the best that can be said for the area with respect to night life is that it's close to New York City. Most visitors, however, should find something to do or see after dinner. *An Evening Dinner Theater* in Elmsford offers familiar musicals and light dramatic fare. Dinner is either buffet of sit-down style. Among area theaters open during the summer are the *Mahopac Farm House,* Mahopac, 628–1169; and the *Cecilwood Theater,* Fishkill, 896–7650.

The *New Westchester Theater* in Tarrytown occasionally features appearances by major popular musicians; 631–9300. The same can be said about the *Mid Hudson Civic Center* in Poughkeepsie; 485–5800.

Summer entertainment programs are popular. The most ambitious is the Pepsico series at the State University of New York at Purchase. The schedule includes theater, dance, music, and film; 253–5900. The *Caramoor Music Festival* in Katonah features classical music concerts outdoors on weekends, 232–4206. Another outdoor series is held on the grounds of Lyndhurst, an estate in Tarrytown; 631–7766.

The bar set often can be found at the chain hotels, such as the new *Mariott* in Tarrytown and the *Holiday Inn* in Mount Kisco.

THE JERSEY SHORE AND
ATLANTIC CITY

by JOHN MAXYMUK

John Maxymuk, a resident of the Jersey Shore, is a contributing editor to Atlantic City *Magazine.*

One of New Jersey's largest industries is tourism, and its main attraction is the 125-mile eastern coastline that stretches from Sandy Hook to Cape May, the Jersey Shore. Diversified recreation is what makes the shore so appealing: it offers boardwalks, amusement parks, beaches, facilities for surf- and deep-sea fishing, swimming, boating, bird sanctuaries, wildlife refuges, historical landmarks and exciting nightlife—particularly in Atlantic City's gambling casinos.

The entire shore is located within a few hours' drive from New York City. To start the tour from the north, take the Garden State Parkway to exit 117 onto Route 36 and head toward Sandy Hook. An exhilarating bird's-eye view of both the Atlantic Ocean and Sandy Hook is available along Ocean Drive in Atlantic Highlands. The well-named Highlands were the setting for James Fennimore Cooper's 19th-century novel *Water Witch.*

The Sandy Hook peninsula arches back toward New York and is divided into two sections. The northern section houses a government installation including Fort Hancock, headquarters for the 52nd Artillery Brigade. Sandy Hook's strategic military importance dates to the pre-Revolutionary days of the Colonies and derives from the fact that the Hook extends into New York Harbor. Whoever controlled Sandy Hook could easily intercept anyone headed for New York.

While the northern section is closed to the public, the southern section is a 460-acre National Park, part of the Gateway National Recreation Area. Originally popular among Indians as a hunting and fishing preserve as well as for its varied vegetation of beach plums, hackberry, holly trees, and even some cactus, Sandy Hook was first purchased by English Colonist Richard Hartshorne for 13 shillings in 1678. It now attracts 30 to 50 million visitors annually.

Besides the wilds, Sandy Hook's public beaches permit both bathing and surf fishing, and the park has picnic tables. Though not open to the public, the Sandy Hook Lighthouse is also on the grounds. It was built at the water's edge in 1762, but since then approximately 1,000 feet of shoreline has accumulated in front of it through tidal action. The beacon is the oldest continuously lit lighthouse in the nation.

On the way back to the mainland, stop at Navesink Twin Lights on Beacon Hill off Route 36. A massive fortress-like structure which you can tour, this lighthouse was built in 1862 (on the site where a previous lighthouse had been built in 1828), and in clear weather affords an unhampered view of the distant New York skyline. In the summer, a marine museum is also open on the grounds.

Traveling south, you'll come upon Long Branch, which has been a forerunner to Atlantic City in two aspects: from the 1870s to the 1890s Long Branch was the nation's leading recreational resort, and in the same time period it featured casino gambling.

The whole idea of summer-resort housing rentals is said to have begun in 1788 in Long Branch when Philadelphian Elliston Perot rented a Long Branch mansion for the summer. Soon others saw the choice business opportunity and began to buy property to rent out in the summer. At that time, Long Branch catered to the elite of Philadelphia and vied with Cape May for their resort trade. Long Branch

SANDY HOOK AREA

0 —————— 5
Scale of Miles

Keansburg.

Gateway
National Recreation Area

Sandy Hook
Bay

Sandy Hook Natl. Pk.

(36)

GARDEN STATE PKY.

Highlands

Navesink R.

Sea Bright

Red Bank

Shrewsbury R.

(520)

(36)

(34)

Shrewsbury

Monmouth Beach

Monmouth Park Race Track

Monmouth
Reservoir

Oceanport

(18)

Eatontown

Long Branch

ATLANTIC
OCEAN

Elberon

was known then (and perhaps admired) for its modest bathing rules: one sex in the water at a time.

By the time President U.S. Grant became a frequent visitor after 1868, the town had loosened up quite a bit. Long Branch became known for its gold-domed gambling casinos (gentlemen only) during this country's Gilded Age. Such New York personalities as Diamond Jim Brady, Lily Langtry, and Lillian Russell were frequent visitors, as well as Presidents Hayes, Harrison and Garfield (who was brought to Long Branch to die after having been shot). Much later President Wilson also visited here.

In some casinos there was gambling even on Sundays until 1894, when Congressman James A. Bradley spearheaded a reform movement and gambling was abolished.

Although Long Branch's salad days are long past, it is still a pleasant resort. It has seven miles of ocean front with five beaches along two miles of boardwalk. In addition to the boardwalk amusements and ocean bathing, Long Branch also has the longest fishing pier on the East Coast (800 feet), open around the clock.

Asbury Park gives the impression of not only the carnival-come-to-town, but of the carnival-become-the-town. Asbury Park is the image of Atlantic City in the 1960s, on the decline, but still attracting people who "knew it when." It was founded in 1870 by the aforementioned Congressman Bradley and named after Methodist Bishop Francis Asbury. Although first termed "Bradley's Folly," because it was then mostly briars, the venture was a rapid success.

Asbury Park's appeal doesn't seem to change: rides for the kids, amusements for teenagers, games of chance, novelty stores, sweetshops, music, and a convention hall. You still walk the mile-long boardwalk, play on the beach, and swim in the ocean (there are locker facilities available at both the Fourth Avenue Bathing Pavilion and the Eighth Avenue Bathhouse).

Entertainment is booked year-round in Convention Hall, which is on the boardwalk and seats 3,500. Band concerts are held every Thursday night from June through August outdoors at the Fifth Avenue Pavilion. Through music the area has achieved a certain amount of new fame in recent years, as contemporary popular musicians Bruce Springsteen as well as Southside Johnny and the Asbury Jukes surfaced in area bars.

Asbury Park holds special appeal to fishermen because of the three freshwater lakes within its boundaries. Not only can local fishermen fish from the beach and from deep-sea boats, as at most resorts, but in Asbury Park freshwater fishing is a viable option.

The neighboring community of Ocean Grove is a small religious resort which used to be notorious for its strict blue laws. Until 1979, not only was there no swimming permitted on Sundays, but there were

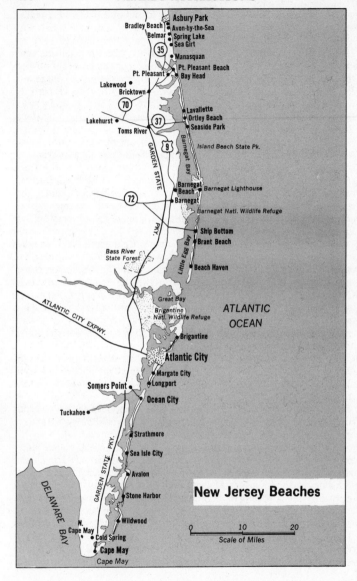

New Jersey Beaches

no automobiles allowed within town limits on the Sabbath. All cars had to be parked outside the front gates of the city from midnight Saturday to midnight Sunday.

The gates are always open now, but this is still a quiet seaside town filled by Victorian-era boardinghouses surrounding the massive wooden Great Auditorium built in 1869 and still the center of the town's activities. Ocean Grove is where Woody Allen shot most of his 1980 feature film, *Stardust Memories.*

Although still far from being densely populated, Ocean County is one of the fastest growing counties in New Jersey, increasing its population by five times since 1950. To get an idea of what it once was like, you can visit two large parks. Inland, near Lakewood off Route 88, is Ocean County Park, one of the largest county parks in the state. Formerly the park's 575 acres of pine groves belonged to John D. Rockefeller, Sr., as a vacation estate. Its vast grounds—on which picnicking is permitted—are impressive and well kept.

Back on the shore is Island Beach State Park, 2,694 acres of remote long-stretching dunes. The state purchased this land in 1953 and opened the park six years later. The park offers the chance to see a natural barrier beach in near-pristine condition. As well as dune grass, briar, and ivy, you'll find beach plum and other rare vegetation covering this "island" (it hasn't been an island since the Cranberry Inlet closed in 1812). There are a few beach houses and parking lots in one area, in addition to picnic tables. The northern section of the park is devoted to guided nature trails. The central section features several beaches where swimming is allowed and lifeguards are on duty. The southern third is for birds and fishermen.

There is only one way to reach Long Beach Island by land—via the Route 72 causeway—and this says something about the resort's style. If you're looking for big-city excitement on your vacation, don't look here. Appropriate to the Philadelphia Quakers who founded it, Long Beach Island offers simpler pleasures. The various towns are virtually indistinguishable. There is no boardwalk, but there is an abundance of clean beaches, boating, sailing, fishing, and bathing.

Both powerboats and sailboats speckle Little Egg Harbor and Barnegat Bay surrounding the island as well as the Atlantic Ocean. The fishing is excellent, both in the bay and in the ocean. You can troll for tuna, bonito, and bluefish, or deep-sea fish for mackerel, porgy, and sea bass, or catch striped bass and weakfish both in the bay and in the surf.

At the northernmost point of the island is the "Grand Old Champion of the Tides," the Barnegat Light State Park. More affectionately known as "Old Barney," the light is on 13 acres of unsoiled and unspoiled beach that has facilities for picnicking, jetty fishing, and bathing. The lighthouse was originally built in 1858 by General George

G. Meade, later a hero at Gettysburg. Thanks to regular maintenance and the structure's durability, the beacon is still in good condition. The walls are 10 feet thick at the base and taper toward the top of the 172-foot structure. From the top you have an excellent view of Barnegat Shoals, the scene of more than 200 shipwrecks. There is an admission charge.

On the way to Atlantic City, two stops are worthwhile: the Historic Towne of Smithville and the Brigantine National Wildlife Refuge. Smithville is located 12 miles north of Atlantic City on Route 9 and is a meticulous restoration of a typical 18th-century southern New Jersey town. Many of the town's buildings have been moved to Smithville from their original South Jersey sites. There are a number of fine inns at which to eat, 30 specialty shops, and many preserved historical buildings to stroll through. The Smithville Inn was originally built in 1787 by James Baremore and used as a one-room stagecoach stop for many years. The shops feature everything from antiques and reproduction furniture to tasty baked goods. The "Old Village" of restored historical buildings transports you to an authentic Colonial atmosphere. By the pond is a 170-year-old grist mill, and on the pond are the popular swan boats, which you can rent.

Another mile south on Route 9 will bring you to the Brigantine National Wildlife Refuge, a coastal sanctuary mostly for birds. Established in 1939, the refuge has over 20,000 acres of preserved tidal marshes, barrier beaches, and wooded areas. Fall and spring are the best times to visit because of the migratory habits of the birds along the Atlantic Flyway, but even at other times you might see snow geese, black ducks, skimmers, and expatriated Canada geese, gulls, terns, brants, and rails. There are well-marked wildlife trails amid the marshy and wooded acreage. There is some hunting in season. Admission is free.

Atlantic City

The greatest tourist attraction on the shore is of course Atlantic City, the aging "Queen of Resorts." Having adopted casino gambling by referendum in 1976, the resort is in a period of transition. Once a sparking jewel on the water, Atlantic City had declined so formidably in the 1960s and '70s that some referred to it as "Newark by the Sea." The injection of the casinos has given the town new life and spirit. "Casino City" will never be what Atlantic City was, but in undergoing its change it is becoming something equally rich.

Until the 1850s, Atlantic City was known as Leeds Point after its first landholder, Jeremiah Leeds. It was then a small community of fishermen, for the most part. In 1852 Dr. Jonathan Pitney and others were

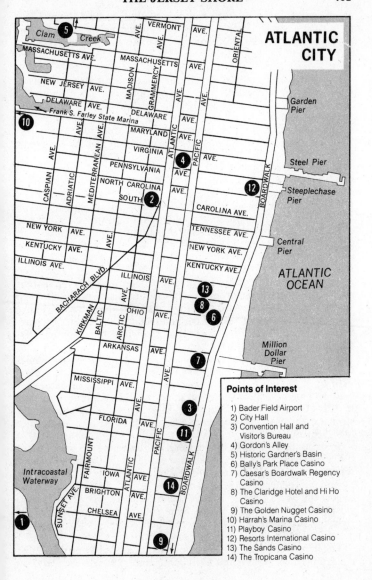

ATLANTIC CITY

ATLANTIC OCEAN

Garden Pier

Steel Pier

Steeplechase Pier

Central Pier

Million Dollar Pier

Intracoastal Waterway

Clam Creek

Frank S. Farley State Marina

Bacharach Blvd.

Points of Interest

1) Bader Field Airport
2) City Hall
3) Convention Hall and Visitor's Bureau
4) Gordon's Alley
5) Historic Gardner's Basin
6) Bally's Park Place Casino
7) Caesar's Boardwalk Regency Casino
8) The Claridge Hotel and Hi Ho Casino
9) The Golden Nugget Casino
10) Harrah's Marina Casino
11) Playboy Casino
12) Resorts International Casino
13) The Sands Casino
14) The Tropicana Casino

able to convince the Camden and Atlantic Railroad to charter a line to transport bog iron from the nearby Pine Barrens to the cities and to promote the shore as a fisherman's haven. In 1854, Leeds Point was incorporated as Atlantic City, and in July of that year the first trains started arriving.

Not too long after a regular trade began, boardinghouse owner Charles McGlade decided to upgrade his house (installing wallpaper, comfortable beds, and stuffed chairs) in order to attract women. Heretofore women had not been interested in coming to the shore and staying in white-washed fishermen's shacks. As McGlade's idea quickly proved successful, other hotelmen followed suit and the resort was born.

In 1870, local businessmen began to clamor about the popularity of beach strolling among the tenants, and the subsequent damage done to expensive hotel carpets from the tenants tracking the beach sand in. A portable boardwalk was devised. Built in eight-foot sections and taken down at the end of the season, it was the first boardwalk the world had seen. Since that time the Boardwalk has been rebuilt five times, each time higher and larger. The present walk was built in 1939 and is six and a half miles long. People flocked to walk the boards, and Atlantic City was fully launched.

In 1881, Colonel Howard built the first Boardwalk pier, but both it and a subsequent one were destroyed by natural disasters. Even though the idea of piers was derided as "Howard's folly," soon there were five piers extending into the sea: the Million Dollar, Central, Steeplechase, Steel, and Garden Piers. Each offered its own combination of rides, amusements, shows and attractions. The Steel Pier became famous as "The Showplace of the Nation," consistently signing the biggest names in show business, be they Harry James, Frank Sinatra, or Fats Waller.

In an effort to extend the summer season to one week beyond Labor Day, an enterprising promoter hit upon the idea of a beauty pageant in 1921. Over sixty years later, the Miss America Pageant is going stronger than ever, still attracting a large national television audience each September.

So many firsts, largests and general oddities have occurred in the "World's Playground." The first postcard in 1895. The origin of salt-water taffy in the 1800s. The long-suffering high-diving horse on the Steel Pier. The term "airport," coined in 1919 at the opening of what is now the world's oldest commercial airfield, Atlantic City Airport. Boardwalk entrepreneur Captain John Young's Italian villa residence right on the Boardwalk, Number 1 Atlantic Ocean. And this is only a short selection.

The hotel district was built up along the Boardwalk, and it featured a magnificent string of hotels, each built grander, more elaborately and ornate than the last. Most of them are gone now. The Dennis grew from a two-room cottage in 1860 to an enormous 450-room hotel in this century. The Marlborough-Blenheim was the first poured-concrete hotel in the country; the process was supervised by its inventor Thomas Edison. (It has been torn down to make way for Bally's Park Place Casino.) The 634-room Ambassador was demolished. The 14-story, twin-domed triumph of Moorish architecture, the Traymore, was dynamited. The St. Charles, The Breakers, and others . . . all gone. Only the Chalfonte-Haddon Hall, remodeled into Resorts International Hotel Casino, and the Claridge, remodeled into the Claridge Hotel and Hi Ho Casino.

Times were tough on the shore just as they were everywhere else during the Depression. In 1941, the island was filled with soldiers preparing to go overseas, and resort business declined. In the post-war period the recreation trade was good and Atlantic City prospered, but the fall was rapid in the developing jet-travel era of the '60s and '70s. Legalized gambling was seen as the salvation.

Resorts International was the first casino to open in May 1978, and things started to turn around again. In the next three and a half years, eight more casinos opened: Caesar's Boardwalk Regency, Bally's Park Place, The Sands, Golden Nugget, Harrah's, Playboy, the Claridge, and Tropicana. The increase in visitors has been remarkable; the crowds have returned and the city is struggling to keep pace. Once again there is nightlife in Atlantic City, and now it's year-round.

And there are other things to do besides gambling. Gordon's Alley is an imaginatively designed Old World mini-mall in a somewhat run-down section uptown. It features small, sophisticated shops and free parking. Gardner's Basin at the Inlet section of town is a re-creation of a 19th-century maritime village. There are large ships, small craft, a marine mammal rescue center, and a saltwater aquarium as well as shops, exhibits, and a restaurant. There is a slight admission charge. The Atlantic City Historical Museum on the Garden Pier burnt down in 1981, but those in charge vow to rebuild.

South Along the Shore

The most interesting way to travel south from Atlantic City is to take the Ocean Drive, 40 scenic miles along the coast over six connecting toll (30 cents) bridges. Just follow Atlantic Avenue through Atlantic City and its neighboring exclusive suburbs on Absecon Island: Ventnor, Margate, and Longport. Margate is perhaps the most well-known due to its cluster of popular summer-season bayside bars which cater mostly to a college-age crowd.

Also in Margate is Lucy the Elephant, a National Landmark. She was originally built in 1881 by a real-estate promoter to attract business, and had two sister pachyderms: one on Coney Island which burned down in 1896, and one in Cape May that was torn down in 1899. Lucy is six stories high, 38 feet long, and 80 feet around. She was a hotel attraction as well as a tavern before she fell into a state of drastic disrepair in the 1960s. She has since been entirely restored and moved two blocks from the original site. For a slight admission charge you can tour her—climb up the inside of her legs, peek out her eyes and stand in her howdah overlooking the ocean.

After leaving Longport, start looking for signs reading "Flight of the Gull"; they will direct you along Ocean Drive into Cape May County. Cape May County is noted for its clean sand, fun boardwalks, and marinas, as well as being rumored as having more *Mayflower* descendants than any other county in the United States.

Over the first bridge you'll come to Ocean City, "America's Greatest Family Resort." Ocean City is the dry town by the water. There is no liquor, beer, or wine sold within its limits. Founded in 1879 as a Methodist resort by three ministers, the Lake Brothers, Ocean City forbids alcohol in its original charter and continues to uphold that spirit.

Eight-mile-long Ocean City's appeal lies in its small-town atmosphere and in its small but active beaches. On the two-and-a-half-mile boardwalk are arcades, shops, candy stores, and eateries. Throughout the summer free concerts are put on nightly by the Ocean City Orchestra on the Music Pier at Moorlyn Terrace. There is also charter-boat fishing, as well as excellent surf casting and plenty of pleasure boating along the very accessible inland waterways.

Ocean City sponsors a number of imaginative events. On the Saturday nearest to August 1, each year for 25 years crowds have flocked to the bayside of the island to watch "A Night in Venice," a parade of brightly decorated boats along the bay. Bayfront houses join in with their own strewn lights. Other recreational activities range from crab races to beauty pageants.

And if you want to buy alcoholic beverages or down a drink in a tavern, just take the Ninth Street Bridge to the causeway to Somers Point. Somers Point has nightlife for everyone, loud raucous bars for the younger crowd, and fine dining for others.

If you continue to follow Ocean Drive southward, you next come to Sea Isle City. Sea Isle is a picturesque fishing village, alive with on-the-water pleasures upon its docks and lagoons.

Avalon is the next town, less developed than the others along the drive. It has a small boardwalk and lovely sand dunes. On the same island, Stone Harbor is known for its mélange of sparkling waterways highly conducive to boating. At its southern end is the Stone Harbor Bird Sanctuary, the only heronry in the United States sponsored by and located within a municipality. Established in 1947, the 21-acre sanctuary is populated by many species of herons: American egret, snowy egret, cattle egret, Louisiana heron, black-crowned night heron, and green heron. The only non-herons are the glossy ibises, which first arrived here in 1958.

Over the next bridge are the Wildwoods. They were originally named for the area's lush vegetation, but most of that has been replaced by a dense covering of motels in this very popular resort. Along with Atlantic City and Asbury Park, Wildwood offers probably the most exciting night life down the shoreline. Atlantic City has the casinos, but Wildwood and Asbury Park have the honky-tonk bars. This is in addition to its beautiful wide beaches, its excellent facilities for fishing, boating, and sailing, and its two-and-a-half-mile-long boardwalk packed with rides, games, and excitement.

More sedate, but no less interesting, is Cape May, at the southern tip of New Jersey. One of the oldest seashore resorts on the East Coast, Cape May's attraction is primarily the past. The town is filled with Victorian-era architecture, particularly in the Victorian village section of town. The upkeep on all that "gingerbread" alone is staggering. Cape May reached its peak before the Civil War, when it attracted a mix of federal officials and wealthy Southern planters to its six gambling casinos. While that era is long gone, the town is still deservedly popular and well maintained.

Besides going to Fisherman's Wharf to eat and Washington Street Mall to shop, you'll also want to explore Cape May's fine beaches. Along them you may find some semiprecious stones known as "Cape May Diamonds." Actually weathered quartz pebbles, these "diamonds" come in different shades and colors and vary from the size of a pea to that of a walnut. Some colorless ones resemble diamonds. When wet, they're bright and clear, but they dull upon drying. Cut and polished, they're sometimes set in rings, necklaces, and bracelets.

On the southernmost tip of the shore is Cape May Point, where the Atlantic Ocean meets the Delaware Bay. Here you can take the Cape May–Lewes Ferry to Delaware and cross the gateway to the South.

PRACTICAL INFORMATION FOR ATLANTIC CITY

 HOW TO GET THERE FROM NEW YORK. *By car:* The easiest way is to get on the New Jersey Turnpike and follow it to the Garden State Parkway. To get to Atlantic City, take exit 38A, and take the Atlantic City Expressway, a toll road, into the city. But parking fees in Atlantic City are exorbitant.

By air: There is regular air service from Philadelphia to Atlantic City on *Allegheny Airlines.* There is also service available from the Newark and New York City airports.

By bus: You can leave the driving to someone else either by conventional bus line runs from Port Authority to the Atlantic City Bus Terminal (the trip takes 2½ hours and costs about $16.00 round trip) or you can reserve a seat on a special Atlantic City bus package. These packages take you right to the door of a specific casino and are run through collaboration of the casinos and different bus companies. You'll get round-trip transportation, a free gift (usually a box of saltwater taffy), and either a meal or eight to ten dollars in quarters. Contact: *Domenico Tours,* (212) 732–0274; *Greyhound,* (212) 594–2000; *Harran Transportation,* (212) 343–6060; *Casser Tours,* (212) 840–6500, and *Trailways.* (212) 563–9432.

TELEPHONE. The area code for Atlantic City is 609.

TOURIST INFORMATION. Contact the Visitors Bureau, 2300 Pacific Ave., Atlantic City, NJ 08401. 348–7044

 HOTELS AND MOTELS. In general, Atlantic City's places to stay are the most expensive along the typically expensive Jersey shore. Yet they are filled, particularly during the summer season, so make plans and reservations well in advance.

Since casino hotels are covered in their own section above, they are not included here. However, the accommodations there are uniformly *Deluxe.* If you're interested in staying at a casino hotel, but don't want to pay upwards of $90 a night, check out the midweek packages many casinos offer. When there's little demand for hotel rooms, you can get free meals, revue tickets, and souvenirs all included in the room rate—itself at a good discount. Such deals are scarce in the summer. Contact casino sales departments.

Double-occupancy rates are categorized as follows: *Deluxe,* $70 and higher; *Expensive,* $55–$70; *Moderate,* $40–$55.

Best Western Inn of Atlantic City. *Deluxe.* Indiana and Pacific. Rooftop pool. Restaurant. 348–9175.

Bala Motel. *Expensive to Deluxe.* 110 S. Illinois Ave. Pool. Restaurant. 348–0151.

The Deauville Hotel and Motor Inn. *Expensive to Deluxe.* Brighton Ave. and the Boardwalk. Pool, sauna, restaurant. Seasonal rates. 344–1251.

Lafayette Motor Inn. *Expensive to Deluxe.* 111 S. North Carolina Ave. Pool, restaurant, cafeteria. 345–3251.

Atlantic City Barbizon. *Expensive.* North Carolina Ave. Pool, air-conditioned. 348–0134.

Midtown Motor Inn. *Expensive.* Indiana and Pacific Aves. Two pools. Coachman Restaurant and Lounge. 348–3031.

St. Moritz. *Expensive.* 134 S. Virginia Ave. Efficiencies available. 344–7186.

Seaside Hotel and Motor Inn. *Expensive.* Pennsylvania Ave. and the Boardwalk. Pool, restaurant. Seasonal rates. 340–3000.

Mt. Royal. *Moderate.* S. Park Place. Pool, restaurant, coffee shop. 344–7021.

 CASINOS. Atlantic City has staked so much of its future on the success of casino gambling that it's not unusual for even long-time residents to refer to their hometown as "Casino City." Whether the casinos will help alleviate many of Atlantic City's urban problems remains to be seen, but the fact that casinos attract visitors is undeniable (13 million in 1980; 18½ million in 1981). Although they all draw customers, each has its own individuality and style.

Resorts International on North Carolina Ave. and the Boardwalk (344–6000) is the largest and oldest. It opened in May 1978 in the remodeled Chalfonte-Haddon Hall, has 727 rooms and plans to more than double that. Its casino is the largest at 60,000 square feet, and it has more slot machines, lounges, and restaurants than any of the others. It draws the biggest names in show business for its shows and features good, exciting live music in all its lounges. It has top-flight eateries including French, Italian, and Japanese restaurants, as well as an oyster bar, a coffee shop, and a fairly priced buffet. The lobby is very small and the casino is always crowded, but as Frank Sinatra says, "Resorts runs a classy saloon."

Caesar's Boardwalk Regency on Arkansas Avenue and the Boardwalk (348–4411) opened in June 1979. The casino is the third largest, with 55,000 square feet, and the hotel has 506 rooms. The style is flashy and decorative. There are five restaurants, three lounges, and a number of shops on the second floor. Caesar's also signs the biggest name performers to appear in its theater and offers live entertainment in its lounges (though usually more pedestrian than the music in Resorts' lounges). The finest of its many restaurants is the Palm Court. Their gourmet menu features French Provincial dishes and seafood. This casino is also usually crowded, but there are always places to sit and rest.

Bally's Park Place on Park Place and the Boardwalk (340–2000) opened December 1979. Outside, the building's smooth curves are easy on the eye, while inside two towering escalators flanked by cascading waterfalls rivet your attention. The casino is spacious (60,000 square feet), elegant, and active. Billy's Pub is the only lounge, but it's large and comfortable. There are a handful of restaurants. Bally's does not book star attractions, though; instead they put together revues of varying quality.

The Sands (formerly The Brighton) on Indiana Avenue and Brighton Park (441–4000) is off the water, being a block from the Boardwalk. It was the first casino built completely from scratch, and opened in 1980. The casino floor is the second-smallest in town, 32,000 square feet, and it has about half the slot machines and blackjack tables as Resorts or Bally's. The idea was to attract the high rollers, those who gamble regularly for high stakes. Last year, new management assumed control, and the casino's fortunes have taken a turn for the better. The theater has started featuring headline attractions, often the same stars who play Caesar's and the Claridge.

Golden Nugget on Boston Avenue and the Boardwalk (347–7111) also opened in 1980. Going to the Nugget is like attending a costume party. The $131 million newly constructed building is designed along Victorian lines with an abundance of brass and marble. There are 80 custom-made chandeliers, gold flaking on the walls, and 50,000 square yards of ceramic tile. Each of the hotel's 520 rooms has a view of the ocean. The casino has 40,000 square feet, and every employee is dressed in costume: doormen are in livery, security guards are fancy-Dan Western marshalls, and the cocktail waitresses are dance hall girls wearing less than a sneeze. There's a fine gourmet restaurant and an excellent buffet. Golden Nugget is ostentatious and overblown, and the taped ragtime Muzak becomes annoying, but it shouldn't be missed. In the off season, weekday parking is free up to three hours.

Harrah's Marina Hotel Casino is a $2.50 cab ride away from the others. It's located on the inlet (1725 Brigantine Boulevard; 441–5000); and opened in 1980. The design is modern and attractive. The casino is open and bright, with upstairs windows looking out on the water. The restaurants are good and the breakfast and dinner buffets are wonderful. Lounge acts are frequently very good. Headliners have included the Beach Boys and the Captain and Tennille. Always on display are vehicles from Harrah's enormous collection of antique automobiles. Parking for your non-antique auto is free for up to three hours.

Playboy at Florida on the Boardwalk (344–4000) opened in the spring of 1981. The casino is on three levels, 50,000 square feet, all overlooking the ocean. All of the games are played on each level. Of course the main attraction to this popular new casino has been the Playboy Bunnies—some of whom are dealers and some of whom are cocktail waitresses. Although Golden Nuggets wear equally skimpy costumes, the Playboy Bunnies seem to hold a particular mystique over casino goers. However, in early 1982 the future was clouded when Hugh Hefner was denied a license by the Casino Control Commission. At press time it is unclear how this will affect Playboy's affiliation with the casino.

The Claridge Hotel and Hi Ho Casino at Park Place and Brighton Park (347–2111) is the casino with the decidedly English accent. Security guards dress like British Bobbies, and cocktail waitresses like cockney wenches, and the restaurants feature English entrées. Housed in the now-restored famous Claridge Hotel left from old Atlantic City, the multi-leveled casino is the smallest (30,000 square feet) in town. It opened in the summer of 1981 and often books headline acts into its intimate theater.

The Tropicana at Iowa Avenue and the Boardwalk (340–4000) opened in the fall of 1981 and will be the last new casino for a while at least. For the first time since the casino referendum was passed, no new casinos are under construction. The Tropicana represents a $330-million investment by Ramada. The casino's ambience is European; it strives to be Atlantic City's version of Monte Carlo. Inside, the feeling is light, airy, and plush, highlighted by the skylight windows above. There is the usual raft of expensive, elegant restaurants, but for a real treat take the glass elevator to the Top of the Trop Lounge on the 22nd floor overlooking a panorama of Atlantic City and Atlantic Ocean.

 OUTDOOR SPORTS. Like so many shore areas, Atlantic City allows for good *fishing* and lots of it. There are party, charter boats, and rowboats. You can fish from the beach and off piers, bridges, or jetties. There is also good crabbing. Trolling for game fishing, you may catch bluefish, marlin, or tuna. Deep-sea fishing you may snag flounder, mackerel, porgy, or weakfish. In the Inlet and Bay are crab, flounder, bass, and weakfish. The best place to head for charter, party, or simple fishing boats is the *Frank S. Farley Marina* at the Absecon Inlet between Huron and Maryland Aves.

As for *tennis* and *golf,* there is an abundance of courts and country clubs in the immediate vicinity. The country clubs are all off of the island however.

 AMUSEMENT CENTERS. The best and most convenient places to take the kids for amusements are the Boardwalk piers. The Million Dollar Pier has burnt down, but Central Pier at Tennessee Ave. and the Steeplechase Pier at Pennsylvania Ave. are both open and offer rides, games, and exhibits. A number of casinos such as *Golden Nugget* and *Harrah's* have game rooms which are filled with the latest and most popular arcade games.

In Brigantine, a popular summer attraction for kids of all ages is *The Brigantine Castle,* a dark and spooky haunted castle. Be forewarned that the castle is very dark and can be quite unsettling, so it's not recommended for the very young.

 DINING OUT. Atlantic City does not lack for excellent places to eat, particularly since the casinos brought new life to the town. Again, the casinos are considered under their own heading and are not included here.

Price categories may be interpreted as follows: *Deluxe,* $12.50 and above; *Expensive,* $10.00–$12.50; *Moderate,* $6.50–$10.00; and *Inexpensive,* below $6.50. These costs include appetizer, main course, and dessert; they do not include drinks, tip, or tax. Credit cards are abbreviated thus: AE, American Express; MC, Master Card; V,Visa; CB, Carte Blanche; DC, Diner's Club.

The Knife and Fork Inn. *Expensive–Deluxe.* Albany and Atlantic Aves. Seafood and meat dishes. Baking on premises. Jacket required. 344–1133. AE only.

Mama Mott's. *Expensive to Deluxe.* 151 S. New York Ave. Authentic Italian cuisine and seafood cooked to order. Major credit cards.

Orsatti's. *Expensive–Deluxe.* Raleigh Ave. and the Boardwalk. Italian specialties and seafood. Bar. Dinner dancing. Jacket preferred. 344–7671. Major credit cards.

Abe's Oyster House. *Expensive.* 2031 Atlantic Ave. Seafood specialties. Liquor. Since 1926. 344–7701. Closed Mondays. Major credit cards.

Flying Cloud Café. *Expensive.* Historic Gardner's Basin. Seafood smorgasbord. Entertainment, dancing. 348–3290. Seasonal.

The Front Porch. *Expensive.* 132 S. New York Ave. French food. Light and airy atmosphere on the second-story porch. 345–1917. Closed Tuesday evenings. Dinner Saturday till midnight. Major credit cards.

Le Grand Fromage. *Expensive.* 25 Gordon's Alley. French *nouvelle cuisine.* Seafood and meat dinners. Baking on Premises. 347–2743. Closed Sunday and Monday. Major credit cards.

12 South. *Expensive.* 12 S. Indiana Ave. Sophisticated sandwich house. Open 24 hours. Major credit cards. Pleasant, comfortable atmosphere. Bar. Dinner menu. 344–1112.

Margate Fishery and Captain's Gallery. *Moderate.* 125 Douglas Ave. Continental-American cuisine. Fine seafood. 822–6100. AE, MC, V.

Los Amigos. *Inexpensive–Moderate.* 1926 Atlantic Ave. Mexican food Mexican atmosphere. Bar. Late-night snacks. 344–2293. Dinner menu till 2 A.M.; Late night menu till 7 A.M. Major credit cards.

The White House Sub Shop. *Inexpensive.* Mississippi and Arctic Aves. A local landmark and still making the best hoagies along the shore. Autographed photos of athletes and entertainers adorn the walls. 345–1564.

NIGHT LIFE. Atlantic City's main reason for being is its night life, but the casinos aren't the only such game in town. There are many fun nightspots for spending either a relaxing or exciting evening.

To hear quiet but contemporary music, try *Camillo's* on 114 South Carolina Ave. It features a cool and comfortable atmosphere with brick walls, dark tables, and an outdoor terrace. There's light gourmet dining and fresh fruit drinks as well as live jazz. At *The Last Resort* at South Carolina and the Boardwalk, live entertainment (again mostly jazz—Thursday is Big Band Night) is the main attraction. The *Jockey Club* at North Carolina and Atlantic Aves. was once a famous jazz club in the old Atlantic City. It has been imaginatively restored and again features exciting live jazz music.

If you want to party heartier visit *Little John's,* a bar-restaurant in a converted stone church once slated for demolition, at Tennessee and Pacific Avenues.

There's dancing nightly and a cover charge. Open 24 hours, *The Lido* at 3006 Atlantic Ave. also has dancing nightly, in addition to late-night snacks and a delightful happy hour. For disco-dancing, there's the *Chez Paree* at New York and the Boardwalk. Atlantic City's foremost disco features flashing lights, continuous 16-minute disco cuts and a heavy cover charge.

Just to go and talk and have a good time, there's *The Easy Street Pub* at 30 S. Florida Ave. It has a casually elegant atmosphere and has fast become a favorite meeting place in town. Lastly, there's *The Irish Pub* on St. James Place and the Boardwalk. A friendly, joyous, old-time party atmosphere enlivens this very Irish pub. Irish music on weekends.

PRACTICAL INFORMATION FOR THE JERSEY SHORE

 HOW TO GET AROUND. *By air:* Newark Airport is a major international air terminal. It is served by most domestic major airlines. Other smaller airfields are at Atlantic City, Teterboro, Caldwell, Morristown, Monmouth County, Princeton, and Trenton.

By Bus: The Jersey Shore: Stretching more than half the length of New Jersey—from Lower New York Bay to the mouth of the Delaware River—are the hundreds of towns collectively called the Jersey Shore. There is bus service to almost every dot along "the Shore." Asbury Park is 1 hour and 40 minutes from the Port Authority Bus Terminal ($10.00 round trip). Point Pleasant is 2¼ hours away ($11.10 round trip). Seaside Heights is 2½ hours ($12.20). Cape May is 4 hours, 10 minutes away ($21.70). *Transport of New Jersey, Atlantic City Transportation Co., Asbury Park—New York Transit, Boro Buses, Greyhound, Trailways, Domenico Bus Service* and the *New York-Keansburg-Long Branch Bus* companies all offer commuter, charter, and special tour service within the state. For information about bus travel to and within New Jersey, contact the Port Authority Bus Terminal at 8th Avenue and 41st St., New York City. Tel. (212) 466-7000.

By car: The most common way of reaching any of these places is by car, however. Take the Lincoln Tunnel out of New York City. Follow Route 3 to the New Jersey Turnpike southbound. At exit 11 pick up the Garden State Parkway. The Jersey Shore begins just a few miles south and continues for about 125 miles. Pick your spot and bring along plenty of quarters for the frequent toll booths on the Parkway.

TELEPHONE. The area code for the Jersey Shore is 609.

 TOURIST INFORMATION. *State Promotion Office,* N.J. Department of Labor and Industry, P.O. Box 400, Trenton 08625. *New Jersey Dept. of Conservation & Economic Development,* Box 1889, Trenton; *Visitors Bureau,* 2300 Pacific Ave., Atlantic City 08401; the *Cape May County Dept. of Public Affairs.* Box 365, Old Court House, Cape May Court House 08204; and *Ocean County Bureau of Public Relations.* Court House Square, Toms River 08753.

HOTELS AND MOTELS. All along the popular shore resort areas the visitor is a captive audience and room rates are usually high and at times exorbitant. Accommodations are generally of standard quality, but remember that you'll be spending most of your time outside the room.

Double-occupancy rates are categorized as follows: *Deluxe,* $60 and higher; *Expensive,* $50–$60; *Moderate,* $40–$50; and *Inexpensive,* below $40. For a more complete explanation of categories see *Facts at Your Fingertips* at the front of this guide.

ASBURY PARK

Howard Johnson's Motor Lodge. *Expensive.* Asbury Park Circle, Neptune. Pool, restaurant adjacent, pets. (201) 776–9000.

Betsy Ross Motel. *Inexpensive.* At junction of Rtes. 66 and 33, Neptune. Pool, air-conditioned. (201) 922-1920.

LONG BEACH ISLAND

Engleside Efficiency Motel. *Deluxe.* 30 Engleside Ave., Beach Haven. Oceanfront. Efficiencies available. Pool. 492–1251.

Mariner Motor Inn. *Expensive.* Bay Ave. and 33rd St., Beach Haven. Gardens. Pool, refrigerators. Seasonal. 492–1235.

Quarter Deck Inn. *Moderate.* 351 W. 9th. Pool, some efficiencies. Seasonal rates. 494–9055.

The Seashell Motel. *Moderate.* Centre and Atlantic Aves., Beach Haven. Pool, restaurant. Seasonal rates. 492–4611.

OCEAN CITY

The Flanders. *Deluxe.* 11th St. and the Boardwalk. American Plan in summer. Social program. Three pools, tennis, golf. 399–1000.

Port-o-Call Hotel and Motor Inn. *Expensive–Deluxe.* 1510 Boardwalk. Efficiencies available. Pool, sauna, dining room. 399–8812.

The Forum Motor Inn. *Moderate–Expensive.* 8th St. and Ocean Ave. Pool, coffee shop, refrigerators. 399–8700.

Harbor House Motor Inn. *Moderate–Expensive.* 2nd and Bay Aves. Bayfront. Pool, marina, fishing, coffee shop. 399–8585.

Sting Ray Motor Inn. *Moderate–Expensive.* 1280 Boardwalk. Pool, restaurant. Seasonal. 399–8555.

CAPE MAY

Cape May is deservedly famous for its guesthouses, large Victorian-era homes which are used as boardinghouses. They are comfortable and unique places to spend a vacation and are no more expensive than hotels (they're often cheaper). Some, like *The Queen Victoria* on Ocean Street, include large country breakfasts in the room rate. Others, like the Victorian Rose on Columbia Avenue, include a continental breakfast. Still others, like the *Holly House* on Jackson Street, don't serve meals, but are less expensive while retaining the Victorian atmosphere. A list of Cape May's guesthouses can be easily obtained by writing the Cape May County Department of Public Affairs, Box 365, Old Court House, Cape May, NJ 08204. If you prefer modern accommodations, they are also available.

Atlas Motor Inn. *Deluxe.* Beach Drive and Madison Ave. Pool, sauna, efficiencies, restaurant with cocktails and entertainment. Toll-free tel.: from New York (800) 257–8513; from New Jersey (800) 642–3766.

La Mer Motor Inn. *Expensive.* Beach and Pittsburgh Aves.; 884–2200. Pool, restaurant, playground, efficiencies available.

The Jetty Motel. *Moderate to Expensive.* 2nd Ave. and Beach Dr.; 884–4640. Pool, restaurant. Efficiencies available.

The Montreal Inn. *Moderate to Expensive.* 1029 Beach Ave.; 884–7011. Heated pool, restaurant, and efficiencies.

 AMUSEMENT CENTERS. Aside from the games and rides provided on so many boardwalks along the shore such as in Asbury Park, Wildwood, and of course Atlantic City, the biggest and most exciting place to take the children is *Six Flags Great Adventure* in Jackson. A high admission charge ($14.95) is the one drawback to this $100,000,000 project open only in the summer. There are two parts to Great Adventure: an enormous amusement park with games, rides, attractions, and live shows, and a 450-acre safari. The drive through safari is the highlight of the park. Over 2,000 exotic animals and birds can be seen virtually in their natural habitats. It is possible to pay admission only to the amusement park ($3.50) or the safari ($5.25).

 CAMPING OUT. One could tour all of New Jersey and camp for the whole trip either at public or private campgrounds. The most consistently nice places to stay near the shore are a handful of state parks not too far from the beaches. *Allaire State Park* in Farmingdale envelops the richly historic Village of Allaire, a Revolutionary-period restored bog-iron community. In the surrounding 3,000-acre park there are picnic tables, tent sites, riding trails, and canoeing.

Part of the *Pine Barrens* (the largest unspoiled woodland in the Northeast), *Bass River State Forest* is 9,400 acres of woods in New Gretna. There are 187 campsites as well as swimming, boating, and fishing on *Lake Absegami. Wharton State Forest* is 100,000 acres, also in South Jersey's Pine Barrens. Wharton can accommodate 1,600 visitors and offers swimming, fishing, and canoeing in and on its plethora of streams. Also amongst the Pines is another historic bog-iron town, *Batsto,* which also features mansion exhibits and craft demonstrations. The 11,000-acre *Belleplain State Forest* in Woodbine has 193 campsites and also offers facilities for swimming, boating, and fishing.

For a free guide to New Jersey's campgrounds, contact the New Jersey Division of Travel and Tourism, CN 384, Trenton, NJ 08625.

FISHING. Traditionally, fishing in New Jersey is second only to the beaches for shore recreation. By the sea there are four ways to go after the fishes. The least productive and least expensive method is surf fishing. Most beaches along the shore permit surf fishing after lifeguards go off duty, though jetties, piers, and bridges are often more lively. *Weakfish, flounder,* and *striped bass* are all catchable. Renting a small boat and fishing or crabbing in the shore's many inlets and bays is another relatively inexpensive option. Rentals are usually motor boats, and rods and reels can also be rented. The four- to six-person boats generally range from $18 to $30 for a full day. *Flounder, weakfish,* and *bluefish* abound in the bays.

Party boats are a third choice available almost everywhere. It's simple; just pay from $15 to $30 for a full-day trip, get on board with the others, and an experienced captain will take you to where the fish are biting. Fish vary according to season, but *weakfish, drum, flounder, bluefish,* and *mackerel* are among the most populous. Charter boats are for high rollers only. You and the rest of your party of six to twelve can expect to pay at least $200 to be chauffeured about the water to fish for whatever you wish. Tackle is supplied and often there will be a mate aboard for general assistance.

Information on shore fishing can be obtained from the Division of Fish and Game, New Jersey Department of Environmental Protection, Trenton, NJ 08625. No license is required for saltwater fishing.

BEACHES. Sun-soaked beaches are the primary draw of the Jersey Shore. Although for the past few years shore sunbathers have had to pay to get on most of the beaches along the whole shoreline, the crowds continue to come. Beach tags are necessary at every beach on the shore aside from those in Atlantic City and the Wildwoods. Tags may be purchased from the local municipality. Generally, for the season they cost around $3.50 if purchased before Memorial Day and $5.00–$7.00 if bought later. Weekly tags usually run from $2.00–$2.50.

New Jersey offers quality beaches to fit a wide variety of tastes. Long Beach Island beaches are not wide, but their jetties and dunes are picturesque, and since there's no boardwalk, these beaches present a more natural appearance. They are also among the best surfing beaches in the state.

Atlantic City beaches are completely different. They're free and filled with hubbub, being on the world's oldest and wildest Boardwalk. They cater largely to a day-tourist trade. On the same island, Ventnor and Margate are much more sedate. They offer wide family beaches which are closed to regular traffic.

Ocean City beaches are small but popular, a bit rowdy, and next to a fun boardwalk. The surfing is good here, too. The Wildwoods are free and are well known for their wide white-sand beaches. The beaches in Wildwood Crest in particular are very pleasant and quiet because there is only a walking boardwalk with no stores. All the way to the south, Cape May offers big, clean, wide beaches attractively dotted with rocks. Contact the New Jersey Division of Travel and Tourism, CN 384, Trenton, NJ 08625, for a free beach guide.

 DINING OUT. Being right on the water, most of the best restaurants along the shore serve good, fresh seafood. In southern Jersey, good authentic Italian dishes are also common. Prices run fairly reasonable.

Price categories may be interpreted as follows: *Deluxe,* $12.50 and above; *Expensive,* $10.00–$12.50; *Moderate,* $6.50–$10.00; and *Inexpensive,* below $6.50. These costs include appetizer, main course, and dessert; they do not include drinks, tip, or tax. Credit cards are abbreviated thus: AE, American Express; MC, MasterCard; V, Visa; CB, Carte Blanche; DC, Diner's Club. A more complete explanation of the categories can be found in *Facts at Your Fingertips* at the front of this guide.

LONG BEACH ISLAND

Morrison's. *Moderate–Expensive.* 2nd Ave., Beach Haven; 492–5111. Seafood. Dining overlooking the bay. AE, V.

The Port-O'-Call. *Moderate-Expensive.* Engleside and Bay Aves., Beach Haven; 492–0715. Traditional seaside atmosphere. Meat, seafood, salad bar. AE, MC, V.

The Village Pub. *Moderate.* Centre St. and Bay Ave., Beach Haven; 492–0192. Italian and American dishes. Bar. MC, V.

The Owl Tree Tavern. *Inexpensive.* 80th St. and the Boulevard, Harvey Cedars; 494–8191. Bar atmosphere. Late-night snacks. Entertainment.

OCEAN CITY/SOMERS POINT

The Culinary Garden. *Expensive.* 841 Central Ave. Ocean City; 399–3330. Beef, seafood, and New York deli sandwiches. Informal. AE, MC, V.

The Salt Box. *Expensive.* 1046 Asbury Ave., Ocean City; 399–9219. Seafood and French cuisine. Comfortable atmosphere in an old converted house. Closed Sundays and Mondays throughout the summer. No credit cards.

Daniel's. *Moderate–Expensive.* 234 Shore Rd., Somers Point; 927–4117. Prime rib, steak, seafood. Bar. Major credit cards.

Dorothy's Olde World Cuisine. *Moderate–Expensive.* 406 14th St., Ocean City; 398–3482. European and American dishes. Small and cozy. Seasonal.

Gregory's. *Moderate–Expensive.* 900 Shore Rd., Somers Point; 927–6665. Broiled seafood. Big Sunday brunch. Bar. Major credit cards.

Mac's. *Moderate–Expensive.* 908 Shore Rd., Somers Point; 927–2759. Steaks, chops, seafood and Italian. Bar. AE, MC, V.

Watson's Restaurant. *Moderate–Expensive.* 9th and Ocean Aves., Ocean City; 399–3482. Traditionally popular. Seafood, meat dishes. Seasonal.

CAPE MAY

The Lobster House. *Expensive.* Fisherman's Wharf; 884–8296. Cocktail lounge on a fishing schooner; dance floor on the dock. Seafood of course. AE, V.

The Mad Batter Restaurant. (at the Carroll Villa Hotel). *Expensive.* 19 Jackson St; 884–5970. Sumptuous gourmet dining. Outdoor Victorian atmosphere. MC, V.

Top of the Marq. *Expensive.* 501 Beach Dr.; 884–3431. Beef, seafood. Baking on premises. Formal. View of Atlantic Ocean from six flights up. Seasonal. Open seven days in summer, weekends only during off-season. Major credit cards.

The Merion Inn. *Moderate.* 106 Decatur St.; 884–8363. Seafood, fresh fruit pies, "make your own" relishes. No credit cards.

The Pilot House. *Inexpensive.* 142 Decatur St.; 884–3449. Seafood. Lunches and dinners. Bar. MC V.

The Ugly Mug. *Inexpensive.* 426 Washington St.; 884–3459. Mall. Jumbo sandwiches. Dinners. Entertainment. Bar. Warm atmosphere.

PRACTICAL INFORMATION FOR THE NEW
JERSEY MEADOWLANDS

 THE MEADOWLANDS. The opening of the Meadowlands Sports Complex (Route 3, East Rutherford, off Routes 3, 17, 20 and Turnpike exit 16W) has revolutionized spectator sports in New Jersey. There is *night trotting* or *thoroughbred racing* all year. The Stadium holds more than 70,000 spectators and has halls where fancy balls are held. The Cosmos *professional soccer* team has drawn crowds of more than 72,000. The Giants *professional football* team uses it as its home field. The new Brendan Byrne Arena is used for special sporting events, concert performances, and other kinds of shows.

 HOW TO GET THERE. To get there by car take the Lincoln Tunnel and go west on Route 3. You can't miss it. There is also bus service from the Port Authority Bus Terminal every 20 minutes; $1.40 each way.

OTHER DAYTRIPS FROM NEW YORK CITY

by
IRA MAYER

First-timers to New York are invariably taken aback by the fact that there are vast parklands within the city, that many streets are tree-lined, that there's any greenery or flowers at all. Those with the time to spend a day outside the city are even more amazed to discover that there are farmlands less than an hour away in almost any direction, mountain ranges to the west and north within a two-hour drive, and that you can get a taste of New England within minutes of the Thomas E. Dewey Thruway by driving northeast into Connecticut.

Herewith, then, are a few possible day-trips (some will fit well with stops at sights mentioned in the "Nearby Attractions" section), all designed with the notion of giving you a sense of the nearby countryside, but with activities or attractions included to keep them from becoming day-long rides. All but the Princeton trip are best taken by car, because an automobile gives you the freedom to stop and go and detour as you please. All are also within an approximate 100-mile radius of the city. Total driving time should be between four and five hours—but remember to add in the time to be spent touring the area, eating, and for weather conditions. Early starts are always recommended, and do be sure to obtain a detailed road map of the area you plan to visit.

A Taste of New England and the Berkshire Mountains

This trip is good all year round, though you might want to check winter driving conditions, as snow accumulations are greater in these parts than they are in Manhattan.

Leave the city by way of the Saw Mill River Parkway (reached most readily by traveling up the Henry Hudson Parkway and continuing north) and the Taconic Parkway, north to Rte. 44 east. Rte. 44 will take you directly into Salisbury, Connecticut—a small quaint New England village with white clapboard colonial homes, eighteenth-century town hall, and library and block-long shopping street. In summer, stop for brunch at the Ragamont Inn in the center of town, where you can dine on the Austrian chef's strawberry pancakes, omelettes, or full luncheon fare, served on an open patio. In winter, warm up by the fireplaces at the Under Mountain Inn (two miles through town on Rte. 41—the left hand of the fork at the White Hart Inn), where the specialties include hot cider, French toast, eggs Benedict, and similar fare.

Leave town retracing your way on Rte. 44 and follow the signs at the junction for Rte. 41 toward Sharon. Then continue onto Local Road 4 to the Sharon Audubon Society—580 forested acres set off by lakes and streams. A $1 contribution is requested, after which you can follow a self-guided trail around the grounds. Departing, take Road 4 east to US 7, stopping at Housatonic State Park for a picnic, fishing, or hiking, or continue on US 7 until Rte. 128, going to the West Cornwall Covered Bridge—a reproduction of an old west bridge that was washed out in 1936. Starting the formal trip home, return to US 7 heading south. Leave plenty of time for this leg of the journey if you enjoy antique hunting, for this road is dotted with home/shops open to browsers. Stop in Gaylordsville at the Fritz and Frank for a late afternoon drink overlooking the Housatonic River before heading onto the Merritt Parkway and back into the city.

There are two other possibilities for the same trip. You'll find many inns with fine restaurants off US 7, one of the most popular (and largest) being the Silvermine Tavern—a particularly good stop for families. Consult *Architectural Digest's* "Country Inns of Lower New England" for detailed descriptions of many of the area's finest inns. Finally, if cost is not a factor and you really want to build the day around a truly memorable gourmet meal, reverse the entire trip by heading north on US 7 at the outset (making all the same stops but skipping Salisbury); once in Great Barrington, Massachusetts (just beyond the Connecticut border), go west on Rte. 23 to the junction at Rte. 22 in Hillsdale, New York. (The distances aren't that great—the Berkshire hills are where the three states intersect.) Here you'll find L'hostellrie Bressane, a French style country inn noted near and far for outstanding food and an excellent wine selection. (Reservations on summer weekends are necessary several weeks in advance, and recommended even at other times.)

Woodstock

Most direct route: New York Thruway north to Exit 19 (Kingston). Follow Route 28 west, then right onto 375 and into town.

The rock festival didn't actually take place in this quaint upstate New York town, but the environs have proved especially attractive to performers, artists, and craftspeople since the turn of the century. The center of town itself is overflowing with galleries, antique shops, and places to eat—the latter including Joyous Lake, a restaurant-cum-nightclub that is a favorite among jazz, blues, and rock musicians residing in the area. During the summer there is a small-scale but respectable performing arts festival at the Woodstock Playhouse (contact the Chamber of Commerce, P.O. Box 36, Woodstock, N Y 12498 for specific schedule).

Once you've made your way browsing through the galleries and shops, pass through the center of town heading another two miles on Rte. 212 to Bearsville. Watch carefully on the left for the Bear Café and pull in for good Continental fare, or ample burgers and salads. In winter, there are crackling fires in the various dining rooms; in summer, you can sit outdoors by a stream. Return by way of Hunter Mountain (continue further west on 212 until you can make a right onto NY 28; then follow NY 214 to NY 23A—don't worry, road signs will guide you), stopping to take the chairlift to the peak before reaching Rte. 32 and the New York Thruway southbound.

The Pocono Mountains, Pennsylvania

Take the George Washington Bridge and follow the signs for Route 80 going west. Exit at Rte. 209, south to Bushkill Falls (open April through November).

This area is dotted with waterfalls, Bushkill having the nickname of Pennsylvania's Niagara, plunging 300 feet. The trails around the area are easy to walk (the map you get at the entrance gives alternates for the few steeper passes), and there are a small zoo and playground for the children. Winona Five Falls is a bit farther south on Rte. 209. Here five cascades are found, with still more hiking trails. Far more commercially oriented is the Pocono's Magic Valley, also at Winona—an amusement park (the falls are within its boundaries, and admission to the park includes the fee for the falls trails) open daily in the summer and weekends in fall and spring. To return, continue south on Rte. 209 until you hit I-80 again, this time heading east. En route you may wish to stop at the Delaware Water Gap, a picturesque wooded area whose mountains rise to an elevation of 1,200 feet, popular for camping, picnics, and hiking.

For those interested in antiquing, the New Hope area of Pennsylvania, just across the Delaware River (via US Rtes. 22 and 202) is prime hunting territory.

Hill-stead Museum, Farmington, Connecticut.

Connecticut Turnpike (I-95) to exit 48; I-91 north to exit 21; Conn. Road 72 to I-84 east. Exit at No. 39, go down a small hill, and watch for the signs.

Hill-stead was once a private residence and remains pretty much as it was, with a surprisingly impressive collection of paintings by Manet, Monet, and Degas, among others, and numerous American and European antiques. The grounds seem to be perennially in bloom and you are invited to stroll about. The museum is open Wednesdays, Thursdays, Saturdays, and Sundays from 2–5 P.M. only, with tours conducted as demand necessitates. Return via I-84 east and 684 south.

An alternate in the same general vicinity is Capriland's Herb Farm, Coventry, Connecticut. Resident herbalist Adelma Grenier Simmons conducts tours of the farm, emphasizing seasonal "attractions" or where you may wander on your own. A daily luncheon program and Sunday afternoon tea, both designed to showcase the value of herbs in cooking, are available for modest fees. For the latter it is best to reserve in advance. Summer and fall are the favored seasons, though the farm is closed only for a few weeks in the spring during planting season.

From Manhattan take I-84, switching to I-86 due north of Hartford. Follow Rte. 31 to Coventry, turn left onto 44A, and make the second right onto Silver Street. The farm is at No. 534. Call (203) 742–7244.

Princeton University

Take either the train or the bus—no car required. By train: From Penn Station, take any train to Princeton Junction (usually the train goes on to Philadelphia). You get off at Princeton Junction and change onto a trolley-like train that goes into Princeton Station, which is right at the southwestern edge of the university. By bus: From the Port Authority Bus Terminal at 42nd St. and Eighth Ave., take the Suburban Transit bus line for Princeton (every half hour 6 A.M. to 2 A.M.); the bus will leave you off at Palmer Square, near the university's main gates at the northern edge of the campus. The wide old building with a clock tower is Nassau Hall, the administration building and the home of the original College of New Jersey dating from 1756.

Inquire at Stanhope Hall, next to Nassau Hall, about guided tours of the campus. Main sights to see are Nassau Hall itself—pockmarked with holes from British bullets shot during the Revolutionary War, the library, the chapel, a small but impressive art museum, and of course the university as a whole—one of the most attractive in the U.S. For lunch, try the Nassau Tavern or Lahiere's, both more or less across the street from the main gates.

Be sure also to see the Eating Clubs on Prospect St., and, a nice stroll away from the university on the Princeton Station side, the Graduate School and the Institute for Advanced Studies (ask for directions).

INDEX

INDEX

The index is divided as follows:
General information for New York City
New York City
Other areas and localities—which are Long Island, Hudson
River Valley, Jersey Shore, Atlantic City and other
nearby attractions.

(The letters H and R indicate Hotel and Restaurant listings.)

OTHER AREAS & LOCALITIES

Localities outside of New York State are indicated: Connecticut (Conn.), Pennsylvania (Pa.), New Jersey (N.J.).

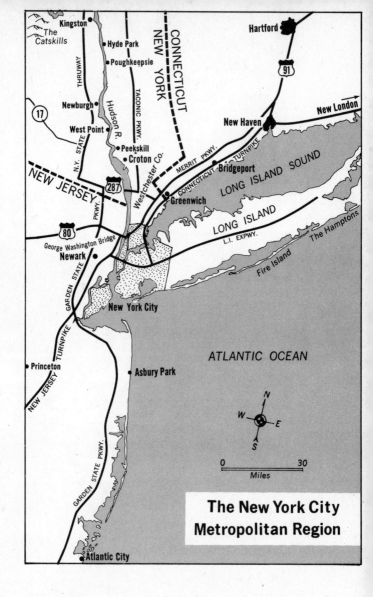

The New York City
Metropolitan Region